CW01182853

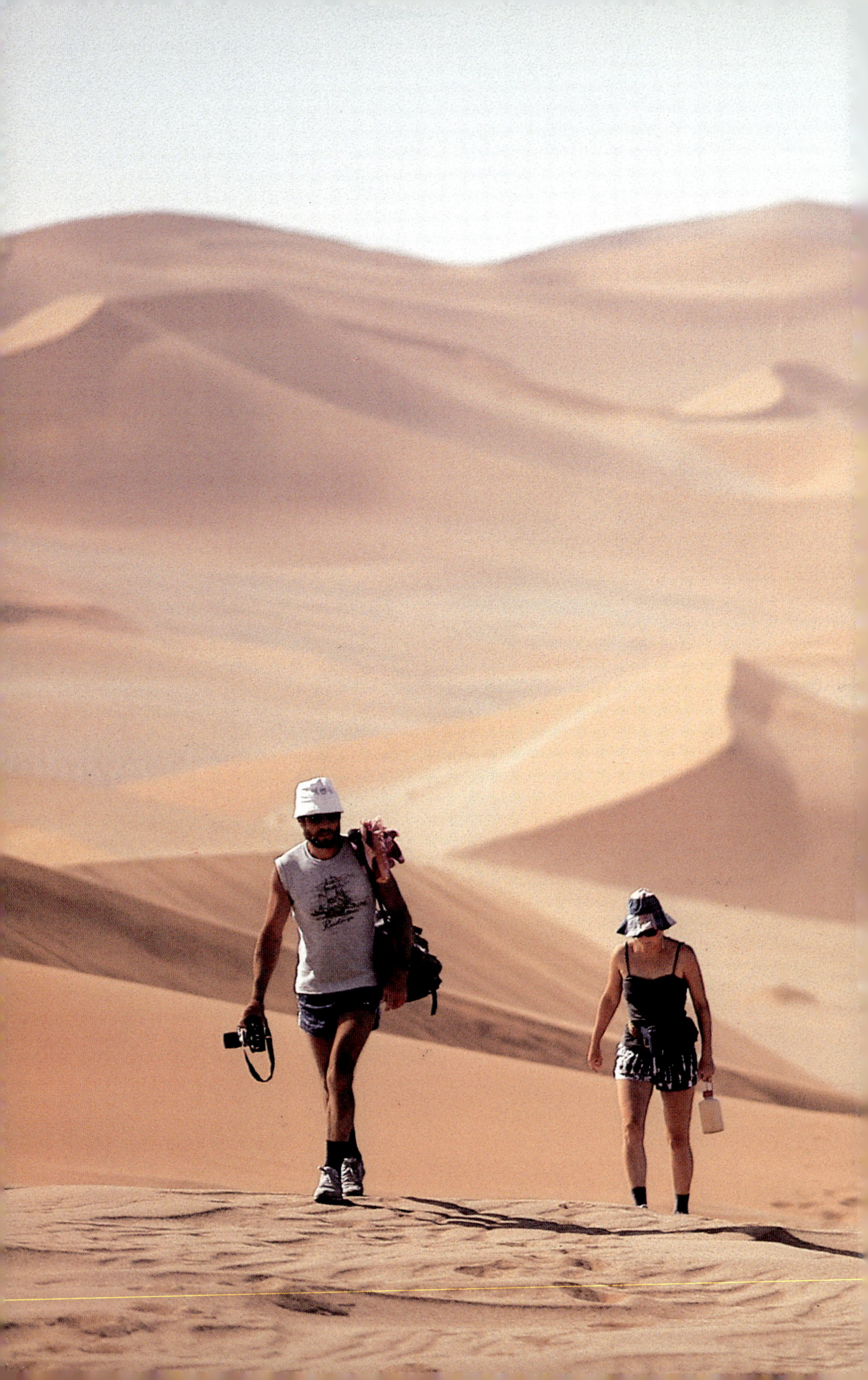

Spectrum Guide to
NAMIBIA

Spectrum Guide to Namibia

Struik Publishers (Pty) Ltd.,
(A member of the Struik Group (Pty) Ltd.,)
Cornelis Struik House,
80 McKenzie Street,
Cape Town 8001
South Africa.

Reg. No. 54/00965/07

First published in 1994

© 1994 Camerapix

ISBN 1-86825-312-0

This book was designed and produced by
Camerapix Publishers International,
P.O. Box 45048,
Nairobi, Kenya

All rights reserved. No part of this publication may be reproduced, stored in a retrieval system, or transmitted in any form, or by any means, electronic, mechanical, photocopying, recording, or otherwise, without prior permission in writing from Camerapix Publishers International.

Printed and bound in Hong Kong.

The **Spectrum Guides** series provides a comprehensive and detailed description of each country it covers, together with all the essential data that tourists, business visitors, or potential investors are likely to require.

Spectrum Guides in print:
African Wildlife Safaris
Ethiopia
Jordan
Kenya
Maldives
Pakistan
Seychelles
South Africa
Tanzania
Zimbabwe

Publisher and Chief Executive: Mohamed Amin
Editorial Director: Brian Tetley
Picture Editor: Duncan Willetts
International Projects Director: Debbie Gaiger
Editor: Tarquin Hall
Associate Editors: Roger Barnard, Amy Schoeman and Jan Hemsing
Photographic Research: Abdul Rehman
Editorial Assistants: Mary-Anne Muiruri and Sophie Brown
Design: Craig Dodd and Liz Roberts

Editorial Board

Spectrum Guide to Namibia is the latest in the acclaimed series of high-quality, lavishly and colourfully illustrated international *Spectrum Guides* to exotic and exciting countries, cultures, flora and fauna.

One of the most spectacular tourist destinations in the world, Namibia constantly invites superlatives. Yet until this book — the product of months of work by a dedicated team of writers and researchers in the *Spectrum Guides* editorial office and in the field in Namibia — there were few, if any, comprehensive guides to its many attractions.

The pictures are from the cameras of *Spectrum Guides* Publisher and Chief Executive **Mohamed Amin** and his colleague, **Duncan Willetts**, both world-renowned photographers. Namibia, with its deserts, rivers, plateaux and game-filled plains, had long been a country they dearly wished to work in, adding both inspiration and challenge to their outstanding photographic skills.

Amin led the team assigned to produce *Spectrum Guide to Namibia*, and was responsible, with International Projects Director British-born **Debbie Gaiger,** for the complex liaison and logistics.

Working closely together, Editorial Director **Brian Tetley**, with more than forty years of editorial experience in Europe and Africa, and Editor **Tarquin Hall**, laboured long and hard to produce a fascinating, in-depth and readable guide book to a country as yet little known to international tourism.

Hall, a young British writer, contributed most of the text by researching and writing Parts One to Three and specialist sections of Part Four.

Associate Editors **Roger Barnard**, British-born Namibian **Amy Schoeman** and Kenya's **Jan Hemsing** edited the text, and undertook responsibility for maintaining Spectrum Guides' in-house style.

Design was by **Craig Dodd** and **Liz Roberts**, while Kenyan **Abdul Rehman** oversaw photographic research.

Finally, Editorial Assistants **Mary-Anne Muiruri** and **Sophie Brown** coordinated the preparation of manuscripts and typesetting.

Above: Contemporary sculpture symbolises the unity and dreams of free Namibia.

TABLE OF CONTENTS

INTRODUCTION

THE NAMIBIAN EXPERIENCE 17
TRAVEL BRIEF & SOCIAL ADVISORY 19

PART ONE: HISTORY, GEOGRAPHY AND PEOPLE

INTRODUCTION 30
HISTORY 33
THE LAND 56
THE PEOPLE 62

PART TWO: PLACES AND TRAVEL

SOUTHERN NAMIBIA 70
ORANJEMUND 72
NOORDOEWER 73
KARASBURG 74
FISH RIVER CANYON 74
AUGRABIES-STEENBOK NR 80
KEETMANSHOOP 81
AUS 87
KOLMANSKOP 91
LÜDERITZ PENINSULA 93
BETHANIE 96
DUWISIB CASTLE 97
BRUKKAROS 98
MUKUROB 100
GOCHAS 101
MARIENTAL 103
HARDAP DAM 103
MALTAHÖHE 106
REHOBOTH 106
GOBABIS 107

CENTRAL NAMIBIA 108
NAMIB-NAUKLUFT PARK 108
SESRIEM & SOSSUVLEI 111
KUISEB RIVER 125
SANDWICH HARBOUR 127
RÖSSING 130

MIDLAND HIGHLANDS 132
GAMSBERG 132
DAAN VILJOEN GAME RESERVE 133
VON BACH RESORT 135
OKAHANDJA 136
GROSS-BARMEN RESORT 138
OTJIMBINGWE 138
USAKOS 139
OMARURU 141
OTJIWARONGO 143

OUTJO 144
WATERBERG PLATEAU PARK 146
GROOTFONTEIN 149
TSUMEB 150
LAKE OTJIKOTO 153
KALAHARI DESERT 155
KAUDOM GAME RESERVE 156

SKELETON COAST 158
NATIONAL WEST COAST 165
HENTIES BAY 166
CAPE CROSS 166
SKELETON COAST 167

DAMARALAND 180
SPITZKOPPE 181
BRANDBERG 184
KHORIXAS 187
TWYFELFONTEIN 189
BURNT MOUNTAIN 190
DAMARALAND WILDERNESS 191
PALMWAG 192
HOBATERE GAME PARK 192
SESFONTEIN 193
KAOKOLAND 193
RUACANA 194

NORTHERN NAMIBIA 199
ETOSHA NATIONAL PARK 199
RUNDU 214
CAPRIVI STRIP (WEST) 218
MAHANGO GAME RESERVE 218
CAPRIVI GAME RESERVE 220
CAPRIVI STRIP (EAST) 221
MAMILI NATIONAL PARK 222
LAKE LIAMBESI 222
KATIMA MULILO 223

PART THREE: THE CAPITAL AND THE TOWNS

WINDHOEK 228
SWAKOPMUND 240
WALVIS BAY 251
LÜDERITZ 255

PART FOUR: SPECIAL FEATURES

WILDLIFE 264
BIRDLIFE 286
FLORA 291
SPORTING NAMIBIA 295
ROCK ART 300
TASTES OF NAMIBIA 302

PART FIVE: BUSINESS NAMIBIA

THE ECONOMY 305
INVESTMENT 309
TAXATION 311

PART SIX: FACTS AT YOUR FINGERTIPS

VISA & IMMIGRATION REGULATIONS 312
HEALTH REQUIREMENTS 312
INTERNATIONAL FLIGHTS 312
AIR FARES 312
DEPARTURE TAX 312
ARRIVAL BY SEA 312
ARRIVAL BY RAIL 312
ARRIVAL BY ROAD 312
CUSTOMS 313
ROAD SERVICES 313
TAXI SERVICES 313
CAR HIRE 313
DRIVING 313
RAIL SERVICES 313
CLIMATE 313
CURRENCY 314
CURRENCY REGULATIONS 314
BANKS 314
CREDIT CARDS 314
GOVERNMENT 314
LANGUAGE 314
RELIGION 314
TIME 314
BUSINESS HOURS 314
SECURITY 314
COMMUNICATIONS 314
MEDIA 315
ENERGY 315
MEDICAL SERVICES 315
MEDICAL INSURANCE 315
LIQUOR 315
TIPPING 315
CLUBS 315

IN BRIEF

HUNTING & TOURING 316
TROPHY HUNTING 316
HERITAGE SITES 317
NATIONAL PARKS, GAME RESERVES 318
MUSEUMS 324
MONUMENTS 326

ANIMAL CHECKLIST 327
REPTILE CHECKLIST 328
AMPHIBIANS CHECKLIST 329
SNAKE CHECKLIST 329
WILDLIFE PROFILE 330
BIRD CHECKLIST 332
BIRDLIFE PROFILE 336
PLANT PROFILE 340
DEMOGRAPHIC PROFILE 341
GAZETTEER 342
PUBLIC HOLIDAYS 343

LISTINGS

AIRLINES 344
AIR CHARTER 344
ART GALLERIES 344
BANKS 344
BOAT CHARTER 345
BUS COMPANIES 345
BUSINESS ASSOCIATIONS 345
CAR HIRE 346
CLUBS 346
NAMIBIAN MISSIONS ABROAD 346
FOREIGN CONSULS AND MISSIONS 347
TOURIST GUEST FARMS 349
HUNTERS' GUEST FARMS 351
ACCOMMODATION 351
REST CAMPS & CARAVAN PARKS 353
MEDIA 353
MUSEUMS 354
TAXIS 354
TRAVEL CONSULTANTS 354
TOUR OPERATORS 355
HUNTING ASSOCIATION 355
CAMPING EQUIPMENT 355
BIBLIOGRAPHY 356
INDEX 358

MAPS

NAMIBIA 14
NAMIBIA REGIONS 15
FISH RIVER CANYON 76
NAMIB-NAUKLUFT PARK 109
SKELETON COAST 159
ETOSHA NATIONAL PARK 200
CAPRIVI STRIP 214
WINDHOEK 229
SWAKOPMUND 241
LÜDERITZ 256

Half title: Sundown over the Namibian veld. Title page: Tourists climb the slopes of one of the great sand mountains of the Namib. Page 8-9: Hundreds of rutting seal bulls and breeding cows gather each southern spring on the rocky shores of Cape Cross, home to more than 80,000 of the amphibians. Page 10-11: Dramatic viewpoint across and into southern Nambia's mighty Fish River Canyon. Page 12-13: Hippos abound in the swamps and hidden deltas of the Caprivi Strip's marvellous wetlands.

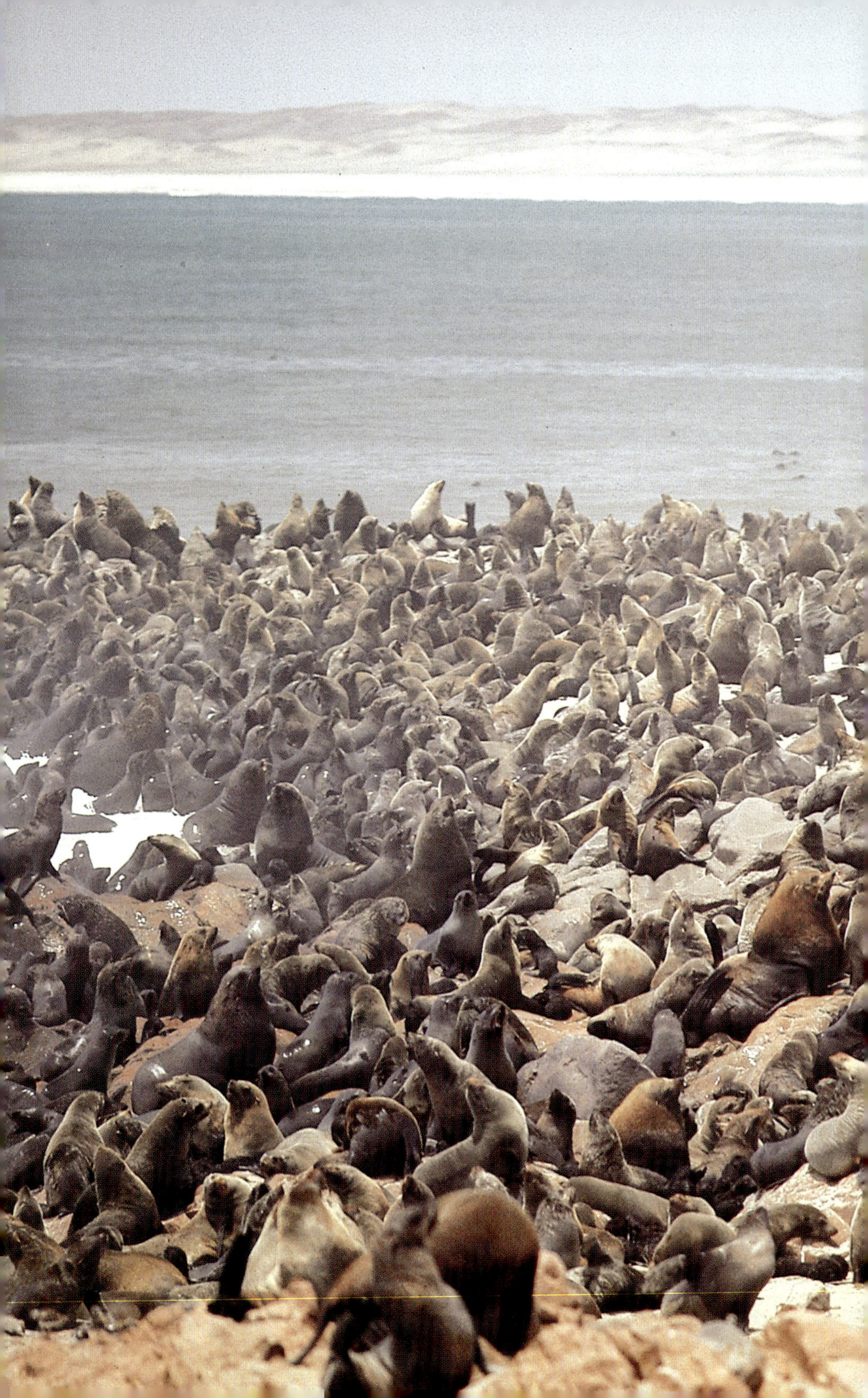

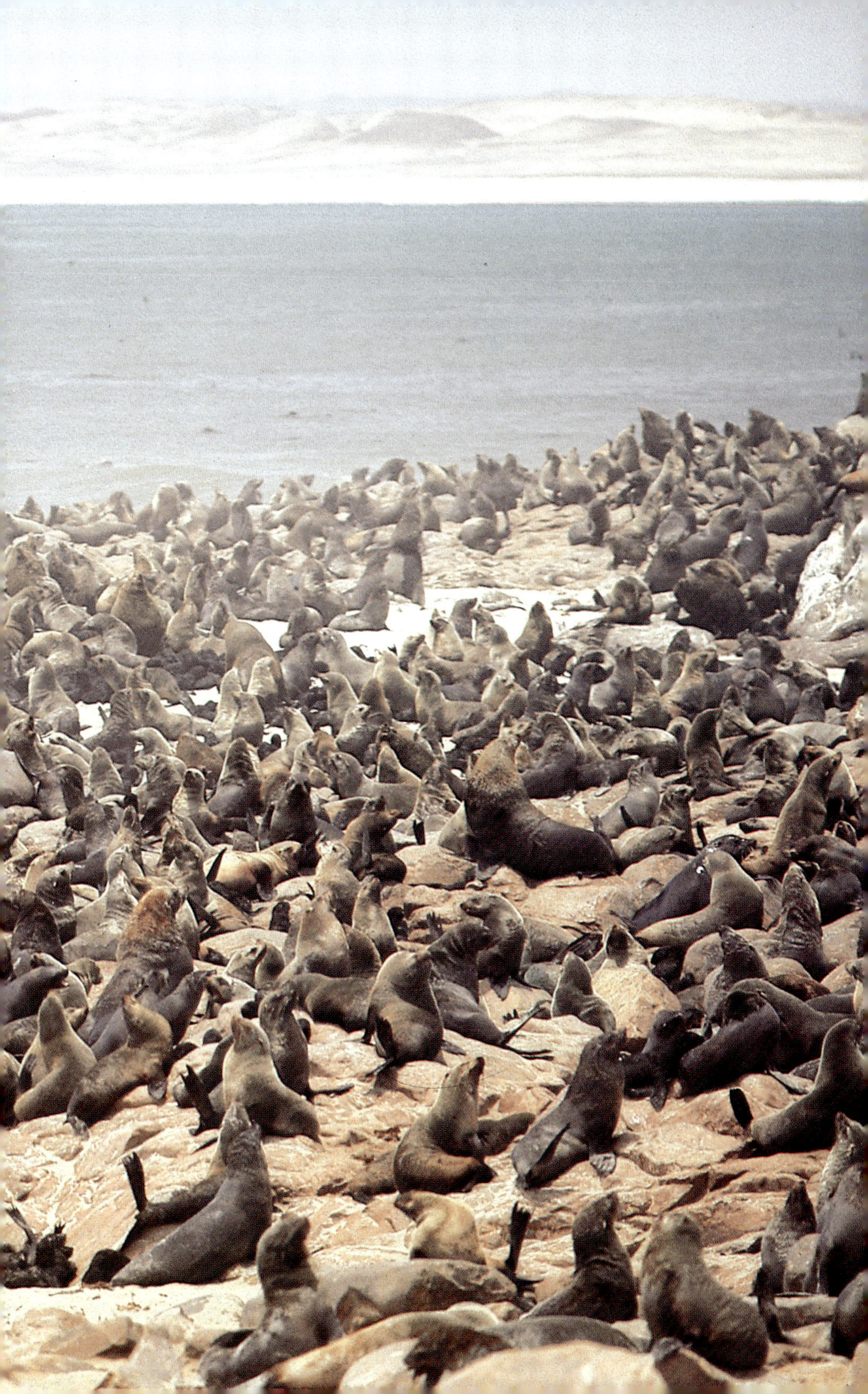

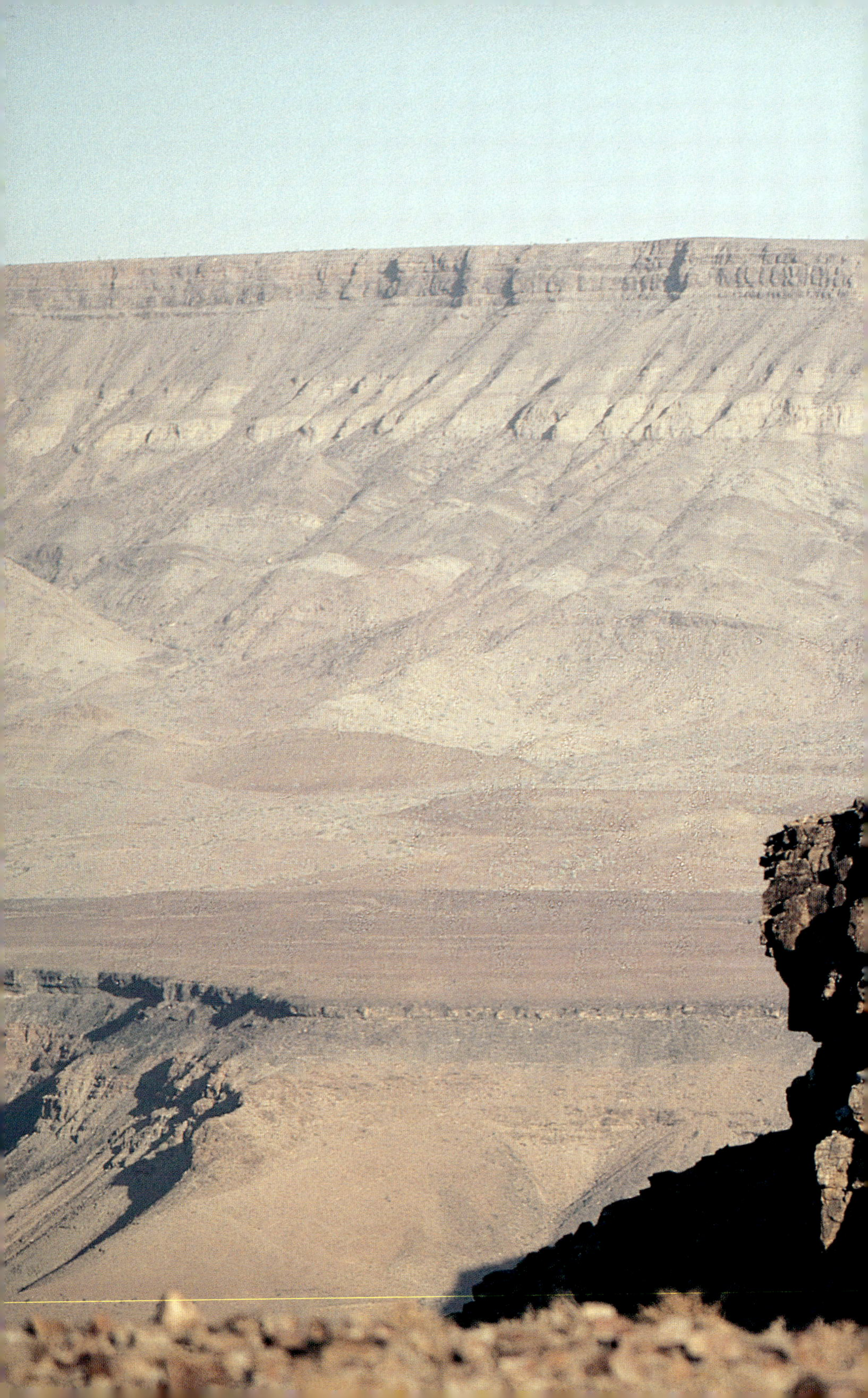

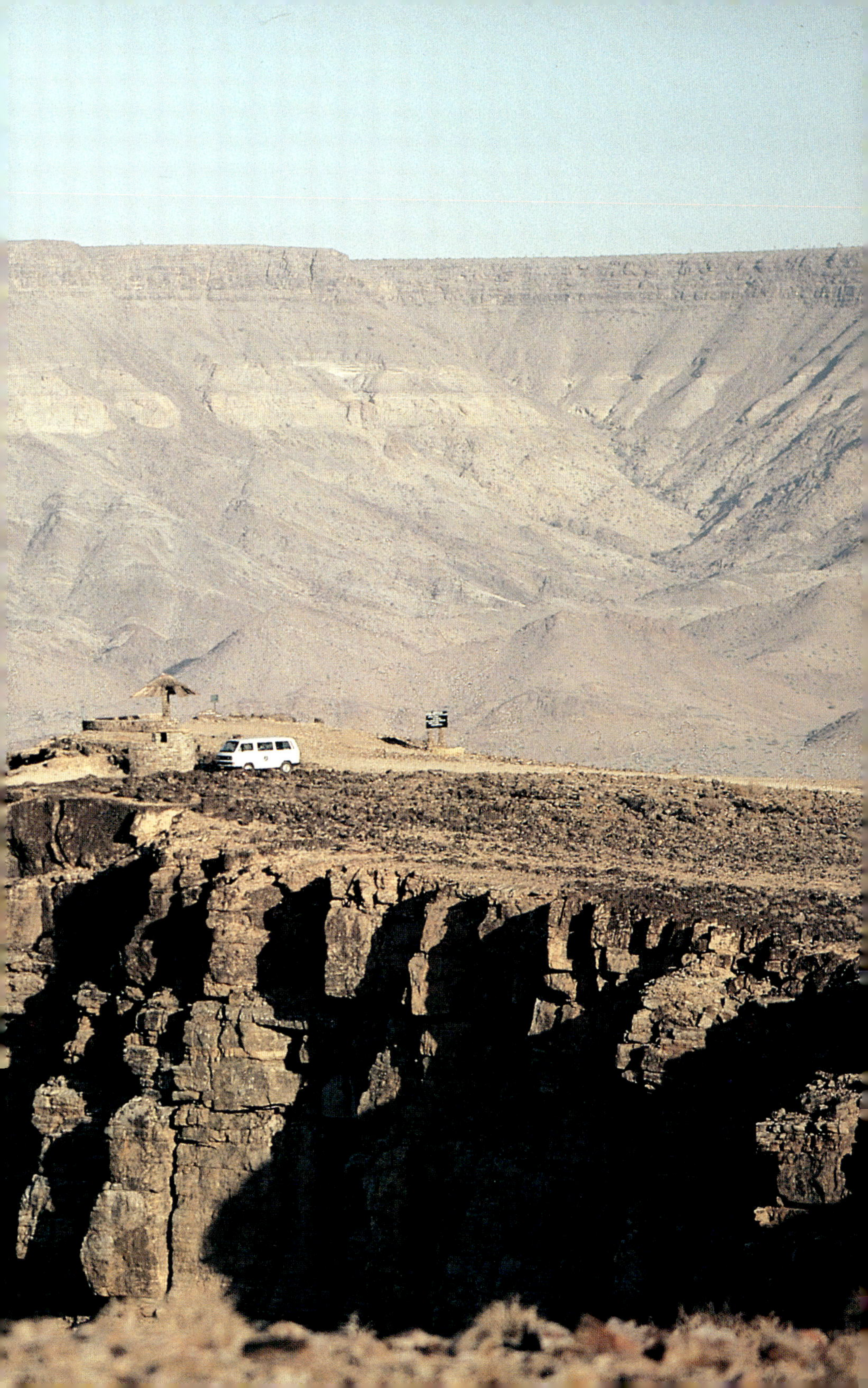

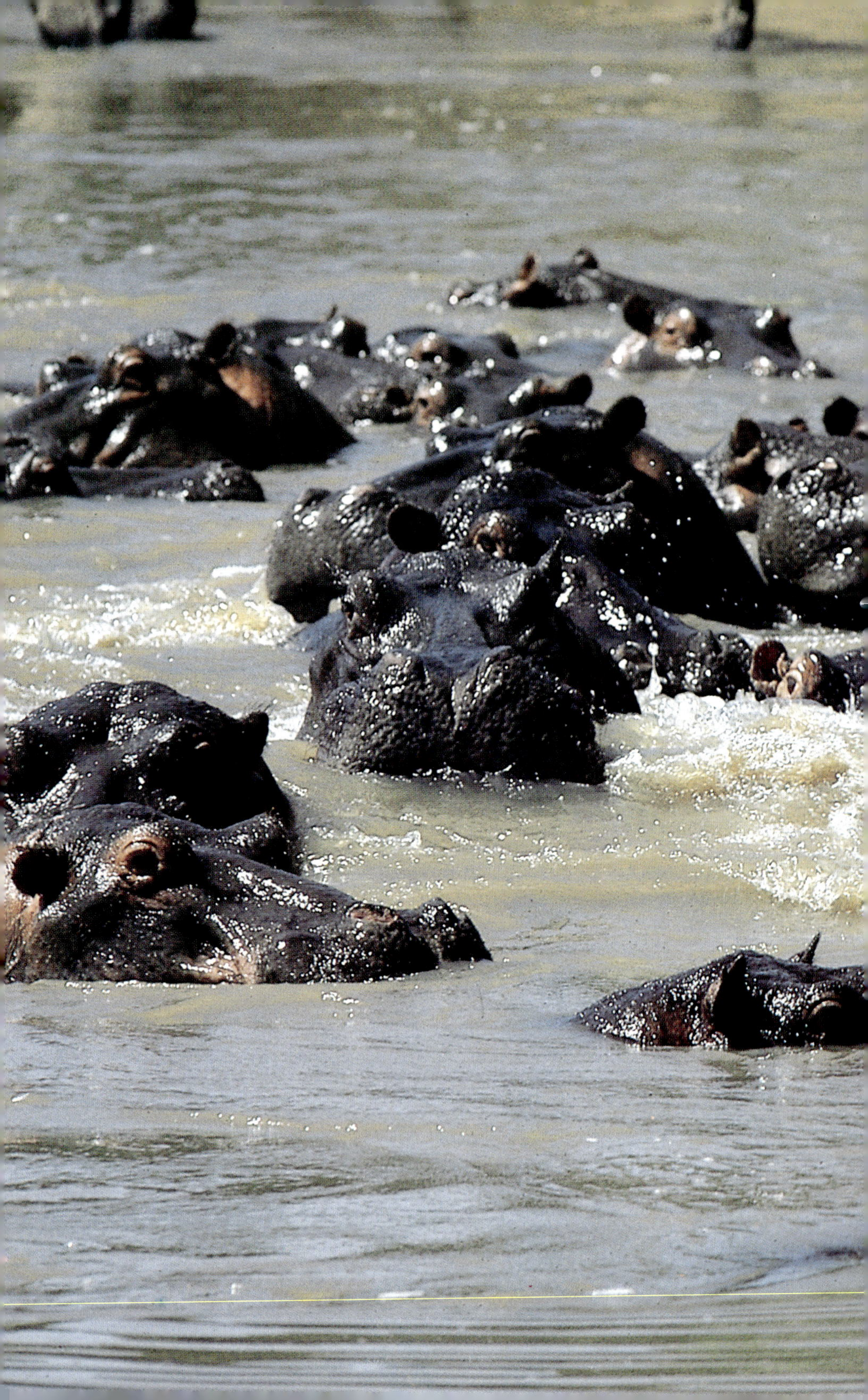

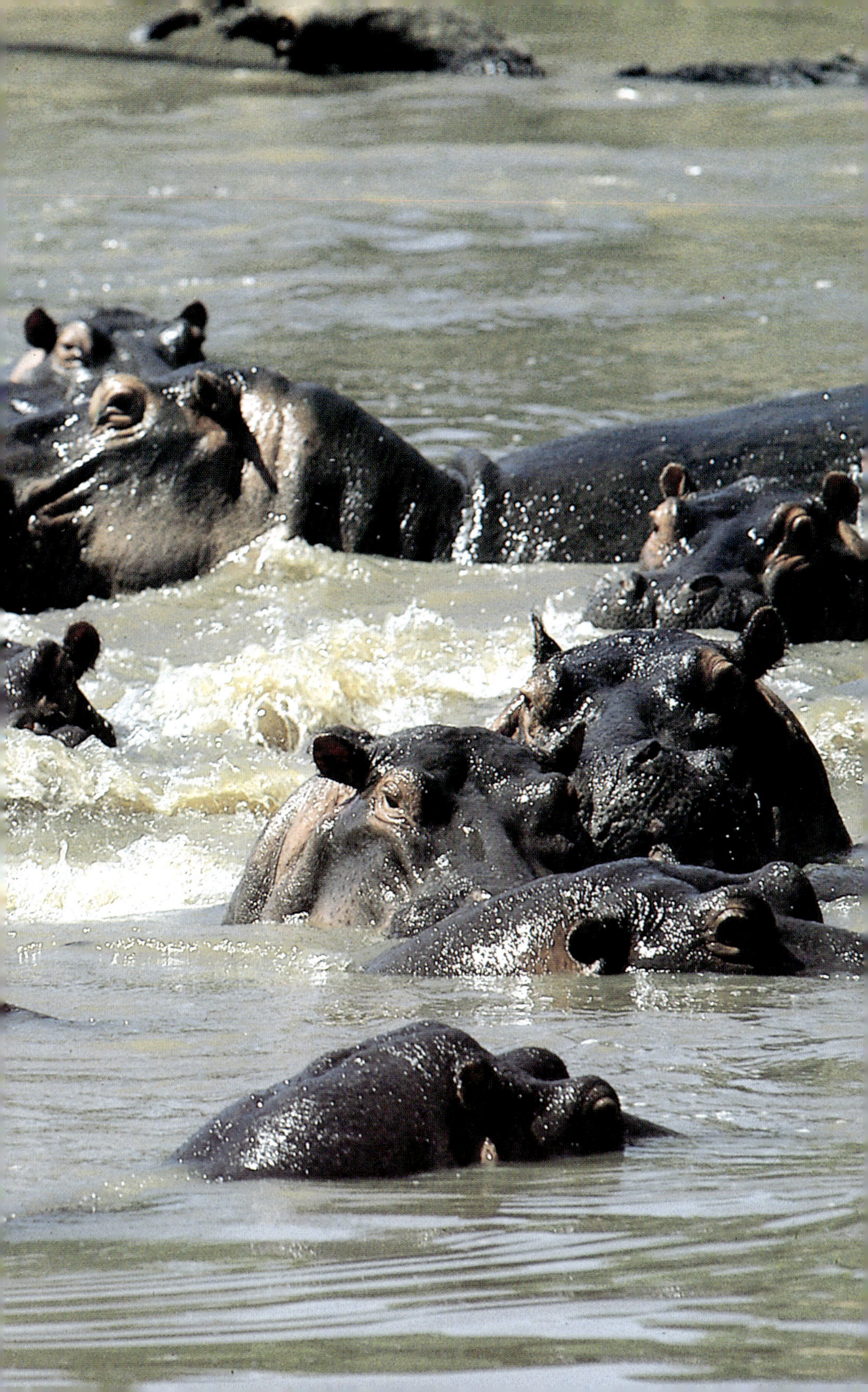

Namibia

The regions of Namibia

© Camerapix 1994

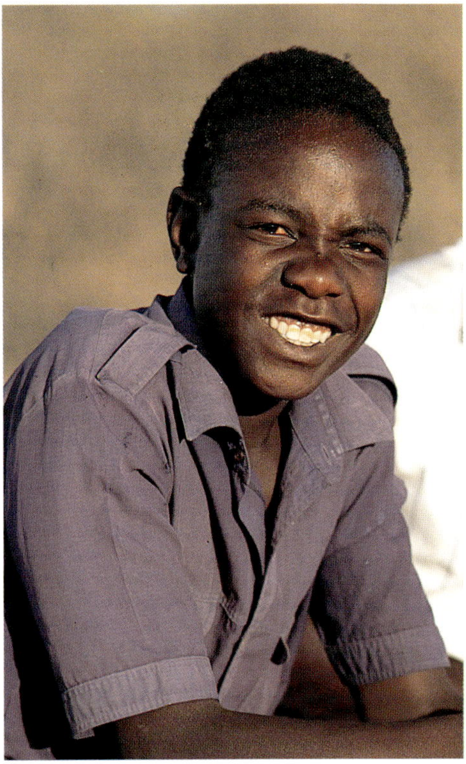
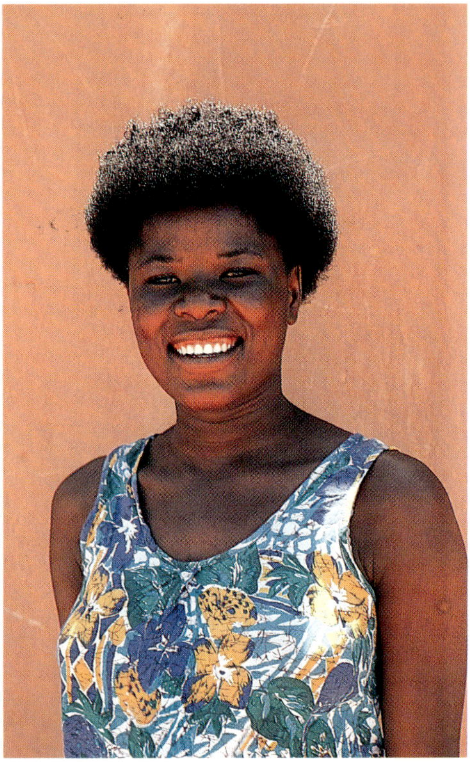
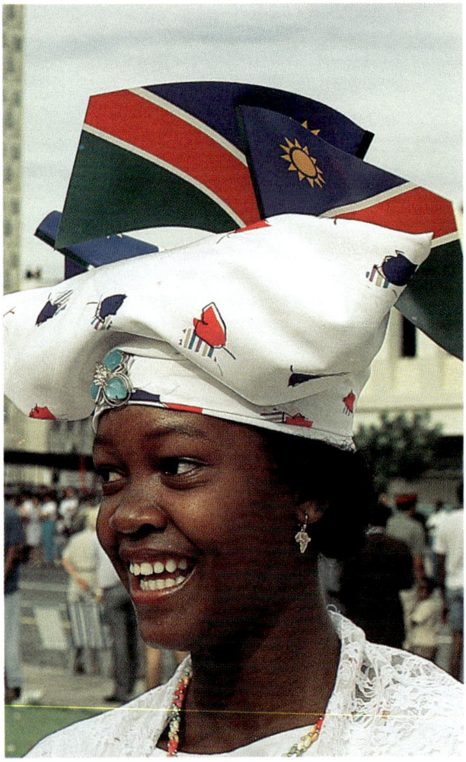
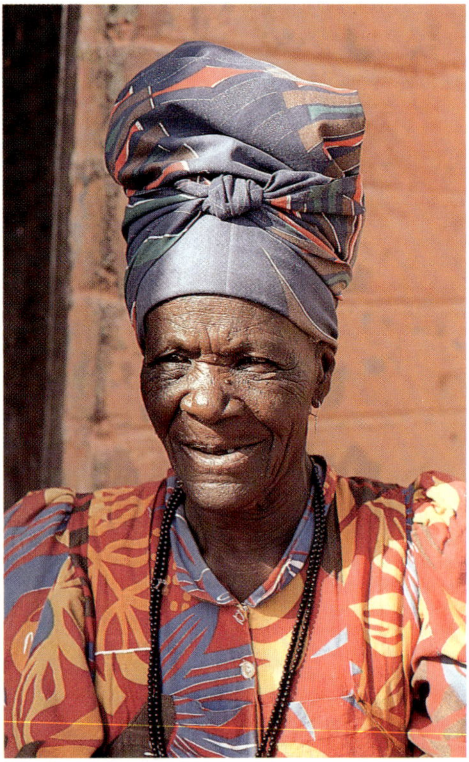

The Namibian Experience

The only sound on Namibia's Skeleton Coast is that of huge waves crashing and pounding against wrecked ships. Roller after roller hammers their steel carcasses as they rust away on the most desolate shoreline in the world.

Many sailors have died there, slowly and agonisingly, from extreme thirst and hunger. Their bones remain half-hidden in the sand — serving as a reminder to visitors not to test this unforgiving place.

Inland, the sand dunes of the mighty Namib Desert roll inexorably over the horizon, seemingly forever. Strange rock formations rise out of the ground, like talons waiting to drag intruders down into oblivion.

An even more unlikely phenomenon crawls across the desert — the thick fogs that descend frequently. But then the Skeleton Coast is a unique place.

When you stand there facing the cold Atlantic, shrouded in fog, at the edge of one of the oldest deserts in the world, it is an eerie but wonderful experience.

Yet Namibia is not all raw and untouched wilderness. It is also a land of scintillating contrast.

Beyond the wide, sandy wastes of the Namib Desert the massive Central Escarpment rises 900 to 2,000 metres (3,000-6,500 feet) above sea level, and undulating plains and sandy valleys make way for mountains with craggy ridges.

Further south is the escarpment's most spectacular natural feature — the Fish River Canyon. At a depth of 550 metres (1,800 feet), it is second in size and grandeur in Africa only to the Blue Nile Gorge in Ethiopia.

Meanwhile the north forms a total contrast to the rest of the country. There lies rich farmland, fed for the most part by the Okavango and other rivers that flow south from Angola.

Over hundreds of years, generation after generation of Africans have adapted to these different terrains and climates — even in the most inhospitable regions where they live on minimal amounts of water.

For wherever you go in Namibia you will find settlements scattered across its huge expanses. From the air these mud and thatch villages look like strings of beads. And for the folk who live in them nothing much has changed since the San nomads first walked across this fascinating country thousands of years ago, leaving a wealth of rock art at sites around the country. Between 2,000 and 1,000 years ago, Bantu-speaking tribes moved into the north-eastern corner of the country, following the wide waters of the Okavango River into the Caprivi Strip and beyond. A succession of tribes followed.

Yet incredibly it was not until 400 years ago that the western world came to know anything about this mysterious land astride the Tropic of Capricorn. It was then discovered by Portuguese explorers who landed there during their search for a sea route to the East.

After them came the Germans and then the South Africans — to form colonial administrations, farm the land and impose apartheid under which blacks and whites were segregated. But on 21 March 1990, Namibia became a free nation and now its people are among the friendliest in Africa. The small population of just 1.5 million people is a melting pot of African and European cultures woven into a complex tapestry. A mixture of African and European language is spoken in most

Opposite top left: Young Damara tribesman brings his ancient heritage to bear on the challenges of the 21st century. Opposite top: Smiling Damara tribeswoman reflects Namibia's rich cultural heritage near Twyfelfontein, Damaraland. Opposite left: Bright colours of a modern but traditional Victorian-style Herero headdress in Windhoek. Opposite: Venerable matriarch in an Herero township close to the Namibian capital of Windhoek.

Above: Air Namibia's 747 makes a final circuit before landing at Windhoek's International Airport.

towns, and the capital, Windhoek, is one of the continent's most cosmopolitan cities.

For most visitors Namibia's cultures and its rich assortment of wildlife — from the Big Five to marvellously adapted reptiles and insects — act as a magnet, drawing them back to the country time and again.

The Etosha National Park, in the north, knows no season. Only scorching heat and desert storms mark passing time as month after month the shimmering sun bleaches the plain into a desolate wasteland.

But with the rains comes life. Overnight, grass grows, plants bloom and water fills depressions in the ground. Later, when the drought resumes, animals congregate around these life-giving pools in hundreds of thousands.

A safari in Etosha and many other places in Namibia is unlike any other. For there you find no evidence of the passage of mankind. When a lion lifts his head and roars, a tingle of excitement hits your spine. And when a cheetah brings down an antelope in front of you, or a rhino bulldozes its way through the bush in sudden anger, you know you are experiencing what will become the memory of a lifetime.

A memory called Namibia. Wild, bewitching and beautiful.

Welcome.

Travel Brief and Social Advisory

Some dos and don'ts to make your visit more enjoyable.

The Road to Discovery

Land of myths and legends, tucked away in the south-western corner of Africa just waiting to be discovered, Namibia is one of the last places in the world where man may still experience the miracle of nature, unspoilt by civilisation. Truly, Namibia is the land of the free.

Many planning an African adventure might assume that because Namibia is such a new nation, it is unprepared for visitors. Nothing could be further from the truth.

You may spend days and nights in the wilderness alongside the greatest and most ferocious natural predators on earth, while enjoying all the luxuries of civilisation with nothing to fear. These include self-contained suites with private bathrooms, air-conditioning, well-stocked cocktail bars and five-course gourmet meals.

Visitors enjoy at least three-star accommodation, often higher, in most major centres and wildlife parks. However, other areas, such as the Skeleton Coast, are only for the truly intrepid and adventurous.

With all this, a Namibian holiday is certain to be the adventure of a lifetime. Nonetheless, even in the most relaxed societies unforeseen problems may arise.

This section, therefore, focuses on both the benefits and the potential pitfalls of travel in Namibia.

Getting There

Windhoek boasts two airports — Windhoek International Airport which lies forty-five kilometres (twenty-eight miles) from the city centre and Eros Regional Airport which is five kilometres (three miles) from the city centre.

Flying time from Europe is between ten and twelve hours. Air Namibia, Lufthansa, South African Airways, Air France, LTU, TAAG the Angolan Airline, Air Zimbabwe, Air Botswana and Zambia Air all operate services into Windhoek International.

Getting Around

By road

Namibia has one of the best road networks in Africa. Tarred roads from Windhoek to the north, south, east and west make travel between the main centres possible in all weathers. And the gravel surfaces of secondary roads are graded regularly and well maintained. However, this does not mean visitors should drive as fast on them as they would on tarmac. Caution is required as it is very easy to skid or roll a car on such loose surfaces.

Vehicles also become covered in layers of dust which creep into everything. So wrap electronic equipment and cameras carefully. If there is air conditioning, close the windows and use it.

A natural surface unique to the country is that of the salt roads of the coast. Gypsum, extracted from the desert, is soaked with brine to create a surface as hard and smooth as tarmac.

Namibians drive on the left-hand side. Seat belts are compulsory and a valid international driving licence is necessary for all visitors, except residents from neighbouring states. Vehicles can be hired in all major centres, but make sure you are equipped to cope with emergencies when travelling off the main routes.

Hitchhiking in Namibia is illegal but the law is not enforced and visitors who thumb lifts are not usually penalised. And since hitching is the only way to get around, everyone does it. But remember that in areas where there are few vehicles — even though truck drivers are usually happy to offer a lift — you run the risk of standing in the searing sun all day. Always keep a tube of sun-block handy.

Above: Tarred road cuts like an arrow through the barren wastes of the Namib Desert from Keetmanshoop to Lüderitz.

Long-distance buses in Namibia are modern and efficient, but they are not available every day, so plan carefully.

Coaches link Windhoek with all major centres. The schedules are available from the main coach station opposite the Kalahari Sands Hotel. There are twice-weekly international coaches from Windhoek, and Cape Town and Johannesburg. Although both are long journeys, you see more of the country than by plane. The comfortable coaches are air-conditioned with reclining seats and videos. Meals are included in the fare. Road maps are available in most major towns. This guide gives approximate distances in miles and kilometres.

Namibia is bordered by South Africa in the south and south-east, Botswana in the east, Zimbabwe and Zambia in the north-east on the Caprivi Strip, and Angola in the north. There are many land entry points from all these countries.

From South Africa there are customs and immigration checkposts at Ariamsvlei on the road between Upington and Nakop, at Rietfontein, Velloorsdrift and Noordoewer. On the border with Botswana there are posts at Buitepos, Ngoma and Mohembo. The only one between Zambia and Namibia is at Wenela, and between Zimbabwe and Namibia the border post is at Kazungula in the Caprivi Strip.

By air

Namibia has a well-developed domestic and international air network. The principal carrier is Air Namibia, whose international network covers London, Frankfurt, Luanda (Angola), Lusaka (Zambia), Harare (Zimbabwe) and Johannesburg. In Namibia, it operates scheduled services from Eros Airport to Katima Mulilo in the Caprivi Strip, Oranjemund, Keetmanshoop and Lüderitz in the south, Etosha, Oshakati, Rundu, Swakopmund and Tsumeb, using Boeing 737 jets and Beechcraft B-1900 twin-engined turbo-prop aircraft. Air Namibia's Windhoek office is in the Kalahari Sands Hotel complex on Independence Avenue.

Namibia Commercial Aviation, founded in the 1970s, operates a charter fleet of

Above: Cream and green livery reflects the pristine glory of Windhoek's mainline station.

single-, twin- and jet-engine aircraft out of Windhoek to all parts of Namibia and to neighbouring countries.

By train

If you want to travel quickly in Namibia then avoid the rail service. Apart from the primary north-south line, all TransNamib rail services run slowly and stop frequently. There are routes from the capital to the west, coast, north and south, and three times a week, a service from Windhoek to De Aar Junction in South Africa which takes between twenty-nine and thirty-four hours.

For steam enthusiasts the highlight is the Diamond Special which runs twice a year from Keetmanshoop in the south to Lüderitz. (See "Southern Namibia", Part Two). However, if you are a railway enthusiast remember that TransNamib often mixes passengers and freight together on ordinary schedule services which may mean an uncomfortable journey.

There are three classes, and reservations for the return half of a journey must be made at the station you wish to return from, not your starting point.

A fully booked train in Namibia is rare as this mode of transport is unpopular. Keep in mind, also, that trains run infrequently and schedules often change from week to week. Check well in advance.

The people

For those hoping to escape from an overpopulated world for a few weeks, Namibia is the ideal place to do so. Four times the size of Britain, the country has only 1.5 million people, and you can go for days literally without seeing another soul.

On the other hand, if you enjoy meeting new people in a new country, none are friendlier. Take a walk in any town — even the capital, Windhoek — and you will find folk with time on their hands only too happy to give directions or talk.

English is the official language, but German and Afrikaans are also widely spoken. German and Afrikaans constitute an important lingua franca. The indigenous African languages and dialects are many, but they fall into two main groups — Bantu and Khoisan. Most people speak either

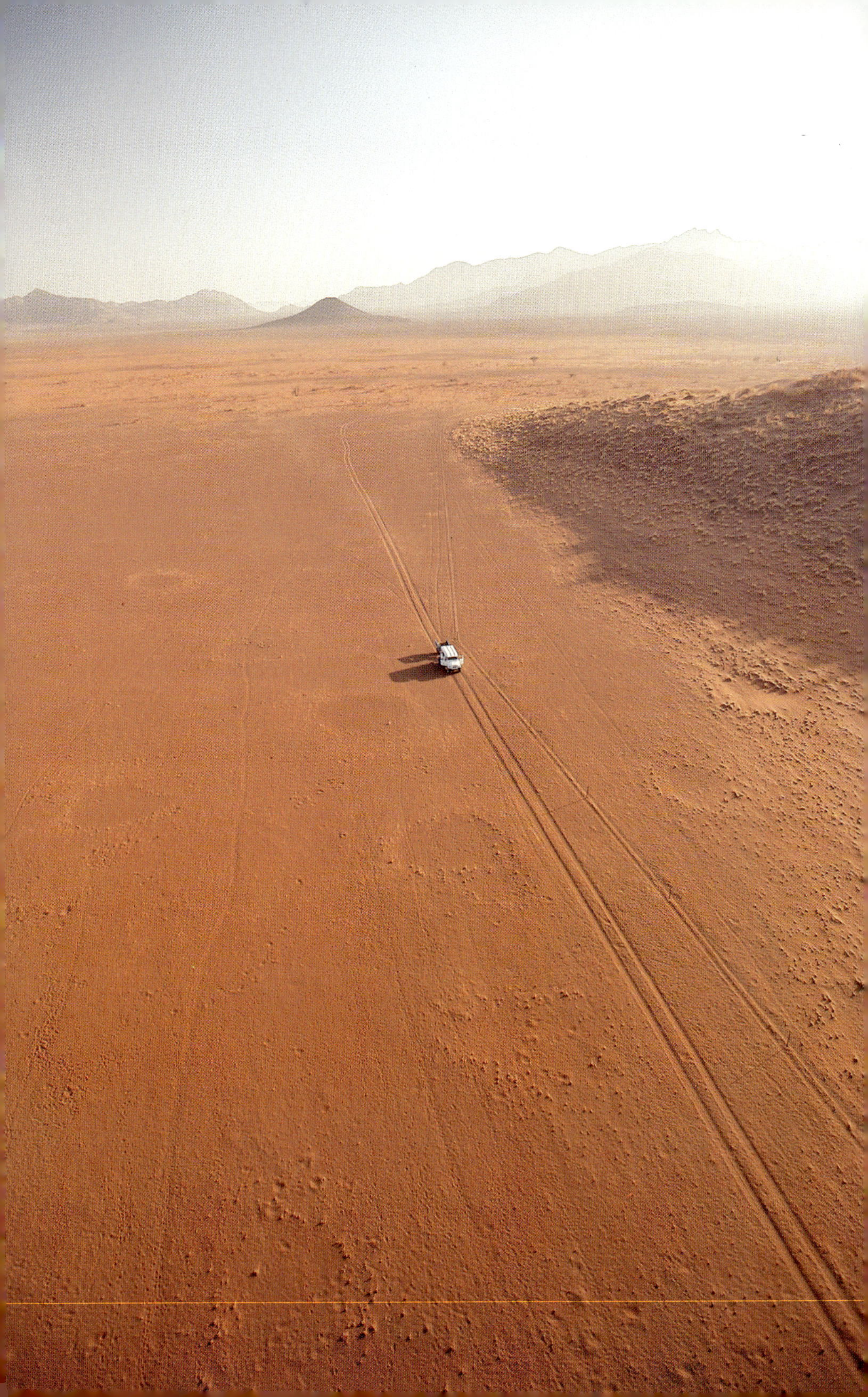

German, Afrikaans or English, and in many cases all three.

Sit for a few moments at a street cafe in the capital and you will notice an amazingly cosmopolitan crowd passing by. (See "Windhoek: City in the Sun", Part Three). Basters mix with Hereros in dazzling dresses and headdresses, along with Namibians of German and Dutch descent — a model of cultural symbiosis for Africa.

Many German and Afrikaaner Namibians have fascinating, epic family histories. It is not unusual to meet someone whose great-grandfather ventured there during the time of the diamond rush, discovered a fortune in the sand dunes, spent it, and eventually settled down to farm.

Strike up a conversation with anyone — white or black — and they talk with pride about how they are building their free country.

Most evident to visitors from other African or third world countries is the Namibian commitment to civic pride and public well-being. There can be few more orderly communities than those in Namibia where queue-jumpers, jaywalkers, and litter-louts provoke glares of disgust and contempt. Indeed, the urban centres are so meticulously clean and well-organised it is difficult to believe this is the 'developing world'.

The police and meter-maids are smart, disciplined, courteous, and always helpful to visitors in need of direction or advice.

Take note, however, that the head of state commands a great deal more respect than leaders in the west; an attitude inherent in most African cultures.

Nonetheless, although strongly conservative in attitudes, social habits, and dress, there remains a remarkable air of freedom and hope about this vibrant young nation.

Safety

While Namibia is essentially a land of innocence, peopled by law-abiding citizens, crime does exist. The country is far better policed, however, than most developing nations and visitors who observe sensible precautions will enjoy a trouble-free holiday.

Do not leave valuables in your car. But if you have no choice, store them out of sight, make sure the vehicle is locked and try to arrange for a security guard to watch it.

Walking at night in major centres is reasonably safe. But there have been instances of muggings, so it may be prudent to take a taxi.

Climate

Although much of the country lies north of the Tropic of Capricorn, the climate is typical of semi-desert country — hot days and cool nights.

Temperatures in midsummer may rise above 40°C. During the winter, days are agreeably warm, although temperatures often drop below freezing point just before dawn.

Along the high central plateau, temperatures are lower than in other inland regions, while along the coast the cold Benguela Current moderates the desert heat, inhibits rainfall and causes fog. Characteristic of the coastal desert during the southern autumn, winter and spring, are dense fogs which occur generally from late afternoon until mid-morning the following day.

The interior has two rainy seasons. The short rains fall between October and early December. The long rains — when fairly frequent thunderstorms occur — fall from mid-January until April. Dry and cloudless conditions mark the rest of the year. In all, the country enjoys an average of 300 days of sunshine a year.

When to go

The fine climate, with its generally dry conditions, permits visits throughout the year. It should be pointed out, however, that Ai-Ais Hot Springs in the Fish River Canyon is closed from November until

---

Opposite: Four-wheel drive vehicle in the almost trackless wastes of the Naukluft Mountains of the Namib-Naukluft National Park.

Below: World's end in the fastness of the great Namib Desert where, even so, farmers are guaranteed service.

Above: In Etosha National Park and the rich grasslands of the Caprivi Strip elephants have right of way.

mid-March. Okaukuejo, Namutoni, and Halali camps in the Etosha National Park are open throughout the year. Some resorts close for a few months.

Others, such as Swakopmund, are extremely busy over Christmas and Easter during the long school holidays, so be sure to book in advance.

The best time to visit the Namib is between May and September when the sun is less intense, although the nights are sometimes cold.

Windhoek is pleasant throughout the year, enjoying an average of 300 wonderful cloudless days.

Clothes

In most places the sun is blisteringly hot and the nights vary from cool to cold. For most of the year the standard safari outfit — tailored shirt or top jacket and trousers — is ideal for bush travel. Carry a hat to avoid sunstroke.

At other times, shorts, casuals and anything you require for sports and swimming should suffice, but bring along woollens for the evenings.

Women may find cotton dresses cooler and more comfortable than trousers, particularly for day time wear during the summer months. 'Baggy' trousers rather than skin-tight jeans are obviously better ventilated. For footwear, comfort should take precedence over style, as much of the terrain is rough.

Drip-dry clothing is ideal, although virtually all hotels have laundry services. Even so, if you plan going into the desert along dusty roads, you will need two or three changes of clothing.

What to take

Most essentials are made in South Africa and are available locally. However, if you are on specific drugs for prolonged periods, carry more than adequate dosages with you. The same applies if you require surgical supplies.

It is also worth taking a spare pair of spectacles or, failing that, at least a prescription that will enable you to obtain another pair.

Sunglasses, suntan lotion, hats and

Above: Off a rugged gravel road in the middle of nowhere, a comforting sign reassures lone travellers.

torches are available in the larger centres. But cameras are extremely expensive.

Health

Namibia is relatively free from tropical diseases, but if you plan on travel, especially to the northern wetlands, you should take precautions against malaria, bilharzia and sleeping sickness.

All visitors should take an antimalarial prophylactic, beginning two weeks before their arrival and continuing for six weeks after their departure.

Doctors recommend sensible precautions — it's better to be safe than sorry — against tetanus, polio, cholera, typhoid, and paratyphoid. A gamma globulin injection provides some protection against possible infection from hepatitis and is well worth it. That said, the incidence of these infections and diseases is low.

There are first-class hospitals in Windhoek and most major towns, as well as excellent dentists and opticians. Medical treatment, however, is expensive and it is wiser to take out medical insurance cover before departure.

There is no shortage of chemists or drugstores, all staffed by qualified pharmacists. Most drugs are available. Pharmacies are open during normal weekday shopping hours and also offer a night service in Windhoek .

Rivers and dams in the north might contain bilharzia, so avoid swimming and drinking from them. All swimming pools are maintained to adequate health standards and are perfectly safe to use.

Tap water in all urban areas, whether from reservoirs or boreholes, is purified and completely safe to drink.

Safari operators always carry sufficient supplies for bush travel but, if you are going into isolated areas alone, it is advisable to carry water purification apparatus or tablets.

There is some prostitution in Windhoek, but only those with a death-wish will ignore the widespread threat of AIDS.

Photography

Most varieties of colour and black and white film are readily available and reasonably priced in Windhoek and major

Above: Service crews check and refurbish Air Namibia's 747 at the airline's HQ at Windhoek International Airport.

centres. However, professionals may wish to bring their own supply from home.

Wherever you are buying film, be sure to check that it has been refrigerated or kept in a cool, shaded place. If it has been sitting on a shop shelf in the sun it may be useless.

Where to stay

An extremely wide range of accommodation is available to suit all tastes and pockets. You will find hotels, guest farms, lodges, campsites and caravan parks from the most expensive to the cheapest.

Camping

Namibia is ideal for those who enjoy the rugged, outdoor life. Many people claim that camping is the only way to enjoy the country, providing an inexpensive and delightful do-it-yourself holiday you will never forget. Most centres have caravan parks, campsites and rest camps. By far the best are in the Caprivi Strip and around Windhoek. It is advisable to book accommodation if you plan on staying in a rondavel or bungalow. Government-run sites can be booked at a central office in Windhoek. Others should be booked directly. (See Listings).

Camping on public land without permission is illegal, but farmers will sometimes allow you to stay if you ask permission.

You may only camp in specific areas in the national parks. Namibia's Directorate of Nature Conservation is manned by dedicated workers. Rangers patrol the country's wildlife parks and have extensive powers. Obey their rules. Wherever you camp, make sure you choose a spot to pitch your tent well before sundown. If possible, choose level ground with some shade. Avoid dried-up river beds: sudden storms may create flashfloods which might sweep you away, vehicle and all.

Where the climate is generally hot — in low country — pitch your tent with the largest windows facing the prevailing wind. Temperatures can become unbearable without adequate ventilation. Do not camp across or near game trails and waterholes. Animals can be dangerous as well as curious.

Ensure adequate control of camp fires.

Clear all dry grass and leaves and place any available stones around the fireplace.

On safari

Many view a safari as some kind of endurance test, highlighted by glimpses of stunning scenery, diverse people and herds of wild animals. You will enjoy your safari more if you scrutinise your itinerary with care and insist on having enough time in each place to enjoy it to the full. Be selective. If it means cutting down the distances you travel each day, do so.

Remember, too, that although some animals have grown used to human beings, they are still wild and should be regarded with caution. Do not feed monkeys or other primates — nor make excessive noise to attract their attention.

Do not leave the designated trails for that closer shot, and do not get out of your vehicle in the middle of the bush. Close all your windows and zips when you leave your room or tent.

Many tourists believe that success is related to the number of animals they check-off in the shortest possible time. But this is not the ideal way to enjoy the unprecedented opportunities for wildlife viewing in Namibia.

Instead, read up on wildlife to help you identify the smaller creatures and the birds. Then, if something catches your eye, spend time observing it and learning its habits and characteristics first-hand. In short, make the most of your safari.

Tell your guide that, despite the watch you wear, you are in no hurry. And remember the slower you drive, the more you see. A lioness crouched in the grass, tail swishing and eyes alert, may be looking for supper. Stop and wait. Before the hour is up you may well witness the unparalleled spectacle of her bringing down a gazelle.

Always keep you camera loaded and ready for use. You never quite know when the action's going to start. But do not stand or sit on top of the vehicle for a better view.

The best time to see wildlife is in the early morning and late afternoon.

National Anthem

Namibia land of the brave
Freedom fight we have won
Glory to their bravery
Whose blood waters our freedom

We give our love and loyalty
Together in unity
Contrasting beautiful Namibia
Namibia our country

Beloved land of savannahs
Hold high the banner of liberty

Chorus:
Namibia our country
Namibia motherland
We love thee.

Above: Namibian flag flutters against the background of Windhoek Airport's air traffic control centre.

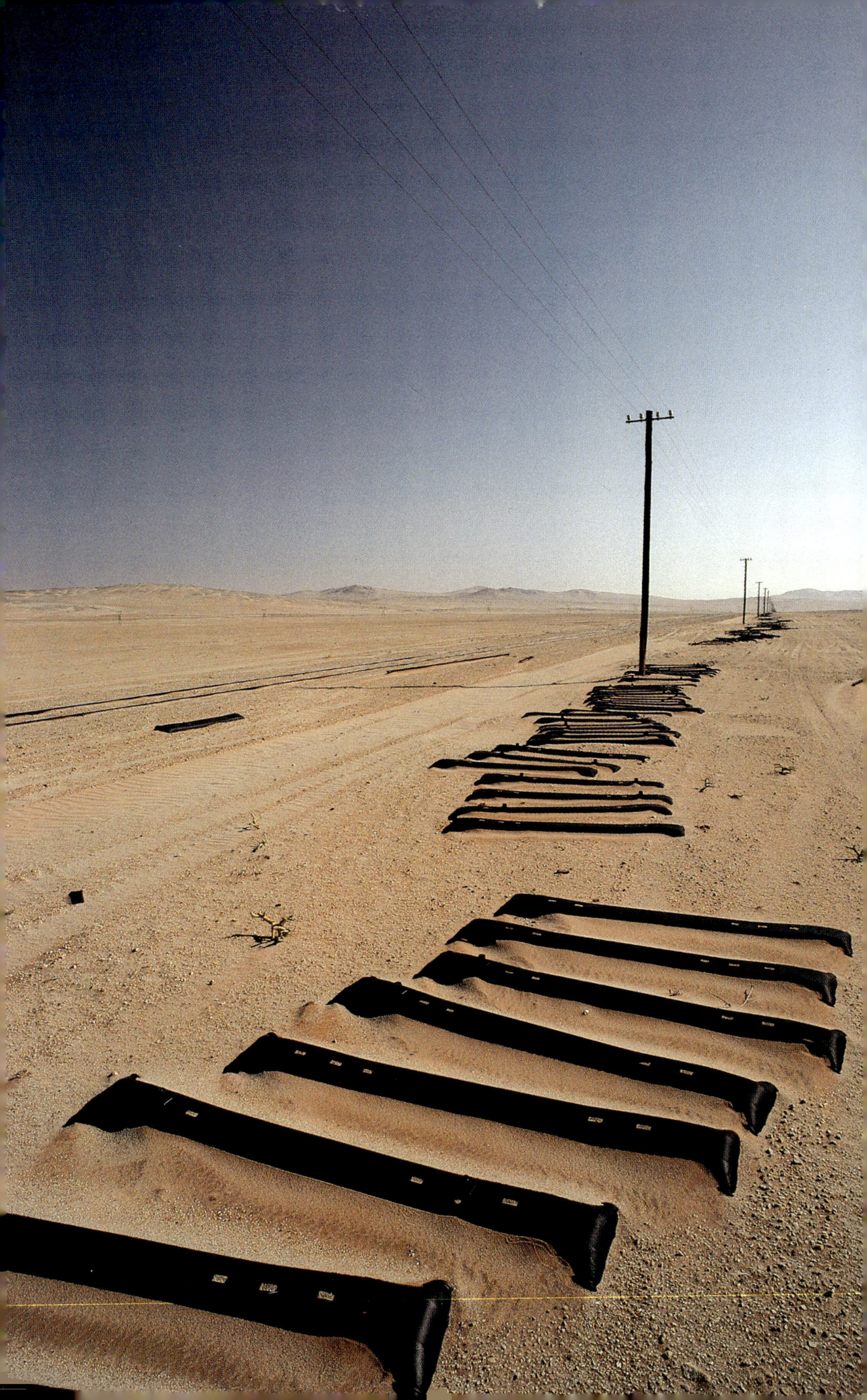

PART ONE: HISTORY, GEOGRAPHY, AND PEOPLE

Above: Scorched and barren Hunsberge Mountains of southern Namibia where the Fish River flows seasonally.

Opposite: Discarded iron sleepers line the track side where the Lüderitz to Keetmanshoop line runs its uninterrupted course across the Namib Desert.

Land of Lost Horizons

From the dawn of time, nature's hand has sculpted Namibia's extraordinary and unique landscapes. To journey across its endless horizons and over its arid lands is to experience contrast after scintillating contrast. Rugged yet fragile, barren but beautiful, haunting Namibia is a country of many faces — a land of legends and myths in a setting of stark magnificence that is home to some of the hardiest plants, creatures and people on earth.

Ancient records from the time of Herodotus indicate that the Phoenicians were the first explorers to circumnavigate the African continent. They were followed, around 600 BC, by a fleet despatched by the Egyptian Pharaoh, Necho II, who ordered his ships to sail along the continent's eastern seaboard.

Not until 2,000 years later did the Portuguese navigators and explorers set out in search of new lands and the sea route to the Indies. In the fifteenth century, King John II of Portugal sent two expeditions under Diego Cão to Africa. History records that the explorer anchored south of what is now Namibia's Skeleton Coast and stepped ashore to set up a stone cross on top of a rocky cape. The cross stood there for more than 400 years until the captain of a German vessel removed it late last century and took it to a museum in Berlin. About two years after Diego Cão left his landmark, Bartholomeo Diaz, another legendary Portuguese explorer, positioned a second cross in a bay he called *Angra dos Ilheos* 'Island Bay', later named *Angra Pequena* 'Narrow Bay', now Lüderitz Bay.

It is on the Namibian coast that the dunes of the great Namib Desert tumble into the icy Atlantic. Among the oldest deserts in the world, some eighty million years, the Namib seems denuded of life — scorched by the noonday sun, frozen by the chill night mists that billow in from the ocean, shutting out the frosty moon. Yet, astonishingly, life exists above and below its surface, as plants and creatures draw sustenance from the wind and moisture, from its misty phantoms. Such life, from tiny beetles to mighty elephants, has shaped itself to this harsh environment. Indeed, many species are found nowhere else in the world. Built by searing multi-directional winds, the highest dunes in the world — mountains of sand — run along the erosional trough of the Tsauchab River to a magical place called Sossusvlei.

East of the Namib stand remnants of the time before man walked these lands — dinosaur tracks and petrified forests, the greatest meteorite on Earth and ancient clay castles. These are among the plethora of natural marvels that adorn Namibia's endless plains.

From the tortured, eroded cliffs of the Fish River Canyon, second in size in Africa only to Ethiopia's Blue Nile Gorge, through Namibia's quaint, colonial-style towns, to the wildernesses of Etosha and the Caprivi Strip, Namibia's bright, brittle beauty is vast even by African standards. Yet, although its 824,268 square kilometres (318,250 square miles) is four times the size of Britain, its population numbers fewer than one-and-a-half million people, giving it one of the lowest population densities in the world with fewer than two people to each square kilometre. This remarkably low number may ensure that the changes that have ravaged much of Africa never affect this one of its newest republics.

Basking in summer temperatures that range from 10-33°C (50-82°F) between October and April and from 6-26°C (43-79°F) in winter between May and September, Namibia's unspoilt splendour makes it truly a land of the free for the free. A developing network of well-maintained tar, gravel and dirt roads allows visitors to reach the farthest corners of what has been called Africa's Gem — from the fallen glory of the Finger of God in the south to the majesty of the Okavango River and the rapids of the Popa Falls in the north; from the mystery of the White Lady of the Brandberg to the raw power of the Namib Desert; from the gigantic fossil woods of

Above: Millennia-old Bushman depictions of giraffe and other wildlife found in a treasury of prehistoric art at Twyfelfontein.

Opposite: Ancient Bushman painting with its highly stylised human figures.

Above: Turn-of-the-century archive picture of traditional Herero women's dress.

the Petrified Forest near Khorixas to the Hoba Meteorite near Grootfontein; from the abundant wildlife of that other Eden, the Etosha National Park, to the fascination of the Skeleton Coast.

And its people, every bit as unique and diverse, include Africa's oldest race, the San Bushmen, whose affinity to the trackless desert and savannahs where they live seems almost miraculous. One of their legends says: 'Now you come, now you go. When you come again you will never go.'

The many African tribes and European settlers live in a country of contrast and vibrant colour, bordered in the west, where the Namib-Naukluft National Park sprawls across more than 50,000 square kilometres (19,305 square miles), an area larger than Denmark, by the Atlantic. The southern border with South Africa is formed by the Orange River. In the north, much of the border between Namibia and Angola is made up of the Kunene and Okavango Rivers. And to the east lies the vast Kalahari Desert which sweeps into Botswana.

Many contemporary aspects of Namibia bear witness to the Victorian Age when the European powers carved up Africa between themselves. Even now, Herero women dress in Victorian fashions, while the charming buildings of both Swakopmund and Windhoek, the capital, reflect nineteenth-century convention and style. And these vestiges extend beyond costume or architecture to the national boundaries where two particular instances remain curious reminders of colonial days. The first is a narrow corridor of land, 482 kilometres (300 miles) long, extending as far as the Zambezi. The Caprivi Strip, also known as the Devil's Finger, was the outcome of the German Kaiser's ambition to join his western and eastern African empires together. The second anachronism, Walvis Bay — midway between the Kunene and Orange Rivers, annexed in 1878 to become part of Britain's Cape Colony — remained under South African jurisdiction until the beginning of 1994.

Namibia forms three distinct topographical regions — the Namib Desert, the central inland plateau's mountains and plains with, most magnificent of all, the Etosha National Park, and finally the

Above: Missionary August Kühlmann and his bride Elizabeth celebrate their Namibian wedding on 15 January 1903.

Kalahari Desert in the south-east reaches of the country. Now, in the first decade of freedom, Namibia's doors are open to all who wish to explore its many natural wonders and fascinating cultures.

History

Written in the granite of Namibia's mountains and the sand of its living deserts is a story of mystery and discovery. And the creation of a country of unique beauty where mankind's earliest ancestors first evolved.

The finding of a fossil anthropoid jawbone in the Otavi Mountains, near the spot where remains dating from fifteen to twelve million years ago had been uncovered, was yet another clue in the unfolding history of Namibia and mankind's evolution.

The fossil skull and backbone of another early man in the highlands to the north of the capital, Windhoek, shaded in more detail to the picture that is being drawn.

And there is extensive evidence, in the form of Stone Age tools and weapons found all over Namibia, including excavations in Windhoek, to show that early man hunted ancient elephant and other wild creatures in the area.

But Namibia has never yielded its secrets easily. Indeed, the hinterland, barricaded by the formidable depths of the Namib Desert all along the south-western seaboard of the continent, remained a secret until recent times.

The Phoenicians are reckoned to have been the first to circumnavigate the African continent. According to Herodotus, the Egyptian Pharaoh, Necho II, sent several ships down the east coast and up the west coast in 600 BC— an extraordinary voyage, since it took place more than 2,000 years before the Portuguese attempted to follow the same route.

Herodotus records that during the three-year journey they landed at various points, sometimes staying long enough to plant crops. Yet it is unlikely these seafarers ever set foot on the Namibian coast. Two thousand years later that honour fell to the Portuguese explorer, Diego Cão, who had been despatched by King John II of Portugal on the first European voyage of exploration down the west coast of Africa. A knight of the Portuguese court, Cão was a navigator of some repute.

The king's ultimate dream was to find the southernmost point of the continent and round it to open the sea route to the Indies.

With him, Cão carried two stone crosses, *padrãos* — one on each of his ships — hewn from the rock of Lisbon, to raise on newfound shores in the name of Portugal and Christendom.

For two years Cão travelled down the west coast, planting one cross at the mouth of the Congo and the second at *Cabo do Lobo* or Seal Cape, the present day *Cabo de Santa Maria*, north of Mossamedes in Angola. But there, out of food and fresh water, he turned back.

However, when Cão returned to Lisbon, King John ordered him to set out once more with two new ships, another pair of crosses, and the warning that this time there could be no failure — he must round Africa.

Once more the vessels set out. But the further south they went the more desolate, dry and inhospitable the landscape stretching along their port bow became.

In *Lords of the Last Frontier*, Lawrence Green quotes the nineteenth-century Swedish explorer and naturalist Charles John Andersson's search for the Kunene River:

"When a heavy sea-fog rests upon these uncouth and rugged surfaces — and it does so very often — a place fitter to represent the infernal regions could scarcely, in searching the world around, be found. A shudder, amounting almost to fear, came over me when its frightful desolation first suddenly broke upon my view. 'Death,' I exclaimed, 'would be preferable to banishment in such a country'."

Cão's hopes of reaching his goal had faded by the time he landed at a small rocky cape on the south-west coast of Africa. In despair he erected one of the crosses. The inscription on it read:

"In the year 6685 of the creation of the earth and 1485 after the birth of Christ the most excellent and most serene King Dom João II of Portugal ordered this land to be discovered and this padrão to be placed by Diego Cão, gentleman of his house."

Cão then reboarded his ship and set sail for home a broken man. Shortly afterwards, he died at sea.

Cão's cross stood atop the cape for almost 400 years, all the world unheeding of its existence until the middle of last century, when another explorer, Captain W Messum, spotted it while he was combing the coastline for guano deposits.

More than thirty years later, in 1879, Captain W B Warren in his cruiser, the *Swallow*, noticed the cross while looking for a place to land. Later, he returned with a German concession to hunt seals and work guano deposits between the mouths of the Ugab and the Omaruru Rivers.

And in 1893 the captain of the *Falke*, a German warship, found the cross which had by then tilted to one side. Realising its importance, the captain removed the cross and positioned a wooden replica in its place. Two years later this was replaced by a granite replica. In addition to the original Portuguese inscription, the Germans added the eagle of the Kaiser together with the inscription:

Erected by order of the German Kaiser and King of Prussia Wilhelm II in 1894 at the place of the original which has been weathered through the years.

Ironically, Cão's original cross had been taken aboard the *Falke* to Cape Town, the destination the Portuguese explorer had dreamed of reaching. From South Africa it was transported to Berlin where it was damaged during World War II bombings. Now restored, it is on display in a Berlin museum. (See "Skeleton Coast: Bleached Bones and Rusting Ships", Part Two).

Opposite top: Officer of the much-feared Schutztruppe which tightened Germany's imperial hold on Namibia.

Centre left: Germany's Theodor Leutwein in ceremonial dress.

Centre right: Missionary Carl Hugo Hahn.

Left: Adolf Lüderitz who vanished at sea shortly after he was ruined financially.

Right: 1890 portrait of Chief Maherero.

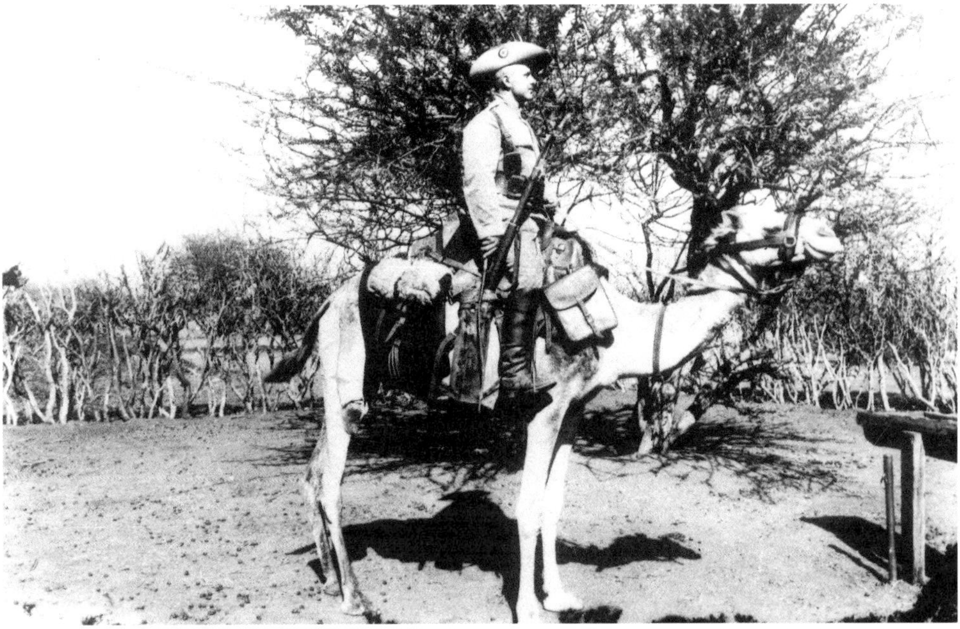
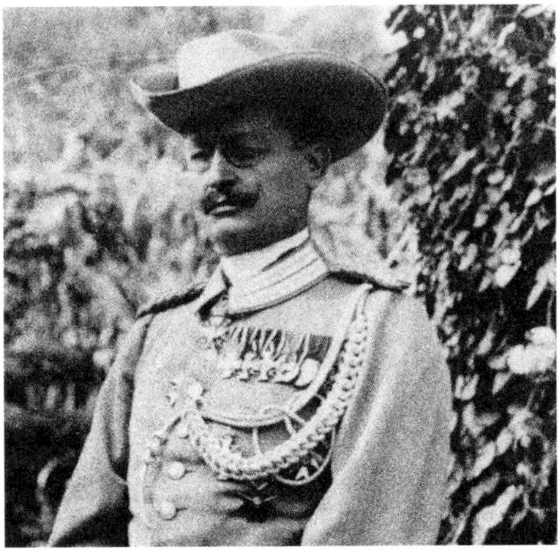
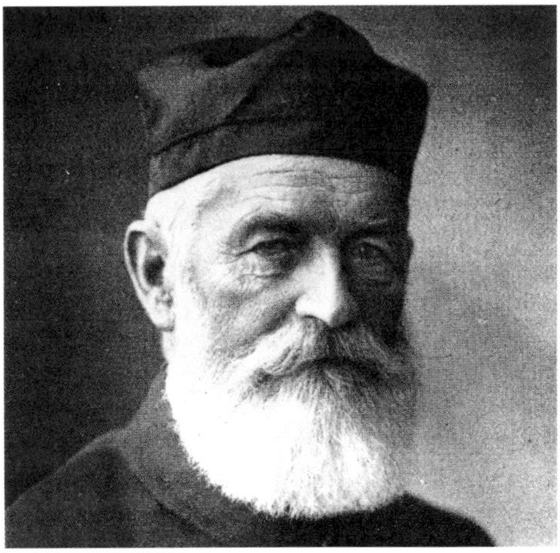
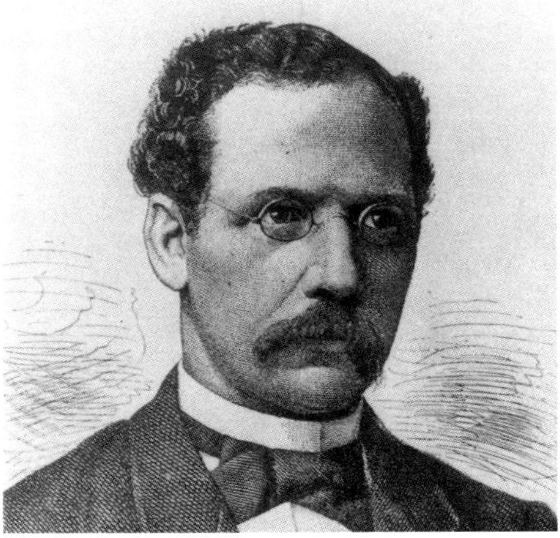
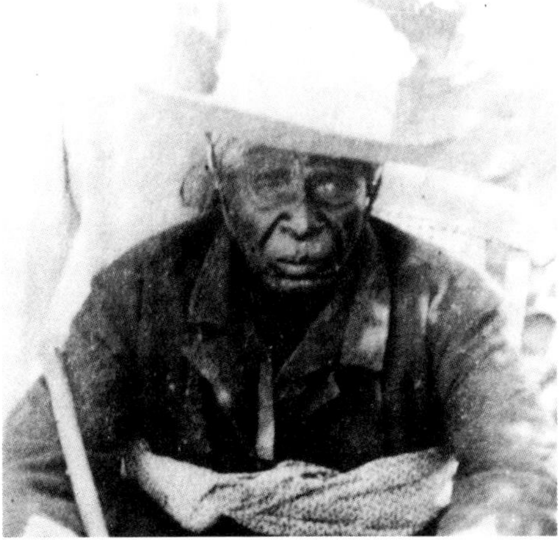

Above: Marble monument in the Old Location cemetery on the western outskirts of Windhoek honours the martyrs who gave their lives protesting the forced resettlement of Namibia's indigenous citizens to the black township of Katutura.

Early settlers

The first inhabitants of the vast wilderness of Namibia were the hunter-gatherers who migrated there in prehistoric times and moved about in groups of about fifty. The San, a semi-nomadic people who lived in caves and rock shelters in the north-central uplands and had highly organised extended families, decorated their caves with lively paintings, many of which may be seen today. Some of the rock paintings found in the Huns Mountains, that detail their nomadic lifestyles, were painted at a time that almost defies comprehension — 27,000 years ago. These peaceful people lived a placid, undisturbed existence for millennia. But when the San came into contact with the Nama pastoralists, descendants of the Khoikhoi of the Cape Province, who pushed northwards from their traditional lands in the Orange River region in the eighteenth century, they found themselves at war.

The Bergdama and the Wambo tribes also migrated into their land not long after the Nama. The Wambo, who journeyed from Central Africa, settled in the northern flatlands. Before long the Bantu-speaking Herero penetrated the Kaokoveld in the north-west, drifting into the midlands.

Finally, large numbers of the Oorlam tribe, themselves Nama who had closer contact with Western influences in the Cape, advanced into Namibia's heartlands under Jager Afrikaner, a military man of mixed loyalties.

He had aided the Cape Dutch government in its efforts to contain the San raiders of the colonial border areas, but later reverted to banditry. When a Dutch expedition was sent to curtail his activities, he retreated far beyond the Orange River.

Jager had a large following, all of whom he armed. But this extraordinary man had a sudden change of heart. He converted to Christianity and thereafter lived peacefully until his death in 1823.

The reformed brigand was succeeded by Jonker and Jan Jonker Afrikaner who played significant roles in the vicious rivalries of the nineteenth century.

Above: Bronze plaque marks grave of a German trooper who died in 1901 while imposing the Kaiser's will on the people of South West Africa.

Finally the Basters, a fiercely independent half-caste people, were the last of the pre-colonial immigrants. Driven north of the Orange in the 1860s by the Boers, the Basters settled in an area south of Windhoek, establishing a settlement called Rehoboth.

This competition for land, water and grazing rights brought troubled years in the middle of the nineteenth century and developed into open warfare. Although their battles were never conclusive, the Nama and the Herero fought each other mercilessly.

By the time the Europeans began their colonisation of Namibia, countless tribes and clans roamed its trackless wastes. It took many long and bloody years for them to retrieve their land and win independence.

Colonialism begins

It was in 1793 that the beginnings of the colonial power struggle began. The Dutch government of the Cape took Walvis Bay, Lüderitz Bay and other coastal areas under their protection to thwart foreign territorial and commercial competition.

Only two years later the British occupied the Cape of Good Hope and inherited the 'protectorates', though formal accession was delayed by almost a century. The

Above: Nama freedom fighter Hendrik Witbooi.

Above: Bell cast in Apolda, Germany, in 1909 now hangs in Windhoek's imposing Christuskirche.

offshore islands were annexed by the Crown in 1867 and Walvis Bay in 1878.

During the eighteenth and nineteenth centuries, a handful of cattlemen, prospectors, Boer trekkers and explorers started arriving, some searching for copper in the south. Among these, the elephant hunter Jacobus Coetse, who crossed the Orange in 1760, became the first European to travel from the Dutch Cape Colony in the south. Hendrik Hop followed, reaching the vicinity of present-day Keetmanshoop.

Later, Pieter Pienaar anchored in Walvis Bay and, following the course of the Swakop River, penetrated far inland. But it was the missionaries who launched the first organised moves into the vast interior. The earliest of these brave evangelists were Abraham and Christian Albrecht, who lived among the Nama.

Meanwhile, in 1815, Heinrich Schmelen founded the Bethanien mission station, establishing a German evangelical presence that prepared the ground for the arrival of the Rhenish Mission Society in 1842. He later took a Nama bride and set her to work translating the Bible into the Nama language. Before the decade was out, these newcomers were teaching and preaching to Jan Jonker Afrikaner's people around Windhoek, Rehoboth, Walvis Bay, and Otjimbingwe on the Swakop River.

Later, more centres were established, most successfully among the Nama, whose cultural origins lay in the Calvinism of the Dutch-ruled Cape. The Hereros, always intensely independent and extremely proud of their traditions, fiercely resisted Christian indoctrination. Lutheran pastors of the Finnish Missionary Society settled among the Wambo in 1870.

But the tribal wars brought widespread havoc, prompting repeated requests for British intervention — mainly from German missionaries, traders and the German government, who felt responsible for their subjects' welfare. The calls were routinely rejected by the British until 1876, when the Cape authorities signed various treaties with local leaders, extending the Cape colonial administration's authority beyond the Orange River.

None of the Cape's efforts brought any degree of stability to the land — there was

Above: Cross erected by order of Kaiser Wilhelm II and a replica of Diego Cão's original on the headland at Cape Cross.

far too much inter-tribal rivalry. And the British had no intention of becoming embroiled in tribal quarrels. Besides, Cape politicians were preoccupied with troubles elsewhere on the subcontinent.

Thus it was that the German Chancellor, von Bismarck, grasped the initiative when Adolf Lüderitz, a Hamburg trader, petitioned the German government for protection. By 1884, they had annexed the entire territory, although the Walvis Bay enclave and offshore islands were retained by Britain.

It was the formal birth of German South West Africa — and the start of a reign of terror and genocide — but most native Namibians had no idea that their country had just come under the German wing.

Early uprising

For the first years the formal administration in Windhoek constituted little more than an Imperial Commissioner, secretary and minor officials. Outside the capital, which was based at first in Otjimbingwe, the wild interior was mainly unknown.

But before long, Germany saw that keeping civil order in a territory at war with itself for more than half a century needed more expertise and greater resources.

In 1889, Captain Curt von Francois set out from Walvis Bay with twenty-three men to restore peace to the countryside. It was a massive task, and in May 1894 the imperial *Schutztruppe* arrived as reinforcements. These crack troops built stone forts across the territory — many of them are still visible — to assert control over South West Africa. Their arrival spurred the growth of colonial communities, and traders and merchant companies started to reap healthy profits. From 1892, white farmers had been moving further and further into the grasslands to settle. Now roads were built and railways followed as the economy prospered.

The country began to take shape. Indeed, in the late 1890s the Portuguese, British and Germans drew a Namibian border — all without consulting the local people. In particular, the Herero and Nama resented Germans taking their land, eroding age-old

HULLE
NAAM
LEEF
TOT IN
EWIGHEID

1914–18

1939

Above: Imperial Eagle of Kaiser Wilhelm II on the stained glass windows the German monarch donated to Lüderitz's Felsenkirche — Evangelical Lutheran Church — which was consecrated in 1912.

rights to common pastures and water resources, and introducing foreign laws and taxation.

Thus, near the end of 1903, under the banner of Hendrik Witbooi, the Nama rebelled. The bulk of the *Schutztruppe* marched south where their most formidable foe was Jacob Morenga. Like his descendants who fought South African forces half-a-century later, he used guerilla tactics. Hit-and-run became the only means of engaging such an organised army as the Germans.

Records from that time report: "The Nama warriors showed unbelievable stamina and mobility, decided skill in the use of the terrain in guerrilla warfare, and last but not least, great personal courage."

Months later, having been relieved of their German watchdogs, the Herero took up arms and began what is undoubtedly the most horrific chapter in Namibia's history.

On 2 October 1904, the German commander, General von Trotha, issued the following proclamation:

"I, the great general of the German troops, send this letter to the Herero people. Hereros are no longer German subjects . . . All the Hereros must leave the land. If the people do not want this, then I will force them to do it with the great guns. Any Herero found within the German borders with or without a gun, with or without cattle, will be shot. I shall no longer receive any women or children; I will drive them back to their people. I will shoot them. This is my decision for the Herero people."

The General, determined to wipe out resistance, did exactly what he had threatened, resorting to genocide by poisoning waterholes and indiscriminate machine gunning.

German losses were insignificant compared with the suffering of the Herero. During eighty-eight bloody clashes, much

Opposite: Memorial to the fallen soldiers of two world wars in Windhoek.

Above: Memorial to those who fell in the 1916 Owambo Campaign stands in a pleasant garden near Windhoek railway station.

of the Herero nation was exterminated. Between 1905 and 1907, thousands of Hereros died from starvation and thirst in the barren desert wastes of the Kalahari. More perished when the survivors were rounded up into concentration camps. Eventually, the remnants were 'resettled' in the inhospitable sandveld region of present-day Hereroland. Soon after — as if the German administration had not done enough — new laws deprived Africans of the right to own land or cattle.

Diamond rush

As early as the 1860s prospectors suspected the existence of large diamond deposits in the Namib Desert. One Cape Town enterprise won a concession from a local chief to explore a large strip north of the Orange River, but without success.

Four decades later, when Zacharias Lewala, a labourer, was shovelling drifting sand from the railway line at Grasplatz, he spotted a small speck glittering in the sand. Lewala reached down and picked up a diamond.

As prospectors converged on the area, the railway siding became a boom town. Within months, thousands of acres were staked out with mining claims.

The secretary of South Africa's giant De Beers conglomerate, claiming that the reports were 'greatly over-exaggerated', predicted the field would yield no more than 1.5 million carats. But within twelve years Namibia accounted for twenty per cent of Africa's entire diamond production.

As more diamond deposits were found along the Namib Desert coastline, the authorities declared it 'forbidden territory', *Sperrgebiet*, and awarded the sole prospecting rights to the *Deutsche Diamanten Gesellschaft*.

Enter South Africa

During the Great War of 1914-18, South West Africa was the first German dominion taken by the western Allies. But victory was delayed until General Louis Botha, Prime Minister of the Union of South Africa, and General Jan Smuts, had quashed a full-scale Boer rebellion in South Africa.

Finally, in February 1915, Botha landed in Swakopmund with a 12,000-man army, while Smut's 6,000 troops took Lüderitz Bay as another force moved north from the Orange River region.

Vastly outnumbered, the *Schutztruppe* put up little resistance, laying mines and poisoning wells as they retreated. In fact, the South Africans' main enemies were the desert heat and hostile terrain.

By July 1915, the campaign had come to a swift and successful conclusion. In the wake of the decisive victory an interim military administration was quickly installed.

Under the 1919 Treaty of Versailles the Germans renounced all rights to their colonial possessions leaving the Allies to set up suitable administrations.

In December 1920, the League of Nations entrusted South West Africa to the Union of South Africa as a mandated territory subject to certain guarantees. The accord, signed in Geneva, gave South Africa power to administer Namibia as an integral part of its own territory. But the guarantees played a crucial role in helping the country gain its independence in 1990.

Firstly, South Africa was prohibited from establishing military bases in Namibia or conscripting the people for military service. Secondly, they were instructed to nurture the economic and social advancement of the native people. But the League made one significant omission — no indication was given as to when or whether Namibia should advance to self-government. Under the new order, German officials, soldiers and police left, but at least half the German population chose to remain. Also in 1920, five years after South African forces occupied German South West Africa, Consolidated Diamond Mines (CDM) bought the diamond concession.

Although native Namibians were excluded from the democratic process, the population recovered some livestock and demanded the return of their lands. Like Germany, however, Pretoria regarded its new territory as a colony, ripe for the settlement of white farmers. Loans and other incentives were made available and immigration from South Africa was encouraged.

Settlers streamed in and were given huge farms on the rich grazing lands of the central plateau. The new administration, following the model being established in South Africa, intensified efforts to force Africans into small and infertile reserves. The Herero were allocated stretches of semi-desert in the east — the same area in which thousands had died during the retreat from the Germans years before.

Little if any economic development took place in these reserves while more money was spent on settling Afrikaaners. Apartheid — segregation — was enforced in urban areas with Africans forced to live in crude ghettos on the outskirts of towns.

While denigrating German colonialism as barbaric, the South African administration continued most of the old policies and invented new, inhuman ones. Africans were forbidden to own land, while livestock ownership was limited by law and restricted by grazing fees.

Soon, curfews were imposed in urban areas and under a new Masters and Servants law, Europeans could inflict corporal punishment on servants simply for trying to desert — or for disobedience. In the same year, a new vagrancy law allowed the authorities to imprison or fine Africans in unofficial employment or housing.

To increase the supply of migrant labour from the populous regions north of the new Police Zone, the South Africans bullied chiefs and kings to cooperate in recruitment. Those who did not comply were simply removed. Missionaries were now required to urge 'all natives under their influence to seek employment'.

Resistance to South African colonialism grew in the south. When the Bondelswarts, who had been confined to a small arid reserve and had been reduced to virtual starvation by taxes and stock controls, defied the arrest of their leaders, South Africa responded by bombing and machine-gunning their defensive positions indiscriminately, killing more than 100 men, women and children.

In 1924 the army was mobilised against the people of the Rehoboth community, who had negotiated limited self-government for a small republic they had established in central Namibia before German colonisation. In response to Rehoboth agitation for full independence, their 'capital' was surrounded. More than 600 Rehobothers, together with Herero and Nama supporters, were arrested, and the Rehoboth Council stripped of its powers.

The continuing resistance of African communities was paralleled by the formation of the first African nationalist organisations and trade unions. In the 1920s hundreds joined branches of the Universal

Negro Improvement Association of Marcus Garvey in Windhoek and Lüderitz.

The South African based Industrial and Commercial Workers Union — ICU — the first mass nonracial trade union, took root in Lüderitz. Meanwhile contract workers from the north formed benefit societies that laid the foundation for future workers' organisations. However, none of them brought much relief from oppression and exploitation.

By 1926 the white population had almost doubled and nearly 1,000 farms covering a large part of the country had been established. The average European farm covered 150 square kilometres (60 square miles) of once indigenous pastures. In 1932, the South African authorities intervened militarily in the north, overthrowing Chief Ipumbu of the Ukuambi. Eleven years later, in 1943, the white legislature was pressing for the territory to be annexed by South Africa.

At the end of the Second World War, when the United Nations was established, General Jan Christian Smuts, the South African Prime Minister, also argued that Namibia should be incorporated into South Africa. But in rejecting the demand, the UN told South Africa to place Namibia under trusteeship, as with other mandated territories.

For fourteen years, however, Pretoria resisted all pressure from the UN to administer Namibia in terms of its mandate, even after the International Court of Justice — ICJ — ruled that it should.

From 1948 the National Party government was more defiant than Smuts, refusing to provide the UN with annual reports on its administration and giving white settlers the right to elect MPs to the South African parliament.

Segregation and discrimination inside Namibia were intensified by the efforts of the National Party government to extend the South African apartheid system.

Meanwhile, in messages to the UN detailing the oppressive conditions, African leaders demanded the country's independence, or pleaded for it to be placed under international control.

Namibians opposed to South African rule were prevented from leaving the territory, and Michael Scott, a clergyman serving in South Africa, was dispatched to petition the UN.

Finally, in the 1950s, Namibian representatives spoke to the UN for the first time in messages smuggled out of the country. And in 1960 the UN received a total of 120 messages and petitions — clear indication of the rising resentment against the South Africans.

The Movement Begins

Traditional leaders such as Hosea Kutako and David Witbooi, grandson of Hendrik Witbooi, played an important part in linking new struggles with earlier resistance, but increasingly the initiative passed to political or educational associations, the churches and organisations representing workers.

Even within the church the call was for independence from overseas influence. In the 1950s, after a series of mass defections and strong pressure, the Rhenish Mission was transformed into the independent Evangelical Lutheran Church, while the other main church, the Finnish Mission Society, became the Evangelical Lutheran Church of Namibia. From this point the churches made an important contribution to the liberation struggle, while the African Improvement Society's adult education branches in major towns were another significant factor.

Namibians studying in South Africa established links with South African organisations, particularly the African National Congress — ANC. And in 1959, on their return to Namibia, some former students formed the South West African National Union — SWANU.

With such a base among the African intelligentsia, SWANU articulated the case for Namibian independence in the late 1950s and early 1960s and gained much support. It was, however, unable to make the transition into a national movement and stood aside from the armed struggle that now developed.

The most significant role in forming a national liberation front was played by the workers. From the early 1950s, Lüderitz

Above: Proud symbols of free Namibia on display in Windhoek's Alte Feste Museum.

had become a centre of trade union activity mainly through the South African Food and Canning Workers Union — but it was suppressed violently by the police.

In December 1959, South Africa outraged the entire country when police in Windhoek opened fire without warning on a demonstration led by women, killing thirteen and injuring fifty-two. Known as the Windhoek massacre and commemorated each year by Namibian Women's Day, the demonstration had started as a peaceful protest against the resettlement of blacks in a new segregated township, Katutura. The massacre intensified the freedom movement, giving it a new urgency. Police reaction was such, however, that the national leadership was forced underground or into exile.

In April 1960, the Owambo People's Organisation — OPO — changed its name to the South West Africa People's Organization — SWAPO. At that time it was a non-violent pressure group led by Andimba Herman Toivo ja Toivo and Shafiishuna Samuel Nujoma, the man destined to become first President of

Above: Bronze logo of the colonial government of German South West Africa in Windhoek's Alte Feste Museum.

REICHSPOST
50 PF
DEUTSCH-SÜDWESTAFRIKA
20 PFENNIG 20
Zuidwest Afrika 1d
South West Afrika 1d
S.W.A. £1
SUIDWES AFRIKA
POSSEEL · INKOMSTE 1d
SOUTH WEST AFRICA
POSTAGE · REVENUE 1d
SUIDAFRIKA Suidwes Afrika 1/ POSSEEL
SOUTH AFRICA South West Africa 1/ POSTAGE
1910 1935 SUIDWES-AFRIKA SOUTH WEST AFRICA 3d POSSEEL - POSTAGE 3d
1937 SUIDWES-AFRIKA POSSEEL 4d
1937 SOUTH WEST AFRICA POSTAGE 4d
SUIDWES-AFRIKA 1/- SOUTH WEST AFRICA
SOUTH AFRICA S.W.A. 1/ POSTAGE
SUIDAFRIKA S.W.A. 1/ POSSEEL
South West Africa 1/3 POSTAGE 1/3
Suidwes-Afrika 1/3 POSSEEL 1/3
SUIDWES-AFRIKA 5/- SOUTH WEST AFRICA
SUIDWES-AFRIKA 1c SOUTH WEST AFRICA
3D SWA SUID-AFRIKA 1947
3D SWA SOUTH AFRICA 1947
SWA 9c
SOUTH AFRICA SWA 1652-1952 4½d SUID-AFRIKA
SUIDWES AFRIKA SOUTH WEST AFRICA
12½c SUIDWES-AFRIKA · SOUTH WEST AFRICA
SWA R1
SWA 10c SCHWERINSBURG
SWA R2
SWA 15c
Namib SWA 20c
SWA 10c WOERMANNHAUS 1977
SWA 20c
SWA 5c VISRIVIERCANYON
SWA 6c Herero
HARDAP SWA 20c
SWA 11c
SWA 50c
SWA 60c Vote for your future Stem vir u toekoms
SWA
45c NAMIBIA
NAMIBIA 25c BARCELONA OLYMPIC GAMES
NAMIBIA INDEPENDENCE 21 MARCH 1990 18c
SPITZKUPPE SWA 25c

Namibia. But not for another thirty years.

Born in Orandjera, Owambo, in 1929, Nujoma was educated at the Finnish mission school there, and at St Barnabas School in Windhoek. As a young man he worked for the South African Railways in Cape Town, where he met and befriended Toivo ja Toivo.

Shortly after, he was dismissed for his trade-union activities and returned to Windhoek to help organise the protest against the forced settlement of the city's African population which ended in massacre.

Under Nujoma, SWAPO set itself the task of uniting Namibians to achieve independence, and a society free from apartheid, discrimination and the migrant labour system. It was a formidable task. The Windhoek massacre and the repressive, intransigent attitude of the South Africans left the SWAPO leadership with few illusions about the likelihood of peaceful independence.

War ahead

Namibian freedom fighters were initially supported by fellow Africans, the African National Congress — ANC — of South Africa and Chief Tshekedi of Botswana. In 1960, Liberia and Ethiopia took South Africa to the International Court of Justice, charging Pretoria with failure to meet its mandate obligations in Namibia. It was not enough.

In 1961 the SWAPO congress in Windhoek endorsed contingency plans for a military struggle. During the next few years, hundreds of SWAPO supporters secretly left the territory to establish military training facilities and prepare for independence.

Meanwhile Nujoma, sponsored by Ghana's Kwame Nkrumah, appeared before the UN's Committee on South West Africa in New York. There, he and Mburumba Kerina organised the reconstitution of SWAPO. Kerina became chairman, Nujoma president.

The first cadres of SWAPO freedom fighters trained in Egypt between 1962 and 1964 before returning to the Caprivi Strip to set up rural bases.

In 1966, after six long years of argument, the ICJ concluded that Ethiopia and Liberia had no legal basis to bring the case of Namibia before them and declined to rule on the issue.

But strengthened in its opposition to colonialism by the new membership of dozens of African and Asian states, the UN General Assembly responded swiftly to the ICJ's prevarication. It terminated South Africa's mandate because South Africa had imposed apartheid and repressed the people. Ordering South Africa out of the territory, it placed Namibia under direct UN responsibility until such time as independence could be achieved.

But South Africa defied the world body, and the exiled SWAPO leadership called on Namibians 'to rise in arms and bring about our own liberation'. The onset of the armed struggle, although foreseen by SWAPO, had a profound effect on the young movement. Many were detained, or imprisoned, while others were driven into exile.

Armed struggle

The first clash between SWAPO freedom fighters and South African forces took place on 26 August 1966, when the police attacked a guerilla base at Ongulumbashe in Owambo. Later that year, guerillas sabotaged government installations and began attacking police patrols.

But guerilla activity was generally restricted to the rainy season when movement was safer and easier, so initially the struggle was low-key.

Freedom fighters were regarded as 'armed political militants' who carried out political organising work as well as military operations. But they were integrated into the local population.

Security forces, however, were swift to carry out reprisals against people suspected

Opposite: Colourful stamps mark the turbulent history of Namibia from the moment it was first colonised as South West Africa.

of supporting guerillas, and SWAPO was largely driven underground, although still not banned. At the end of 1969, the movement regrouped at a conference at Tanga in Tanzania, attended by delegates from inside and outside Namibia.

A Youth League and a Women's Council were formed and an Elders' Council was establised to link traditional leaders with the modern liberation struggle. But, most importantly, the military wing was restructured and renamed the People's Liberation Army of Namibia — PLAN.

The same year, the UN Security Council affirmed the termination of South Africa's mandate and demanded its withdrawal from Namibia. In June 1971, confirming the UN's direct responsibility for Namibia, the ICJ also declared that South Africa's presence was illegal and ordered it to end its occupation. The ICJ added that UN member states should refrain from any acts which would imply recognition of South Africa's administration or presence in Namibia.

Predictably, South Africa rejected the court's opinion; within Namibia the decision precipitated mass resistance, leading to a general strike at the end of 1971 which brought most mines, the railways, and fishing and construction industries in Walvis Bay and Windhoek to a standstill. Strike leaders were prosecuted and a state of emergency was declared in the north.

Striking contract workers, especially Wambo, returned to their homes in the north where they united with local people in order to resist police attacks and repression by officials who had been given greater powers by the South African authorities. In the months that followed the struggle became more intense and generalised.

The struggle intensifies

Early in 1972, the UN Security Council requested the Secretary-General, Kurt Waldheim, to 'enable the people of Namibia to exercise their right to self-determination and independence'. But Waldheim made little progress.

Frustrated by this failure, SWAPO warned that continued mediation would be disastrous and could only sustain a South African presence in the country.

The UN sent a special envoy to tell Pretoria that there had to be unequivocal clarification of South Africa's policy of independence for the people of Namibia and an end to all discrimination.

South Africa's counter proposal to establish an 'advisory council' with representatives from regional governments and authorities was immediately rejected by the National Convention of Non-Whites, a coalition of nine African political organisations including SWAPO.

Increasingly weary of South Africa's attempts to buy time, the UN Security Council gave up hope of 'meaningful talks' with South Africa.

Now South Africa intensified its dictatorship. In January 1972, South African defence force troops imposed martial law in Owambo, thus escalating the liberation movement. The next year, the South African government tried to foist 'self-governing' status on the Wambo and Kavango to undercut UN demands for independence for the territory as a whole. Organising support from contract workers in the south, and in the townships themselves, SWAPO — especially its Youth League — led a boycott of the elections.

Despite the imposition of a state of emergency, mass detentions, the suppression of SWAPO meetings and the deployment of thousands of police and troops, the boycott was an overwhelming success in Owambo.

Afterwards, SWAPO leaders and supporters were rounded up and publicly flogged. Youth League members were detained, tried and imprisoned. There were political demonstrations, and protests against the South African occupation and its system throughout Namibia.

As new recruits strengthened SWAPO's military force, South Africa dispatched large numbers of conscripts to contain the uprising. But in December 1973 the UN acknowledged SWAPO as the 'authentic representatives of the people of Namibia'.

From mid-1974, the South African regime modified its strategy, attempting to build opposition to SWAPO by establishing a pseudo-independent adminstration. New elections were held in Owambo after thousands of troop reinforcements were sent in.

Leaders and representatives of political organisations participating in apartheid structures were selected to represent each of the twelve groups into which the Namibian people had been divided in what became known as the Turnhalle Conference. SWAPO organised rallies and united with other political organisations to oppose the South African scheme.

But when the Portuguese government in neighbouring Angola collapsed during l974-75, South Africa was faced with an entirely new set of circumstances, which meant positioning SADF units along the entire Namibian border with Angola and Zambia — an extensive area to guard.

Extreme pressure was also placed on the Wambo tribal authorities and the other northern administrators for their immediate participation in the 'fight against terrorism'. Meanwhile, in Owambo, 'tribal police' were forcibly trained to use firearms.

The Portuguese colonial collapse, however, created conditions which meant that SWAPO could transform the popular uprising of the early 1970s into a military offensive.

It opened the whole of Namibia's northern border to PLAN. Now the guerillas, whose bases inside Namibia had been raided by South African forces, had a haven from which to operate.

Despite the SADF operations in Angola, PLAN began large-scale operations in Kavango and Owambo. Tens of thousands of South African troops occupied northern Nambia, but PLAN retained the military initiative. They mined patrol roads, laid ambushes and attacked military bases.

South Africa responded with force, and thousands of Namibians fled to Angola, Botswana and Zambia to seek protection from SWAPO or to join PLAN. To cater for the needs of tens of thousands of exiles, schools, health centres and agricultural projects were set up by SWAPO.

The UN Security Council then set May 1975 as the deadline for South Africa to announce its withdrawal from Namibia. But Pretoria stated emphatically that it was not intent on withdrawing, although it conceded that the territory did have separate international status.

Meanwhile, in the latter part of 1975, South Africa launched military offensives into southern Angola, squeezing SWAPO and PLAN units between their columns in a classic pincer movement.

SWAPO and PLAN were rapidly joined and aided by the *Movimento Popular de Libertacao de Angola* — MPLA. As the military balance turned, South Africa had no option but to announce its withdrawal from southern Angola. And while the Nambian resistance had won a decisive victory, more importantly, the South Africans had been outflanked.

The South African attack on southern Angola was a direct violation of the UN mandate, which clearly forbade South Africa from using Namibia as a military base, making its position with the UN more vulnerable — to the delight of SWAPO.

Soon, the MPLA was recognised as the legal government of Angola and SWAPO was allowed to establish military bases along the border. South Africa's attempts to crush the resistance before it could gain firm ground in Angola brought further disaster both domestically and internationally.

In the next twelve months the number of guerilla attacks and 'contracts' reported by the SADF was more than three times that of the previous ten years. And in May 1976, SWAPO organised a national conference at Walvis Bay, which reaffirmed the unity of the internal and external leadership and stated the principles on which the movement would negotiate with the South African regime.

The movement's drive to national unity was also considerably strengthened when several traditional leaders and political groups in the south and central areas of the country formally joined SWAPO. Among them was Pastor Hendrik Witbooi, grandson of Hendrik Witbooi, who had led the campaign against the Germans. Thus the political mobilisation which had earlier taken place in the north now occurred in the south and central areas. Students

Above: Joyous proclamation of freedom after a liberation struggle lasting more than a century.

Above: Old Namibian soldier celebrates the birth of free Namibia.

boycotted South African schools, workers were organised in the NUNW, and SWAPO's Youth League and Women's Council gained wide popular support.

But hundreds were arrested for resisting the South African police. Many were detained, others flogged. Not surprisingly, by December 1976, over 5,000 Namibians were officially reported to have fled to neighbouring Angola.

In September 1977, when South Africa established the post of Administrator-General in Windhoek, his role was announced as supervisor of a South African-controlled election. To lend credibility to this move, and avert international criticism, some Namibian laws, including the 'pass' laws, were revoked. But to the international community it was nothing more than an endeavour to delay independence, and SWAPO instantly launched a campaign to defy Pretoria's plans.

The government responded to this failure by greatly enlarging its counter-insurgency forces. There followed a massive mobilisation with an estimated

45,000 troops pouring into northern Namibia during 1977 alone.

In November 1977, South Africa imposed the Democratic Turnhalle Alliance — DTA — on Namibia, under the leadership of Dirk Mudge. It was composed of several narrowly-based ethnic parties.

Backed by the army, the police and most businesses, the DTA received substantial funding. Pensions, jobs and other facilities were made dependent on DTA membership, and armed bands of DTA supporters were transported to different parts of the country to intimidate opponents.

Although open organisation was no longer possible, the liberation movement was able to build popular resistance.

Throughout Namibia, people openly defied the authorities, while organisations representing workers, students, women and local communities grew in strength. SWAPO organised mass rallies in various centres, but many of these were banned or broken up by DTA supporters.

Contract workers in Windhoek staged a one-day strike to protest against DTA-brokered violence. SWAPO leaders at national, regional and branch level were detained.

Following the assassination in March 1978 of Chief Clemens Kapuuo, leader of the Herero and a prominent member of the DTA, wide emergency powers were assumed by the Administrator-General and a number of prominent SWAPO supporters were detained without trial.

April 1978 saw South Africa consider outline plans for a UN-supervised election of a Namibian constituent assembly which would draft a constitution in preparation for independence — all by the end of 1978.

The South Africans, however, insisted on one proviso — that South African troops should remain in the country pending a complete cessation of hostilities by SWAPO.

Despite this apparently positive diplomatic move, South African forces raided a SWAPO refugee camp in May, killing many Namibians. Yet SWAPO decided to continue negotiating the western plan which had been accepted by South Africa in April. Adopted as Security

Below: Founding father of Namibia, President Sam Nujoma.

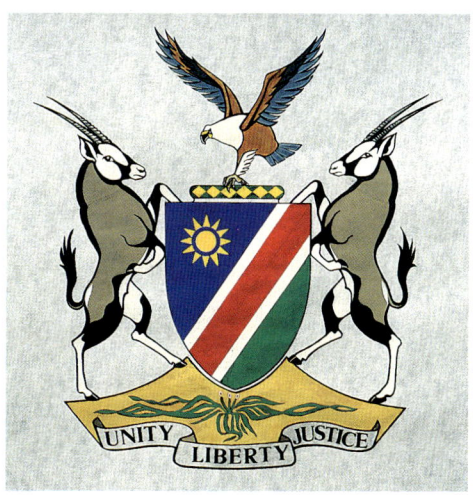

Above: Coat of Arms of Namibia.

Council Resolution 435 in September 1978, it provided for cessation of hostilities, the withdrawal of South African troops and the holding of free elections to be overseen by the United Nations Transition Assistance Group — UNTAG.

But in a complete turn-around, South Africa suddenly withdrew its support and said that it would implement its own internal settlement by staging December elections for a Namibian constituent assembly. Five parties contested seats while SWAPO and the Namibian National Front staged a boycott. Although the DTA won forty-one of the fifty seats in the assembly, the west considered the elections invalid. Dozens of cases of bribery, fraud and intimidation were recorded by the Namibian churches, who acted as self-appointed observers.

At the end of the 1970s the Namibian economy entered deep recession. Coupled with the war and a six-year drought, it exacerbated unemployment and deprivation. The 1980s saw the political struggle intensified by SWAPO in the face of South Africa's refusal to implement the UN peace plan.

During this period, SWAPO broadened its political support inside Namibia by forging alliances with other political groups. Increasing support also came from within the churches, while the militant SWAPO Youth League gained a massive following. By the end of the decade the movement was genuinely national, representing a cross-section of Namibian society in all geographical areas.

Final initiatives

The UN started 1981 with a new initiative, and convened a conference in Geneva attended by SWAPO, South Africa, the 'contact group' — Canada, France, Germany, the UK and USA — with several sub-Saharan African states behind the scenes.

Within a week the talks broke down, the South African representatives unwilling even to put their signatures to a 'declaration of intent'.

During 1982, however, the western 'contact group' continued meeting and consulting with the Pretoria government and SWAPO. But then South African acceptance of resolution 435 became conditional upon the withdrawal of Cuban troops from Angola. The policy, known as 'linkage', was fervently supported by the USA. Indeed, the very concept had been introduced by the White House in 1981, following a visit to Washington by Roelof (Pik) Botha, the South African minister for foreign affairs.

Botha had persuaded President Ronald Reagan that the wars in Namibia and southern Angola were a deterrent to Soviet expansion in southern Africa.

Washington's move created a severe setback for the 'contact group' which did not share this view. France, in particular, reacted very strongly and withdrew, condemning Reagan's move.

Meanwhile, South African troops launched the most extensive raids across the frontier into southern Angola since the 1975-6 conflict. By 1983, entire areas of Namibia's northern neighbour were effectively occupied. Pretoria openly admitted that its forces were 200 kilometres (125 miles) inside Angola.

Thanks to the Washington linkage agreement there was little to stop the South African forces, except Namibian and Angolan resistance. Eventually, however, the invaders experienced heavy retaliation from the Angolans.

As the SADF attacked PLAN's bases in Angola, the Namibians increasingly relied on support from within Namibia. They established permanent bases inside the territory and were active throughout the year.

In Namibia the focus of the war was in Owambo, by far the most populous area, but it soon spread to Kavango and the harsh Kaokoveld, especially during 1983. PLAN sabotage actions were also carried out in the south and central areas, and in Windhoek itself.

An assessment by South African military-intelligence officers in 1984 noted that SWAPO 'had an intensive intelligence-gathering network whereby the public, especially the hundreds of *cucca* (trading) shops in Owambo and Kavango, are involved and keep it informed as to the movement of the security forces'.

Information on the fighting was rigorously suppressed by the SADF. Official information consisted of little more than tallies of the number of PLAN fighters the 'security forces' claimed to have killed.

However, PLAN regularly released 'war communiques' documenting operations and reflecting far higher South African casualties than officially admitted.

The information blackout enabled the South Africans to carry out a sustained propaganda campaign portraying the SADF as winning the war. They continually claimed to be on the brink of breaking the Namibian resistance.

In 1984 a ceasefire was concluded in Angola. US government officials were sent to observe the South African withdrawal, while Angola agreed not to let either SWAPO or Cuban forces into the south. South Africa finally withdrew in April 1985.

By this time, it had become clear in Namibia that South Africa had failed to build the DTA as an alternative to SWAPO. The administration had been abolished and the country was again ruled directly through the South African Administrator-General.

Yet in June 1985, Pretoria tried again. This time they installed a 'Transitional Government of National Unity (TGNU) in Windhoek, pending independence'. Condemned in advance by the USA and other governments who were still members of the 'contact group', it was proclaimed 'null and void' by the UN. Thus the liberation movement continued to gain support, and by 1986 it was operating openly inside Namibia.

During this period there was an increase in fighting. Groups of freedom fighters penetrated the commercial farming areas south of Owambo, attacking armed white farms and engaging police and military forces.

The struggle took the form associated with guerilla warfare — small groups of fighters sabotaging communcations networks and government facilties, while larger groups laid ambushes and attacked army and police bases, usually at night.

But PLAN was vastly outnumbered by the South African occupation forces and unable to establish major bases inside Namibia, while South Africa's military operations intensified. The recruitment and conscription of Namibians into the armed forces increased markedly, so that by 1988 more than 20,000 were involved.

Special mobile units, *Koevoets*, which took over responsibility for the fight against PLAN, were even more ruthless than regular troops.

Peace at last

Now Angola seized the initiative. Early in 1987 it opened bilateral negotiations with the USA and Cuba, and in 1988 they agreed, in principle, to the withdrawal of Cuban troops from Angola. There was one proviso however — the agreement would only go into effect upon the implementation of the UN independence plan for Namibia.

In March, the proposal presented by Angola and Cuba was rejected by Pretoria as being 'insufficiently detailed'. But South Africa did enter into tripartite negotiations with Angola and Cuba, while the USA acted as mediator. The USSR, long supporters of SWAPO, also played a prominent if indirect part in the lead up to independence.

In 1988 when Gorbachev and Reagan met in Moscow, the two presidents set a target date of 29 September for a settlement of the Angolan and Namibian conflicts. Although early in May South Africa stated the deadline was unrealistic, it made a commitment to 'implement the resolution to the letter' — provided, of course, that an agreement for the withdrawal of Cuban troops was reached.

Finally, all the parties involved in the negotiations accepted a document containing fourteen 'essential principles' for a peaceful settlement, and in early August it was confirmed that the implementation of UN Security Council Resolution 435 would begin on 1 November.

Shortly afterwards Angola, Cuba and South Africa announced a cease-fire, and South Africa undertook to withdraw all its forces from Angola.

Above: Herero tribal dancers in the traditional voluminous Victorian gowns introduced last century by Christian missionaries.

Although there was a failure to agree upon a precise schedule for the withdrawal of the Cuban troops, in December 1988, South Africa, Angola and Cuba signed a formal treaty naming 1 April 1989 as the implementation date for UN Security Council Resolution 435. They established a joint commission to observe its implementation. It meant that a constituent assembly would be elected on 1 November 1989. In the meantime, South African forces in Namibia were confined to their bases and their numbers were reduced to 1,500. In fact, a total withdrawal of South African forces was completed one week after the November election. A multinational military observer force, the UN Transition Assistance Group (UNTAG), monitored the South African withdrawal, while PLAN forces were confined to their bases in Angola where they were disarmed and then repatriated.

Early in June 1989, all racially discriminatory legislation was thrown out and an amnesty granted to all refugees and exiles. Over the next few months nearly 42,000 Namibians, including the national hero Sam Nujoma, flocked back to their homeland. It was an emotional time, as many families separated for years were reunited.

Throughout the period before the election, accusations of intimidation were exchanged between the supporters of SWAPO and DTA. When the elections came, however, they were conducted calmly with more than ninety-five per cent of the electorate voting.

Ten political parties and various alliances contested the seventy-two seats which make up the Namibian constituent assembly. In the end, SWAPO received 57.3 per cent of the votes, winning forty-one seats. While this was an overall majority, it did not give SWAPO the two-thirds majority which would have allowed the party to draw up its own draft constitution for Namibia.

But in December 1989, all the parties in the constitutional assembly introduced proposals for a draft constitution, and a spirit of compromise prevailed. Executive power was vested in a president who was permitted to serve a maximum of two five-year terms.

By the end of January 1990, they declared that Namibia would become independent on 21 March 1990. Later that month the assembly elected Sam Nujoma as Namibia's first leader.

Independence celebrations

At midnight on 20 March 1990, at Independence Stadium, thousands of Namibians jostled to obtain a better view of the hoisting of the Namibian Flag, the swearing-in of President Sam Nujoma by UN Secretary-General, Dr Javier Perez de Cuellar, the lighting of the Freedom Flame, a parade by the Guard of Honour and a massive fireworks display followed by a procession of schoolchildren with the Namibian flag.

Everywhere you travel in Namibia, people of all colours still celebrate and relish their newly-earned independence, and Namibia's symbols — the flag and coat of arms — are proudly displayed wherever the visitor turns.

The colours of the flag are arranged diagonally. The top left-hand corner is blue, the middle red and the bottom right-hand corner green. The colours are separated by thinner bands of white. In the blue area is a golden sun with twelve triangular rays.

The blue represents the Namibian sky, the Atlantic Ocean and the country's precious water resources. The sun represents life and energy. The red is for Namibia's most important resource, its people. It refers to their heroism and their determination to build a future of equal opportunity for all. White stands for peace and unity, and green symbolises vegetation and agricultural resources.

Similar themes are represented in the national coat of arms, which represents its people, and is also the official government emblem.

Various national symbols are represented on the coat of arms, including the national flag. Two animals and a plant are used symbolically. The African fish eagle with its excellent vision is seen as symbol of the far-sightedness of the country's leaders, while the oryx antelope is renowned for its courage, elegance and pride.

The *Welwitchia mirabilis*, a unique desert plant, is a fighter for survival and is therefore symbolic of the nation's fortitude and tenacity. The headband refers to Namibia's traditions, and the diamond to its natural resources.

The motto 'Unity, Liberty, Justice' enshrines the key principles embodied in the constitution and in the hearts of the people, for the legacy that the Namibian freedom fighters left was one of peace and hope.

Building upon this foundation the government has achieved varying degrees of success in meeting the aspirations of Namibians. The 'red line' is a fence extending across Namibia from east to west, some way south from the Angolan border, to keep disease-ridden game and cattle from the north from contaminating healthy game and cattle in the south. The fence also divides communal and commercial agriculture. Moreover it is a symbol of the rift between the two Namibias at opposite ends of the economic spectrum, a barrier the government has vowed to remove.

At independence, the white population, approximately five per cent, was mostly urban and enjoyed the amenities of a modern western European country, while the black population, ninety-five per cent of the people, lived in abject poverty. With this inequality, the main task of the government has been to dismantle an economic and social system built on apartheid.

Redirecting public expenditure to meet the health and educational needs of the majority was a necessary first step. Other priorities tackled by the new administration were housing and rural development.

The most difficult challenge, however, was to create enough employment opportunities to absorb everyone into the labour force.

Four years after independence the new nation is a shining example to the rest of the continent — and perhaps most importantly to South Africa — as its ethnic groups work together in peace.

The Land: Sun and Diamonds

It is said that nature is a great teacher of colour and beauty and thus it is not surprising that visitors to Namibia don the cloak of the artist. In addition to its wildlife, the country has some of the most spectacular desert ecosystems on earth.

No one who beholds the blade-sharp dunes of the Namib, the lava fields of Damaraland, the lunar-like canyons of the south, the treachery of the Skeleton Coast or the wild drama of Etosha can fail to be inspired by this land of a thousand faces.

Yet much about Namibia is indefinable. It is harsh and haunting, yet the savagery of wind and time sweeten the landscape with gentleness.

Namibia has four distinct natural regions: the eighty- to 120-kilometre-wide (fifty to seventy-five mile) belt of the Namib Desert stretching along the entire coastline; the semi-arid mountainous plateau — varying in altitude from 900 to 2,000 metres (3,000-6,500 feet) and covering the central part of the interior; the low-lying north-eastern and south-eastern areas, extensions of the dry Kalahari and Karoo regions of Botswana and South Africa; and the bush-covered plains to the north of the Etosha Pan, including the fairly high rainfall areas of Kavango and the Caprivi Strip.

Oldest desert in the world

The sand dunes around Sossusvlei are said to be the highest in the world — rising 350 metres (1,150 feet) in a feast of constantly-changing colours, from ivory-white to apricot and gold.

The Namib is the most fascinating desert in the world because of its unique and diverse plant and animal life — from the *Welwitschia mirabilis*, a plant that has been on earth much longer than most plants known today, to the dancing white lady, a strange spider of the dunes.

Long and narrow, extending some 1,900 kilometres (1,180 miles) from the Olifants River mouth in the Cape Province of South Africa to the Namibe in Angola, the Namib Desert is widely thought to be one of the world's oldest deserts. It is crossed by two west-flowing perennial rivers, the Kunene and the Orange, which form the northern and southern borders of Namibia.

To the south of the Orange, the Namib Desert is no wider than fifty kilometres (thirty-one miles). But the central part, the most arid, stretches about 200 kilometres (125 miles) inland. The terrain rises steadily until, at an altitude of around 1,000 metres (3,280 feet), it reaches the edge of the central plateau.

The Namib region has a landscape of great diversity: immense gravel plains, dune fields, inselbergs, chains of rocky hills, massive mountains to the east, salt flats, dry river-beds, as well as two permanent river mouths.

To the south, the Namib Desert is a sea of sand, of massive, regimented, shifting dunes. Here and there among them lies an odd salt pan or mudflat, and relics of sporadic streams that failed to make their way to the ocean. Underground rivers cross the wasteland, their dry beds refreshingly, but incongruously, mantled in greenery.

Farther north, the land levels to a harder plain from which the occasional isolated granite mountain rises, the bedrock of which is slashed by deep gorges. What little soil there is tends to be confined to the area's few flood plains and river estuaries.

There, too, are the desolate shores of the Skeleton Coast, graveyard of a thousand ships and named for the many mariners who survived the wrecks only to perish in its desert wastes.

Above the Atlantic Ocean a permanent anticyclone causes southerly winds to blow north along the Namib coast. The wind generates surface currents and, as a consequence of the relatively stable meteorological conditions, a surface current flows between six and thirty kilometres (three and nineteen miles) an hour north-north-west up the Namib coast. It's one aspect of the Benguela system which is also characterised by powerful upwellings of deep, cold water that significantly lower the

Above: Giant boulders in the craggy Erongo Mountains.

surface temperature below that of the water further offshore. This mass of water profoundly influences the climate of the Namib Desert, creating the dense fogs that nourish the plants and animals of the desert.

Thus the Namib is a partly temperate desert, where temperatures rarely exceed 40°C in the shade and the annual average maximum temperature is about 30°C. Yet at ground level, temperatures frequently exceed 60°C and at times 70°C. Then, by the end of the night in the central desert, temperatures drop below zero. These drastic extremes render life particularly difficult for both plants and animals.

The Namib is also extremely arid. The wettest region at the foot of the great escarpment to the east receives little more than 100 millimetres (four inches) of rain a year. The southern sector receives winter rainfall, while the north is distinguished by summer showers. In the central area, where rainfall is scarce and unseasonal, it is usual for several consecutive years to pass without rain and then for several times the yearly average to be delivered in a single deluge.

The fog is a vital source of water in the coastal areas and, in fact, is more predictable and reliable than the rain. At its densest at ground level the fog produces condensation on the hillsides. During the night it extends up to fifty kilometres (thirty-one miles) inland, often lingering during the morning but normally dissipating before noon.

The prevailing southerly winds, which blow between forty and sixty per cent of the time, are also the strongest, being responsible for the transport and accumulation of sand in the dune fields and the sand seas. But the more moderate westerly winds push the fog far inland. Easterly and northeasterly winds are hot. When they gust in the central part of the desert, the humidity level falls precipitously within minutes, while the ambient temperature rises several degrees. Such winds are more frequent in winter.

The winds of the Namib Desert fulfil an important function both in the shaping of the landscape and in the ecology. It is the wind that carries and accumulates the sand and blows the fine elements from the

Above: Desert succulent, a diminutive euphorbia, struggles for existence in the barren granite hills of Damaraland.

surface of the plains, leaving behind only rocks and gravel.

Loaded with sand, the wind erodes and polishes the rocks. The wind also distributes detritus or organic matter into the heart of the desert, providing food and nutrients for animals, even in areas devoid of vegetation.

The plateau

To the east of the Namib are the highlands of the central plateau, a hardveld tableland varying in height from 900 to 2,000 metres (3,000-6,500 feet).

A region of wide geophysical diversity, the countryside ranges from broken veld through sandy valleys and undulating plains to mountain massifs and jagged peaks.

In the central segment, the hills around Windhoek are especially noteworthy, while in the west, when not veiled in mist, the majestic massif of the Brandberg is visible from a considerable distance. Its principal peak, the Königstein, 2,573 metres (8,442 feet), is the highest in the country. The mountain has been a focal point and challenge to climbers and explorers for decades, but its chief claim to fame lies in the rock painting known as the White Lady of the Brandberg.

Among the many prehistoric rock paintings in the valleys and ravines of the mountain, this one — part of a great frieze in the Tsisab Gorge — has excited the most attention, as well as controversy. (See "Damarland: Land of Light", Part Two).

The Khomas Highland, the Eros and other ranges combine to form Namibia's highest tract of territory, a central watershed from which headwaters drain to all points of the compass. Much further to the south is the plateau's most spectacular natural feature, Fish River Canyon.

The northern section of Namibia is a distinctive region, quite different in character from the rest of the plateau. For the most part it comprises a great alluvial plain created by the Okavango and other rivers that flow southwards from Angola to feed the wetlands of northern Botswana and the huge shallow known as the Etosha

Pan. This upland country is generally well-watered and blessed with good grazing.

The highlands are the economic, as well as the geographic, heart of the country. They enjoy relatively generous summer rains that sustain nutritious ground cover, flocks of karakul sheep and — in the north — cultivated land and herds of beef and dairy cattle.

Kalahari Desert

This mighty territory is part of southern Africa's great interior plateau, covering more than 1.2 million square kilometres (500,000 square miles).

It extends into Angola and across Botswana to Zimbabwe and Zambia. It accounts for a large portion of eastern Namibia extending some 400 kilometres (248 miles) into the north and eighty kilometres (fifty miles) into the south.

The Kalahari is commonly termed a desert because its porous, sandy soils do not retain surface water. In reality, however, much of it is a life-sustaining wilderness and its sparsely grassed plains are home to huge herds of game and other animals.

Mining

Namibia is rich in minerals and it is small wonder that mining is the most important economic sector of the country. Archaic basic rocks were penetrated during the geological epochs by magma. Some of these deposits of raw material cannot be mined economically, either because they do not occur in sufficient quantities, or the deposits are too unfavourably situated for mining. In this regard South Africa is better off, because similar and equally old deposits are more readily accessible.

Nevertheless, the country has a number of economically viable minerals, the most lucrative being diamonds, uranium, copper and iron.

New diamond deposits discovered in the north will ensure the viability of the diamond industry for another fifty years.

The most important mining centre in the north is in the Tsumeb-Grootfontein-Otavi region where the mining of zinc, copper and lead ores dates back to colonial times.

Since 1978, uranium oxide has been mined between Swakopmund and Usakos by Rössing Uranium. The deposits of this important base mineral are said to be so vast that uranium could eventually even replace diamonds as the country's leading mineral resource.

Although Namibia is no longer a country where prospectors seek their fortunes, it does have much to offer amateur geologists, whatever their angle or approach may be. Collecting is in many people's blood, and rocks and minerals are particularly satisfying. Finding out about them is an infinite source of interest, and picking them up takes you to out-of-the-way places and gives you the opportunity of meeting interesting people.

It is not possible to give precise information about localities in many instances, particularly in the case of materials which have a side distribution. Besides this, collecting grounds change from time to time; some become incorporated into prohibited areas, some may become subject to concession rights and, of course, there is always the exciting possibility of new sources turning up. Your best plan is to take local advice wherever you are.

In small places, try the staff at the local police station first. If they do not know details themselves they will invariably know someone who does, and will be able to answer questions regarding permits or permission. In larger centres, museums are usually helpful and will know if there are any local gem clubs and how to get in touch with them.

There are also permanent geological exhibits in most of the museums and these may help with problems of identification. Mines vary in their reception of amateurs. Many are helpful, some not so welcoming, and some, out of necessity, have rigid security regulations. It should be borne in mind that searching in disused mines can be dangerous — likewise, caves may be unsafe and do not offer much.

The geological map of Namibia, which shows the mines and farm boundaries, is invaluable since it shows the distribution of the main rock types.

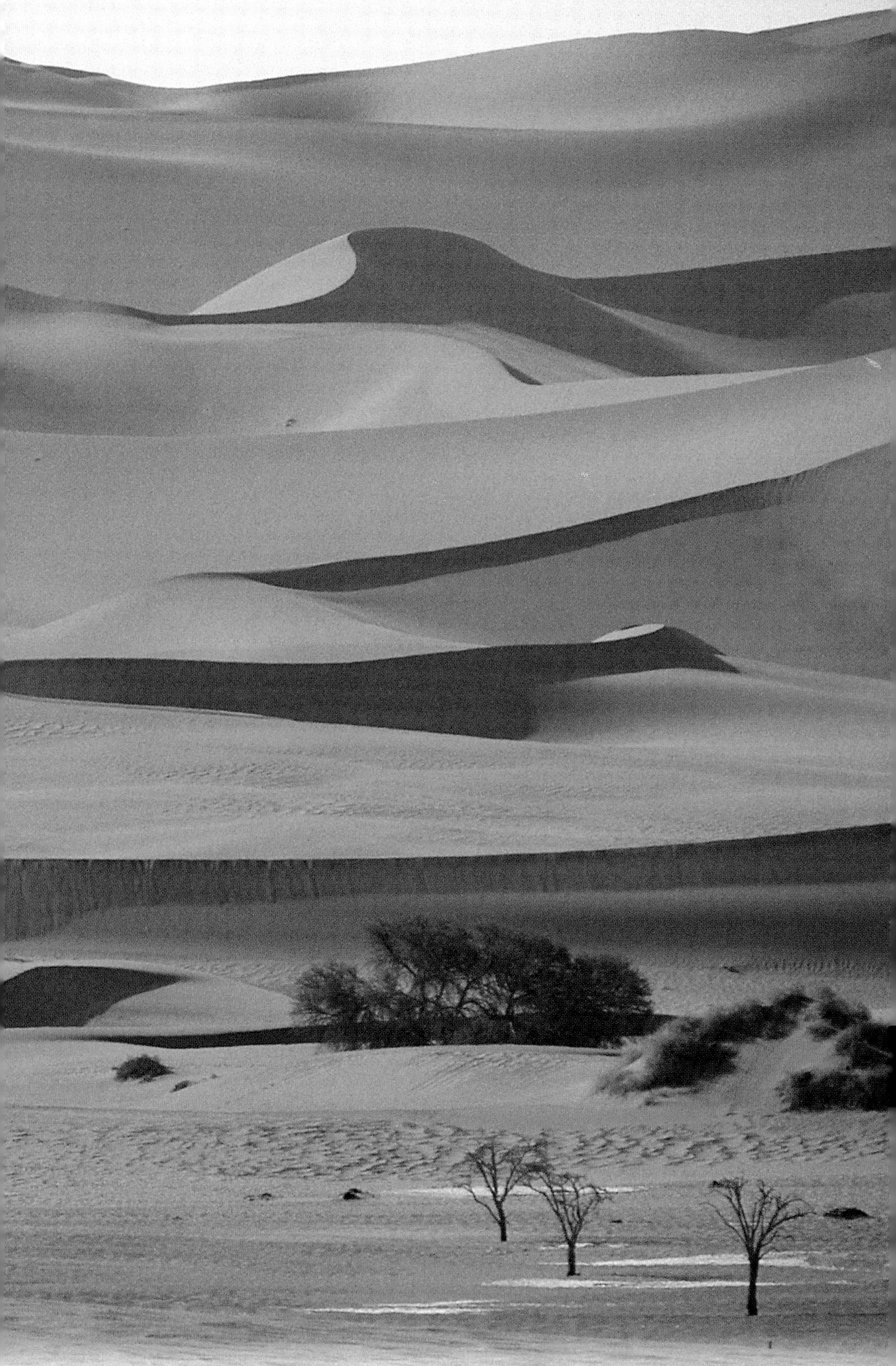

The People: A Kaleidoscope of Colourful Cultures

Diverse, charming and welcoming — all these adjectives conjure up images of Namibia's friendly people who hail from all corners of Africa and Europe. Truly, they are a kaleidoscope of peoples.

Each group has brought with it individual skills and experience, methods and ways which are now being used to forge a bright destiny for this new nation of many living as one. Geographically, Namibia is the fifteenth-largest African state: two-thirds the size of its southern neighbour. And yet even sparsely populated South Africa has more than thirty times as many people.

For Namibia's 1991 population was approximately 1.5 million — an average of less than two persons to each square kilometre, a remarkable statistic when you consider the population problems elsewhere in Africa. It is a statistic that may go some way to reflect the barren character of the land itself of which only one per cent is arable.

Thus, close to one in every four Namibians lives in urban societies of which the capital, Windhoek, is the largest. And with an estimated annual birthrate increase of about three per cent, the urban centres are increasing by nearly twice that rate in a constant drift from the country to town.

Despite the relatively small population, Namibia has a rich cultural mosaic — a melting pot of African peoples in which each group has its own individual characteristics and traditions.

Most Africans come from the north, the largest ethnic group being the Wambo — consisting of eight different tribes, each with its own territory and dialect. The other major tribes are Kavango, Herero, Damara, Nama, East Caprivian, Kaokolander, Bushmen, Rehoboth Baster and Tswana.

Spread across this vast land astride the Tropic of Capricorn, Namibians have adapted their cultures and customs to the terrain in which they live — mostly arid and desolate.

But all those who have migrated to this land in the past thousands of years have absorbed something from those who were already there — even the colonials.

The Basters

Numbering 30,000, the Basters are a racially mixed, westernised, Afrikaans-speaking people who arrived from the Cape Colony in the late 1860s. They brought with them their Calvinist religion and a fierce independence. Their largest settlement is Rehoboth, south of Windhoek.

The Bushmen

One of the most fascinating groups in Namibia is the San Bushmen, of which there are an estimated 30,000. Only a small number — an estimated 2,000 — maintain their ancient way of life, hunting and gathering. Nowadays most Bushmen work as farmworkers, although they continue to live in their traditional homelands between the Kavango, Herero and Botswana borders.

Natural conservationists in an ever more polluted world, Bushmen take great care of their harsh habitat, at home in a terrain where few other human beings could survive. Their incredible bushlore unfailingly leads them to water, and they live off the desert's trees and shrubs, including the starch-containing veld onion.

Those who continue the tribe's 20,000 years of traditions even use utensils that have not noticeably altered during the past few thousand years.

The Dzuwazi San are a sub-group of the Kung San, possibly the only Bushmen who still live to some extent as hunter gatherers. Although these fascinating people are able to identify more than 250 plants, one single

Previous page: Hardy desert plants cling tenaciously to life at the foot of the great sand mountains of Sossusvlei.

fruit contributes fifty per cent of their total nourishment. With fewer wild animals, hunting, the second sphere of activity for the Bushmen, has become less central to their lifestyle. When they do hunt, however, they use arrows tipped with poison obtained from plants, snakes or the larvae of certain beetles.

San bows are small and consequently only have a maximum range of some twenty-five metres (eighty feet) which means they have to stalk the game as closely as possible. During the freedom war South African defence forces recruited these skilled trackers to track down Namibia's freedom fighters.

Caprivians

The East Caprivian communities of the north-eastern extension of Namibia bordering Angola, Zambia and Botswana, totalling about 40,000, are closely related to the Lozi of Barotseland, a region of Zambia which is seasonally flooded by the waters of the Zambezi River. To a degree, fishing and hunting are significant but by no means exclusive elements of the local economy. Caprivians also keep cattle and cultivate the land.

Those living in the eastern segment of the Caprivi Strip lead a less permanent existence as they are displaced for some months each year by floodwaters.

The Damara

The 90,000-strong Damara (or Bergdama), concentrated in the hinterland of the north-western seaboard, are something of a mystery as they speak a Khoikhoi language yet, in appearance and culture, are more akin to the Bantu people of west and central Africa. Their origins are obscure. All that is known with certainty is that they brought with them pottery and iron-making which they supplied to the dominant Herero and Nama.

The Damara were organised in small migratory groups, each controlled by a chief advised by elder male kinsmen. Like the Wambo, they hold fire sacred. Other traditional religious beliefs encompass a Supreme Being responsible for the coming of the rains and the renewal of the earth.

Above: Herero mother and child in colourful adaptation of the tribe's traditional Victorian costumes.

European origin

There are about 75,000 European inhabitants, two-thirds of whom are Afrikaans-speaking and one-quarter German-speaking. The majority live in urban centres in central and southern Namibia. Most are involved in commerce, manufacturing, farming and, to a diminishing extent, the civil service.

The Herero

The Herero and their cousins live in the arid, eastern sandveld areas bordering Botswana. The offshoot Himba live in the Kaokoveld region of the north-west. Together the three groups total some 90,000.

The primary religious figure of their culture is known by the three names, Nyadambi, Karunga and Huku, titles common among many tribes of south-western Africa.

He is the creator of the world, but does not intervene in the affairs of men. The first missionaries and ethnologists reported hearing the title *Makuru* as the figure to whom the Himba often made reference, but this term means 'the ancient one', rather than god.

As an impersonal force, *Makuru* leads a concrete hierarchy of spiritual powers — ancestors — who are endowed with the power to make their presence felt in the lives of their descendants.

A sacred fire is fundamental to Himba rituals, constituting the spiritual life of a lineage and symbolizing continuity between the dead and the living. The fire is traditionally kindled by two sacred sticks.

Only the chief of the clan is authorized to cut and handle these sacred sticks which he guards in his hut. The fire must never die, preserving as it does a link between ancestors and descendants. Any breach in the ritual is perceived as a sign of future misfortune and an offence against the ancestors.

Every Himba village has a wooden bowl in which the chief mixes together water and leaves. These he holds in his mouth and then spits out. The ritual is repeated each time the chief wants to attract the attention of the ancestral spirits and make a request. Apart from religious practices, the Himbas deal in magic. Divination is the prediction of the future, or explanation of past events, by inspection of animal entrails. When a goat is killed or a steer sacrificed, an old woman analyses the veins and configurations of the stomach to make predictions.

Until early this century the Herero were nomadic, living fairly comfortably off the meat and milk of the large herds of cattle, goats and sheep that grazed the pastures of Namibia's central upland region. Bloody battles with the German colonial forces, however, decimated them and they became impoverished and were translocated.

Cattle nurtured by boreholes are still central to their living, but many Herero also raise sheep and poultry and grow subsistence crops of maize and millet. Rural groups are traditionally organised around an extended family.

Visually, the most remarkable Herero characteristic is the traditional costume worn by the women — a long colourful Victorian-type dress adapted from the styles favoured by the wives of early European missionaries.

The related Tjimba and Himba, whose home is the Kaokoveld, are highly distinctive sub-groups. The forebears of the latter were in fact the Herero herders who were dispossessed by Nama warriors during the nineteenth century and fled to the remote and inhospitable north-western region. There they became known as the Ova-Himba which means beggars. Over the ensuing decades these semi-nomadic pastoralists have clung tenaciously to their traditional ways, shunning the trappings of civilisation.

The Kavango

Numbering more than 110,000, the Kavango live in the north-east, south of the Okavango River. It is a parklike region of tall grasses interspersed with scrub and patches of woodland, some 1,100 metres (3,600 feet) above sea level, that thicken into forests of mahogany, blackwood and teak towards the east. More than 200 trees and bushes have been identified there. This is

Top: Symbol of young Namibia's vitality and hope.

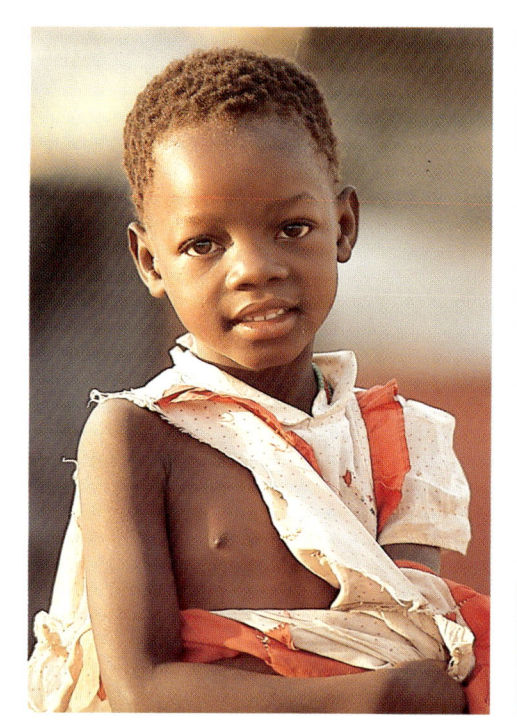

Above: Young Baster girl serves as drum majorette in one of the many colourful annual celebrations held in Windhoek.

Top: Youngster in the Lizuali homelands of Caprivi.

Above: Veteran of colonial Namibia displays his military honours in a country where bitterness has been laid aside to build a united nation.

65

Above: Roadside vendor displays hides of springbok gazelles.

big game country and the animal life includes elephants and buffalo, along with large buck. In the river lurk crocodile, hippo and tigerfish. (See "Kavango and the Caprivi Strip: Where Four Nations Meet", Part Two).

The Kavango are divided into six tribal groups. Most rural families subsist on their cereals and livestock and on river fish. Many are river dwellers, their most prized possession being a dugout canoe. Woodcarving is a flourishing local industry.

Nama

The 50,000 Nama, many of whom live in the central region south of Windhoek, are among the last substantial groups of the true Khoikhoi, once called Hottentot.

By tradition, these semi-nomadic pastoralists originally occupied the country to the north and the south of the Orange River, living a peaceful enough existence in the southern interior of today's Namibia, in Great Namaqualand or Namaland. But after the arrival of the Herero in the latter part of the eighteenth century, competition for grazing lands led to decades of bitter warfare. Later came the mixed-descent Oorlam groups, whose presence initially intensified the conflict, but who eventually assumed the leadership of the Nama and carried on the struggle against the Herero.

Later still, first under German and then under South African colonial rule, the Nama were confined to certain areas of the south-central region and their pastoral rights were guaranteed.

The Nama have much in common with the San, sharing with the latter their linguistic roots and to some degree their physical appearance. They are light-skinned and fine-boned, though the Nama tend to be taller. Individual families still follow their old wandering ways, but most Nama now live in permanent settlements and work within the formal economy. Most, too, have adopted Western lifestyles and the Christian religion.

The Wambo

The Wambo and its eight sub-groups totalling about 600,000 make up just over one-third of Namibia's population. They live mainly in the north in an area that stretches east from the Kaokoveld to Kavango. The region, which saw continual fighting during the liberation struggle, was known as Owambo and has, since Independence, been divided into four provinces.

Man-made irrigation canals bring life to the area, flat savannah crossed by watercourses, *oshanas*, sustaining animals and agriculture.

The Wambo probably settled in this region in the sixteenth century, but only vague myths and legends are known about their origin. Although traditionally polygamous, today only monogamy is practised.

When babies are four days old, they are taken to the entrance of the hut where they are shown their immediate environment and the tasks they will have to perform are demonstrated to them.

From birth onwards, they are segregated according to sex. During the childhood years children belong to the family of the mother. Surprisingly, the mother's brother has more influence on the child than the actual father. The children are heirs of the uncle, not the father. Like the Herero, the Wambo also have a holy fire.

Traditionally, a Wambo village is enclosed by a pole fence, within which fenced-off areas delineate sleeping quarters, food stores, kitchens, cattle pens and so forth. Central to the larger village unit is the open 'reception area' where feasts are held, visitors entertained and the 'holy fire' — sometimes a log — burns ceaselessly.

The Wambo's ancient body of religious belief involves a Supreme Being, *Kalunga*, and the veneration of ancestors. But today, the majority are Christians of the Finnish Mission, which arrived in force in 1870. The remainder are either Roman Catholic or Anglicans.

Below: Youngsters of all races are the proud inheritors of free Namibia.

Above: Farm youngster enjoys the outdoor life in spring pastures near Windhoek.

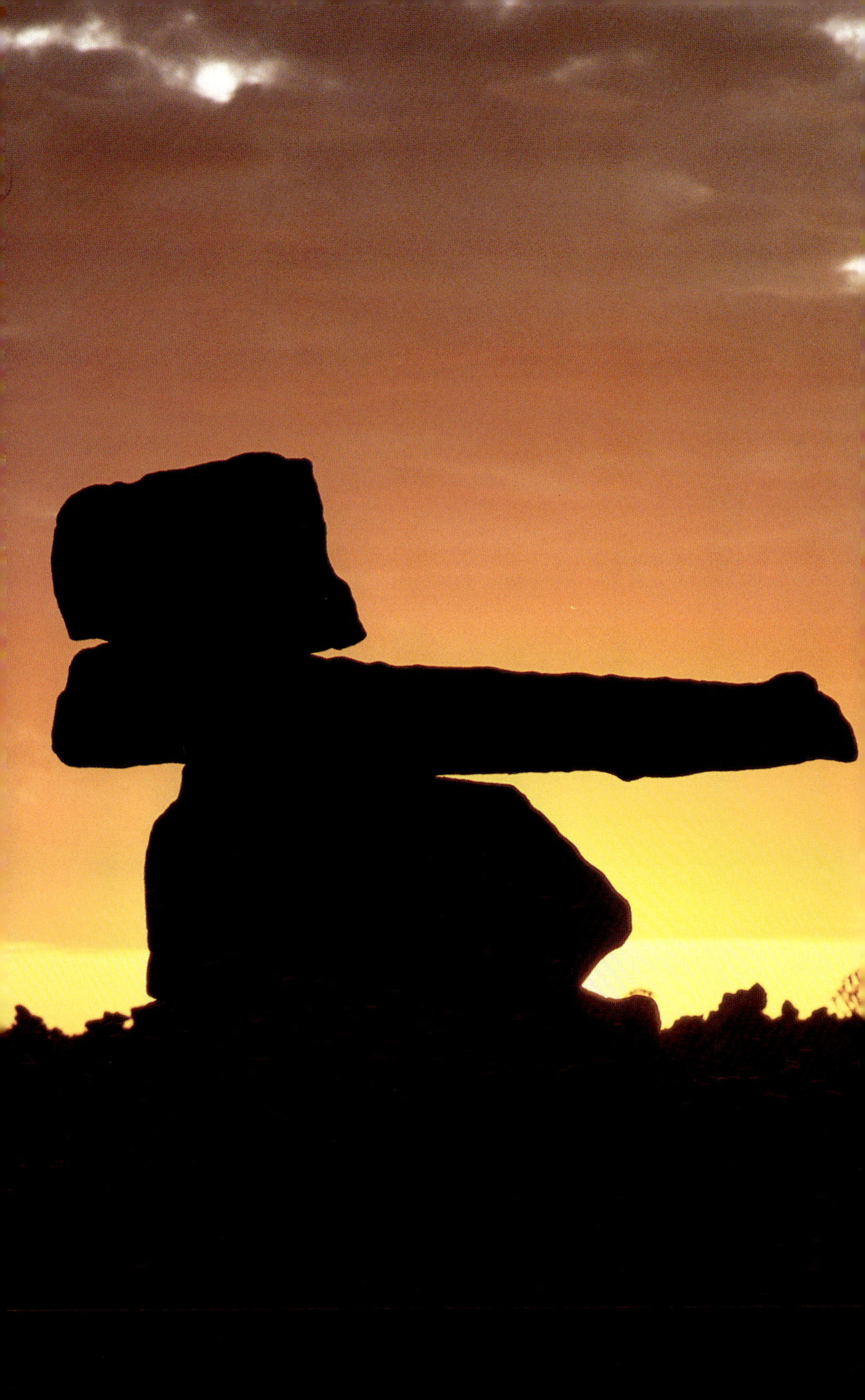

PART TWO: PLACES AND TRAVEL

Above: SWA Safari tour buses beside the limestone column known as the Vingerklip which rises out of the barren wastes east of Khorixas.

Opposite: Sundown over the Giant's Playground with its balancing rocks near Keetmanshoop in southern Namibia.

Southern Namibia: Quiver Trees and Granite Forts, Desert Horses and Diamond Mines

Few areas of the world encompass such a stark but beautiful setting as the mountains, desert plains and drifting dunes of southern Namibia. Yet despite its aridity there is a rich geophysical and cultural diversity.

There you will find a diamond rush town half-consumed by the drifting sands of the desert, fork-branched quiver trees, odd-looking, fat-tailed sheep, desert roses that crystallised out of salt and sand, the world's only breed of desert horses, and much more to excite the imagination. Unlike any other place in so many aspects, the region stretches north from the banks of the Orange River to the Disney-like town of Lüderitz and beyond.

And within the folds of its stark, rugged mountains, stony plains and roaming sand dunes, is a unique natural treasure where scrubland gives way to undulating hills, sandy valleys, and age-old volcanoes and their debris. One main road runs over the Orange River from the South African border through this stunning scenery like a huge, black python — from Cape Town in South Africa, through Noordoewer on the Namibian border, to Keetmanshoop. And from there the B1 thrusts all the way through Namibia to the Angolan border, in faultless condition with no potholes, cracks or ditches to worry about, but only the marching dunes of the powerful Namib, which often cover the way in the south. It is along this road, or just off it, that many of Southern Namibia's attractions lie.

To the west stretches Diamond Area One — starting in the extreme south on the banks of the Orange River and reaching north beyond Lüderitz — where a fortune lies buried beneath the sand.

But it is a restricted area, the Forbidden — *Sperrgebiet* — Coast, controlled by the South African giant, Consolidated Diamond Mines (CDM), and anyone who strays into this area without permission is certain to be prosecuted.

Visitors with proper authorisation are allowed. Such permits are obtainable from the CDM offices in Windhoek or Lüderitz for those who apply at least a month in advance. The application must be accompanied by a report from a local police station to the effect that the applicant is not a criminal. The process, though, is slow and laborious but well worth it.

Namibia's diamonds were formed millions of years ago in the interior of southern Africa, and over the millennia, carried to the Atlantic by the Orange River. There they were left on ancient beaches which have now become part of the mainland.

Namibia's ore body, in which the diamonds are embedded, is nearly 100 kilometres (sixty miles) long, in the shape of an attenuated triangle three kilometres (one-and-three-quarter miles) wide at its base near Oranjemund, in the south, narrowing to 200 metres (650 feet) at its apex in the north. Although the grade improves towards the north, the volume of the ore and the size of the diamonds decreases. For planning purposes, the ore body was originally divided into some 3,000 blocks. Roughly two-thirds have already been mined, while the remainder are continuously analysed for viability by on-site computers. In the event, grade is the only measure of a diamond's value.

Since World War II, CDM has introduced plant and machinery capable of handling more and more tonnage at lower costs. Meanwhile, unique problems have been overcome. In the process, the company has developed ways to mine deep deposits inundated by the pounding surf of the Atlantic Ocean. Thus, previously inaccessible ore has been added to available reserves. With a population of 8,000 the company headquarters of Oranjemund, on the South African border, is the eighth-largest town in Namibia.

The Orange River, which flows more than 2,000 kilometres (1,243 miles) from its

Above: Bedrock is exposed down to the water line where huge concrete walls hold back the Atlantic breakers from the men working to sweep up castaway diamonds.

source in the Drakensberg Mountains of South Africa, forms Namibia's southern boundary with South Africa. The old name of the Orange River was Gariep. It doesn't take its new name from the muddy colour of its water but from Holland's Prince William V of Orange in whose honour the Boer settlers of South Africa renamed the river in 1779. Nonetheless, its waters have the consistency of a thick paste — it contains five times as much silt as the Nile. But its shallows, cataracts and outcrops of rock make it particularly dangerous, especially when in spate. It was on the South African banks of the river in 1866 that a young boy, Erasmus Jacobs, discovered a diamond. He had no idea what it was but, after he was found playing with it, diamond fever swept southern Africa and a series of finds fuelled a frenzy of greed, excitement and prospecting.

As early as 1897, the master of a sailing vessel, Captain R Jones, sailed into the harbour at Cape Town clutching a packet of diamonds which he said he had picked up on one of the many islands along the southern coast of South West Africa. But he died before he could return. Again, in 1905 and 1906, a few diamonds were found in guano which had been mined on the same offshore islands. Two years later the first diamond fields were discovered, well north of the Orange River, at a remote spot called Kolmanskop on the Atlantic fringes of the Namib.

Diamonds brought rapid change and swift development. Hamlets turned into villages, villages blossomed into towns, and roads and railways were laid. When the diamond seams around Kolmanskop began to run out during the late 1920s, operations were transferred to the diamond fields at the south-eastern edge of the Namib while prospecting moved south to the Orange River. As diamonds had been discovered at Alexander Bay, on the Orange River's southern banks, it was thought that the seam should extend to the northern banks. The theory became fact in 1928 when geologists discovered more diamond coastal terraces north of the Orange River. Production began in the 1930s.

Now Oranjemund, complete with airport, rail and bus terminals, verdant

Above: Five thousand carats of uncut diamonds — one day's production from CDM at Oranjemund.

municipal parks and immaculate golf course, is the closest thing to heaven in a harsh and intimidating land, a town without jobless or homeless people where no one ever goes hungry, and all medical treatment is free.

Getting there

Oranjemund is 1,086 kilometres (675 miles) from Windhoek via its only road link through Lüderitz, from which it is a 270-kilometre (168-mile) distance. There is an airport with frequent company and charter flights.

When to go

Oranjemund is part of the Forbidden Coast and visitors require special permission from Consolidated Diamond Mines to go there.

Where to stay

There are no tourist facilities.

Sightseeing

The **Orange River** and the **Namib Desert** have been generous with their bounty, holding on to precious gems, cast there by ancient tides, for man to recover by strip mining. The Forbidden Coast where the diamonds lie is a daunting barrier of black, craggy **cliffs** with razor-sharp **ridges** and spectacular **rock formations**, including the sixty-metre-high (197-foot) natural arch of **Bogenfels rock**. **Dykes** are built to form **lagoons** to recover diamonds below the tideline when the waters are pumped dry. Mechanical diggers remove some thirty million tonnes of earth, sand and rock a year at Oranjemund alone. The diggings, spread over several hundred square kilometres, form the world's largest opencast **mine**.

Few sights anywhere are as awesome as those of the giant excavators, the largest and most spectacular earth-movers in the world, gouging great chunks of sand and rock out of the earth down to a depth of twenty-five metres (eighty-two feet), protective dykes holding back the ever-threatening waters of the Atlantic. When the sand and rock are pulled away, the diamond-bearing gravels are revealed. A task force of Wambo labourers, armed with simple brooms, industriously sweep forward to search the surface for diamonds lodged in tiny cracks and crevasses — retrieving an average of 6,000 carats of diamonds a day. The scale of the operation may be perceived in the fact that for just 200 milligrams of diamond, at least thirteen-and-a-quarter tonnes of sand, gravel and conglomerate have to be cleared away. These operations cost in the region of a million US dollars a day.

The biggest diamond ever recovered weighed 246 carats. Such wealth creates its own temptations and security within the forbidden territory is a continual battle. The theft of uncut diamonds is a massive industry on its own. For every US $3,000,000 of stolen gemstones recovered, experts estimate another ninety per cent find their way onto the market.

Thieves use all manner of means to smuggle out their loot. Once, X-ray machines detected a condom containing 200 stones, while cut-away heels in shoes, hollow books and luggage handles have become familiar hiding places to blasé security staff. When a homing pigeon was seen fluttering on a ten-foot **security fence**, closer examination showed it was carrying a pouch so heavy with diamonds that the bird was unable to take off.

Other discoveries have been diamonds stashed in **soccer balls** which have been kicked over the fence, empty **bottles** thrown there — and even **tunnels** under the fence.

So tough is security that since 1927 no vehicle or machine has ever left the Oranjemund Diamond Mine. In fact, a vast **dump** — the **disused equipment park** — contains row upon row of **lorries, trucks, bulldozers, cranes,** some of the largest earth-moving equipment ever built, and acres of old **tyres,** all spread out over kilometres of barren landscape.

Almost 100 per cent of the **stones** are of gem quality, mainly colourless or pale yellow. Namibia's rare numbers of **'fancy' diamonds**, varied in colour but often pink, are unequalled for quality.

CDM is Namibia's major taxpayer, contributing between sixty and sixty-four per cent of its profits to the national exchequer. Indeed, in 1981 the company accounted for ninety-seven per cent of all tax revenue.

But production remains strictly controlled. CDM is a subsidiary of the South African De Beers conglomerate run by the Oppenheimer dynasty. When overproduction threatened prices in the 1970s, the company closed down most of the Namibian mines — the world's sixth-largest producer. De Beers continues to control the market, although in the early 1990s, when world markets were flooded by cut-price diamonds from the former Soviet Union and illicitly-mined stones from Angola, the traditional structure was close to collapse.

Consolidated Diamond Mines were also angered when an American entrepreneur was given a concession to mine diamonds between the high and low tidemarks along the Forbidden Coast. While the company initiated legal action, the American put a fleet of costly dredging barges to work sucking gravel from the sea-bed. In the end, CDM took over the operation but the potential for offshore diamonds has never been really viable. Meanwhile, the southern shores offer another fascinating oddity.

All the way along the Forbidden Coast a string of curiously named islands, stretching north beyond Lüderitz, underlined the strange anomaly of South Africa's continued role in independent Namibia, even as late as 1993. For if **Roast Beef** and **Black Rock Islands** were part of the country's sovereignty, others such as **Plum Pudding, Sinclair's, Pomona, Albatross, Possession, South Long, North Long, Halifax, Penguin, Seal, Ichaboe** and **Mercury Islands** remained marked on the map as South African territory — with no word to explain why one should be different from the other. (See "Lüderitz: Between Dunes, Diamonds and Ocean", Part Three).

North-east of Oranjemund, the Orange River cuts a dog-leg through the mountains and barren land of the harsh southern wilderness to the main points of entry from South Africa, and Cape Town in particular. **Noordoewer**, in fact, lies some 120 kilometres (seventy-five miles) directly south-east of the diamond headquarters.

Getting there

Noordoewer is 1,144 kilometres (711 miles) from Swakopmund, 786 kilometres (488 miles) from Windhoek, 707 kilometres (440 miles) from Cape Town and 304 kilometres (190 miles) from Keetmanshoop. It is served by coach services from Cape Town and Windhoek.

When to go

Noordoewer is unpleasant at any time of the year but most bearable in the southern spring, between September and November, and autumn, between March and May.

Where to stay

Camel Lodge is the town's only hotel. See Listings for "Hotels".

Sightseeing

Little more than a one-street border town, Noordoewer nonetheless has a certain fascination as gateway to Namibia and also for its dominating position on the banks of **Orange River**.

Adventurers can organise canoeing and rafting expeditions down to the river's lower reaches.

Apart from its **border post** complete with **customs** and **immigration**, Noordoewer boasts a **hotel**, **shop** and **filling station**.

From Noordoewer, the main **B1 road** cuts through well-irrigated farmlands — sometimes ablaze with orange blossoms and filled with a variety of vegetables — to **Grünau** where it links up with the **B3 highway** from South Africa which enters Namibia at the **border post** of **Nakop**.

Fifty-one kilometres, (thirty-two miles) south-east of Grünau is **Karasburg,** southern Namibia's third-largest community.

Getting there

Karasburg is 1,281 kilometres (800 miles) from Johannesburg, 303 kilometres (189 miles) from Upington, on the border with South Africa, 690 kilometres (430 miles) from Windhoek, and 208 kilometres (130 miles) from Keetmanshoop. It is linked to Windhoek and other major centres by road, rail and air services.

When to go

Karasburg is pleasant all year-round.

Where to stay

Kalkfontein Hotel (1-star) and Van Riebeeck Hotel (1-star). See Listings for "Hotels".

Sightseeing

Quieter and smaller than Keetmanshoop, and much further south, **Karasburg** has a bustling **high-street**, **filling station**, **post office**, **railway station**, **hospital**, **airport** and **two hotels**. It's an ideal base from which to explore Namibia's southernmost reaches.

Thirty-six kilometres (twenty-three miles) **south** of the town, along a **minor road** that runs past the airport, is the **settlement** where Namibia's first **mission post** was established early in the nineteenth century.

The station was built around the **hot springs** of appropriately named **Warmbad** in 1805 but it later became more famous for its spa waters than its historic significance.

All that marks the place today is a **plaque** commemorating its founding father, missionary Edward Cook. The **ruins** of its **old fort** and the **spa buildings** are now the subject of a restoration programme.

From Grünau, the B2 runs north under the lee of the 2,187-metre (7,175-foot) high **Karas Mountains** to Keetmanshoop.

Natural Wonder

But there is more to southern Namibia than deserts, diamonds and the Orange River. In fact, it is the dried-up course of another once-mighty river of the south that lingers in the mind when other memories may have faded. A winding trail leads eighty kilometres (fifty miles) west of the B1 highway between Noordoewer and Grünau through a bleached, burnt-out wasteland to one of Africa's greatest natural wonders.

Over thousands of years the Fish River cut a 550-metre (1,800-foot) deep chasm in the rocky, barren plain that is twenty-seven kilometres (seventeen miles) across at its widest. Twisting 161 kilometres (100 miles)

Above: Balancing rocks in the fascinating Giant's Playground near Keetmanshoop.

through tortured, eroded cliffs, staggering in their rugged beauty, the Fish River Canyon is surpassed in size in Africa only by Ethiopia's Blue Nile Gorge. There is one road which runs along the edge of the canyon to a series of viewing points where its sheer cliffs plunge to the billion-years-old river bed. Truly, this is a marvel of living antiquity.

In an area often plagued by drought, the well-watered canyon, with its fish and game, was an oasis for early inhabitants. In 1981 more than forty Stone Age sites were recorded, increasing in size where the canyon begins to widen in the south. Fish River Canyon was proclaimed a national monument in 1962, became a game reserve in 1968 and a conservation area in 1969. The reserve was expanded in 1987 to include the Huns Mountains in the west and land to the south.

Whether you arrive by foot or road, nothing detracts from the wonder of this pristine wilderness. The canyon headquarters are at the hot springs of Ai-Ais, a truly life-sustaining oasis. Bubbling up from the river-bed, rich in fluoride, sulphate and chloride, the water, which has an average temperature of 60°C, is piped into indoor pools, jacuzzis and an outdoor swimming pool. Many suffering from rheumatism and nervous disorders claim to find relief in the waters.

The springs are likely to have been known to the Stone Age inhabitants of the canyon for thousands of years, for Ai-Ais is the local vernacular for 'fire-water'.

At the beginning of the twentieth century, during the Nama war against the Herero, the Germans made Ai-Ais their base camp. And when the South African forces under General Louis Botha invaded South West Africa in 1915, German soldiers sought refuge in Ai-Ais to recover from their wounds.

After World War I, the South West African administration leased the spring to a Karasburg entrepreneur who built the beginnings of the present resort. The modern rest camp was opened officially on 16 March 1971, and almost exactly a year later the Fish River came down in flood and washed away nearly everything — except the main building which is on high ground.

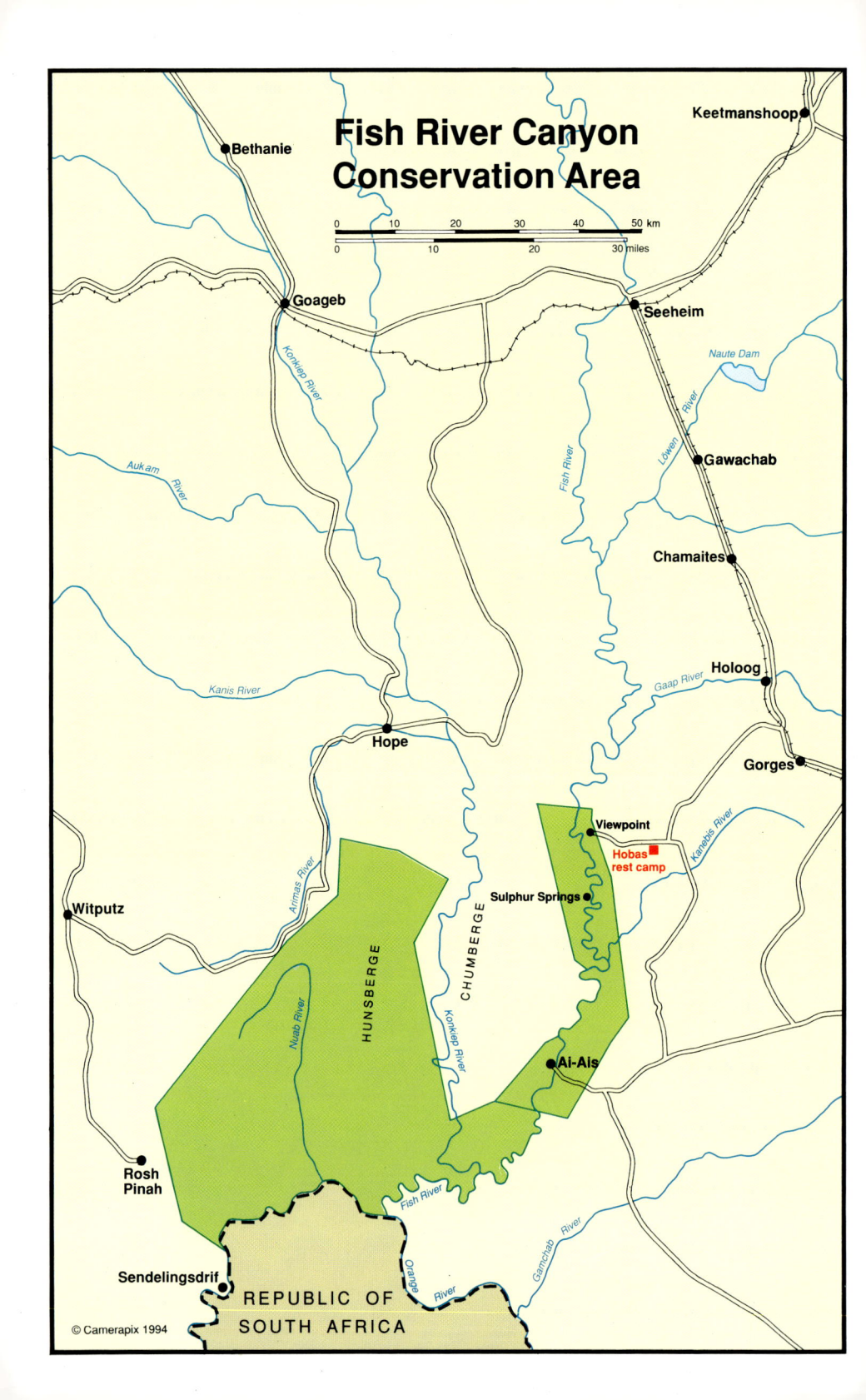

Fish River Canyon Conservation Area

Above: Lone Quiver Tree, the Kokerboom, stands on the escarpment overlooking Fish River Canyon.

Now restored, Ai-Ais is safe from the powerful torrents. Today it is a bastion of relaxation amid the wilderness.

Getting there

Ai-Ais, 1,102 kilometres (684 miles) from Swakopmund, 1,033 kilometres (641 miles) from Walvis Bay, 744 kilometres (462 miles) from Windhoek, 596 kilometres (370 miles) from Lüderitz, and 262 kilometres (163 miles) from Keetmanshoop, is served by road and air.

When to go

The cliffs of Fish River Canyon may be visited all year round, although the canyon floor is open only between May and September. Due to the intense heat of summer and the threat of flashfloods, Ai-Ais is closed from the end of October to mid-March.

Where to stay

Hobas Rest Camp is ten kilometres (six miles) from the canyon. Ten camp-sites are available for a maximum of eight persons each. There is also a kiosk with basic supplies as well as a swimming pool.

Ai-Ais Springs is a resort with everything from flats and guesthouses to caravan parks and campsites. Make bookings for both Hobas and Ai-Ais well in advance. See Listings.

Sightseeing

The depth of the **Fish River Canyon** ranges between 457 and 549 metres (1,499-1,801 feet). In Africa, only Ethiopia's Blue Nile Gorge is deeper and longer, and at Fish River Canyon the visitor is faced with nature at its most impressive, for nothing infringes upon the majesty of the canyon.

The **view** is awe-inspiring. Inevitably, as you stand close to the edge, a rock, pebble or flurry of shale cascades down the **cliffs** and the mind becomes confounded by the kaleidoscope of colours and images reflecting from the myriad cliffs and bends, bluffs and crags. It is a hypnotic world of eroded rock.

A cold wind whips across the **plain** and over the cliffs, evoking an atmosphere that may have existed from the beginning of time. For these menacing **slopes** of sandstone, shale and lava were laid down almost 1,800 million years ago. Condensed, squeezed and folded while heated to more than 600°C, they metamorphosed, re-crystallised and changed appearance. The rocks and intrusive granites form the Namaqualand Metamorphic complex.

The almost **black streaks** running through this complex are fractures plugged by lava which, unable to force its way to the surface, solidified about 900 million years ago. Now the **strata** began to erode, baring the rocks and smoothing them into a vast plain which, some 650 million years ago, became the floor of a shallow sea that covered southern Namibia.

About 150 million years later the earth's crust fractured and a small valley formed near the Fish River. Slowly, the uppermost sections of the Nama Group wasted away. And then, nearly 300 million years ago, glaciers moving south deepened the valley even further, followed by more fractures.

Within the most recent faults and fractures, deep in the earth's crust, ground water is heated to emerge on the surface as **hot springs**.

Raging torrent

The often dry **river-bed** writhes along the bottom of the canyon like a snake. Indeed, the Fish is the longest river in Namibia. From its source, it flows more than 800 spectacular kilometres (497 miles) to its **confluence** with the Orange River, 110 kilometres (sixty-eight miles) **east** of the Atlantic Ocean.

For the first few hundred kilometres it makes barely any incision into the escarpment, but where it begins its descent **south** of **Seeheim** — at the junction of the **Gaap River** — it reaches approximately fifty metres (165 feet). Further **south**, it drops over two **waterfalls** in quick succession and enters the canyon.

The Fish River is one of only a few in the country to have permanent **pools** in its lower and middle reaches outside the rainy season. But in flood it becomes a raging 100-metre-wide (300 feet) torrent, flowing in places at between twenty and twenty-five kilometres (twelve to sixteen miles) an hour. The river flow varies with the rainfall, usually from mid-November to the end of March.

In an area plagued by drought, it's little wonder that the well-watered canyon with its fish and game became an oasis to Namibia's early inhabitants. Archaeological surveys have uncovered nine Stone Age sites which date back 50,000 years.

The larger settlements are located in the **west** near **Ai-Ais Springs** where the canyon is wider. More recent settlements from the later Stone Age are located mainly on the inside of the river bends.

But Fish River Canyon also plays host to a vast variety of flora and fauna. Search the skies overhead and you may see a **white-backed mousebird** or **dusky sunbird**. The birdlife of the canyon is prolific, with well over sixty species.

Along the river, **grey heron**, **hammerkop**, **Egyptian goose**, **blacksmith plover** and **Cape wagtail** are common while the **reedbeds** are the habitat of the **purple gallinule** and **African marsh warbler**. The **red-eyed bulbul**, **Cape robin** and **bokmakierie** live in the riverine **forest**. And the **rocky slopes** and **cliffs** are the habitat of such species as **rock kestrel**, **rock pigeon**, **mountain chat**, **sickle-winged chat** and **pale-winged starling**.

As for wildlife, visitors may be lucky to spot a dainty **klipspringer**, **rock dassie** or **chacma baboon** on the rocky outcrops surrounding the canyon.

The canyon proper is home to the secretive **leopard**, **kudu** and **Hartmann's mountain zebra**. But all are shy and come out only at night to hunt or quench their thirst. Often, the zebra's horse-like **spoor** and dung in the lower reaches of the canyon are the only indications of its presence.

Reeds grow in dense clumps on the river banks along with trees and shrubs such as **camel thorn** — easily recognised by its characteristic grey, crescent-shaped seed-pods — **sweet thorn** and **wild tamarisk**, which favours the river-bed and river-bank. Other tree and grass species in the canyon include the **quiver tree** (*Aloe dichotoma*), **noorsdoring** (*Euphorbia virosa*), silky **Bushman grass** (*Stipagrostis uniplumis*) and tall **Bushman grass** (*Stipagrostis ciliata*).

Only after the rains do the **flowers** reveal themselves in all their glory. Suddenly, and only briefly, the canyon is blanketed from top to bottom in a sea of yellow-flowering **devil's thorn** (*Tribulus zeyheri*) and yellow **cleome**, which grows up to a metre (three feet) high.

During May and June the white, trumpet-like flowers of the exotic ***Datura innoxia*** colour some areas. At these times, the canyon looks as if a giant artist has painted vivid white and yellow patches along the river's course.

Several **viewing points** lie along the **road** that follows the **edge** of the canyon. The main one, **west** of Hobas, eight kilometres (five miles) **north** of Ai-Ais, affords visitors superb vistas of **Hell's Bend** — a classical example of a meander formed when the river was still young.

Further **south** there are viewing spots above **Palm Springs**, but the best views of all are from the **Sulphur Springs lookout point**. Although fairly rocky, it's generally in good condition and suitable for cars.

In truth, however, there is no better way to see the canyon than by walking through it. Only then is the visitor able to appreciate its true grandeur. Backpackers cover the eighty-five kilometres (fifty-three miles) between the northernmost viewpoint and Ai-Ais in four to five days. No facilities have been provided and the wilderness is experienced in its barest — and most exciting — form.

The **first section** of the descent into the canyon is rather steep, but fortunately there are **chains** along the path. It is advisable to move down this section at an easy pace. It takes anything between forty-five and ninety minutes. The route on the first day follows the **left bank** of the **river**, passing along large **boulders** interspersed with stretches of soft, loose sand.

Palm Springs

Palm Springs is one of the popular **overnight camps** in the canyon. There, weary hikers soothe aching muscles in **pools** fed by **thermal springs** — a welcome luxury after the first day.

The origin of the **palm trees** at Palm Springs has given rise to many stories, the

Above: Restored church in Keetmanshoop, 'capital' of southern Namibia, is now preserved as a museum.

most popular being that they grew from date stones discarded by two German runaways who sought refuge in the canyon during World War I.

One was said to be suffering from skin cancer, the other asthma — yet after bathing in the springs both were miraculously cured.

The hot springs are forced to the surface from a depth of some 2,000 metres (6,560 feet) at a rate of about thirty litres (six-and-a-half gallons) a second. The temperature of the water — rich in fluorides, chlorides and sulphates — averages 57°C.

South of Palm Springs, the boulder-strewn route gives way to **sandy beaches** alongside sweeping **river-bends**. These wide meanders involve frequent river crossings which save a considerable distance. Thirty kilometres (nineteen miles) from the starting point stands the familiar landmark of the **Table Mountain**.

After a short ascent, the impressive **Four Finger Rock** comes into view. Some two to three kilometres (one-and-a-quarter to two

Above: Bleached shores of the lake formed by the Naute Dam, south-east of Keetmanshoop.

miles) further on the trail crosses the river again and leads up a slope to the **west**.

Rest there awhile and watch **lizards** scuttle across granite rocks. The late afternoon sunlight strikes through the billowing clouds like a celestial ray to cast shadows near pools of glistening water.

German grave

From this point the canyon opens out. About two kilometres (one-and-a-quarter miles) further **south** is the **grave** of Lieutenant Thilo von Trotha, a German officer who was killed in a skirmish with the Nama in 1905 and was buried where he fell. The grave blends into the **western bank** at the **mouth** of the valley leading from the Four Finger Rock and is difficult to distinguish. From there, Ai-Ais is a good day's walk further south.

The **pools** on the canyon floor are usually well-stocked with fish: **small-mouthed yellow fish**, **large-mouthed yellow fish**, **barbel**, **carp** and **blue kurper**. Fishing permits are available at Ai-Ais.

When it comes to cooking the fish, visitors may build fires wherever they choose, although they are encouraged to use existing spots made by other hikers so as not to scar the environment.

Hikers should also bear in mind that it's advisable to take along a small stove as wood is scarce at the head of the trail. When you do find timber, never break branches off seemingly dead trees.

If, after the five-day hike, you still feel that you have yet to come to grips with Fish River Canyon, and are still searching for that feeling of conquest, the one thing left to do may be to fly over it. Light aircraft may be chartered from Ai-Ais or Keetmanshoop Airport. An airborne excursion may put a dent in your bank balance, but when you look down on all 160 kilometres (100 miles) of the canyon, basking in the shimmering heat, you may feel it well worth the cost.

Augrabies-Steenbok Nature Reserve

There is no visitor accommodation in this small reserve in southern Namibia **north-west** of **Grünau**, but camping is allowed and there are basic toilet facilities. It is an area of small trees, shrubs and succulents and home to **Hartmann's mountain zebra, klipspringer, gemsbok** and **chacma baboon.**

Getting there

Take the C28 (C12) to Seeheim from Grünau and eleven kilometres (seven miles) beyond the Fish River Canyon viewpoint turnoff take the left turn and follow the signposts for another ten kilometres (six miles).

When to go

The reserve is open throughout the year from sun-up to sundown

To Keetmanshoop

Back on the B1, continue another 200 kilometres (125 miles) to the capital of southern Namibia, Keetmanshoop.

The town bore witness to the arrival of the first Europeans from the Cape. They came to trade, hunt and explore the riches of this new and mysterious land. In 1791, an expedition under Hendrik Hop reached as far as Hainabis on the Löwen River about twelve kilometres (seven-and-a-half miles) from where Keetmanshoop now stands. At the time, the Nama settlement there was known as "black mud", *Nugoaes*.

The first missionaries to South West Africa were sent by the London Missionary Society. Although they had established many stations in South Africa's Cape Colony, they found conditions in South West Africa so severe they promptly left.

The German Missionary Society, however, also sent representatives to South West Africa. And in April 1866, preacher John Schroder built a canvas shelter at Keetmanshoop. It is said the two trees he used to support the shelter are still alive. Later he constructed a hut for himself and his family, and built a church from reeds plastered with mud. Since he lacked funds he appealed for help to a rich industrialist, Johan Keetman, chairman of the German Missionary Society. Keetman sent 2,000 marks to build a church. In appreciation, Schroder named his settlement Keetman and eventually it became Keetmanshoop. But the man whose generosity inspired the name never saw 'his' town.

The Reverend Thomas Fenchel who succeeded Schroder is remembered, in fact, as the father of the town. He served the community for thirty-three years, building the mission station and a school which is still in use. At the turn of the century the first German garrison in Keetmanshoop built a fort, which was later demolished and replaced by a police station. Soon after, the town became the administrative capital of the south. In 1960, a brewery and ice factory were established there along with four hotels. Keetmanshoop has since grown around its old buildings and is perfectly positioned for visitors who wish to explore southern Namibia.

Getting there

Keetmanshoop, on the banks of a seasonal river, is 1,489 kilometres (925 miles) from Johannesburg, 1,011 kilometres (628 miles) from Cape Town, 482 kilometres (300 miles) from Windhoek, 334 kilometres (207 miles) from Lüderitz, and 221 kilometres (137 miles) from Mariental. The town is at the hub of the region and is served by scheduled road, rail and air services from all major centres.

Where to stay

The Canyon Hotel (3-star) and Travel Inn (2-star). There is a campsite on Agtstelaan and Aubstraat Street, off Kaiser Street. In Grünau, Grünau Hotel (1-star). In Lüderitz, Bay View Hotel (2-star), Kapps Hotel (1-star), Zum Sperrgebiet Hotel (1-star). In Maltahöhe, the Maltahöhe Hotel, (1-star). In Mariental, the Sandberg Hotel (1-star). See Listings for "Hotels".

Sightseeing

At the crossroads of southern Namibia, Keetmanshoop, which stands 1,000 metres (3,280 feet) above sea level, has a fascinating **museum**, near the **campsite** on the **corner** of **Sewendelaan** and **Kaiser Street**, where there is much information and history about the town and the surrounding areas.

81

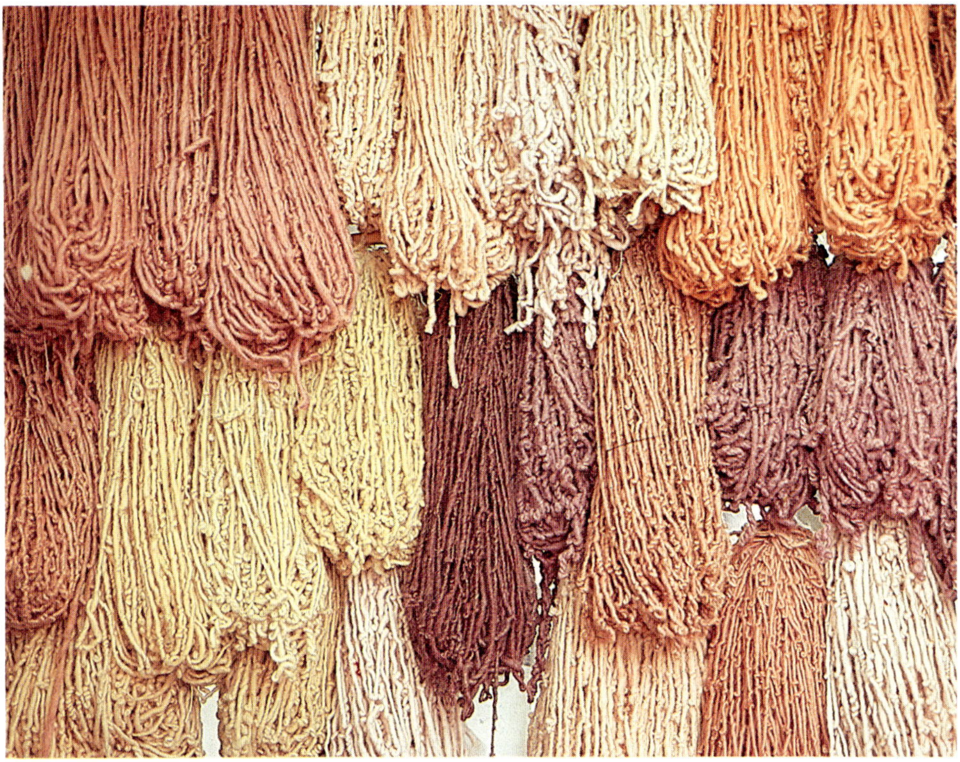

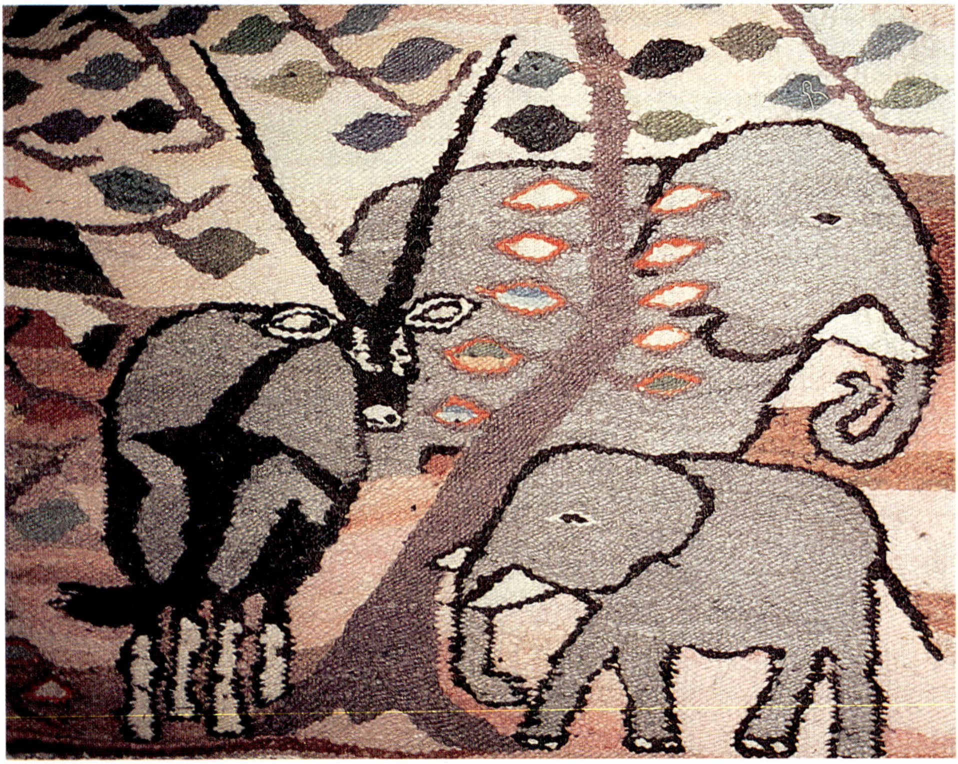

The museum is in the picturesque **church**, the oldest building in Keetmanshoop, which was completed in 1895 and seated 1,000 worshippers. But between 1950 and 1960 it fell into disuse and was used by vagrants and squatters. The legacy of their vandalism can be seen in the blackened **ruins** of two **wooden pillars** under the **gallery**. Now the Monument Committee and town council have saved this little gem for posterity.

The interior boasts an elegant **pulpit**, **gallery** and fine **masonry**. And the church's original and unusual corrugated **iron roof** remains intact. Take note of the **bell-tower**, constructed without mortar, or any other binding material for that matter.

There is a fascinating **collection** of old **photographs**, period **silverware**, Afrikaner **furniture**, **gramophones**, period **dress**, old **rifles** and much more.

Just around the corner is the old **Post Office**, built in 1910 to the design of the government architect Gottlieb Redecker. The handsome **facade** joins a pronounced, pointed gable to a wide, rectangular **tower** that supports a telegraph **mast**. Declared a **national monument** in 1987, the building houses the offices of the **Southern Tourist Forum** and **Air Namibia**.

There is also a fascinating **station**. Twice a year, at Easter and July, Namibian Railways celebrates the pioneering days of steam when a **Diamond Train** special, hauled by a majestic Class 24 **locomotive**, steams the 334 kilometres (208 miles) from Keetmanshoop to Lüderitz. The journey begins as a cloud of white doves are released into the bright blue of the Namibian sky while the train passes under a ceremonial arch at Keetmanshoop station.

Aboard the train, 200 or so passengers are entertained by a **band** whose repertoire includes a Diamond Train Song composed by Crispin Clay, the bard of Lüderitz, while the **dining** and **lounge cars** are decked out in the livery of the early days of the diamond rush — together with archive **pictures**. And each coach carries a legendary name — such as Kolmanskop, Pomana and Edatal.

Keetmanshoop is also the centre of Namibia's karakul sheep industry. This hardy species from Bokhara in Uzbekistan, Central Asia, thrives in the dry, warm climate and landscape of southern Namibia.

They were imported in 1907 by German trader Paul Albert Thorer who had shipped thirty-six of the creatures to Germany in 1902. But the central European climate was unsuitable for most of the sheep, which died off. So Thorer shipped the twelve survivors to Namibia where they thrived.

After World War I, South Africa established an experimental karakul centre at Neudam, near Windhoek, where researchers succeeded in breeding a karakul with a pure white skin, and another one with a pelt with a shallow 'water silk' curl pattern.

Karakul skins come from lambs killed twenty-four hours after birth. Only these are of value for the skin hardens as it grows older. About twenty-five pelts are required to make a jacket, thirty-two for a coat.

The karakul industry expanded rapidly and by 1937 one million skins had been sold. Today the skins are sold at the London Fur Fair with sales influenced by swings in the fashion industry. The main buyers are the USA, Canada and Germany. Karakul wool is also exported but it is inferior to Merino fleece and used mainly for making carpets.

Those interested in finding out more should visit the **Gellap Ost Karakul Farm** just outside Keetmanshoop, along the **northern airport road**. Research on the 137-square kilometre (fifty-two-square-mile) farm centres on refining the pattern and quality of the skins, as well as improving pastures.

There are many other excursions from Keetmanshoop to nearby fascinating places.

Opposite top: Dyed strands of fleecy karakul wool are sundried before weaving.
Opposite: Wildlife images woven into a colourful karakul rug.
Overleaf: Namibia's unique herd of wild desert horses forage for scant grazing by the railway line in the gravel flats of the Namib Desert near Aus, halfway between Keetmanshoop and Lüderitz.

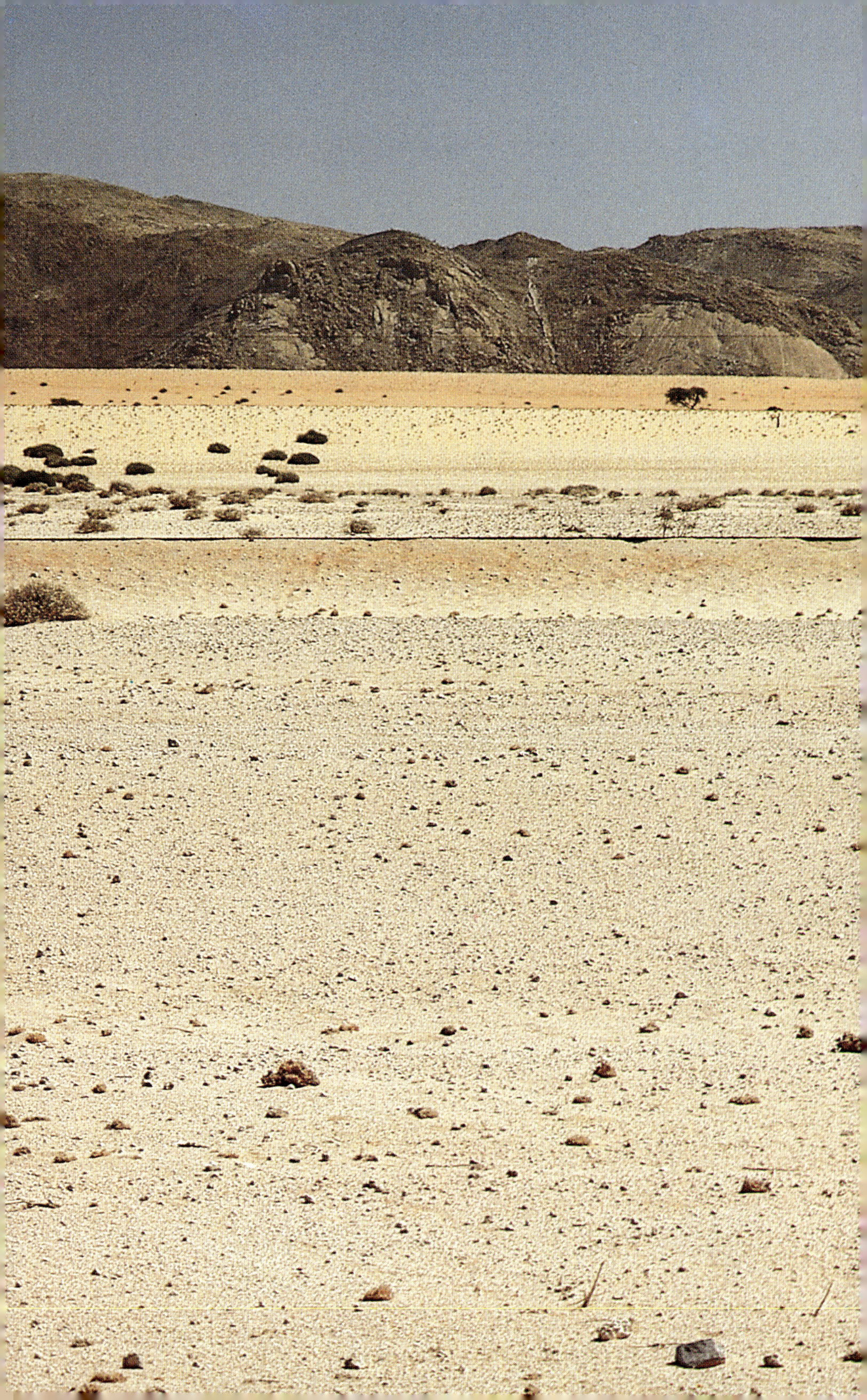

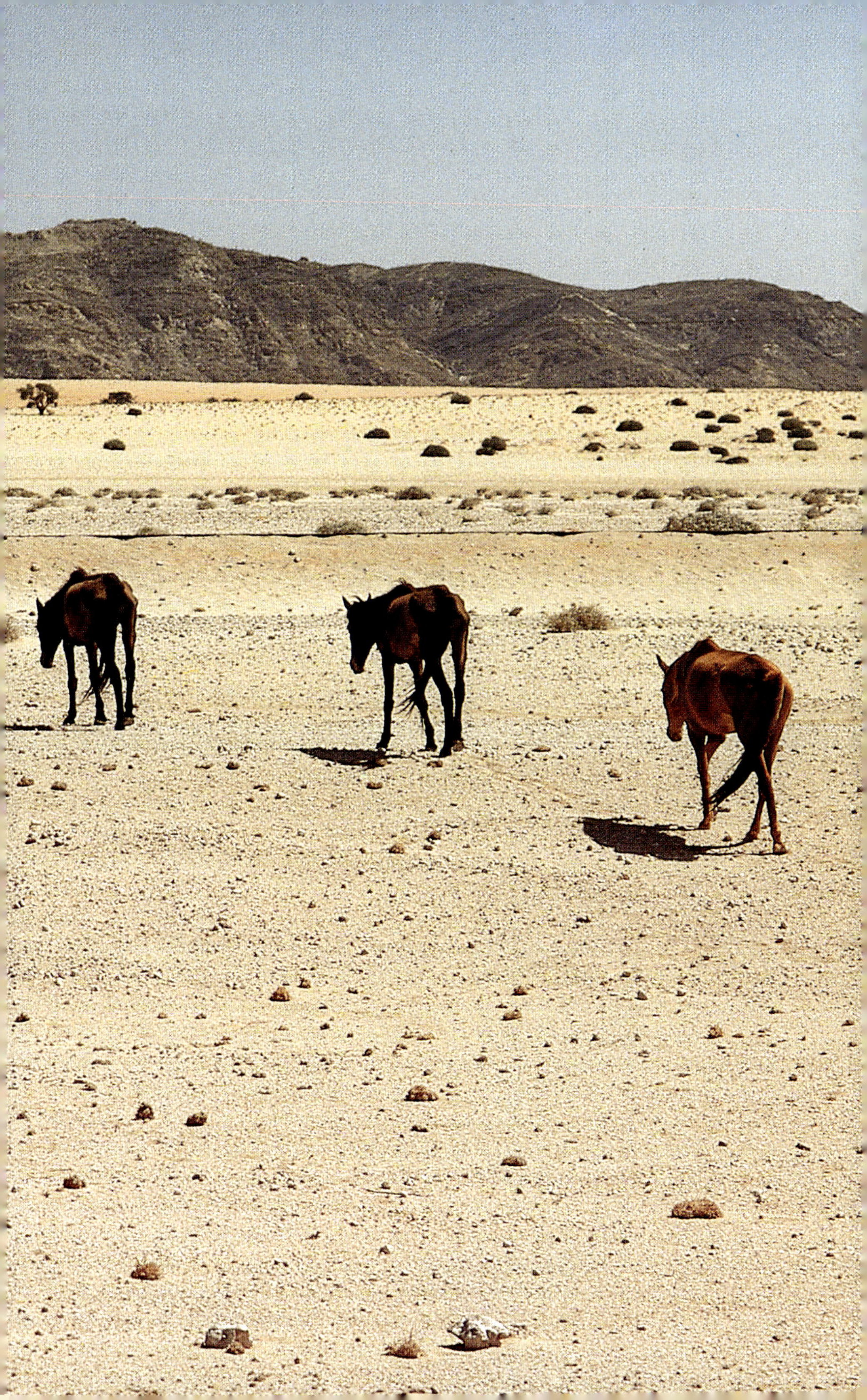

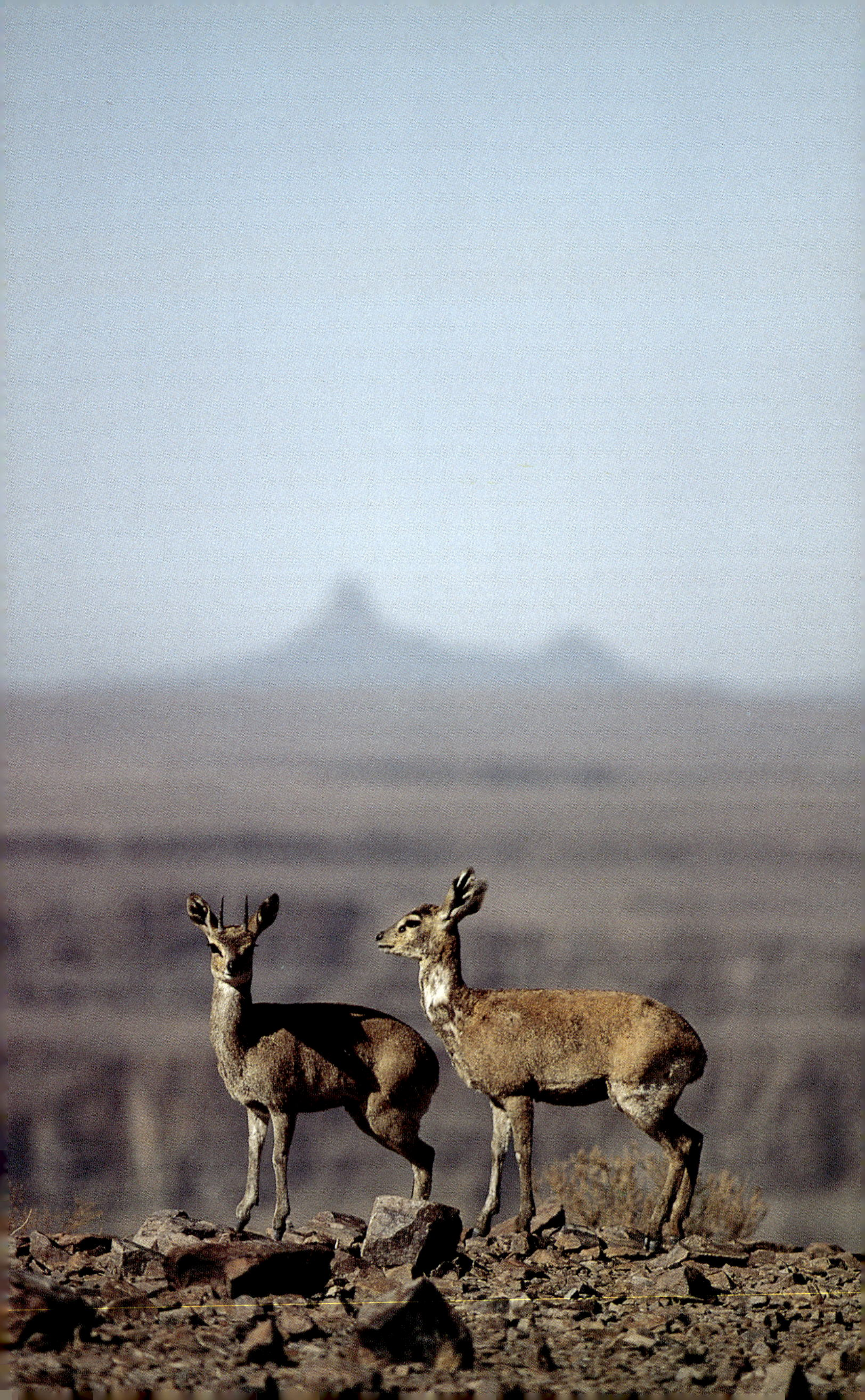

For example, the unusual **Quiver Tree Forest** on Gariganus Farm, fourteen kilometres (nine miles) north-west of Keetmanshoop, is like a backdrop to a science fiction film. About 300 trees, their alien-like forked branches rising almost straight into the air, grow there. Their trunks seem unnaturally smooth among a landscape of black rocks. Like so much of Namibia, it is a strange, out-of-this-world kind of place. It was declared a **national monument** on 1 June 1955. The quiver tree or kokerboom is one of Namibia's most distinctive plants. (See "The Great Survivors", Flora, Part Four).

It is extremely rare to find such a large group of quiver trees since the plant usually grows in solitary isolation. Some trees in the forest are between 200 and 300 years old. While most are between three and five metres (nine to sixteen feet) tall, occasional specimens reach as high as nine metres (thirty feet).

The **Giant's Playground**, across the road from the Quiver Tree Forest, was opened to the public in 1990 and is one of Namibia's most unusual attractions. Follow the **trail** through stacks of volcanic **balancing boulders**, weathered by the elements over millions of years. But take care for it's easy to get lost in this extensive rock labyrinth.

Westward Ho! Of Desert Horses and Strange Delights

From Keetmanshoop the **B4** leads west to the southern turnoff to the **Naute Dam**, thirty-two kilometres (twenty miles) from the town. Situated in glorious surroundings in the **Löwen River**, a tributary of the Fish River, the dam is favoured by water sports lovers and fishermen.

The main road then passes the **railway siding** at **Seeheim**, eight kilometres (five miles) further west, after which there is a **bridge** over the Fish River which affords a super view of where the river begins nudging and carving its way into the escarpment — the beginnings of the great Fish River Canyon.

Eleven kilometres (seven miles) along the main road a **national monument signboard** marks the starting point of a one-kilometre (half-a-mile) **walk** to an **old fort**, built between 1905 and 1906 to protect traffic on the road from Keetmanshoop and Lüderitz against marauding bands of Nama. For until the small contingent of soldiers arrived, the nearby **waterhole**, where travellers stopped for refreshment, was constantly attacked.

The fort, built from local slabs and rocks, merges remarkably well with the surroundings — as do the nearby **graves** of two soldiers.

Back on the main B4 road, after another fifty kilometres (thirty-one miles) there is a turn **north** at **Goageb** to **Bethanie**. (See "Missionary Heroes, Eccentric Settlers"). From Goageb the road continues another 100 kilometres (sixty-two miles) **west** to Aus.

Prison camp

At first glance, **Aus** seems like a ghost town. Literally in the middle of nowhere it merges into the side of a hill along the main road to Lüderitz. The buildings on its extremely dusty **high street** are constantly covered in a cloud of grey silt.

In July 1915, the German forces at Khorab, just north of Otavi, surrendered to South Africa and two prisoner-of-war camps were established. German officers were held at Okanjande, near Otjiwarongo, while the **camp** at Aus was for non-commissioned officers and other ranks.

Aus was ideal as a prisoner-of-war camp for there was no link between South Africa and South West Africa, and much of the railway line from Aus into the interior had been blown up. Supplies were therefore shipped from Cape Town to Lüderitz, and from there by train to Aus.

By August 1915 more than 1,552 prisoners were held captive at Aus.

At first, the men were housed in bell tents which offered little shelter from the

Opposite: With the monolithic outline of Hohenzoller Mountain in the background, klipspringer — antelope of cliff and rock — haunt the Fish River Canyon.

Above: Baroque grandeur of the ruins of a once-wealthy diamond industry on the outskirts of the desert ghost town of Kolmanskop near Lüderitz.

elements, and the severe extremes of temperature made conditions unbearable for both the Germans and their sixty South African guards. Yet, despite repeated pleas, the administration did nothing to ease the conditions.

So the PoWs began to make their own bricks and build houses. The construction was ingenious. Flattened tin cans were joined together to make tiles for roofs. The houses were generally one-roomed (some semi-detached), giving the impression of a small, closed neighbourhood. And many were underground, with their roofs just visible. By April 1916 the Germans had abandoned their tents.

They took great pride in their houses, even constructing attractive front gables, while others kept gardens. Their South African watchdogs, however, made no effort to improve their own lot.

Even when the Germans offered them building materials for construction of barracks the South Africans rejected the offer and most remained in pitiful huts made from sacking.

After the Treaty of Versailles was signed the first German prisoners left the camp in April 1919 and in May it was officially closed.

Seven decades later all evidence of these curious German structures had vanished beneath the desert sands.

Today the one-street town is notable only for the **Bahnhof Hotel**, which may only have one-star but exudes much character. The locals at the bar know a great deal about the desert and prospecting.

Free spirits of the desert

Further **west**, between Aus and Lüderitz, the road touches the southern fringes of the imposing Namib. It's there that you gain the first glimpses of the oldest desert in the world in all its golden glory. Signboards at the side of the road warn against vehicles stopping or alighting. For there the road runs through the forbidden land — *Sperrgebiet* — otherwise known as Diamond Area One. This vast treasury, blasted by the Atlantic gales, scorched by the relentless sun, runs north in a 100-kilometre (sixty-

Above: Sand sweeps into a mansion where fortunes were counted in rough diamonds plucked from the same desert sands near Kolmanskop.

two-mile) wide belt along the Namibian coast from the Orange River to Lüderitz.

Keep your eyes peeled for groups of wild horses on the plains at the edge of this sea of sand. You might think that in such an open wilderness any animals would stand out like sore thumbs. Yet it is only when they venture near the tarmac that you gain a close-up view of these bedraggled beasts, so thin their rib cages protrude through their coats. Amazingly they are able to go without water for as long as five days. By moving slowly, they sweat less.

Their only permanent source of water is an artificial pan at Garub, fed by a borehole. Their numbers vary according to the condition of the surrounding veld, although generally their population is between 150 and 160.

Many theories exist about the origins of the only wild desert-dwelling horses in the world. Some suggest that they were once owned by local farmers, others that they are descended from a stud established by a German aristocrat Baron von Wolf, at Duwisib Castle, many kilometres to the north. (See "Missionary Heroes, Eccentric Settlers"). According to another story, one horse was found with a German regimental insignia branded on its thigh. This supports a theory that they are offspring of mounts abandoned by the German cavalry who fled from the South Africans in 1915.

Feeding voraciously during the all too rare rainy seasons, the animals build themselves up to survive the lean, mean years of drought. And even this has its advantages. So dry is the area there are almost no parasites.

Splinters of stars

Diamonds are coveted by women. And men will kidnap, seduce, lie, cheat — and kill for them. Ancient Greeks believed they were the splinters of stars that had fallen to earth. These precious stones have been surrounded by intrigue and legends ever since they were first mined in India 2,500 years ago. One such legend is written in the sands around a clutch of abandoned buildings 116 kilometres (seventy-two-and-a-half miles) west of Aus. Passing along the

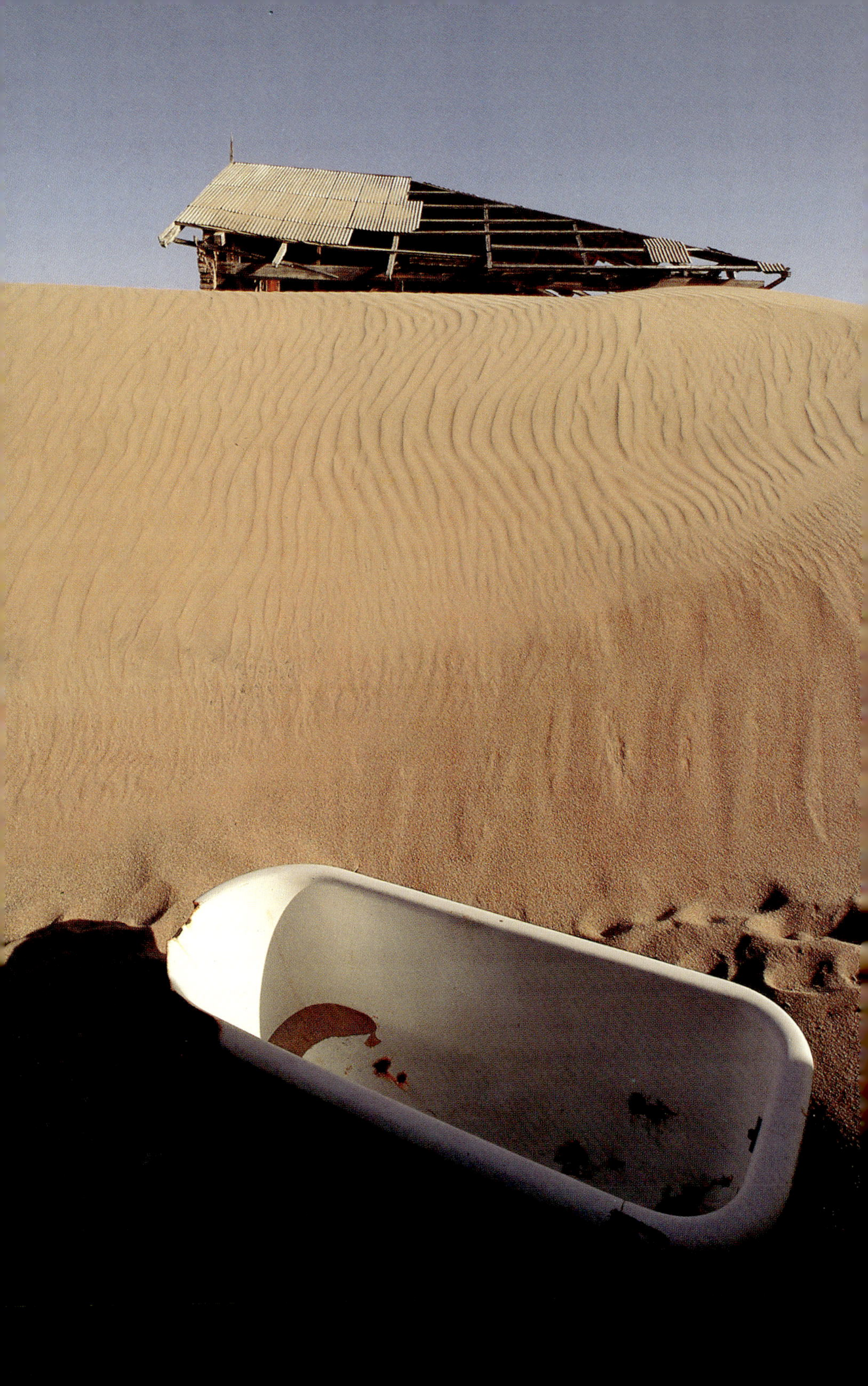

road today you may initially have little desire to stop and explore. But the closer you get, the more the contrast of the ruined turn-of-the-century German buildings, grand houses, baroque theatre and stately offices in the middle of the sea of sand kindles the imagination.

Even the name of this ghost town evokes visions of wealth lost and found. Kolmanskop, however, was named after a transport driver, Jani Kolman, who was rescued from the spot after a vicious sandstorm trapped his voortrek of ox-wagons.

The South West African diamond rush began in 1908 long before diamonds were discovered by August Stauch, a German railway supervisor. He was destined to become richer than most ever dream of. Yet, separated from his beloved family, he died a pauper.

Stauch arrived in what is now Namibia in May 1907, and was based at Grasplatz not far from Kolmanskop. One day in 1908, when he was leading a work team, one of the labourers, shovelling the desert sands away from the railway line, returned with an armful of wood.

Stauch told him jokingly: "Don't look for wood. Look for diamonds." Not long after, the man, Zacharias Lewala, spotted a telltale sparkle in the sand and, remembering Stauch's admonition, bent down and picked it up. Later he gave the stone to his foreman who sent it to Stauch.

When the German ran it over the glass of his watch the stone cut it. Stauch, convinced it was a diamond, quit his job and began staking claims around Kolmanskop.

At that time, Kolmanskop was just a siding nine kilometres (five-and-a-half miles) east of Lüderitz. When Stauch took the stone to a laboratory in Swakopmund for assay, an analyst gave a cursory, disinterested look, pointing out that diamonds didn't "just lie around in the desert". Stauch walked away only to be called back excitedly by the analyst shouting: "Herr Stauch! It is a diamond!" Not only that, it was a diamond of outstanding quality, even though small. Later observers were not surprised. Diamonds lay on the desert literally "like plums under a plum tree".

The news sparked diamond fever as sailors deserted ships, traders their shops, and men their wives to converge on Kolmanskop. And while prices soared, water ran out and prospectors quarrelled over ownership.

Stauch soon discovered the diamonds were larger and more plentiful in the valleys that ran between the sand dunes, and Kolmanskop became a bustling centre boasting everything that could be found in a modern European city — butchery, bakery, furniture factory, soda-water and lemonade plant, daily ice and milk deliveries, four skittle alleys, public playground and even a swimming pool.

Large, elegant houses were built for the mining executives and a grand community-centre, complete with theatre and an orchestra that played at tea dances. Later the town fathers founded a well-equipped hospital and imported the country's first X-ray machine. But as the diamond deposits in the immediate vicinity became depleted the good times came to an end and people began to move away in search of fresh finds further south.

Within the span of forty years Kolmanskop lived, flourished and died. By 1950 all mining in Kolmanskop had ended. As for Stauch, he became a millionaire many times over.

But the great depression of the 1920s brought his empire crashing down and he was forced to sell all his assets. When he died in Germany at the age of sixty-nine in May 1947 all that he had to his name was two marks and fifty pfennigs.

Getting there

Kolmanskop, 1,814 kilometres (1,127 miles) from Johannesburg, 1,336 kilometres (830 miles) from Cape Town, 807 kilometres (501 miles) from Windhoek, 722 kilometres (450 miles) from Swakopmund and 325

Opposite: Relics of a boom that flourished, withered and died — haunting reminders of the glory that was once Kolmanskop's.

Above: Old boilers used to process whale blubber slowly rust away on the beach at Grasplatz near Lüderitz.

kilometres (202 miles) from Keetmanshoop, is served by road and rail.

When to go

The ghost town lies in the Diamond Area and visitors require a special pass which is available at any time of the year from CDM offices in Lüderitz or Windhoek. CDM also run guided tours.

Where to stay

At Lüderitz, nine kilometres (five-and-a-half miles) from Kolmanskop. (See "Lüderitz: Between Dunes, Diamonds and Ocean", Part Three and Listings).

Sightseeing

Now only the skeletons of Kolmanskop's grand elaborate buildings remain, although there is still a certain dignity about their ravaged **ruins**. Many **doorways** are blocked by **sand**, but you enter by climbing the dunes and through the windows — sometimes those on the second floor. Inside, the only sounds are those of the wind whistling through the rotting roofs and empty window frames and the creaking of rickety floorboards underfoot. Yet it is easy to picture a German family sitting down to enjoy a banquet under the chandeliers in one of the grand rooms. The memories are so recent and rich you feel you can almost reach out and touch them.

Most buildings have been preserved as they were when they were abandoned, but the romantic atmosphere is perfectly retained — proud remnants of a glorious past.

In April 1983, the seventy-fifth anniversary of the discovery of the first diamond, Consolidated Diamond Mines restored many more buildings, including the **casino**, **skittle alley**, and **retail shop**.

The area around Lüderitz is also well-known for **'desert roses'** — crystals of sand and salt formed under damp, moist conditions. Not long ago digging these up was prohibited, but now enthusiasts may obtain a permit to do so, together with a map, from the CDM office in Lüderitz. There are, however, restrictions to be observed. You may only take away three 'roses' to a total of one-and-a-half kilos (three-and-a-quarter pounds) and you are

Above: Replica of the cross raised by Bartholomeo Diaz at Diaz Point overlooking Halifax Island near Lüderitz.

given only two hours in which to find and remove them.

The Lüderitz Peninsula

Heading north-east as you leave Kolmanskop the road crests a hill and there, stretching out below you, is the Atlantic, an iridescent blue against a faultless sky. With the town of Lüderitz in the background, surf breaks over black rocks as penguins and seals dive beneath the waves.

Far out on the horizon, fishing boats bob up and down on the swell while the crisp ocean air is refreshingly strong. Lüderitz lies to the north of an intriguing peninsula where many delightful bays await ex–ploration. (See "Luderitz: Between Dunes, Diamonds and Ocean", Part Three).

Getting there

Lüderitz, 1,823 kilometres (1,113 miles) from Johannesburg, 1,345 kilometres (836 miles) from Cape Town, 816 kilometres (507 miles) from Windhoek, 731 kilometres (454 miles) from Swakopmund, 762 kilometres (474 miles) from Walvis Bay, 334 kilometres (207 miles) from Keetmanshoop, is linked by rail and air services to Cape Town, Windhoek and Walvis Bay.

When to go

The weather is unpredictable and often foggy and cold. This is a welcome relief when you have been in the hot desert.

Where to stay

Bay View Hotel (2-star), comfortable with swimming pool, Kapps Hotel (1-star), Zum Sperrgebiet Hotel (1-star), charming. See Listings for "Hotels". There are also some holiday chalets behind the Strand Cafe and a campsite. See Listings.

Sightseeing

Radford Bay is named after the first white settler to live there without water. David Radford collected dew every morning to survive. Occasionally he traded with passing ships, exchanging water for dried fish, shark-liver oil and ostrich feathers.

Continue to **Second Lagoon** rich with cultivated **oyster beds**. From there to the

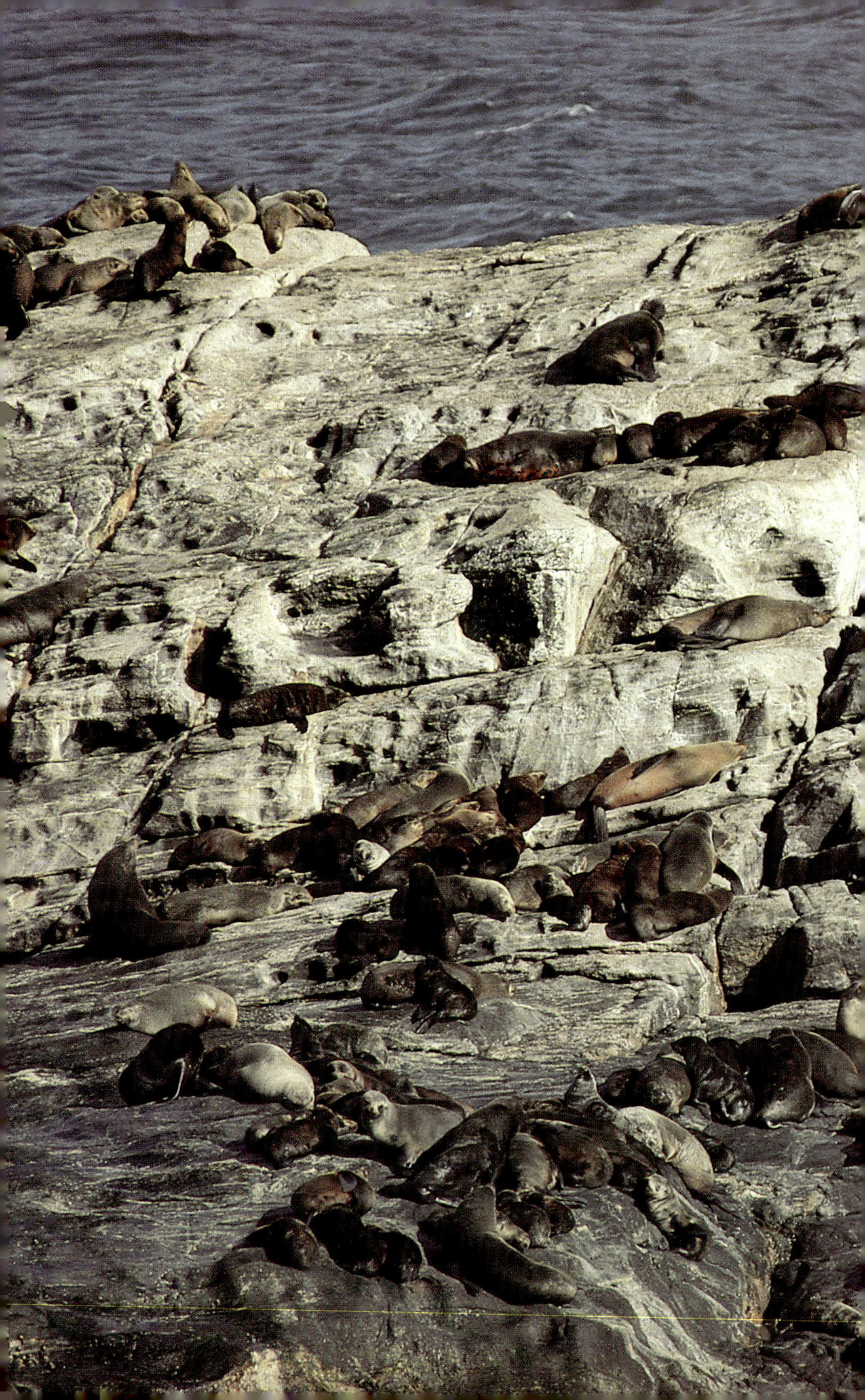

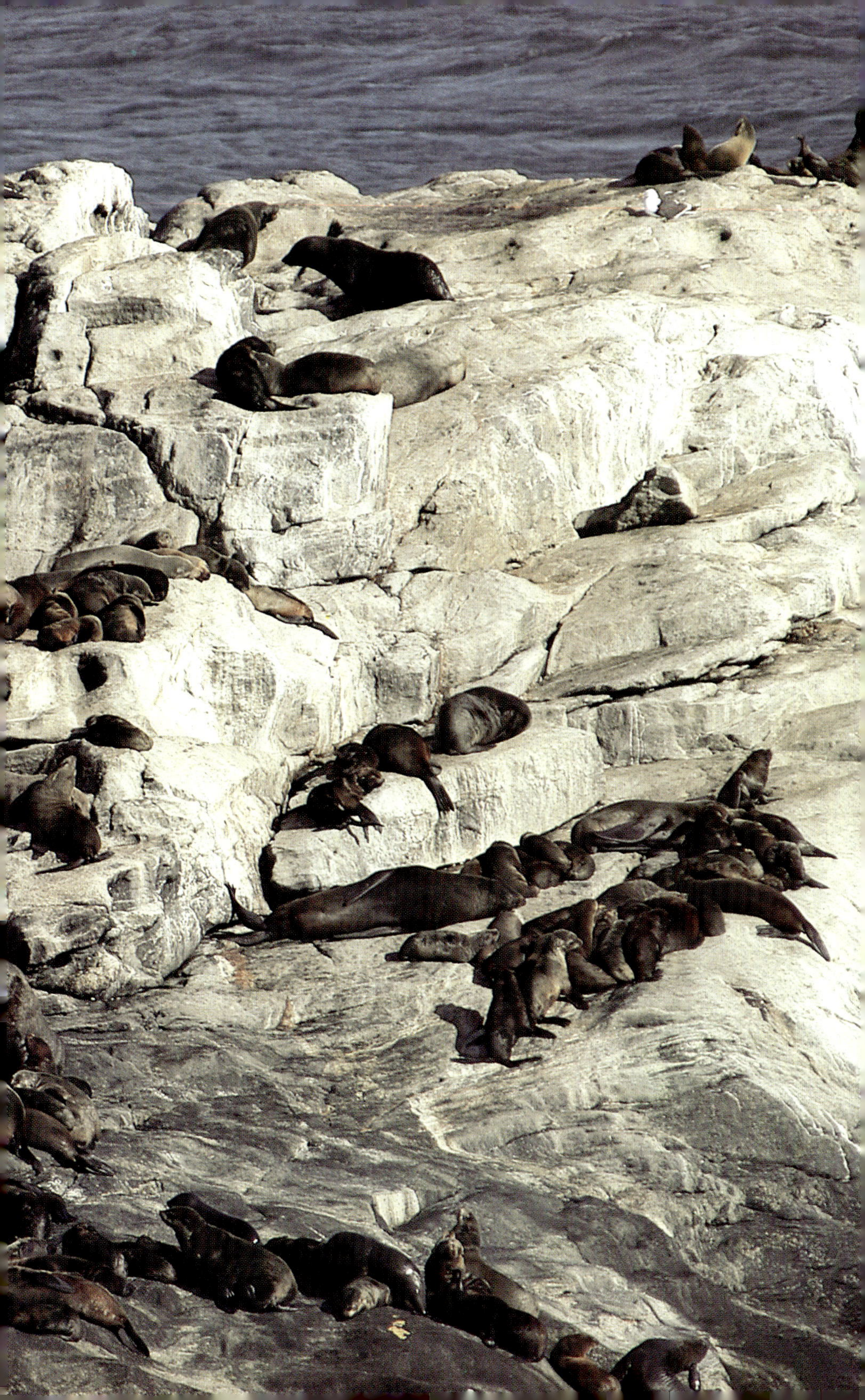

harbour, the coastline is often crowded with birdwatchers for **greater flamingo** are common — although the chances of seeing them depend on the tide.

Several kilometres past Second Lagoon take the turnoff to **Grosse Bucht, Large Bay** — the only sandy stretch on the peninsula, apart from **Agate Beach**.

The road leading northwards from Grosse Bucht takes the visitor to many **bays** and **clifftops**. Among these, **Guano Bay** offers a striking view of **Halifax Island**. Continuing to **Diaz Point**, you may notice a **grave** with a **wooden cross** that reads: "George Pond of London, died here of hunger and thirst in 1906."

A little further on, where a **lighthouse** dates back to 1910, a **wooden bridge** crosses a rocky gully to **Diaz Point**. Built in 1911, the bridge once served a steam-operated foghorn.

From Diaz Point the road runs past the old **landing strip** and leads to a short detour to **Sturmvogelbucht** where the remains of an old German **whaling station**, dating back to 1913, may be seen.

Nearby **Griffith Bay** takes its name from an American sailor who sought refuge in Lüderitz during the American Civil War. But he was later shot as a traitor by a crew member of another visiting American ship.

Return to Lüderitz to cross onto **Shark Island** by way of a **causeway** where a plaque reminds visitors of the German merchant, Adolf Lüderitz, founder of Namibia's oldest harbour town. Finally, move on to Agate Beach for a late walk, before a crayfish meal in downtown Lüderitz. (See "The Capital and the Towns", Part Three).

Missionary Heroes, Eccentric Settlers

One particular diversion in southern Namibia seems to encompass all that is heroic and eccentric about its missionary-colonial past. The journey of discovery begins at the start of the C14 which runs north-west off the B4 from Goageb.

Getting there

Some twenty-nine kilometres (eighteen miles) along this road is Bethanie where Heinrich Schmelen established Namibia's first mission station in 1814. Forced to abandon it after six years of constant inter-tribal conflicts, he later tried to re-establish it but was again beaten by warfare, horrific drought and locust plagues. In 1840, however, when the rights of the London Missionary Society were consigned to the Rhenish Missionary Society, the Reverend Hans Knudsen came to Bethanie.

Sightseeing

Schmelen House stands in the grounds of the Evangelical Lutheran Church. Built by Schmelen in 1814, it was burnt down shortly after he abandoned Bethanie. It has since been rebuilt, the only parts dating back to the original being the **stone walls**. Now a **national monument**, it houses a captivating photographic history of the mission and Bethanie. Ask at the **hotel** or **vicarage** for the **key** so that you may have a look around.

Along **Keetmanshoop Street** stands a handsome **house** that was declared a **national monument** in 1951. Built in 1883 by the Nama leader, Captain Joseph Fredericks, it was there in October 1884 that the first protection treaty between the Germans and the Bethanian Nama was signed by the Captain and the German Consul General, Dr Friedrich Nachtigal.

The 1899 **Rhenish Mission Church** is in **Quelen Street**. In the nearby **graveyard**, lie the remains of the dedicated missionaries who lived, worked, and died in Bethanie. The **twin towers** of the 1859 church — one of the oldest in Namibia — had to be torn down when they became unstable. Until 1970, the remainder of the building served as a school.

Previous page: Basking seals on one of the rocky islands off Lüderitz.

Above: Duwisib Castle, monument to the magnificent folly of a German aristocrat and his ambitions to tame the wilderness at the edge of the Namib Desert.

To Duwisib

The main C14 through Bethanie carries on north to **Helmeringhausen**, a quaint settlement which, in fact, is nothing more than a farmstead with a neighbouring **museum**, general dealer **store**, **filling station**, **hotel**, **chapel** and **graveyard**.

Adjacent to the Helmeringhausen Hotel is an interesting open-air **farm museum** with a large number of old German implements on display. Among these is a beautiful Lüderitz **fire-engine** and a sturdy **ox-wagon** that once laboured across the sandy wastes, transporting building materials and furniture from Lüderitz to Duwisib Castle. The museum was established in 1984 by the Helmeringhausen Farmers' Association.

Helmeringhausen was originally known as Chamis and during the German colonial period a military station was established there. In 1899 a prefabricated wooden house was shipped from Germany to Lüderitz, whence it was transported east by ox-wagon. Erected on the northern bank of the Konkiep River, the building served as a barracks and mess for the German troops. It was later replaced by a permanent, double-storied structure which was converted to the single-storey building now serving as a **farmhouse**.

The graveyard is surrounded by an attractive **stone wall** which forms a half-circle on one side. There, in small alcoves, are the **tombstones** of German troops who died during the Nama wars. In the centre of the graveyard is a **memorial** in the form of a **chapel,** while nearby is a set of heavy **iron gates** forged from the rims of several ox-wagon wheels.

Duwisib Castle

Sixty-two kilometres (thirty-eight-and-a-half miles) further **north** from Helmeringhausen turn **west** onto route 831 where **signposts** show the way to one of Namibia's more unlikely surprises. You would hardly expect to find a **castle**, surrounded by scrubland, at the very edge of a haunting desert. And **Duwisib**, turrets and all, is a real castle encircled by a rich variety of trees and lawns, striking contrast to its backdrop of desert browns and oranges. Such is the castle's authenticity that you half expect a beautiful young maiden with long, golden hair to lean out of one of the small windows and a fire-breathing dragon to emerge from a moat.

The story behind Duwisib Castle is also like something out of a fairy-tale. It was completed in 1909 by a dashing captain, Baron Hans-Heinrich von Wolf, a member of the Saxon nobility, born in Dresden in January 1873. After completing school he followed his father's footsteps and entered military service, later becoming an artillery captain in the Royal Saxon army at Könisbruck, Dresden.

In 1904 he was sent to South West Africa to serve with the *Schutztruppe*. Following the end of hostilities in 1907, von Wolf returned to Germany and married an American, Jayta Humphries, the step-daughter of the American consul in Dresden. The couple settled in South West Africa and by the end of 1908 owned eight farms covering 1,400 square kilometres (540 square miles).

Von Wolf envisaged a home similar to the castles built by the *Schutztruppe* at Gibeon, Namutoni and Windhoek. Soon the renowned architect, August Sander, was commissioned to design a building to serve as both home and fortress.

Stone for the castle came from a quarry some three kilometres (two miles) from the building site, while other material was imported from Germany. The ambitious nature of this project can best be appreciated when considering the logistics of transporting material from Swakopmund overland by ox-wagon. Twenty were used on the 640-kilometre (397-mile) journey — half of it across the Namib Desert.

But — perhaps most amazing — skilled craftsmen were recruited all over Europe: stonemasons from Italy, carpenters from Scandinavia and building labourers from Ireland. Their combined efforts resulted in a building which has been described as surpassing any comparable project in taste, craftsmanship — and cost.

Duwisib consists of **twenty-two rooms** arranged in a **U-shape**, enclosed by a high **wall**. From the **entrance** you pass through an **arch** into the main hall or *Rittersaal*. A narrow wooden staircase leads up to a **minstrel's gallery** and the *Herrenzimmer* — a room reserved exclusively for men. Central to the design of Duwisib is the way it was built to withstand any attack. Most rooms have **embrasures**, not windows.

Downstairs, the **main hall** is flanked by **sitting rooms**, both with beautifully embellished **fireplaces**. In a country as hot as Namibia it's a surprise to find fireplaces in most rooms. The thick stone walls, small windows and south-west aspect, however, necessitate some form of heating, especially during the winter when the building becomes extremely cold. During the summer, however, it remains pleasantly cool.

The castle was lavishly appointed with family **heirlooms**, fine **furnishings** and **fittings**, which von Wolf bought during a visit to Germany in 1908. The walls of the castle were decorated with **paintings**, **etchings** and family **portraits** as well as **swords** and **rifles** — and reflected von Wolf's passion for horses.

But like most fairy-tales, their story has a sad ending. The same passion for horses sent the couple to England in August 1914 to buy fresh bloodstock for their stud. However, while they were at sea, World War I broke out and their ship was diverted to South America.

In Rio de Janeiro, Jayta succeeded in obtaining a berth on a Dutch vessel bound for Scandinavia, while von Wolf and a companion smuggled themselves aboard as stowaways. From Scandinavia they went to Germany, where von Wolf joined the army, only to be killed in 1916 during the battle of the Somme. Jayta never returned to Duwisib. She settled in Switzerland during World War II and the property was eventually sold to a Swedish family.

King of the plains

The volcanic peak of Brukkaros constantly dominates the western horizon along the B1 on the 221-kilometre (138-mile) drive between Keetmanshoop and Mariental. Shrouded by billowing morning clouds, the peak forms an unforgettable picture of eternal splendour. The volcano's vernacular

Above: Lone quiver tree provides little shade but welcome presence atop the rim of Brukkaros volcano.

name, *Geitsigubeb*, refers to the mountain's likeness to a large leather apron worn by Khoikhoi women. The German name, Brukkaros, derives from a combination of *karos*, vernacular for 'leather apron' and the Germanisation of *broek*, the Afrikaans for trousers.

Getting there

The turnoff to the volcano's base south of Tses is accessible only to 4WD vehicles.

When to go

You do not need a permit and there are no facilities.

Where to stay

Visitors camp wherever they choose, although the nicest spot is among the boulders near the end of the road. Make sure you have enough firewood if you plan to spend the night as none is available nearby.

Sightseeing

From the road's end, a well-maintained **footpath** leads to the **crater** via the eroded **southern rim**. It is an easy thirty-minute walk up a slight gradient. The trail was carved in 1930 when the American Smithsonian Institute installed an **observatory** on the **western rim** to examine the sun's surface.

Continue along the path to the rim where you will find the observation station is still intact if not functioning. A brief scurry up the final slope brings you to the edge. It is well worth the effort for the incredible **view** over the plains. Deep incisions on the volcano's flanks radiate out from Brukkaros like a huge fan to the point where plains spin out in all directions to the horizon.

Indeed, many groups, as well as the Smithsonian, have taken advantage of its supreme position 650 metres (2,133 feet) above the plains. At the turn of the century, the Germans maintained a **heliograph station** on the **eastern rim**. Recently, a **VHF radio mast** was placed on the **northern rim**. But there is little shade and the heat deters even the most hardy hiker. Nevertheless, if you have the time, continue down onto the **crater floor** where hidden **cavities** await discovery and there are more **kokerboom trees** to marvel at.

The observer finds no evidence of lava, yet this is a volcano. This is because it began life eighty million years ago when kimberlite-like magma — molten rocks — intruded into rocks lying about a kilometre (half-a-mile mile) below the earth's surface. In its upward journey this magma probably met and reacted with underground water. The result was steam, creating inordinately high amounts of pressure, causing the overlying rocks to literally swell up into a dome 400 metres (1,312 feet) high and ten kilometres (six miles) across.

As the rocks were raised upwards, more magma invaded higher and higher into the heart of the dome, encountering more water. The lid of overlying rock was now much thinner and the superheated steam — as if inside a giant pressure cooker — blew off the dome in what must have been a sudden, cataclysmic explosion. When water poured into the gaping hole it met more encroaching lava. Subsequent explosions followed at progressively deeper levels. Finally, from two kilometres (one-and-a-quarter miles) below the surface, rock was blasted skyward, building a rim of debris and ash around the crater.

When the explosions eventually stopped, rain washed the finer material onto the crater floor. Hot springs spurted out around the edge, depositing substantial amounts of fine-grained quartz, which gradually cemented into tough, weather-resistant rock.

Brukkaros's volcanic stage was short-lived, most probably only continuing for a year or two, but sedimentation lasted many hundreds of thousands of years. Since then, the elements have steadily removed any loose rocks, leaving cemented sediments in the form of the crater.

Finger of God

Further along the B1, a slight detour **east** at Asab takes the visitor to **Mukurob** — the remains of a single **rock pinnacle**, thirty-four metres (112 feet) high, the narrow neck of which for centuries balanced precariously on a base of shale. But early in December 1988 the towering 637-tonne obelisk was blown over and tumbled down, shattering into thousands of pieces.

The pinnacle, known as the Finger of God, was a relic which resisted the elements moving from the Weissrand Plateau immediately to the east. The upper nine-and-a-half metre (thirty-one feet) of the 'head' consisted of sandstone, followed by a three-metre (nine-foot) layer of conglomerate. The obelisk was also known as the Vingerklip and as *Hererovrou* on account of its resemblance to the face and headdress of a Herero woman.

The origin of Mukurob can best be understood when surveying the landscape east of the formation. As a result of erosion of the softer shale and vertical seams, the sandstone escarpment of the **Weissrand Plateau** has been broken down into large blocks which have mostly collapsed, though Mukurob defied nature for much longer. Some 200 metres (219 yards) **north-west** of the formation are two other **relic columns**.

Meteorites

The landscape on either side of the road gives some feeling of the vastness of Namibia. For there the **horizon** seems all encircling. Barely anything infringes upon this perfect line, making visitors from cramped cities feel insignificant, yet revitalised at the same time.

Look out for **ostriches** in the fenced areas to the **west** and **east.** Many **farms** raise these birds for eggs and meat.

Further north, at **Gibeon railway station**, a small **graveyard** testifies to one of the bloodiest battles of the 1914-15 German South West African campaign. The battle was fought there on 27 April 1915, between a 1,500-strong force under Brigadier-General Sir Duncan McKenzie and a German force of 800 men commanded by General von Kleist. Twenty-nine South Africans were killed and sixty-six wounded.

The German losses were twelve dead and thirty wounded, with 188 taken prisoner. A train with arms and ammunition was also captured by the South Africans.

Gibeon is also famous for the fact that it

was at the centre of one of the world's largest meteorite showers. The **Gibeon Shower** fell over some 20,000 square kilometres (7,722 square miles) with the highest concentration in the Gibeon area scattered across 2,500 square kilometres (965 square miles).

On account of their dense and pure metallic structure, relatively young age, and the arid climate of the Gibeon area, only minor corrosion took place after they struck the earth.

Thirty-seven **fragments**, with a total mass of more than twelve tonnes, were collected between 1911 and 1913 by a German state geologist, Dr P Range.

Altogether, seventy-seven meteorites with a total weight of twenty-one tonnes have so far been recovered. Many may be seen at **Meteor Fountain** in the Post Street Mall, Windhoek. (See "The Capital and the Towns", Part Three). The largest, one of 650 kilos (1,433 pounds), however, is in the South African Museum, Cape Town.

From Gochas to Stampriet

The C18 road to **Gochas** turns **east** almost directly from Gibeon railway station. At the far end of the four-way **crossing,** the **grave** of the first missionary of Gochas, **Heinrich Rust**, may be found. It sits under a large **camel thorn tree**. Take the **signposted turnoff** at the intersection and then turn **right** again a few hundred metres on.

After Gibeon was declared a district in 1894, a non-commissioned officer and three soldiers were stationed at Gochas, on the banks of the **Auob River**, to maintain law and order. A fort completed in 1897 has long since disappeared. In the **cemetery**, a short distance beyond the village **post office**, are the **graves** of a large number of soldiers killed in many battles with the Witbooi Nama along the Auob.

Two **monuments** on the **Haruchas Farm** are further reminders of the battles fought there in January 1905 between the Nama and the German forces under *Hauptmann* Eugen Stuhlmann.

Drive **north-west** along the **C15**. The area, with its artesian wells, is an important fruit and vegetable growing centre with large **orchards**, bursting with colour and variety — a pleasant change from the scrubland further **south**. About fifty kilometres (thirty-two miles) on, a **granite monument** to the **east** of the road marks the **spot** where a German patrol of fourteen men were killed during a surprise attack on 4 March 1905.

Top: Worker tends young chicks hatched on an ostrich farm near Mariental.

Above: Farm-reared ostrich near Mariental.

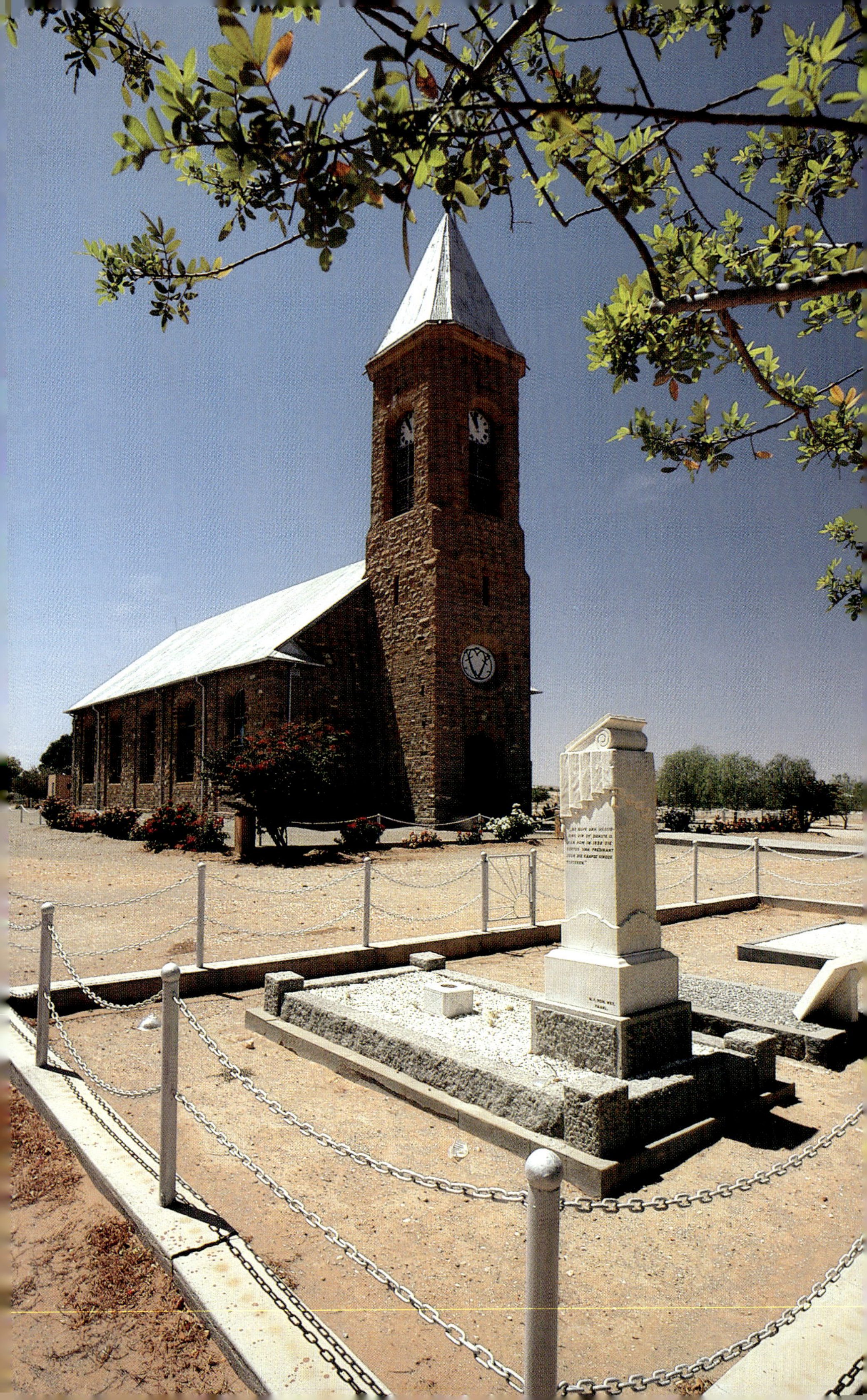

Just before **Stampriet**, turn into **Gross Nabas Farm** where a fairly inconspicuous **monument** serves as a reminder of one of the bloodiest battles fought during the Nama rebellion. In January 1905 the Witbooi Nama inflicted heavy losses on a German force. The **main C20 road southwest** from Stampriet takes you to Mariental and Hardap Dam.

Mary's dale

Before the arrival of white settlers the site of the present town of Mariental was known to the Khoikhoi as Zaragaebis — 'dusty' or 'dirty face'. The name has its origins in the heavy dust storms that often occur there in summer.

Hermann Brandt was the first white farmer to settle in the area after purchasing a farm in 1890 from the Nama chief Hendrik Witbooi. He named the farm *Enkelkameeldoring*, Solitary Camel Thorn, but three years later renamed it *Mariental* — 'Mary's dale' — in honour of his wife, Anna-Maria Mahler.

In 1894 a non-commissioned officer and fourteen soldiers were stationed there and the following year a police station was established on the Mariental farm. During the Nama uprising of 1903 to 1907 about forty whites were killed in the vicinity. Police Sergeant E. Stumpfe later bought the Koichas farm for five cents a hectare and, in 1914, asked the German Administration to establish a village there. But nothing was done until Stumpfe donated land to the Dutch Reformed church and repeated his request to the new South African military magistrate at Gibeon. The cornerstone of the first Dutch Reformed church in the country was laid on 11 September 1920, and Mariental was officially proclaimed two months later.

Getting there

Mariental, 1,710 kilometres (1,063 miles) from Johannesburg, 1,232 kilometres (765 miles) from Cape Town, 650 kilometres (404 miles) from Walvis Bay, 261 kilometres (162 miles) from Windhoek and 221 kilometres (137 miles) from Keetmanshoop, is served by road and rail services.

When to go

The weather is pleasant all year-round.

Where to stay

The Sandberg Hotel (1-star). See Listings for "Hotels". There are bungalows, dormitories, guest rooms, caravan park and campsite at the nearby water resort of Hardap Dam. See Listings.

Sightseeing

Although Mariental may never claim to be the centre of the universe it has an extraordinary number of petrol filling stations for such a small town — one on virtually every street.

There is an **information centre** in the middle of town but the only other place of any interest is the **Dutch Reformed church**, around which much of the history of the area hangs.

Hardap Dam: Paradise Found

Just a few kilometres north of Mariental, an east turn leads to the recreation resort of Hardap Dam. After the heat of desert scrubland, the shores of the inviting lake, stretching into the distance amongst craggy outcrops, are a haven not only for birds and wildlife, but also visitors and locals.

Walk down to the shoreline in the lengthening shadows of late afternoon to watch the kudu and springbok mingle with pelicans and ostrich as a breeze whips across the semi-desert. While the sun slowly sinks below the horizon, the colour of the sky changes every few minutes from purples to reds, from yellows to oranges. No setting could be more perfect for a few days' relaxation.

The man-made Namibian oasis was created between 1960 and 1963, although the idea of a dam on the Fish River was first

Opposite: Elegant lines of Namibia's first Dutch Reformed church at Mariental, midway between Keetmanshoop and Windhoek.

Above: African butterfly alights on flowering shrub.

proposed by a German professor as long ago as 1897. Behind the thirty-nine-metre-high (128-foot) dam wall, stretching 865 metres (946 yards) between two cliffs, lies a 323-million cubic metre (11,405 million cubic feet) capacity lake spread over twenty-five square kilometres (nine-and-three-quarter square miles). When full, more than four-and-a-half million litres (one million gallons) of water a second cascade down the spillways of Namibia's largest and most spectacular dam.

The lake is popular for boating, windsurfing and angling. Seven fish species include the small-mouth yellow fish, carp, barbel, mud mullet, mudfish and blue kurper. Angling licences are available at the tourist office, but fishing from the dam shore is restricted to special sites on the north-eastern bank. Fishing from boats is allowed anywhere in the areas indicated on the resort map available at the tourist office, and in the river below the dam.

The Hardap Game Reserve is divided into two sections — one of eighteen square kilometres (seven square miles), the other 237 square kilometres (ninety-two square miles) on the south-west side of the dam wall.

The area's topography consists of wide plains interspersed by *koppies* and stony ridges, especially near the upper reaches. The reserve's vegetation has been classified as dwarf shrub savannah. Scattered trees, such as camel thorn, grow mainly in the river courses along with wild green-hair trees and buffalo-thorn.

Hardap is home to an abundance of game, including gemsbok, kudu, red hartebeest, springbok, Hartmann's mountain zebra, eland and ostrich. Cheetah used to live there but when their numbers increased to the detriment of the other game they were removed. And some 260 bird species have been recorded within the reserve. The numbers of white pelican fluctuate with the availability of water elsewhere, but at times more than 1,000 form a white blanket on the lake.

Between October and April keep an eye open for osprey. The Goliath heron, green-backed heron, kelp gull and Caspian tern can be seen outside their normal range. The fan-tailed cisticola favours the grassland.

Above: Gold sun lifts veil of night from the waters of Hardap Dam.

The dam is also the habitat of white-breasted and reed cormorant, darter, African spoonbill, Egyptian geese and red-knobbed coot. If you stay there you might even be fortunate enough to hear the challenging cry of the African fish eagle.

Getting there

The nearest town is Mariental which is 650 kilometres (404 miles) from Walvis Bay, 261 kilometres (162 miles) from Windhoek, and 221 kilometres (137 miles) from Keetmanshoop. The turnoff to the Hardap Recreation Resort is signposted fifteen kilometres (nine miles) north of Mariental.

Where to stay

There are bungalows, dormitories, rooms, a caravan park and campsites. See Listings for "Accommodation".

Sightseeing

Many fish species found in the **dam** and in the country's major rivers such as the Fish, Kunene and Kavango, may be observed in the **aquarium** next to the **tourist office**. It is the only public freshwater aquarium in the country but unfortunately the **tanks** are unlabelled, making it difficult to identify the various species.

There are also excellent **displays** on fish biology and a fish **distribution map** of Namibia. Below the **dam wall** the Fresh Water Fish Institute of the Directorate of Conservation and Research carries out studies into fish production, breeding and conservation problems.

A network of roads, covering eighty-two kilometres (fifty-one miles), leads the visitor to **viewpoints** overlooking the dam and the appropriately named **Crater Hills**. The more energetic can explore the park by way of two circular **trails**, one nine kilometres (five-and-a-half miles) long, the other fifteen kilometres (nine miles). It is an invigorating and satisfying hike along the **lake shore**, through **hidden valleys** and up rocky **slopes** and **hills**, and certainly helps build an appetite. By far the best way to round off a day at Hardap is to visit the **restaurant** with its large bay window at the edge of the dam overlooking the lake.

The food is excellent and the service exemplary. If, however, you prefer to cook for yourself, a shop next to the restaurant stocks groceries, frozen fish from the dam, souvenirs and liquor. Other facilities include a **swimming pool**, protected by a natural cliff, **tennis courts**, **children's playground** and **filling station**.

To Maltahöhe

From Hardap Dam return to Mariental and take the **C19** to **Maltahöhe**, established at the turn of the century and named after Malta von Byrgsdorff, the wife of the commander of the garrison at Gibeon.

More than **forty graves** of German soldiers who died in the many battles during the campaign against Hendrik Witbooi in 1894 and the Nama rebellion of 1903-7, are in the **graveyard** to the **east**.

North of Maltahöhe, route C14 passes through the **Nomtsas Farm** where a **signboard** indicates the **turnoff** to the Ernst Hermann **graveyard**, now a **national monument**. Namibia's pioneer wool farmer, Hermann started Namibia's first wool farming operation at Kubub, near Aus. After Kubub was destroyed by Hendrik Witbooi in 1893, Hermann continued the operation at Nomtsas which, with an area of more than 1,000 square kilometres (386 square miles), was the largest sheep farm in the country.

In 1904, Hermann and others were killed by the Nama and buried in the graveyard. Nearby are the **ruins** of his **house**, the old **shearing shed** and the original **waterhole**.

Spa town

In the 261 kilometres (162 miles) between Mariental and Windhoek on the **B1** the only place of any real note is the town of **Rehoboth**, eighty-seven kilometres (fifty-four miles) south of Windhoek, renowned for its spa complex at a thermal spring originally known as *aris* — vernacular for smoke — which refers to the steam rising off the spring on cold winter mornings.

Like so many towns in Namibia, Rehoboth developed around a mission station, established in 1844 by the missionary, Heinrich Kleinschmidt. Abandoned in 1864, it was rebuilt when the Basters settled there around 1870 under Hermanus van Wyk.

The Basters, a half-caste group of mixed European and Khoikhoi blood, originated in the Cape Province of South Africa whence they gradually migrated northwards, settling along the Orange River towards the end of the eighteenth century. Following 1865 legislation requiring all settlers to prove their right over property, a large number crossed the Orange River and eventually settled at Rehoboth around 1870. The Basters are proud of their heritage and although their name — meaning simply half-caste — is considered derogatory elsewhere, they insist on being called Basters.

Getting there

Rehoboth, 1,884 kilometres (1,171 miles) from Johannesburg, 1,406 kilometres (874 miles) from Cape Town, 787 kilometres (489 miles) from Rundu, 445 kilometres (277 miles) from Swakopmund, 395 kilometres (245 miles) from Keetmanshoop and eighty-seven kilometres (fifty-four miles) from Windhoek, is served by road services. The railway station is some kilometres from the town.

When to go

Rehoboth has a delightful climate all year-round.

Where to stay

Rio Monte Hotel (1-star) and Suidwes Hotel. See Listings for "Hotels". There are guesthouses, caravan parks and campsites. See Listings.

Sightseeing

Rehoboth is a sprawling, well laid-out town with a sense of spaciousness. The only hotel in the centre of town, the **Rio Monte**, however, is to say the least functional and its rooms are above the social focus of the town — its **noisy bar**.

The main attraction is the **spa resort** which has an outdoor, warm water **swimming pool**, **thermal bath** with a temperature of 39°C, and **restaurant**. The **Rehoboth Museum**, opened in December 1986 next to the **post office**, is housed in the

1903 residence of the town's first postmaster.

Its external exhibits include **relics** of the short-lived **narrow-gauge railway** that ran between the **mainline station** and the **town centre** between 1911 and 1915 and a traditional **Damara mud-and-thatch house**.

Inside there are fascinating **displays** of archive **photographs** taken between 1893 and 1896, a three-dimensional **model** of the three topographical regions of Namibia, which merge in the area around Rehoboth, and displays depicting the evolution of man and prehistoric times in the area.

It is also possible to make excursions to the **Oanab Dam Nature Reserve** — an area of just over seventy square kilometres (twenty-seven square miles) of rugged broken country which **kudu, eland, gemsbok, springbok** and **Hartmann's mountain zebra** make their home. **Oanab Dam,** completed in 1990, covers two-and-a-half square kilometres (one square mile) with **picnic sites** and **lookout points**, and an ancient **burial site**.

Ranch capital

Eastward, all along the southern half of the B1, stretches the endless scrub desert of the Kalahari, punctuated only by a few large-scale farms and ranches. And **Gobabis**, the **eastern terminal** of the **B6** which runs 205 kilometres (127 miles) from Windhoek, is indeed the ranching capital of Namibia.

Although extremely hot during the summer, Gobabis is a pleasant town. It is said the name means 'place of the elephant' but according to others it is a vernacular name meaning 'place of arguing or discussion'. The town also serves as an administrative centre for the country's smallest tribal group, the Tswana, numbering about 10,000.

Gobabis grew up around a **mission station** established there in 1856 by a Rhenish missionary. In 1865, the missionary was driven out when he tried to establish peace between the Khoikhoi and the Damara and missionary work was only resumed in 1876. But when hostilities broke out between the Khoikhoi and Herero once again, the evangelists were forced to abandon the station.

A military unit under the command of Lieutenant Lampe occupied Gobabis in March 1895 on the orders of Major Theodor Leutwein and in May the following year, a rebellion by the Herero and Khoikhoi was put down. Shortly afterwards the foundations for a fort, completed in 1897, were laid. However, the fort was later demolished.

Getting there

Gobabis is 2,176 kilometres (1,352 miles) from Johannesburg, 1,698 kilometres (1,055 miles) from Cape Town, 905 kilometres (562 miles) from Rundu, 563 kilometres (350 miles) from Swakopmund and 205 kilometres (128 miles) from Windhoek.

When to go

Gobabis is dry and warm all year-round.

Where to stay

Central Hotel (1-star) and Gobabis Hotel (1-star). See Listings for "Hotels".

Sightseeing

For most of the way from Windhoek the tar road shadows the **Black Nossob River** which drains out of the Neudamm highlands **east** of the capital to disappear in the drylands of the **Kalahari**.

There are optional stops at the **Karakul Carpet Weaving Centre** on **Ibenstein Farm** and **Pepperkorrel Farm**, **south** of Omitara, but visitors must make prior arrangements.

The old **hospital** in Gobabis is now a **national monument** and the only remaining nineteenth-century building in town. It is at the **junction** of **Lieutenant Lampe Street** and **Lazarette Street** on the town's **southern periphery**.

Ten kilometres (six miles) **east** of Gobabis the tar ends and the remaining 111 kilometres (sixty-nine miles) to **Buitepos** on the **Botswana border** is gravel and fit only for 4WD vehicles. From there it is roughly another 500 kilometres (310 miles) or so to the **Okavango Delta**.

In 1993, however, work was still progressing on the **Trans-Kalahari Highway**, which began in 1991. When complete, it will link the capitals of the two nations.

Namib-Naukluft Park: Colour and Contrast

From Maltahöhe, the C14 leads south a few kilometres to a turnoff along a minor gravel road that heads west and north-west to the Naukluft Mountains of the Namib-Naukluft Park. The largest of Namibia's nature conservation areas, covering 49,768 square kilometres (19,215 square miles) — the size of Switzerland — the park is one of the most unusual wildlife and nature reserves in the world. The Naukluft area, proclaimed a sanctuary in 1964 to conserve Hartmann's mountain zebra, was integrated into the Namib Desert Park in 1979.

Part of the high escarpment marking the western edge of Namibia's interior highlands, the flat, plateau-like top of the Naukluft Mountains is separated from the adjacent highland plateau to the south by impressive near-vertical cliffs, while in the north-west and west its highest peaks loom almost 900 metres (3,000 feet) above the Namib plains.

The plateau consists mainly of dolomite and limestone formations. Over many millennia floodwaters have cut deep gorges and created an extensive underground drainage system. In some deep-cut ravines, underground water reservoirs spring to the surface as crystal-clear pools and streams.

The basement, found mainly to the west of the mountain, consists of meta-sedimentary and volcanic rocks, gneisses and granites, varying from two billion to a billion years in age. The overlying Nama sediments, consisting mainly of black limestone, were deposited about 600 million years ago when south-west Africa was covered by a shallow tropical sea.

Because of the variety of soil and water levels, the Naukluft vegetation is a mosaic of five main plant communities, the most common being the *Commiphora, Acacia and Euphorbia* species. It also includes a number of protected plants, such as *Lithops schwantesii* and *Trichocaulon*. Aloes such as the small *Aloe sladeniana*, restricted to the mountains of the western escarpment, flourishes mainly in the Naukluft and Zaris mountains in dense groups in rock crevices, producing pale pink flowers in January and February. The *Aloe karasbergensis* may be distinguished by its thornless, yellow-white leaves, with its pale pink and reddish flowers blooming towards the end of the year.

The ten or so gorges in the park are rich in vegetation with more than 150 species recorded along the Naukluft River alone. A characteristic tree of the river-banks is the common cluster fig which attracts large numbers of birds when in fruit.

Most mammal species in Naukluft are either nocturnal, like the leopard, or small and thus easily overlooked. Visitors, however, are likely to come across kudu, Hartmann's mountain zebra, springbok, klipspringer, steenbok, chacma baboon, rock rabbit, and dassie rat, while gemsbok and springbok are common inhabitants of the gravel plains and sand dunes to the west.

At least 190 bird species, many of which need specialised habitats, including the black eagle, augur buzzard, lanner falcon, Gray's lark and Bradfield's swift have been recorded. Bird watching in the Naukluft is always rewarding as the area lies in the southernmost limit of several species indigenous to the north of Namibia, such as Ruppell's parrot, Monteiro's hornbill, Herero chat and chestnut weaver.

Mountain chat, Layard's tit-babbler and dusky sunbird are also seen on the slopes. Rock runner are restricted to the northern and eastern slopes, while the plateau is the habitat for species such as Ludwig's bustard, sabota lark and bokmakierie, whose loud onomatopoeic call often pierces the eerie silence.

The black cuckoo, European bee-eater and lesser grey shrike often visit in the summer, while cuckoo and Didric cuckoo are more often heard than seen.

Namib-Naukluft Park

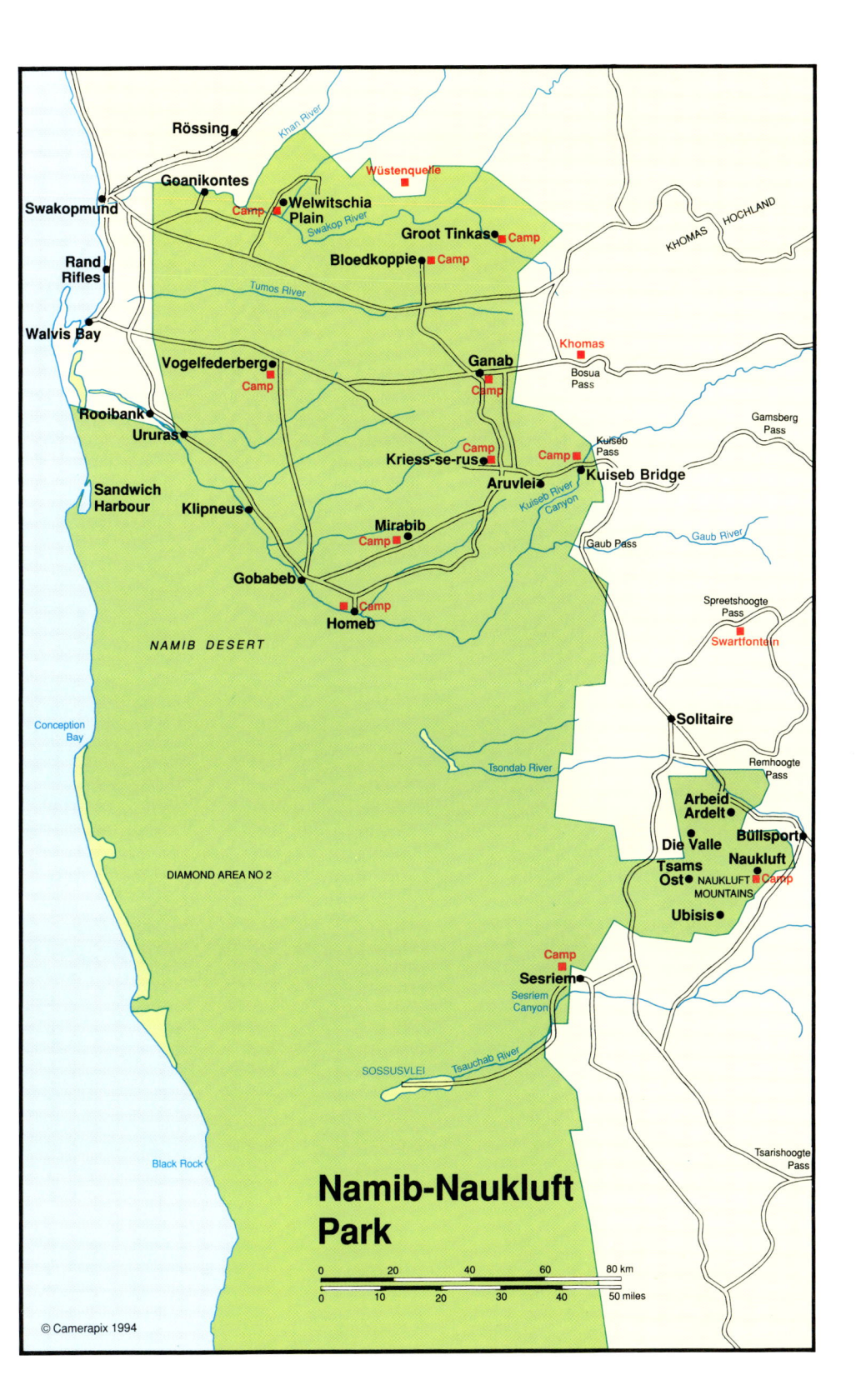

Above: Borehole supplies vital water to desert wildlife such as springbok in the eastern hinterlands of the Namib Desert.

Getting there

The nearest town is Maltahöhe, 111 kilometres (sixty-nine miles) from Mariental, 332 kilometres (206 miles) from Keetmanshoop, 372 kilometres (231 miles) from Windhoek, 374 kilometres (232 miles) from Lüderitz and 1,072 kilometres (666 miles) from Rundu. The park may be approached along route C14 between Solitaire, Büllsport and Maltahöhe.

When to go

It is best to avoid the extreme heat of summer, between late November and January.

Where to stay

There are four campsites. See Listings.

Sightseeing

Early in the morning, as the blues and blacks of night slowly fade, an orange glow rises in the **east** behind rugged **mountains**. To the east, huge **sand dunes** drop breathtakingly onto a vast desert plain.

Moving imperceptibly, a **balloon** drifts through the clear air above the mountains where animals, reptiles and birds begin to move across the earth's surface.

From 1,800 metres (6,000 feet) the world unfolds in timeless patterns of pink-grey granite mountains, yellow-brown desert plains and contoured sand dunes. Flying in a balloon along the **border** of the Namib-Naukluft Park is the best way to see one of the oldest deserts in the world, for only from a balloon does the visitor gain a true perspective of the massive expanse.

Lift-off points vary with every flight, according to weather conditions and the wishes of the passengers. The flight area encompasses the **Naukluft Mountains**, sand dunes of **Sossusvlei**, and flat **Namib plains**.

Because of extreme temperatures, flying is restricted to the cool of morning, particularly in the summer and this means an early start. For those who prefer their feet firmly on the ground, an eight-day **hiking trail** through the Naukluft Mountains affords the opportunity to discover one of the most beautiful parts of Namibia on foot. Deep **ravines**, **caves** and perennial **springs** characterise this seemingly arid country.

The **trail** begins at the **Naukluft Hut** near the **campsite**. Except for two fairly steep ascents the first day's hike covers easy terrain, following a **zebra path** with an easy gradient. The hiker is rewarded with spectacular views of the side of the valley, some 300 metres (984 feet) below. The overnight stop, **Putte**, takes its name from the nearby **well** which is equipped with a **hand-pump**, enabling you to obtain water and enjoy a shower.

The second day's hike of fifteen kilometres (nine miles) mainly traverses the **undulating plateau**, and requires about six hours to complete. Nearly half way along the trail you reach **Bergpos** and descend into the spectacular **Ubusis Kloof**. Several **chains** have been anchored at steep points which are difficult to negotiate. The **Ubusis Hut** used to be a **holiday cottage** before the park was established.

From Bergpos there is an easy route across the plateau to the **Adlerhorst Shelter**. **Mountain zebra** and **kudu** are often seen in the area.

The fourth day, seventeen kilometres (ten-and-a-half miles) takes you to **Tsams Ost**. Initially, the route leads over fairly level terrain before branching off into the stunning **gorge** carved by the **Tsams River**. After following the ravine for some distance the trail leaves the river, climbing steeply to bypass a **waterfall** before winding down to the river, where an enormous **moringa tree** offers welcome shade.

You pass a number of pretty springs shortly before reaching the **campsite** at Tsams Ost, while the final two kilometres (one-and-a-quarter miles) to the shelter is along a **gravel road**.

The fifth day's hike leads to **Die Valle**. From the shelter, a trail climbs steeply up **Broekskeur** and traverses undulating terrain covered with patches of **euphorbia**, **quiver**, and **moringa trees** to **Fonteinpomp**. The final eleven kilometres (six-and-three-quarter miles) are along a **river valley**. On the sixth day, the trail leads to the **Die Valle Waterfall**, a magnificent sight, despite usually being dry.

For a short while you climb up a steep **contour path** to the top of the 200-metre (656-foot) high waterfall. From there the trail follows the narrow gorge carved by the river and continues to climb, before descending to the **Arbeid Adelt Valley**.

Day seven begins with a steep climb up an overgrown **ravine** where a **chain** helps hikers to scale another **waterfall**. After about three hours you reach the **plateau** and from **Bakenkop** the hiker is rewarded with magnificent vistas of the valley carved by the **Tsondab River** some 600 metres (2,000 feet) below. The trail then winds over **Kapokvlakte**, where **springbok**, and sometimes **gemsbok**, are seen before reaching **Kapokvlakte Shelter**.

The final day's hike covers about sixteen kilometres (ten miles). After following a jeep track the trail traverses a **watershed** before descending to the **Naukluft River** by way of a **tributary**. There you may wish to cool off in any number of crystal-clear **pools**. From the first pool it's about a forty-minute walk to the **Naukluft Hut**.

Sesriem and Sossusvlei: Golden Glory

As in most countries of Southern Africa you have to travel a fair distance to reach the places that challenge your senses the most. And in the Namib you have a fair stretch of wilderness to cover to reach Sesriem Gorge and the sand dunes of Sossusvlei, the highest in the world. In a feast of constantly-changing colours, from ivory-white to apricot and gold, they dominate the environment.

The views of the wind-driven sands are exquisite and it is difficult to resist tumbling down the side of a dune only for

---

Overleaf: Sculpted by the winds of centuries, mountains of sand roll to their meeting place at Sossusvlei in the Namib Desert.

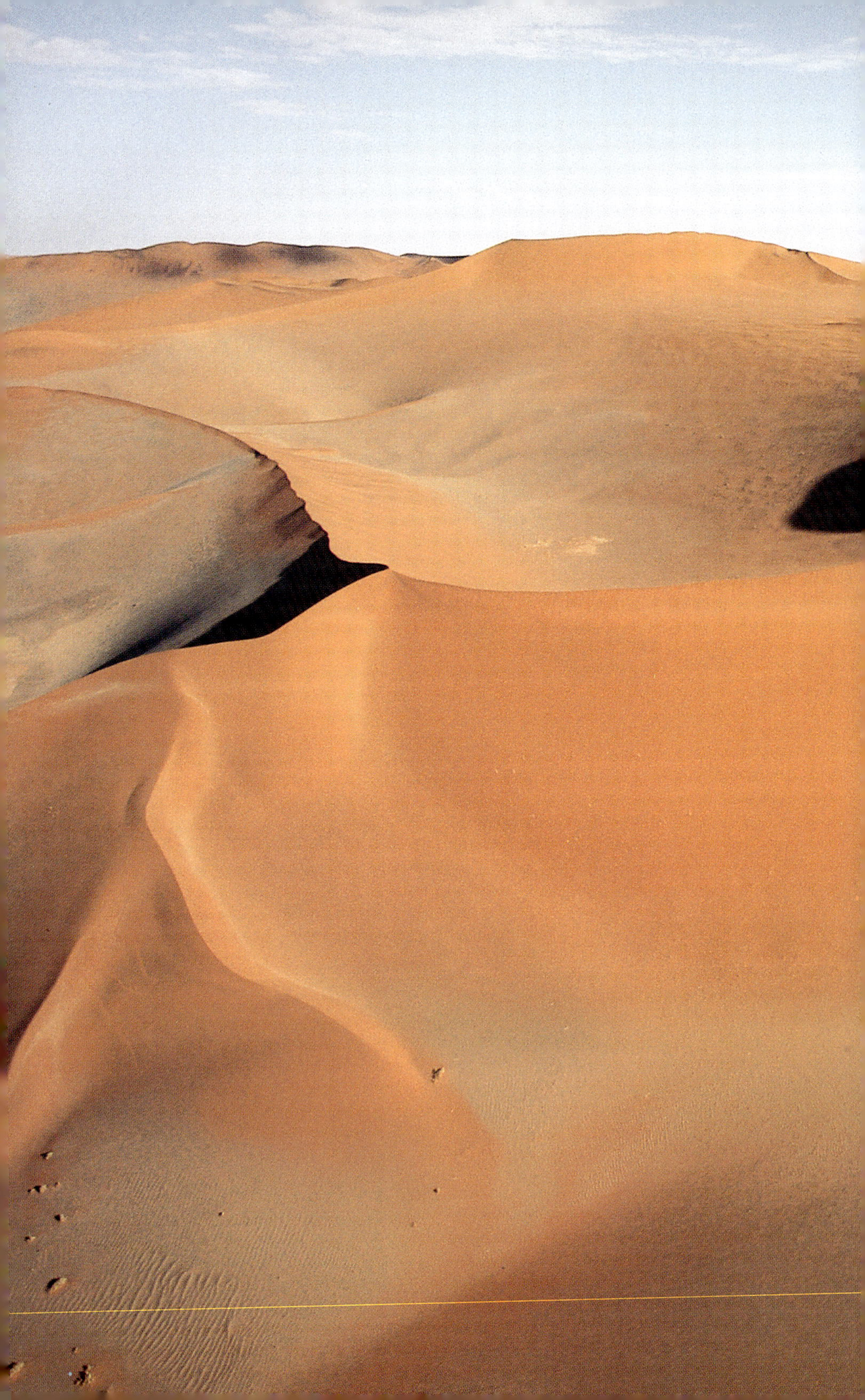

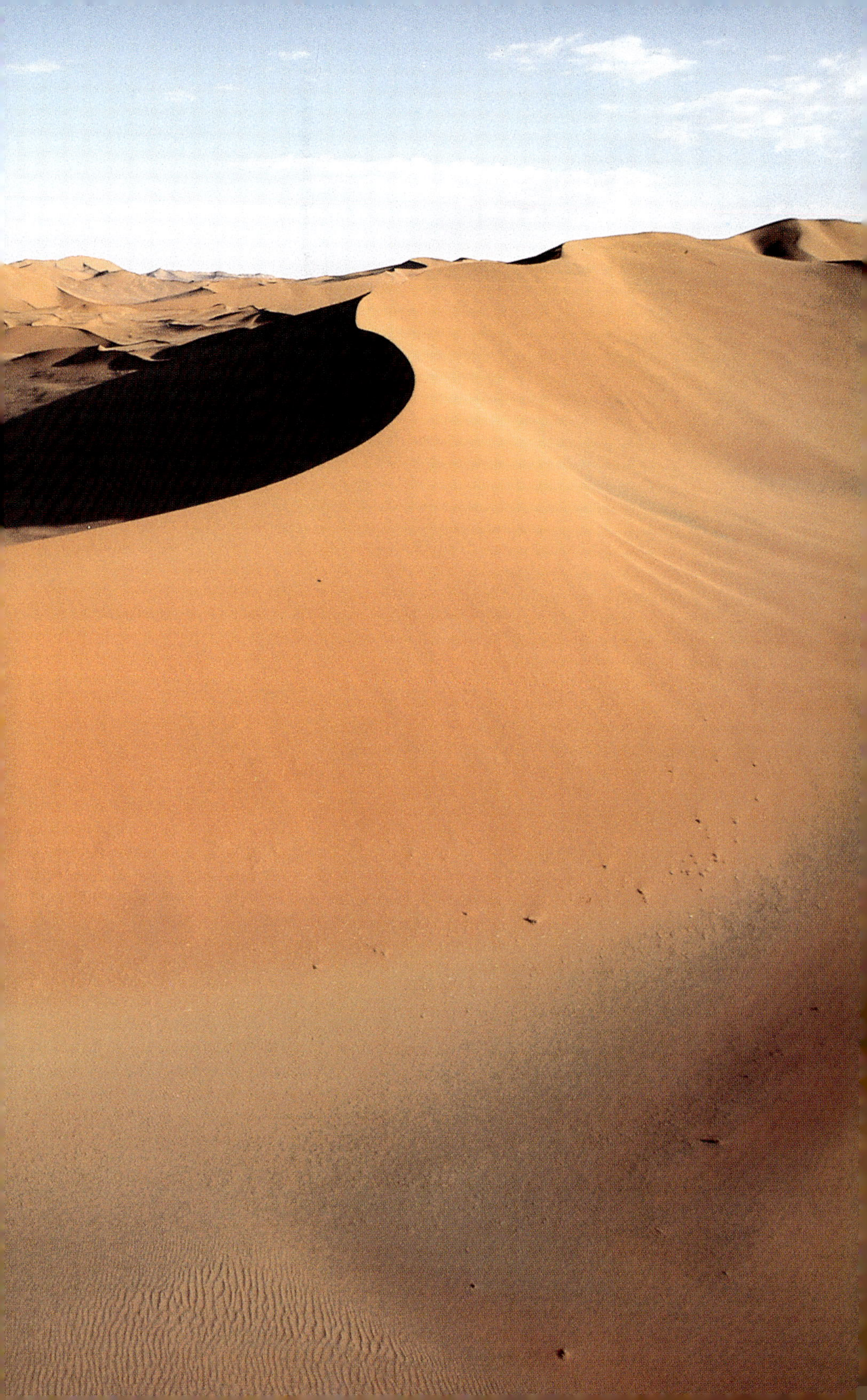

Above: Hardiest of the world's desert antelopes, oryx graze the sparse vegetation of the Namib Desert — masters of survival.

the rolling sand to cover your tracks in matter of minutes.

But most striking is that the dunes seem to go on forever. Indeed, the dune sea covers widely dispersed patches from the Orange River in the south, expanding north to Angola unless abruptly stopped by the barrier of the Swakop, Hoarusib, Kuiseb and Kunene rivers.

Relatively narrow, less than 200 kilometres (124 miles) wide, the Namib Desert stretches about 2,000 kilometres (1,200 miles) north from the Orange River to San Nicolau, Angola. Geographers divide the region into three sections: the transitional Namib Desert in the south; the central Namib; and the gravel plains of the northern Namib.

The rewards of making the slow climb to the top of a dune are worth the slog. The silence is overwhelming, the space immense. Vast and brooding, the dunes march inexorably into the distance beneath the searching sun, refusing to reveal their secrets. They bow only to the wind which changes their peaks like cresting waves.

Shaped by the wind, their nature is influenced by the amount of sand around them and their position in the dune sea. They vary in height — in places up to 340 metres (1,120 feet), reputed to be the highest dunes of any desert in the world — width, colour, shape, and composition. All Namib dunes are composed principally of quartz sands with small amounts of heavier minerals such as ilmenite.

The terms to describe dunes come from Arabic. For example, barchans, siefs, silks, transverse, star and linear. Parabolic or multi-cyclic dunes, caused by winds of similar strengths blowing from many directions, are common around Sossusvlei. The slipface of a dune is an area of cascading sand near the top where insects and other creatures forage.

And beneath the active dunes are 'tertiary-age dunes', solidified through the passage of time. These petrified relics can be seen at Dieprivier near Solitaire.

The Namib is a true desert in the sense that it receives little or no rain. It does, however, have an important alternative source of moisture — the fog which rolls inland from the sea where it is created by the cooling of moisture picked up by westerly winds as they blow across the Benguela Current.

The dense mists usually extend about 110 kilometres (sixty-eight miles) inland, covering the Namib and providing much-needed water through condensation. Located approximately sixty kilometres (thirty-seven miles) from the coast, Sossusvlei is well within the fog belt.

The fog supports a wide variety of life forms. There you will find unusual plants such as the *lithops* and *euphorbias*, the well-documented *Welwitschia mirabilis* — a living fossil plant endemic to the Namib which collects water through its leaves and may live for 2,000 years — and *Stipagrostis sabulicola*, a common dune grass that absorbs water through its shallow roots which grow just below the surface of the dune.

Ingenious in their survival these plants may be, but they lead a precarious life. Indeed, everything in the Namib lives by its fingertips — from the flora and fauna to the very ecosystem.

"Take only photographs, leave only footprints," has special significance when applied to the Namib Desert because its fragile landscape is slow to heal. On the gravel plains, major scars such as vehicle tracks leave its surface permanently damaged. But in the sandy areas the tracks soon disappear. The Namib is also an uncompromising environment, a pleasure to those who understand and take precautions, but a nightmare to those who enter unprepared.

Above: Oryx exploit every opportunity to maintain their cool.

Lost in the mists of time

The age of the Namib Desert has long been a topic of controversy. Although the final word has by no means been spoken or written, contemporary thinking concludes that the climate of the narrow coastal tract between the southern Atlantic and the Great Western Escarpment has varied between arid and semi-arid for at least eighty million years. It does not mean the

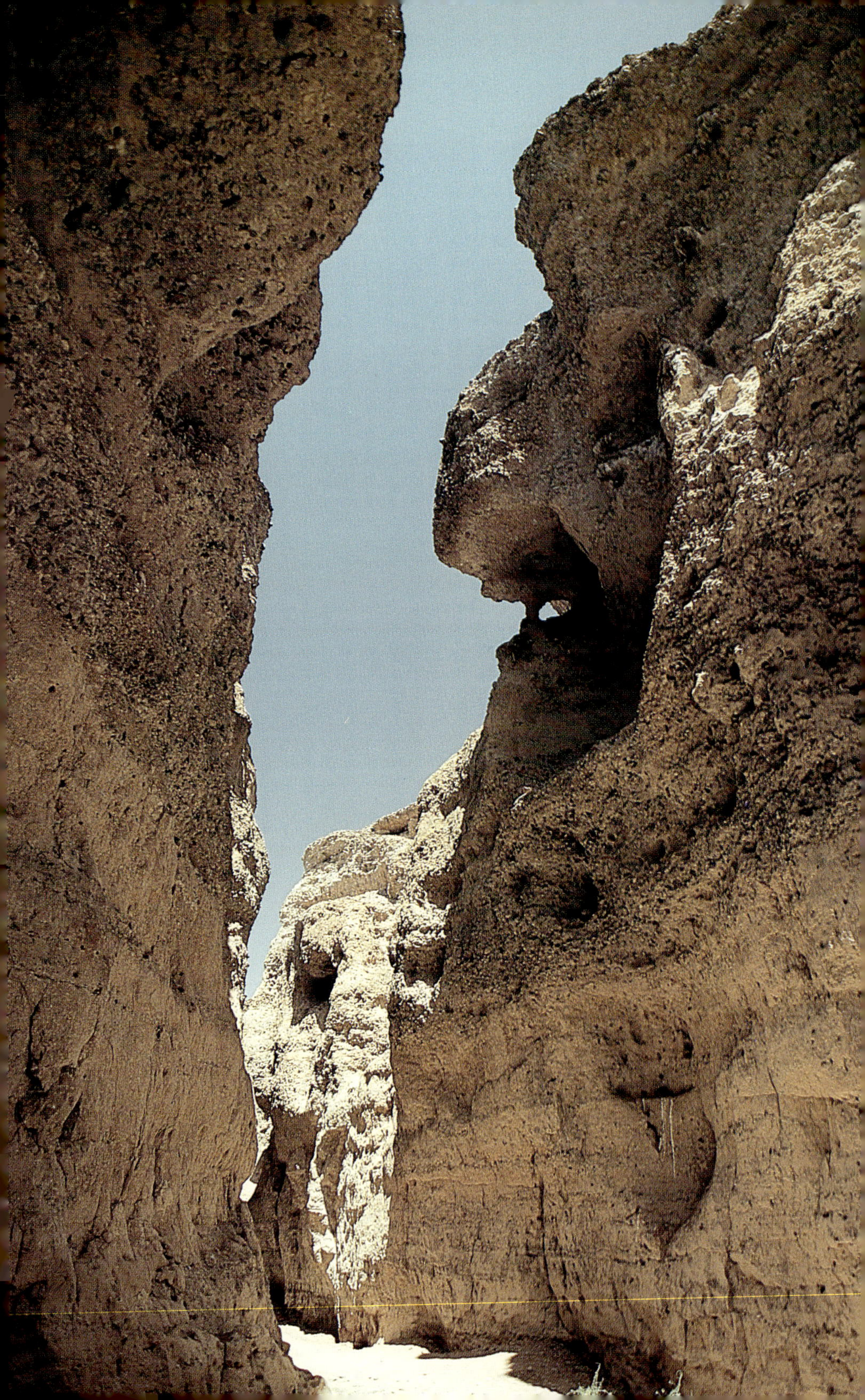

dunes are as old as that, or that any of the features seen today looked the same then. Indeed, the landscape is constantly changing under the influence of episodic rainfall and occasional water flowing into the desert from further inland.

The Benguela Current plays a major role in maintaining these arid conditions. The southern dune field between Lüderitz and Swakopmund probably only formed after the Benguela Current, with its associated upwelling, was established. Certainly the foggy conditions that characterise the Namib, and the fascinating climatic range, are no older than the Benguela Current itself.

Many strange features suggest that not too long ago the climate was much wetter — perhaps during the Pleistocene ice ages — and that the last 30,000 years has seen fresh dune fields. Most of these unusual patterns and geomorphologic formations, however, may be due to the extremely occasional rainfall of the Namib or its long, narrow shape with vegetated river-beds crossing the desert reaches.

The Namib climate

Deserts are characterised by their paucity of rain and the Namib is no exception. Not only is rainfall minimal, varying from an average of less than fifteen millimetres (half an inch) on the coast to about 100 millimetres (almost four inches) on the eastern border, but it is also irregular. Thus, in some years such as 1934 and 1976, the average rainfall was exceeded by several hundred per cent, while in other years there was no rain at all.

The Namib, however, has an extremely important alternative source of moisture — and that is the fog that extends inland for tens of kilometres on many mornings and is densest between 300 and 600 metres (1,000-2,000 feet), at least in the heart of the desert between the Kuiseb and Swakop Rivers.

Any small hill or other obstacle — rocks, plants, and soil — catches the condensation. When this 'fog-water catchment' is large enough, for example, on smooth, west-facing rocks, succulents and other desert vegetation germinates and thrives.

Coupled with the fog is the high humidity along the coast. Even when there is no fog, this provides moisture for lichens and other specialised vegetation. Inland the humidity drops sharply, while temperatures increase rapidly.

As a result, the foggy, cool zone lying along the coast is replaced further inland by an area where fog and high humidity frequently occur in the morning, only to vanish well before noon.

This part of the desert, between thirty and sixty kilometres (twenty to forty miles) inland, experiences daily fluctuations and is by far the most extreme climatic zone of the central Namib.

Wind is also an important and extremely noticeable component of the desert climate. West winds blow fog onshore and east winds carry tiny pieces of organic material, an important food source for many animals, reptiles, insects and birds.

Most of the year, a strong south-westerly blows, resulting in a layer of cooler air lying below a layer of warmer air which reduces the turbulence necessary for cloud development, thus preventing rain from occurring.

In winter, the dominant east wind, following soon after rain, is extremely noticeable to humans and other animals. Thus, small, newly germinated plants have only a short time to establish themselves before the desiccating wind stunts their growth.

In central Namib the influence of the climatic gradient on the diversity of vegetation is particularly noticeable in the desert between Usakos and Swakopmund where an endless variety of trees disappear from the landscape to be replaced by small shrubs and lichens in the west.

A fragile world

At first glance the desert looks barren, harsh and hostile. But it is a fragile environment, easily disturbed.

While perennial plants grow slowly,

Opposite: Noonday sun strikes the bed of the seasonal Tsauchab River where it cuts the Sesriem Canyon.

annual ones grow only in years of adequate rain. More important than the vegetation is the desert surface, totally barren or covered with a crust of curious plant-like organisms known as lichens. When this sensitive surface is disturbed it may never recover, providing instead another place for erosion to begin when the infrequent rain does eventually fall. Tyre tracks on the gravel plains last for decades, leading to an ugly array of crisscross trails that impoverish desert life.

The most easily disturbed parts of the desert lie within about fifty kilometres (thirty miles) of the coast, where the surface consists largely of gypsum, and fog-dependent lichens often constitute the dominant plant growth. Archaeological and palaeontological sites are also extremely sensitive to disturbance, as are the waterholes upon which many animals depend.

Not all the Namib is highly sensitive, however. Some areas, with well-planned, moderate usage, are easily sustained. Tracks on the surface of the eastern Namib are not as long lasting as those on gypsum, while those on sand dunes generally blow away quickly. Any desert, however, should be treated with care.

While there is no list of Namib endangered species of plants or animals, many lichens and other endemic organisms in the foggy coastal area have a localised range and could easily die out. Some succulents are already at risk from persistent collectors. Certainly the number has been reduced in some areas.

The Namib Desert is appreciated best when walking rather than driving. In this way, neither the plant and animal life nor the soil surface are unduly disturbed. And walking allows visitors to notice many plants and animals of the little-known world under their feet.

In ages past, vast quantities of sand were carried into the Atlantic Ocean by the Orange and Fish Rivers. The material was subsequently deposited northwards by the vigorous longshore drift under the influence of the strong coastal south-westerly wind regime. The spectacular results of this deposition are best seen at Sossusvlei.

The sensational crested dunes, known as star dunes, are normally formed where the wind varies in direction. In the Sossusvlei area, the dunes reach up to 340 metres (1,115 feet) above the Tsauchab River, although free-standing examples may be only about twenty-two metres (seventy two feet) high.

The dunes are the habitat of several species of tenebrionid beetles, lizards, spiders and other creatures which derive their water requirements from dew, light rain and especially fog. Amongst these are the colourful, translucent, web-footed gecko, *Palmatogecko rangei,* which moves rapidly over the soft sand. It is exclusively nocturnal and feeds on small insects and, in turn, is preyed upon by the 'dancing white lady of the Namib', *Orchestrella longpipes,* a spider living in tunnels constructed in the sand dunes. To prevent these from being covered with loose sand, *Orchestrella longpipes* lines its tunnel with a cobweb while digging.

Another interesting inhabitant is the sand-diving lizard, *Aporosaura anchietae,* found on the dune slip faces. Studies of this species show that the males maintain a well-defined hierarchy, defending their territory from lower-ranking subordinate males. In this way, the dominant male increases the chances of breeding with the females.

Living in the cool, moist, deeper layers of sand, the lobed feet of the *Comicus* dune cricket allow it to move with ease over the soft sand while feeding at night. The largest reptile, the side-winding adder, *Bitis peringueyi,* averages twenty to twenty-five centimetres (eight to ten inches) in length. It conceals itself in the sand with only its eyes and the tip of its tail exposed. In doing so, the adder protects itself from the extremes of temperature while waiting to ambush its prey.

Grant's golden mole, *Eremitalpa granti*

Opposite: Weaver bird nests in the Namib Desert.

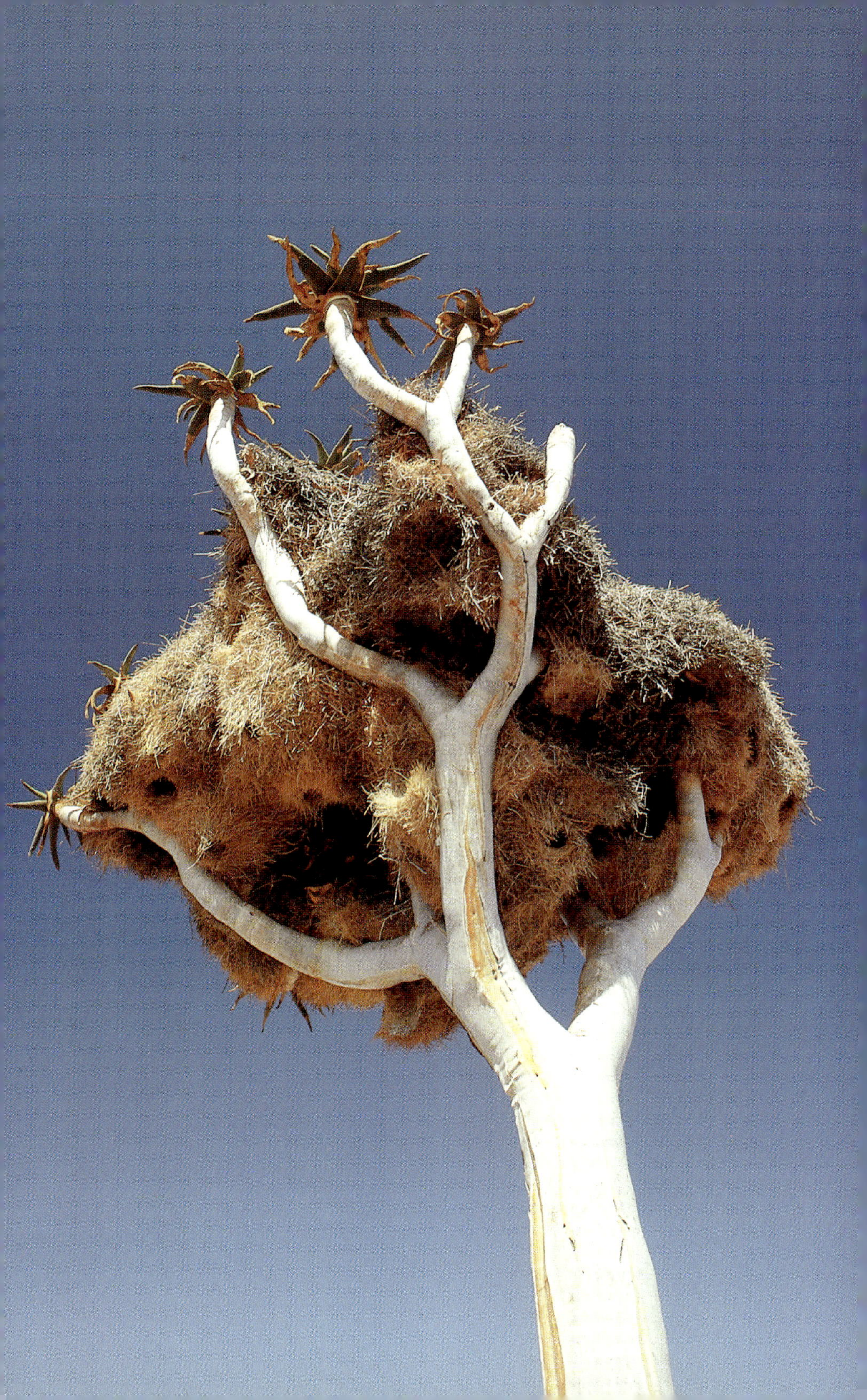

Above: Camel trekking through the Namib Desert.

---

namibensis, is the most lovable of the dune sea's inhabitants. First discovered in 1837 by Captain James Alexander, the animal was lost to science for 126 years until 1963 when it was rediscovered in the Kuiseb River. (See "Wildlife: Just Out of This World", Part Four).

With neither ears nor eye-sockets, the golden mole is dormant during the day, usually at the base of a grass tuft or hummock, emerging at night to feed on insects and their larvae.

An intriguing feature of the Namib is Sesriem Canyon, where the Tsauchab River has carved a gorge up to thirty metres (100 feet) deep through the gravels deposited some eighteen to fifteen million years ago during a wetter phase in the history of the Namib.

The canyon dates back some four to two million years when continental uplift caused the incision not only of the Tsauchab River, but also of most of the other westward-flowing rivers in the Namib.

The name, Sesriem, is said to derive from the fact that early travellers collected water by joining six ox thongs, *riems*, to lower a bucket from the top of the canyon to the pools at the bottom. The west of the canyon gradually becomes shallower until the river broadens out into a valley on its way to Sossusvlei.

Getting there

Sesriem is reached by taking the turnoff signposted about sixty-nine kilometres (forty-three miles) south of Solitaire. The entrance gate is twelve kilometres (seven miles) beyond the turnoff.

Where to stay

There is a campsite at Sesriem. Advance bookings must be made. See Listings.

Sightseeing

From the parking area at Sesriem a **track** leads into the **canyon** where various conglomerate layers of rock can be seen clearly. After good rains the canyon holds water for several months and it is possible to swim in the deep **pool** where the track reaches the floor. As you walk up into the canyon it gradually becomes narrower until in some places it's a mere two metres (seven feet) wide.

An early start is advisable if you are continuing to Sossusvlei as the **sand dunes** are seen at their best immediately after sunrise when the orange contrasts sharply with the dark shadow side. Confirm departure and return times at the **tourist office** at **Sesriem**, as these vary according to sunrise and sunset. The sixty-kilometre (thirty-seven-mile) journey is usually covered in one-and-a-quarter hours.

Twenty-four kilometres (fifteen miles) from Sesriem the **road** crosses the **Tsauchab River** and from there the road continues along the broad river **valley**. Numerous dead **camel thorn trees** indicate an old river course and provide evidence that the river once followed a more southerly route.

The Tsauchab once flowed into the Atlantic Ocean, until its course was blocked by encroaching sand dunes. Indeed, archaeological and geomorphological evidence show that a decreasing water flow, coupled with obstruction by sand dunes, blocked its flow some seventy kilometres (forty-three miles) inland about 60,000 years ago. Nevertheless, over thousands of years the Tsauchab River has managed to keep its course, ending in a **clay pan** sixty-five kilometres (forty miles) south-west of Sesriem at **Sossusvlei**.

Cars stop at a **point** three kilometres (one-and-three-quarter miles) from Sossusvlei, while 4WD vehicles may continue to the **parking area**. But remember: the landscape is ecologically sensitive and it is an offence to leave the track, which is demarcated by stakes.

Where the trail ends, there's a walk of four or so kilometres (two-and-a-half miles) over a low **sand ridge** to the wonder of Sossusvlei. All around, the sleek, contoured ridges of rolling mountains of sand rise up more than 300 metres (1,000 feet) like a towering and flamboyant range of alpine peaks set down among a dazzling necklace of salt pans.

Just before sunrise, as the first fragile fingers of pink that herald the desert dawn bring promise of another memorable day, these magnificent star dunes, reputed to be the highest sand dunes on earth, their colours and shadows changing by the hour from beige to rust-red to purple, make Sossusvlei a graceful and secret place, privy only to a favoured few.

West of Sossusvlei lies a sixty-kilometre (thirty-seven mile) wide belt of linear dunes, the largest area of the Central Namib sand sea. The **north**-to-**south**-trending dunes lie diagonal to the prevailing south-westerly winds and reach lengths of up to fifty kilometres (thirty-one miles). They're lower than those at Sossusvlei, being some sixty to 100-metres (200-330 feet) high, and are separated by **valleys** up to one-and-a-half kilometres (one mile) wide.

Above: Hardy desert survivor in close-up.

Overleaf: Scrub plants mark the subterranean aquifers beneath one of the Namib's dried-up water courses.

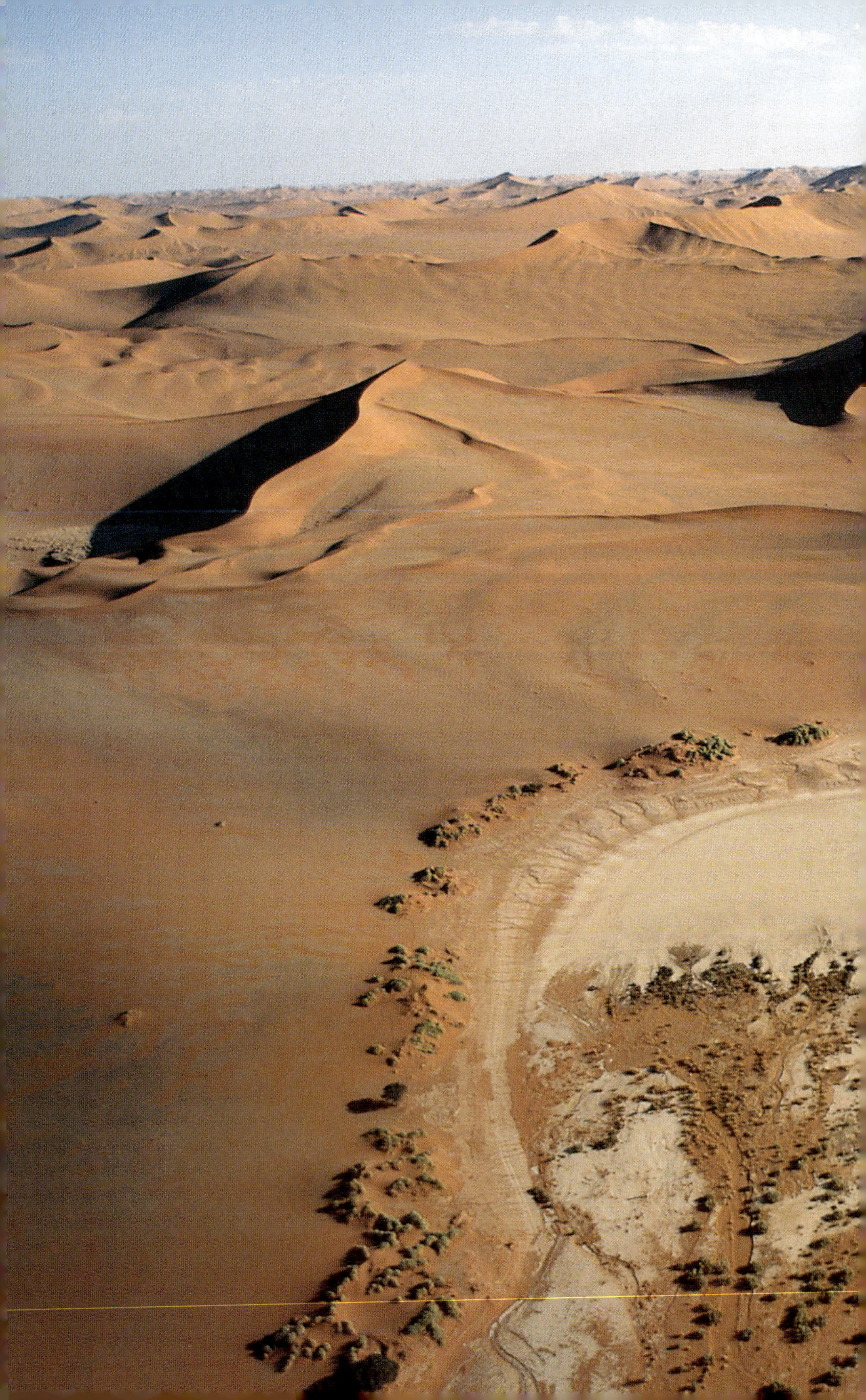

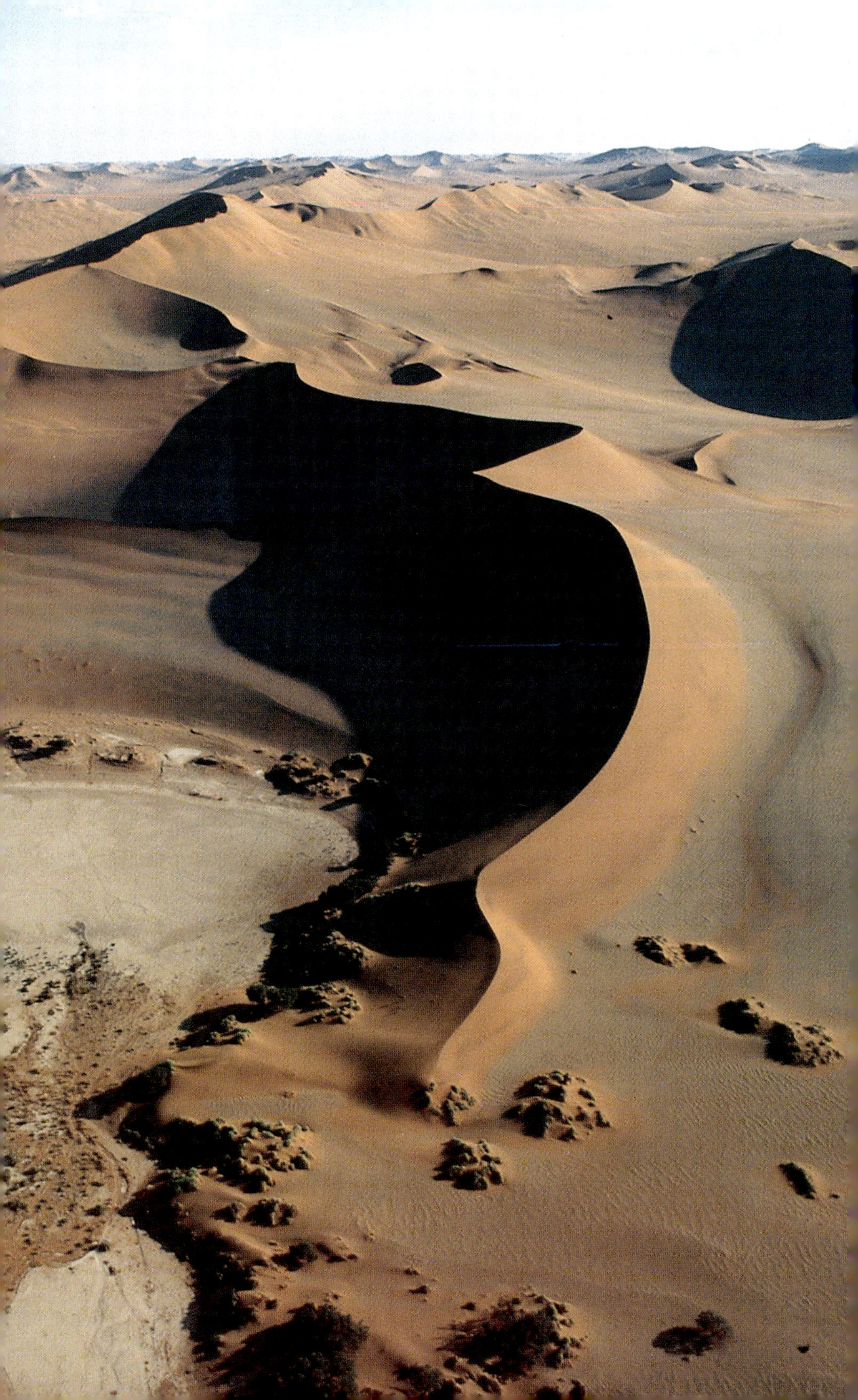

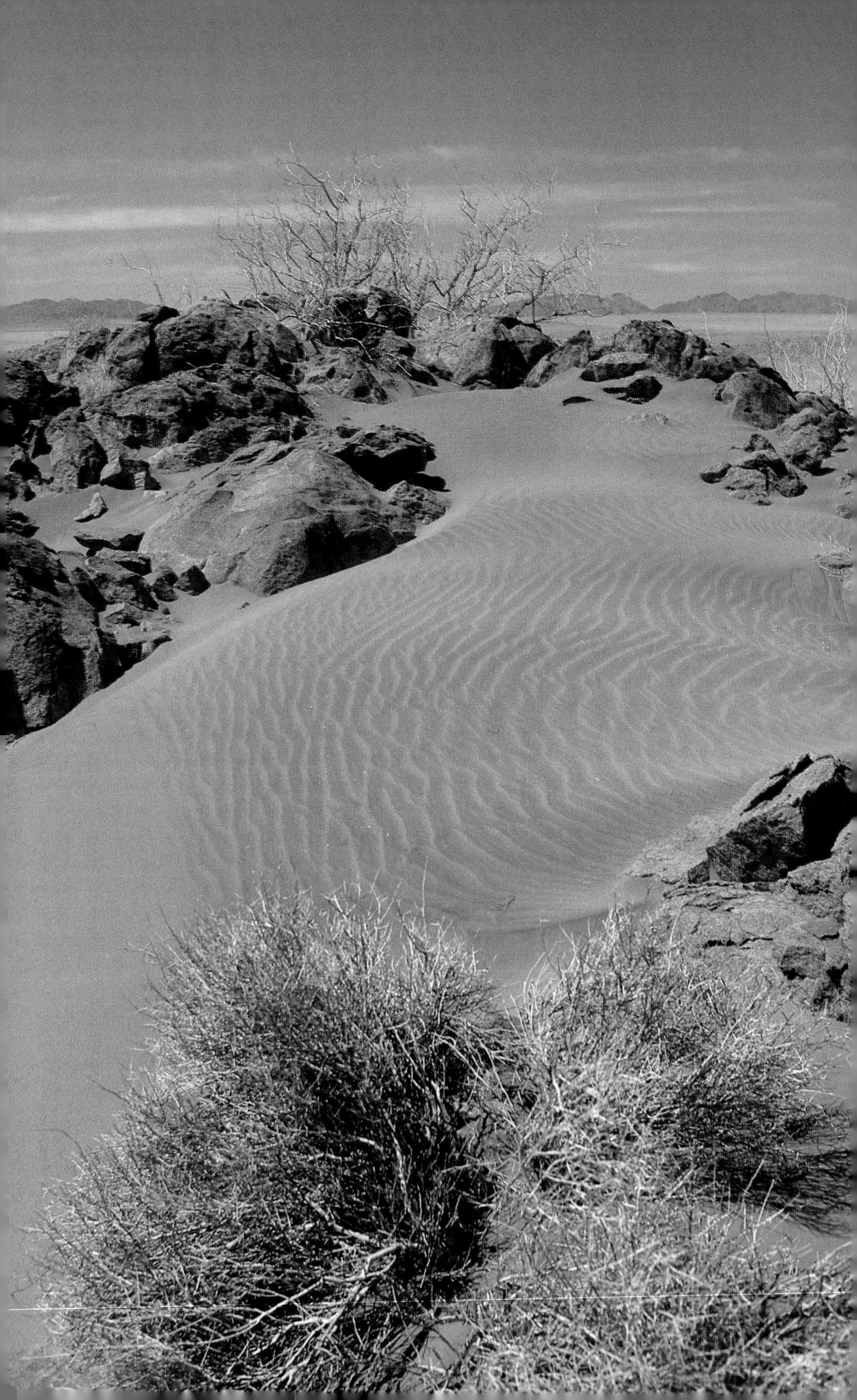

Above: Footsteps lead along a rippled ridge in the sand mountains of Sossusvlei.

Closer to the coast lies a ten- to twenty-kilometre (six to twelve miles) wide belt of crescentic dunes, including transverse and barchan types. These lie roughly perpendicular to the path of the south-west wind, dominant along the Namib coast.

One of the most fascinating aspects of the dune areas is the way in which the plants that live there have adapted to their inhospitable environment.

The dune grass, *Stipagrostis sabulicola*, forms small dunelets on the main dunes, which are the centre of life for plant-dependent species. During the early morning hours the fog precipitates on the live and dead plants, thus supplying the only source of water for the greater part of the year.

From Sesriem, backtrack along the trail to the **minor road** and **north turn** to **Solitaire**. From Solitaire the road traces the **eastern boundary** of the **Namib-Naukluft Park**.

Central Namib: A Magic Panorama

Further north, the road descends into the valley of the Gaub River, a tributary of the Kuiseb River, before travelling into the centre of the park. Some seventy-three kilometres (forty-five miles) north of Solitaire the C26 road joins the C14 from the east and descends the Gamsberg Pass. Then, after another few kilometres through the deeply scarred landscape, the road descends to the Kuiseb Pass over the Kuiseb River.

Where to stay

There are campsites at Kuiseb Bridge, Kriess-se-Rus, Ganab, Homeb, Mirabib, Vogelfederberg, the Swakop River, Bloedkoppie and Groot Tinkas. See Listings.

Opposite: Namibia's characteristic desert scenery — sand, rocks and stunted shrub.

Above: Weathered limbs of an acacia that may have died 500 years earlier mark the trail to Sossusvlei.

Provided you have a permit, the campsite below the bridge is ideal for a break.

Sightseeing

The **Kuiseb River**, rising in the Khomas Hochland near Windhoek, plays a vital role in preventing the northward encroachment of the dunes. Owing to the relatively high rainfall in its catchment area, it is one of the largest rivers to cross the desert between the Orange and Kunene rivers.

About twenty kilometres (twelve miles) west of the **Kuiseb Canyon** is the turnoff to the **Carp Cliff viewpoint**, with awe-inspiring views of the Kuiseb Valley and **Gamsberg** section of the **Great Escarpment**. As you stand on the **canyon rim** at Carp Cliff, some 180 metres (590 feet) above the present **river**, it is hard to believe that you are actually inside one of the Kuiseb's ancient river-beds — abandoned millions of years ago. Sections of the Canyon, however, clearly illustrate that this river system represents a valley within a former valley. At the Carp Cliff viewpoint, the well-rounded boulders and cobbles on the canyon rim were laid down in an enormous alluvial fan that stretched from the Gamsberg area to Sandwich Harbour on the coast.

At that time, some eighteen to fifteen million years ago, they were deposited by streams over an even earlier Kuiseb drainage system, probably dating from forty to twenty million years ago. It is represented by the greyish brown to whitish sandstone underlying the gravels at Carp Cliff. During that period the Kuiseb Canyon did not reach the Atlantic Ocean as it was blocked — as the Tsauchab River is today at Sossusvlei — by dunes of an ancient sand sea. Geologically the deeply incised course of the Kuiseb is, therefore, a youthful feature.

About one-and-a-half to one million years ago the bed of the Kuiseb was choked with its own sediments. Subsequently these deposits were cemented by lime-charged underground waters. Now they are seen as terrace deposits lining the river's course. Significantly, wedges of linear-type dunes are also incorporated into these conglomeratic terrace deposits, providing the first

Above: Namibia's curious flora has adapted to desert conditions to sustain remarkable life styles.

evidence of an association between the Kuiseb River, as it is today, and the main Namib sand sea.

A short **walk** leads to a large overhanging **cliff** where two German geologists, Henno Martin and Hermann Korn, who feared internment during World War II, lived for more than two years with their dog. During their stay there they found carp, probably washed downstream by floods, in one of the shallow pools of the Kuiseb River. Their classic story, *The Sheltering Desert*, relates how they and their dog, Otto, managed to survive against all odds in this inhospitable area. It was made into a movie in 1990.

Many tree species grow along the **Kuiseb** and **Swakop Rivers**, the most conspicuous being the **ana**, **camel thorn**, **ebony** and **needle bush**, while grasses of the genera *Stipagrostis* and *Eragrostis* form dense clumps on the **eastern plains** after rains.

Further **west**, the vegetation of the dry **gravel** consists of plants such as the *Salsola* species and *Arthraerua leubnitziae*, and the ana tree, camel thorn and buffalo-thorn.

Among the predators found in the Central Namib are black-backed **jackal**, which prefer the ravines, and **leopard**, which live in the Kuiseb and Swakop canyons and the mountainous areas of the north-east. **Spotted** and **brown hyena** are seen in the park's **eastern areas**.

Namib Excursions: From Sandwich to Welwitschia

From the Kuiseb Pass the C14 arrows west to Walvis Bay and the minor trail south to Sandwich Harbour, undoubtedly one of the most sought after scenic attractions of the Namib coast. Forty-two kilometres (twenty-six miles) from Walvis Bay, and accessible only by 4WD vehicle, Sandwich Harbour is a large sand-lined lagoon, haven for huge numbers of coastal and freshwater birds, and a major breeding area for many fish species. It is not just the romance of an isolated and inaccessible lagoon that sparks the imagination — although this certainly plays a part — but also some of the most

Above: Flight of flamingos rises into lowering night from the waters of Sandwich Harbour.

spectacular scenery along the Namib coast, combined with an unusual history.

Originally dubbed *Port D'Ilheo*, Sandwich is said to be a corruption of the Dutch name, *zandvisch*. It was used as a deep-water anchorage by early navigators who considered it safer than Walvis Bay where there was more fog. But the shoreline changes continuously and turn of the century maps mark this stretch of coast with dots rather than solid lines.

When the area was surveyed in 1880 by Lieutenant Oldham of HMS *Sylvia* the northern end was open, with a depth of five fathoms (approximately nine metres or thirty feet). However, some twelve years later, a sandbar blocked the mouth.

Sandwich served many diverse purposes over the centuries. Early whalers sheltered there from storms and, in the mid-1800s, De Pass, Spence and Company established a trading station to export cured fish, shark liver, sealskins and guano to Cape Town and Mauritius.

At the turn of the century the South West Africa Company operated a meat canning factory at Sandwich, the cattle being obtained from the Khoikhoi. Between 1904 and 1906 the harbour found yet another use — as a backdoor for gun-running to the Herero and Nama uprising against the Germans.

From 1910 large quantities of guano were collected from the natural sand islands of the lagoon by the *Deutsche Kolonialgesellschaft* and then shipped to Germany, but the company sold its rights in 1923. During the following thirteen years a variety of companies exploited the rich deposits.

In 1937 the concession was seized by Fisons Albatross Fertilisers, which promptly decided to enlarge Long Island. A diesel sand-pumping machine and other equipment was imported from the Netherlands and, by the end of 1938, nearly four hectares (ten acres) had been added to the island. The work, however, was interrupted by the outbreak of World War II and the operation was seriously jeopardised in 1943 when the mouth of the lagoon silted up and jackal moved in, causing birds to leave.

But after the mouth was washed open by

the first spring tide in April 1944, the water level in the lagoon rose to normal and the birds returned. After the war, large quantities of guano were again harvested, but the mouth soon silted up again. By 1957 the sea and sand dunes had reclaimed their rightful places, leaving only a few pieces of rusty machinery as testimony to man's activities at Sandwich Harbour.

Today the lagoon covers about twenty square kilometres (seven-and-three-quarter square miles), stretching roughly fifteen kilometres (nine miles) in a south-north direction, with a maximum width of three-and-a-half kilometres (two miles). On its eastern side the lagoon is flanked by 100-metre high (330-foot) dunes.

Getting there

A tarmac road follows the coast south from Walvis Bay. (See "The Capital and the Towns", Part Three). At the checkpoint it is about twenty kilometres (twelve miles) to Sandwich Harbour. You may also drive all the way along the beach if you wish.

When to go

The area is closed on Sundays. You may only explore the bird sanctuary on foot.

Sightseeing

A number of enclosed reed-lined **pools** back directly onto the **Namib dunes** at the **northern end** of the **beach**. These lagoons are fed by the sea, via narrow channels which fill at high tide, and by freshwater seeping from a subterranean **watercourse** of the Kuiseb River under the dunes. Percolating through the inland dunes, this helps to reduce the salinity in the lagoon, hence the reeds and grasses that clothe its edges.

It is worth making the effort to climb at least a little way up one of the enormous dunes for, from such a vantage point, you can see all over the deep lagoon, protected from the ocean by a **sand-spit**, and the extensive tidal **mudflats** to the south.

The wetland is of international importance as a reserve for migratory waterbirds in Africa with 113 species recorded. **Greater** and **lesser flamingo** are often seen, along with such uncommon

Above: In a remarkable demonstration of natural chemistry, sand and salt crystalise to form a desert rose.

species as the **ringed plover**, **Kittlitz's plover**, **turnstone**, **common** and **marsh sandpiper**, **Caspian tern**, **whiskered tern**, **white-winged tern** and **swift**. **Dabchick**, also uncommon, are residents of the lagoon, while South African **shelduck** and **moorhen** favour it above other areas of the coast.

The shores are also the habitat of small numbers of **black-backed jackal**, **brown hyena**, and **gemsbok**.

To Rössing

Twelve kilometres (seven miles) along the B2 east of Swakopmund (See "The Capital and the Towns", Part Three) an unusual castle-like **building** around the **ruins** of a police station and customs post dating back to 1892 is now in business as the **Burg Hotel**.

It is a fascinating repository of the history of the German colony. In the old building a **bar** displays numerous museum pieces. **Photographs** of the ruins before the restoration add to its atmosphere and take you back a hundred years.

Further **east** along the B2, between the hotel and the **Rössing Country Club**, there is a **camel farm** which operates desert treks. Camels were a common form of police transport at the turn of the century. The camels graze along the **Swakop River** during the morning. The **Rössing Uranium Mine**, a few kilometres south of **Arandis** on the B2, may be visited by joining a bus tour that operates every Friday. Reservations can be made at the Swakopmund Museum.

The geological history of the Rössing deposits goes back some 1,700 million years when the Namib Desert was part of the sea. Sediments from higher-lying areas were deposited on the sea-bed, causing further accumulation of deposits which sank deep into the earth's crust. The rocks were then folded and metamorphosed while underlying molten matter was forced upwards and became embedded in the sedimentary rock.

Discovered in the 1920s by Captain Peter Louw, a prospector, the uranium deposits are the largest of their kind in the world — three kilometres (one-and-three-quarter miles) long and one kilometre (half-a-mile) wide. The low-grade uranium, however, is contained in tough, abrasive granite known as alaskite. Each week a million tonnes of rock are recovered from the **open pit**, mined in fifteen-metre-deep (fifty-foot) **trenches**, using about 300 tonnes of explosives. The rock is then loaded into 150-tonne trucks and transported to two crushers with a capacity to process 40,000 tonnes a day and turned into a yellow paste, *Ammonium diuranate*. In the final stage it is dried and roasted at a temperature of more than 6,000°C to form uranium oxide.

Masters of the desert

In the nearby plains is one of Namibia's great natural curiosities, the intriguing *Welwitschia mirabilis,* a well-documented botanic oddity, continually studied by scientists from around the world. (See "Flora: The Great Survivors", Part Four).

Most visitors attracted to Namibia by the abundant and diverse wildlife don't realise that without the even greater array of desert-adapted plants which feed the animals and provide them with life-sustaining water contained in leaves, stems and trunks, there would be no game. The drier parts of Namibia support an amazing variety of plants which have managed to establish themselves in one of the earth's most extreme environments.

Sightseeing

Thirteen **stone beacons** mark points of particular interest in the **Welwitschia plains** of the **northern part** of Namib-Naukluft Park. The first beacon marks a **lichen field**. Look carefully at these small plant-like organisms, the result of a symbiotic relationship between an alga, producing food by photosynthesis, and a fungus, providing a physical structure. You will see many different types, some hundreds of years old, and all exceedingly fragile and vulnerable.

The **tenth beacon** at the **Swakop River Valley**, with a profusion of small trees

Above: One of the great natural wonders of the plant world, the long-lived *Welwitschia mirabilis*.

around it, is a good spot for lunch. Indeed, you may find it difficult to believe that you are in the middle of the desert. **Beacon number eleven** brings you to several *Welwitschia* on the gravel flats and the **last beacon** marks the largest of these, estimated to be more than 1,500 years old.

Also on the **B2 east** of Swakopmund a **road sign** indicates the **turnoff** to a military **cemetery**. Continue along the **gravel road** towards the **railway line**, cross over, and turn east to the fenced **graveyard** marked by a large tree, almost opposite the **old station building**. There, German and South African soldiers killed in the Battle of Trekkopje on 26 April 1915, are buried.

After the invasion of Swakopmund by South African forces in January 1915, the retreating Germans destroyed the Otavi line between Swakopmund and Usakos, as well as the state line sixty-two kilometres (thirty-eight miles) east of Swakopmund.

While rebuilding the Otavi line, the construction camp of the South Africa Engineering Corps at Trekkopje was attacked by Germans. Although outnumbered, the South Africans, in Rolls Royce armoured cars with revolving machine-gun turrets, defeated the enemy. Another reminder of the South West Africa World War I Campaign may be seen by taking another **turnoff** — indicated by a **national monument sign** — forty-seven kilometres (twenty-nine miles) **east** of Swakopmund. Follow the **track** to the **railway line** from where it is a short distance on foot to a raised **platform**. From that, there is a splendid view over the twenty-seven metre (twenty-nine-and-a-half yards) by twelve-metre (thirteen-yard) **regimental insignia** of the 2nd Durban Light Infantry which was laid out in white quartz chips and dark brown rocks by some South African soldiers assigned to patrol the railway line to prevent the Germans sabotaging it.

They occupied themselves by skilfully setting out their names, initials and regimental symbols. Further to the **right** is the incomplete **thistle** of the Transvaal Scottish Regiment. You can just make out the Gaelic motto, *Alba nam buadh*.

Midland Highlands: Undulating Hills, Mountains, Rock Paintings and Passes

To the east of the Namib the highlands of the central plateau climb to a hardveld tableland, varying in height from 900 to nearly 2,000 metres (2,950-6,560 feet), to form a region of wide geophysical diversity, the countryside ranging from broken veld, sandy valleys and undulating plains, to mountain massifs and jagged peaks.

The highlands, with their generous summer rains, sustain nutritious ground cover for flocks of karakul sheep in the south and cultivated land and cattle in the north. Whereas the mountains consist of massive rock, the plains of the plateau are filled with the erosion rubble of the geological epochs of the past; rivers have gradually scoured the surface and only the more substantial masses remain.

The Khomas Hochland, an upland region forming part of the interior plateau of central Namibia, between 1,750 and 2,000 metres (5,750-6,560 feet) above sea level, formed some 650 to 750 million years ago when sediments accumulated on the floor of a massive sea which covered southern Africa.

These subsequently metamorphosed during a mountain-building phase to form schists which, in turn, folded and tilted. During several major geological periods, the mountain chain has been reduced to its roots — as it is today. Extending eastward from the great escarpment to the Windhoek area, the terrain is deeply dissected with abundant seasonal river valleys, sharp ridges and rolling hills.

Getting there

Windhoek is 2,027 kilometres (1,260 miles) from Pretoria, 1,971 kilometres (1,225 miles) from Johannesburg, 1,493 kilometres (928 miles) from Cape Town, 816 kilometres (506 miles) from Lüderitz, 700 kilometres (435 miles) from Rundu, 533 kilometres (330 miles) from Namutoni, 482 kilometres (299 miles) from Keetmanshoop, 357 kilometres (222 miles) from Swakopmund and 389 kilometres (241 miles) from Walvis Bay. There are several major routes and passes through the central plateau from Windhoek. The B1 from Noordoewer on the South African border runs north and connects with the B2 to Swakopmund. The Bosua Pass (the C28) connects the capital with Swakopmund via a more direct route, while the Gamsberg Pass takes a south-easterly route through the northern edges of the Namib-Naukluft Park. All are well-maintained.

When to go

The area is pleasant all year-round.

Where to stay

In Windhoek, the Kalahari Sands (4-star), Hotel Safari (3-star), Hotel Thuringer Hof (2-star), Continental Hotel (2-star), Hotel Fürstenhof (2-star), Hotel-Pension Cela (2-star), Aris Hotel (1-star), Tuckers Tavern (1-star). See Listings for "Hotels". There are many guest farms, caravan parks and campsites throughout the area. See Listings.

Sightseeing

Of the three **Khomas Hochland** routes to the coast, the route via the **Gamsberg Pass**, also known as the 'Garden Route of Namibia', is the most popular. As you travel further **west**, the scenery is increasingly dominated by the 2,347-metre-high (7,700-foot) **Gamsberg**, a large tabletop mountain. It consists of granite a million years old with a conspicuous horizontal capping of weather-resistant sandstone twenty-five metres (eighty-two feet) thick.

It was formed about 200 million years ago when this area was covered by sediments washed into the shallow sea which covered large parts of the subcontinent. The Gamsberg has been protected from the ravages of subsequent erosion by its sandstone cap.

The name is said to derive from the local vernacular for 'shut' or 'closed', a reference to the fact that the mountain obscures any view. It is worth stopping at the **top** of the **pass**, however, to enjoy a magnificent **panorama** of rolling hills and deep valleys. From its **summit**, the pass snakes down the escarpment to continue along several stunning valleys until it reaches the **inner Namib**, with its level plains. About 175 kilometres (109 miles) out of Windhoek the road joins **route C14**, just ten kilometres (six miles) from the **gateway** into the Namib-Naukluft Park.

The **Bosua Pass** on the **C28** through the Khomas Hochland highlands is the most direct route to **Swakopmund** through the Namib Desert.

Getting there

From Windhoek, follow the turnoff signposted Daan Viljoen at the intersection of Curt von Francois and Republiek streets.

When to go

The Khomas Hochland highlands have a year-round pleasant climate.

Where to stay

There are bungalows and a campsite, together with a restaurant and swimming pool. Reservations should be made in advance. See Listings.

Sightseeing

Daan Viljoen Game Reserve, fourteen kilometres (nine miles) from Windhoek, makes a perfect day trip from the capital. Within half-an-hour of the city centre, visitors may drive through the undulating **hills** of the Khomas Hochland, watching an abundance of wild animals in their natural habitat.

Even around the **guest bungalows**, **eland** and **blue wildebeest** often wander, while **red-billed francolin** and **helmeted guinea fowl** frequently look for scraps.

There is a **circular drive** and two **nature trails**. The three-kilometre (two-mile) **Wag 'n Bietjie Trail** is ideal for the family group or those seeking an easy ramble. It starts near the **park office** and follows the **Augeigas River** upstream for one-and-a-half kilometres (one mile) to the **Stengel** and **Koch und Schultheiss dams**.

The nine-kilometre (six-mile) **Rooibos Trail** follows a more strenuous, circular route, starting near the **swimming pool** and ending at the **restaurant**. As there are no dangerous predators you may, however, also follow any of the numerous **game tracks** crisscrossing the park. Provided you remain downwind, you should be able to stalk close to the wildlife.

Daan Viljoen is home to mammals typical of the Khomas Hochland, such as **eland**, **gemsbok**, **Hartmann's mountain zebra**, **blue wildebeest**, **red hartebeest**, **springbok** and **kudu**. Smaller species include **klipspringer**, **steenbok**, **rock dassie** and **chacma baboon**. (See "Wildlife: Just Out of This World", Part Four).

The **lake** is stocked with **barbel**, **kurper**, and **black bass** and permits to fish in the dam are available at the rest camp. Daan Viljoen Game Reserve lies within the Highland Savanna Veld and the hills are thick with **mountain thorn**, **Namibian resin tree**, **red bushwillow** (known locally as *koedoebos*) **candle thorn**, **wild camphor bush**, and *Elephantorrhiza suffruticosa* (known locally as *looiwortelbos*).

Camel thorn, **sweet thorn**, **karree**, and **buffalo-thorn** grow in the valleys, while *Antephora*, *Enneapogon*, and *Stipagrostis* are the main grasses. The green-flowered *Aloe viridiflora*, which normally grows singly, is endemic to the reserve, as is *Euphorbia avasmontana*.

To date, more than 200 bird species have been recorded in the reserve and, if you're experienced, you should be able to tick off between sixty and ninety species a day, among them **Monteiro's hornbill**, **rock-runner**, **white-tailed shrike**, **green-backed heron** and **pin-tailed whydah**.

Daan Viljoen, proclaimed a reserve in 1962, was named after a former Administrator, D T du P Viljoen.

Copper Mine

Further along the C28 a **signpost** marks the turnoff **south** to the **Matchless Mine** now, unfortunately, closed to the public. Archaeological excavations at several sites in the Khomas Hochland provide evidence of indigenous copper smelting going back 300 and 200 years. Large-scale commercial

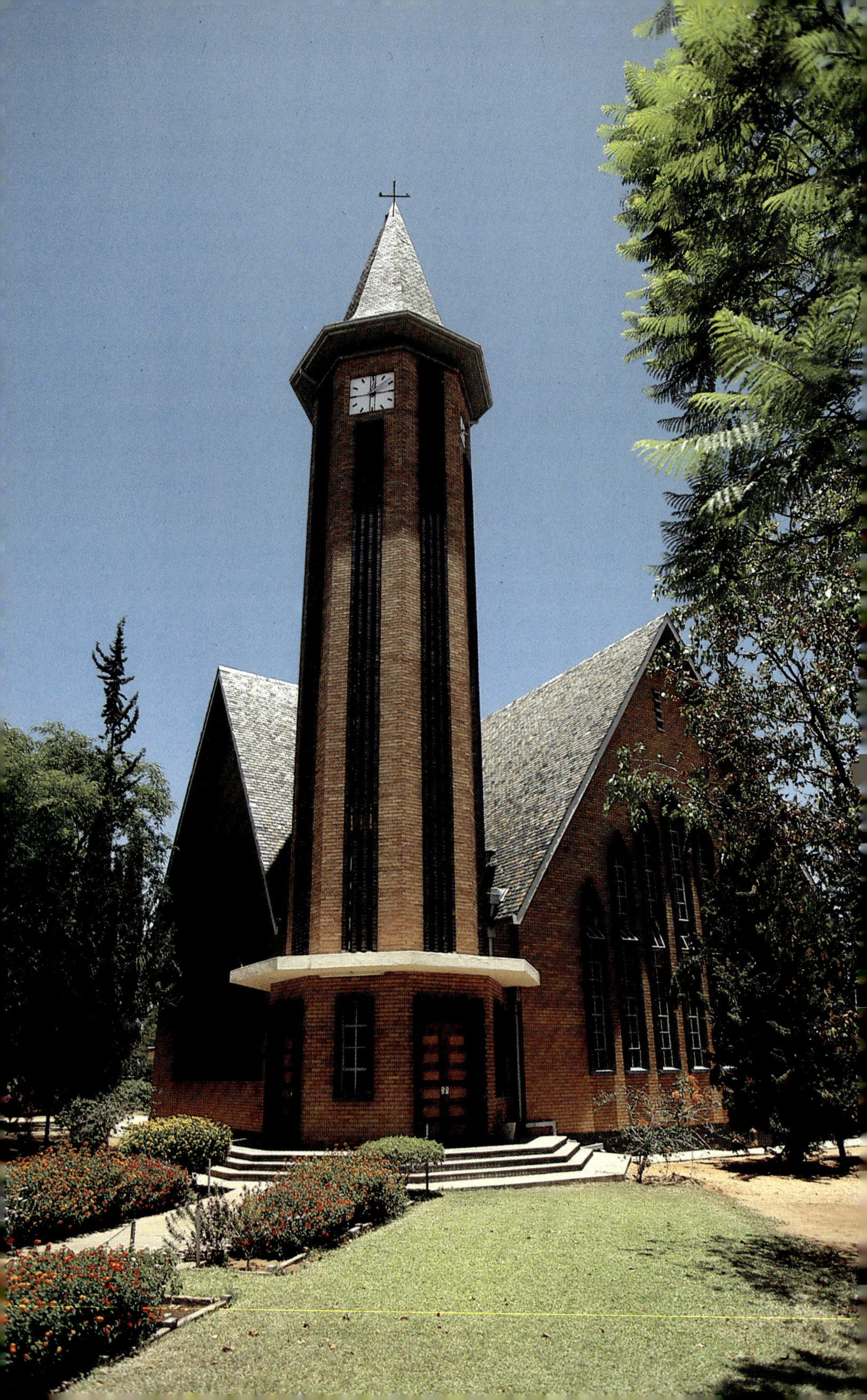

exploitation of the Matchless Mine dates back to 1856 when the Walvisch Bay Mining Company began operations in central Namibia.

The mine's first manager was the renowned traveller, explorer and trader, Charles John Andersson, who supervised the operation between 1856 and 1858. But in 1860 the company abandoned the site and it was well over a century before an extensive drilling programme was carried out by the Tsumeb Corporation, resulting in renewed mining, between 1970 and 1983, of copper and sulphur.

Sixteen kilometres (ten miles) beyond the mine, a decaying and dilapidated turn-of-the-century **house** rises incongruously above the hills shadowing the C28. Strangely out of context with the dry ruggedness of its surroundings, **Liebig House** has the reputation of being haunted. It was built around 1912 on the **New-Heusis Farm** of the Deutsche Farmgesellschaft. Take a stroll though the unusual colonial double-storey **building** where, with a little imagination, you will be able to picture the once-lavish life-style of the occupants.

A **fountain** in a large room downstairs must have been the focal point and a row of beautifully patterned **tiles** decorates some of the **walls**. Upstairs you can but envy the past occupants the expansive view they awakened to each morning.

Further west, at Karanab, the C28 passes the **ruins** of the **von Francois Fort**, named after Major Curt von Francois, the founder of modern Windhoek. With a force of twenty-one men, disguised as a scientific expedition to conceal their military objective, von Francois landed in Walvis Bay in June 1899, making his temporary headquarters at Tsaobis, south-west of Otjimbingwe.

The following year, he moved his headquarters to the site of the present-day Windhoek and established a series of military posts. The von Francois fort was built to protect the route between Swakopmund and Windhoek, but later served as a drying-out-post, *Trockenposten*, for alcoholic German troops. Built of local flat stones, the fort blends so well with its surroundings that you will miss it unless you keep your eyes peeled. The fort's mortar has not weathered the years, thus revealing how the natural stones were skilfully placed on top of one another to form the walls. From the 'windows', there is a view of the **Heusis River Valley** and the surrounding hills — underlining the fort's strategic position.

To Von Bach Recreation Resort

North of Windhoek along the B1 the country is nothing short of stunning. Distant mountains hang hauntingly above the plains, topped by cotton-wool clouds, stretching across a blue sky.

The first stop in this area, thirty kilometres (nineteen miles) north of Windhoek, is at the Düsternbrook Farm. There you will find half a dozen leopards in a large enclosure — a photographer's dream — and there is also horse riding so it makes an excellent day out from Windhoek.

Further north is Von Bach Recreation Resort, created around a dam nestling in the north-eastern flanks of the Auas Mountains and the upper reaches of the Swakop River drainage system.

Completed in 1968, Von Bach is Windhoek's main water source. It forms part of the first phase of a master water plan to meet projected water requirements for Namibia's central areas. Covering some forty-three square kilometres (sixteen square miles), the reserve is divided in two when the lake is full — the south-eastern portion covering approximately two-thirds of the area, the remainder occupying the north-western section.

The surrounding terrain is extremely hilly, the highest point being 300 metres (984 feet) above the dam wall in the south-western corner.

Opposite: Soaring, graceful lines of the modern Lutheran church at Otjiwarongo.

Above: German-built 1912 narrow-gauge locomotive stands as monument to pioneering past outside the station at Otjiwarongo.

When to go

The resort is open throughout the year.

Where to stay

There are overnight campsites and huts and a picnic site.

Sightseeing

The **lake** is surrounded by savannah vegetation with **ringwood tree**, **blue thorn**, **black thorn** and **red bushwillow**, while the river course has abundant **camel thorn** and **sweet thorn**.

When it was proclaimed a reserve, only a few **kudu** and **baboons** lived there but since then, **Hartmann's mountain zebra**, **springbok**, **eland** and **ostrich** have been introduced. Game viewing is limited, however, as the only **tourist road** leads to the campsite on the **south-eastern bank**.

Visitors may water-ski, windsurf and go yachting. Open from sunrise to sunset, the reserve is also popular with anglers as it's stocked with **large-mouth bass**, **blue kurper**, **small-mouth yellowfish**, **carp**, and **barbel**. Angling permits are available at the gate.

To Okahandja

Much of the history of the Herero people is closely connected with Okahandja, a small pleasant town, north of Von Bach.

In 1843 two Rhenish missionaries, Carl Hugo Hahb and Heinrich Kleinschmidt, visited the springs and named them *Schmelens Verwachting* after Heinrich Schmelen of the London Missionary Society, who had been there sixteen years before. But it was not until 1849 that the first missionary, Friedrich Kolbe, settled in Okahandja. Just three months later, tribal fighting forced him to abandon the mission station and it did not reopen until peace returned to the area.

Getting there

Okahandja is on the B1 seventy-one kilometres (forty-four miles) north of Windhoek.

When to go

Okahandja has a pleasant climate all year-round.

Where to stay

Okahandja Hotel (1-star). See Listings for "Hotels". Guest Farms: Haasenhof, J&C Lievenberg, Matador, Okomitundu, Otjisazu and Otjisema. See Listings. Hunting Farms: Moringa and Okatjuru. See Listings.

Sightseeing

At the **southern** end of **Church Street**, which runs parallel to **Main Street**, you will find the **Rhenish Mission Church**, in use until 1952 and now a **national monument**. It was built between 1871 and 1876. The **graves** of several German soldiers, missionaries, and Herero leaders — including those of Trougoth and Willem Maherero — fill the pretty **graveyard**.

Immediately opposite the **church** are the graves of Jonker Afrikaner, leader of the Nama until his death in 1861, and the Herero chiefs Clemens Kapuuo and Hosea Kutako.

Kutako, first president of the Democratic Turnhalle Alliance, was assassinated in 1978 at Katutura, Windhoek. Having made the first direct petition to the United Nations against South African rule, he is considered by many to be the father of Namibian black nationalism.

In a final demonstration of his commitment to unity, Kutako chose to be buried near Jonker Afrikaner, a former enemy of the Herero people, and not, as is customary, in the cemetery of his ancestors.

Further along **Church Street**, slightly obscured by trees, a **signpost** indicates the footpath to the **communal grave** of Tjamuaha, and Samuel Maherero.

It is there that the Hereros pay homage each August to their forefather. The stately procession from these graves to those of Afrikaner, Kutako, and Kapuuo has become a significant event in the Okahandja calendar.

On the main **road** half-a-kilometre (one-third of a mile) **north** of the **turnoff** to **Gross-Barmen**, lies the site of **Moordkopppie** where, on 23 August 1850,

Above: Sign outside Otjiwarongo picnic site.

a large number of followers of the Herero chief, Kahitjenne, were killed by a group of Nama. Although a **national monument**, the site is fenced off and not signposted.

Thermal springs

Twenty-four kilometres (fifteen miles) south-west of Okahandja, along a tarred road, the Gross-Barmen resort stands on the banks of a tributary of the Swakop River and is well-known for its thermal springs.

Where to stay

Gross-Barmen offers luxury bungalows, caravan park and campsites, a shop and petrol station. There is an indoor thermal bath with six private baths and a swimming pool.

Sightseeing

The **springs** bubble up between the outdoor pool and the restaurant complex at a temperature of about 65°C.

The surrounding hillsides and the **dam** offer superb opportunities for bird watching and a **path** has been cut through the dense **reedbeds** where many wooden **benches** form excellent vantage points over the **lake**. Those in need of more strenuous exercise may walk either along the **river** or among the rocky **outcrops**.

Originally known as Otjikango, a vernacular phrase meaning 'a spring flowing weakly through rocky ground', the **resort** is built on the site of Namibia's first Rhenish **mission station** which was founded in October 1844 by Carl Hugo Hahn and Heinrich Kleinschmidt after the spring at Okahandja dried up. Five days after their arrival, Jonker Afrikaner arrived unexpectedly and encouraged them to settle there. They named the station Neu-Barmen after the headquarters of the Rhenish Missionary Society at Barmen in Germany. It later became Gross-Barmen.

As it was on the battleground between the warring Herero and Nama, the mission was abandoned several times and after 1890 no more missionaries were stationed there. Sadly, all that remains are the **ruins** of the **church** and **mission house**.

Former capital

If history is what you are after in Namibia, take the B2 west from Okahandja to Karibib where you turn south-east off the beaten track, to Otjimbingwe. Although a visit to this historic settlement, once the capital of the country, requires a special detour from Karibib, it is well-signposted.

Situated at the junction of the Swakop and the Omusema rivers, halfway between Windhoek and Walvis Bay on the gold oxwagon route, Otjimbingwe became the most important settlement in the country after Reichs-Kommissar Dr Heinrich Göring established it as the administrative seat of German South West Africa.

In 1849, the Rhenish missionary, Johannes Rathm, built a station there for the Herero. And in 1854, following the discovery of copper deposits in the area, the Walvis Bay Mining Company — WBM — made Otjimbingwe its headquarters. The same year, a trading store began selling arms, ammunition and liquor, offering credit for Europeans and bartering with the locals. Suddenly transformed into a boomtown, Otjimbingwe quickly degenerated into a den of iniquity.

From the 1860s, an increasing number of unscrupulous traders, dealing in liquor, arms and ammunition, were active in the area, seriously interfering with missionary work. To counter this, the *Missionshandelsgesellschaft* was founded in January 1871 to promote more constructive trade. Otjimbingwe served as the local headquarters, while branches were established at Okahandja and Rehoboth.

Namibia's first post office, housed in a tiny hut in the vicinity of the trading store, was opened in Otjimbingwe in July 1888 — a week after the country joined the Universal Postal Union. Two years later the Germans transferred their headquarters to Windhoek and when the railway line, following a more northerly route between Windhoek and Swakopmund, was completed early this century, Otjimbingwe lost all significance.

When the copper boom came to an end in 1860 the explorer, Charles John

Above: Elegant archways curve over the gateway of the Gross-Barmen Spa.

Andersson, bought the WBM Company's assets and established his headquarters there. More than a century later, the store, purchased by Eduard Halbich, is still in business. The town, however, is but a shadow of its former self.

Sightseeing

The main part of the Rhenish **church** dates back to 1867. The **tower** was added in 1899. It was built for the Herero even though their Chief, Zeraua, was not a Christian. On more than one occasion, during attacks by the Nama, its thick walls served as a refuge for women and children. Near the church stands a **tower** built in 1872 by the *Missionshandelsgesellschaft* to protect its trading venture from the Nama. No less than thirty assaults were hurled against the eight-metre-high (twenty-six-foot) tower, none of them successful.

Facing the tower is the 1896 **wind motor**, erected by the Halbich family to generate power to the adjoining wagon factory. The nine-metre (thirty-foot) diameter **windmill sail** turned a driving shaft attached to a gear on the ground. From there, a belt ran to another horizontal driving shaft inside the building. The eight horse-power motor generated enough energy to drive a saw, turntable, iron drill and waterpump at the nearby **spring**.

To Usakos

From Otjimbingwe, it is a few kilometres west to the Tsaobis Leopard Nature Park on the south bank of the Swakop river high on the escarpment overlooking the Namib. From there the C32 leads north back to Karibib. The park, comprising thirty-five square kilometres (fifteen square miles) of rugged mountainous country, was established as a leopard sanctuary in 1969. As leopards are mainly nocturnal creatures the chances of sighting them are only fair. Other game more likely to be seen are springbok, kudu, gemsbok and Hartmann's mountain zebra.

Where to stay

Hotel Erongoblick (2-star), Hotel Stroblhof (1-star). See Listings for "Hotels". Guest

Farms: Albertshöhe, Audawib. See Listings. Hunting Farm: Khomas. See Listings. At Tsaobis Leopard Nature Park there are ten fully equipped bungalows. Booking in advance is imperative.

Sightseeing

Thirty kilometres (nineteen miles) **west** of Karibib, the town of **Usakos** stands on the **southern bank** of the **Khan River**. Travellers often pass through the town without realising the important role it played in the history of Namibia's railways. For Usakos developed around the railway **workshops** built there early this century to service locomotives on the narrow-gauge Otavi Line.

By 1907 it boasted two **hotels** and a population of 300 and, in time, the workshops were rivalled only by those at De Aar in South Africa.

In 1960, when steam was replaced by diesel, a modern workshop opened in Windhoek, resulting in the depopulation of Usakos. More recently, however, this trend has been reversed and the commissioning of a **gold mine** in the hills to the **south-east** has attracted more people and revived the town's business.

Just **east** of Usakos, a **secondary road** leads off the B2 at the **signpost** marked **Ameib Guest Ranch** — famous for its **rock paintings** — where visitors may stay overnight. For those opting for something more basic, there is a **campsite**. Hours may be spent exploring the area, although at midday the heat among the granite masses often becomes unbearable.

Rock formations

In addition to the many **rock paintings** in the **Erongo Mountains,** the ranch's rock formations are also a great attraction. The **Bull's Party**, in particular, is a collection of more-or-less round boulders positioned in such a way as to create the impression of a number of bulls engaged in conversation — hence the name.

Nearby another rocky outcrop has been named, appropriately, **Elephant Head**. And keep an eye open for an enormous, sixteen-metre-high (fifty-two-foot) **boulder** that seems to have dropped out of the sky.

Provided you set off in the cool of early morning or late afternoon, the walk from the car park to the guest farm's star attraction, **Phillip's Cave**, is enjoyable. At this **national monument** you will be enthralled by the **painting** of a large white elephant on the facing wall. Other animals easily distinguishable include giraffe, zebra and ostrich, as well as a red antelope superimposed on an elephant.

The paintings are detailed in the Abbé Breuil's *Phillip Cave*. His theories as to the Mediterranean origin and age of the paintings, however, were rejected by later archaeologists.

Anibib Farm

Further north, **Anibib Farm** boasts one of the largest **collections** of **rock paintings** in Namibia as well as the greatest concentration of different animals and human figures in a variety of positions. These are spread over twenty square kilometres (eight square miles) and are well preserved. Anibib conducts a maximum of two guided tours a day for parties of no more than six.

Besides the beautiful scenery, the tours afford a glimpse into the way of life of earlier inhabitants of the area. **Stone Age tools**, including grinding stones, have been left untouched, as have **beads** and **ostrich egg shells**.

Neighbouring **Etemba Guest Farm**, on the northern perimeter of the Erongo Mountains, is named after the vernacular word for 'halting place'. It was a favourite resting place for travellers from Swakopmund as water was always available in the sandy river-bed of the Omaruru River. Following the severe drought of the early 1980s, however, when the boreholes ran dry, the farm was forced to close. It has since been re-opened and offers accommodation in **bungalows**. There is a **swimming pool**, **restaurant** and **campsite**.

The farm's real attractions are the countless **rock paintings north** of the main Erongo massif. Especially interesting are those in the **Etemba Cave**. With its beautiful view of the **Omaruru River** it is easy to understand why Stone Age artists chose to paint from this platform. There are other **rock painting sites** in the area and a **map** available at the farm will help you to locate them. Do not miss the **Mushroom Rock** — a boulder resting precariously on a smaller one, created by erosive action.

To Omaruru

Back at Karibib, the C33 leads north through Omaruru, eventually to link up with the B1. Omaruru was where the Swedish trader and hunter, Alex Eriksson, established his trading headquarters in 1879, the same year that a mission station was built on the shady banks of the Omaruru River.

Omaruru, which means 'bitter thickmilk', is a reference to milk produced by cows grazing on the bitter-bush, *Pechuelloeschae leubnitziae*, which remains green long after most others have grown unpalatable. But the meat and milk of animals feeding on the bitter-bush itself becomes bitter.

Where to stay

Central Hotel (3-star), Hotel Staebe (1-star). See Listings for "Hotels". Guest-farms: Boskloof, Erindi Onganga, Immenhof, Okosongoro, Otjandue, Otjikoko, Otjumeost, Schönfeld. See Listings.

Sightseeing

The **Franke Tower**, at the southern end of the town, declared a **national monument** in 1963, was raised by the residents in 1908 to honour Captain Victor Franke. In January 1904, he was suppressing an uprising in Gibeon when he heard that Okahandja and Omaruru were under siege by the Herero. Given permission by Governor Leutwein to relieve the siege he made a forced march north. Nineteen days and 900 kilometres (560 miles) later, they reached Omaruru where the German troops were greatly outnumbered by the Herero.

Nonetheless, on 4 February 1904, Franke led a gallant cavalry charge, causing the Herero chief, Manassa, and his followers to flee. He was honoured with Germany's highest military honour — awarded by the Kaiser himself.

The tower is kept locked but you may collect the key at either the **Central Hotel**, **Main Street**, or the **Hotel Staebe**, **Monument Street**. In the **grounds** of the tower stands a **cannon** which claimed the lives of 100 Herero and nine Germans. The nearby **battlefield** was declared a **national monument** in 1972.

Another famous **monument** in the town is the **mission house** — this is the oldest building in Omaruru. Built with raw clay bricks, it was completed in 1872 by the Rhenish missionary, Gottlieb Viehe, who had established a mission station there two years earlier. Inside, in 1874, Viehe translated the New Testament, the liturgy, prayers, and catechisms into Herero.

In the years that followed, the house served as a temporary military post where several highly placed officials, including the special envoy of the Cape Government, W C Palgrave, and Hauptmann Curt von Francois, held meetings with Herero chiefs.

The old **graveyard** opposite is the resting place for a number of Germans and a Herero chief, Wilhelm Zwraua. Each October, the Herero pay homage to their leader, and the procession from the **Ozonde** residential area to the graveyard and back is colourful and lively.

Hunting

Just **north** of Omaruru on route C33, **Epako** lies to the **west** immediately after crossing the railway line. A **farm** of undulating hills, mountains and plains, it covers approximately 110 square kilometres (forty-two square miles).

Blue and **black wildebeest**, **impala** and **black-faced impala**, **eland**, **giraffe**, **Burchell's zebra** and **red hartebeest** roam free and there is also a huge variety of birdlife. There are extensive facilities for visitors — including guided tours — although Epako is primarily a hunting farm. See Listings.

Further north, again on the C33, is Kalkfeld. There you should follow the signs on the secondary road that leads east out of the town to Otjihaenamaparero Farm where you will find several fossilised dinosaur tracks which were declared a national monument in 1951.

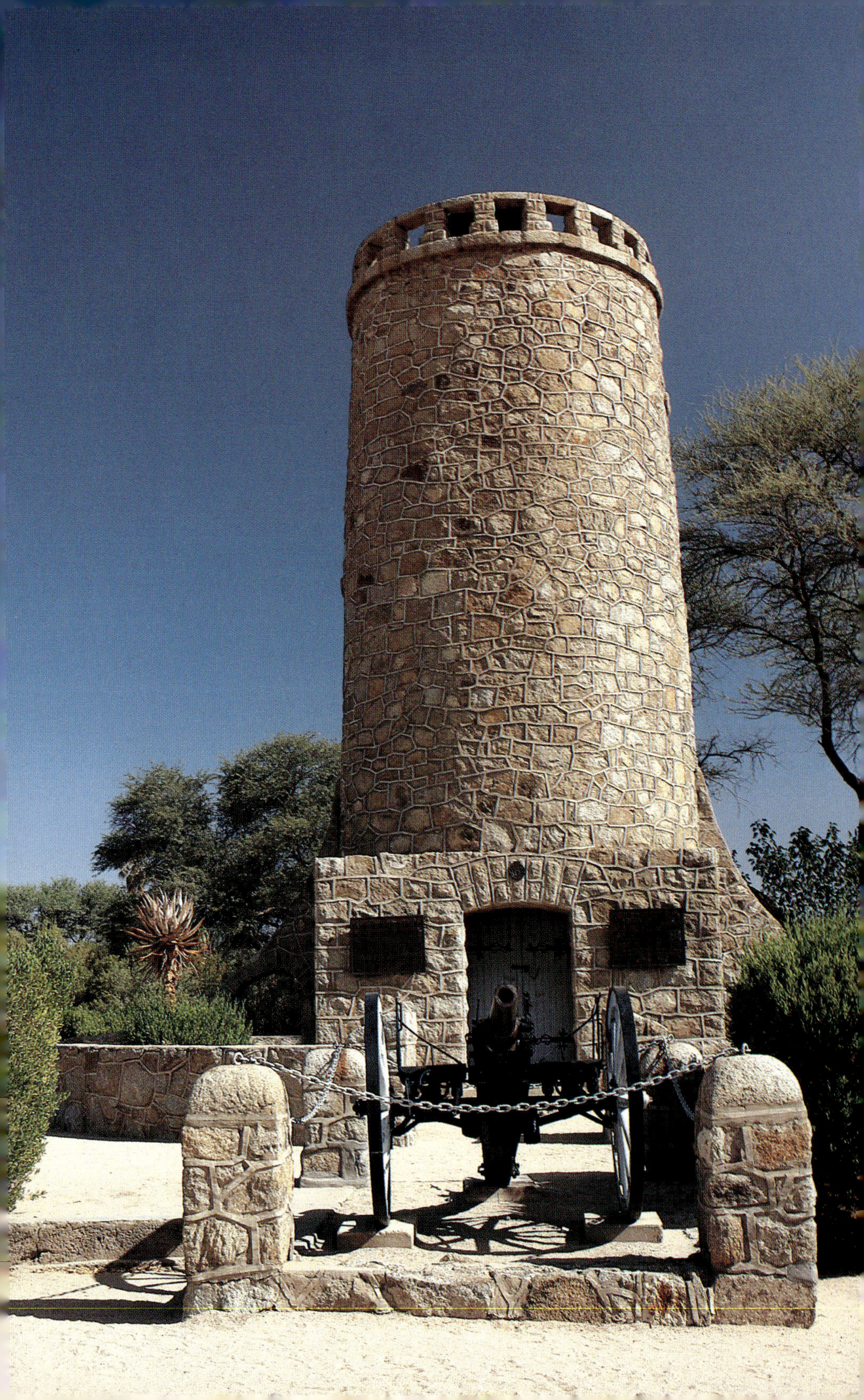

Sightseeing

The age of the **footprints** stamped in the red Etjo sandstone is estimated at between 150 and 185 million years. Perhaps the most striking are those of a two-legged, three-toed animal, the **tracks** of which cover a distance of some twenty-five metres (eighty-two feet).

With powerful hind legs and comparatively short forelimbs, the dinosaur ran like an ostrich, and for a long time experts confused their footprints with those of birds.

Further along the road you will find **Mount Etjo Safari Lodge**, a private nature reserve where guests view game either on foot or from open safari vehicles, under the guidance of an experienced ranger. Visitors may also while away time at one of the **waterholes** where hidden **huts** have been strategically placed with special facilities for professional photographers.

You are likely to see **cheetah** and **leopard**, **elephant**, **white rhino**, **giraffe**, and several antelope species, such as **roan**, **eland**, **gemsbok**, **red hartebeest**, **kudu** and the dainty **Damara dik-dik**. The waterholes are also rewarding for bird-watchers. But the undoubted highlight of a visit to Etjo is a close-up view of lions feeding. An antelope carcass is used as bait and there are excellent floodlit views from the **hides**. Mount Etjo's hotel-style rooms are close to a **dam**. Guests who prefer to spend a night close to nature, however, may do so in a comfortable **tree-top hide**.

Otjiwa Game Ranch, adjacent to the B1 between Okahandja and Otjiwarongo, is open throughout the year. It is typical Namibian thornveld country where **white rhino**, **kudu**, **eland**, **gemsbok**, **Burchell's zebra** and **waterbuck** will be found. Visitor facilities include four-person **cottages** and two exclusive self-contained **camps** which can accommodate up to eight people. See Listings.

To Otjiwarongo

If you are driving directly from Windhoek, the main B1 passes through Otjiwarongo north of Okahandja. Originally known to the Herero as Kanubes, the name — 'place of the fat cattle' — is an apt description, for the area is well-known for its cattle ranches.

Where to stay

Hotel Brumme (1-star), Hotel Hamburger Hof (2-star), Otjibamba Lodge (3-star). See Listings for "Hotels". Guest farms: Okonjima (2-star), Waterberg Big Game Hunting Lodge (3-star). See Listings.

Sightseeing

A Rhenish **mission station** was established at Otjiwarongo in 1891 under an agreement with the Herero chief, Kambazembi. And, in 1904, a **military post** was built at Okanjande, a few kilometres south of the present town.

The date the **railway station** was completed — 2 April 1906 — is recognised as the date on which Otjiwarongo was established. The station is on the **Swakopmund-Tsumeb** line, built to export copper from the north-east of the country.

In front of the **station** you will find **Locomotive No.40**, one of three heavy-duty locomotives built in 1912 by Henschel and Son of Casel, Germany. They were used on the narrow-gauge Otavi line between Kranzberg, about twenty kilometres (twelve miles) west of Karibib, and Tsumeb and Grootfontein until 1960 when the gauge was standardised.

The town's first **post office** was housed in a tent when it opened in April 1906. It was replaced by a permanent building in 1907, the same year as a **police station** was built. The town received municipal status in 1939. Namibia's first **crocodile farm** is on the outskirts of the town.

Opposite: Franke Tower raised in Omaruru in 1908 to honour Captain Victor Franke who marched 900 kilometres in twenty days to put down a rebellion.

Above: Early German water tower is now a Namibian national monument.
Opposite: Magnificent rock formation at Vingerklip.

To Outjo

North-west of Otjiwarongo, eighty kilometres (fifty miles) along the main route to the Okaukuejo Rest Camp in the Etosha National Park, lies Outjo, a perennial spring. The town there was founded by Tom Lambert, a trader, in 1880. Five years later a German military force arrived. They built a wind generator.

Where to stay

Hotel Onduri (2-star), Hotel Etosha (1-star), Bambatsi Holiday Ranch, Borgplaas Safari Lodge, Otjitambi (2-star), Toshari Inn. See Listings.

Sightseeing

The German-built **windmill** first went into use in March 1902. Power from the nine-and-a-half-metre-high (thirty-one-foot) stone and clay tower drove a pump which piped water into a cement dam for use by the barracks, hospital and stables.

In the old German **cemetery**, a **monument** was raised in 1933 to the memory of the German officials and soldiers murdered on 19 October 1914, by Portuguese at the Naulila Fort near the Kunene River, Angola. The monument also remembers the soldiers who died or went missing during the punitive 1914 expedition led by Major Victor Franke against Naulila.

An old **stone house**, dating back to around 1899, was one of the first houses in Outjo. Sometimes referred to as the **Franke House**, it was built on the instructions of Major von Estdorff for the commander of the German troops.

Some 130 kilometres (eighty-one miles) **west** of **Outjo**, **signposts** lead the way to the **Vingerklip**, an impressive lone relic of prehistoric erosion. The approach to the base of the column is steep, with loose gravel.

Also known as the *Kalk Kegel* — limestone skittle — the thirty-five-metre (115-foot) column of limestone conglomerate sits atop a small hill. Its base has a circumference of roughly forty-four metres (145 feet).

It is estimated that the column was

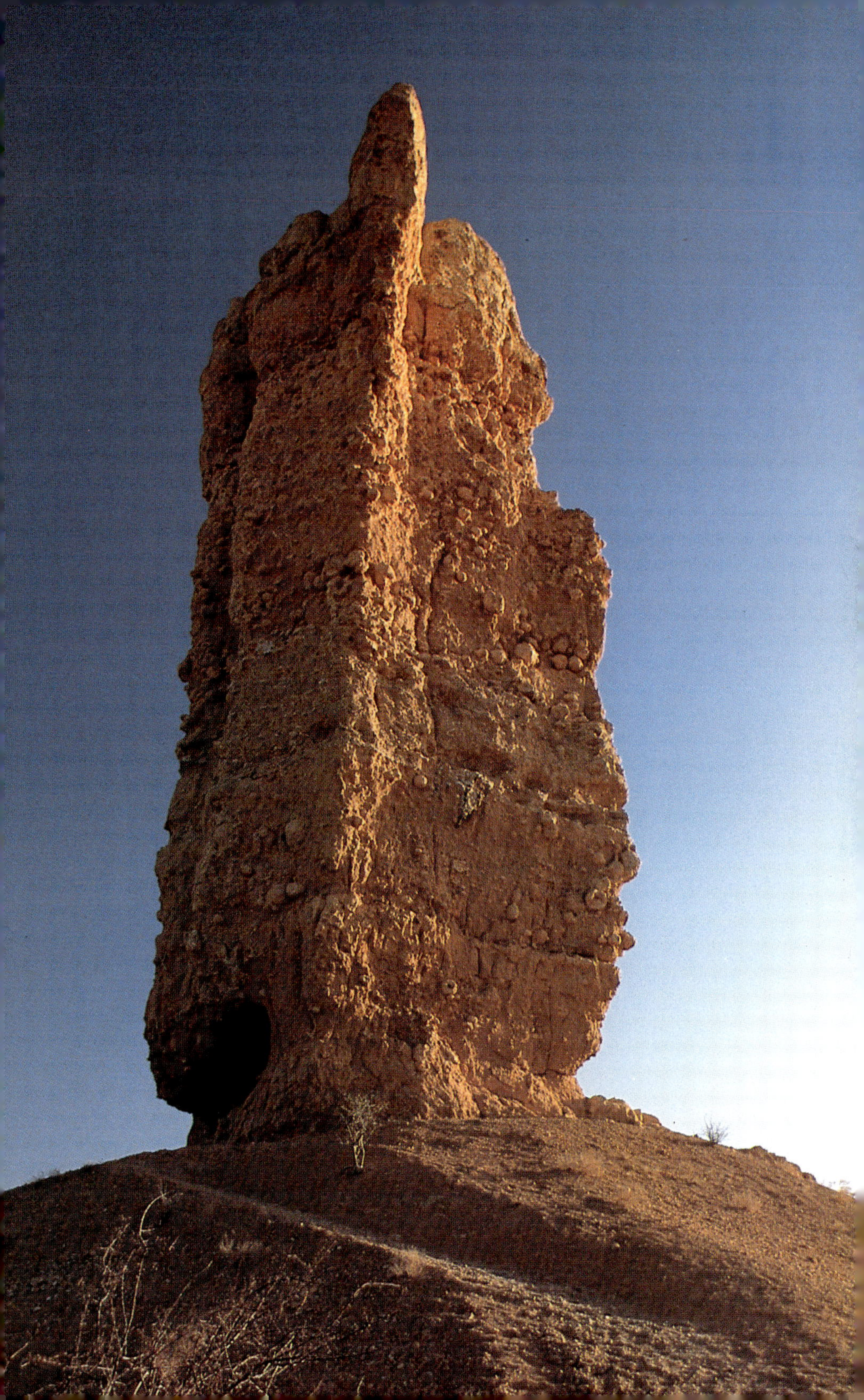

formed some fifteen million years ago, at the same time as the Sesriem and Kuiseb canyon.

During the Lower Tertiary Period, the Ugab River carved out a wide valley but, in drier times about thirty million years ago, the river filled the valley with silt. The Vingerklip is an eroded remnant of the silt deposits.

The first recorded ascent was by an American climber, Tom Choate, in 1970 and it was the earliest climb in Namibia using mechanical aids. The first free climb was made three years later, when a party led by Udo Kleynstuber ascended the **eastern face**.

Waterberg Plateau Park

The Waterberg Plateau Park, east of the B1 between Otjiwarongo and Otavi, was originally created as a sanctuary for the rare and endangered game species of the Caprivi Strip.

Rising above a surrounding sea of African bush and savannah, the Waterberg Plateau, with its flamboyant brick-red sandstone formations and lush green vegetation, presents an island of vibrant colour, in vivid contrast to the pastel dune seas of the Namib and the white expanses of the Etosha Pan. Within three hours drive of Windhoek, the park is a sought-after weekend retreat and convenient stopover for travellers.

The Waterberg complex lies in a south-west to north-easterly direction and may be divided into three sections: the Small Waterberg in the south; the Omuverume Plateau, which has the highest elevation and is saddled to the main plateau; and the Waterberg Plateau proper, which is roughly forty-eight kilometres (thirty miles) long and varies from eight to sixteen kilometres (five to ten miles) in breadth.

With the exception of its northern side, the plateau is surrounded by a wall of cliffs, which become steadily lower and more broken towards the north. The highest point on the main plateau is at the Okarakuvisa range, and it is there the column-like erosion of the Waterberg sandstone is at its most spectacular.

The vegetation of the Waterberg Plateau Park changes dramatically from an acacia savannah at the bottom of the plateau to a lush green sub-tropical dry woodland with tall trees and wide grassy plains at the top. Of the large variety of trees on the plateau, the silver terminalia is the most dominant, giving a silver-green glow to the landscape in the summer months. In the spring, the weeping-wattle, shaped like a jacaranda, bears heavy clusters of yellow flowers. Other common trees are the Kalahari apple-leaf, with its soft purple blossoms, the bush willow, silver bush willow, wild syringa, wild plum, flame acacia and coffee mimosa.

Common shrubs are the lavender-bush, cork-bush and the attractive coffee-bush, or white bauhinia, with its white orchid-like flowers. Below the cliffs where the fountains seep through, lush green Waterberg ferns flourish among wild fig trees. On top of the plateau, among grasses such as swartvoet, velvet, finger- and stick-grass, an occasional bright red flame lily may catch the eye.

The vegetation of the Waterberg area is similar to that of the Caprivi. Consequently, when the Odendaal Commission recommended that the West Caprivi Game Park be deproclaimed, the Director of the then Division of Nature Conservation and Tourism, Bernabé de la Bat, recommended that the area be set aside as a reserve for eland and as a refuge for the scarce and endangered species of the Caprivi. In 1970, the Namibia Administration started buying up farms at Waterberg and, in 1972, the park was proclaimed. In the same year, the Division embarked on an ambitious translocation programme to populate the new park with game.

From locations as far afield as Natal and Addo, a large variety of species including white rhino, eland, giraffe, buffalo, roan and sable antelope, tsessebe, blue wildebeest, red hartebeest, impala and duiker were translocated into the park. These animals all formerly occurred at the Waterberg. Other animals found at Waterberg are gemsbok, kudu, baboon, brown hyena, leopard and cheetah, and smaller animals such as wart hog, steenbok,

Above: Detail of Bushman engravings uncovered in the Waterberg Plateau Park.

klipspringer, dik-dik, rock hyrax, Cape hunting dog, black-backed jackal and caracal.

The abundance of trees and large quantities of natural food sources at the Waterberg support a particularly rich bird life of 200 species, some of which occur in only a few other locations in Namibia. Examples of these are Bradfield's hornbill, pallid flycatcher, Hartlaub's francolin and the alpine swift which breeds in the cliffs at Waterberg.

Of the ethnic groups, the yellow Bushmen were the first inhabitants of the Waterberg. All that remains of them today are their engravings of animal tracks on the rocks surrounding the large waterhole at Okarakuvisa. Towards the middle of nineteenth century, a group of Damara cohabitated with them and, at about this time, the first Hereros moved into the area. The explorers Andersson and Galton were the first Europeans to visit the Waterberg.

In 1873, a Rhenish mission station was established on the Waterberg Plateau but it was destroyed seven years later during the Khoikhoi and Herero war, only to be rebuilt in 1891. It was on the plateau that the deciding battle of the Herero uprising of 1904 took place. Communication between the five German forces, with a combined strength of ninety-six officers, 1,488 men, thirty cannons and twelve machine guns, was hampered by the dense vegetation. Their victory was largely due to the heliograph station above Otjozonjupa. The battle of Waterberg is commemorated every year, on the second Sunday in August, at the cemetery near the battle site, where more than seventy *Schutztruppe* lie buried.

When to go

The best time to visit is during the dry season between April and November.

Where to stay

Bernabé de la Bat Rest Camp consists of luxury chalets, small bungalows, a swimming-pool, shop, campsite, restaurant and bar complex with beer garden. The latter is situated in the restored 'Rasthaus', originally built as a police station in 1908 and subsequently used as a guest house for tourists until the 1960s. Waterberg Big

Above: National monument atop the Waterberg Plateau honours the seventy members of the *Schutztruppe* who fell in a 1904 battle against Herero freedom fighters and are buried there.

Game Hunting Lodge, Okonjima Guest Farm. See Listings.

Sightseeing

The **reserve** was established primarily to resettle and breed the rare and endangered species which have been introduced. You will also see **common duiker, wild dog, side-striped jackal, lesser bush baby** and **rock dassie.**

Experienced bird-watchers may count on spotting anything up to 115 species in a two-day period covering all habitat types — plateau top, scree slopes, cliffs and the *acacia* woodlands at the base of the plateau.

The only **breeding colony** of **Cape vultures** in Namibia is located on the **Okarukuvisa cliffs** to the **west** where you will see the birds gliding effortlessly over the surrounding plains in search of carrion.

In the late 1950s, the colony numbered about 500 but, as a result of indiscriminate poisoning by farmers, their numbers were down to fewer than twenty by 1980. In an attempt to save the birds from extinction, the Directorate of Nature Conservation launched a programme of controlled burning to transform bush grassland and parkland. In addition, carcasses of common species such as gemsbok and kudu are laid out regularly enabling the birds to supplement their diet.

Other vultures found in the park are the **white-backed vulture, lappetfaced vulture** and **white headed vulture.** The park harbours eight eagle species, including **black eagles** and **booted eagles**.

The park has many other bird species which are near endemic to Namibia, with seventy-five per cent or more of their world population occurring in this country. These include **Rüppell's parrot, Monteiro's hornbill** and **rock runner**.

The geology of the Waterberg is of particular interest. The plateau is an erosion relic that consists of sedimentary rock from the Karoo System. The rock can be divided into two sections; a lower, the **Omingonde Formation**, which consists of approximately 350 metres (1,148 feet) of reddish-brown mud-, silt-, sand- and gritstone and conglomerate, and an upper, the **Etjo Formation**, of brown sandstone which

148

forms the **perpendicular cliffs** of seventy to seventy-five metres high (200-246 feet) directly under the crest.

The lower rock formations are probably fluvial, deposited by rivers in a shallow lake, whereas the upper formations have an aeolian origin, in that sand that was blown over the lake by wind gradually settled in the water. The plateau has its elevated position as the result of the resistance of the Etjo sandstone to weathering, and to pressure tension in the earth's crust which, millions of years ago, lifted the Karoo layers south of Omaruru and Grootfontein.

It was partly due to this tension that, over the centuries, pillar-like seams developed in the Etjo sandstone. Rainwater which falls on top of the plateau flows into the seams and seeps down until it is stopped by the impermeable mud-and-siltstone of the **Omingonde Formation**, to flow down the mountain slope from numerous fountains.

The sandy nature of the plateau, the rocky scene surrounding it and its vegetation form an effective sponge. The top of the plateau is dry for most of the year. For game to survive, water is pumped up from **boreholes** at **Onjoka**, where the nature conservators are based, to **watering points** and **dams** on the plateau.

Fossils of mammal-like reptiles which occur in the Omingonde Formation, and tracks of **two-** and **four-footed dinosaurs** which occur in the Etjo sandstone, indicate that the rock formations were deposited during the upper Triassic period and vary in age from 200 million to 180 million years. According to their tracks these dinosaurs were mainly herbivores.

The Waterberg Plateau Park has a variety of hiking possibilities, for the experienced hiker as well as the casual walker. In the wilderness section on top of the plateau there are two **small camps**, **Antephora** and **Huilboom,** for use by hiking parties. Such a group leaves from Onjoka situated **north-east** from the main camp, and is accompanied by a ranger.

From the main rest camp, there is a one- to three-day unaccompanied hiking **trail** up onto the plateau, where there is an **overnight hut**. A number of **walking trails** have been laid out in and around the camp, the principle being that once visitors have arrived they move around on foot and refrain from using their vehicles. One of these trails leads up to a **lookout point** on the **escarpment**.

Because of the roughness of the terrain and absence of proper roads, only specially equipped 4WD vehicles supplied by the Ministry of Wildlife, Conservation and Tourism are used for game viewing on top of the plateau. For the smaller and more adventurous groups there are open vehicles, and for larger groups enclosed buses. Much care has been taken to ensure effective game viewing by the provision of lookout points and submerged **hides**.

To Grootfontein

Continuing north-east along the B1, the main road reaches the fascinating town of **Otavi**. Just **north** of the town an unobtrusive **monument** marks the spot where Germany surrendered to the Commander of the Union Forces, General Louis Botha, on 9 July 1915. The Governor of South West Africa, Dr Seitz, and the Commander of the German forces in South West Africa, Colonel Victor Franke, were the German signatories.

Although often referred to as the Khorab Treaty, it was signed at Otavi probably because most of the German forces surrendered at Khorab, some thirty kilometres (nineteen miles) north. The 1920 monument was erected at the request of the Governor-General of the Union of South Africa, Lord Buxton.

From Otavi, the main road to Grootfontein crosses a valley between the Otavi Mountains and the Kupferberg, passing Gross Otabi where Damara miners are known to have smelted copper during the 1800s, possibly even earlier.

Kombat, formerly known as Asis, is forty kilometres (twenty-five miles) east of Otavi. Copper, lead and silver are produced at the Kombat Mine, which was operated between 1911 and 1925 by a German company and re-opened in 1960 by the Tsumeb Corporation.

Giant meteor

Further **east** is the **turnoff** to the 50-tonne **Hoba Meteorite**, the largest in the world. It was discovered in 1920 by Jacobus Brits who was hunting in the area when he spotted an unusual rock. Surrounded by limestone, only the upper portion of the cubed meteor was visible.

He chiselled off a piece and the South West Africa Company at Grootfontein confirmed that it was a meteorite which struck the earth some 80,000 years ago. The ore consists of 82.4 per cent iron, 16.4 per cent nickel and 0.76 per cent cobalt. Other trace elements include carbon, zinc, copper, sulphur, chromium, iridium, germanium, and gallium.

It has been suggested that it broke into several fragments when it hit the atmosphere and that other fragments could well be in the vicinity, waiting to be discovered.

In 1921, Mr T Tonnesen, general manager of the South West Africa Company, sent a photograph and a letter to the head office in London saying he intended to mine the meteorite's nickel. Fortunately he never did. Yet, despite being declared a **national monument** in March 1955, it has suffered badly at the hands of vandals and trophy hunters. In 1985, Rössing Uranium joined the National Monuments Council in a scheme to protect the meteorite. The surrounding **trees** and **shrubs** were numbered and listed in the **information hut** and the smart new complex was officially opened in July 1987.

Where to stay

Meteor Hotel (2-star), Nord Hotel (1-star). See Listings for "Hotels".

Sightseeing

Many of Grootfontein's **stone** and **limestone buildings** date back to the German period and tall, shady **trees** give the town its distinctive character.

During September and October, when the blue-purple jacarandas and the red flamboyants create a blaze of colour, the town is especially attractive. Grootfontein takes its name from a **fountain** on the **northern perimeter** of the town, surrounded by a charming **tree park**, planted by the South West Africa Company.

In the mid-1880s, a group of Dorsland Trekkers established the capital of the Republic of Upingtonia there after buying land from an Owambo chief. The short-lived republic lasted only two years and was then abandoned. In 1893, the South West Africa Company established its head office at Grootfontein and won a concession to prospect for minerals. The population increased in 1896 when a number of Afrikaner families from the Transvaal settled there to farm.

Soon after, the German troops built a **fort** and administrative **post**. At the time, Grootfontein was part of the Outjo district. It became a town in 1907. In 1908, a ninety-one-kilometre (fifty-seven mile) narrow-gauge **railway line** to Otavi was built. In 1915, the fort was occupied by a military magistrate and in 1922 a limestone extension was added after which the building was used as a boarding school until the late 1960s. Subsequently it fell into disuse and was threatened by demolition but, after a 1974 public appeal, the **fort**, between **Upingtonia** and **Eriksson Streets**, was restored. Today it serves as a **museum**. Exhibits concentrate on the early history of the area, featuring the Republic of Upingtonia, the Dorsland Trek and the German colonial period.

The **graves** of several soldiers in the **cemetery**, past the **turnoff** to the **showground** on the **Grootfontein-Rundu** road, also serve as reminders of the colonial period.

To Tsumeb

North-east of Otjiwarongo the B1 runs 181 kilometres (112 miles) to Tsumeb. The last town before Etosha National Park, Tsumeb's history is closely linked to the minerals and metals mined there. Iron Age smelting sites at Gross Otavi, Otjikoto and Tsumeb provide evidence of the exploitation of the copper resources over thousands of years. During the second half

Above: Iron-clad roof of elegant 1914 Roman Catholic church of St. Barbara, patron saint of miners, dominates Tsumeb's main street.

Right: Palm trees provide welcome shade in Tsumeb's verdant municipal gardens.

Overleaf: Old steam engine stands in sun outside Tsumeb Museum.

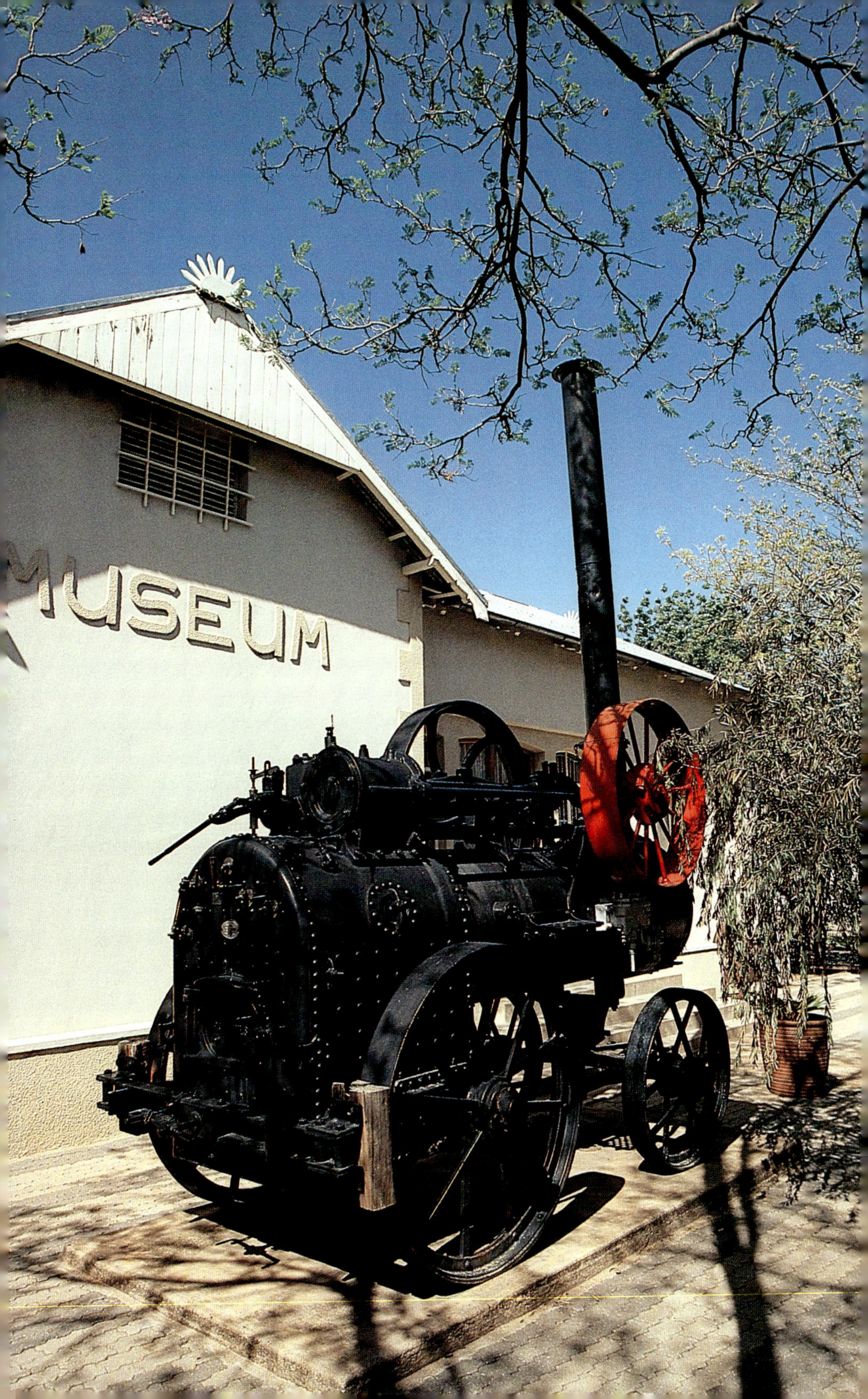
MUSEUM

of the last century the ownership of these areas was in dispute. While various tribes laid claim to the mineral-rich resources, several white traders were given concessions. Among these was an 1892 concession granted to the South West Africa Company. OMEG was founded in April 1900 to obtain more capital for the exploitation of the ore deposits and, in August that year, the chief engineer, Christopher James and thirty-three miners arrived in Tsumeb. They built a road to the existing shafts, sank two new pits and, by 28 December 1900, nine tonnes of copper ore left by ox-wagon for Swakopmund.

In May 1903, OMEG signed an agreement with the South West Africa Company for a railway from Fort Alexander in Angola to Otavi and the Witwatersrand goldfields. The plan, however, was thwarted by the Anglo-Boer War.

Work on a railway line between Swakopmund and Tsumeb began in November 1903 and was completed in August 1906. Later, mining operations were nearly brought to a standstill by World War I. The 1930s depression caused the mine to close for a time, then it reopened only to close once again during World War II. Today it is a major producer of copper, lead, silver, cadmium, and arsenic trioxide.

Getting there

Tsumeb is 308 kilometres (192 miles) from Rundu, 426 kilometres (265 miles) from Windhoek, 552 kilometres (343 miles) from Swakopmund, and 907 kilometres (564 miles) from Keetmanshoop. There are road, rail and air services to the town.

Where to stay

Hotel Eckleben (2-star), Minen Hotel (1-star), Mokuti Lodge (3-star). See Listings for "Hotels". Guest farms: La Rochelle. See Listings.

Sightseeing

The **museum**, which reflects the town's early mining days, is housed in a 1915 **school building** on **Main Street**. The school was built three years after missionary Ferdinand Lang began teaching in a skittle alley behind the **hotel**. Within weeks of completion the school was turned into a German military hospital. It reverted to a school between 1920 and 1950.

German World War I armaments recovered from **Otjikoto Lake** are on display in the **Khorab Room** as well as an interesting collection of **rocks** and **minerals**.

The **OMEG Minenburo** on Main Street is one of the most attractive buildings in Tsumeb, easily mistaken for a church. Built in 1907 by Joseph Olbrich, its **tower** symbolises the importance and economic power of the OMEG company.

The **second director's residence**, on the corner of **3rd Street** and **8th Road**, dates back to 1912 and is characterised by the **turrets** used for ventilation.

Around the corner, **St Barbara Roman Catholic Church** — consecrated in 1914 — is named after the patron saint of mine workers. For thirteen years it was the only church in Tsumeb. The unusual **tower** above the main entrance is particularly eye-catching.

Lake Otjikoto

Some twenty-four kilometres (fifteen miles) **north-west** of Tsumeb lies another natural wonder of Namibia — **Otjikoto Lake**, a vernacular name which translates as the 'place too deep for cattle to drink'. The first known whites to cast their eyes on the lake were the explorers Charles Andersson and Sir Francis Galton who camped on its banks in May 1851.

Andersson recorded: "Otjikoto, one of the most wonderful of Nature's freaks, is situated at the northern extremity of those broken hills which take their rise in the neighbourhood of Okamabuti, and in the midst of a dense coppice. So effectually is it hidden from view, that a person might pass within fifty paces of it without being aware of its existence. Owing to its steep and rugged sides, cattle have no access to the water; and even a man can only approach this enormous well by means of a steep and slippery footpath."

Situated in an area of porous limestone, it was an underground cavern until the roof collapsed to create a fifty-five-metre-deep

Above: Acacia and succulents line the banks of Lake Otjikoto near Tsumeb.

(180-foot) lake. It has given birth to its own unique endemic species of fish.

The Karstveld is pitted with depressions and sinkholes which extend from the towns of Tsumeb, Otavi and Grootfontein westward through the Etosha Park, then northward to Owambo. Dolomite rocks are a characteristic feature and when these rocks are fractured through earth movements, allowing water to enter and create cavities in the rock, caves form. Gradually, these grow into underground caverns that usually contain water. In some cases, the roof of the cavern collapses to form open sinkholes like Otjikoto and Guinas.

Lake Otjikoto lies along the **main road from Tsumeb** to **Etosha** and **Owambo** and consequently is visited by many people. Now, great numbers of fish are visible from the shore, practically all of them different from those collected there years ago.

One species present today is known as the **Otjikoto tilapia**, but in fact the species is none other than *Tilapia guinasana* whose natural home is **Lake Guinas**. Another species is the well-known **Mozambique tilapia**, *Oreochromis mossambicus* and there is also the **southern mouthbrooder**, an original inhabitant of Lake Otjikoto. Tilapia were introduced to this lake some time ago by an unknown person.

In 1915, the retreating Germans dumped most of their weapons and ammunition into the lake to prevent them from falling into South African hands. In 1916, a diving team recovered five cannons, ten cannon chassis, three machine guns, and other arms and ammunition.

Fifty-four years later, in a joint salvage operation by the South African Army, the Tsumeb Corporation and the Windhoek State Museum, three divers from Windhoek came across the **wheels** of what was taken to be a cannon and a Krupps **ammunition wagon** was recovered in almost perfect condition. It can be seen at Windhoek's Alte Feste Museum. (See "The Capital and the Towns", Part Three).

Nearby, **Lake Guinas** has a different appearance from Otjikoto, in that it is deeper and the water dark and inky compared with Otjikoto's bright turquoise blue. No alien fish have been introduced into Lake Guinas. There the remarkable colour range of *Tilapia guinasana* is truly revealed. The colour and colour pattern of virtually every individual is different, ranging from entirely black to almost white.

Many individual fish have spectacular arrays of blue, black, yellow, white, green and red. It may be that this species was present before the lake became a sinkhole, and genetic control was upset. In the absence of competition or predation, there was little need for a distinctive coloration for mate recognition, general communi‐ cation or for camouflage.

The home of the **cave catfish** *Clarias cavernicola*, the only true cave fish known in southern Africa, is a fascinating cave on the **Aigamas Farm**, **north-west** of Otavi. The cave is like a deep gash in the side of a hill. The **lake** at the bottom of the cave has been a source of fresh water for ages, and the steeply-sloping cave floor is worn smooth.

Early this century, a large **steam pump** was installed to irrigate the **citrus orchard** on the farm. Some **pipes** were either discarded or fell accidentally into the lake and are still on the lake bed.

During the Herero War, the cave was used as a shelter by German patrols.

The Land of the Bushmen

The north-west extremity of the Kalahari, the greatest unbroken expanse of sand in the world, thrusts eastward from Tsumeb, beginning at the banks of the Omatako River.

Now part of the massive new region of Otjosondjupa, the ancestral homelands of the San Bushmen lie in these arid expanses which extend across Namibia, north of Gobabis and Rietfontein, into Botswana. (See "The People: A Kaleidoscope of Colourful Cultures", Part One).

Fable says that, lost somewhere among the sands of the Kalahari are the ruins of a great city. One who claimed to have found them was a nineteenth-century conman, William Leonard Hunt, who later wrote *Through the Kalahari Desert*.

"We camped . . . beside a long line of stone which looked like the Chinese Wall after an earthquake, and which, on examination, proved to be the ruins of quite an extensive structure, in some places buried beneath the sand, but in others fully exposed to view. We traced the remains for nearly a mile, mostly a heap of huge stones, but all flat-sided, and here and there with the cement perfect and plainly visible between the layers. . . . The general outline of this wall was in the form of an arc, inside which lay at intervals of about forty feet apart a series of heaps of masonry in the shape of an oval or obtuse ellipse, about a foot and a half deep, and with a flat bottom, but hollowed out at the sides for about a foot from the edge. Some of these heaps were cut out of solid rock, others were formed of more than one piece of stone, fitted together very accurately. . . . On digging down nearby in the middle of the arc, we came upon a pavement about twenty feet wide, made of large stones. . . . This pavement was intersected by another similar one at right angles, forming a Maltese cross, in the centre of which at some time must have stood an altar, column, or some sort of monument, for the base was quite distinct, composed of loose pieces of fluted masonry."

Although it was impossible to have made the journey in the short time given, the account and illustrations inspired many to search for this desert Atlantis. As did the poetry:

A half-buried ruin — a huge wreck of stones
On a lone and desolate spot;
A temple — or a tomb for human bones
Left by man to decay and rot.
Rude sculptured blocks from the red sand project,
And shapeless uncouth stones appear,
Some great man's ashes designed to protect,
Buried many a thousand year.
A relic, may be, of the glorious past,
A city once grand and sublime,
Destroyed by earthquake, defaced by the blast,
Swept away by the hand of time.

Taunted throughout summer by the dark clouds which march across the sky, always promising, rarely delivering, the Kalahari, cut by seasonal rivers, receives little more than 150 millimetres (six inches) of rain a year.

Sightseeing

Some fifty-five kilometres (thirty-four miles) **north-east** of **Grootfontein** the main **B8** road touches the **junction** with the minor C44 road which leads 220 kilometres (137 miles) east to **Tsumkwe**. From the junction it cuts through semi-arid country dotted with large-scale cattle **ranches** and the small settlement of **Maroelaboom** with its **police station**.

Forty-five kilometres (twenty-eight miles) beyond this hamlet, the **border** between Bushmanland and cattle country is marked by the first traces of the **Kalahari Desert** which soon becomes deep sand.

All that inhabits these badlands, apart from the nomadic San, is an occasional **giraffe** and a few **antelope** and **gazelle**. Deeper into the Kalahari, the desert is characterised by **seasonal pans** and occasional **baobab trees**.

Tsumkwe lies at the very heart of Namibia's old Bushmanland, 143 kilometres (eighty-nine miles) from the border with the ranchlands.

Getting there

Tsumkwe, the former capital of what used to be Bushmanland, is 275 kilometres (171 miles) from Grootfontein, 413 kilometres (257 miles) from Rundu, 727 kilometres (452 miles) from Windhoek, 853 kilometres (530 miles) from Swakopmund, 1,209 kilometres (751 miles) from Keetmanshoop, 2,220 kilometres (1,380 miles) from Cape Town, 2,698 kilometres (1,676 miles) from Johannesburg and is served by road and charter flights in light aircraft.

When to go

The area is open all year-round.

Where to stay

There is no tourist accommodation and no facilities for tourists. Visitors need to carry camping equipment and plentiful supplies of food, water and fuel.

Choose campsites carefully and clear up and carry away all waste. Remember, too, that only 4WD vehicles can negotiate this region which has few recognised roads or trails.

Sightseeing

Tsumkwe has a number of administration **offices, police post, filling station, clinic** and **shop**.

From Tsumkwe, a **dirt road** leads **north** to one of Namibia's newest game reserves, **Kaudom**, which lies in a remote and arid area of the Kalahari Desert along the **Botswana border**.

There is a **campsite** near a small San village, **Tjokwe** — unusual because campers can sleep inside the **hollow trunk** of a 700-year-old **baobab tree**. An even bigger **baobab** — thirty-five metres (115 feet) in circumference — stands by the trail some way **north-east** on the way to Kaudom.

Kaudom Game Reserve

Little-visited Kaudom, Namibia's remotest wildlife sanctuary, covers 3,840 square kilometres (1,483 square miles) of sere, semi-desert plain dotted with dry fossil river-beds — *omurambas* — along which roam wild dog, tsessebe, kudu, wildebeest, endangered roan antelope and elephant.

During the testing months of the dry season the elephant tap down into the underground streams that filter west from the Okavango Delta system in Botswana. Their presence under the parched surface is marked by the occasional waterhole which they feed.

Well away from the established tourist trails, facilities in this game reserve, which opened in the middle of the 1980s, are sparse and basic.

But although Kaudom's herds are smaller than those in Etosha, this remote and timeless sanctuary remains as pristine as the day mankind was born in the Great Rift Valley of Eastern Africa.

No fences bar the ageless game trails and Kaudom's animals are free to roam wherever instinct leads, from one season to the next, in search of pastures new. The reserve is enriched by varied and interesting birdlife.

Getting there

Follow the B8 north of Grootfontein for fifty-seven kilometres (thirty-five miles) to the east turnoff on the gravel C74 (C44) and follow this for 222 kilometres (138 miles) to Tsumkwe. Then turn north and follow the signposts to the reserve. It is fifty kilometres (thirty-one miles) from Tsumkwe to Sikeretti.

When to go

Kaudom is open throughout the year from sun-up to sundown.

Where to stay

There are a few campsites and basic wooden-hut accommodation at Sikeretti (Sigaretti) in the south and at Kaudom in the north, for which it is essential that bookings are made in advance. Water is available but nothing else, so the traveller intending to stay overnight should be fully self-sufficient. For those who have not made bookings there is accommodation at Popa Falls in the Caprivi Strip. See Listings.

Sightseeing

From the **Sigaretti** campsite a **track** follows the dry **course** of the **Nhoma Omuramba**, reaching a turnoff to **Elandsvlakte** after twenty-four kilometres (fifteen miles). There you can either follow the route via **Elandsvlakte** and the **Tsau waterhole** to **Kaudom Camp** or continue to **Tari Kora**.

From there, a **track** heads **north**, reaching the **Leeupan waterhole** from where you can continue to **Tsau** or **north** to **Kaudom Omuramba**.

Wild **seringa**, **Zambezi** and **wild teak** and **manketti trees** grow on the plains, as well as **copalwood**, or large false mopane, sometimes referred to as 'bastard' mopane. Extensive **reed beds** and **grasslands** flourish in the **Nhoma** and **Kaudom Omuramba** system, while *Acacia* belts grow along the margins of the **sand dune valleys**.

Good summer rains result in tall grasses, making game spotting difficult, but at other times visitors see **lion**, **wild dog**, **leopard**,

Above: Leopard up a tree in Kaudom Game Reserve.

spotted hyena, and **black-backed** and **side-striped jackal**.

Game numbers vary considerably. However, **kudu**, **roan** and **gemsbok** live there in abundance as well as **blue wildebeest**, **tsessebe**, **eland**, **red hartebeest**, and **reedbuck**.

Your chances of spotting **elephant** are good. Indeed, you can sometimes come very close to these animals when they browse around the park's two unfenced **campsites**.

Skeleton Coast: Bleached Bones and Rusting Ships

Twelve headless skeletons lying on a beach, the bones of a child in an abandoned hut, and a weather-beaten slate buried in the sand in 1860 with the message, "I am proceeding to a river sixty miles north, and should anyone find this and follow me, God will help him", are evocative examples of the many hapless people who came to their end on what must be the loneliest stretch of coastline in the world. The slate was not found until 1943.

Once feared and shunned by seafarers because of its treacherous coastline flanked by bone-bleaching desert wastes, the Skeleton Coast is now prized as a place of beauty, tranquillity, and magnificent solitude.

Situated in the far north-west of Namibia, this part of the Namib Desert is one of Africa's most intriguing and pristine wilderness areas. Essentially, its attraction lies in the colour, changing moods and untouched profile of its landscape, the diversity of its desert-adapted flora and fauna and the variety of its geological features.

No wider than fifty kilometres (thirty-one miles) at any point, the Skeleton Coast extends 600 kilometres (373 miles) from the Kunene River to Cape Cross, with the western sections of Kunene and Erongo — formerly Kaokoland and Damaraland — forming its hinterland. In former years, before the countless skeletons of ships and men along its shores gave rise to the evocative name Skeleton Coast, the area was known as the Kaokoveld coast.

Where the icy Atlantic waves tear at Namibia's jagged coastline, a great cross, chiselled from black rock, looks out to the storm-tossed horizon. The crucifix is a replica of the one placed there more than 500 years ago by the Portuguese navigator-explorer, Diego Cão. He was ordered by King John II of Portugal to round the southern cape of Africa and discover a sea route to the spice centres of the East. Thus, six years before Columbus stepped ashore in the New World, Diego Cão sailed from Lisbon.

A knight of the Portuguese Court and a great seaman, Cão was given two stone crosses, *padrãos*, hewn from Lisbon's finest rock, to raise up on new-found shores — in the name of Portugal, King John II, and Christianity — and told not to return until his mission was accomplished. (See "Land of Lost Horizons", Part One).

It is easy to imagine the horrific conditions at sea in the fifteenth century when whole crews perished from scurvy, plague, or lack of fresh water, and although Cão's small fleet braved the stormy waters of the South Atlantic for well on two years, his expedition ended in failure.

But, fearful of the monarch's wrath, the explorer contrived to pitch one cross at the mouth of the Congo River, while the other was raised on the coastline at *Cabo do Lobo*, now *Cabo do Santa Maria* in Angola.

There, out of food and drinking water, the barren shores seeming to stretch forever southwards, Diego Cão turned round and headed home to face the anger of King John II. Failure, however, was not in the royal lexicon and Cão was handed another pair of crosses, given two new ships and sent on his way again.

The navigator embarked on this second voyage with heavy heart as he once more charted his way southwards through the storm-tossed Atlantic, eventually arriving at the barren stretch of forbidding land whose endless, hostile shores seemed ever-increasing in their emptiness and solitude.

History records that by this time Cão was a broken man. Choosing a rocky cape that jutted out into the dark seascape, he anchored there briefly in January 1486, to step ashore and set up one of the crosses before returning, despondent and humiliated, to die aboard ship on the voyage home to Portugal.

The Portuguese inscription on the cross

Skeleton Coast Park & Kaokoland

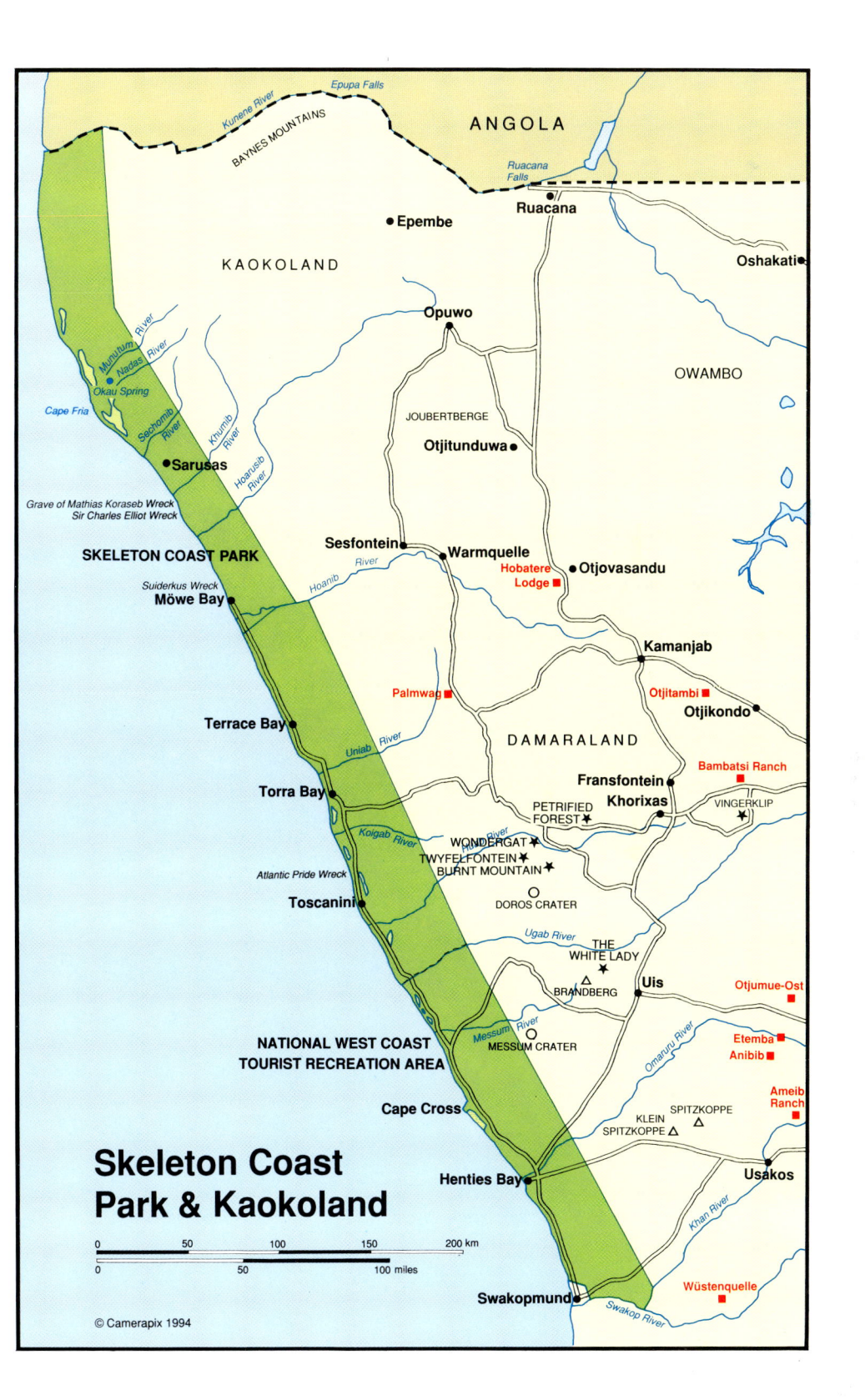

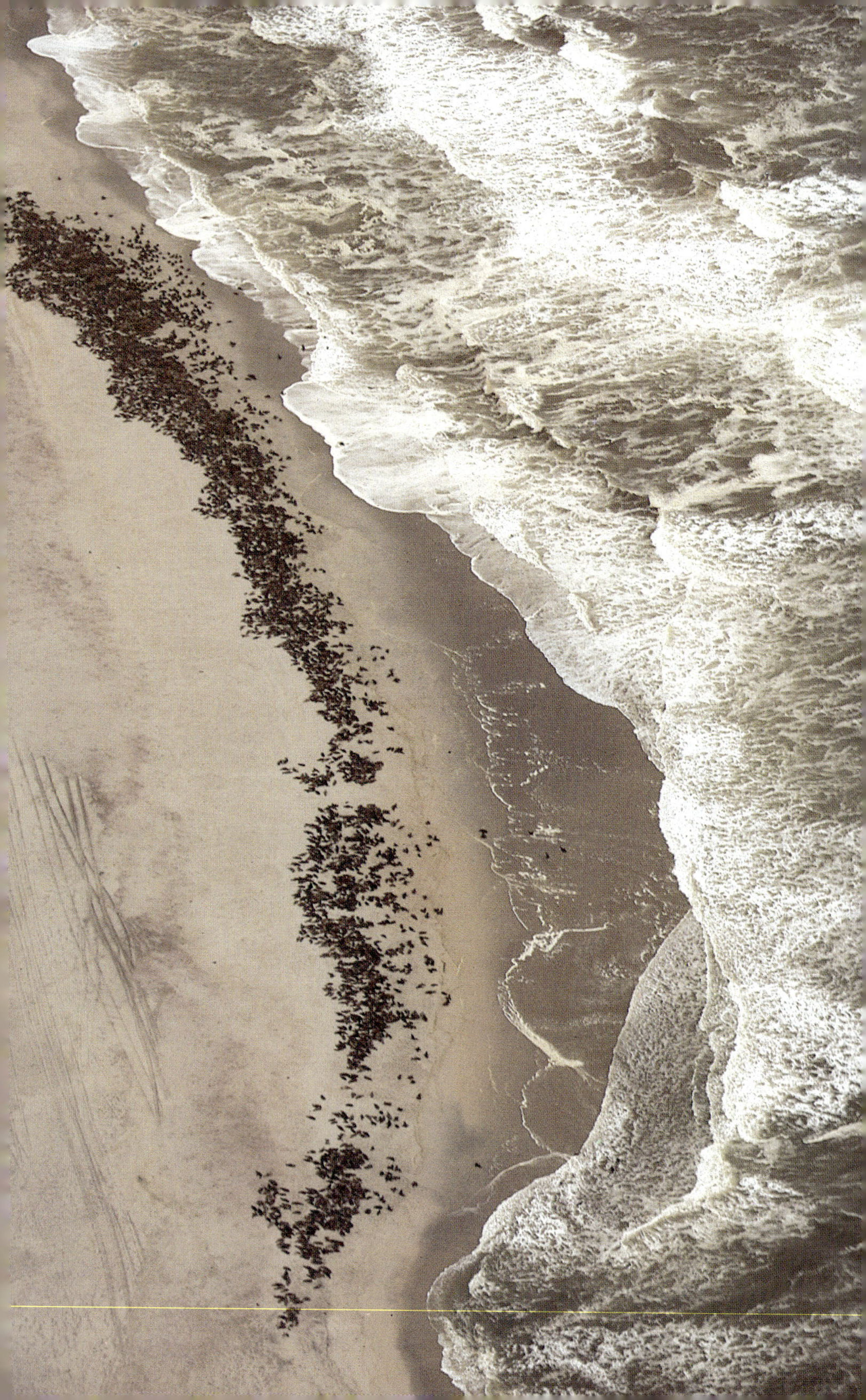

reads: "In the year 6685 of the creation of the earth and 1485 after the birth of Christ the most excellent and most serene King Dom João II of Portugal ordered this land to be discovered and this *padrão* to be placed by Diego Cão, gentleman of his house".

The cross stood atop the barren cape to which it gave its name, all the world unheeding of its existence, for almost 400 years, until the middle of the last century.

It was then seen by Captain W Messum, who was combing the seaboard for guano deposits. These led to an influx of European sailing ships along Namibia's coast, hauling away tons of the fertiliser, in a 'guano rush' akin to the gold rush of Johannesburg.

The captain went ashore at Cape Cross and explored inland towards the Brandberg massif. Subsequently, the circle of mountains west of the Brandberg was named the Messum Crater.

Thirty years later, in 1879, W B Warren, captain of the cruiser *Swallow*, was searching for a place to land when he saw Cão's cross. The skipper had a German concession to work the guano deposits and hunt seals along the coast between the Ugab and Omaruru rivers.

In 1895, sixteen years after he first landed, he laid a small railway near Cape Cross which presented its builders with an extraordinary challenge. It fell into disrepair in 1906 but its remains on the salt-pans of Cape Cross are still visible.

After facing centuries of cruel winds, Cão's stone cross developed a severe list and was in danger of collapse. Early in 1893 the captain of the German cruiser *Falke*, however, recognised its historical importance and took it away, leaving a wooden replica in its place.

Two years later the wooden cross was replaced by a granite replica bearing the original Portuguese inscription, plus another in German, under the Kaiser's eagle, which read: "Erected by order of the German Kaiser and King of Prussia Wilhelm II in 1894 at the place of the original which has been weathered through years". Ironically, the *Falke* carried the cross to Cape Town, the destination that Diego Cão had striven to reach but failed. From there, it was taken to a Berlin museum.

During 1894 and 1900 a German geologist in the employ of the South West Africa Company, Dr George Hartmann, undertook several surveys of the Skeleton Coast, the most extensive of which was in 1896.

The objective was to map the Kaokoveld coast between Cape Cross and the Kunene River to find possible locations for a harbour — and to discover guano deposits.

In the early 1950s, the well-known author and traveller, Lawrence G Green, visited the Kaokoveld and the Skeleton Coast with what was later to become known as the Carp expedition. Although the convoy did not travel along the coast as planned, after making its way down the Khumib River from Orupembe, it did reach Rocky Point. Green gives an account of his experiences in *Lords of the Last Frontier*.

In 1954 the feasibility of a harbour on the coast, with a view to developing Namibia's fishing industry, was once again considered. Thus, for the first time, all the coast from Swakopmund to the Kunene River was explored in motor vehicles in a trip lasting twelve days. This epic journey subsequently became known as the Van Zyl expedition.

The creation of the Skeleton Coast Park dates back to 1963, when, for political reasons, the narrow coastline, approximately thirty to forty kilometres wide (nineteen to twenty-five miles) and 500 kilometres long (371 miles), between the Ugab and the Kunene Rivers, was set aside as a future nature reserve. Formally proclaimed in 1971, the park has since been managed by the Directorate of Nature Conservation as a wilderness reserve — where development is kept to a minimum and the public has limited access.

There is ample evidence of the many ships wrecked on this lonely stretch of coastline. The sand and wind-blasted remains of tugs, liners, galleons, clippers, gunboats and trawlers, and their pitiful flotsam and jetsam, lie strewn untidily for

---

Opposite: Cape seals basking along the shores of the Skeleton Coast.

Above: Seal colony at Cape Cross in the National West Coast Tourist Recreation Area.

endless miles of desolate beach along with the bones of those cast ashore to die.

But the skeletons are not only those of men. Bleached bones of countless whales, exploited by the whaling fleets, lie scattered among the wreckage on the beaches, while the skeletons of myriad trees washed down from the interior by the floods of many past seasons form tangled heaps at abandoned river mouths.

The main cause of the Skeleton Coast's justifiable reputation as a marine graveyard is the fast-flowing Benguela Current with its deadly cross-currents, heavy swell and dense sea fogs. In an instant, these become all-enveloping, reducing visibility to virtually nil. They combine with gale-force winds that build mountainous waves, treacherous reefs of coastal rocks, and unexpected shoals and sandbanks that reach into the sea to make the coast a navigator's nightmare.

Castaways

The one hope of survival for castaways — apart, perhaps, from the slim chance of being found and rescued — was to find one of the few 'linear oases' formed by the seasonal rivers running westward through the immense dune sea to the Atlantic. These rare ribbons of life play host to a surprising number of plants and animals. Rising in the highlands of the Kaokoveld plateau, they flow as subterranean streams, below the surface of ancient river-beds.

Periodically, these hidden life-sustaining rivers emerge onto the bone-dry surface and flow briefly above ground — perhaps bypassing impassable rock formations below the surface — only to disappear as suddenly into the thirsty sand.

Such stretches are scarce, but they are vital to local inhabitants and wildlife. For the Himba, a secluded tribe of the Namib, they are life-sustaining, enabling groups to remain in any area without visible water. They also support the populations of desert elephant and rhino while during the dry season giraffe, zebra, gemsbok, springbok, lion and cheetah travel many kilometres to these oases.

The dry river-beds are also major desert thoroughfares along which animals, people and even rescue parties travel through the

Above: Seal cow gives shade to newly born calf at Cape Cross.

desert. Such a party went to the aid of castaways from the Skeleton Coast's best-known wreck, that of the *Dunedin Star*, a British cargo liner of 13,000 tonnes, which has all but been pounded into atoms. The vessel ran aground late on the night of 29 November 1942, some kilometres off the shore about forty kilometres (twenty-five miles) south of the Kunene mouth. On board were twenty-one passengers, a crew of eighty-five, mail, war stores consisting mainly of explosives and a mixed consignment of military equipment.

On the morning of 30 November the captain decided to abandon ship. He had only one motor-boat, rendered useless after three trips, during which all the passengers and forty-two crew were taken ashore. The remaining crew were taken off by volunteers of the *Téméraire*, transferred safely aboard the *Manchester Division*, and taken to Walvis Bay.

Tragic force

The story of the rescue of the castaways reads as a long and frustrating series of endless disasters, involving a large number of vehicles, vessels and aircraft and the tragic loss of two lives. The last of the castaways arrived at Windhoek on Christmas Eve, a long and gruelling twenty-six days after the *Dunedin Star* ran aground.

Although subsequently the Skeleton Coast has become more accessible as a result of modern technology, the elements still gain the upper hand from time to time. In December 1976, the *Suiderkus,* equipped with the most up-to-date navigational equipment, ran onto the rocks at Möwe Bay on her maiden voyage. Even today, however well-equipped and technically advanced, the danger of a 4WD vehicle becoming bogged down, whether on beach, river-bed or salt-pan, is ever present.

This is one reason why the Skeleton Coast Park is managed as a wilderness area. The other is that overexposure of such a fragile ecological system to tourism will inevitably be detrimental. Tourism in an arid region is self-limiting, for large numbers of visitors endanger its easily disrupted ecosystem. The defacement that goes hand in hand with the building of an

Above: Seal enjoys the sun at Cape Cross.

— is no different than a thousand, ten thousand or even a million years ago. This sense of timelessness pervades as perspectives take on new dimensions and horizons expand into infinity.

Beyond the river valleys, the panoramas transform into a conglomeration of colours and forms that assail the eye — gravel plains stretching to the horizon, challenged only by towering sand-dunes while, farther inland, razor-sharp peaks and hills jut through the silky sand to form strange, unearthly landscapes. The gravel plains are covered by ancient lichens and specially adapted bushes — some species even forming their own mini-dunes as an aid to survival — and everywhere you search you find small tenebrionid beetles.

North of the Hoarusib River, sandwiched between the dune-fields and the wide sandy beaches, pools of reed-fringed water defy one of the oldest deserts in the world. These are well worth seeking out.

The Skeleton Coast is flanked in the west by the Atlantic Ocean and in the east by the rugged, semi-desert regions of Kunene and Erongo — formerly Kaokoland and Damaraland — and divided into three separate regions: the National West Coast Recreational Area, the Skeleton Coast and the Wilderness area.

Getting there

Swakopmund is 2,327 kilometres (1,446 miles) from Johannesburg, 1,849 kilometres (1,149 miles) from Cape Town, 1,144 kilometres (711 miles) from Noordoewer, 840 kilometres (522 miles) from Keetmanshoop, 826 kilometres (513 miles) from Rundu and 356 kilometres (221 miles) from Windhoek.

An excellent tarmac road, the C34 runs along the coast from Swakopmund to Möwe Bay. Charter flights operate to specified resorts and landing strips. These two resorts are reached along the main coastal road from Swakopmund, passing through the Ugab Mouth gate, or from the interior, via the Springbokwasser gate. Visitors to the park need either a day permit or proof of reservations at one of the resorts.

infrastructure would soon destroy the very thing that tourists set out to enjoy.

In the south of the park, tourism is restricted to two angling resorts — Torra Bay, a campsite, and Terrace Bay, a small self-contained rest-camp — where visitors must remain within the boundaries.

The north may be visited only by fly-in safaris undertaken by a private tour operator with a concession to run tourism. Visitors are accommodated in rustic camps with only basic facilities, and taken around in 4WD vehicles under the supervision of expert guides.

The first impression when flying along the Skeleton Coast is that the land — with its diversity of colour, texture and form, the components exposed and uncluttered by vegetation or urban and rural development

When to go

The coast may be visited all year round, but most mornings are foggy and cold.

Where to stay

There are campsites in the National West Coast Recreation Area, the Cape Cross Seal Reserve, and Skeleton Coast Park. South of the Hoanib River, Terrace Bay, a former diamond mining and processing plant, is now a small, self-contained rest-camp with shop and restaurant. Torra Bay has a camping-caravan site with basic amenities which is open for the Namibian summer school holidays, from 1 December to 31 January. See Listings.

Visitors are allowed into the extreme northern part of the Skeleton Coast Park only as guests of a private concession holder.

Fly-in safaris of up to five days depart from Windhoek throughout the year. Guests sleep in small tents equipped with camp beds, foam-rubber mattresses, sheets, pillows, sleeping bags, lamps and torches. Washbasins and chemical toilets are also provided. See Listings.

Sightseeing

The enormous **National West Coast Tourist Recreation Area** extends 200 kilometres (125 miles) northwards from **Swakopmund** to the **Ugab River**, stretching inland for approximately fifty kilometres (thirty-one miles).

This stretch of coast is acclaimed by surfers for its breakers and highly-favoured by anglers for its catches of **galjoen**, **cob**, **steenbras**, **geelbek**, and **blacktail**. It is also popular with bird-watchers, for the coastline between Swakopmund and Terrace Bay is a breeding-ground for seventy per cent of the world's population of **Damara tern**. Worldwide, their entire breeding population is probably fewer than 2,000 pairs.

They migrate from lands as far north as the Gulf of Guinea, reaching the Namibian coast between September and October. **Kelp gulls**, **crows**, **black-backed jackal** and **brown hyena** are their principal enemies. To safeguard their eggs and chicks, the Damara tern nest on the **gravel plains** and **salt pans** inland from the coast.

Their breeding time coincides with the height of the tourist season and their habitat is gravely threatened by thoughtless and reckless off-road driving.

The first point of interest along the coast is the **salt works**, seven kilometres (four miles) **north** of Swakopmund. Production of the concentrated brine at the salt pan, known as **Panther Beacon**, began in 1933 but by 1952 the salt source was exhausted.

Since then, seawater has been pumped into evaporation ponds from which the crystallised salt is removed by mechanical scrapers. Impurities are taken out in the washing and screening plant, and the salt is graded into various grain sizes. The salt is used mainly in the plastic, chemical, and paper industries in South Africa and the 180,000 tonnes produced annually supplies more than ninety per cent of South Africa's needs.

Situated near the salt works, the **Richwater Oyster Company** started cultivating oysters in 1985. Every year, about half a million seed oysters are imported from Guernsey in the English Channel Islands and initially cultivated in a shallow, thirty-five-hectare (eighty-six-acre) **seawater pond**. Conditions are ideal, for not only does the pond offer protection, but the temperature is warmer.

In addition, the seawater along the west coast is highly nutritious. The oysters are kept in the nursery pond until they reach a length of about twenty-five millimetres (one inch), when they are transferred to open shelves in cement channels.

Also near the salt pans is the **Mile 4 Caravan Park**, said to be the biggest of its kind in southern Africa.

Some twenty-five kilometres (fifteen miles) beyond the park the road sweeps through the one-street fishing resort of **Wlotzkasbaken**. Seventy-six kilometres (forty-seven miles) from Swakopmund, just over half way to **Cape Cross**, is the sleepy resort of **Henties Bay**, at the mouth of the Omararu River. The town's population increases tenfold during the summer season for it is rated as Namibia's top fishing resort.

Above: Misty phantoms of Namibia's Skeleton Coast drape themselves across the Namib Desert's ochre-coloured dunes.

Getting there

Henties Bay is 2,402 kilometres (1,493 miles) from Johannesburg, 1,924 kilometres (1,196 miles) from Cape Town, 1,219 kilometres (757 miles) from Noordoewer, 915 kilometres (568 miles) from Keetmanshoop, and 431 kilometres (268 miles) from Windhoek.

When to go

The Skeleton Coast is cool and refreshing all year round.

Where to stay

Hotel De Duine (1-star). See Listing for "Hotels". Die Oord Rest Camp. See Listings.

Sightseeing

Henties Bay is a typical small seaside resort. The social hub of the town is in the bar of the **Hotel De Duine**. There are two **filling stations** and several **shops**, including some which specialise in fishing and fishing equipment.

It is also a good base from which to explore the Namib's unique **lichen fields** which lie a little way inland from the town.

Seals

Situated seventy kilometres (forty-three miles) along the coastal road, **north** of **Henties Bay**, the **Cape Cross Seal Reserve** is open every day except Friday. Cape Cross is home to between 80,000 and 100,000 Cape fur seals — one of three species of fur seals living along the southern African coast. (See: "Wildlife: Just Out of This World", Part Four).

The rocks below Cape Cross are alive with a multitude of writhing Cape fur seal cows whose cries and barks fill the air.

Around 90,000 creatures, there to give birth, jostle for a precious but precarious flipper hold on the rocky shore.

When the males travel far off into the South Atlantic at the end of each breeding season, they are 190 kilos (420 pounds) and twice as heavy as the cows. Eating the equivalent of eight per cent of their body weight each day, the bulls take full advantage of the Atlantic's rich marine life to virtually double their weight to 360 kilos (794 pounds).

Then, as the October winds south of the Equator carry the first nascent promise of southern spring, the great bulls begin to arrive at the end of their 1,600-kilometre (1,000-mile) odyssey from the **south** — deep in rut, ready to establish a harem of between five and twenty-five cows and to protect their domains. Although sleek and elegant in the water, on land the great bulls are cumbersome and awkward.

In the next six weeks they burn the extra fat away in vicious fights with their rivals — snarling and rearing up aggressively, lunging their heads and snapping their teeth in an awesome display of might. At the end, the beaten ones squirm away in shame.

Most Cape pups are born in late November and early December, after a nine-month gestation.

The tiny black, new-born blubbery forms wriggle helplessly in all directions while the waters teem with female seals catching fish for their offspring. Left alone, the pups are tempting prey for the Namib's hungry hunter-scavengers — **black-backed jackal** and **brown hyena**. In addition, the unwieldy and careless movements of the great bulls leave hundreds more squashed in their wake.

Every December, dozens of dead calves litter the shore in a feast for the Cape's scavengers. When the cows return from fishing, they trace their offspring through a combination of wailing and scent.

Within days of giving birth, the cows mate again with the bulls. For many observers what lingers most is the appalling stench that emanates from this mass of blubber. Nonetheless, it does nothing to deter the hunters who cull the seals each year.

Cape Cross seals have been exploited for their skins and other products since 1895, when 2,000 skins were exported. The industry, however, experienced mixed fortunes over the years which followed. Today, the seal population is controlled by culling.

Cape Cross was also of economic value for another reason — guano. In 1895, 6,000 tonnes were collected from islands in the **salt pans** south of Cape Cross. The concession holders, the Damaraland *Guano-Gesellschaft*, faced many problems and, by 1902, guano production was down to 500 tonnes and ceased operation the following year.

Cape Cross is also of special historic interest for it was there in 1486 that Diego Cão, the first-known European to set foot on the coast of Namibia, raised a two-metre (seven-foot) high limestone cross and, in time, the site became known as Cape Cross.

Now visitors are surprised to see **two crosses**, one a **replica** raised on the instructions of Kaiser Wilhelm II. In 1974 the **area** around the site was landscaped and a number of **paved circles** and **semi-circles** built at different levels, each depicting part of the Cape history. The circles and semi-circles represent the Southern Cross — symbol of the direction in which Cão sailed.

The **stones** on the **terrace** have been laid out to form a **star**, symbolic of their importance to early navigators.

The **other cross**, on a second **terrace**, is a **replica**, commissioned by the National Monuments Council, which was unveiled in 1980 on the very spot where the original stood.

Based on a plaster cast of the original, the cross was cut from Namib dolerite — the hard stone which forms the rocky outcrop at Cape Cross. The Cão family crest and the wording of the original in Latin and Portuguese, together with English, Afrikaans, and German, is engraved on the other three levels. (See "Land of Lost Horizons", Part One).

Skeleton Coast Park: Land of Linear Oases

From the Ugab to the Kunene River, on the border with Angola, the Skeleton Coast Park covers roughly one-third of Namibia's coastline, encompasssing the transition zone from the higher Kaokoveld interior to the foggy ocean shore.

Drought-ridden

Paradoxically, although the Namib Desert has one of the most humid atmospheres in the world, the moist air is so thin it cannot make rain. Annual rainfall is between fifteen to twenty-five millimetres (half to one inch), the rain falling in different locations in different years.

While temperatures inland rise sharply during the day, the coast itself is cool throughout the year, except on winter days when bergwinds blow and it becomes warmer than in summer.

Throughout the year, the prevailing winds at the coast are south and south-westerlies. The *Ostwind*, a typical bergwind which blows between April and July, brings the life-giving detritus from the interior, providing food for the small and uniquely adapted creatures of the dunes.

The regular inflow of moisture brought by the dense fogs has enabled an extraordinary plant community with a large number of endemic species to evolve. Subject to extremes of temperature, strong winds and encroaching sands, the plants ensure their survival through ingenious adaptations to catch and store moisture.

Above: Masters of desert survival, hardy oryx graze the sparse grasses on the floor of a Namib dune valley.

Opposite top: Wind-driven barchan dunes march north along the Skeleton Coast.

Opposite: Uniquely adapted to survival in the Namib, Namibia's desert-dwelling elephants have dwindled almost to extinction because of poaching.

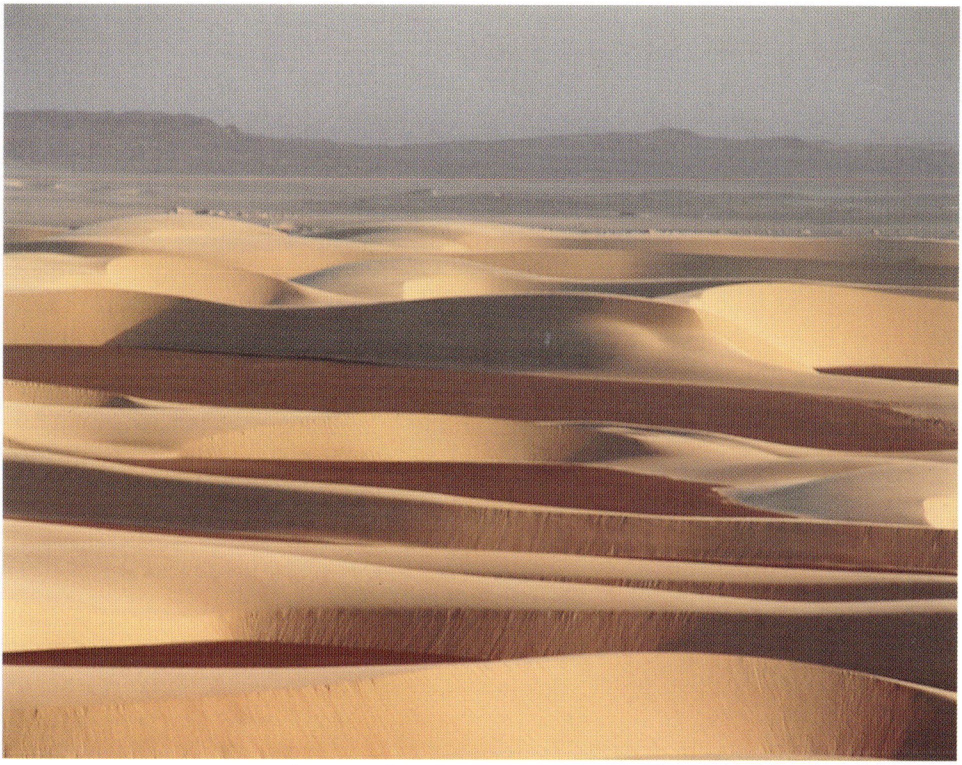

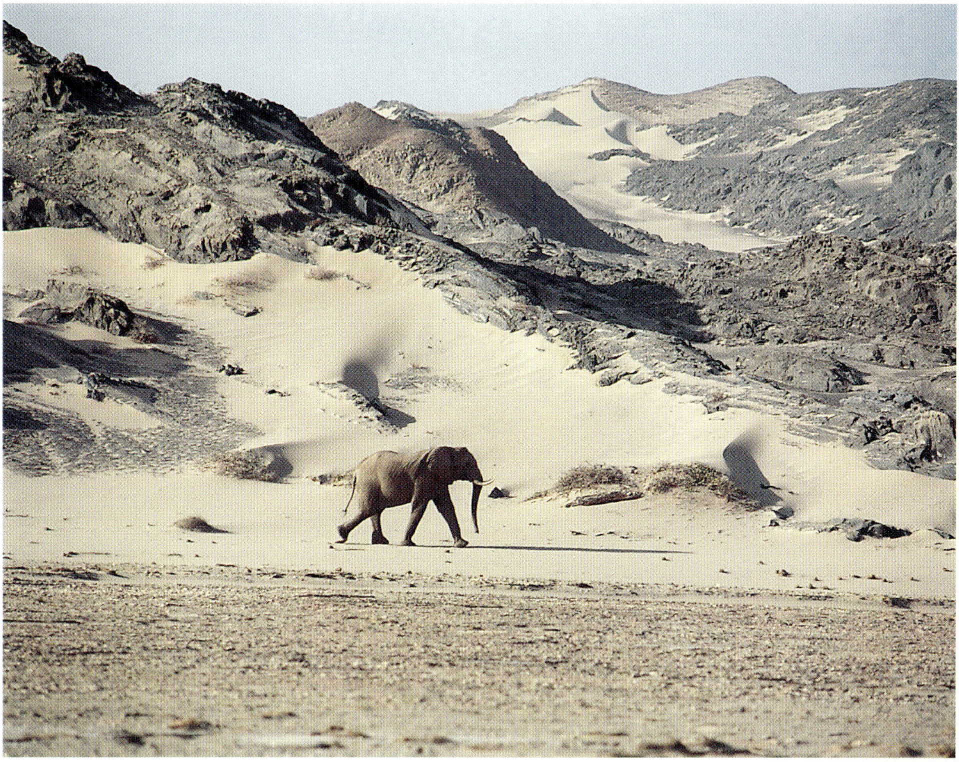

Getting there

No direct roads lead to this region. All travel is by 4WD or light aircraft. Safaris into western Kunene include visits to the Himba people. See Listings.

Where to stay

Accommodation is in small igloo tents or wooden huts in different overnight camps equipped with basic facilities.

When to go

The coast climate tends to be cool even in summer. Although warm during the day, the interior usually starts cooling off in the late afternoon. Nights are cold.

Sightseeing

Visitors are driven around the area in 4WD vehicles under the supervision of expert guides. Destinations include such features as the **roaring dunes**, **Rocky Point**, the white **clay 'temples'** of the **Hoarusib Canyon**, the **seal colony** at **Cape Frio**, the **Agate Mountain** and the **Kunene River**, where visitors explore some of its spectacular gorges by motorboat.

Long treks are impracticable because of distances, climate, harsh conditions and lack of water. Supervised walks, however, are conducted by Directorate of Conservation officials along the course of the **Ugab River**, the **southern border** of the park.

The **northern** wilderness section is restricted to fly-in safaris. Over the past fifteen years this area has become internationally known as one of the most scenically beautiful and ecologically interesting wilderness areas in the world.

The safaris are conducted by a concessionaire, under contract to the government, who has the sole right to take visitors into the area in groups of no less than four and no more than fifteen people.

Travelling **north** from the **border** of the National West Coast Tourist Recreation Area the landscapes become more interesting. The oldest rocks found at the Skeleton Coast are mica-schist, gneiss and granite, part of the Damara sequence, deposited between 1,000 and 700 million years ago.

Today the granites — molten rock which crystallised deep within the bowels of the earth — are clearly visible at **Möwe Bay** in a striking mosaic of grey granite, sectioned by darker grey dolerite dykes and pink feldspar gravels.

In younger Mesozoic times, about 170 to 120 million years ago, the supercontinent of the southern hemisphere, Gondwanaland, began to break apart as the African and South American continents slowly drifted away from each other.

During this rifting, deep fissures opened in the crust of the earth and vast quantities of lava, squeezed out of its bowels, spread like a large flat cake over the Namib platform. These lavas are identical to those found in Brazil.

Gemstones

The brick-red, brown, grey and black lavas contain **agate, carnelian, jasper, moss agate** and **amethyst**, the latter found in several growth layers of large hollow geodes. At one time amethysts were mined at **Sarusas**, but although the quality was high, mining never became profitable because of high costs and limited demand.

Alluvial **diamonds** occur sporadically in marine terraces at several locations along the coast. Although of good quality, they are generally small. Because they occur only in small pockets, they are not profitable to mine. **Garnets** are also found at the Skeleton Coast, usually in the same locations as diamonds.

Visually interesting is the fine garnet sand which covers long stretches of beach in washes of dark maroon. Blown into sandy areas, this garnet sand forms a colourful coating on the backs of dunes, creating intriguing patterns on the slipfaces. Minerals found in association with garnet sand are magnetite and ilmenite, tiny black particles which add to the colourful, surreal patterns characteristically seen on the backs of the Skeleton Coast dunes.

Opposite: Birds roost on the rusting remains of a 1975 shipwreck on the Skeleton Coast.

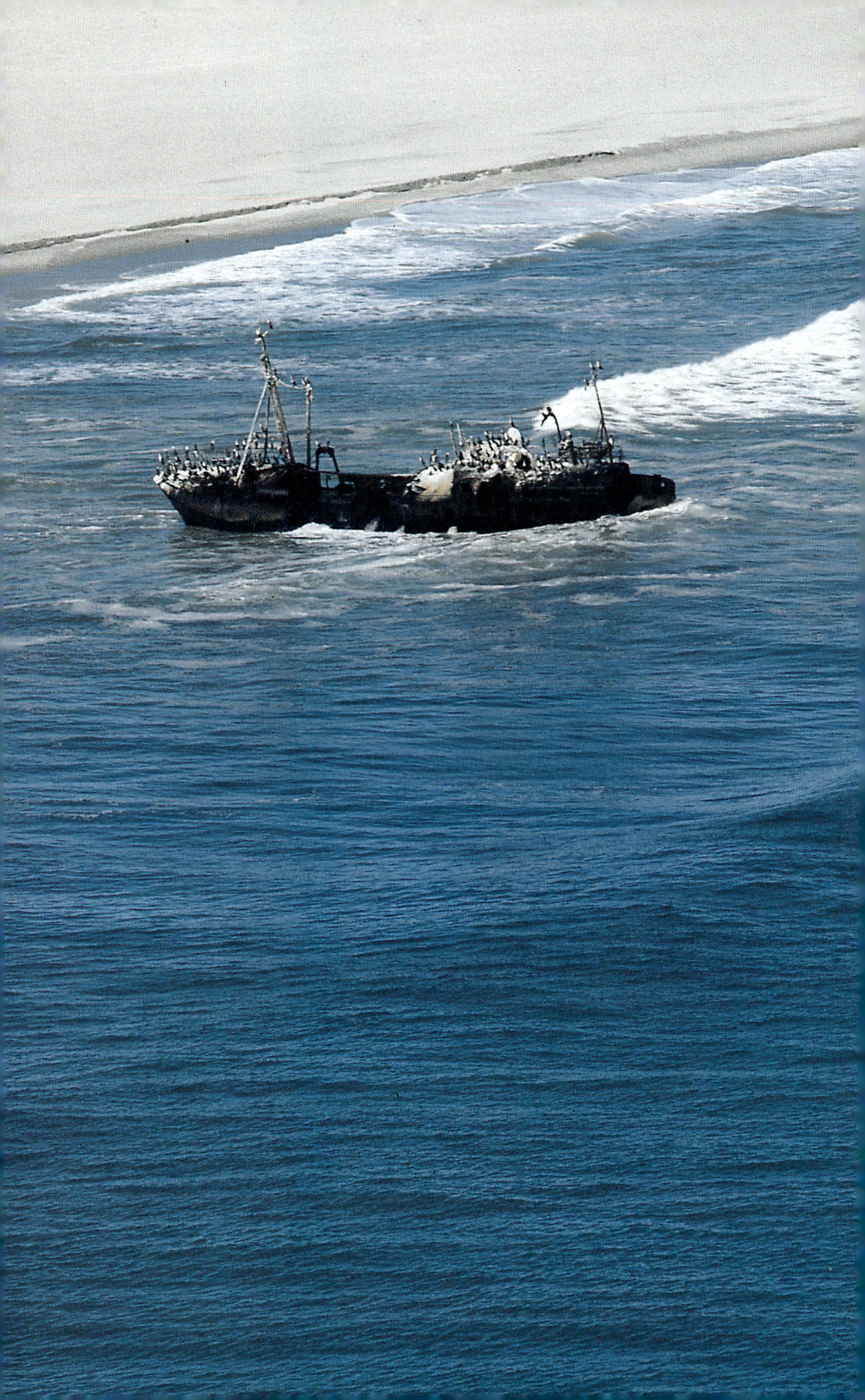

Above: Weathering through the millennia these surreal rock formations were sculpted by the floodwaters of the Kunene River.

Roaring dunes

Sprawled like massive pieces of modern sculpture over the desert surface, **dunes** are a living and integral part of the Skeleton Coast. Formed by the deposition of sand churned out onto the beaches by Atlantic waves and seized by the prevailing south and south-west winds, they roar, rumble, smoke and wander in an ever-changing cosmos of colour and contour.

One of the most captivating formations is the **barchan**, a crescent-shaped dune which occurs where sand is relatively scarce. Formed by the prevailing south-west wind, these dunes move in a north-easterly direction at average speeds of between two and three metres (six and ten feet) a year.

An interesting phenomenon prevalent in the larger barchans is that they make a roaring or rumbling sound when sand build-up on the crest slides down the slipface. The warmer and drier the dune, the greater the roar, and the larger the dune, the louder the roar.

Shrub-coppice, or **hump dunes** are familiar, especially near the coast and in dry river courses. In effect, they are mounds of sand which accumulate around vegetation and are relatively small, on average up to one to two metres (three to seven feet) high.

Lending an exotic touch to the **Hoarusib Canyon** are the so-called **white temples**, or castles of clay — impressive formations of yellowish-white sedimentary clay. These remnants of ancient river silt deposits are thought by geomorphologists to have been formed when the dunes dammed the river less than 100,000 years ago.

The Skeleton Coast is very much the product of its climate. The dense coastal fogs and cold sea breezes caused by the icy Benguela Current and the hot bergwinds from the interior foster both its singular ecosystem and its aura of mystery and impenetrability. Contrary to popular belief, temperatures at the Skeleton Coast are relatively cool and moderate, rarely exceeding 30°C (86°F).

Natural curiosities

Some of the most curious plants grow on

mountain slopes, such as the strange hedgehog-like **elephant's foot**, which anchors itself among the rocks with its long taproot; the conspicuous *Hoodia*, with its large, reddish-brown plate-like flowers; the small well-camouflaged *Trichocaulon*, which spreads flat on the ground with knobbly, finger-like leaves and the **Bushman's candle** with its pink and white flowers and resin-like bark which can be burnt as incense.

Truly outlandish are the stunted low-spreading **Commiphora trees** with their thick swollen stems.

Vegetation, which grows in association with the dunes, is widely distributed. Common examples are the **ganna** or **brackbush**, **narra**, **dollar-bush**, **desert parsley** and **dune lucerne**. Although these bushes appear to grow on top of the dunes, it is the other way round — the dune 'grows' around the bush, which remains on top by extending its roots.

Despite its straggly, untidy and rather nondescript appearance, ganna provides valuable fodder for the animals of the desert. **Springbok, gemsbok, ostrich** and many other **birds**, as well as **insects**, feed off its highly nutritious small dusky grey-green leaves.

But while ganna is dependent on fog for survival and grows virtually all along the coast, the narra plant, endemic to the Namib, only grows close to rivers and old river courses where its roots can reach subterranean water. The nutritious pips and watery pulp of the round and prickly narra fruit are eaten especially by porcupine, gemsbok and hyena.

Two common species of **euphorbia** occur in the Skeleton Coast; the **plains euphorbia**, which grows in flat areas, and the cactus-like **candelabra euphorbia**, which can be seen growing among rocks on mountain slopes.

One of the most interesting forms of plant-life in the desert is **lichen**, of which more than 100 species grow on the **gravel plains**, **rocky outcrops** and **mountain slopes**. A lichen is a complex symbiosis of an alga and a fungus.

Normally hard and brittle, lichens come to life, or 'bloom', when water is sprinkled

Below: Rare flora, such as desert parsley, *Merremia querichii*, cling tenaciously to life in the arid immensity of the Namib Desert.

Above: Softly-shaded perfection of the desert edelweiss, one of Namibia's unique species of desert plant.

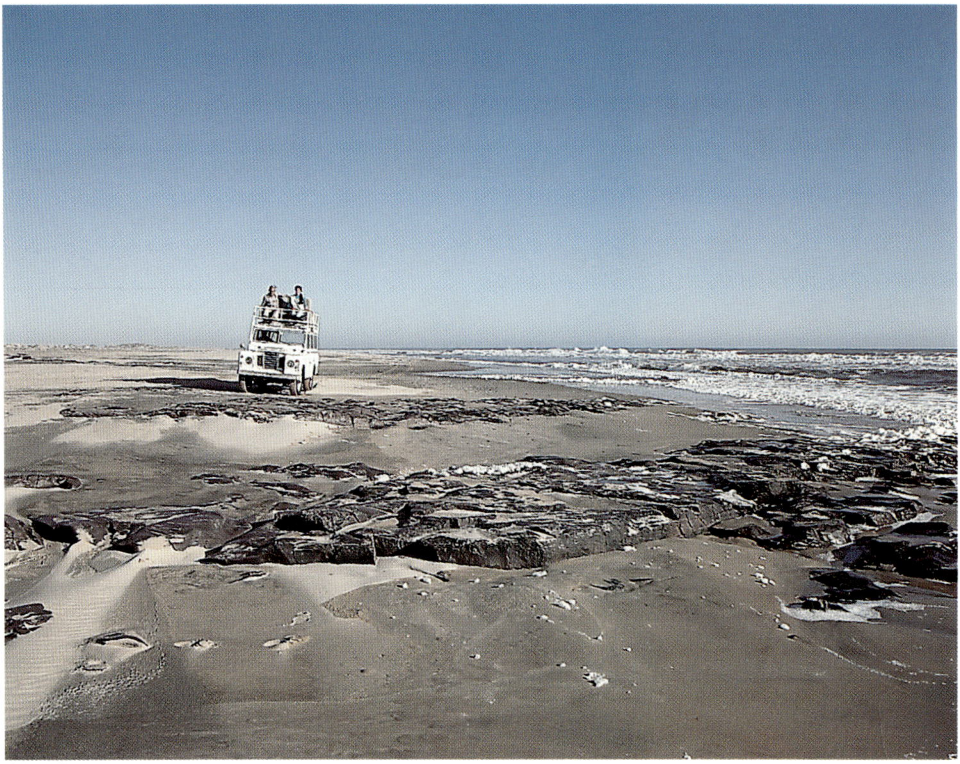

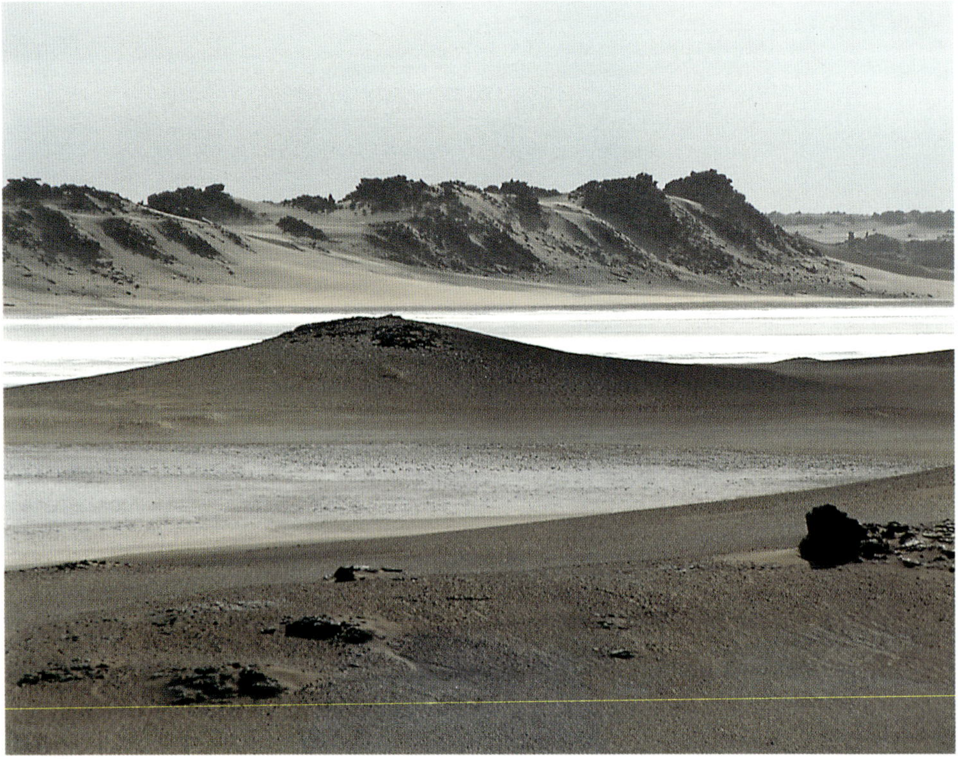

over them, moving visibly and becoming soft and leathery to the touch. Like other desert vegetation, lichens depend on the fog for survival, although they manage without moisture for long periods.

Living fossil

Possibly the most unusual plant in the Namib is the living fossil plant, *Welwitschia mirabilis*. In effect a tree turned dwarf by the rigours of the desert, welwitschias produce only two leaves throughout their long lifetime.

These grow up to three metres (ten feet) long. Constantly worn away by desert sun and searing winds, the tough, leathery leaf-blades are torn into long, thong-like shreds, causing the plant to resemble a dishevelled mass of wire wool.

The welwitschia produces separate male and female plants. The female produces up to 100 cone-like flowers in one season, while the male plant has smaller, branched flowers which produce an abundance of pollen. Often the cones are brightly coloured — the males salmon pink, the females greenish-yellow to reddish-brown.

These plants of ancient origin are extremely long-lived, and among the oldest in the world. The age of one specimen on the Welwitschia Plain near Swakopmund is thought to be at least 2,000 years, while average ages determined by carbon-dating are between 500 and 600 years.

A major component of the character and ecology of the Skeleton Coast are the rivers that drain westwards towards the sea, carrying plant forms normally foreign to such an arid environment from the interior into the desert. Sustained by subterranean water, the comparatively rich vegetation supports a wide spectrum of animal life, including large and small mammals, birds, reptiles and insects.

Underground water

Transverse rock barriers force some water to the surface, creating permanent and semi-permanent **waterholes**. **Sand-holes** under the surface which contain water are opened up by **elephant** and **gemsbok**. These are called *gorras*.

The largest river is the Hoarusib, which comes down in flood at least once a year, while from time to time the **Hoanib**, **Huab**, **Khumib**, **Koichab**, **Uniab** and **Ugab** Rivers reach the sea. The **Sechomib**, **Nadas**, **Munutum** and **Odondojengo** rarely flow and — when they do — peter out in the sand.

Animals which live in dry river-beds are not always typical of the desert, as they have regular access to water and feed on vegetation that also occurs in the interior. Larger species such as **elephant**, **black rhino** and **lion** are migratory, moving up and down the **river courses**, often increasing in numbers when food becomes scarce in the interior.

Giraffe are also occasionally seen in the river-beds, as well as **chacma baboons**. Smaller animals which commonly occur are **Cape hare**, **crested porcupine**, **genet**, **caracal** and **African wild cat**.

An impressive bird sometimes seen in the river courses is the **lappet-faced vulture**, which nests on the tops of large acacia trees. Smaller birds commonly seen are **Cape sparrows**, **mountain chats**, **bokmakieries**, **tit-babblers**, **red-eyed bulbuls** and **mousebirds**. Several species of birds are found at the waterholes, such as **Egyptian geese**, **avocets**, **red-knobbed coots** and **Cape teals**.

Larger mammals seen most commonly on the plains are **springbok** and **gemsbok**. In years of good rain, numbers increase and even **zebra** move in from the interior, followed by predators such as **hyena**, **lion** and **leopard**.

Birds and game

There is a surprising variety of birds on the open plains. Larks, of which the diminutive **Gray's lark** is very much in evidence, are extremely common. One interesting bird,

Opposite top: Dangerous solitude of the Skeleton Coast is best explored by 4WD in the company of skilled escorts.
Opposite: Gaunt rock outcrops guard the alkaline wastes of a Cape Frio salt pan along the Skeleton Coast.

Below: Prickly, melon-like fruit of the Namib Desert's narra bush provides refreshing succour for man and beast alike.

Above: Fragile lichen fields of the Namib plains are a treasure of nature's antiquities.

the **Namaqua sandgrouse**, occurs in considerable numbers on the gravel flats.

The birds feed almost exclusively on small dry seeds and therefore have to drink regularly. About two hours after sunrise they gather at waterholes in their hundreds, sometimes thousands. Newly hatched sandgrouse chicks have to be provided with water daily.

It is brought to them by the male, whose uniquely modified breast feathers absorb drinking water when he wades into the shallows at waterholes. He then flies back and exudes it in droplets for the chicks to drink.

Large birds often seen on the plains are **Ludwig's bustard, Rüppell's korhaan** and **ostrich**. Another typical bird seen there, as well as among the dunes, in the river courses and on the beaches, is the ubiquitous **pied crow**, also referred to as the parson's crow.

Black-backed jackal, which patrol up and down the beaches scavenging on dead **seals**, **birds** and **fish**, are a familiar sight at the Skeleton Coast. Competing with them for the refuse and carrion cast up by the tides are **brown hyena**, also self-appointed health officials of the coast.

Other scavengers are the **ghost crabs**, fair-weather creatures which live under the surface along the beaches, emerging when the sand is warmed by the sun. At the slightest provocation they scuttle away frenetically towards the sea with their curious sideways gait, sometimes in large squadrons.

Most numerous of the coastal birds are **Cape cormorants** and **gulls**, while small flocks of the rare **Damara tern** are a familiar sight. Coastal lagoons and waterholes are frequented by **lesser** and **greater flamingo**.

Another colony of **Cape fur seal** occurs along the Skeleton Coast at **Cape Frio**, where there are about 50,000.

The **sand dunes** harbour unusual and highly specialised insects and other small creatures. The all-important fog generated by the Benguela Current and the detritus consisting of dried-out animal and plant material blown in from the interior by the hot easterly bergwinds, maintain an established pattern of food and water chains.

This sustains the many primary dune-dwellers such as **termites**, **beetles**, **fish moths** and **ants**, which are preyed on by **lizards**, **snakes**, **spiders**, **crickets**, **flies**, **scorpions**, **chameleons** and **wasps**.

Unique to northern Namib are the unusual coloured 'white' **Tenebrionid beetles**, which are active on the dune surface after their black relatives have dived into the sand to avoid overheating.

Sidewinder

On closer inspection an apparently smooth dune slipface reveals an intricate network of many different **tracks**. Those of the **sidewinding adder**, a diagonal series of broken transverse lines, are especially distinctive. The sidewinder drinks by sucking droplets of condensed moisture from its body. It hides in the sand during the daytime, with only its eyes above the surface.

An interesting lizard of the dunes is the colourful, translucent **Palmatogecko**, or web-footed gecko, exclusively nocturnal and ethereal in appearance, with salmon-pink and chalky-white body, large, dark protruding eyes, white lids and turquoise blue spots on the head.

The large vegetarian sand-diving **Skoogi**, or desert-plated lizard, endemic to the northern Namib, is characterised by its glossy orange and creamy yellow skin, the male having a shiny black chin and throat.

The **shovel-nosed lizard**, with its delicate mother-of-pearl sheen, is smaller and easily identified by its unusual flattened snout.

When temperatures are high, these lizards perform a footlifting dance, holding the tail above the surface of the dune to keep cool. If disturbed they dive beneath the sand in a rapid cork-screwing movement.

Another intriguing inhabitant of the dunes is the **trapdoor spider**, also known as the **dancing white lady**. It builds its home by digging a hole in the sand, covering the walls with a cobweb lining and constructing a kind of trapdoor over the

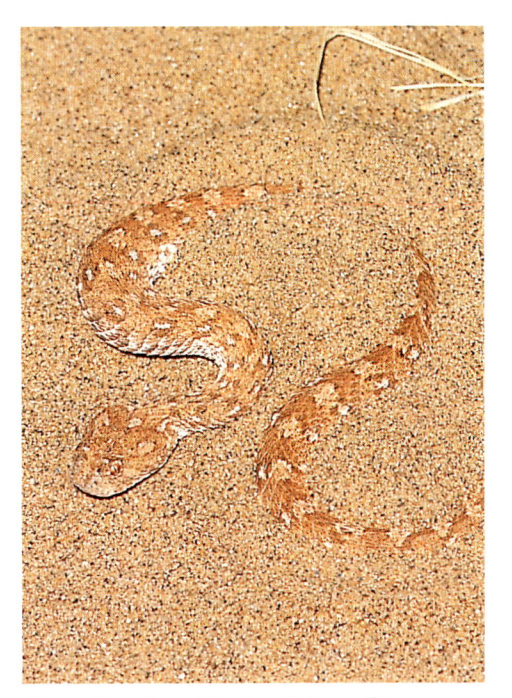

Above: Guardian of the desert dunes, the sidewinder adder survives by drinking the condensation that forms on its skin.

opening. Black **dune wasps** prey on these spiders. When threatened, the spider forms itself into a tight ball and rolls rapidly down a dune slope to escape.

Step by step

The **southern** Skeleton Coast Park lies between the Ugab and Hoanib rivers, but entry is carefully controlled. Visitors need a day permit to drive through the park, available from the Directorate of Nature Conservation offices in Windhoek, Swakopmund and Okaukuejo.

Covering more than 16,000 square kilometres (6,178 square miles), it is a fisherman's paradise. Of the four species most eagerly sought, **cob** and **galjoen** account for more than half the annual catch, the balance being made up mainly by **steenbras** and **blacktail**, **mackerel**, **white stump-nose** and **strepie**. Galjoen and blacktail tend to be caught in the turbulent surf or rocky areas. Cob and steenbras, on the other hand, favour sandy or pebble beaches.

The coastline is level, only occasionally

broken by scattered rocky outcrops. Inland, the southern flat gravel plains make way for the high dunes **north** of **Terrace Bay** which literally stretch into the ocean in places. Crossing the park are several linear oases in the form of dry river-beds.

The first of these is the **Ugab River**, one of the longest to cross the Namib, its waters coming from as far east as **Outjo** and **Otjiwarongo**. Its valley forms an important corridor for animal movement between the interior and the coast.

The dense vegetation is made up of various indigenous plants, but mostly **wild tobacco** — a foreign import which has run riot.

There is a three-day **hiking trail** up the valley organised by the Directorate of Nature Conservation. It is tough going but should leave those who undertake it with an understanding of the complex ecosystem present — and they may even spot an **oryx** or two.

About thirty-eight kilometres (twenty-four miles) **north** of the Ugab River, the **coast road** crosses the **Huab River** and there is a small **loop road** off to the **east** that explores the **valley** further inland.

It is worth getting out and wandering around on foot among the dollar bushes with their thick, fleshy leaves. Notice how they occur on the leeward side of small mounds of sand, appearing to grow out of them.

Inland, to the north of the river-bed, are a few crescent-shaped **barchan dunes** emerging from the river's sands and 'marching' northwards. Further north still, the **wreck** of the *Atlantic Pride* lies just off shore.

The **Koigab Valley** contains one of the smallest rivers. It still supports perennial vegetation and even flows occasionally. It is a good place to look for what are possibly the world's only white beetles — the focus of much scientific study since their discovery.

Their unique coloration is thought to be an adaptation to reduce their absorption of heat, and hence allow them to forage above the sand's surface during the middle of the day. If this is the case, however, then it remains a mystery as to why they are only found in the northern Namib, and why the majority of other desert beetles are black.

Torra Bay, between the Koigab and Uniab rivers, lies just **south** of the first dunes in the Namib's great northern dune-field. There the first low barchan dunes start migrating northward, eventually forming a sand sea stretching as far as the **Curoca River** in Angola.

Visitors may notice some of the dunes have purple crests, contrasting with the lighter coloured sand below, caused by a high proportion of purple-brown garnet crystals in the sand. Being less dense than the quartz sand grains these collect on the surface. Those who have a magnifying glass should look closely at a handful of the sand — they will find a kaleidoscope of colours sparkling in their palm.

Though fairly short, as far as wildlife is concerned, the **Uniab Valley** contains one of the most important rivers to cross the Namib. Its headwaters come from around **Palmwag**, an area of relatively abundant game, and its lower reaches have formed an impressive, well-vegetated **delta**. In between, a wide **valley** supports rich flora and fauna, flanked along some of its course by dunes.

The **roadside** is a fascinating area to explore on foot for a few hours, so park the car, take along binoculars and, most importantly, a flask of water.

It seems that in the past the Uniab's mouth formed a large delta, subsequently raised up above sea level, only to be cut into again by the river to form a series of five alternative routes to the sea.

At present only one of these has water flowing through it, although most have freshwater pools fed by underground seepage — forming small verdant **oases** dotted around the watercourses that provide a home to water birds and an important stop-over for migrants, including the delicate black and white avocets.

In the early 1990s it was the **second course** from the **north** that hosted the flow and, upstream, there is often an overground trickle through the canyon, carved smooth by the water. **Springbok** or **gemsbok** may be grazing there — and visitors may catch a glimpse of a **brown hyena**.

The **dune belt** around Terrace Bay widens to stretch down to the ocean. The crests of these dunes are ideal places to search for the highly unusual beetles which perform 'headstands' or dig trenches in order to drink, but only before sunrise.

The beetles may be seen high on the dunes with their backs to the wind and their heads down — 'fog basking' — a little before sun-up. Fog condenses on their bodies, dripping down in droplets below their mouths, providing all the water they need to survive.

The large, round beetles of the *Lepidochora* genus illustrate another way of collecting moisture. They dig small **trenches** near the dune crests, perpen-dicular to the prevailing wind, and collect the condensation from the trench walls.

Sparse vegetation

The vegetation between the Ugab and Huab rivers falls within the Central Namib Type — north of the Huab it is relatively sparse, the most common species being dollar-bush, **brakspekbos** and occasional stands of ganna.

Mammals are not present in large numbers along the coast, mainly black-backed jackal, brown hyena, and occasionally Cape fur seal.

One unusual inhabitant is **lion**, of which perhaps only five live along the entire Skeleton Coast. These have adapted to coastal resources and feed on **white-breasted** and **Cape cormorants**, **seals** and even **beached whales**. They move between the coast and the interior along the river courses cutting through the Namib.

Far more prolific is the coastal birdlife. The nutrient-rich Atlantic draws large numbers of sea and shore birds. The coastline and wetlands attract at least seventeen Palaearctic migrants and more than 203 birds have been recorded in the park.

The most common waders along the coast are **white-fronted plover**, **grey plover**, **turnstone** and **sanderling**, while **curlew sandpiper** and **little stint** are abundant in the wetlands. Elsewhere **terek**, **marsh**, **white-rumped** and **broad-billed sandpiper**, and **whimbrel** are the most common.

Below: Ghost crab in aggressive defence posture.

Above: Desert-dwelling tenebrionid beetles have become masters at tapping the Skeleton Coast's early-morning fogs to quench their thirsts.

Damaraland: Land of Light

The arid north-western area of Namibia encompasses Damaraland and Kaokoland, part of the mosaic of ethnically based homelands that make up the country.

This region, named Kaokoveld by Captain G C Shortridge in his monumental 1934 work on the mammals of South West Africa, describes the area stretching from the Ugab River to the Kunene, inland to where Damaraland touches Outjo, Otjiwarongo, Omaruru, and Karibib. Until recently, it was a remote, primeval region of undeveloped landscapes and abundant wildlife, where people lived in a way unchanged for centuries.

Stretching for about 600 kilometres (372 miles) from north to south, the untamed mountain scenery and uniquely adapted animal life have something to offer all visitors, whatever their interests.

Unique Kaokoveld features such as the Spitzkoppe, Petrified Forest, Burnt Mountain and Twyfelfontein, managed by the Directorate of Nature Conservation as conservation areas, are accessible to cars along well-maintained roads.

It is a wildlife paradise, home to endangered rhino and elephant, even though small in number, for they have adapted uniquely to this harsh land.

Studies on the feeding behaviour of the black rhino show that they have the ability to eat plants such as *Euphorbia virosa*, which normally has a strong chemical defence against herbivores, and *Welwitschia mirabilis*,

Although there are many waterholes, the rhino travel up to twenty-five kilometres (fifteen miles) at night, usually over extremely rocky terrain, to reach water. The area is also famous for its desert-adapted elephants.

Elephants are wonderful gardeners — some seeds that pass through their digestive tracts have a germination success rate of up to fifty-seven per cent compared with natural germination of twelve per cent.

During periods of drought, seeds in elephant dung are an important source of food for birds such as guineafowl, francolin, and rock pigeon. (See "Wildlife: Just Out of This World", Part Four).

During the 1970s and 1980s, the elephant and black rhino were slaughtered dramatically by poachers. In mid-1983 local game guards appointed by area headmen began patrolling the Kaokoveld under the direction of conservationist Garth Owen-Smith, who headed the Namibia Wildlife Trust's Damaraland-Kaokoland Desert Project, in conjunction with another conservationist, Chris Ayre.

By 1986 more than sixty poachers had been convicted and now the system is considered one of the world's most successful anti-poaching operations.

Damaraland encompasses the entire Namib hinterland in a north-east crescent from Rössing that curves back to the coast along the Hoanib River. It is a vast and fascinating region of Namibia, since divided by the new regions drawn up for the 1993 local authority elections.

Getting there

Two roads lead into Damaraland from Henties Bay — one running east through the Omaruru River Game Park around the southern base of the Spitzkoppe to join the B2 between Ebony and Usakos. The other road runs north-east in the southern lee of the Brandberg massif to join the Omaruru-Khorixas road. 4WD vehicles are recommended for extensive travel.

When to go

The region is open all-year-round but the southern spring is the ideal time to visit this arid hinterland region.

Where to stay

At Walvis Bay: Casa Mia Hotel (2-star), Flamingo Hotel (1-star), Hotel Atlantic (2-star), Mermaid Hotel (1-star); at Swakopmund: Atlanta Hotel (1-star), Hansa Hotel (3-star), Hotel Europa Hof (2-star), Hotel Garni Adler (2-star), Hotel Gruner Kranz (2-star), Jay Jay's (1-star), Hotel Shutze (1-star), Strand Hotel (2-star), Pension Deutsches Haus, Pension Dig by See, Pension Prinzessin-Ruprecht-Heim, Pension Rapmund, Pension Schweizerhaus, Pension d'Avignon; at Usakos: Usakos

Above: Granite boulders in the dramatic wastelands of the Damara hinterland.
Overleaf: Rocky wastes at the summit of Brandberg, Namibia's highest mountain massif.

Hotel, Wustenquell Desert Lodge (2-star), Ameib Ranch (3-star); at Henties Bay: Hotel de Duine (1-star); at Karibib: Hotel Erongoblick (1-star), Hotel Stroblhof (1-star); at Omaruru: Central Hotel (1-star); Hotel Staebe (1-star); Guest Farms: Boskloof, Erindi Onganga, Immenhof, Okosongoro, Otjandue, Otjikoto, Otjumue-Ost, Schon-feld; at Kamanjab: Habatere Lodge (3-star). See Listings for "Hotels" and accommodation.

Sightseeing

Namibia's most prominent and best-known landmark is the **Spitzkoppe**. As you travel on the **Usakos-Hentiesbaai Road,** or on the **B2** to Swakopmund, it is ever-present on the **northern horizon** — the first of the myriad attractions and wonders of this marvellously fascinating region which contains so much of what makes Namibia unique.

Known as the Matterhorn of Africa, the Spitzkoppe rises 1,784 metres (5,852 feet) above the flat surrounding plains. Immediately to the **east** lies the dome-shaped **Pondok Mountain**, and about ten kilometres (six miles) **south-west**, the 1,572-metre-high (5,157-foot) **Klein Spitzkoppe**.

Geologically, the area dates back some 750-500 million years. During the break-up of Gondwanaland, large parts of southern Africa were affected by volcanic activity and vast amounts of lava burst out of the **Spitzkoppe**, **Brandberg**, and **Erongo** volcanoes. Subsequent erosion has exposed the granitic cores as typical *inselbergs*, islands of rock in the plains.

The Spitzkoppe was first climbed by its **north-west face** in 1946, and then stood inviolate for more than ten years before the second successful ascent was made in 1960, when a three-man party pioneered a route up the precipitous **west face**. The mountain remains popular with local and overseas climbers.

Among many fascinating rock formations in the area, one resembles a **shark's mouth** and another forms a dramatic **natural arch**. Early man, too, found refuge in these mountains and covered the caves with his art.

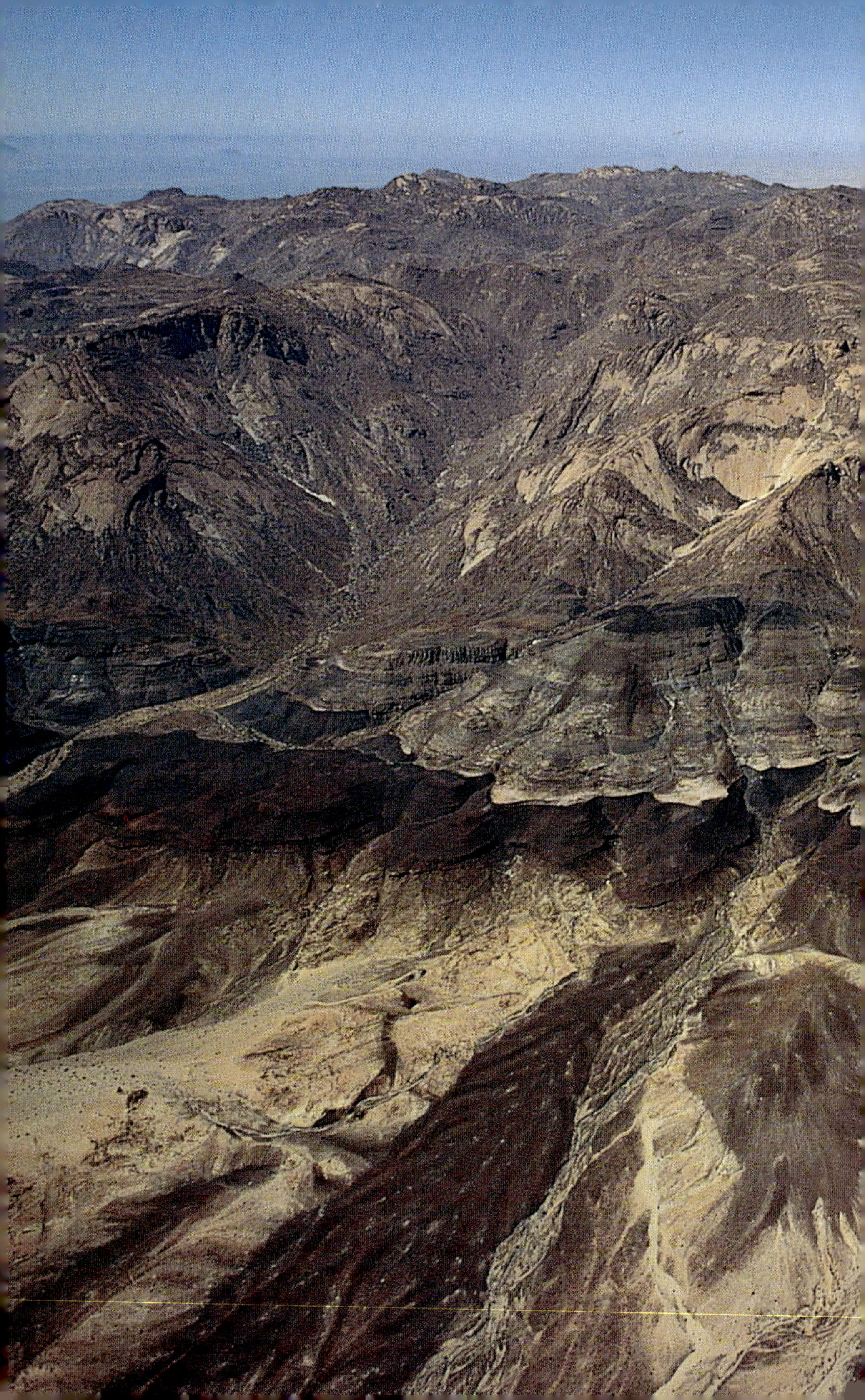

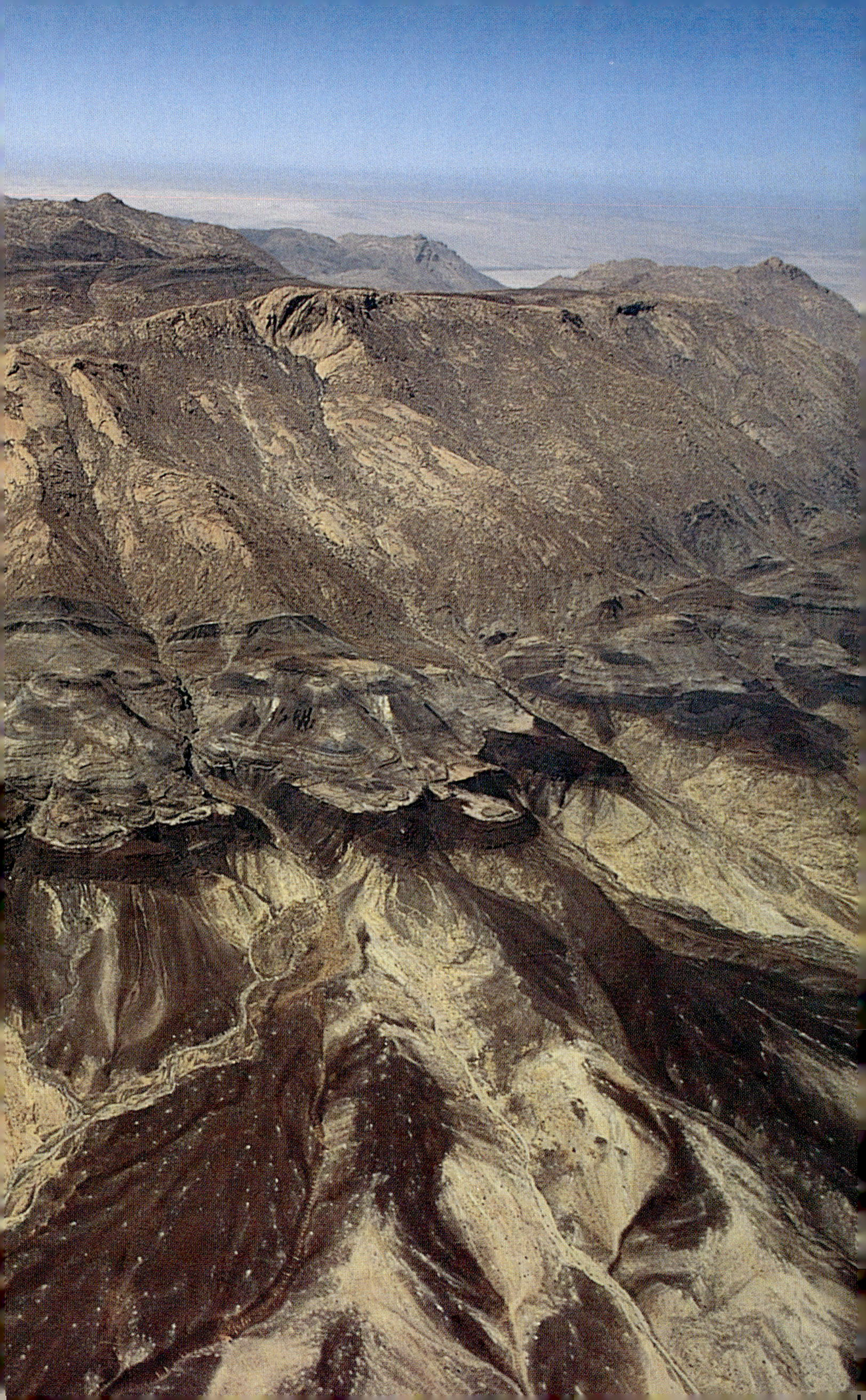

Above: Fossil tree trunks in the Petrified Forest of Damaraland.

One famous group of rock paintings may be found at **Bushman's Paradise** in the **Pondok Mountain**, east of the **Spitzkoppe**. En route there is a small **stone dam**, fed by runoff from the smooth boulders when the area occasionally receives its meagre rainfall. The dam was built in 1896 to water a German farm near Spitzkoppe.

At the top of the ascent to Bushman's Paradise there is a superb **view** over the surrounding countryside. After a short scramble, visitors come to the edge of a natural **amphitheatre** so well endowed with plants that it is a botanist's dream.

The paintings are under an overhang by the **cliff edge**. Despite the fact that they were declared a **national monument** as long ago as 1954, they have been so vandalised that there is not much left to see. It is still worth visiting the site, however, just to view the area, aptly named 'Bushman's Paradise'.

An alternative route to the top takes about three-quarters of an hour. Continue down the valley, following a fairly worn path which leads to a narrow cleft. After a short distance the trail reaches the **base** of Pondok Mountain and follows it round to the **starting point** about ten minutes further on.

To the Brandberg

Returning to the road which lies to the **east**, it is about 100 kilometres (sixty-two miles) to the turnoff **north** to the small mining village of **Uis**. There, in 1922, Etemba Schmidt established a **tin mine** on the banks of the **Kartoffel River**. But it was not until 1951 that any large-scale mining was carried out. It is now operated by ISCOR, the South African iron and steel giant.

From Uis, the Brandberg Mountain is reached by taking the C35 nineteen kilometres (twelve miles) **north-east** to the **signpost west** to **Witvrou** — Afrikaans for White Lady. There are myriad **tracks** to be explored by 4WD vehicle, but by far the most popular attraction is the White Lady rock painting, requiring a fairly strenuous walk there and back of about three hours. The route is well-marked.

The paintings were discovered in 1918

Above: Boulders at the foot of the Spitzkoppe — the 'Matterhorn of Africa'.

by Reinard Maack, a surveyor, Professor A Griess, a Windhoek high school principal, and Lieutenant George Schultze of Keetmanshoop. Maack was convinced that they had Mediterranean characteristics, an interpretation shared by a world authority on rock art, Abbé Henri Breuil, who was shown a watercolour copy of the painting, made by Maack. The Abbé believed the central figure was that of a white woman.

Thirteen years later, Breuil showed photographs of the paintings to a colleague, who said that the central figure was reminiscent of a young woman athlete of Cretan origin.

Soon the White Lady became known internationally and the Mediterranean origins of the paintings were accepted for a number of years, although not without criticism from other archaeologists.

Since then, detailed research has led modern archaeologists to conclude that the paintings represent indigenous people. Several interpretations of the local origin of the art and the gender of the subjects have been advanced.

The absence of breasts and the hunting bow are thought enough to indicate, in fact, that the White Lady is a male. Furthermore, the white colouring is thought to represent body paint commonly used by medicine men.

Within a one-and-a-half kilometre (one mile) radius of the White Lady there are ten major and seven minor **rock painting sites** — including **Jochmann Shelter** which takes its name from *Oberleutnant* Hugo Jochmann who first found the rock paintings in the Brandberg in 1909.

These include a **snake** with ears, a **lion** — a species seldom depicted in paintings in Namibia — and a two-metre-long (seven-foot) unidentified **animal**.

In a nearby cave there are vivid **paintings** of **ostriches,** while **giraffes** feature in **paintings** in other shelters.

Art treasury

Several hundred other sites on the massif were painstakingly traced by rock art expert, Harald Pager. He spent almost eight years in the Brandberg but died before he could complete his work.

Above: Curator at Twyfelfontein examines priceless rock engravings.

On its **southern face** the mountain boasts one of Namibia's densest concentrations of **stone-walled** sites. There is clear evidence that the pastoralists who lived in them retreated seasonally to the mountain plateau as the plain's grasses began to wither. There, at 2,187 metres (7,175 feet), flocks of 100 sheep could survive on ten hectares for six months — while needing 500 hectares to survive at sea level.

Indeed, it is hard to imagine that animals can live in such a harsh environment. **Steenbok**, **gemsbok** and **springbok**, however, inhabit the **plains** surrounding the Brandberg, while the more rocky areas attract **klipspringer** and **Hartmann's mountain zebra**.

The animals depend for water on a few perennial **springs** rising in the valley's lower reaches. **Leopard**, **black-backed jackal** and **aardwolf** also live there but are seldom seen because of their nocturnal behaviour. **Rock dassies** and **elephant shrews** scurry over rocks.

Two colourful birds in the area are the **rosy-faced lovebird** and **Rüppell's parrot**, which flies noisily between trees. Other species include **scimitar-billed woodhoopoe**, **red-eyed bulbul**, **mountain chat**, and **dusky sunbird**, while the **Herero chat** is endemic to a narrow band of land stretching from the Naukluft Mountains to south-western Angola.

To reach **Numas Ravine** and **Messum Crater west** of the Brandberg return to Uis and continue along the C35 for fourteen kilometres (nine miles) to the **north turnoff** to **Brandberg West**. Forty kilometres (twenty-five miles) further on the road crosses the dry **bed** of the **Messum River**. After another fourteen kilometres (nine miles) an indistinct **track** turns **west** and, after nine kilometres (five-and-a-half miles), it comes to a **fork**. Keep **north-east** for **Numas** and continue up the **valley**, past a **pool** in the river-bed where some large **fig trees**, **rushes**, and an African **star-chestnut** grow. Keeping to the **north-side** of the ravine, the **trail** leads to a permanent **spring** well-concealed by vegetation.

The area was popular with Stone Age man who left many finely executed **rock paintings** on the boulders and overhangs and which are well preserved.

Above: Large mouth-like rock formation near Khorixas.

Now follow the **south bank** of the Messum River and after about forty kilometres (twenty-five miles) cross over and turn onto the **D2342** from **Henties Bay.** Another eleven kilometres (seven miles) further along, the Messum makes a wide loop and the road leaves the river, continuing **south-west** to the edge of the **Messum Crater.**

There, continue three kilometres (two miles) **west** to a track down into the crater. Head **south** for about seven kilometres (four miles) to a **campsite** by a **rock outcrop** and an excellent view of the massive crater. The **marker poles** west of the outcrop indicate the **eastern boundary** of the National West Coast Tourist Recreation Area.

Follow the track **west** and turn **south** just beyond the boundary poles to another opening at the **southern end** of the crater. From there, continue **south** for a short distance before heading for a prominent **brown outcrop of rocks.** When the rocks are struck, they make all kinds of strange, musical sounds.

A well-defined **track** crosses several river courses during the next thirty-two kilometres (twenty miles). Do not leave the trail: it leads through **lichen fields** which are soon damaged irrevocably by tyres or footprints.

The plants unfold and change colour when water is sprinkled over them. Finally, some kilometres **north** of **Cape Cross,** the track joins the coastal route between **Swakopmund** and **Terrace Bay.**

To Khorixas

For more ancient art and stupendous geological wonders, continue north-east from Uis along the C35 to the junction with the C39 and turn west for a few kilometres to Khorixas, the administrative centre of Damaraland. The town is ideally situated for exploring northern Damaraland and the Kaokoveld.

For it is from Khorixas that the way to the wonder of the Petrified Forest, Twyfelfontein rock paintings, the Organ Pipes and Burnt Mountain — better known as Verbrandeberg — is well signposted.

Above: Once thought to be of Cretan origin, these carvings at Twyfelfontein are believed to have been executed at least 15,000 years ago.

Khorixas Rest Camp where there are forty bungalows, restaurant and swimming pool. See Listing for "Hotels". Ameib Farm, Anibib Farm, Etemba Farm. See Listings.

Sightseeing

The **turnoff** to the **Petrified Forest,** which lies a few kilometres **north** of the **C39,** is some seventy kilometres (forty-three miles) or so along the C39 **west** of **Khorixas**.

Despite being declared a **national monument** in 1950, the Petrified Forest has been badly vandalised. However, now the area is well-policed, and it is against the law to remove or damage even the smallest fossil.

The forest covers about 800 metres (half-a-mile) by 300 metres (328 yards) on a small sandstone rise in the **Aba-Huab River Valley**.

It is thought that the trees were carried there by floodwaters, an assumption supported by the fact that there are no roots or branches. The trees were probably stranded on sandbanks or shoals, for many lie parallel to each other.

Subsequently embedded in sand — also deposited by the rivers — opal-filled cracks in the logs suggest that they dried out. Such an oxygen-depleted environment prevented decay and created ideal conditions for petrifaction. This was enhanced when silica-rich water penetrated the logs, filling the cells, bark, and other parts.

Over time, the sediments gradually hardened. And then, nearly 200 million years later, after the uplift of the entire area, erosion in a warm, often arid climate removed the overlying rocks and finally exposed the petrified trees.

There are at least **fifty tree-trunks** on the plateau — some only partly exposed, others fully. One partially exposed trunk measures more than thirty metres (ninety-eight feet) and has a circumference of six metres (nineteen feet).

The **growing rings** and the texture of the **bark** are so well-preserved that the petrified trees have been identified as belonging to the *Gymnospermae*, or cone-bearing plants, a group which flourished between 300 and 200 million years ago — not as a single species, but in at least four varieties.

Getting there

Khorixas is 2,419 kilometres (1,503 miles) from Johannesburg, 1,941 kilometres (1,206 miles) from Cape Town, 630 kilometres (391 miles) from Rundu, 448 kilometres (278 miles) from Windhoek, 259 kilometres (161 miles) from Swakopmund, and 130 kilometres (eighty-one miles) from Outjo.

When to go

The area is open all year-round.

Where to stay

At Kamanjab, Hobatere Lodge (3-star) or at

Above: Vivid mural decorates a Damara hut marking the gateway to the priceless rock paintings and engravings found at Twyfelfontein.

Twyfelfontein

Central to this region is Twyfelfontein.

Getting there

Twyfelfontein lies to the west of the C39. The turnoff is some eighty-five-kilometres (fifty-three miles) west of Khorixas and is well signposted.

When to go

It is best to visit early in the morning or late in the afternoon as the heat is intense and, in the direct sunlight, the rock engravings are not seen to their best advantage.

Sightseeing

The slopes above the largest known concentration of Stone Age **petroglyphs** in Namibia are littered with large **rock slabs**. The barren surroundings and rock-strewn slopes seem a most unlikely place for any human habitation, but a **small spring** near the base of the hill has provided animals with water for thousands of years.

The abundance of game also attracted Stone Age people. Crude stone tools and the remains of huts and pottery reveal that they were followed by the Damara, who named the fountain Ui-Ais — The Spring.

In 1947, the land was bought by D Levin who named it **Twyfelfontein — Doubtful Fountain** — as he doubted whether the spring could truly have supported man and game for so long. Many **paths** crisscross the area and visitors are advised to allow at least two hours for sightseeing, if not more. Some rock slabs have as many as **seventy engravings**.

Two of the larger engravings are of **rhino,** measuring ninety-two centimetres (three feet) by fifty-five centimetres (twenty-one inches), and an **elephant,** measuring fifty-seven centimetres (twenty-two inches) by seventy-three centimetres (twenty-eight inches).

More than 2,500 engravings have been recorded. The earliest include **signs** and **symbols**, carved nineteen millimetres (three-quarters of an inch) deep in the rock.

Illustrations of antelope and their spoor

Above: Unusual rock formation near Twyfelfontein known as the Organ Pipes.

were also produced by rubbing and polishing within the outline. Some petroglyphs were engraved by cutting the outline and then chiselling away the space within. Many animals, such as **rhino**, **antelope**, **giraffe** and **ostrich**, were depicted in this way.

One interesting **petroglyph** shows a lion sporting an unusually long L-shaped tail with a paw-print at the end and spoor instead of paws. The lion appears to have an antelope in its mouth, but closer inspection reveals that it is not actually eating it. The image was superimposed many centuries later. In this particular slab there are at least thirty other engravings including snakes, giraffe, rhino and zebra.

With the exception of the northern Cape, where engravings and paintings are found together, rock art in South Africa is generally geographically separated, giving rise to the belief that the two art forms were the work of different peoples. In Namibia, however, both forms often occur together, perhaps the best examples being at Twyfelfontein and the Grosse Dom Ravine in the Brandberg.

Analysis of more than 16,400 Namibian rock engravings has shown that animals, animal spoor and abstract motifs are represented more or less equally, namely thirty-two, thirty-one and thirty per cent, respectively. Human figures only comprise two per cent.

Organ pipes

It is just a few kilometres **south** along the same **4WD trail** to the impressive and fascinating **Organ Pipes** and **Burnt Mountain,** both well **signposted** and each with a **parking area**.

Descend one of the paths to the Organ Pipes, a mass of perpendicular dolerite pillars, with a maximum height of five metres (sixteen feet) exposed in a **gorge** roughly 100-metres (320 feet) long.

Formed by the intrusion of dolerite, a plutonic rock, into the shales of the Karoo Sequence some 120 million years ago, they shrank during cooling and split at joints in angular columns. Subsequently, after the erosion of the overlying rocks, they were exposed to weathering.

From the **parking area** there is an

Above: Millennia-old Bushman engravings of wildlife at Twyfelfontein.

excellent view of the **Burnt Mountain**, part of a twelve-kilometre-long (seven-mile), **east**-**west ridge** some 200 metres (656 feet) above the surrounding area.

During the day's heat the mountain is stark and uninviting, but in the early morning and late afternoon it presents a kaleidoscope of colour. The Karoo shales and limestone which formed the mountain were deposited some 200 million years ago.

Eighty million years later they underwent a wide-ranging metamorphosis giving the rocks their distinctive coloration.

Closer examination reveals an amazing number of shades ranging from red to orange, black, grey, white and purple.

Another fascinating feature of the area is a slag-like **heap of rock** and coarse-grained sand about one kilometre (half a mile) **east** of the Organ Pipes.

And then, ten-and-a-half kilometres (six-and-a-half miles) **north-west** along nearby route D3254, a **track east** leads half a kilometre to another natural marvel, the **Wondergat**, a deep **hole** created when a subterranean river swallowed a chunk of earth. On one side it is possible to scramble onto a ledge for a view into the seemingly bottomless pit. But take care.

Damaraland Wilderness Reserve

Elephant, **rhino**, **lion**, **hyena**, **jackal**, **Hartmann's zebra**, **gemsbok**, **springbok** and **ostrich** are all seen in the low-altitude 1,600-square kilometre (618-square mile) **Damaraland Wilderness Reserve** just east of Damaraland and west of Kamanjab in what is now the Kunene region.

Getting there

By charter flight to the airstrip or by safari concessionaire.

When to go

The reserve is open between March and December.

Where to stay

There is tented accommodation with toilets, bucket showers and dining tent.

North-Western Damaraland: The Unspoilt Wilderness

West of the Burnt Mountain, the **Doros Crater concession area** in the trackless wastes of **western Damaraland** may only be explored by a 4WD vehicle. The main attraction is the area's fascinating scenery and interesting geology, which includes the Doros Crater, the **Krone Canyon** and another **petrified forest**.

In north-western Damaraland, stones packed in circles near the **Gai-Ais fountain** provide evidence of an early settlement, while structures dating back to the German pioneers are also on view.

Getting there

Few trails lead through the awesome wilderness of central and north-western Damaraland where indiscriminate off-road driving has disturbed the sensitive plains. Visitors must now be accompanied by a guide. See Listings.

Palmwag Lodge

North-east of Khorixas, Palmwag Lodge is the base for adventure safaris into the Kaokoveld desert. The approach to the camp is through an animal disease checkpoint, the so-called 'Red Line'.

Getting there

An experienced guide and 4WD vehicle are needed to reach Palmwag.

Where to stay

Situated among shady fan palms alongside a perennial spring in the Uniab River, Palmwag is a delightful rest camp with comfortable three- and four-bed reed huts. There are two swimming pools and also a campsite.

Sightseeing

Among the area's many highlights is **Van Zylsgat**, a deep **pool** carved in the solid bedrock of the **Uniab River**. Even months after the summer rains, the water is up to six metres (twenty feet) deep and animals such as **giraffe, springbok, Hartmann's mountain zebra, gemsbok, kudu** and **steenbok** drink there.

Palmwag is also renowned for its **elephant** and **black rhino**, uniquely adapted to survival in an extremely arid environment.

Hobatere Game Park

North-east of Palmwag, bordering on the Etosha National Park, lies Hobatere Game Park.

Getting there

Kamanjab is 2,439 kilometres (1,516 miles) from Johannesburg, 1,961 kilometres (1,218 miles) from Cape Town, 950 kilometres (590 miles) from Keetmanshoop, 468 kilometres (291 miles) from Windhoek and 650 kilometres (404 miles) from Rundu.

From **Kamamjab** follow the C35 **road** to **Ruacana** for seventy kilometres (forty-three miles) where a **signpost** marks the **west turnoff** to **Hobatere Game Park**.

When to go

The area is open all year-round, but the heat of the high summer months is extremely harsh.

Where to stay

Hobatere Game Lodge, See Listings.

Sightseeing

One of five concession areas in Damaraland, Hobatere caters for upmarket visitors on photographic safaris, the emphasis being on personalised service.

There are **elephant, gemsbok, giraffe, kudu, springbok, black-faced impala, Hartmann's mountain zebra** and **lion** throughout the park.

West from the park the road crosses the **Hoanib River** on the **southern border** of **Kaokoland**. After another nine kilometres (six miles) it reaches **Warmquelle**, a settlement that derives its name from the **hot springs** there.

Turn off at the **signpost** to the **school** and follow the road for about half a kilometre (one-third of a mile) to the springs, surrounded by large, shady **fig trees**. The water is considerably cooler than other hot springs in the country.

Gardens

The **gardens** below the springs were laid out by Dr C A Schlettwein who bought the forty-square-kilometre (fifteen-square-mile) **Warmbad farm** at the turn of the century.

Schlettwein assumed that the colony would build its own harbour, as Walvis Bay was a British possession, and was convinced it would be in the north. His hopes were thwarted by World War I.

Before that, however, he set about cultivating vegetables, tobacco, maize, and lucerne for the German garrison at nearby **Sesfontein**. The cultivated area grew, gradually demanding better irrigation methods and, around 1910, an Italian named Oldani designed and built an **aqueduct**, the remains of which can still be seen.

After World War I, Warmquelle was acquired by the government to enlarge the reserve created for the Khoikhoi in exchange for a farm in the Kamanjab district.

Visitors may have a refreshing dip at the **Ongongo Waterfall**. From the aqueduct the falls are reached by following a **track** past the **school** for about three-and-a-half kilometres (two-and-a-quarter miles).

There, park the car and walk **upstream** for about 800 metres (half-a-mile). Alternatively, those in 4WD vehicles may cross the river to follow the track on the **western bank**. The surrounding area is in a concession controlled by **Desert Adventure Safaris**. See Listings.

Sesfontein

A few kilometres **north-west** of Warmquelle, the road reaches **Sesfontein** which owes its name to **six springs**. An historic German military barracks may be reached by taking the turnoff opposite the **primary school**.

After the rinderpest cattle plague in 1896, the German authorities established a number of control posts in the north, of which Sesfontein was the most westerly.

The road, built between Outjo and Sesfontein in 1901, made it possible to transport material there to build a military garrison. During 1905-6 it was converted into a **fort**, accommodating forty soldiers and twenty-five horses.

A five-hectare (twelve-and-a-half acre) **garden** was laid out where wheat and dates were cultivated. Some **palm trees** still flourish. The gardens were irrigated by an extensive system of furrows leading from a **spring** a few hundred metres **west** of the fort.

In 1909, Sesfontein ceased to be a military base but continued as a police post until it was abandoned in 1914. The fort fell into disrepair until 1987 when the local authority began a restoration project. Now it is a **museum** and **offices** for the local tribal leaders.

Kaokoland

Sesfontein is close to the southern borders of the 48,982 square kilometres (18,911 square miles) of what, until 1993, was Kaokoland, a mountainous tract of largely unspoilt wilderness and uniquely adapted wildlife now incorporated into Namibia's Kunene Region. It is also home to the Himba, a tribe little affected by civilisation.

In the entire region there are no more than 16,000 people, most of whom live in what was eastern Kaokoland.

The Himba number about 6,000 and their small settlements are fairly frequent.

The Himba's beehive huts are made from saplings, usually mopane, covered with a mixture of mud and cattle dung. Many settlements are deserted as these pastoral people wander continuously with their herds in search of grazing.

Visitors sometimes meet a family on the move. It is difficult to conceive that all their worldly possessions are wrapped in the animal skins carried with them.

The Himba women, their bodies covered in butterfat to which powdered oxides have been added to protect their skin from the harsh climate, are physically striking.

Married women are distinguished by their leather headdresses and other adornments, including necklaces, belts and wide copper bracelets. (See "The People: A Kaleidoscope of Colourful Cultures", Part One).

Visitors who want to photograph these people should offer sugar, maize meal and tobacco. Money has little value.

Central to the new northern region of Kunene is what was known as Ovamboland (now Owambo), home of the Wambo, a cultural group formed by eight distinct sub-groups, totalling well over 600,000.

These proud people are spread out over Namibia's vast north-west savannah. With its luxuriant vegetation, watered by many rivers and abundant rich rainfall, Owambo is a lush contrast to the stark aridity of the Namib and Kalahari deserts in the south. The land, where drought was unknown until recently, yields a rich harvest of maize, millet and other cereals, pumpkins and other vegetables, melons and other fruit.

Besides tilling the land and planting, the Wambo use traditional wicker nets to fish their rivers for barbel. Their extended, matrilineal families live in stockaded compounds in beehive-shaped mud and wood huts, with separate pens for livestock and grain stores under the same thatched roof. When Wambo society came into contact with the Europeans in the mid-nineteenth century their lifestyle was changed irrevocably and ancient rituals, centred around a sacred fire, were abandoned in favour of Christianity introduced by missionaries. But from time immemorial the Wambo believed in one God, the supreme creator.

The area, which includes what was Kaokoland and Ovamboland, has become increasingly popular with tourists eager to get off the beaten track. From the road map, which indicates a network of district roads, potential visitors may think that Kaokoland is easily travelled. Be warned, however, none are signposted and most are mere tracks, barely maintained and fit only for 4WD vehicles. Trips are undertaken to such places of interest as Ruacana Falls.

Getting there

Ruacana is 2,831 kilometres (1,759 miles) from Johannesburg, 2,353 kilometres (1,462 miles) from Cape Town, 1,342 kilometres (834 miles) from Keetmanshoop, 860 kilometres (534 miles) from Windhoek, 700 kilometres (434 miles) from Rundu, and 684 kilometres (425 miles) from Swakopmund.

There are three main routes to the area: the D3706 through Sesfontein; from the south along route C35 via Kamanjab and Opuwo; or from the north-east along the B1 and route C46 via Oshakati and Ruacana.

The Namibia Department of Transport topographical map shows most major tracks, springs and settlements, and it is vital in planning a trip to be sure you also carry enough fuel. Do not plan on covering a great distance in a day as progress is often slow. An average of twenty-five kilometres (fifteen miles) an hour is usual. Remember, too, that petrol is available only at Palmwag in the south, and Opuwo and Ruacana in the north-east.

When to go

Any time of the year

Where to stay

At Oshakati, International Guest House. See Listings for "Hotels".

Sightseeing

The administrative seat of Kaokoland, **Opuwo** is the only town in the entire region. There you can stock up with such necessities as cold drinks and fresh bread, obtainable from the **bakery** next to the **filling station**.

The **Hoarusib**, which comes down in flood at least once a year, starts its journey westwards from the **Otjihipa** and **Etorocha Mountains** in the northern highlands of **Kaokoland** in dramatic fashion, twisting through a **narrow gorge**. As it plunges down to the sea through a spectacular array of scenery, the river cuts through a **canyon** dominated by incredible castles of clay, known as **White Temples**.

Composed of yellow-white clay that crumbles at a touch, these eroded pinnacles, each with its own distinctive shape, were formed from the silt deposits of this once-mighty waterway. Perched high above the river banks, they are reminiscent of the ancient fortresses and palaces of the Middle East. One or two even suggest the pyramids of old Egypt.

Above: Mighty castles of clay formed from silt eroded through the centuries dominate the dramatic Hoarusib River valley.

Juxtaposed in front of the sheer wall of the canyon, they have a startling, almost supernatural quality. They are thought by geomorphologists to be the result of the damming of the river by the dunes within the last 100,000 years.

Little more than twenty years ago Kaokoland was a wildlife paradise. Sadly, large-scale poaching has decimated the area's elephant and black rhino populations. And now the future of the few elephant which still roam along the beds of the Hoanib and Hoarusib rivers is threatened by tourists.

Camps are often made at **springs** in the **river-beds**, denying the creatures water, often at the end of a long journey. The animals are then forced on to the next waterhole, perhaps thirty to forty kilometres (nineteen to twenty-five miles) away. Also, when elephants are sighted, many visitors attempt to get as close as possible to take photographs. Often the elephants have no way of escaping and experience severe stress and trauma.

Giraffe are frequently seen along the river courses, which also offer food and shelter to **kudu**, while **springbok**, **gemsbok** and **ostrich** inhabit the plains. The more mountainous areas sustain herds of **Hartmann's mountain zebra**.

During their epic journey from the Transvaal to Angola, between 1874 and 1881, the Dorsland Trekkers travelled through Kaokoland and settled for a short while at **Kaoko Otavi** and **Otjitunduwa**, also known as **Rusplaas** in central Kaokoland. The **ruins** of a two-roomed **house** built at the **Otjitunduwa fountain** were declared a **national monument** in 1951. Several **houses** and a **church** — since gone — were built at **Kaoko Otavi** but, after eighteen months, the trekkers moved further north.

At the eastern edge of Kaokoland and western Owambo, the **Kunene River** plunges over the **Ruacana Falls** in a foaming, crystal-white column of water. Some kilometres westward, as it races through the **Baines Mountain** along the Namibian-Angola **border**, it takes yet another leap towards the Atlantic over the **Epupa Falls** before cutting through the remote and little-visited **Otjihipa** and

Above: Source of life and abundance in the arid land of Namibia's north, the Kunene River is also a potent source of hydroelectric power upstream at Ruacana.

Hartmann Mountains into the ocean.

All along its course, lush riverine **forest** coats its banks with a cloak of verdure and its waters teem with the most aggressive **crocodiles** in Africa. But the great herds of wildlife — elephant, hippo, rhino and impala — which once roamed along its course were almost wiped out early this century.

Where the river's **estuary** empties into the Atlantic, the crocodile, a species which has endured through 130 million years, is joined by one of the marine world's oldest creatures, the **leather-backed turtle** which swarm there to breed.

Many species of fish, including the **fighting tiger fish**, **leather fish** and **springers**, flourish in the Kunene's fast-flowing waters which also sustain colonies of **freshwater shrimps**.

The power potential has not gone unacknowledged, however, and the waters have been harnessed by a **hydroelectric** **development** near Ruacana which provides half the entire country's energy needs.

Until recently the river's very existence was shrouded in myth and legend and doubted by western observers. C J Andersson noted in his 1856 book *Lake Ngami*: "Many years previously to our visit to the Ovambo, a French frigate discovered the embouchure of a magnificent river, known as the Cunene, between the seventeenth and eighteenth degrees of south latitude. Other vessels were sent out to explore it, and to ascertain its course, but, strange to say, they searched in vain for it!"

Ruacana, a strategic town on the Angolan border, today shows signs of stress and trauma as this pleasant place was a linchpin in the freedom struggle and continued to suffer in 1993 from Angola's ongoing civil war.

Visitors find out how sensitive the area is when taking innocent photographs. It is best to check with officialdom beforehand.

Opposite: Early-morning light bathes sparsely vegetated sand dunes on the banks of the Kunene River.

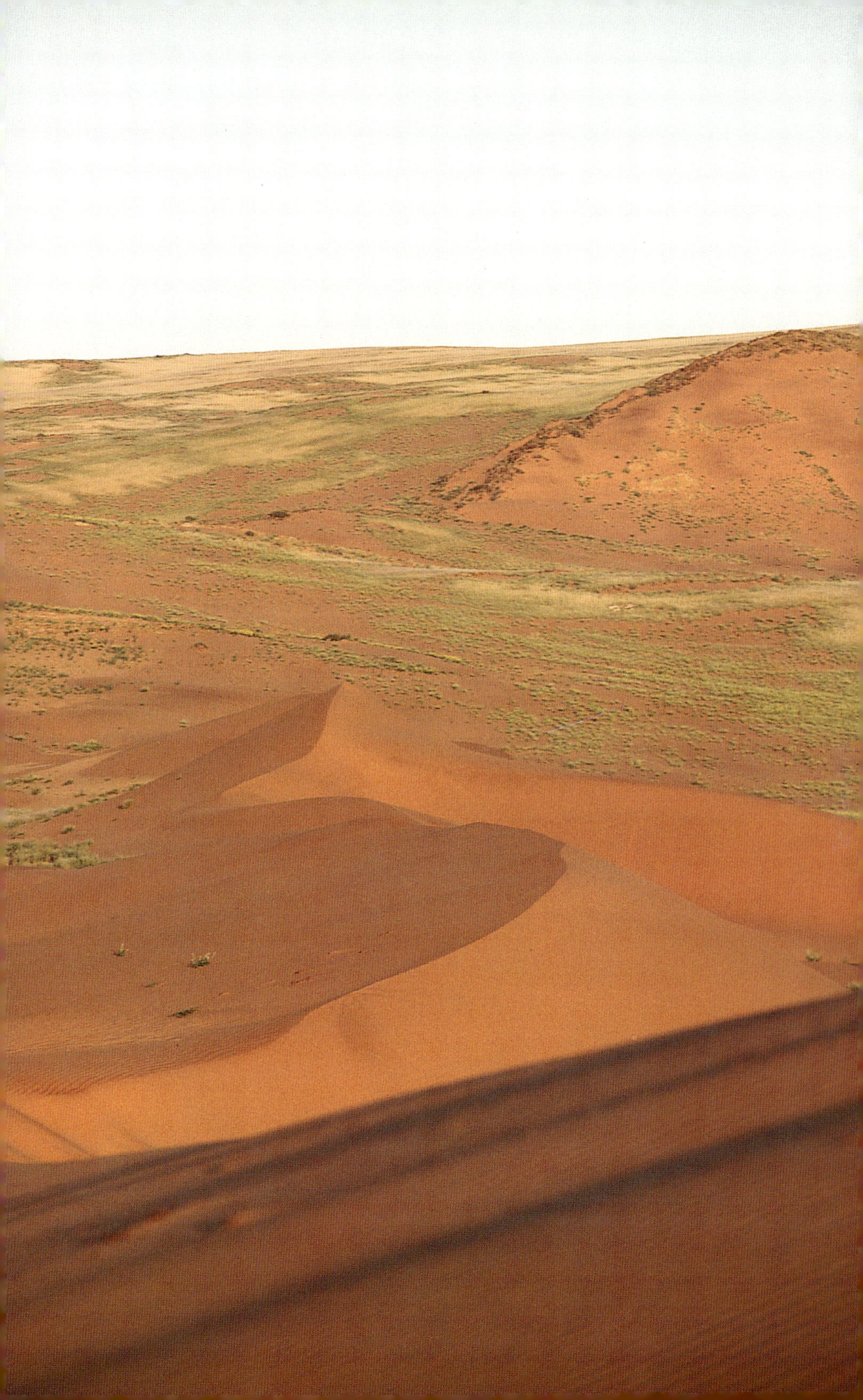

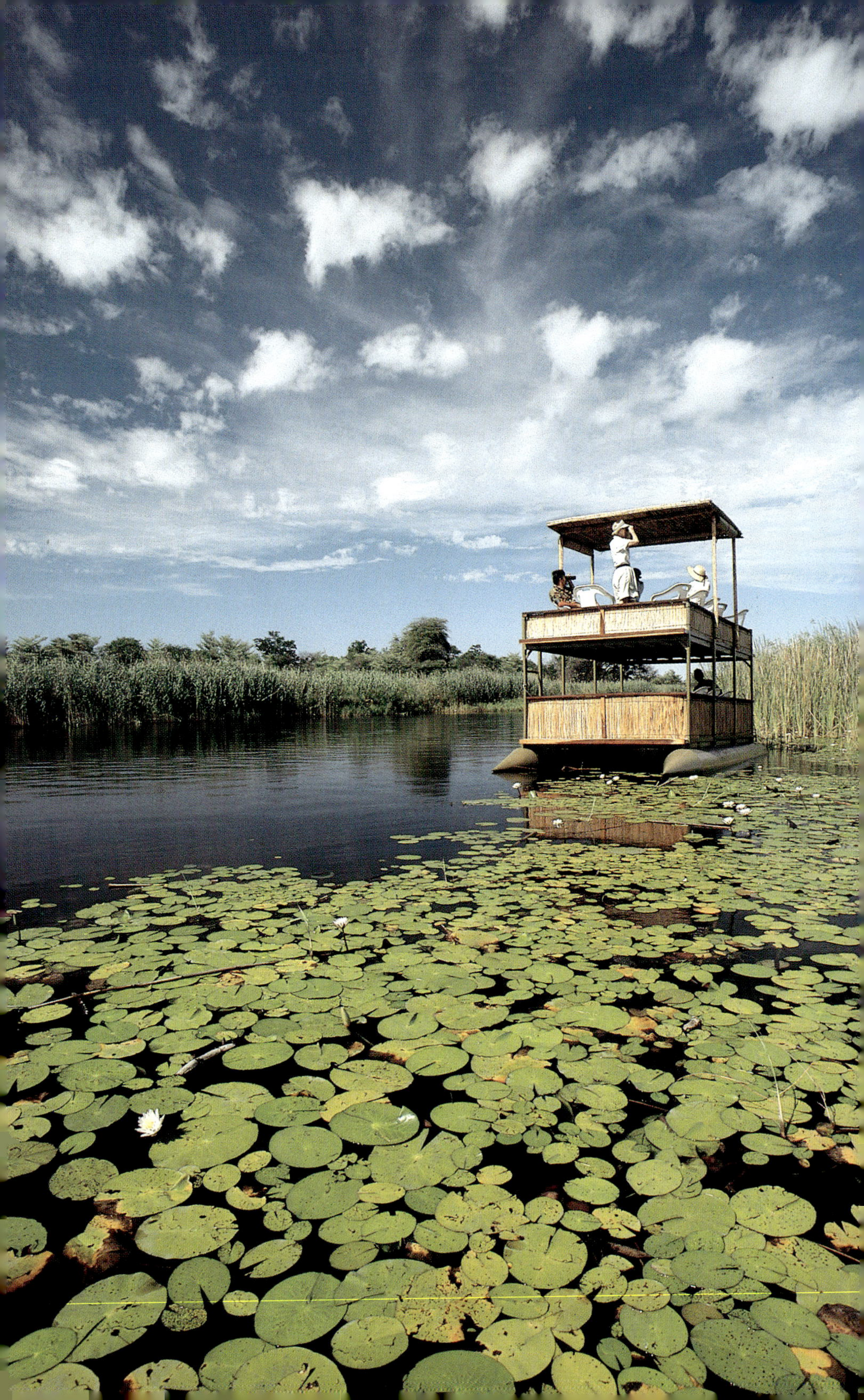

Wildlife Edens: Etosha National Park, Land of Dry Water

Covering 22,270 square kilometres (8,600 square miles), Etosha National Park ranges from dense bush to large open plains where herds of animals roam as free as they did in the days when the world was new. Conservationists regard it as one of the greatest and most important game parks in the world.

As a game park, Etosha excels during the dry season when huge herds of animals can be seen amid some of the most photogenic scenery on the continent. During that time, as the small bush pools dry up and the grass grows sere, the game moves closer to the springs at its edge.

Before it was fenced, the animals migrated between Etosha and Kaokoland, but now they are forced to stay within the park. Hence, the months between August and late October are ideal for game viewing.

At its heart is the Etosha Pan — a gigantic 6,133-square kilometre (2,368-square mile) shallow depression. In exceptionally rainy periods it fills with water, usually no more than a metre (three feet) deep. Perennial springs on its verges attract concentrations of birds and game.

The origins of the pan are not known, but geologists believe that millions of years ago it was an inland lake, about the size of Holland, fed by a mighty river. During the physical uplifting of southern Africa the river changed course, the lake dried up and shrank to its present size and, because of its massive salt deposits, became a highly saline, desert plain.

The first recorded descriptions of Etosha were made by travellers Sir Francis Galton and Charles Andersson, who camped at Namutoni in 1851. The latter described the pan as 'covered with saline encrustations, and having wooded and well-defined borders. The surface consisted of a soft, greenish-yellow, clay soil, strewed with fragments of small sand-stone, of a purple tint.'

The abundance of game attracted hunters and traders and, following the outbreak of rinderpest in 1886 — which resulted in the extermination of large numbers of animals, steps had to be taken towards their protection. Hunting regulations were promulgated as early as 1892.

Although Etosha is Namibia's oldest national park, its boundaries have been constantly reshuffled since its establishment. In 1907, three game reserves were created by the German Governor of South West Africa, Friedrich von Lindequist, of which Etosha formed part of the 93,240 square kilometres (36,000 square miles) of Game Reserve Two, comprising the Etosha Pan and the Kaokoveld from the Kunene River in the north to the Hoarusib River in the south. In 1947 the Kaokoveld portion was given to the Herero, while Etosha was reduced by 3,406 square kilometres (1,315 square miles), the excised land being divided into farms — an area known today as the Gagarus block.

Following the recommendations of the Elephant Commission of 1956, however, its size almost doubled to nearly 100,000 square kilometres (38,610 square miles) while Game Reserve One, north-east of Grootfontein, was abandoned. Instead, the park was extended westwards by adding unoccupied state land between the Hoanib and Ugab rivers.

Six years later, the Odendaal Commission brought about a drastic reduction in size. No consideration was given to ecological boundaries or traditional game migration routes, and game reserves had to be created elsewhere for the relocation of scarce and endangered species. At the same time three farms near

Opposite: Game viewing from a pontoon on one of the many delightful, hidden waterways of the Caprivi Strip — at Lianshulu where the Okavango flows across the border into the Okavango Delta of Botswana.

Etosha National Park

Above: Lion takes the sun at an Etosha waterhole.

Otjovasandu, the bergveld in the west and the sandveld north of Namutoni, were added.

Today the park, although little more than a quarter of its original size, remains one of the world's most impressive game sancturies.

During the boundary changes a control post was established at Okaukuejo — one of four designed to combat the spread of foot-and-mouth disease and contain illegal hunting and gun-running on the north. The others were at Sesfontein, Namutoni and Karakuwisa.

Although Okaukuejo Fort, built in 1901, has long since disappeared, the post still serves as the administrative headquarters of the park and is also the centre of the Etosha Ecological Institute, founded in 1974 to conduct research on various aspects of Etosha's ecology.

Getting there

Namutoni, 533 kilometres (330 miles) from Windhoek, 659 kilometres (409 miles) from Swakopmund, 691 kilometres (429 miles) from Walvis Bay, 1,015 kilometres (630 miles) from Keetmanshoop, 1,349 kilometres (838 miles) from Lüderitz, 2,026 kilometres (1,259 miles) from Cape Town and 2,504 kilometres (1,556 miles) from Johannesburg, is serviced by road and air.

When to go

Etosha is open all year-round. Between August and late October is best for game viewing.

Where to stay

Mokuti Lodge (3-star) is situated on the eastern border of the park beside the von Lindequist Gate. Luxury chalets have double beds, a lounge area and mini-bar. The main building has conference facilities, two restaurants and an open-air swimming pool. There are hotels at Outjo, Otavi and Tsumeb. See Listings for "Hotels". There is accommodation in Namutoni Fort and a campsite, and guesthouses and campsites at Okaukuejo and Halali, on Etosha's southern boundary. See Listings.

Sightseeing

Known variously as the 'Place of Mirages',

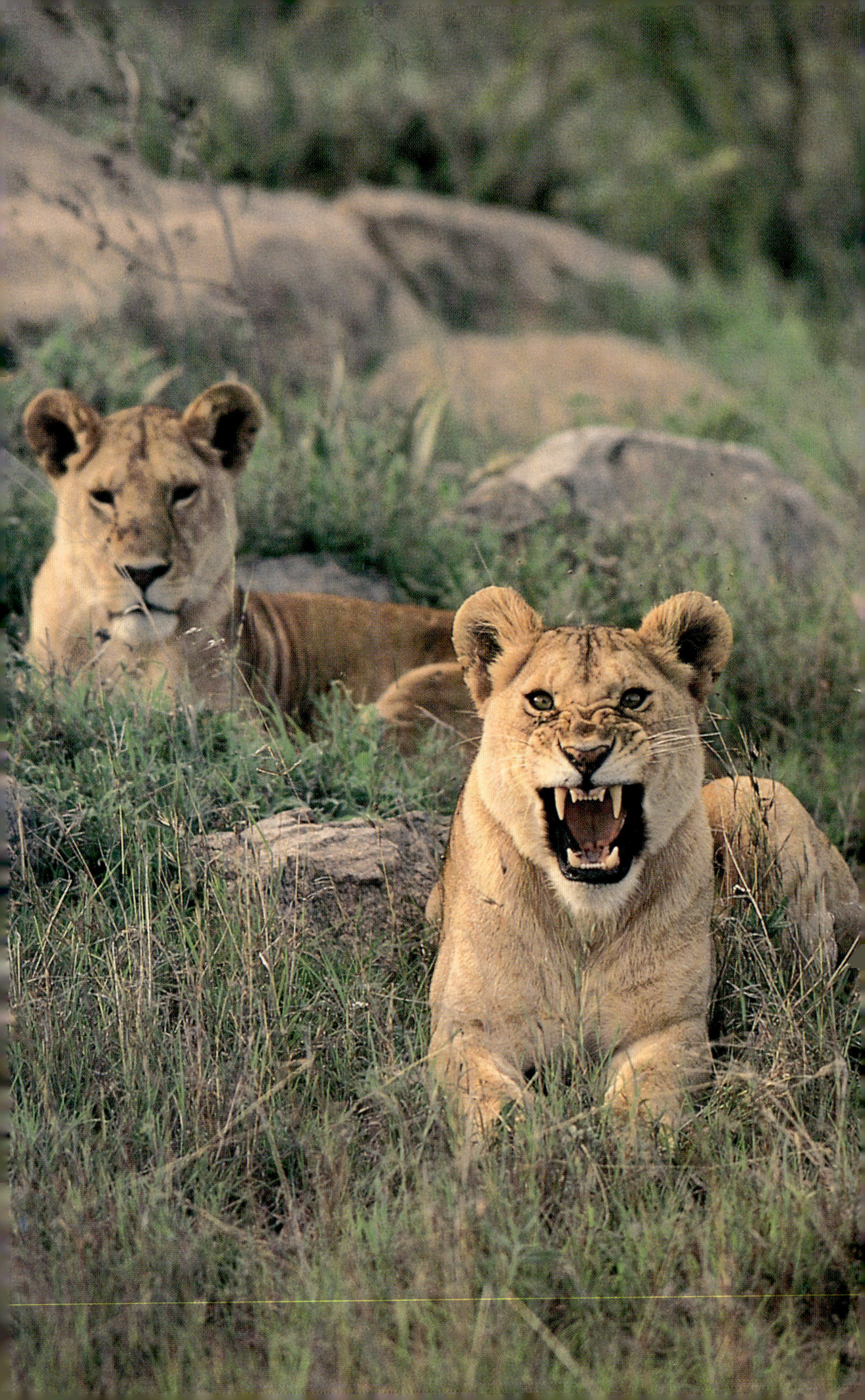

Above: Lion pride sleeps out the midday heat in Etosha.
Opposite: Lioness and adolescent cub in Etosha National Park.

'Land of Dry Water' and the 'Great White Place', **Etosha** is an apparently endless pan of silvery-white sand where dust devils play and mirages blur the horizon. All the **roads** are motorable although they are never really busy compared with those of other crowded parks in the rest of Africa.

In January it is hot and fairly damp, with an average temperature of around 27°C (80.5°F) and heavy cloud cover. This gradually disperses until the rains cease, around April. During this time, the plants are bright and green and the park loses some of its stark beauty.

From May to July it becomes cooler and dries out. Some winter nights are quite chilly. After August, however, the flora shrivels as the heat builds up towards the coming of the rains in November — when again the skies cloud over.

During and after the rains the game disperses and moves away from the waterholes to surface water elsewhere in the park.

Stretching 120 kilometres (seventy-five miles) at its longest and a maximum of fifty-five kilometres (thirty-five miles) from **north** to **south**, the Etosha **salt pan** covers almost a quarter of the park.

It is seasonally inundated with water from the **Ekuma** and **Oshigambo Rivers** to the **north** — the extent of the flooding being determined by the summer rainfall in its catchment area — but most animals are unable to drink the water as the salt content is often double that of seawater.

They are attracted to the **waterholes** at the edge of the pan which are fed by subterranean **springs** and supplemented annually with rainwater.

Broadly speaking, the vegetation of the park may be classified into two subtypes, namely **tree savannah** in the **east** and **shrub** and **thorn-tree savannah** in the **west**.

Several *Acacia* species such as the **water thorn**, **red umbrella thorn**, **umbrella thorn**, and **hairy umbrella thorn**, as well as **mopane**, and a number of *Combretum* species, varying from shrubs to trees, characterise much of Etosha. And most of the grasses are *Anthephora*, *Enneapogon*, *Aristida* and *Stipagrostis*.

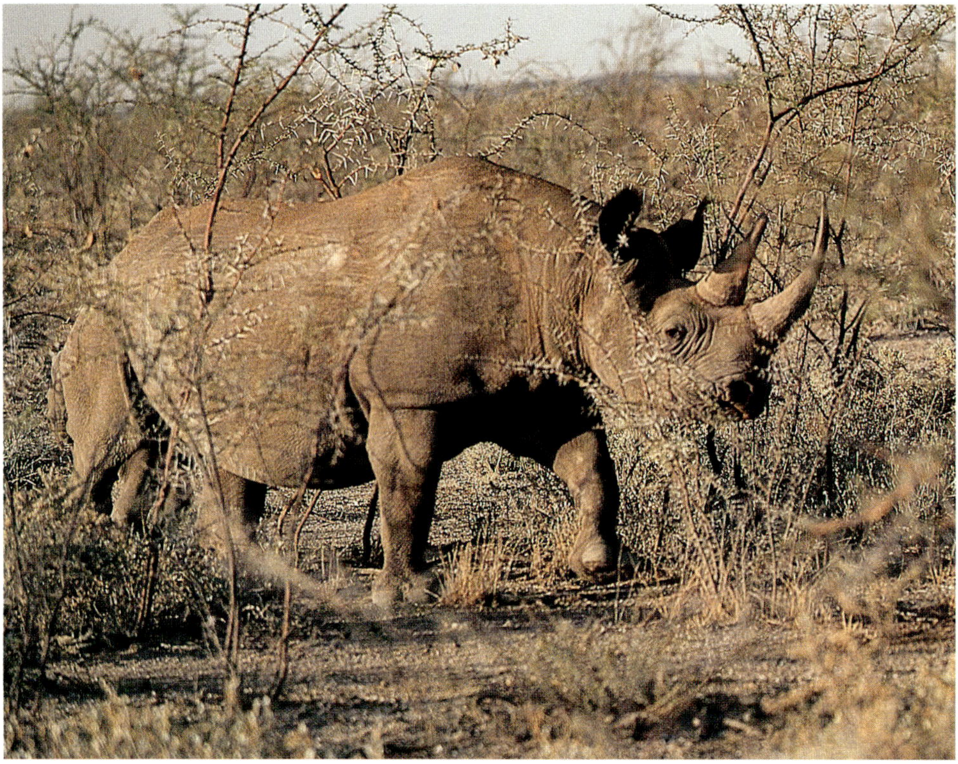

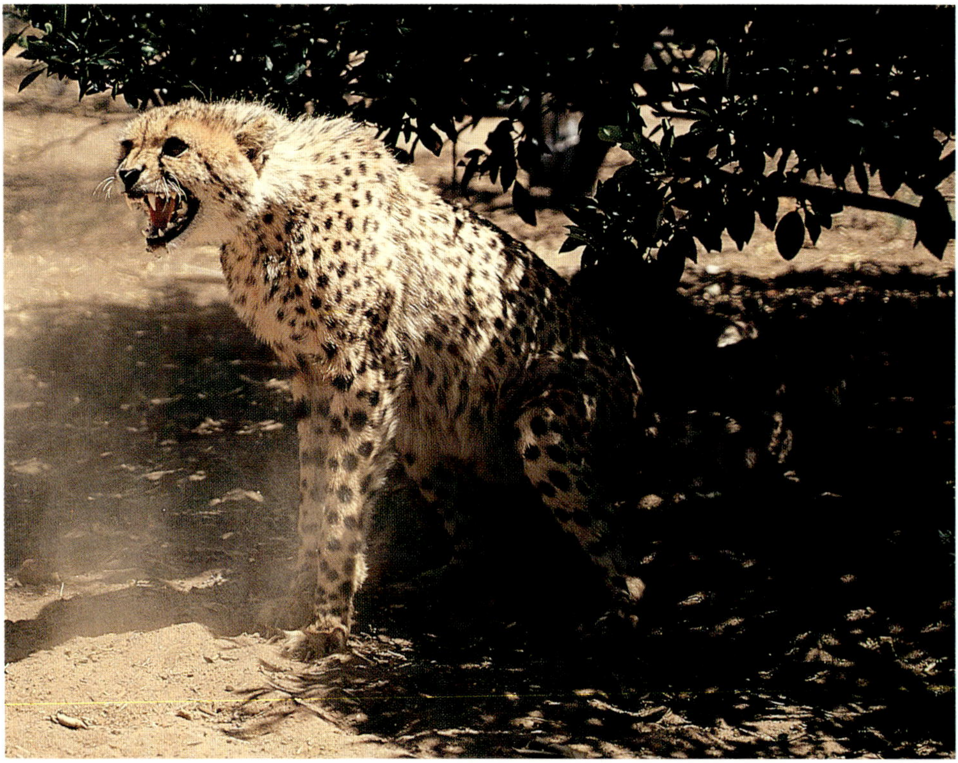

Above: Kudu seeking shelter in scattered bushland.

Opposite top: Etosha is the last remaining stronghold of the black rhino with more than ten per cent of the world's surviving creatures.

Opposite: Namibia and Botswana in southern Africa share places with Tanzania and Kenya in eastern Africa as the last refuge of cheetah — the world's fastest land animal.

Haunted forest

A species arousing the curiosity of visitors is *Moringa ovalifolia*, sometimes referred to as the **phantom tree**, found in the **Haunted Forest**, *Spokieswoud*, thirty kilometres (nineteen miles) west of **Okaukuejo**.

These trees usually grow on hills, yet there are about 900 in the Haunted Forest. (See "Flora: The Great Survivors", Part Four). The ends of their branches are enjoyed by Etosha's **elephant, gemsbok** and **giraffe**. The waterholes in this area had to be sealed many years ago to prevent elephants from destroying the forest.

Etosha's animals are typical of those found in the southern savannah plains of Africa. Five rare or endangered species, the **black** (hook-lipped) **rhinoceros, black-faced impala, Hartmann's mountain zebra, Roan antelope** and the diminutive **Damara dik-dik** live in this habitat. (See "Wildlife: Just Out of This World", Part Four).

Burchell's or plains **zebra, springbok, gemsbok** and **elephant** roam the reserve in abundance, while **kudu**, **blue wildebeest** and **giraffe** are fairly common. **Red hartebeest**, **eland**, and **steenbok** are found in smaller numbers.

Etosha's carnivores include **lion**, **cheetah**, **leopard**, **spotted** and **brown hyena**. **Black-backed jackal** are frequently seen during the late afternoons and early mornings.

The distribution of animals is related largely to the availability of food and water. Some species, however, prefer certain areas. For example, large numbers of kudu are frequently found in the Namutoni area, while common **duiker** remain in the grassland and shrub cover **north**. The Namutoni area is also one of the best places to spot **Damara dik-dik**, and **red hartebeest** favour it between midnight and dawn.

At Okaukuejo

Visitors unfamiliar with animal spoor may walk past the entrance of the **Etosha Ecological Institute** where the **cement walkway** has been decorated with the

Above: Giraffe seek afternoon revival at an Etosha waterhole.

Opposite top: Seasonal rains bring a rare flush of green grass to Etosha's withered wilderness — and mudholes where young elephant enjoy a frolic.

Opposite: Game-watching tourists study herd of zebra at Etosha.

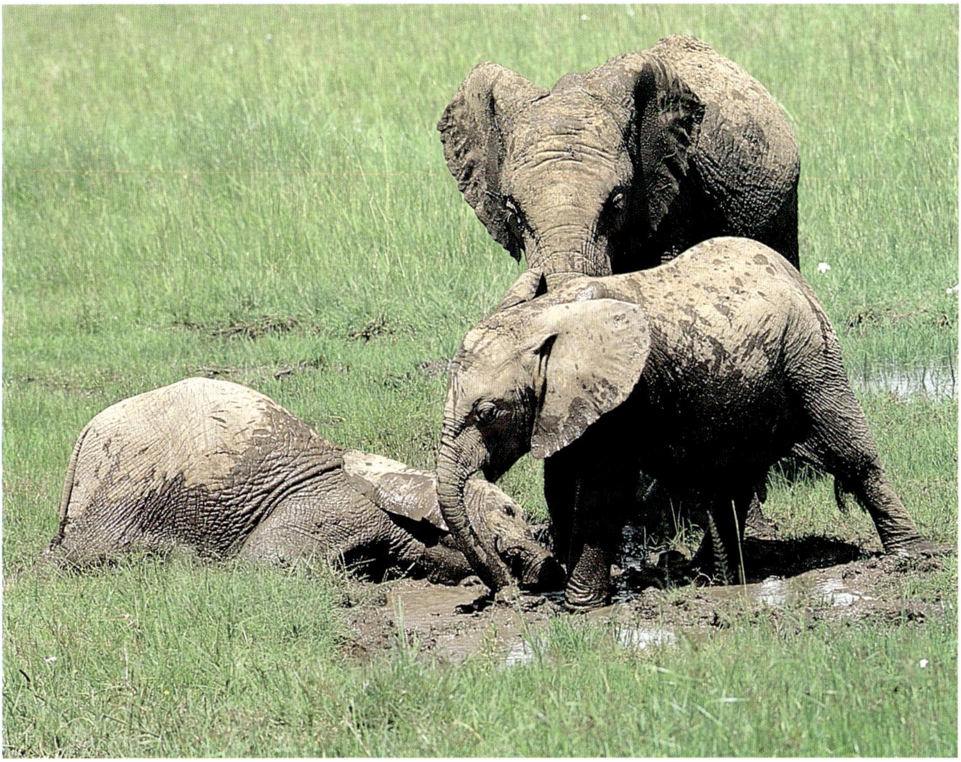

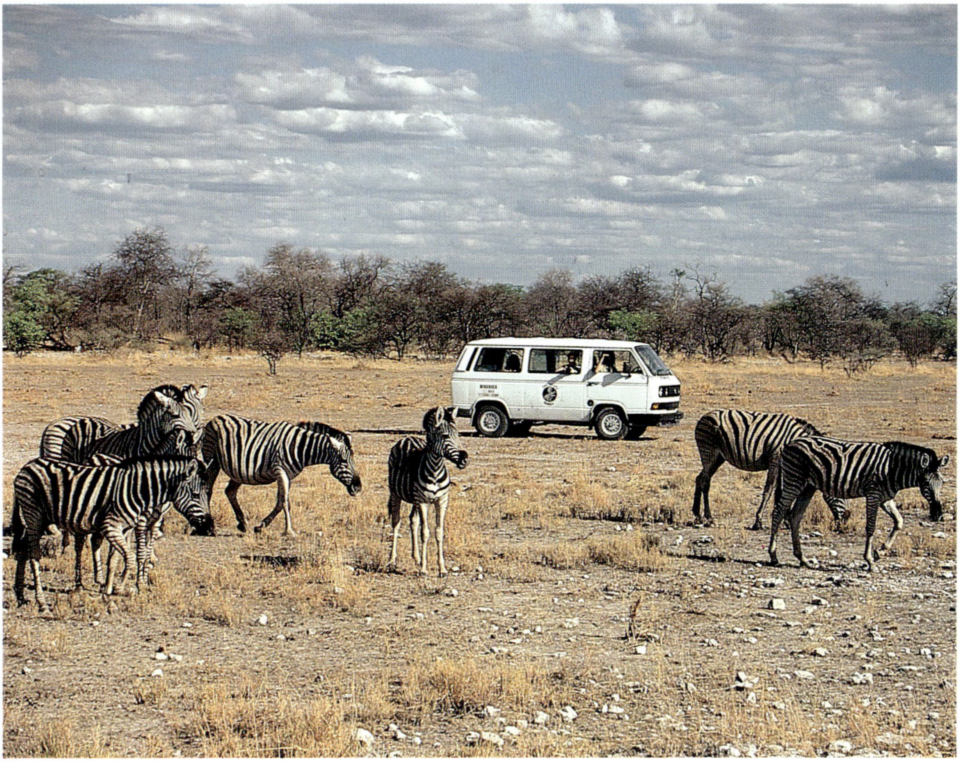

Top: Bird nests cover dead tree at an Etosha waterhole.

Above: Castle of clay — termite hill in the arid wastes of Namibia's Kalahari Desert.

footprints of various animals. While the institute is not open to the general public, visitors are welcome at the **information centre** next to the **post office**, and at the **tourist centre**.

Etosha's most popular **rest camp** is at Okaukuejo where the nearby waterhole is floodlit at night, giving visitors the opportunity to watch animals not often seen during the day.

It is perfectly placed for exploring the **northern part** of the great Namibian plateau: a distinctive area, quite different in character from the rest of the country.

For the most part it comprises a great alluvial plain created by the **Okavango** and other rivers which flow southwards from Angola to feed the wetlands of northern Botswana and the huge shallow known as the Etosha Pan.

Etosha's **western area** is one of the few places in Namibia where both **Burchell's zebra** and **Hartmann's mountain zebra** live together — the latter preferring the mountainous area around **Otjovasandu**. Another species frequently seen roaming the west is **eland**, while **gemsbok**, although seen throughout the park, also show a preference for this drier territory.

Blue wildebeest, Burchell's zebra and **springbok** follow annual migration routes in search of grazing and rainwater and, after the first good summer rains, large herds congregate on the plains north and west of Okaukuejo, where they remain until about April.

As the water diminishes and the grazing decreases, the animals move closer to the waterholes near Okaukuejo before adjourning to the **Gemsbokvlakte plains** to the **east**. This cycle is completed when the animals return to the plains **north** and **west** of Okaukuejo a few days after the first heavy rains of the following wet season.

One million flamingos

More than 320 bird species have been recorded in Etosha National Park, probably the most important breeding area in the southern African population for lesser and greater flamingo. The largest numbers of birds may be seen between October and April when the summer migrants are present. The variety of species and their numbers, however, depends on the extent of flooding.

During exceptional rains, up to a million **flamingos** congregate on the pans, but nature is not always so bountiful. When the pan dried up earlier than usual in June 1969, the lack of water forced the adult birds to depart, leaving the chicks to perish.

In the ensuing weeks 20,000 chicks were caught and released at Fischer's Pan near Namutoni. But when the pan dried up again two years later, an estimated 30,000 young birds marched thirty kilometres (nineteen miles) **north-west** to the nearest water at **Poacher's Point.**

They were fed, en route, by the adult birds flying to and from the water. Then, in August, the chicks set out on the second leg of their trek to the **Ekuma River Delta.** During the early stages of their march, their parents continued feeding them by making a round trip of 100 kilometres (sixty miles). At the end of the month most of the chicks reached the safety of the Ekuma River.

Another fascinating aspect of these birds is their ability to conserve energy. The secret lies in their diet of nutritious, energy-rich algae which absorb energy directly from the sun.

In addition, when flying at night, the cooler, denser air gives greater impetus to their wing thrusts, reducing energy expenditure. A flock of flamingos has been known to fly from Etosha to Walvis Bay — a journey of about 500 kilometres (310 miles) — between sundown and sun-up.

Among the rarer bird species seen at Etosha are **Wahlberg's eagle, Montagu's harrier, gymnogene, Klaas's cuckoo, greyhooded kingfisher** and **white-bellied sunbird**.

Halfway between Okaukuejo and Namutoni is the **Halali rest camp**. The word 'halali' is of German origin and is derived from a single call traditionally sounded on horns by foresters to mark the end of a successful hunt.

Lengthening shadows

When the sun sets over **Namutoni**, and the gates of the world's most romantic **fortress** slam shut, visitors may stand on the

Above: Okakuejo watchtower inside the splendour of Etosha National Park.

ramparts and watch the flat plains disappear into the horizon as the lengthening shadows move over Etosha's grazing **wildebeest**. At such a time it seems as if all the ghosts of Namutoni's past hover about its **battlements** and **walls**.

The fort represents everything historical about northern Namibia. The Wambo built their first kraal near the swampy watering place they called *Omutjamatunda*. Its limestone basin is fed by a spring and birdlife abounded, just as it does today, in the surrounding reeds.

The Swiss botanist, Hans Schinz, named the spot 'Amutoni' soon after the country came under German rule in 1884. It only became known to outsiders after the rinderpest outbreak in 1886 when a cordon hundreds of kilometres long was thrown across the northern territory to protect cattle

Above: Hyena cubs warn off potential intruders to their Etosha den.

against the plague. Thus, Namutoni became a control post.

Sheltered only by reed huts, a garrison of five lived, worked, drank and played cards there. They had to wait until the end of 1903 before the fort was finished. Situated close to the spring, it was a small, rectangular structure, measuring ten metres (thirty-two feet) by twenty-four metres (seventy-eight feet), with six rooms, fortified walls, and two towers.

On 28 January 1904, it was attacked by 500 Wambo. At the time one of the five soldiers was ill with malaria. It was left to the other four, later joined by three ex-servicemen, to defend themselves and the fort. They held on until the Wambo retreated late in the afternoon. Under cover of darkness the Germans managed to escape. Next morning, when the Wambo discovered the fort was empty, they completely destroyed it.

Following the Herero Uprising of 1904, the administration decided to rebuild Namutoni Fort in an asymmetrical quadrangle, approximately sixty metres (197 feet) by sixty-eight metres (223 feet), with a large **watchtower** at the **north-eastern corner**.

It was no easy task. The bricks — 2,000 a day — had to be made on site; but once it was completed Namutoni and its surroundings officially became a district. In February 1906, the garrison commander found himself looking after an area about the size of Ireland.

Game reserve

In 1907, Kaokoland and Etosha were proclaimed a game reserve and the station commander, a Lieutenant Fischer, who loved the area, became the first game warden, studying the animals and plants. After the tribal wars ended, however, Namutoni lost its strategic and administrative status and was closed.

At the outbreak of World War I, a brigade of South African troops was detailed to seal off the north-eastern escape route of German troops. They travelled across Okaukuejo and Rietfontein, and 190 German officers and troops surrendered to them at Namutoni without a single shot being fired.

Kavango and the Caprivi Strip: Where Four Nations Meet

By the time visitors begrudgingly leave Namibia they have been in nearly every environment known to man, have wandered through landscapes they may never have dreamed existed and are left with a treasure trove of experiences and images to take home.

Namibia is full of surprises, a land of contrast where complete opposites meet and co-exist, harmonising and creating unique environments which send the blood pumping through the veins.

Such a place is the Caprivi Strip — a slender finger on Namibia's north-eastern hand, extending between Angola, Zambia, Zimbabwe and Botswana.

Driving from the Etosha National Park, the rugged Waterberg Plateau or the Namib Desert, with images of the dune sea still firmly fixed in mind, few visitors expect to enter such a massive area of lush greenery — kilometre after kilometre of verdant, grassy and sylvan landscape fed by the magnificent Okavango, mighty Zambezi, Kwando and Chobe rivers and other lesser tributaries.

Of these, Africa's fourth-largest and least-spoilt river, the Zambezi, rises on the slopes of a small, remote and little-known hill just over 300 kilometres (186 miles) from the source of the Zaire (Congo) River in the Mwinilunga District of north-western Zambia, where the Zaire border meets Zambia and the easternmost boundary of Angola.

Although the two rivers originate so close together, they soon travel their separate ways; the Zaire flowing north and then west, the Zambezi flowing south and then east. Indeed, almost as soon as this nascent, sunbright stream leaps and bounds down the hill, it enters Angola and flows there for 300 kilometres (186 miles).

From Angola, the river continues its cross-country wanderings, re-entering Zambia at Angola's Capripande border

Above: Distinctive bird of the African plains, a kori bustard.

Overleaf: Sundown over Etosha National Park.

In the following years the fort was used by the South African police, but its condition continued to deteriorate. A campaign was launched to restore the building after one of its towers was destroyed by lightning in 1938. Twelve years later it was declared a **national monument** and, in 1951, the South West African Administration made funds available for its full restoration. It opened its gates officially for tourism in 1958 and, in 1983, more renovations were made.

Built for war, but preserved for peace, Namutoni gives visitors a glimpse of romance and fantasy. It flies its flag of hospitality for guests from around the world who come to revel in the magic of nature and leave captivated by the magic of history.

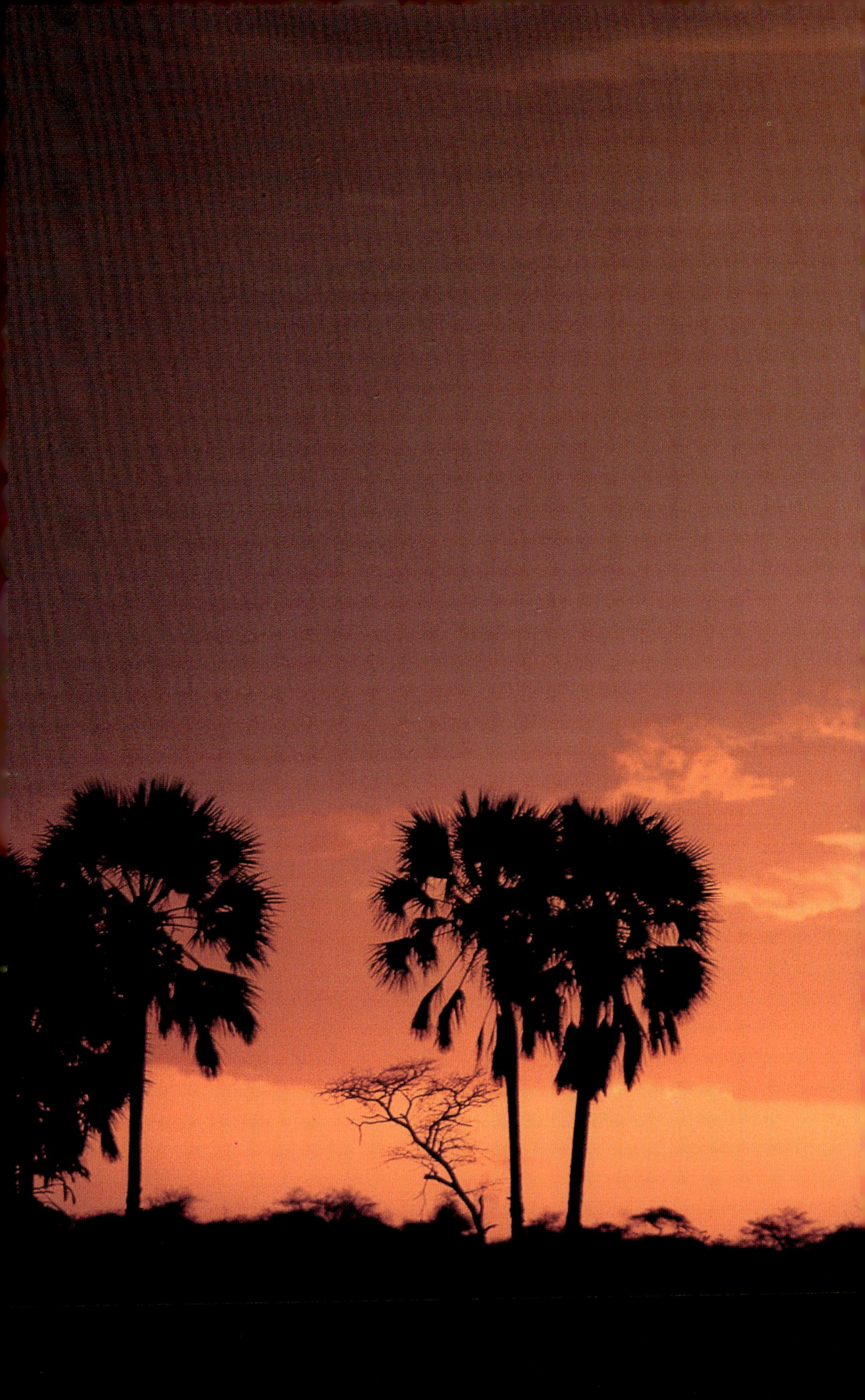

post, then raging downstream over the Chovuma Falls and through the rapids of the Nyamboma Gorge before slowing down to meander across the Luena Flats, on past Senange to Kazungula. There, where rich riverine forests spring to life along its banks, it enters the Caprivi Strip.

Meanwhile, sweeping 400 kilometres (248 miles) down the Angolan border from the north, the Okavango River, which rises in Angola's central highlands and comes into spate in February and March spilling onto the floodplain, flows east to meet its desert destiny in the inland delta of Botswana's Okavango Swamp.

And where Namibia's broad Kavango plains reach into the Caprivi Strip along the Zambian border to the banks of the legendary Zambezi River, the Zambezi and Okavango touch them with the gift of life.

The 110,000 people of the Kavango tribe, Namibia's second-largest, which takes its name from the river, represent one-tenth of Namibia's population.

During Angola's long-running civil war many southern Angolan tribes crossed the river to add to their numbers. By far the greatest proportion of the Kavango's people live in this narrow belt and, once the water has subsided, they are able to cultivate sorghum, millet and maize on the fertile ground.

Not surprisingly, fish is the staple of those Kavango who live on the Okavango's southern banks, along which fisherwomen set their conical wicker traps. Their menfolk simply harpoon the fish from their dugout canoes, *watu*, driven forward by the paddle of a single oarsman.

The tribe, which is matrilineal, tracing its ancestry through female descendants just like their Wambo neighbours, is also renowned for its attractive wood carvings seen by the road.

The Kavango capital of Rundu, welcome outpost in a remote and isolated land, stands above the fertile floodplains on the south bank of the river, 250 kilometres (156 miles) north-east of Grootfontein. The town is on the main access route (the B8) to the Caprivi Strip and the Mahango Game Reserve, Caprivi Game Reserve, Mudumu National Park, Mamili National Park and Lake Liambesi inside the Strip and Kaudom Game Reserve outside it.

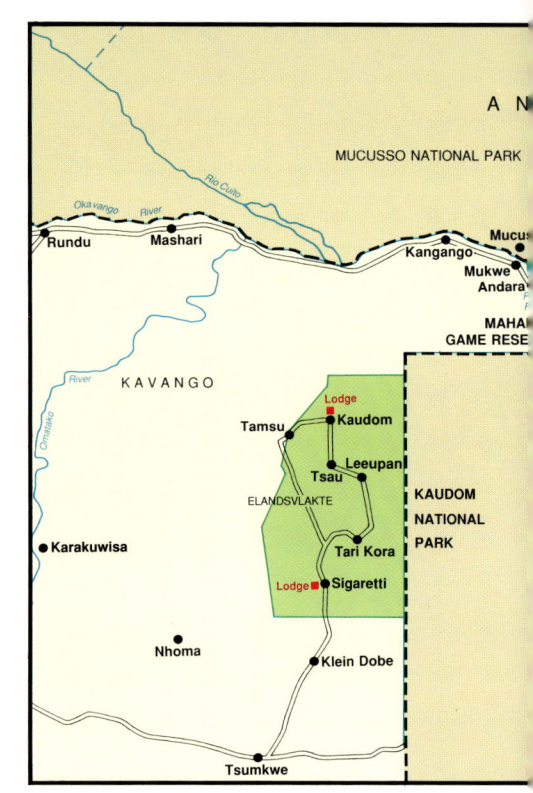

Getting there

Rundu is 308 kilometres (191 miles) from Tsumeb, 661 kilometres (411 miles) from Katima Mulilo, 700 kilometres (435 miles) from Windhoek, 826 kilometres (513 miles) from Swakopmund, 1,182 kilometres (734 miles) from Keetmanshoop, 2,133 kilometres (1,325 miles) from Cape Town, and 2,671 kilometres (1,660 miles) from Johannesburg, and is served by road and air links.

When to go

Year-round, but best between the end of April and early December.

Where to stay

Sarasunga Lodge. See Listings for "Hotels". Kaisosi Safari Lodge (1-star) and Mayana Camp, both outside the town. See Listings. There is also a municipal rest camp with campsites and caravan park. See Listings.

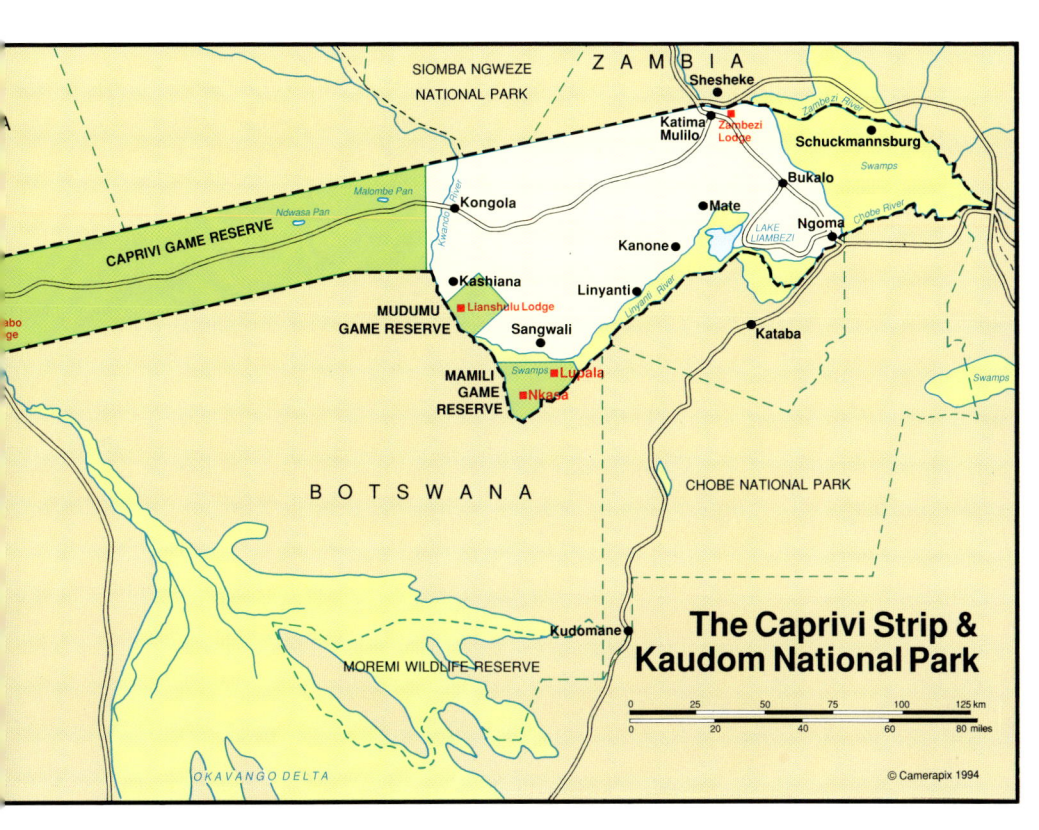

At Tsumeb, Hotel Eckleben (2-star) and Minen Hotel (2-star).

Sightseeing

Rundu, a pleasant, attractive town which swiftly recovered from the trauma of the long, drawn-out freedom struggle, is the capital of the Kavango people and the new region of Okavango, which was delineated in 1993. Its streets are filled with ever-smiling Kavango tribesfolk — fishermen, pastoralists and farmers all. (See "The People: A Kaleidoscope of Colourful Cultures", Part One).

There are local administration **offices**, a fine **hospital**, **abbatoir**, **post office**, two **filling stations**, splendid **supermarket**, and **bars**. The frontage on the **banks** of the **Okavango** is also a pleasant place to watch the local **fishermen** in their **dugout canoes** and witness the impressive sunsets and sunrises.

The surrounding countryside is lush and green and burgeons with rich **crops** of **cereals**, **groundnuts**, **citrus fruit**, **melons** and **cotton**. All along the **B8** to the **Caprivi Strip**, the sides are lined with **stalls** offering **produce** and **handicrafts** for sale to passing motorists.

Into the Caprivi Strip

During the 175 kilometres (108 miles) from Rundu to Andara, where the Caprivi Strip begins, the B8 road hugs the banks of the Okavango River. Andara is the western gateway into the curious 500-kilometre (311-mile) long, fifty-kilometre (thirty-one-mile) wide panhandle of the Caprivi Strip which opens out across sixty-four kilometres (forty miles) at its eastern end and covers 11,520 square kilometres (4,448 square miles).

There, Namibia, Botswana, Zambia and Zimbabwe meet in a permanent reminder of Africa's European legacy.

It was the start of the final decade of the nineteenth century when the Caprivi Strip was first drawn on the map at the Berlin conference of the European super powers which divided Africa's ancient nation states between them.

On 1 July 1890, Britain traded Heligoland and the Caprivi panhandle for Zanzibar and parts of Bechuanaland, now Botswana. The Caprivi Strip was named after the German Chancellor, General Count Georg Leo von Caprivi di Caprara di Montecuccoli.

Almost quarter of a century later, at the very outbreak of the Great War, it was back in British hands — the first German territory to fall. The German governor had been taking tea with a senior British official from Rhodesia, now Zimbabwe, when the Briton was handed a note to say that war had begun.

At once, he placed the German under arrest and annexed the Strip.

At the end of the war it was incorporated into Bechuanaland but at the onset of the Second World War South Africa assumed control.

From 1960, SWAPO established strategic guerilla strongholds in the Strip and it became a key battleground in the freedom fight against South Africa. (See "Land of Lost Horizons", Part One).

Now all is peaceful and the two main cultures — the Subiya and the Mafwe, who share many similarities with the Kavango — survive unchanged in an area whose remoteness has served as barrier to modern influences.

The citizens of East Caprivi are also closely related to neighbouring communities in Zambia, Zimbabwe, Angola and Botswana. As well as common tribal customs and traditions, many also speak the same language. Hunting, fishing, herding cattle and tending crops such as cassava, maize and cereals are central to the Caprivian economy. In the east, the Zambezi's seasonal floods often displace villagers for several months but deposit a rich loamy silt on these marshlands.

The eastern sector near the Zambezi is the most heavily populated area with more than 40,000 people. Many live in and around the regional capital of Katima Mulilo on the banks of the Zambezi River, in small villages of mud-and-wood thatched huts, in a culture which has changed little in hundreds of years.

Long before the Strip came into existence the area was home to a multiplicity of warring cultures. The Subiya, who occupied the land in the east between the Chobe and Zambezi rivers, dominated the region 400 years ago. At the end of the seventeenth century, Sundano, the Subiyan ruler, set out to enlarge his kingdom. He seized large parts of what is now southern Zambia and founded the ruling dynasty which continues to this day.

The Yezi clan, which broke away from their Botswana kin to settle in the Strip, also wielded considerable influence during the eighteenth and early nineteenth centuries. The Scottish explorer and missionary Dr David Livingstone records that in 1849 they were ruled by a chief named Lechulatebe.

Of all these tribes, however, only the Fwe live solely within the borders of the Caprivi Strip. Although their culture is similar to the Kavango, little else is known except that they are believed to have migrated from the north, through Kavangoland.

The region's martial history is still recounted by tribal elders who recall the heroic deeds of such warriors as Mwanambinyi, who ruled Barotseland 300 years ago after defeating Lukonga of the Mbukushu, the echo of his victory ringing down through the centuries across the emptiness of Caprivi's open prairies.

Known as Itenge before, East Caprivi was ruled almost continuously by the Lozi who commanded twenty-five tribes at the start of the nineteenth century. The greatest of all Lozi kings was Mulambwa, the great commander, king of kings, lawmaker and judge.

Stability came to an end in 1820, the Time of Troubles, *Difagane,* when an influx of refugees from Shaka the Zulu moved northwards across southern Africa's highveld.

At the same time, marauding invaders also moved northwards across the Limpopo, leaving havoc in their wake. The Kololo, a Sotho tribe, were among the most aggressive, wandering for years across southern Africa waging war against everyone they met.

When they marched through the Okavango Delta into East Caprivi they were led by the great Sebitwane. After over-

Above: Honeycomb of carmine bee-eater nests eats into the banks of the Kwando River which flows from Angola across the Caprivi Strip into the Okavango Delta.

---

throwing the Lozi king, forcing the Lozi into the swamps of Zambia, Sebitwane appointed sub-chiefs and built new villages in his kingdom.

He then invited Livingstone to bring the word of God to the Caprivi Strip. When the king died in 1851, Livingstone was with him. Soon after, the Lozi returned and slaughtered Sebitwane's successor.

Today the Lozi language, which is to a large extent based on Rotse, is the lingua franca of Caprivi. Furthermore, it is officially used as a medium of instruction in the schools.

In 1935 a Superintendent Britz, the only direct representative of the South West Africa Administration, moved to Katima Mulilo from Schuckmannsburg and, in 1929, Pretoria took over the administration. At this stage a mere three people administered the entire Caprivi area.

There were only three schools with a total enrolment of 162 and an average attendance of fifty per cent. The chiefs in the area collected taxes from their people, to be used for tribal interests. The main forms of transport were carts drawn by oxen, and barges on the river, the latter requiring a crew of twelve to fourteen oarsmen.

World War II brought great changes almost everywhere but, in keeping with its earlier history and geography, the Caprivi was slow to be affected in any significant way.

In 1962 when South African officials visited the territory and were treated with hostility, South Africa put a police force in the Caprivi.

During these years SWAPO grew in support in the area, its aim being to oust the South African Government. After Zambian Independence, PLAN stepped up operations in the area and the war escalated.

It was not until 1990 that the last South African Security Forces left the Strip and peace returned.

Green, fertile floodplains and perennial wetlands mark much of the Strip, beautiful contrast to the dusty face of the Kalahari that distinguishes its other areas. It is extremely narrow and flat. Wherever you go no part rises more than forty-seven metres (154 feet) higher than the rest.

Mahango Game Reserve and Caprivi Game Reserve lie in the western section of the Caprivi Strip, west of the Kwando River. East of the Kwando lie the Caprivi Strip's capital town of Katima Mulilo, the Mamili and Mudumu National Parks and Lake Liambesi.

Getting there

Katima Mulilo, capital of the Caprivi Strip, 661 kilometres (411 miles) from Rundu, 909 kilometres (565 miles) from Grootfontein, 1,361 kilometres (846 miles) from Windhoek, 1,485 kilometres (923 miles) from Swakopmund, 1,873 kilometres (1,164 miles) from Keetmanshoop, 2,854 kilometres (1,773 miles) from Cape Town, 3,332 kilometres (2,070 miles) from Johannesburg, is served by road and air. A minor road south from Katima Mulilo passes through Bukalo where Route 60 loops south-west to Lake Liambesi.

When to go

The Caprivi Strip is open all year-round. However, during the rainy season, from December to April, roads and trails are often flooded and difficult to traverse. It is better to visit between late April and early December.

Where to stay

At Katima Mulilo, Zambezi River Lodge, Zambezi Queen riverboat (sailings between February and May), Hippo Lodge, nine kilometres (six miles) downstream on the Zambezi. At Mudumu National Park, Lianshulu Lodge and Mvubu Camp. See Listings for "Hotels". There is accommodation and campsites at Popa Falls, a forty-guest camp on the banks of the Okavango River and in other areas of the Caprivi Strip. See Listings.

Sightseeing

The B8 road from **Rundu** to the **Zambezi** snakes along the banks of the **Okavango** through an always flat but never monotonous landscape, lush with vegetation including tall elephant grasses. The entire region is virtually one enormous game reserve where you may expect around any bend to come across anything from a herd of elephant to a pride of lion.

Caprivi Strip (West)

Some forty kilometres (twenty-five miles) from Andara, signposts mark the way to **Popa Falls** where the **Okavango** races over **rapids** descending twenty metres (sixty-five feet) in a series of **rocky steps** over the course of fourteen kilometres (nine miles) as it cuts across the Caprivi panhandle to drain into its remarkable **delta** in the **Kalahari**.

There is a **rest camp** of rustic cabins on the river bank built from wild teak planks with thatch roofs, unobtrusive amongst the riverine vegetation.

From the camp it is a short **walk** to the falls where a **wooden bridge** crosses the first of the rapids.

At this point the river divides into several **courses** and the falls are not visible. Upstream, on the main bank, there is an impressive view of the river before it spills over the rapids.

To Mahango Game Reserve

Twenty-five kilometres (sixteen miles) south-east of the Falls, a tributary of the Mahango River marks the northern boundary of the 246 square kilometres (ninety-five square miles) of Mahango Game Reserve.

Squeezed between the Botswana border and the Okavango River, it was opened in 1986.

Getting there

Mahango Game Reserve is 252 kilometres (156 miles) from Rundu and twenty-five kilometres (sixteen miles) from Bagani. From Bagani follow the signposts to Popa Falls and Botswana.

The entrance to the Mahango Game Reserve is nineteen kilometres (twelve miles) south-east of Popa Falls. 4WD is recommended.

Above: Kavango fisherman in dugout canoe on River Kwando.

When to go

The reserve is open all year-round but the best time to visit is between late April and early December.

Where to stay

There is no accommodation other than self-service guesthouses at Popa Falls, and huts and campsites to rent at Suclabo, seventeen kilometres (eleven miles) from the entrance.

Sightseeing

Visitors explore the reserve on foot. The **river** is unsafe as not only is it inhabited by **hippo** and **crocodile**, it is also infested with the deadly liver worm which causes bilharzia.

Bordered in the east by the **Okavango River**, its fertile **floodplain** is covered by **papyrus** and **reeds** and extensive **grasslands**. More than sixty species of mammals, fifteen species of **lizard** and eight species of **snake** are known to make the reserve their home. There are also more than 300 recorded species of bird, many of them water birds.

Among the most outstanding avifauna are the rare **western-banded snake eagle, Pel's fishing owl, white-rumped babbler, African skimmer, swamp boubou, chirping cisticola, finfoot, rock pratincole** and the **coppery-tailed coucal**.

The reserve's wildlife includes **elephant** which migrate along the Strip from **Angola, Botswana** and **Zambia** during the dry season to form the largest remaining herds in Africa.

There are also many **hippo, crocodile, clawless otter** and some of southern Africa's most distinctive plains animals, **blue wildebeest, cape buffalo, kudu, gemsbok, tsessebe, impala, red lechwe, sitatunga,** tiny **reedbuck, roan** and **sable,** whose magnificent, long, sweeping horns curve backwards.

There are also good numbers of **wart hog, baboon, ostrich, vervet monkey, wild** dog, lion and leopard. (See "Wildlife: Just Out of This World", Part Four).

Visitors can explore Mahango on foot. The **main route** through the park links **Bagani** in **Namibia** with **Shakawe** in **Botswana** and a **circular drive** leads down to, and then along, the river.

To Caprivi Game Reserve

Mahango Game Reserve is also the western border of the 6,000 square kilometres (2,316 square miles) of Caprivi Game Reserve which stretches along the panhandle between Angola in the north and Botswana in the south, as far east as the Kwando River.

A vast expanse of densely-wooded country, recently resettled by many of the San Bushmen who were moved away in the 1970s and 1980s (See "The People: A Kaleidoscope of Colourful Cultures, Part Four"), the park serves as a sanctuary for Africa's largest surviving elephant herds, buffalo and many species of antelope.

Together with two smaller reserves, the flat, fertile floodplains serve as the stage for some of the world's greatest wildlife spectacles — alive with prolific numbers of roan antelope, kudu, blue wildebeest, giraffe, hippo, and Burchell's zebra.

Getting there

Caprivi Game Reserve's western entrance is some 250 kilometres (156 miles) from Rundu on the main B8 road which runs right through the park.

When to go

While the park is open all year-round, the best time to visit is between late April and early December (before the rainy season).

Where to stay

There is a camp that can accommodate up to forty guests on the banks of the Okavango River and a campsite. See Listings. The nearest luxury accommodation is at Lianshulu Lodge. See Listings for "Hotels".

Sightseeing

Although many species browse in the

Above: Puff adder — one of Namibia's most lethal snakes.

park's **woodlands**, the largest congregations assemble around the **Kwando River** in the **east** which flows across the Caprivi Strip into the **Okavango Delta** at the point where the panhandle broadens out to its widest.

The **Malombe** and **Ndwasa pans** in the centre of park lure animals during the dry season. The village of **Kongola** lies on the **eastern border** of the park.

Caprivi Strip (East)

The north-west border of Mudumu National Park's 1,010 square kilometres (390 square miles) of rare wetlands and large woodlands, established in 1990, just touches the southernmost boundary of the Caprivi Game Park.

As well as its western wetlands, this northern extension of the magical Okavango Delta is every bit as fascinating as the main delta — treasured ecosystems in arid southern Africa. Mudumu has extensive mopane and terminalia woodlands.

Getting there

The main gate into the Mudumu National Park is about thirty-five kilometres (twenty miles) down the 3511 road which branches off the main B8 Grootfontein-Rundu-Katima Mulilo road and is signposted to Sangwali and Linyanti. Prospective visitors should report to the Directorate of Nature Conservation offices in Windhoek. Charter flights serve Lianshulu landing strip. See Listings.

When to go

The park is open all year-round but subject to unannounced closure, so check with the DNC in Windhoek. The best time to visit is between late April and early December, avoiding the rainy season when much of the park is under water.

Where to stay

Lianshulu Lodge. Accommodation is in twin-bedded en suite thatched chalets. See Listings for "Hotels". Mvubu Camp, six twin-bedded cottage tents. See Listings.

Above: Basket work for sale in craft market at Katima Mulilo.

Sightseeing

Visitors explore **Mudumu** by 4WD vehicle, boat and on foot, wandering along its sylvan **trails** in search of herds of **elephant**. **Buffalo, kudu, sable, hippo, bushpig, wart hog, lion, leopard, spotted hyena** and **wild dog** also inhabit the park and there is a marvellous variety of **birds** in the enchanting **forest** along the banks of the Kwando and in its reed-lined **backwaters**.

There are also small numbers of **marsh antelope** — **lechwe** and **sitatunga** — **buffalo** and **wild dog**. But it is Mudumu's **bird life** — more than 400 species — which is the park's real attraction.

To Mamili National Park

The Kwando River feeds Linyanti Swamp downstream in neighbouring Mamili National Park, part of the Okavango Delta.

Few people, however, realise that Namibia has its own region of waterways and islands similar to Botswana's famous Okavango Delta. Where the Kwando winds east out of Mudumu National Park for twenty kilometres (twelve miles) it abruptly swings north-east, dividing into a series of narrow channels at the point where it hurries to its meeting with the Linyanti.

There it enters the 320 square kilometres (124 square miles) of the Mamili National Park which extends into the Okavango Delta in Botswana. Established in 1990, the park is largely wetlands and in exceptional years of rain is accessible only by boat.

In more arid times much of it may be explored by 4WD vehicle.

Getting there

Some 100 kilometres (sixty miles) off the B8 in a trackless land, Mamili National Park may only be reached by 4WD. Potential visitors should report to the Directorate of Nature Conservation offices in Windhoek. See Listings.

When to go

Although uncomfortably hot and humid in summer, Mamili is at its best during the rains between December and April.

Where to stay

There is no tourist accommodation in Mamili. Kalizo operate a fishing camp about forty kilometres (twenty-five miles) from Katima. See Listings.

Sightseeing

Built around two large **islands** — **Nkasa** and **Lupala** — **Mamili National Park** is mainly marshland veined by a network of reed **channels, lagoons** and **backwaters** rich in bird- and wildlife. Regarded by many as Namibia's most exciting sanctuary, **islands** of trees — **date palms** and **apple leaf** — spring up during the rains.

Hippo and **crocodile** abound in the **pools** that hold water throughout the year while **elephant, red lechwe, sitatunga, lion, leopard, spotted hyena** and **wild dog** all frequent the park. Bird species include **wattled crane, fish eagle, swamp boubou, collared palm thrush**, Bradfield's hornbill, Pel's **fishing owl, white crowned plover** and **slaty egret**.

To Lake Liambesi

South of Katima Mulilo on the Botswana border of the eastern sector of the Caprivi Strip lies Lake Liambesi which is fed by two rivers that give eastern Caprivi, which has the nation's highest rainfall, its distinctive character. The two rivers, Linyanti and Chobe, form the border with Botswana.

The shallow depths of Lake Liambesi, which covers more than 100 square kilometres (thirty-nine square miles), are never deeper than five metres (sixteen feet) and are surrounded by 200 square kilometres (eighty square miles) of swampland.

The thirsty sun is always threatening to suck it dry. Lake Liambesi loses large surface areas — two metres (seven feet) — every year to evaporation. In fact, during the savage drought of 1985 the lake vanished altogether and the local fisherfolk, used to harvesting a tonne of fish a day, were suddenly starving.

Visitors may go boating with the locals on Liambesi. But beware of crocodile and hippo of which there are many. The lake is also fed by the floodwaters of the Zambezi which spill over onto the western floodplains when the river is in spate — between 1955 and 1975 the lake received such an inflow every two or three years.

When to go

The best time of year to visit the lake is during the rainy season between December and April when it is at its largest.

Where to stay

At Katima Mulilo, Zambezi River Lodge, Zambezi Queen riverboat (sailings between February and May), Hippo Lodge, nine kilometres (six miles) downstream on the Zambezi. See Listings for "Hotels". At the Mudumu National Park, Lianshulu Lodge. See Listings for "Hotels". At the Mamili National Park, tented camps. See Listings.

To Katima Mulilo

Eastern Caprivi with its rich variety of typical African habitats — savannah grasslands, dense woodlands and riverine forests, wetlands and swamps — has become increasingly popular as a tourist destination since independence.

The region has its own legislation and administrator, a legacy of South Africa's domination, but is gradually being brought into the national framework.

Katima Mulilo, with a population of about 40,000 taking into account its rural environs, stands on the banks of the great Zambezi and is one of the most fascinating towns in Africa.

Above: Unusual throne room in a baobab tree at Katima Mulilo, 'capital' of the Caprivi Strip.

Getting there

Katima Mulilo, capital of the Caprivi Strip, 661 kilometres (411 miles) from Rundu, 909 kilometres (565 miles) from Grootfontein, 1,361 kilometres (846 miles) from Windhoek, 1,485 kilometres (923 miles) from Swakopmund, 1,873 kilometres (1,164 miles) from Keetmanshoop, 2,854 kilometres (1,773 miles) from Cape Town, 3,332 kilometres (2,070 miles) from Johannesburg, is served by road and air. There are nearby border posts with Zambia

Above: One-tusked elephant roams grasslands of the Caprivi Strip.

at Wenele, four kilometres (two miles) north of Katima Mulilo where the crossing is by ferry; with Zimbabwe at Kazungula but has to transit through Botswana; and with Botswana via Ngoma, sixty kilometres (thirty-seven miles) south-east of Katima Mulilo.

When to go

For much of the Caprivi Strip the best time is the southern autumn, between February and May, and spring, between September and November, avoiding the excessive heat of mid-summer. Caprivi's wetlands, lakes and lagoons are at their most spectacular during the rainy season (between December and April). River cruises from Katima Mulilo operate between February and May when the Zambezi is in spate.

Where to stay

At Katima Mulilo, Zambezi River Lodge, Zambezi Queen riverboat (sailings between February and May), Hippo Lodge, nine kilometres (six miles) downstream on the Zambezi. At the Mudumu National Park, Lianshulu Lodge. See Listings for "Hotels". There is also a tented camp. See Listings. There are campsites and accommodation at Popa Falls and in other areas of the Caprivi Strip. See Listings.

Sightseeing

Katima Mulilo's colourful **market**, with its fresh **produce**, **clothes** and **handicrafts**, is as vibrant as only an African market can be. Produce on sale includes fish, fresh food, brightly-coloured garments and crafted **soapstone curios** and **wood carvings**.

There is a **filling station, supermarket, police post, administrative offices, schools** and **hospital**.

But it is the town's location — on a broad sweep of the **Zambezi** — that provides its real magic.

The **tourist lodge**, complete with verdant **golf course, swimming pool** and **cottages**, has a **floating bar** moored out in the great river where visitors may enjoy their sundowners while watching the **crocodiles, hippo**, river life and the wonderful variety of birds.

Glance skyward and you might spot an **African fish eagle, white-crowned plover,**

Above: Elephant in the Caprivi's lush undergrowth.

half-collared kingfisher or **white-fronted bee-eater** and, in the **woods** along the river banks, there lurk **green-spotted dove, pied barbet, fork-tailed drongo, white-browed robin, three-streaked tchagra, white-helmet shrike** and **blue waxbill**.

The lodge actually began life as a simple boarding house for visiting engineers. It was built by Gert Visagie, a construction engineer who settled at Katima Mulilo in the late 1970s, after undertaking a nine-month contract there. It quickly grew into the luxurious Zambezi Lodge, beside the river's tree-shaded banks.

Since then Visagie has played a major role in the region's development, building an **arts centre** which he gave to the local artists under the management of playwright, potter, artist and folklorist Moses Nasilele. Gert has also been behind the construction of **schools**, a **hospital**, **post office** and **bush clinics**. He is also the new Mayor of Katima.

But his real triumph must be the floating restaurant that became the forty-five-metre (148-foot) river boat, *Zambezi Queen*. Designed by Gert, it took a year to build.

Now it is the only holiday cruiser on southern Africa's inland waters. The *Zambezi Queen* has thirteen **staterooms**, an exotic **bridal suite**, two **lounges, dining room, casino** and even its own **bakery**.

When the river rises during the rainy season from December to April, Gert becomes skipper on four- to eight-day cruises with his crew of eight, eighty kilometres (fifty miles) south down the Zambezi to the top of the magnificent Victoria Falls between Zambia and Zimbabwe.

The boat cruises over waters that teem with some of the finest freshwater game fish in the world — **tiger fish, western bottlenose, tilapia** and **brownspot largemouth**. The tiger fish, related to Latin America's flesh-eating piranha, gives a real fight — sometimes leaping several metres out of the water on occasion.

However Katima Mulilo's unique claim to fame is one that should inspire caution. It is the only town in the world where elephants have the right of way as they parade daily through the streets.

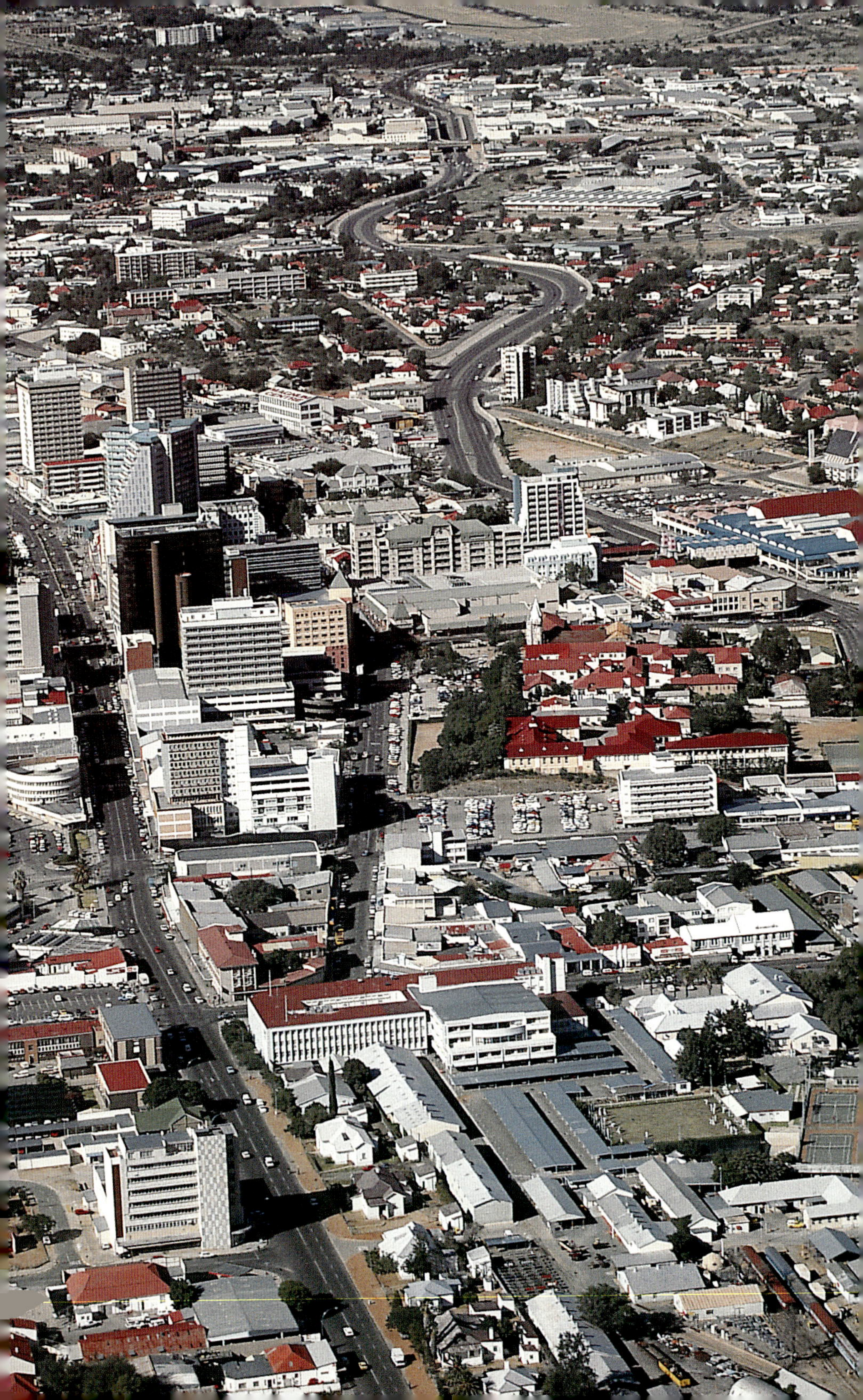

PART THREE: THE CAPITAL AND TOWNS

Above: Kalahari Sands, Windhoek's top hotel, dominates a downtown shopping mall.
Opposite: Bird's eye view of the capital, Windhoek.

Windhoek: City in the Sun

Windhoek International Airport is forty minutes from the city it serves. That is a prospect you may not relish after endless hours in the air, but you will change your mind the moment the air-conditioned bus leaves the airport.

Those forty minutes on the road are an eye-opener. Instead of impatient, hooter-blasting streams of traffic and scurrying pedestrians it is a foretaste of what is to come. For Namibia is a land of wide open spaces, diverse vegetation, prolific bird and wildlife, and tranquillity.

Gaze skywards from the bus and you may spot a majestic eagle on the wing. Or a colourful lilac-breasted roller perched on a fence beside the road. Or dozens of chattering finches disappearing into the bush.

If you are fortunate enough, these first few minutes in Namibia may even bring kudu, eland or duiker to the roadside. Signs warning motorists to beware of kudu on the highway are no idle warning.

The final leg to Windhoek through the outskirts passes the famous German Lutheran Church surrounded by flower beds and lawns basking in the sun.

As you alight from the vehicle, you are left in no doubt that you are in Africa with curio sellers sitting among their baskets, beads and carvings in an outdoor curio bazaar at the heart of the tourist centre.

Blessed with a warm, sunny climate, Windhoek's pavements are happy gathering places. Strolling along the pedestrian malls and shopping arcades visitors enjoy an ever-changing scene and varied attractions. And the population reflects the multitude of the country as a whole.

By international standards Windhoek may be small but it is growing — and at a marvellously controlled pace. High-rise buildings have sprung up all around the centre, although the new structures are not unsightly or dominant.

Windhoek, surrounded by a sea of undulating hills, stands 1,630 metres (5,348 feet) above sea level, making it hot by day and cold at night. Nevertheless, in contrast to other places on the same latitude, it enjoys a temperate climate. Thanks in part to its comfortable atmosphere the area has played host to settlements of one sort or another for many centuries.

Jonker Afrikaner, a Nama chief, gave the city its present name. (See "History: Land of Lost Horizons", Part One). The surrounding mountains reminded him of a farm in the Cape Province called Winterhoek, near Tulbagh, where he spent some time before trekking into the unknown desert land that is now Namibia.

But his choice of name was by no means the first. Indeed, before he settled there, already there was a long list.

The Herero called it *otjomuise*, 'place of the smoke'. The Hottentots referred to it as *ai-gams* 'steam'. Then, in 1837, Captain James Alexander renamed the settlement 'Queen Adelaide's Bath' in honour of the British Queen.

Soon after this, it earned yet another name, this time 'Elberfeld', as ordained by two missionaries. And, to complete this list in 1844, the Wesleyan mission dubbed present-day Windhoek, Concordiaville. After that, until his death in 1863, Jonker Afrikaner made it his headquarters.

It was not until 1890, when Captain Curt von Francois took control of the territory, that modern Windhoek began to take shape.

When the railway across the desert linking Windhoek with Swakopmund was completed in 1902, the nascent capital's potential was instantly realised. Windhoek became the seat of the German colonial government until the South African takeover. Today many historic monuments, mostly colonial, retain their place in Windhoek's architectural legacy, among them the Owambo Campaign Memorial, the Hottentot Memorial and the Reiterdenkmal.

The capital is so steeped in history and culture, and so impressive are the modern

228

Central Windhoek

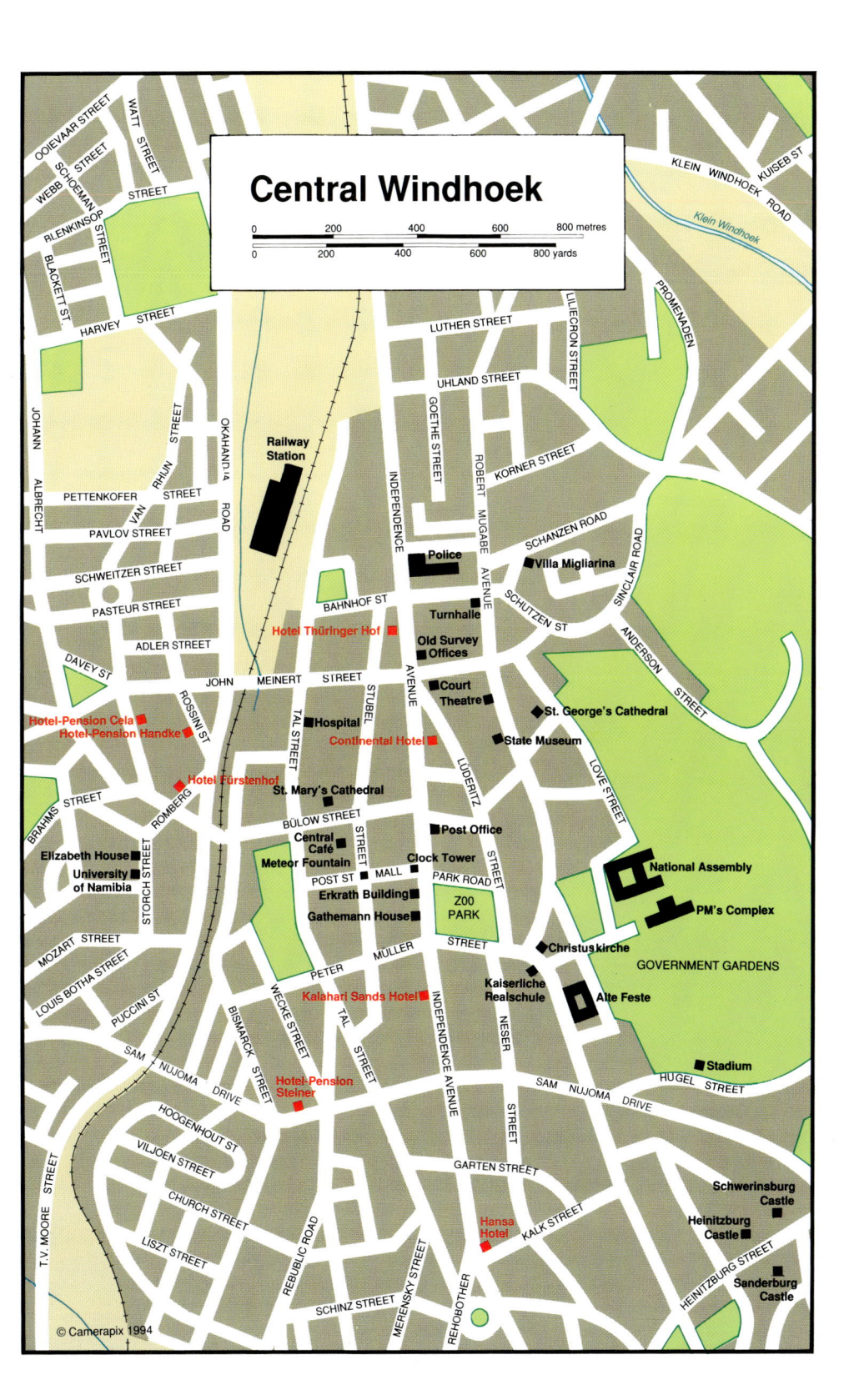

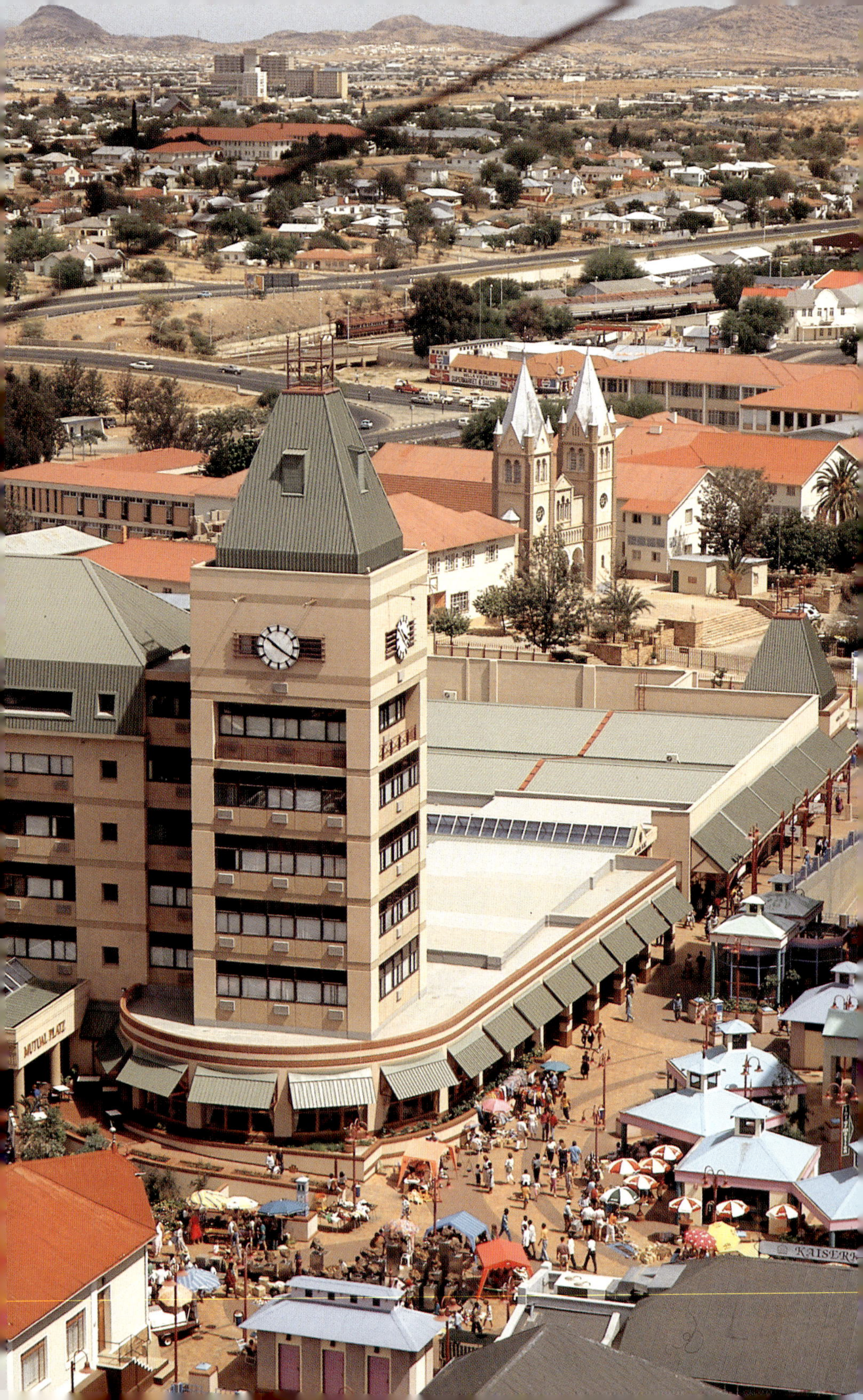
MUTUAL PLATZ

buildings and general efficiency, that visitors may safely conclude that a glorious and prosperous future lies ahead for Windhoek.

Indeed, as Namibia entered its fourth year of independence, the city was growing swiftly, its population approaching 160,000, with new suburban estates extending the city's borders.

Careful planning should ensure that the spaciousness and cleanliness of Windhoek's broad and sunny streets will endure all change — to add more than a measure of delight, not only to its ever-increasing number of citizens but to the burgeoning number of visitors which it welcomes each year.

Getting there

Windhoek, 357 kilometres (222 miles) from Swakopmund, 389 kilometres (241 miles) from Walvis Bay, 482 kilometres (299 miles) from Keetmanshoop, 533 kilometres (331 miles) from Namutoni, 816 kilometres (507 miles) from Lüderitz, 1,493 kilometres (928 miles) from Cape Town, and 1,971 kilometres (1,225 miles) from Johannesburg, is well-served by international flights. Domestic and regional air, rail and road services link it with all major centres in Namibia and southern Africa.

When to go

The city is pleasant all year-round.

Where to stay

Kalahari Sands (4-star), Hotel Safari (3-star), Hotel Thüringer Hof (2-star), Continental Hotel (2-star), Hotel Fürstenhof (2-star), Hotel-Pension Cela (2-star), Aris Hotel (1-star), Tuckers Tavern (1-star), Hotel Kapps Farm (1-star), Hotel-Pension Handke (1-star), Hotel-Pension Steiner (1-star), South West Star Hotel (1-star). See Listings for "Hotels".

There are also guest farms, caravan parks and campsites on the edge of the city. See Listings.

Sightseeing

Independence Avenue — Windhoek's main street — is the **showcase** for the enormous development that has occurred in most places in Namibia since it became self-governing in 1990. Where it fronts on the imposing German colonial buildings, the always busy pedestrian area has been widened several times.

The **Gathemann Restaurant**, on Independence Avenue, is a nice place indeed — the food is good although the service is sometimes a little light on the ground. There you can sit on a balcony overlooking the Avenue.

The restaurant in the **Fürstenhof Hotel**, however, has perfected the art of dining out. There are many other restaurants throughout the city, where nearly every kind of ethnic dish may be sampled.

If it is a good night out that you are looking for, **Casablanca** is the place to head for at a late hour. The spot is held in high regard by Windhoek's youth and young at heart and is open until the early hours. Conveniently, right behind is the excellent **Sam's Restaurant** where the food is superb and the atmosphere relaxed.

After dark, pay a visit to one of the city's fine restaurants or savour some of Windhoek's fine brew in quaint little pubs tucked away in the heart of the city. Comfortable hotels, emphasising personalised service, welcome the visitor who has come for a few days.

Over the Avenue, at the head of **Post Street Mall**, stands a colourful and distinguished **clocktower**. It is a striking new landmark, the focal point for vistas along the avenue and up the mall.

The **Bistro** below the clocktower is one of Windhoek's newest landmarks and has quickly become the place where everybody meets. During the day it has a typically continental atmosphere, with people mixing and mingling inside and outside.

In the evening, however, as if somebody

Opposite: Pedestrian mall and market in Windhoek — with the modern drawing inspiration from the ancient.

Above: Flame trees burst into vivid colour along the streets of Windhoek.

waved a magic wand, the ambience switches from street café to trendy bar. The atmosphere is relaxed and casual, and the menu offers anything from quick snacks to specialist dishes.

Not far away, a new **parking area** at the back of the **post office** adds to the existing municipal off-street parking spaces in the area.

Fast-food wagons dot the nearby **Justice Square**, selling tasty hotdogs of German sausages and mustard. Wash this lot down with some of South Africa's refreshing fruit juices or even an ice-cold Windhoek beer. Nothing else quite hits the mark.

The **railway station** runs almost parallel to Independence Avenue — from **north** to **south** — dividing the **old city** to the **west**, from the newer, mainly **residential areas** of the **east**.

Diagonally between the railway line and Independence Avenue, **Post Street Mall**, now the city centre's major business and shopping area, gently declines past new imposing office **blocks**, shopping areas and a **transport terminal** two blocks away.

Two **bridges** separate the vehicles and pedestrians. One over **Stübel Street**, in the middle of the **mall**, has created a **square** for large gatherings, where a **crafts market** is held twice a month.

A multi-million dollar renewal project for smart **shopping precincts,** with wide **pavements**, interesting **balustrades** and lively continental-style **cafés**, won several design accolades for its use of colour and space.

The 60,000 square metre (71,760 square yard) mall truly revitalized this surprisingly compact city. Furriers offer stylish Swakara karakul pelts. Curio shops and innovations such as the new **Crafts Centre** sell Namibian craftwork. There are many upmarket **jewellery** and **gemstone shops**, as well as clothing **stores** where outfits for safaris-in-style await you.

And there, in the middle of the city's most modern architecture, stands a constant reminder of Namibia's ancient past — **Meteor Fountain**. Atop steel pillars, amid a **fountain** of water, are fixed the largest-known collection of meteorites in the world. Estimated at 600 million years old, the thirty-three fragments came from the

Gibeon Meteorite Shower, the largest such shower ever recorded, which was discovered in 1838 by an explorer, J E Alexander. (See "Missionary Heroes, Eccentric Settlers", Part Two).

Today you can sit beneath these objects from other worlds and ponder the unsolved mysteries of the universe, marvelling at their age and composition. Alternatively, admire the fountain as a unique work of modern art.

Zoo park — across Independence Avenue, where office workers, children and idle day-dreamers rest on benches or well-watered lawns, soaking up the sunshine under **palm** and **jacaranda trees** — has been re-styled. Although in the city centre, no more relaxing environment could be found anywhere.

Opposite Zoo Park are three distinguished buildings designed by Willi Sander, best appreciated by viewing them from across the road. One is the 1910 **Erkrath Building**. It has a common feature reminiscent of the period — business premises downstairs and a residence above.

Next door is the 1913 **Gathemann House**, commissioned by mayor Heinrich Gathemann. It incorporates a **step roof** — a feature to prevent a build-up of snow.

The word 'Kronprinz' and the year, 1902, remain on the single-storey section of the building next door, once the **Hotel Kronprinz**, but converted in 1920.

Standing near the avenue and Zoo Park is a **Soldier's Memorial**, *Kriegerdenkmal*, crowned by a gold eagle. It honours the German troops who died fighting the Nama chief, Hendrik Witbooi, between 1893-94. It was unveiled on 5 April 1897.

Colonial architecture

From Zoo Park the visitor may tour the old city. And what better place to begin than the **Hauptkasse**, on the corner of **Peter Müller** and **Lüderitz Streets**. Completed in 1899, the building once housed the finance section of the colonial government and was later used as a school hostel. Now it houses the Ministry of Agriculture, Water and Rural Development.

The 1891 **Reference Library** across the street was uncomplicated until a pleasant

Above: Jacaranda in bloom at Windhoek.

verandah was added at the turn of the century. Ludwig von Estorff, commander of the *Schutztruppe,* lived in the house between 1902-10.

Standing sentinel over the city is the **Christuskirche**. Its pretty tower is the pride of the local parish — and, indeed, the country as a whole. Late afternoon and early evening, when the setting sun in the west softens its local sandstone, are the best times to photograph this pearl of pearls.

Designed by Gottlieb Redecker, it was a token of thanks for the peace which followed after 1907.

In design it is much like a basilica, with influences of neo-Gothic and Art Nouveau. The **stained glass altar windows** — as with the Lüderitz church — were donated by Kaiser Wilhelm II.

The **Bible** was given by his wife, Augusta. The firm of Schilling in Apolda cast the **brass bells**, as well as those of the Evangelical Lutheran Church in Swakopmund.

The church's poor acoustics and ventilation have lately been improved, along with the terrazzo floor and the tiled

Above: Colourful lights adorn the capital during the Christmas season.

roof. Visitors interested in exploring the interior may obtain the **key** from the **church offices** at 12 Peter Müller Street.

Built between 1907 and 1908, the **Kaiserliche Realschule**, opposite the church, originally served as the first German high school, opening its doors in January 1909. The post World War II years saw the building transformed into an English-medium school. Appropriately it now houses part of the Ministry of Education and Culture.

Next door sits the **Officer's House** (1906-7), an exquisite masterpiece which was restored during the 1980s. Originally designed by Gottlieb Redecker, the decorative **brickwork** around the windows, arches and doorway are characteristic of the architecture fashionable in Germany at the time. It was the first building of this style in Namibia. The **stables** now serve as a garage and outbuildings.

Most Windhoek streets retain their original German names. Indeed, wherever you turn, the German imprint is indelibly stamped on this city.

Nowhere is Windhoek's mixed Afro-European heritage more evident than around the **Alte Feste**, the **fort**, which is Windhoek's oldest building and now a **museum**. A century ago it served as the **headquarters** for the first *Schutztruppe* contingent which arrived in Windhoek in 1889 under Curt von Francois.

Surrounding the Alte Feste is an almost complete neighbourhood of German turn-of-the-century buildings with painted wooden panels and romantic round turrets with bay windows. At sundown, tender tones of yellow, pink and orange, wash across their walls, endowing the city with a warmth that belies the cool evening air.

However, magnificent as some of Windhoek's architecture undoubtedly is, nothing quite compares with the Alte Feste. The massive structure, boasting **turrets** and long, high **white walls**, commands a strategic position over the valley below.

The Alte Feste plays on the imagination. If you close your eyes, you almost see a contingent of German soldiers in spotless uniforms marching along the battlements.

The historical section of the **State Museum** is now housed in the Alte Feste.

234

Above: Traditional Herero dolls on display in Windhoek.

Displays concentrate on the country's history from the arrival of the first missionaries to the end of the German administration. There is also a new **Independence Exhibit** along with a room that houses Namibia's **national symbols**. The turret above the museum affords a panoramic view of the city.

In the **courtyard**, a restaurant serves tantalising barbecued food, while inside a lively **bar** is adorned with **flags** of the **German Reich** and other such Teutonic memorabilia. A **narrow-gauge train**, including the **engine** and **coaches**, may be found on the **south side** of the building.

The **Rider Memorial** on the **embankment** outside the fort was unveiled on 27 January 1912 — birthday of Kaiser Wilhelm II. It is a **statue** of a mounted soldier and honours those killed in the Nama and the Herero wars between 1903-07.

For the artistically inclined, a visit to the murals and works of art in copper, ceramics, paint, wood and marble in the **Office of the Prime Minister complex** would be a memorable experience. They depict various aspects of the country's minerals, fishing industry, agriculture, history and nature, in a highly imaginative and captivating way.

The **National Assembly**, or **Tintenpalast** — Ink Palace — adjoining the Legislative Assembly, dates back to 1912. Built as administrative offices for the German colonial government, its name reflects the large volume of bureaucratic processes which took place there.

Completed in November 1913, the building was used by the local authority for its first meeting on 11 May 1914, only to be disbanded in July the following year with the surrender of the German forces to the South Africans.

The surrounding **gardens** were laid out in the 1930s. One hundred **olive trees** were planted in 1934 and the **bowling greens** were cultivated towards the end of the same decade. With many birds in the **trees** and **shade** for the weary walker, it is a beautiful place,

State House on **Lüderitz Street** was the South African Administrator-General's official residence until independence. In 1958, the former Colonial Governor's

Above: Namibia Commercial Aviation runs a seventeen-aircraft fleet which operates throughout Namibia and to all the neighbouring countries.

residence was demolished to make way for the palatial building where President Sam Nujoma now lives.

If you have a moment, walk up **Sinclair Road** and admire **Villa Migliarina**, now a private home, which stands upon the **hill**.

The **Old Survey** Offices, on the corner of **John Meinert Street** and **Independence Avenue,** date back to 1902. They were built by the German Government to house the **survey office**, with a large drawing office, fire-proof archives where the maps were stored, and rooms for survey equipment.

Behind this, on **Bahnhof Street**, is the **Turnhalle** — Town Hall. The first sitting of the Constitutional Conference on independence for Namibia took place there on 1 September 1975. For this reason it is better known as the Turnhalle Conference.

Before crossing Independence Avenue towards the **railway**, stop at the **Kudu Memorial**, a fine statue built in 1960. It's worth taking note of where this landmark stands, as Windhoekians often offer directions saying, 'Take the first left at the kudu' — or words to that effect.

Station

Sadly, the heyday of the Namibian railway has long ended. And yet the station building still holds its air of romanticism.

The middle and southern wings date back to 1912. Although it is uncertain who was responsible for the design, the handsome building is an amalgamation of various building styles. The sole complaint at the time of completion was that it didn't have a restaurant. Today it houses a 'greasy café'. South African Railways added the northern wing in 1929, in the same style.

'**Poor Old Joe**', a **locomotive** imported from Germany and assembled in Swakopmund in 1899, stands in the **parking area** outside the station building. More than 100 of these locomotives were deployed in the country by 1906.

Almost opposite the station, a 1919 **stone obelisk** serves as a reminder of the turbulent history of Namibia. The Owambo Campaign Memorial is set among tall palms and jacarandas which burst into bloom in spring.

Above: Namibia's State Museum in Robert Mugabe Avenue, Windhoek.

Half camouflaged by trees on a north-eastern hill of the city, between **Sperlinglust** and **Schwerinsburg Streets**, **three castles** stand defying the elements. **Schwerinsburg Castle** was built in 1913 and **Sanderburg Castle** in 1917. They are now both private homes. The third, **Heinitzburg Castle**, built in 1914, is an **art gallery**.

Two attractions not to be missed before leaving the centre of Windhoek are the **Francois Statue** and the **H-shaped house**.

The Curt von Francois Statue, again on Independence Avenue, is the work of Hennie Potgieter and was unveiled on 19 October 1965, the seventy-fifth anniversary of Windhoek's founding, when the town was proclaimed a city.

Further west is the unique Ten-Man house, an H-shaped building completed in 1906. As the name suggests, ten unmarried administration officials were housed there in what was originally a fortress-like building. Much later, the military tone was lightened by adding wide verandahs and decorative turrets. Each corner contained one-bedroom flats with bathrooms, while one-bedroom flats without bathrooms were built in the centre of the H.

Museum

The **Owela Museum,** sometimes referred to as the Natural Science and Cultural Museum, is on **Leutwein Street**, now renamed **Robert Mugabe Avenue**. Perhaps its most fascinating attraction is demonstrations of the African game, Owela, also known as Mbau. Just watching and trying to figure out how it is played may give you a headache. And so, fortunately, a rule book in English is provided. It is a sophisticated form of African 'backgammon'.

The 'board' may be made either of sand, mud, stone, cement or wood. It has forty-two depressions. Marbles, round pebbles or stones from fruit may be used as pieces. The aim is to capture as many of your opponent's stones as possible.

Players move anti-clockwise, although only in their own two rows. Learning this complicated game is difficult as it is played

Above: Windhoek brewery produces lager to ancient German standards of purity.

at great speed with players seemingly moving simultaneously.

Windhoek's cultural attractions do not stop there. The **Windhoek Theatre,** also on Robert Mugabe Avenue, has regular performances of drama, ballet and musicals and the **Warehouse Theatre** in the **Old Brewery Building** on the corner of **Tal Street** and **Sam Nujoma Drive** hosts theatre with music and one-man shows.

The **Standard Bank Space** at the **University of Namibia** on **Storch Street** offers *Sjordés* during lunch hours. Meanwhile, the **Windhoek Conservatoire** on **Peter Müller Street** occasionally stages ballet, modern music and dancing.

Windhoek is also endowed with some first-class galleries (see "In Brief") and the recently established **Namibian Crafts Centre** on Tal Street, in the **Old South West Breweries**, provides a permanent showcase for handicrafts.

There you will find Baster leatherwork and animal skins, wall-hangings, cushion covers, and Bushmen amulets, jewellery, musical instruments, bows, arrows and quivers as well as toys and basketry. Then there is Damara leatherwork, glass and metal, clay pipes and bowls and 'township art' such as wire cars; Herero dolls dressed in African-Victorian style; Nama jewellery and tortoiseshell powder containers; and the famous Kavango basketry, instruments and headdresses.

Excursions

Situated on the **eastern outskirts** of Windhoek, off the road to **J G Strijdom Airport**, **Avis Dam** offers excellent opportunities for bird-watching. The best time to go is just before the first summer rains, when between 100 and 120 species may be seen in a single day. The dam is leased to the Wildlife Society of Namibia.

Goreangab Dam, north-west of the city, is popular with local windsurfers and sailboaters, though swimming is prohibited. Picnic facilities are provided. The dam is reached by driving from Windhoek along the **Okahandja Road**. The turnoff is signposted opposite the **Van Eck power station** on the northern outskirts. From there it is another seven-and-a-half kilometres (four-and-a-half miles) to the dam.

Top: Modern Namibian art on display in Windhoek Design Centre.

Above: Contemporary Namibian art expressed in a large mural in Windhoek.

Swakopmund: Bavarian Seaside Town in Africa

Some mornings the mist rolls in, encircling Swakopmund's graceful old turn-of-the-century buildings. At other times, the town is alive with nothing but sunshine, making the sea sparkle and bathing the beach in golden light.

Whatever the weather, Swakopmund — Namibia's famous seaside resort — is a place of great charm. Nestling between the Namib Desert and the wild Atlantic seaboard, this engaging town boasts lush green lawns, graceful palm trees and carefully tended, colourful public gardens.

The visitor may enter a picturesque coffee shop frequented by little old German women wearing floppy hats, gossiping about their neighbours. It is highly likely they will be eating *Schwartzwald-Torte* with whipped cream and drinking filter *kafee* from delicate white porcelain cups. The coffee shop will be complete with gauzy lace curtains, starched tablecloths and a welter of pot-plants.

Indeed, Swakopmund is just like a small Bavarian village — except for its year-round sun, the sea and sand, desert dunes with exciting excursions, faultless beaches, superb angling, cosmopolitan atmosphere, solitude if required, and no overcrowding. It also boasts one of the best golf courses in southern Africa. In short, Swakopmund is perfect.

Built on flat coast, open to the sea, the town has a population of just over 18,000. It is situated at the mouth of the seasonal Swakop River, which is almost always bone-dry.

For Namibians, generally, the town and its environs represent a place of ease and relaxation — a welcome escape from the relentless inland heat at the year's end, a place to stroll through the town gardens and along the historic Mole, originally a harbour breakwater built between 1899 and 1903.

Swakopmund came into being after the German Reich resolved to build a port along the Namibian coast.

The British had already declared the Walvis Bay enclave to be one of their protectorates and other potential locations for a port along the often treacherous coastline were unacceptable.

Swakopmund was born on 4 August 1892, when Captain Curt von Francois landed just north of the mouth of the Swakop from the gunboat *Hyena*. There, he and the crew raised two beacons to indicate their landing site.

By the end of the following month the first building had been completed. Most appropriately, it was a barracks for the crew and troops. Swakopmund was now protected and ready to receive its first settlers. Forty arrived on 23 August 1893, along with 120 soldiers on the ship, the *Marie Woermann*. By 1897 Swakopmund had 113 settlers. They worked hard to build the new town, using wooden prefabricated buildings, imported from Germany.

Meanwhile, several attempts were made to create landing facilities. A quay was built at the Mole, but the harbour soon silted up. A wooden jetty was then constructed a little further south, and later an iron jetty, the remains of which still stand.

Swakopmund soon became the major port for imports and exports for the newly-founded German Protectorate of Deutsch Sudwestafrika. In 1909, it was one of six towns which received municipal status. Many departments of the central government set up offices while trading and transport houses from Germany established agencies or branches. New companies were also founded and many built permanent offices which still exist.

But in 1915, after German South West Africa was taken by South Africa, all harbour activities were transferred from Swakopmund to Walvis Bay. Many government services were also re-located. Businesses closed down, the citizens left, and the town sank into decline.

The natural potential of Swakopmund as a holiday resort, however, subsequently revitalised the town. Today tourism-related services form a vital part of the economy.

The discovery and development of uranium at Rössing, sixty-five kilometres (forty miles) east of the town, also had an

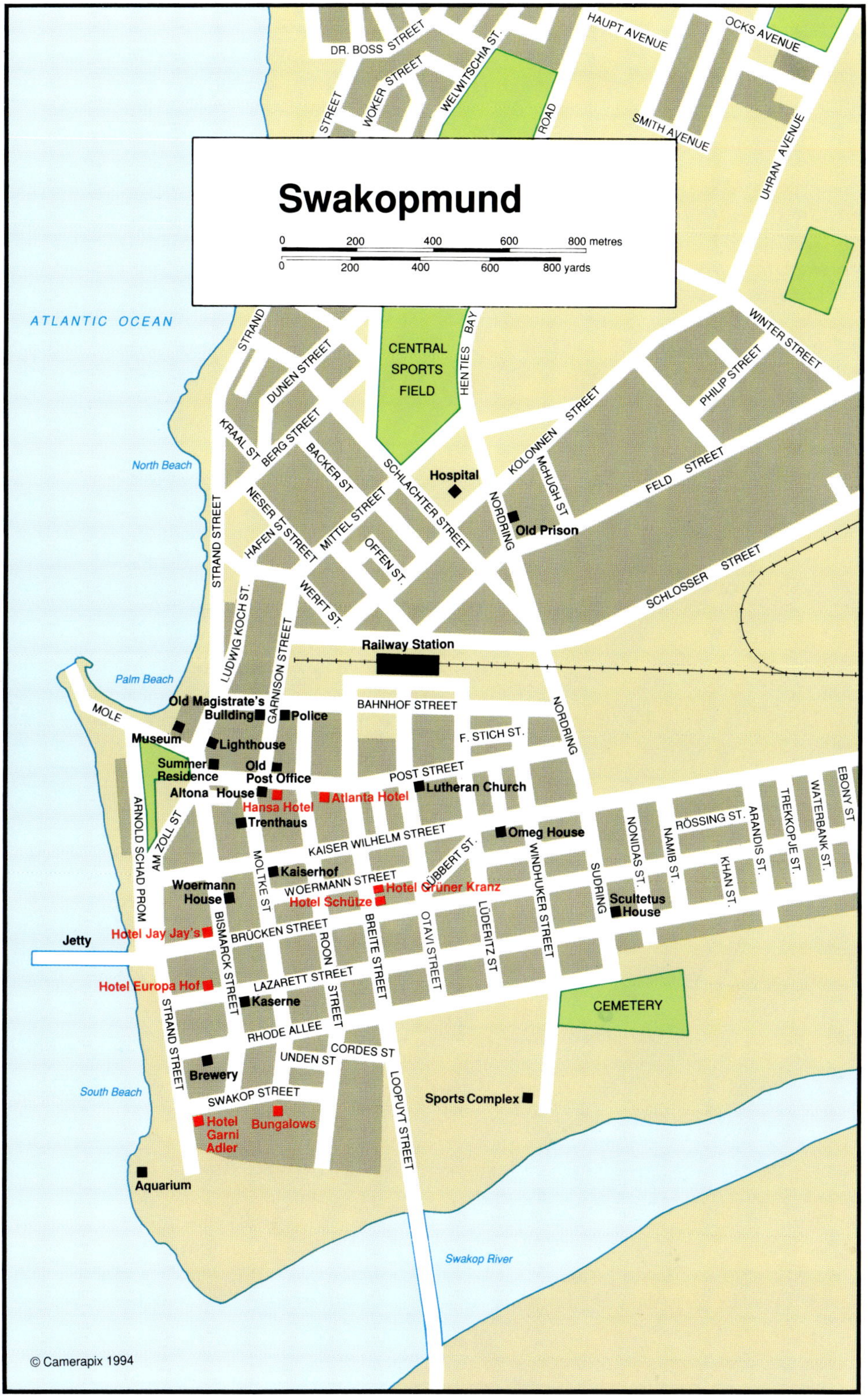
Swakopmund
0 200 400 600 800 metres
0 200 400 600 800 yards
ATLANTIC OCEAN
North Beach
Palm Beach
South Beach
Swakop River
DR. BOSS STREET
WOKER STREET
WELWITSCHIA ST.
ROAD
STREET
HAUPT AVENUE
OCKS AVENUE
SMITH AVENUE
UHRAN AVENUE
WINTER STREET
PHILIP STREET
STRAND
DUNEN STREET
HENTIES BAY
CENTRAL SPORTS FIELD
KOLONNEN STREET
FELD STREET
KRAAL ST
BERG STREET
BACKER ST
SCHLACHTER STREET
Hospital
McHUGH ST
NORDRING
Old Prison
NESER ST
HAFEN ST
STREET
MITTEL STREET
OFFEN ST.
STRAND STREET
SCHLOSSER STREET
WERFT ST.
LUDWIG KOCH ST.
GARNISON STREET
Railway Station
BAHNHOF STREET
Old Magistrate's Building
Police
MOLE
Museum
Lighthouse
F. STICH ST.
NORDRING
Summer Residence
Old Post Office
POST STREET
Altona House
Hansa Hotel
Atlanta Hotel
Lutheran Church
Trenthaus
ARNOLD SCHAD PROM
AM ZOLL ST
KAISER WILHELM STREET
Omeg House
RÖSSING ST.
EBONY ST
WATERBANK ST.
TREKKOPJE ST.
ARANDIS ST.
KHAN ST.
NAMIB ST.
NONIDAS ST.
SUDRING
WINDHUKER STREET
Kaiserhof
GÜBBERT ST.
MOLTKE ST
WOERMANN STREET
Hotel Grüner Kranz
Woermann House
Hotel Schütze
Scultetus House
Hotel Jay Jay's
BRÜCKEN STREET
BISMARCK STREET
ROON STREET
BREITE STREET
OTAVI STREET
LÜDERITZ ST
Jetty
LAZARETT STREET
Hotel Europa Hof
Kaserne
CEMETERY
STRAND STREET
RHODE ALLEE
CORDES ST
UNDEN ST
Brewery
SWAKOP STREET
LOOPUYT STREET
Sports Complex
Hotel Garni Adler
Bungalows
Aquarium
© Camerapix 1994

enormous impact necessitating the expansion of the infrastructure to make the town one of the most modern in the country (See "Namib Excursions: from Sandwich to Welwitschia", Part Two).

Getting there

Swakopmund, 356 kilometres (221 miles) from Windhoek, 659 kilometres (409 miles) from Namutoni, 619 kilometres (384 miles) from Mariental, 731 kilometres (454 miles) from Lüderitz, 840 kilometres (521 miles) from Keetmanshoop, 1,849 kilometres (1,149 miles) from Cape Town, and 2,327 kilometres (1,446 miles) from Johannesburg, is served by road, rail and air services.

When to go

Swakopmund has a year round temperate climate with occasional dry, hot spells. Christmas and Easter holidays are particularly busy, so reservations should be made well in advance.

Where to stay

Hansa Hotel (3-star), Hotel Europa Hof (2-star), Hotel Garni Adler (2-star), Hotel-Pension Schweitzerhaus (2-star), Strand Hotel (2-star), Rapmund Hotel-Pension (1-star), Atlanta Hotel (1-star), Hotel-Pension Deutsches Haus (1-star), Hotel Schütze (1-star), Hotel Jay-Jay's (1-star). See Listings for "Hotels". There are two campsites. See Listings.

Sightseeing

Palm Beach offers safe — if somewhat cold — swimming, and there is sheltered sunbathing in the lee of the old **Mole**. For the more adventurous there are magnificent beaches with excellent angling. Indeed, the climate is ideal for all kinds of activities.

There are restaurants, pubs and shops aplenty: boutiques, goldsmiths offering exquisitely crafted jewellery featuring Namibian precious and semi-precious stones, bakeries and sports shops. The town's colourful history is so recent that a visit to the **Museum**, **east** of the Mole, is enlightening. By far the best museum in the country, this well-kept Swakopmund institution started as the scientific collection of Dr Alfons Weber in 1951. It was transferred to the present site in 1960.

Special **exhibits** include panoramas of desert and sea life, a **collection** of **semi-precious stones**, an extensive **historical exhibition**, and a modern technical display of the largest **open-cast uranium mine** in the world at **Rössing**, which is not far away.

The museum itself was originally the harbour **customs shed**. But when Swakopmund was bombarded by the British auxiliary cruiser, the *Kinfauns Castle*, on 24 September 1914, it was destroyed by fire. Some forty years later the ruins were renovated to house the museum.

If the museum whets your appetite for more history and information, stroll along to the **Swakopmunder Buchhandlung**, a **bookshop** which has a vast collection of literature on the town and the country.

There, or in the museum, you will discover that Swakopmund's original name was Tsoakhaub — a Nama concoction of the words *tso* and *xoub,* two words that refer to the muddy colour the river turns the sea on the rare occasion when it comes into spate.

The source of Swakopmund's unique continental atmosphere is its historic buildings. A number of Namibia's artists have settled in the town, relishing the space, solitude and the ever-changing faces of the surrounding desert. Some of their work is featured in the old **Woermann House** in **Bismarck Street**.

Boasting graceful panelled walls and stucco ceilings, Woermann House was designed by Friedrich Höft as the offices of the Damara and Namaqua Trading Company. Completed in 1905, it included the 'Damara Tower' from which observers anxiously scanned the ocean for ships and the desert for ox-wagons.

In l909, Woermann and Brock, a trading company, bought the building renaming it Woermann House. After the Great War it

---

Opposite: One of the many architectural wonders in Swakopmund.

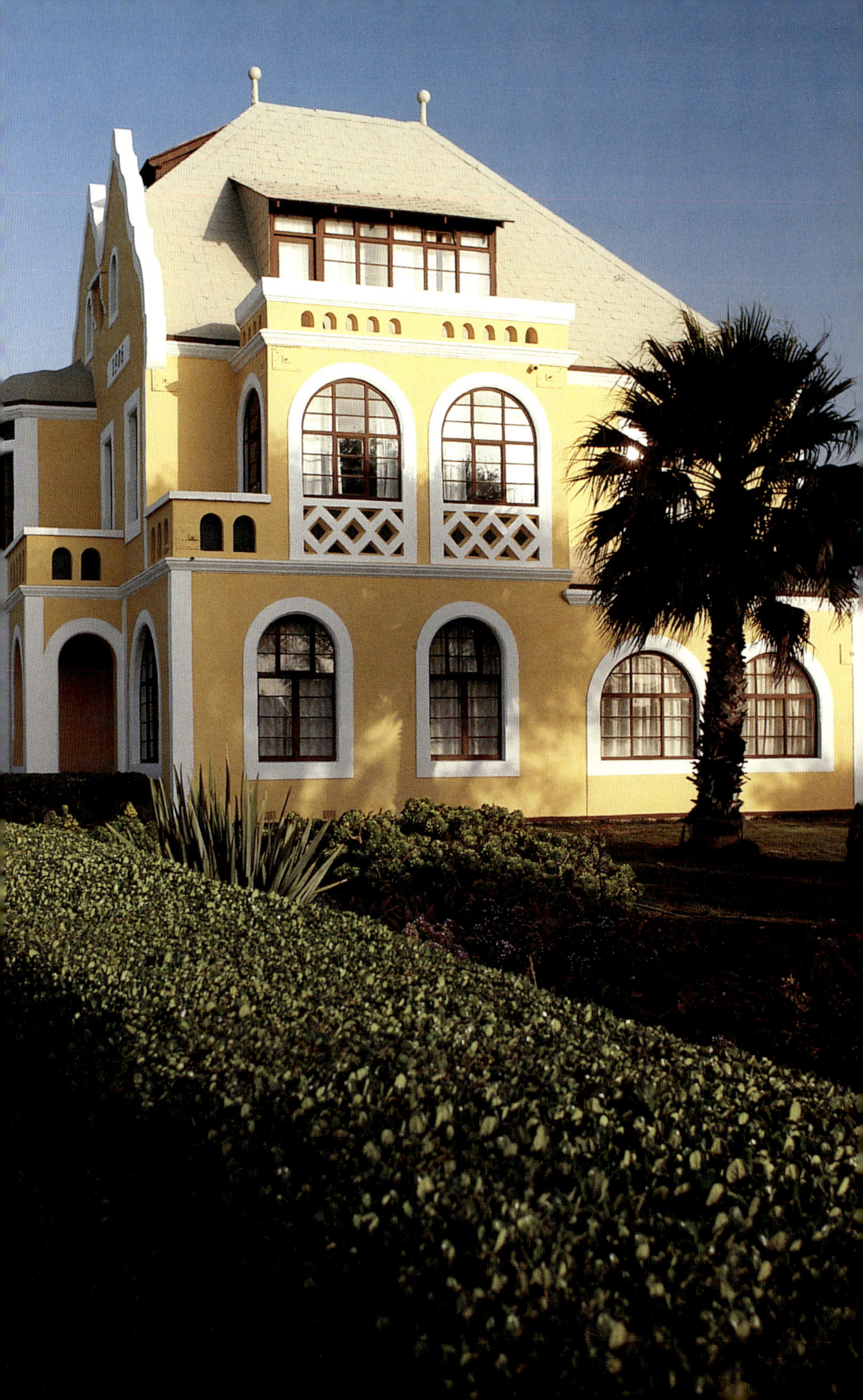

Above: One of Swakopmund's earliest and most magnificent buildings.

was converted into a school hostel and served in this capacity for a full forty years. Slowly, however, it fell into disrepair. By the 1970s it was virtually derelict. Now restored it houses an excellent **public library**.

From the **tower** there is an interesting perspective of Swakopmund and its layout. Indeed, Woermann House is the best starting point for exploring the hidden corners of this inspiring town. Next door is the **art gallery** with work by local artists.

Further south, across **Brücken Street**, are the **M. C. Human Flats**, built by the Bause brothers. They were responsible for many houses in the town from 1902 onwards. Their designs are mostly characterised by their interesting façades which were decorated with a wide variety of embellishments.

Down **Bismarck Street** and across **Lazarett Street**, the 1905 **Kaserne**, in typical German colonial style, is on the corner. It provided living quarters for the engineers' regiment sent to Swakopmund to fight the Herero uprising and build a landing pier and railway line into the interior. The **entrance hall** is decorated with the **crests** of the turn of the century **German states** along with a **plaque** with the names of the men who died in action.

Sea-front

On the seaboard, a **jetty** juts out into the Atlantic. The original 1905 wooden version was seriously damaged by spring floods and borer beetle which found their way into the structure. In 1914 it was dismantled by the South African occupation forces.

Construction of a solid iron pier began in 1911. But, at the outbreak of World War I, only one-third was complete. Then, in 1919, somebody had a brilliant idea. Planks were laid along the **north** side of the **pier** for pedestrians and anglers. Finally, an entire **promenade** was built, along which visitors may take in the ocean air.

A stroll along **Arnold Schad Promenade** brings you to the Mole, situated at the spot where Swakopmund was founded by Hauptmann Curt von Francois. Today pleasure boats are launched there. Swimming in the Mole basin is recommended. The beach is safe, with

Above: Steam engine, the 'Martin Luther', outside Swakopmund marks the failure of a curious humanitarian project.

faultless white sand ideal for sunbathing. There is a **children's pool**, a **play-park** and **hydro-slide** to keep young folk amused.

Next to the Mole basin is an Olympic-size indoor **swimming pool** with heated water and sliding roof, which is opened during sunny weather. There are also **two saunas** in the **basement**. And, as if this were not enough, there is excellent surfing and board sailing to be enjoyed.

The **Old Magistrate's Building** nestles on **Bahnhof Street**. Its fine gables and turrets are similar to those of the jail. Both buildings, designed by Otto Ertl, were built between 1907-8.

The Old Magistrate's Building was intended to be a school, but money for the project ran out and the state finally completed this landmark. It was then used as a court. At the edge of the **municipal gardens** is the **memorial** honouring those who died in World War I.

Warning over the Atlantic

Every town or city has a structure that stands out. The one building that stands head and shoulders above the others in Swakopmund is the 1910 **lighthouse**.

Stretching upwards for twenty-one metres, (seventy feet), its red and white stripes are a striking contrast against the faultless blue sky. Its role was to alert ships, in the fogs and mists of the dangerous Namibian coast, to the presence of rocks and land.

Next to the lighthouse is the *Kaiserliches Bezirksgericht*, built as a magistrate's court but which has served over the years as the summer residence of top government officials and is now the **Presidential holiday home**.

To the **east**, on **Am Zoll**, is the **Marine Memorial**. A Berlin sculptor was responsible for the work which was dedicated to the first Marine Expedition Corps who took part in the suppression of the Herero uprising. It was unveiled in July 1908.

Turn **south** down **Molkte Street** and you will find the **Trendthaus**, restored in 1974, yet another example of Swakopmund's beautiful colonial architecture. The **window boxes** give it Bavarian appeal.

Above: Sheltered sands of the holiday resort of Swakopmund with Strand Hotel in background.

On the corner of **Molkte** and **Post streets** are **Altona House** and **Ludwig Schröder House**, two well-preserved business and residential buildings, as appealing now as they were on the day they were completed. Altona House was the headquarters of the Woermann Line Shipping Company.

Almost directly across the street is the classically symmetrical **Old Post Office** which opened in April 1907, with just 120 post boxes. It served faithfully as the Post Office for sixty years until modern offices were built nearby in 1967. The town council now makes good use of this testimony to the German colonial period.

St Antonius Hospital, on Post Street, opened in March 1908. Originally staffed by sisters of the Franciscan order, the complex continued to serve as a Catholic hospital until 1987.

On the corner of **Post and Breite streets** stands the **Advertising Pillar**, one of many which became familiar sights throughout Swakopmund from 1905. They were named after the printer, E Litfass, who introduced the concept in Berlin in 1855. Businesses, shops and hotels — even the administration — displayed notices on the pillars. This is the only one that remains.

Further **east** down Post Street are several more German buildings. The one on the corner of **Otavi Street** served as a doctor's consulting room from 1910. Opposite stands the **old schoolhouse**, completed in 1913, which harmonises with the baroque style of the **Lutheran Church** and **parsonage** across the road.

On the corner of **Otavi** and **Kaiser Wilhelm streets** the 1911 **Villa Wille** is one of the most beautiful buildings in Swakopmund. The **decorated tower** is particularly eye-catching. Hermann Wille, a builder of note, was killed in action in 1915.

Early in the 1900s Swakopmund was connected to the interior by two railway lines — the Otavi Line to the Tsumeb copper mine and the State Line to Karibib, later extended to Windhoek. Each line had its own station, **OMEG House** in **Kaiser Wilhelm Street** and the state railway station, respectively. OMEG House served as goods sheds for the *Otavi Minen-und Eisenbahn-Gesellschaft* until 1910, when the state took over the line. It proved inadequate, however, and the railway line was diverted to the state station, the **roof** of which — typical of the period — is of particular interest.

Situated on the corner of **Kaiser and Molkte streets**, the **Hotel Kaiserhof** opened in May 1905. Sixteen rooms on the first floor accommodated twenty-six guests, with additional accommodation available on the ground floor. Fire destroyed the hotel in 1914 but it was rebuilt.

The **Deutsche-Afrika-Bank**, which opened in 1909, is on the corner of **Molkte** and **Woermann streets**. Further **south** on **Molkte Street** is the **Hohenzollern building**, undoubtedly the finest example of Victorian baroque in Swakopmund. Built between 1905 and 1906 as a hotel for Hermann Dietz, it later housed the council offices and has since been turned into flats

On the other side of Swakopmund the **old prison** on **Nordring Street** is still used. But it is easy to pass this building without realising it is a jail.

First communications

Near the **beach bungalows** on the **bank** of the **Swakop River** three interesting **towers** were the **radio mast** anchor points of the German radio station built in 1911. The radio station was for communication with Windhoek, ships passing along the west coast, and with Douala in the Cameroon, another German possession. But at the outbreak of World War I the Germans demolished the transmitter because of its strategic importance.

A little further **south** up the Swakop River the **ruins** of the **1926 railway bridge**, washed away during flash floods in 1931, are still visible.

Steam engine

Before the railway line was built, transport to the interior was by ox-wagon. At times there was not enough grazing or water along the way and the oxen perished from hunger and thirst.

Lieutenant Edmund Troost of Germany's Imperial Colonial Troops, who resolved to find an alternative, discovered a steam tractor in Germany. Such was his

Above: Swakopmund memorial to the German dead of World Wars I and II.

Overleaf: Hundreds of flamingo take to the air.

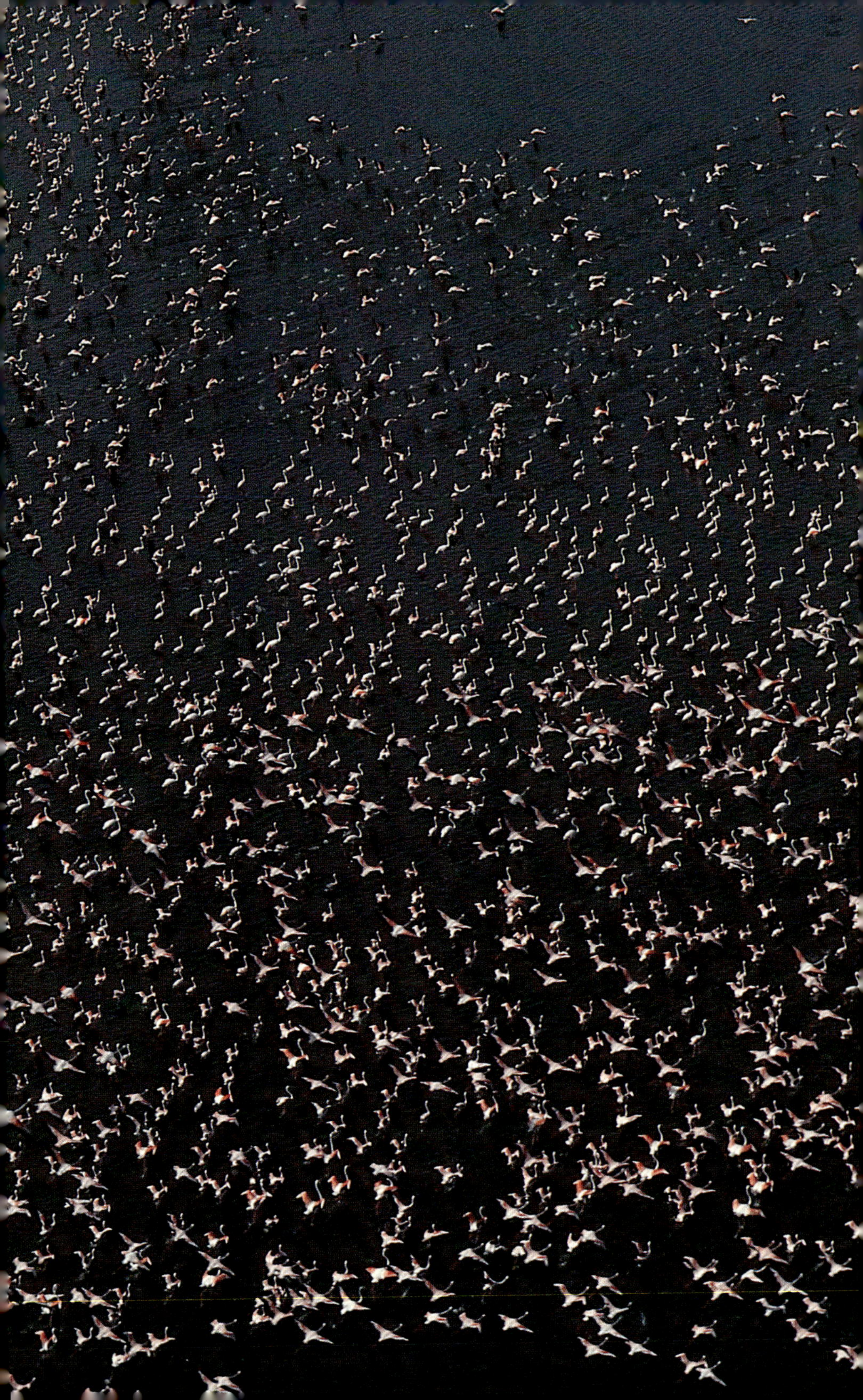

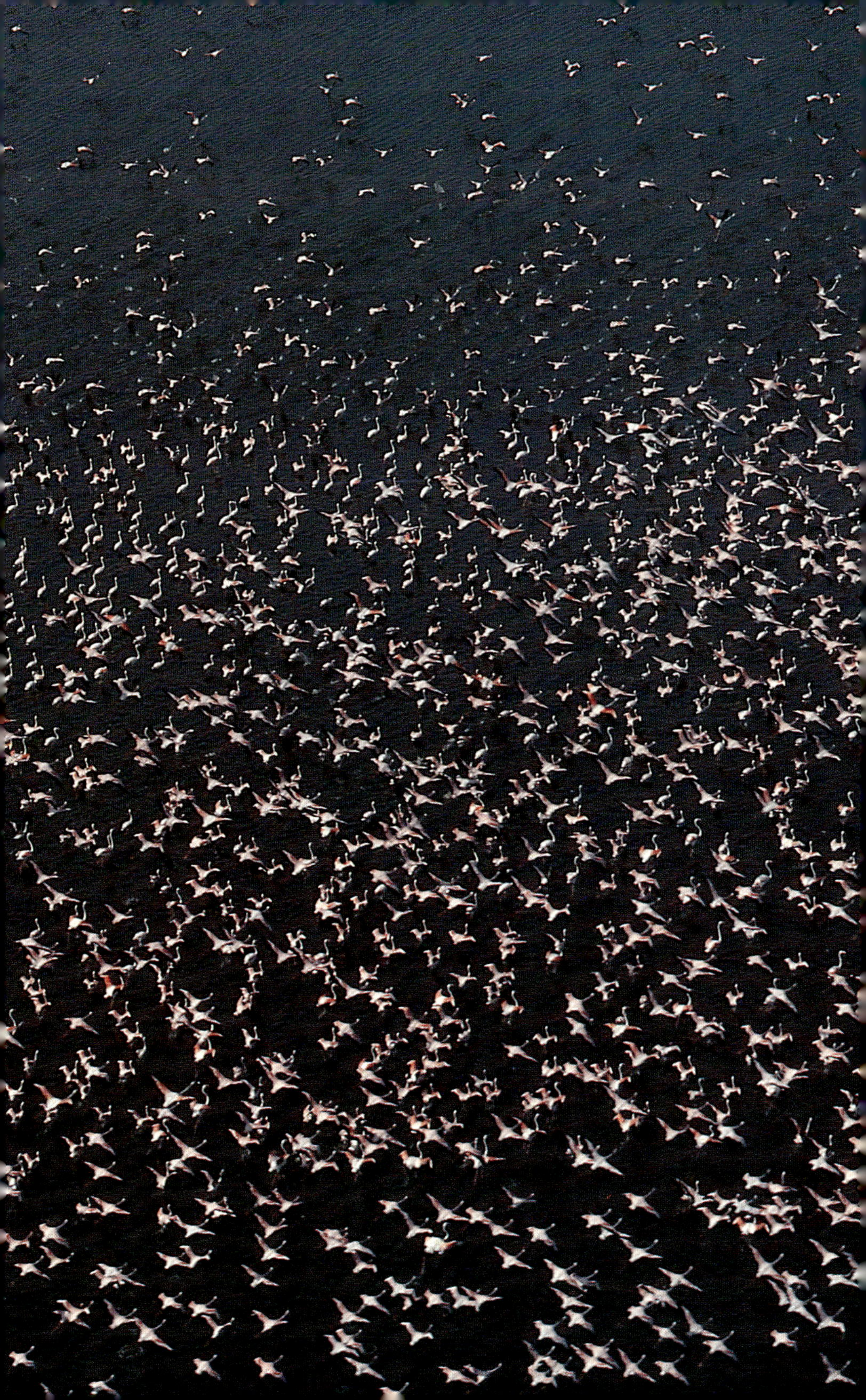

Above: Sundown over Guano Platform at Walvis Bay where the many artificial islands are used for the collection of guano.

determination to make his mark that he paid for it out of his own pocket. The fourteen-tonne machine was unloaded in Walvis Bay in 1896.

But after five months it was still stuck on the quayside, and the engine driver, his contract expired, departed.

Months later, after many difficulties, the engine began running only to become bogged down at the spot where it now stands, mounted on a plinth, just outside Swakopmund alongside the B2.

It was given the name **Martin Luther** because of the evangelist's famous statement: "Here I stand; God help me, I cannot do otherwise." The engine was restored and declared a **national monument** in 1975.

Taking it easy

From **south** of **Walvis Bay** to as far **north** as **Terrace Bay** on the **Skeleton Coast**, the coast is widely renowned for its excellent fishing. (See "The Skeleton Coast: Bleached Bones and Rusting Ships", Part Two). Steenbras, galjoen and kabeljou (Cape cod) are the most common catches.

Access to the beaches in the **National West Coast Tourist Recreation Area** — from **Swakopmund northwards** as far as the Ugab River — is virtually unlimited. In many places you can literally drive to the edge of the beach in an ordinary car.

The weekend edition of the *Namib Times* normally carries tips and advice on the most favoured angling spots. **Tackle** and **bait** may be bought at **supermarkets** and **filling stations**.

There are several **skiboats** for deep-sea angling trips. Divers also take out crayfish and black and white mussels.

Legal restrictions on the size and numbers of fish, mussels and crayfish are strictly enforced by inspectors. Before you go fishing check with the Directorate of Nature Conservation in the Ritterburg building, **Bismarck Street**.

The **Sports Club** and **Rössing Country Club**, fifteen kilometres (nine miles) **east** of the town, offer a great variety of facilities and temporary membership. An **eighteen-hole golf course**, en route to the country club, has well-tended greens and fairways of a high standard.

Walvis Bay: Bird Watcher's Eden

Walvis Bay is the only fully developed harbour on the Namibian coast. Despite the fact that Namibia gained its independence in 1990, Walvis Bay remained an enclave of South Africa until the end of 1992.

In 1993, the port was administered jointly by South Africa and Namibia and in 1994 South Africa relinquished all claims. Now visitors no longer need a South African visa to visit Walvis Bay. The town lacks Swakopmund's graceful architecture and lazy holiday ambience, its numbered streets and roads forming an unexciting grid. In fact, apart from its harbour and abundant birdlife, Walvis Bay has little of interest.

The deep-sea harbour is protected by a spit of land which ends at Pelican Point in the north. Where the spit joins the mainland the shallows are home to a remarkably diverse collection of birds. Indeed, the wetlands are easily the most spectacular and important in southern Africa.

Nevertheless, it was the natural harbour, not the prolific bird life, that attracted early navigators. The first-known ship to reach Walvis Bay was that of Bartholomeo Diaz on 8 December 1487, on his voyage to discover the southern tip of Africa and a route to the east.

The Portuguese, who found the area unattractive because of the lack of fresh water, took note of the abundance of fish, especially sardines, and named this coast *Praia dos Sardinha* — Coast of Sardines.

The high nitrogen content of the Benguela Current creates favourable conditions for plankton, food for whales and pilchards. The area is also ideal for seals and it is no wonder that American and British whalers flocked there during the seventeeth century. Later these seafaring activities, and rumours about the possibilities of copper deposits and herds of livestock in the interior, attracted Dutch settlers from South Africa's Cape Province.

In 1793, the *Meermin,* under Captain Duminy, was sent out to survey the area. The result was that Walvis Bay was annexed by Holland. But when the British occupied the Cape as allies of the Dutch in 1795, Captain Alexander was sent to hoist the British flag over Walvis Bay as well.

The first European settlers arrived in 1844 after an eight-month overland journey from the Cape. They founded new homes there, trading for livestock.

Then, in 1845, the first missionaries arrived, including one who immediately founded a Rhenish mission station at Rooibank in the Kuiseb Valley and preached to the Topnaar Hottentots.

Because of the cattle trade, and the copper mines opening up in the interior, the town flourished. The first road in the territory was built in 1844 at the instigation of the Nama chief, Jan Jonker Afrikaner.

In 1880 the British established an administration. Two years later they began collecting guano deposits from the island of Ichaboe. Now bird droppings are 'harvested' from artificial islands in the bay.

Fishing plays a major role in Walvis Bay's economy, especially anchovy and pilchard catches. But during the last two decades of the twentieth century the fishing grounds were over-exploited by foreign fleets. Pilchard catches have decreased since 1978 and fishermen are now forced 640 kilometres (400 miles) out into the open sea to make their catches.

One major problem for Walvis Bay was the supply of fresh water. An 1899 water condensation plant produced the most expensive water in the world and the demand for water by ships and locomotives soon exceeded capacity. In the following years, wells were sunk upstream in the Kuiseb at Rooibank.

Nonetheless, gardeners in Walvis Bay have a special problem. The groundwater level only three metres (ten feet) below the surface contains four-and-a-half times as much salt as seawater. Thus only shallow-rooted or salt resistant plants and trees, such as the casuarina which is indigenous to Australia, grow there.

In contrast to Swakopmund, only a few Germans live in Walvis Bay. Generally, the number of inhabitants varies according to the fishing season.

Above: Long a port, Walvis Bay remained wholly a South African enclave until 1994 when Namibia took over the administration of its major gateway to the world.

Getting there

Walvis Bay is thirty-one kilometres (nineteen miles) from Swakopmund, 389 kilometres (241 miles) from Windhoek, 814 kilometres (505 miles) from Keetmanshoop 758 kilometres (471 miles) from Lüderitz, 1,882 kilometres (1,170 miles) from Cape Town, and 2,360 kilometres (1,466 miles) from Johannesburg. There are road, rail and air services.

When to go

Walvis Bay is accessible all year round.

Where to stay

Casa Mia Hotel (2-star), Hotel Atlantic (2-star), Flamingo Hotel (1-star), Mermaid Hotel (1-star). See Listings for "Hotels". Golden Fish Guest House. See Listings.

Sightseeing

Walvis Bay may not be much of a tourist destination in the 1990s, but to bird lovers the world over it is a magical place.

The **wetland** comprises three sections — the **lagoon**, the **intertidal areas** and the **saltworks**. Each area supports at least a third of the bird population during the annual cycle, including half the world's **chestnut-banded plover**, as well as eighteen per cent of the southern African race of **blackened grebe**, forty-two per cent of southern Africa's **greater flamingo** and sixty per cent of **lesser flamingo**.

Resident species include the **kelp gull, white pelican, grey-headed gull, Hartlaub's gull, Caspian tern, swift tern** and **Damara tern**.

It is estimated that over 120,000 **wading birds** from northern Eurasia migrate to the Namib Coast each year and almost 50,000 make Walvis Bay their winter home.

The number of migrant Palaearctic waders often exceeds 234,000 with **curlew, sandpiper** and **sanderling** in great

Opposite: Flamingos wading shallows of Sandwich Harbour, one of the world's great natural bird sanctuaries guarded by the mighty dunes of the Namib Desert.

Above: Salt wagons leaving the salt pans north of Swakopmund where more than 180,000 tons of salt a year are recovered by evaporation.

numbers. Other fairly common species include **grey plover**, **knot** and **little stint**.

Among the more uncommon species are the **terek** and **marsh sandpipers**, and **whimbrel**. Often seen is the **white-fronted plover**, while occasionally **black-winged stilt** and **African black oyster-catcher** show themselves. Birds which, although rare, are regularly recorded at the wetland, are the **European oyster-catcher**, **Mongolian** and **sand plovers**, and **common redshank**.

There is a bird paradise at the **sewage disposal** works alongside **Rooikop Road**. To get there, turn into **Thirteenth Street** when entering the town from **Swakopmund**.

The **turnoff** to the Bird Paradise is **signposted** half-a-kilometre (one-third-of-a-mile) further on. Water is pumped into the ponds further inland in an attempt to reduce the mosquitoes.

The 1880 **Rhenish Mission church** was the **earliest building** in Walvis Bay. Originally a prefabricated 'kit' made from Hamburg timber, it arrived in 1879 and was erected the following year. When activity in the harbour increased the building was dismantled and moved to its present site. The walls were then plastered to prevent wood rot.

Railway across the sands

Nearly five kilometres (three miles) to the east of Walvis Bay, on **route C14**, the weathered remains of the **narrow-gauge line** built during the previous century are by the side of the road. The line was built to transport goods to and from the harbour and the terminal at **Plum**. Plum station was simply a store, a cottage and stable.

The first **locomotive**, offloaded in Walvis Bay in 1899, was used in the harbour for some time until attempts were made to take it on the line. Because of shifting sand, however, the experiment was abandoned.

In March 1905 the acting magistrate of Walvis Bay reported that some abandoned sections of the line were buried under mountains of sand more than nine metres (thirty feet) high.

The locomotive, named *Hope*, is now a **national monument**.

Lüderitz: Between Dunes, Diamonds, and Ocean

The historic harbour town of Lüderitz, with its quaint German-style architecture, rugged black rocks and deep blue waters where fishing boats ply their trade, evokes myriad images and memories.

Lüderitz now has a flourishing holiday resort enchantment in its quiet wind-and-sand-scoured streets, old German colonial buildings, and the morning mists that roll in from the sea, bringing life-giving moisture to the plants and animals of the Namib Desert.

Such ambience is perhaps due to its remote and unique location. Lüderitz, surrounded by hundreds of kilometres of desert, is self-contained. The streets are small and familiar, the walls neatly whitewashed, and the air filled with the sweet, rich smells of the shores where the Atlantic laps along the beaches and crashes against menacing boulders in the bay.

Lüderitz's weather is moderated by the ocean and is generally mild — though with occasional morning fogs and strong south-westerly winds from August to July.

The weather has not altered measurably since Bartholomeo Diaz first landed there in 1487. The renowned explorer named the bay *Angra dos Ilheos*, meaning 'Island Bay', although at a later stage it was called *Angra Pequena* — Narrow Bay. Before leaving, Diaz erected a cross on the peninsula as a sign that Portugal had taken possession of the country. Today, a replica marks the spot on Diaz Point where the original cross stood. (See "Land of Lost Horizons", Part One).

Despite occasional Dutch expeditions to the coast during the next 300 years, no settlement was founded until 3 January 1793, when the *Meermin* sailed into *Angra Pequena*. Captain Duminy, afraid another European power would steal a march on Holland, annexed the bay and surrounding islands.

But Dutch dominion was short-lived. In 1795 the British took possession of the newly founded settlement after the *Star*, under Captain Alexander, was dispatched to *Angra Pequena*. On landing, Alexander hoisted the British flag and fired three salvoes.

British whalers flourished there and in 1842, clearing of guano began attracting prospectors in the same way the discovery of diamonds did in later years. Hundreds of thousands of tonnes were removed from a twenty-two-metre (seventy-two-foot) thick layer accumulated over millennia.

Meanwhile, the British never officially proclaimed the Bay as their protectorate and, in May 1881, Heinrich Vogelsang bought the area on behalf of Adolf Lüderitz for 10,000 Reichsmark and 260 rifles from Joseph Fredericks, chief of the Bethanien Hottentots.

The British responded by blocking the harbour with a warship, effectively preventing fresh water being landed. Thus, Lüderitz appealed to Germany for help and by August 1884, the German flag flew over the settlement. South West Africa was born.

The birth of the new colony saw the end of Adolf Lüderitz. He was virtually bankrupt and the South West Africa Company took over his rights. He sailed to the Orange River in October 1886 to investigate its possibilities, but died on the way in mysterious circumstances.

The new town of Lüderitz grew very slowly but, by 1908, the railway line to Keetmanshoop was completed.

The same year August Stauch, a station master, discovered diamonds in the desert just outside the town. Lüderitz was transformed into a boom town.

Thanks to this period, Lüderitz is the only town in Namibia that can truly boast an almost uniform style of German colonial architecture. Bay and bow windows, gables with timber trim, stair-wells, verandahs, turret rooms and many other beautiful features — mostly in the Art Nouveau and German Imperial styles — decorate the buildings.

Unfortunately, the Namibian diamond rush soon ended and the town rapidly declined, only to be 'rediscovered' at the end of the 1970s. Despite a new awareness of its cultural heritage, the precarious prosperity of its 17,500 inhabitants is based

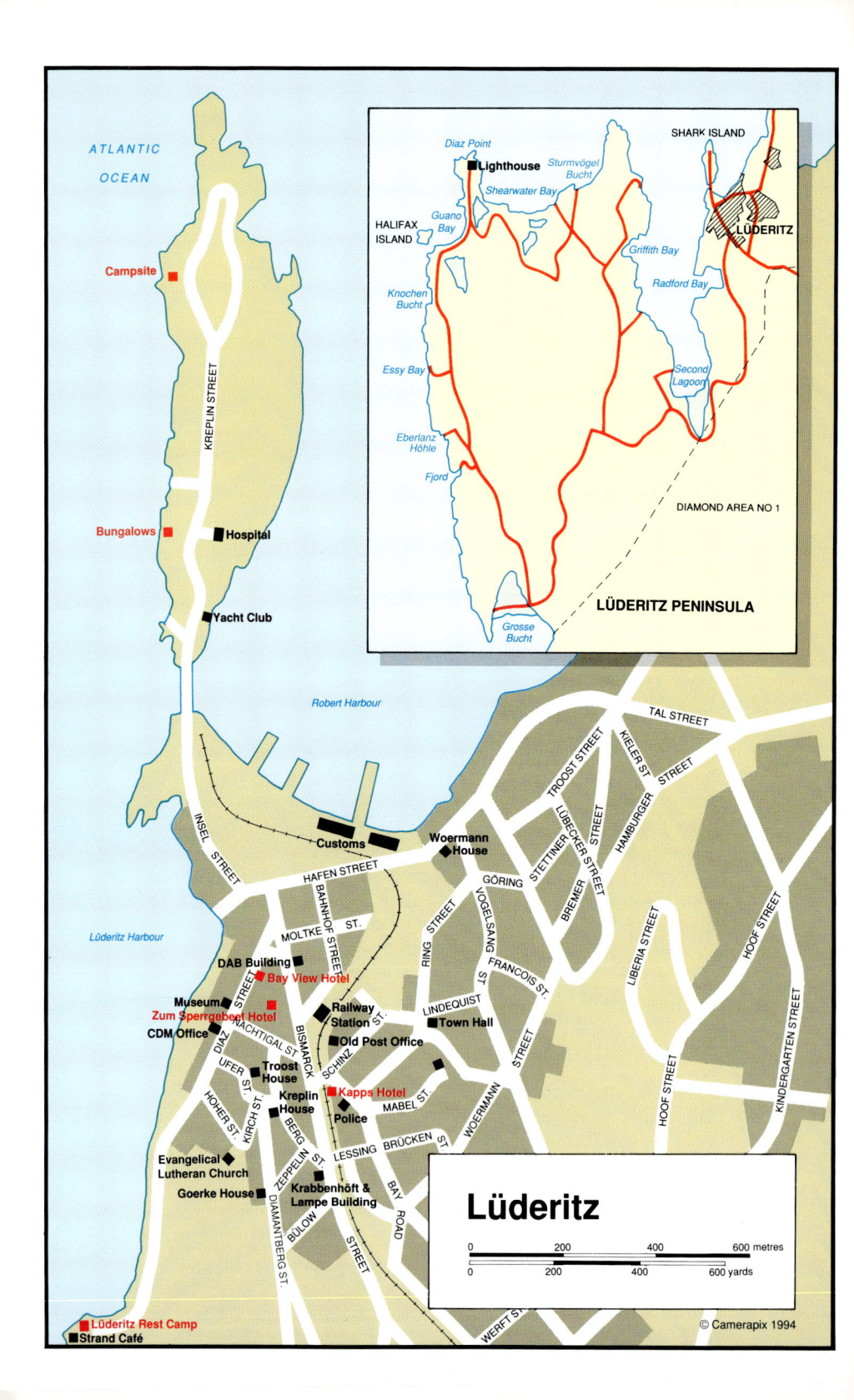

Lüderitz

Lüderitz Peninsula

- Diaz Point
- Lighthouse
- Sturmvögel Bucht
- Shearwater Bay
- Shark Island
- LÜDERITZ
- Halifax Island
- Guano Bay
- Griffith Bay
- Knochen Bucht
- Radford Bay
- Essy Bay
- Second Lagoon
- Eberlanz Höhle
- Fjord
- Grosse Bucht
- DIAMOND AREA NO 1

Lüderitz town

- Atlantic Ocean
- Campsite
- Kreplin Street
- Bungalows
- Hospital
- Yacht Club
- Robert Harbour
- Lüderitz Harbour
- Customs
- Woermann House
- Insel Street
- Hafen Street
- Bahnhof Street
- Moltke St.
- DAB Building
- Bay View Hotel
- Museum
- Zum Sperrgebiet Hotel
- CDM Office
- Diaz Street
- Nachtigal St.
- Bismarck St.
- Ring Street
- Vogelsang St.
- François St.
- Göring Street
- Stettiner Street
- Lübecker Street
- Bremer Street
- Hamburger Street
- Troost Street
- Kieler St.
- Tal Street
- Railway Station
- Lindequist St.
- Town Hall
- Old Post Office
- Liberia Street
- Hoof Street
- Kindergarten Street
- Ufer St.
- Schinz St.
- Troost House
- Kreplin House
- Kapps Hotel
- Mabel St.
- Police
- Woermann Street
- Hoher St.
- Kirch St.
- Berg St.
- Zeppelin St.
- Lessing St.
- Brücken St.
- Bay Road
- Evangelical Lutheran Church
- Goerke House
- Krabbenhöft & Lampe Building
- Diamantberg St.
- Bülow St.
- Werft St.
- Lüderitz Rest Camp
- Strand Café

0   200   400   600 metres
0   200   400   600 yards

© Camerapix 1994

mainly on the seasonal crayfish harvest and, increasingly, on tourists from both home and abroad.

Getting there

Lüderitz is 334 kilometres (207 miles) from Keetmanshoop, 356 kilometres (221 miles) from Swakopmund, 816 kilometres (507 miles) from Windhoek, 938 kilometres (583 miles) from Walvis Bay, 1,345 kilometres (836 miles) from Cape Town and 1,823 kilometres (1,133 miles) from Johannesburg.

The road from Keetmanshoop between Goageb and Aus is gravel. Drivers should take great care, especially at night. Watch out for marching sand dunes which constantly cover the road.

For those coming from the north there is a scenic drive via Helmeringhausen along route C13 which joins the trunk road at Aus. But no deviations are permitted as it runs through a restricted area.

Afternoon sandstorms are extremely powerful, sometimes literally sand-blasting vehicles of all their paint.

Road, rail and air services connect Lüderitz with Cape Town, Windhoek and Walvis Bay.

When to go

Lüderitz is accessible all year-round.

Where to stay

Bay View Hotel (2-star), Kapps Hotel (1-star), Zum Sperrgebiet Hotel, (1-star). See Listings for "Hotels". There are holiday chalets and a campsite. See Listings.

Sightseeing

A healthy way to kick off the morning in **Lüderitz** is to take a stroll down to **Robert Harbour** and greet the new-born day at the end of the **pier**. In the distance the dunes of the **Namib Desert** roll down to the choppy blue waters.

Yacht trips leaving from Robert Harbour, weather permitting, last between two-and-a-half and three hours, with a close-up view of the **penguin colony** on **Halifax Island**. The trip affords beautiful views of Lüderitz and its many bays. **Dolphins** frequently sound near the bow of the yacht.

Bismarck Street, between **Molkte** and **Bahnhof streets**, is home to the **Deutsche-Afrika-Bank building**. Part of the upper, and all the lower, storeys are built of stone. The architects, the Bause brothers, incorporated an elaborate form, designing a belltower and Renaissance-style gable.

Station

Even today, despite the roads which stretch defiantly across the sands, the **railway station** remains the focal point of Lüderitz. It is easily found on the **corner** of **Bismarck Street** and **Bahnhof Street**. The station is built in a combination of architectural styles and was not completed until 1914 — seven years after the railway began.

Continuing up Bismarck Street, turn into **Schinz Street** for the **Old Post Office** building for which the first plans were drafted by a railway commissioner. However, Oswald Reinhardt, a successor, altered the design to include an **upper storey** with a **tower**.

A **public clock** was later placed on the tower, ringing for the first time on New Year's Eve, 1908. But it was transplanted in 1912 to the church tower, where it has remained. The offices of the **Directorate of Nature Conservation** are now housed there.

Cross from **Bismarck Street** into **Nachtigall's Street** and then into **Berg Street** for the **Altstadt area** — the older part of Lüderitz. There is nothing quite like it anywhere else in Namibia.

Troost House (1901) is a semi-detached **residence** in typical colonial-style. Edmund Troost paid a king's ransom to have it built but never spent a single night there. Architecturally, it blends in well with its neighbours, especially the **house** to the **south**, also built by the same architect, Hermann Metje.

Double-storeyed **Kreplin House** on the corner of **Berg** and **Diamantberg streets** has a symmetrical façade dating back to the close of 1909. It belonged to swashbuckling Emil Kreplin, who began his career in Namibia as the manager of the railway, became director of a diamond company and was later the first mayor of Lüderitz.

Built by Friedrich Kramer, Kreplin

Above: Stained glass windows of the Church on the Rock at Lüderitz were donated by Kaiser Wilhelm of Germany.

House is one of the few examples belonging to the second period of the Wilhelminische style similar to Woermann House in Swakopmund.

Further south, down **Berg Street**, is the **Krabbenhöft and Lampe shop** built by Kramer after he completed Kreplin House. The shop and adjoining residence were owned by the trading firm of Krabbenhöft and Lampe which also had branches in Gibeon, Helmeringhausen and Keetmanshoop.

With its **symmetrical façade** and **two storeys**, this masterpiece reflects the style of the neo-Renaissance. The **windows** of the first storey, however, are not positioned directly above the arches on the ground floor.

Karakul carpets

The **Karakul carpet mill** inside produces thick, luxurious carpets which are extremely dense and tight. Customers order according to their preferences and tastes.

Turn back on **Berg Street** and onto **Zeppelin Street**. Almost straight in front, up on **Diamond Hill**, is **Goerke House**. The **top window** affords one of the best views of the town, especially of the **Evangelical Lutheran Church**. Hans Goerke lived there from 1890 until he returned to Germany at the end of February 1912.

Goerke was manager and shareholder of three different companies although, before his rise to riches, he had been a store inspector in the German army. The eye-catching **sundial** is unique — a Wilhelminische decoration unknown in Namibia at the time.

In April 1930 Consolidated Diamond Mines (CDM) bought the house and, in February 1944, it was acquired by the South West Africa Administration. The magistrate occupied the Goerke House during this period — hence the other name by which it is known — **Old Magistrate's Residency**. In February 1983, CDM bought the property and restored the building to its original state. It is now a **guest house** for CDM officials and important visitors and when occupied is closed to the public.

Above: Lonely grave of George Pondo marks the Atlantic shores near Lüderitz.

Church on the rock

The **Evangelical Lutheran Church** lies below Goerke House on **Kirch Street**, dominating the much-photographed view of the town from the bay. *Felsenkirche* — the church on the rock — was built in 1906 and its first minister arrived from Germany in December 1909. The **parsonage** was built by Heinrich Bause the following year. His brother, Albert, was responsible for the design and construction of the church. One of the beautiful **stained glass altar windows** was donated by Kaiser Wilhelm II, and the **Bible** by his wife.

The architecture is more in keeping with Victorian Gothic because the Bause brothers came to Namibia from the Cape with its strong Victorian influences.

The church is normally locked, but is open to the public on Saturdays and Sundays at 1800 hours when the bells are rung. However, it can be visited at other times — the best being sunset — by arrangement with the church council.

On the other side of town, on the corner of **Vogelsang** and **Hafen streets**, is **Woermann House**. The Woermann Line established offices there after they began transporting German troops to Lüderitz.

The **hill** on the site had to be levelled before construction could begin. The rocks that were broken up were used in building the foundations and ground floor. Although the design is simple, the building is rendered unusual by the presence of a water condenser — then a brilliant and inspired technical innovation.

Walk **south** along **Vogelsang Street**, turn into **Lindequist Street** and at the **T-junction** with **Ring Street** stands the 1912-13 **Turnhalle**. Like the Town Hall in Windhoek, the building began life as a gymnasium. Its simple lines are broken by a curved gable with matching semi-circular window. Rectangular windows, separated by pillars, break the monotony of the side walls and allow light to enter the building.

Museum

Wherever visitors go in this handsome town, history constantly comes to life and

Above: Late afternoon sunshine bathes the streets of Lüderitz.

confronts them. The **museum**, located on **Diaz Street**, focuses on the early days of Lüderitz and the surrounding Namib Desert. It was founded by Friedrich Eberlanz as a private collection. He arrived in Lüderitz in 1914 and, fascinated by the local vegetation, discovered new species of succulents, some of which are named after him.

During his wanderings around the town he also came across stone implements and other items. Scientists and other interested people wanted to view his collection and that was the start of the museum.

Crayfishing

One of the major industries of Lüderitz is crayfish, for which it is famous. During the season, which extends from 1 November to 30 April, the factories may be viewed by arrangement with the management.

Left: Colourful flowers in a Lüderitz garden.

Opposite: Westering sun catches facade of Lüderitz's *Felsenkirche* — church on the rock — consecrated in 1912.

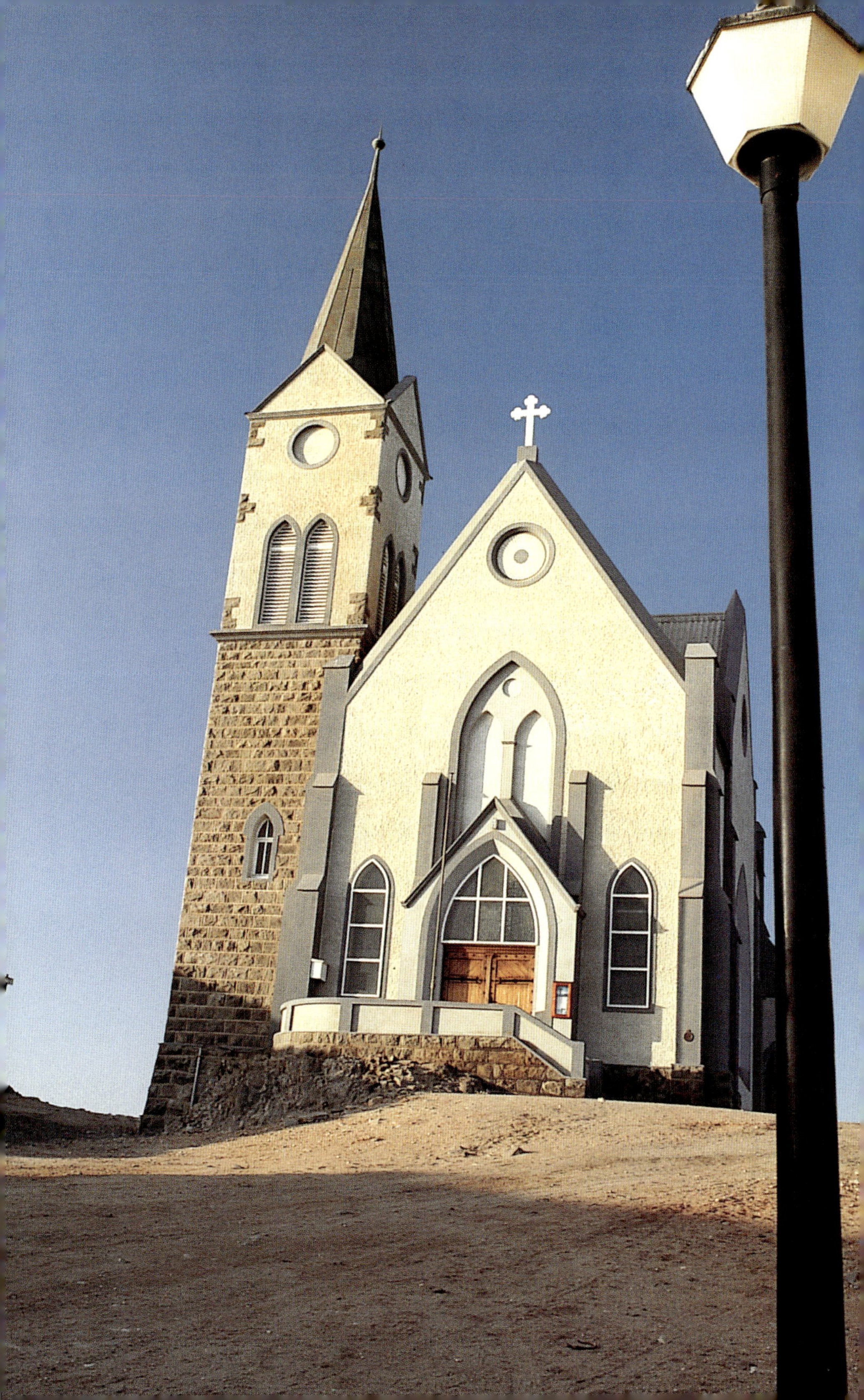

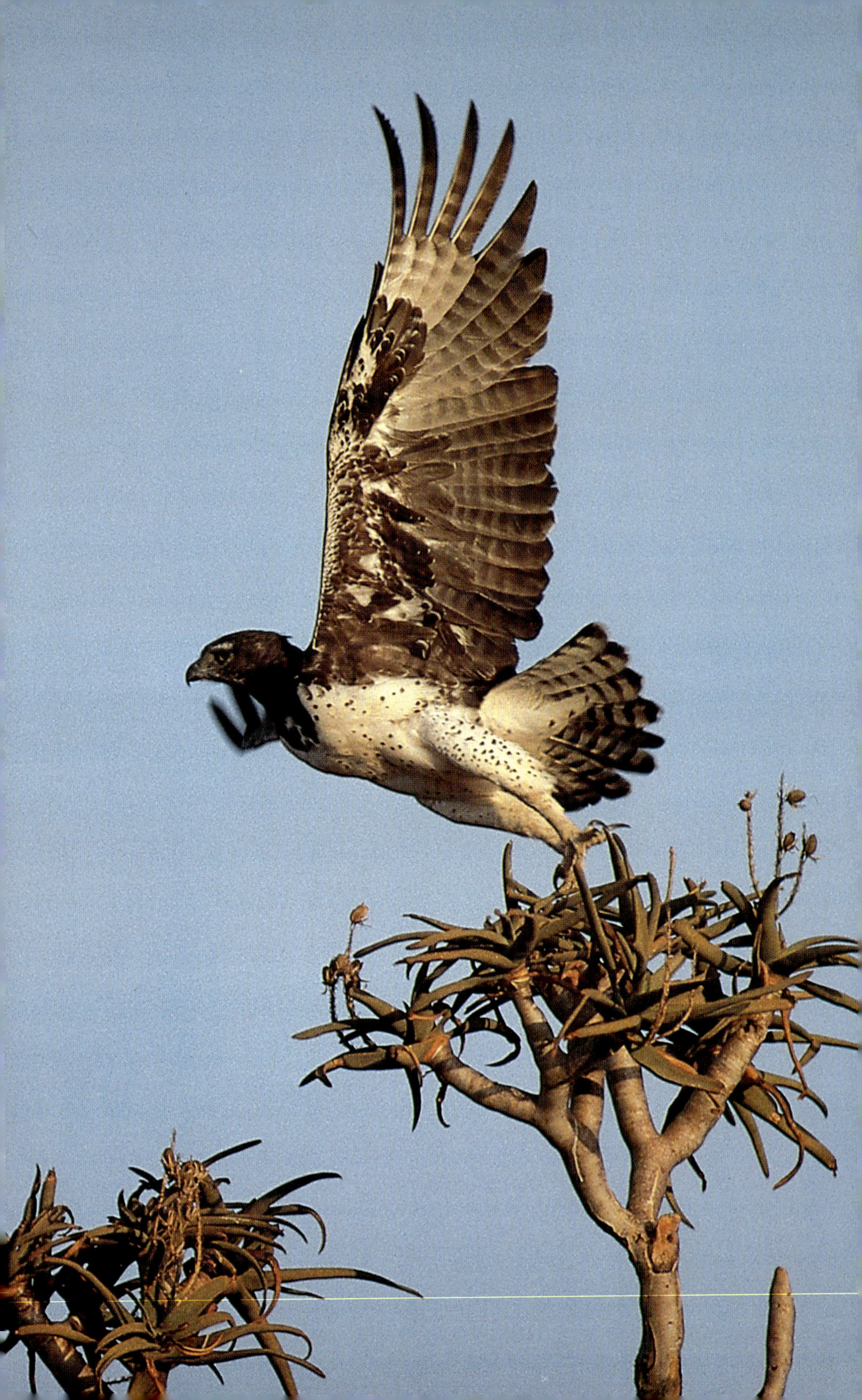

PART FOUR: SPECIAL FEATURES

Above: Study in composition — cheetah gets itself into focus.
Opposite: Young martial eagle leaves its desert perch.

Wildlife: Just Out of This World

Since Independence, Namibia has gained a justified reputation as one of the finest wildlife countries in Africa. With twenty-three wildlife and nature sanctuaries covering 112,236 square kilometres (43,334 square miles), more than thirteen per cent of its total land area is set aside solely for conservation of natural resources.

With few exceptions, virtually all indigenous species of mammal, bird, reptile and insect are well represented. Indeed, Namibia boasts one of the greatest wildlife populations in the world — some species of which are truly unique, many rare, and a few whose lineage goes back long before the first ancestors of mankind evolved.

Ivory Kings

The Kunene and Erongo regions, the Etosha National Park, the Kalahari Desert and the Caprivi Region are home to Namibia's elephant populations.

Elephants were absent for a long period from the **Etosha National Park**, reappearing there in the early 1950s after almost half a century. A large number of boreholes were subsequently sunk to attract more of them from the surrounding farmland, and this programme, combined with fencing the park, resulted in a massive increase to the extent that 535 had to be killed between 1983 and 1985 to bring their numbers closer to the carrying capacity of the land.

Although elephants no longer migrate between Etosha, Kavango, Damaraland and Kaokoland, their movements within Etosha are monitored by radio collars beamed to a satellite.

The desert-dwelling elephants of Kaokoland and Damaraland are thought to be possibly unique.

The **eastern population**, which roams between **Kavango** and the edges of the Etosha National Park in a region where there is between 250 and 300 millimetres (ten and twelve inches) of rain a year, are seen also in Owambo, now part of Kunene and three smaller regions, and also in the area around **Outjo**.

The desert-dwelling elephants trek long distances between the fringes of **Etosha National Park** and the **Namib Desert's Atlantic seaboard**.

In this area, where annual rainfall is between 150 and 200 millimetres (six and eight inches), elephant travel between twenty-five kilometres (fifteen miles) and seventy kilometres (forty-three miles) a day in search of food and water. During the long dry season they often go as long as four or five days without water.

These elephants differ from others elsewhere in Africa which uproot trees — regularly turning woodlands into grasslands. Namibia's desert-dwelling elephants have never been observed to uproot or fell a tree — an indication, perhaps, that they realise the value of any form of vegetation in such an arid land.

The African elephant weighs anything from three-and-a-half to six-and-a-half tonnes. An average elephant eats between ninety and 270 kilos (200-600 pounds) of fodder and drinks between 200 and 300 litres (forty-four and sixty-six gallons) of water a day when available.

It depends almost entirely on its trunk, which it uses for scent and communication, washing and cleaning, carrying and clearing, drinking and eating. The tusks, upper incisors, are simply secondary — but important — lifting, carrying and clearing tools.

An elephant's life span depends on its lower teeth, which are highly adapted to its mode of living. As one is worn away, the next one moves down the jaw to push it out. When the last one has come forward, at any age between fifty and seventy years, the elephant will eventually die of starvation.

Gestation takes close to two years and calves weigh between 120 and 135 kilos (265-300 pounds). During labour, the mother is attended by two other females — 'midwives' — which accompany her when she withdraws from the herd to give birth in discreet privacy. Although their sight is

Above: Lion cubs with mother.

poor, elephants have an excellent sense of smell and well-developed hearing. An elephant's brain is three-and-a-half times heavier than that of a human being — weighing between three-and-a-half and five kilos (eight and eleven pounds).

Rhino

In the Etosha National Park, and other sanctuaries, there is a small but growing population of **white rhinoceros**, *Ceratotherium simum*, a species long close to extinction throughout Africa.

It is not easy to distinguish at a glance between white and **black rhinoceros**, *Diceros bicornis*, for the distinction is not one of colour. The white rhinoceros derives its name from the Afrikaans, *weit*, meaning wide-mouthed, while the black rhinoceros has a hook-lipped mouth. The white rhino is a grazer, not a browser.

White rhino are more docile and gregarious than black rhino, moving in families and groups of between two and five. Much more solid than the black, it is normally a good fifteen centimetres (six inches) higher at the shoulder and weighs between 2,000 and 4,000 kilos (4,400-8,820 pounds), making it the biggest of all land animals after the elephant.

The black rhino, under threat everywhere and down to around 2,000 for the whole African continent in 1990, is under close guard in the **Etosha National Park,** which has the world's largest single surviving population. (See "Wildlife Eden: the Etosha National Park", Part Two).

It weighs between 907 and 1,364 kilos (2,000-3,000 pounds). The average size of its horn varies between fifty and ninety centimetres (one and three feet) for the front horn and just over fifty centimetres (two feet) for the rear horn. With its relatively small feet, three-toed hooves and pointed, prehensile upper lip, the black rhino is a browser and not a grazer.

Buffalo

Buffalo are the largest bovids in Namibia. Cattle-like in appearance, males are larger than females and weigh up to about 800 kilos (1,764 pounds). Both sexes have wide, curving horns but these are more massive in males.

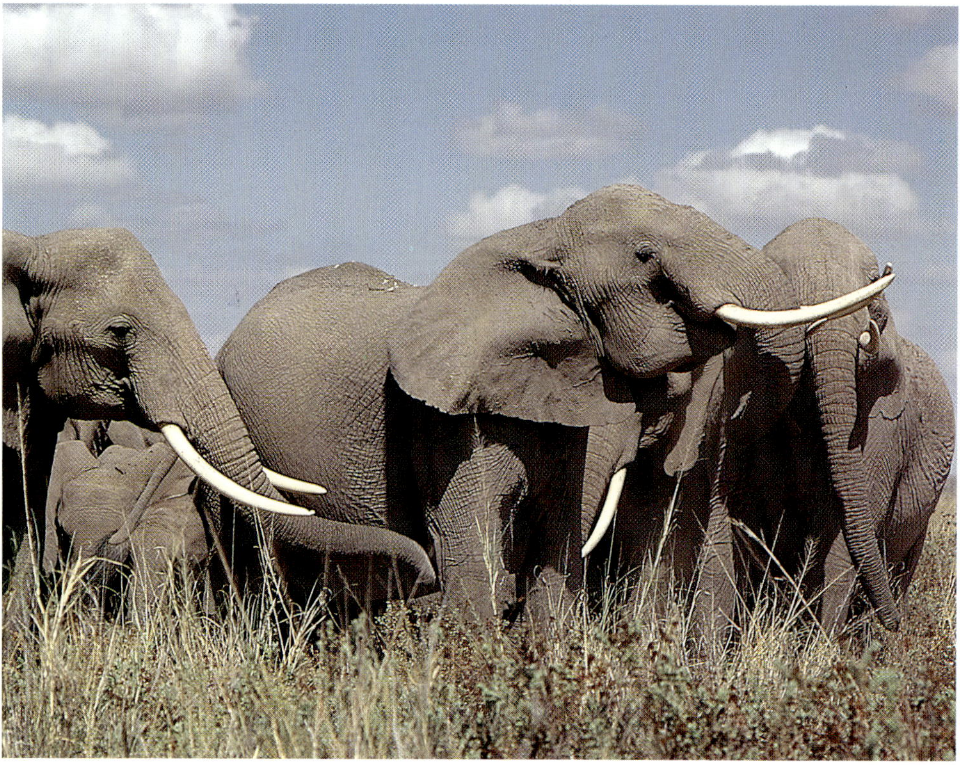

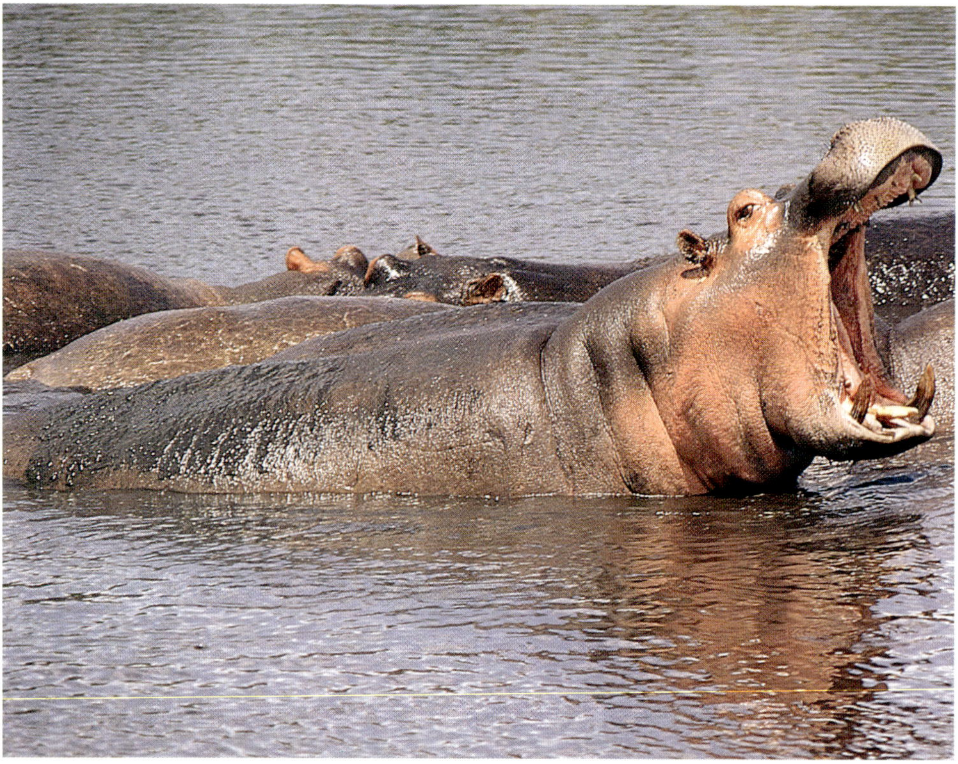

They are almost entirely grazers, dependent on water, and often form huge herds ranging between 500 and 2,000 individuals. Old males, however, frequently live alone or in small bachelor groups, and although often killed by lions, they are formidable animals. It is not uncommon for a lion to be killed in such an attack.

Giraffe

Many other large mammals occur in good numbers throughout Namibia's magnificent **wildlife sanctuaries**. **Giraffe** are particularly plentiful in the **Etosha National Park**.

Nature has given the giraffe, the world's tallest creature, several systems to help it cope with the high life — including a prehensile upper lip and a forty-five centimetre (eighteen-inch) tongue, the longest of any animal.

They also have a complex and unique system of canals and valves that maintain constant blood pressure whether the giraffe is standing tall or stooping to drink.

Giraffe, more closely related to the deer family than any other living creatures, run with a curious and fascinating lope at speeds of up to fifty-six kilometres (thirty-five miles) an hour.

Measuring anything from four-and-a-half to five-and-a-half metres (fifteen to eighteen feet) from the tip of toe to the top of head, giraffe weigh up to 1,270 kilos (2,800 pounds).

River dwellers

Namibia's three perennial rivers, the **Kunene**, **Okavango** and **Orange**, along with the **wetlands** of the **Caprivi Strip,** are home to the country's **crocodile** and **hippopotamus** populations.

Weighing up to four tonnes, the hippopotamus, the third-largest land animal, is sensitive to sunlight and remains in the water throughout the day. Hippo can stay submerged for as long as six minutes. True amphibians, they eat, mate and give birth under water, and spend most of the day sleeping and resting there, coming up frequently to blow air and recharge their lungs.

Their passive appearance belies a potential for aggression that makes them as deadly as buffalo, as many canoeists can testify. Hippo are especially dangerous out of water, and cause many injuries and deaths each year.

Crocodile also lurk in Namibia's waterways. For all its sinister-looking teeth, however, the crocodile is unable to chew. When it eats large prey, the reptile clamps its jaws on its victim's limbs and threshes around in the water, often rotating several times until the limb is wrenched from the body.

To swallow, it raises its head and lets the food fall to the back of its throat. Bodies recovered from dead crocodiles fifteen hours after being consumed have been virtually unmarked.

These cold-blooded saurians, the first species of which evolved more than 130 million years ago, depend entirely on external temperatures to maintain their own — and so regulate their body heat according to the time of day. They leave the water early in the morning to warm up in the sun, returning to escape the excessive heat of high noon, and resurface later in the cool of the afternoon to bask once more in the sun.

Crocodile are caring parents and tenacious of life — the heart of one crocodile continued to beat sixty minutes after it was cut out of the body.

The cats

There are seven species of cats in Namibia, namely lion, leopard, cheetah, caracal, African wild cat, black-footed cat (or small-spotted cat) and serval. Of these only the black-footed cat is endemic to southern Africa.

The largest African carnivore is the **lion,** a species whose range has shrunk since historical times. They were exterminated in Greece in about AD 100 and today are extinct

Opposite top: Elephant in Etosha National Park.

Opposite: Hippo's yawn is a warning to potential enemies.

in Europe. The Asian population is endangered. They are also extinct in North Africa.

In Namibia they are virtually confined to the major **national parks** and sanctuaries, and areas such as **Kaokoland** and the **Kalahari Desert**, where human populations — and their cattle — are low.

The lion weighs up to 280 kilos (620 pounds). Its amber-coloured eyes, like those of the leopard, differ from most cats in that they are circular not oval.

Inherently lazy (some say to conserve their strength) the lion is nevertheless extremely powerful. At one leap it can clear barriers almost four metres (thirteen feet) high, or a chasm up to twelve metres (forty feet) across.

Lion hunt communally by running down their preferred prey — zebra, hartebeest, wildebeest and springbok — at a top speed of around sixty-four kilometres (forty miles) an hour.

Their favourite method is to pounce on the victim's back, drag it to the ground and seize it by the throat. On average, in an ordinary year, a lion or lioness accounts for nineteen head of game at a weight of about 115 kilos (253 pounds) for each kill.

Prides, which number up to thirty animals, mostly females and young, mark their range — up to 160 square kilometres (sixty-two square miles) — by urination.

The lion's roar, rarely heard during daytime, carries as far as eight kilometres (five miles) and signals territorial ownership. So powerful is this roar it stirs the dust two metres (eight feet) away.

There is a balanced population of lion in Namibia's wildlife sanctuaries. And some are even seen along the **Skeleton Coast**, making their way with other creatures down to the linear rivers that cut across the **Namib Desert**.

Prime areas for the lion include the **Etosha** and **Mudumu National Parks**. At Etosha's **Mokuti Lodge** visitors watch them feeding at night under the light of artificial moons.

Night cat

Many areas — such as the **Fish River Canyon**, the **Waterberg Plateau Park** and **Tsaobis Leopard Nature Park** in the Khomas Hochland west of Windhoek — are home to **leopard**. The hoarse rasping cough of the leopard, repeated at intervals, alarms all but the bravest.

In spite of centuries of persecution the leopard has one of the widest geographical distributions of any terrestrial mammal, occurring from China and India and all across Africa to Namibia. Its capacity to adapt to changes enables it to survive in developing Africa with more success than any other large wild animal.

Despite this, visitors who see a leopard are extremely lucky, for they are solitary and secretive as well as nocturnal and shy. They can be seen at close range in a large enclosure on the **Düsternbrook Farm**, north of Windhoek.

Much smaller than a lion, the leopard weighs anything between thirty and thirty-eight kilos (sixty-six and eighty-four pounds). Its sandy fur is exquisitely patterned with dark rosettes.

Superb hunters, these cats prefer to kill by leaping from the branches and seizing the neck or throat of their prey. What they cannot eat immediately, they haul up a tree, out of reach of scavengers. In this way, leopard monopolise their kills — even if towards the end the meat becomes rancid.

Leopards prey on anything from small rodents to fairly large gazelle and antelope. They even eat fish and come readily to carrion.

Fast cat

The **cheetah**, fastest animal on earth and the most stunningly graceful of all big cats, as well as the most tractable, was once common worldwide but now its numbers are dwindling fast. Namibia is home to the largest single remaining population of these slender, graceful creatures.

In fact, the cheetah's greatest hope of

Opposite top: Crocodile are found in abundance in the Okavango and Caprivi Strip and in the River Kunene.
Opposite: Jackal on kill in Namibian wilderness.

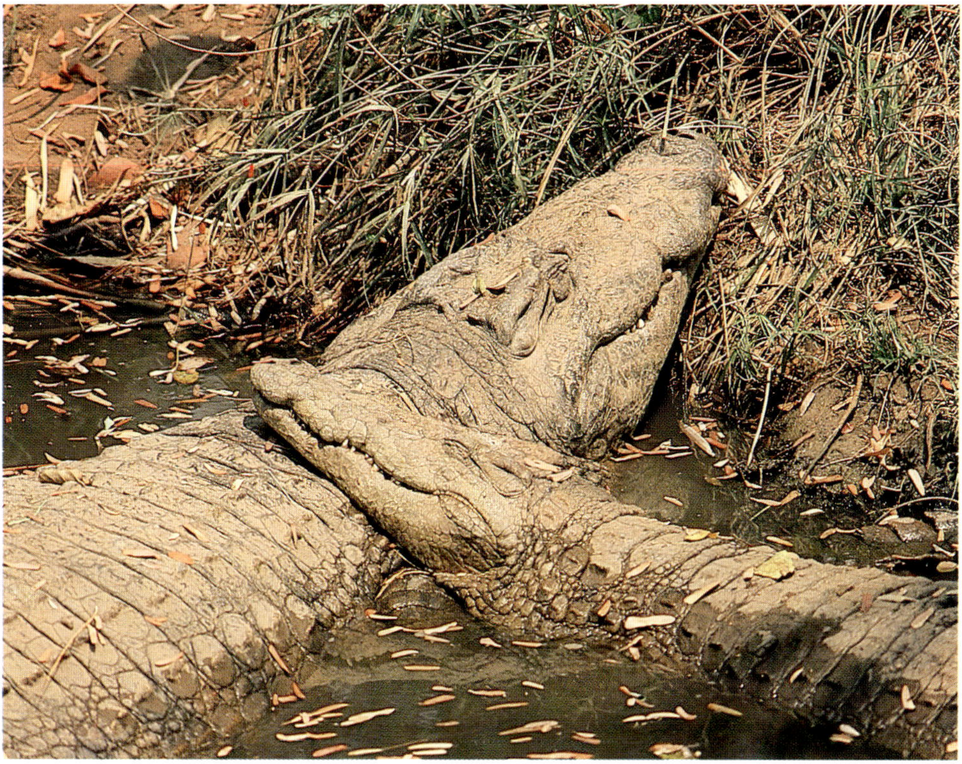

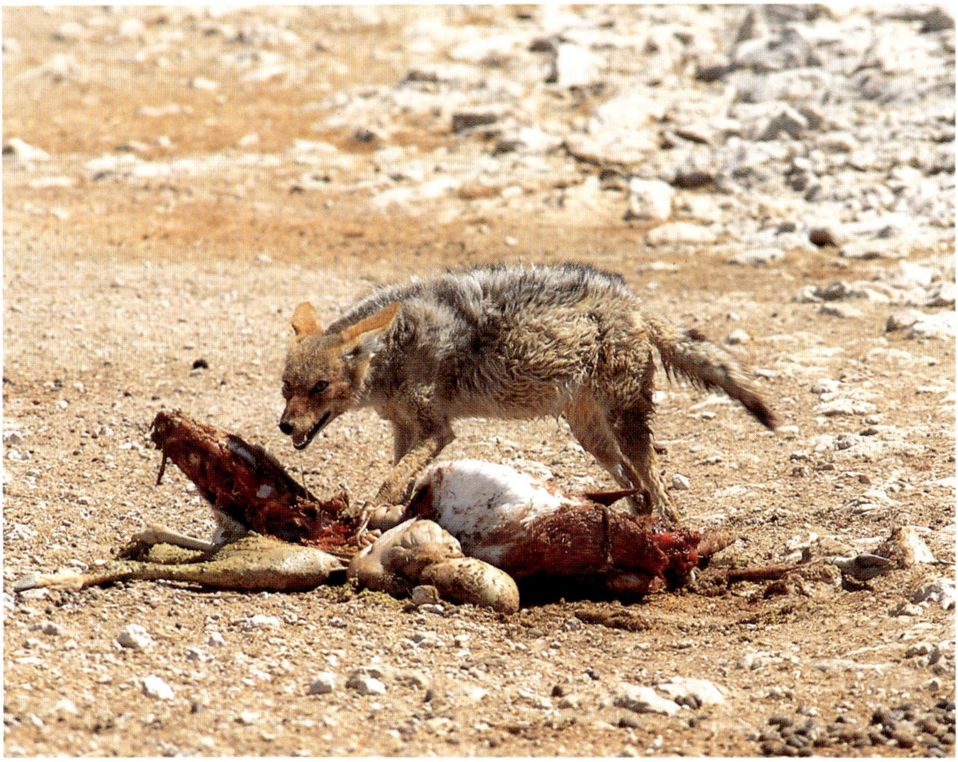

Above: Male kudu are distinguished by their magnificent lyrate horns.

survival lies in Namibia's pristine countryside, although even there its numbers slumped by half in the penultimate decade of the twentieth century, leaving an estimated population of no more than 3,000.

With its tall, slender body, spotted coat, distinctly rounded head and small rounded ears set wide apart, the cheetah has endeared itself to the public. Famed as the fastest animal on earth over short distances, in full stride a cheetah epitomises grace and elegance.

This cat weighs between forty-five and sixty-five kilos (100-143 pounds) and has recorded speeds of more than 112 kilometres (seventy miles) an hour.

In hot regions, such as Namibia and the Kalahari Desert, cheetah have to cope with an entirely different and harsher ecosystem than that found in East Africa.

In a region where air temperatures in summer can be up to 40°C (104°F) and the open ground temperatures above 70°C (158°F), cheetahs are largely inactive between 0900 and 1600 hours.

Thus, the cheetah has taken to making greater use of the hours of darkness when it can prey more successfully on nocturnal species such as spring hares.

Smaller felines

Of the smaller cats, the **caracal** looks like a shrunken lion. The most powerful of the small cats, it is capable of great speed and agility — it is capable of leaping as high as three metres (ten feet) into the air after prey. Its most striking feature is its large pointed ears with long pointed tufts of hair almost the length of the ear itself. Caracal prefer arid regions and are widespread in Namibia.

Because of the **serval's** preference for well-watered country, it is confined to northern Namibia. Its graceful lines, long legs, large oval ears and light, spotted coloration make it one of the most handsome of the small cats.

Above: Leopard, most stealthy of the big cats.

Of medium build, serval weigh between thirteen and fifteen kilos (twenty-eight and thirty-three pounds) and feed on rodents, occasionally taking lizards, fish, vegetables, birds and small antelope — depending on what is available.

Serval are often seen in the late afternoon as they leap above the grass searching for food.

The **African wild cat** is a similar, light sandy colour to the serval, with a series of narrow reddish-black bands on the thighs and throat. Its key characteristic, however, is a rich reddish coloration on the back of the ears. They also have a wider range of habitat, although they need rock cover to rest during the day.

The **black-footed cat** — or small spotted cat — is endemic to **southern** and **western Namibia**. Being nocturnal, highly secretive and the smallest of the cats, far less is known about this relatively scarce cat than any other species of Namibian cat. They prey on rats, mice and hunting spiders.

The hyenas

The Hyaenidae is the smallest of the carnivore family and is represented in Namibia by the aardwolf, brown hyena and spotted hyena. These carnivores are highly specialised, with massive bone-crushing teeth. The exception is the **aardwolf**, an insect eater, which concentrates on termites, and has only vestigial teeth.

Widely distributed in Namibia, except along the Namib Desert coast, aardwolf are predominantly nocturnal and search in pairs or family parties for termites, their principle food. During the day they lie up in burrows, using either old antbear or enlarged springhare holes.

Like all hyenas, aardwolf have anal glands and are assiduous scent markers. Important sites such as their middens and dens are heavily marked with secretions from the anal glands which have a sweet musk-like odour and vary in colour from dark brown to yellowish and orange.

The **brown hyena** with its massive head, neck and shoulders, is also predominantly nocturnal.

In Namibia the brown hyena is also known as the **'Strandwolf'** (translated as 'Beach Wolf') because of their characteristic habit of frequenting beaches in search of carrion. Found only in southern Africa, they also occur in central Namibia and the Namib Desert.

Brown hyena are generally smaller, more secretive and less aggressive than spotted hyena, although their shaggy brown coat, heavy mane and bushy tail make them appear larger.

They are indifferent hunters, only killing small prey such as rodents, birds, reptiles and insects. In the **Kalahari Desert** ostrich eggs feature in their diet, as do wild melons and cucurbits which have a high water content.

The first hour after sun-up is a good time to look for **spotted hyena**. This freak of the bush which shuffles along to its own awful song will then be returning from a hunting and scavenging foray. The spotted hyena is reviled everywhere. According to African legend it carries witches around on moonlit nights.

Yet spotted hyena are impressive animals. Massively built, with particularly heavy forequarters, their immense power is best appreciated when an individual is seen running away from a kill carrying the hind leg of an antelope — or some other heavy piece of meat — high off the ground.

The pack's social organisation is based on a matriarchal system of clans which mark and defend their territories with aggression and much whooping. In fact they have the most sophisticated range of sounds of all the large carnivores — from soft groans to whimpers, whines, squeals, whoops and, of course, the chuckles that sound like human laughter. It is the cascade of maniacal laughter that visitors remember most among the sounds of the African night.

Ancient family

The Viverridae, an ancient family of creatures originating in Eurasia some forty-five million years ago, are represented in Namibia by the **civet**, **genet** and **mongoose**.

The largest viverrid, the **civet,** weighs between nine and twenty kilos (twenty and forty-four pounds). They are found in **savannah** and sometimes **dense forest**, although they hide during the day in old burrows. Civet, which are confined to the wetter parts of **north-eastern Namibia**, have a low-pitched growl and cough.

The two genets — **small spotted genet** and **large spotted genet** — are similar in appearance and habits. Both have short legs, an elongated body and a white ringed tail which is almost as long as the body. Both species are nocturnal, feeding on small rodents, birds, reptiles and insects.

The small spotted genet is widespread, while the large spotted genet only occurs in the extreme **north-east** of Namibia.

In colour, the small spotted genet has a spotted body and a black strip running down the centre of the back. The large spotted genet has larger spots which vary in colour from black to rust.

They are larger generally than the small spotted genet, but the telltale difference between the two is the small spotted genet's white-tipped tail.

The **suricate** — or **meercat** — is diurnal. In fact, the sight of a dozen or more of these late risers sitting on their haunches outside their burrows as they take the mid-morning sun is one of the charms of Namibia's wildlife scene.

Suricates are open, arid country animals and are thus confined to the arid parts of Namibia. Being diurnal, they have to be continually alert. The best place to see a colony of these fascinating animals is along the fringes of dry pans where they build warrens with many entrances in the hard calcareous surface.

When all is safe, they forage nearby, often stopping to dig with their long front claws, or turning over stones and debris in search of insects which are their principle form of food.

There are ten species of **mongoose** in Namibia: **Selous' mongoose, bush-tailed, yellow, large grey, small grey, slender, white-tailed, water, banded** and **dwarf mongoose.**

The largest is the white-tailed mongoose

Above: The dainty bat-eared fox roams in small groups by day and night.

and the smallest is the dwarf mongoose. Probably the most widespread is the slender mongoose, which is often seen darting across the road — the slender, brown body and black tip to the end of the tail being the give-away.

Banded mongoose sometimes occur in groups of up to seventy-five animals. They are very vocal, constantly chatting to their nearest neighbour while scratching around inquisitively for food. Occasionally a few members may sit upright on their haunches to ensure that no danger threatens the troop and one alarm call will send them scurrying for cover.

The dogs

A number of '**foxes**' occur in Africa, but the **Cape fox** is only found in the semi-desert regions of Namibia. About the size of a jackal, their winter coat has a silvery appearance. These solitary animals feed on insects and mice, and are most active at night when one can hear their high-pitched howl, sometimes dueting with other foxes nearby.

With its narrow muzzle, light build and slim legs, the **bat-eared fox** is the daintiest member of Namibia's dog family. They occur widely in Namibia where groups of up to six can be seen during the day or night — moving around in an apparently aimless way.

Their sense of hearing is acute, their characteristic large ears continually twisting and moving as they listen for the faintest sound of beetle and termite movements.

When the exact location of the prey is pinpointed, it is quickly dug up with the forepaws. The bat-eared fox has more teeth, forty-two to fifty, than any other mammal.

So relentlessly has the **wild dog** been persecuted since the turn of the century, it is in real danger of extinction. A few packs roam Namibia's **north-east** wildernesses.

Wild dogs rely on sight rather than smell in hunting and make no attempt to get close to their prey by stalking. They simply run the creature to a standstill.

Prior to a hunt and at the time of the kill, wild dog become very excited and a loud twittering is heard from the whole pack. It is an astonishing display of the close-knit nature of the pack. Adults also indulge in a

Below: Damara — also known as Kirk's — dik dik.

Above: Small grey mongoose.

ritual ceremony of whining, face licking and nudging of the corners of the mouth that results in the regurgitation of food, especially to the sick and lame, and to the young pups of the pack.

Wild dogs play their role in the maintenance of the natural balance. They are not wanton killers and will normally only kill what they require. Through their close-knit social structure, no member of the family goes hungry.

The **side-striped jackal** is so called because of the light-coloured bands on its flanks. Yet its most distinguishing feature is its white-tipped tail. The **black-backed jackal** has a broad dark saddle and black-tipped tail.

Side-striped jackal occur marginally in **north-eastern Namibia,** while black-backed jackal prefer the drier regions. Although side-striped jackal are more strictly carrion eaters, vegetable matter, in a variety of forms, is also an important food item.

Black-backed jackals may be seen during the day, either returning to their rest holes or trotting along paths. Their senses are acute, and unlike the side-striped jackal, they rely mostly on insects for food. In Namibia, however, they are frequently encountered on isolated **beaches** where they scan the shore for dead fish, seal carcasses and other carrion.

They also often capitalise on the abundant and varied marine organisms that are associated with clumps of stranded kelp. There, and elsewhere through their range, their long, drawn-out call, followed by a staccato *ya-ya-ya* is one of the characteristic sounds of the African night.

Tortoises and turtles

Namibia has a great diversity of land tortoises, some of which are endemic. The **mountain**, or **leopard tortoise** is the largest and most common, weighing up to forty kilos (eighty-eight pounds).

Specimens from South Africa's Cape Province are often regarded as a separate subspecies, because males appear to grow slightly larger than the females, whereas elsewhere the females are much larger than the males.

There is a relict population of this large

Above: Largest and most common of Namibia's land tortoises, the leopard tortoise weighs up to 40 kilos.

subspecies, in southern Namibia. The colour pattern is variable, but is generally brighter in juveniles.

The **angulate tortoise**, endemic to southern Namibia, is a medium-size tortoise, unusual in that males are larger than females. Combat between males is marked, the object being to overturn rivals.

The **Namaqualand speckled padloper** is the world's smallest terrestrial tortoise. An adult weighs only 140 grams (five ounces) and lives in rocky areas, its shape allowing it to take refuge in crevices. It also gives the tortoise more stability in the steep, rocky areas where it is found.

There are three species of **hingeback tortoise** in Namibia, two of which are found in the **Caprivi Strip**, while the other is endemic to **southern Namibia**.

The most widespread species of terrapin in Namibia is the **Cape terrapin**, found everywhere except the deserts and mountains. It appears to prefer dams, pans and vleis to streams and rivers. When the water dries up, they readily move overland to another pan, or bury themselves in the mud until the rainy season. They are capable of surviving in this manner for many months.

Namibia's other species of terrapins all belong to the genus *Pelusios*. All have a hinged flap to the front of the plastron which securely and completely seals the front of the shell after the legs and head have been withdrawn.

Soft-shelled terrapins, closely related to terrestrial tortoises, are easily recognised by their soft shells, and the three claws on each foot. The neck is elongated and the nostrils project considerably. Two species are found in the region.

In Namibia, the soft-shelled **Nile turtle**, found in the **Kunene River**, is a monster terrapin, weighing up to forty kilos (eighty-eight pounds) and able to deliver a severe bite. It is also capable of short marine journeys, travelling from one river mouth to the next.

Turtles, or marine tortoises, are represented by five species in the marine waters of the region. The marine turtles are great wanderers, often travelling long distances between continents. All species must come to shore to lay their eggs.

275

Above: Seals bask in the sun on the beach at Cape Frio.

The largest turtle — the world's heaviest reptile — is the **leatherback turtle**, found at the mouth of the **Kunene** and **Orange Rivers**. It weighs up to 750 kilos (1,653 pounds) and has a carapace almost three metres (ten feet) long.

Loggerhead turtles, found off the Namibian coast, are carnivorous, feeding on jellyfish and bluebottles. They weigh up to 150 kilos (330 pounds). The other turtle found off Namibian shores, but only rarely, is the **Hawksbill turtle**.

The seals

Seals return to land to breed and raise their young. The males are the first to arrive at the breeding colonies, signifying the start of intense and ferocious territorial battles to establish space on the crowded beaches for the harem of females which follows. There are three species of fur seals in southern Africa — the **Cape Fur Seal**, **Antarctic Fur Seal** and **Sub-Antarctic Fur Seal**. Commonly known as eared seals, to distinguish them from the true seals which have no external ears, the only one you are likely to see is the Cape Fur Seal, which breeds in twenty-three colonies along the **Namibian coast**. Some of the better known colonies are small offshore islands such as **Seal Island** just off **Lambert's Bay**.

The biggest is at **Cape Cross** on the shores of the **National West Coast Tourist Recreation Area** with between 80,000 and 100,000 animals. In mid-October, the colony becomes a hive of activity as the bulls begin to establish their territories, vigorously defending them against would-be intruders.

About ninety per cent of the pups are born within a thirty-four day period, beginning late November and early December, after a gestation of nine months.

It is extremely unlikely that any of the earless seals, such as the enormous elephant seal, will be seen, since they prefer the cold climates of the Antarctic.

Whales and dolphins

While all whales and dolphins have teeth, at least during their foetal stage, in baleen whales the teeth never erupt above the gums, even after birth. Instead, they are replaced by plates of baleen which grow from the palatine ridges on the roof of the mouth and serve as food collectors.

Baleen whales are therefore highly specialised feeders, relying on the vast quantities of 'krill', a small crustacean found in the cold Antarctic waters. Some, such as the **beaked whale**, are only known from a few specimens found stranded along the Skeleton Coast.

Sperm whales, which were hunted until recently, are now the subject of intensive research, especially since they visit the coastal regions to give birth and raise their calves, thus giving an opportunity for scientists to monitor the recovery of these magnificent creatures.

The best-known members of this group are **killer whales**, known for their predatory habits, and **dolphins**.

Several species of dolphin occur off southern Africa. The **common dolphin** is aptly named for it is probably the most frequently encountered, often as it rides the bow waves of ships, accompanying them for long distances.

Primates

Primates are represented in Namibia by **man, bushbabies, monkeys** and **baboons**.

Bushbabies, or galagos, are small, nocturnal primates which live and feed in trees. Their human-like hands and feet are well-adapted for climbing and for manipulating their food, which comprises fruit, tree gum and some insects.

Both species found in Namibia are very agile, and the **lesser galago** — more widely spread than the **greater** — is well known for its spectacular leaps.

The **vervet monkey** is the most common monkey in Namibia where, in savannah and riverine woodlands, troops of ten to twenty forage during the day, both on the ground and in trees, for fruit, seeds, shoots and some insects. At night groups sleep high in large trees.

Vervets are never as serious a pest as the ubiquitous **chacma baboon**. These large baboons regularly raid agricultural crops such as maize, and have been known to kill small domestic livestock and poultry. They often form loose associations with antelope such as kudu and impala.

Above: Vervet monkey are perhaps the most common species of monkey throughout sub-Saharan Africa and are found in northern, north-eastern and southern Namibia, feeding mainly on wild fruits, leaves, seeds and seed pods.

Antelope and gazelle

There are many species of antelope in Namibia and, like buffalo and giraffe, they are all ruminants. Four species are found nowhere else.

Blue wildebeest, which weigh 250 kilos (550 pounds), are well-known for their large numbers, and occur across Namibia. They are relatively sedentary, normally found in herds of about thirty animals. Although dependent on water, they are animals of the drier areas, favouring short grass plains and avoiding expanses of long grass.

Research at the **Etosha Ecological Institute** has shown the dramatic decline in blue wildebeest in the Etosha National Park since 1955. Then their numbers were estimated at about 25,000. By 1978 only 2,200 remained.

Hartebeest are widespread in Namibia, occurring in as many as twelve subspecies which are known by a variety of names, such as the Western hartebeest, Swayne's hartebeest, Jackson's hartebeest, Tora hartebeest and Coke's hartebeest.

One subspecies, **red hartebeest**, which weighs about 150 kilos (330 pounds), occurs in the drier parts of Namibia, and is normally found in herds of up to twenty.

A species which has close relatives to the north is the **tsessebe**, similar in appearance to the korrigum, tiang and topi of West, Central and East Africa. Tsessebe, which weigh 140 kilos (309 pounds), are not widespread and occur in small populations in **north** and **north-east Namibia**.

Renowned for their spectacular leaps, graceful **impala** are found in **north-east Namibia** and are slightly smaller, at around fifty-five kilos (120 pounds), than the East African subspecies with smaller horns.

During the rut, which extends from about February through to June, with slight geographic variation, the males fight fiercely over territory, 'roaring' loudly.

One subspecies, found only in a small area of northern Namibia, is the **black-faced impala**. As the name implies, they differ in having a dark mask on the face and also have longer and bushier tails.

Springbok, the national emblem of South Africa and classified as gazelles, weigh about forty kilos (eighty-eight pounds) and are highly gregarious animals, living during the dry season in herds of up to 100. During summer, after localised rain, they may form much larger aggregations. They are mixed feeders, eating grass when it is available in the wet season and feeding on shrubs during the dry season.

Allied to the springbok the klipspringers are a group of small antelopes with widespread distribution. **Klipspringer** walk on the tips of their hooves and, like the European chamois, have great mobility across the rocky hillsides that they inhabit. In Namibia, only the males have horns.

The only dik-dik found in Namibia is a subspecies. The **Damara**, or **Kirk's dik-dik** inhabits the drier parts of Namibia, isolated by some 2,000 kilometres (1,242 miles) from its nearest relative, an indication of the change in climate that occurred in the Pleistocene epoch to separate the species.

Oribi and **steenbok** occupy more open habitats and are similar in appearance, rufous in colour with white underparts. Oribi, found only in the extreme **north-east**, are predominantly grazers, and prefer open short grass areas, where they are found in small groups.

The slightly smaller steenbok are generally solitary, but may also be seen in pairs in most parts of the country where there is more cover in the form of tall grassland or scattered bushes.

Three species of duiker are found in Namibia. The **blue duiker** is the smallest. Both the blue duiker and the slightly larger **red duiker** are browsers, inhabiting forests, thickets or dense bush in the east and south of the region. Both sexes have short spiky horns. Larger, and with a much wider range of habitat, is the **common, grey** or **bush duiker**, found throughout Namibia wherever cover exists and browse is available, even in close proximity to human habitation. In contrast to the forest duikers only the males have horns.

The *Reduncinae* are medium-size or large antelopes, never far from water. The largest, **waterbuck**, which weigh 260 kilos (570 pounds), are grazers, normally found in small groups near rivers.

Above: Klipspringer, which walk on the tips of their hooves, are very agile on the rocky hillsides which they inhabit.

The Namibian species is the common waterbuck, with a white ring on the hindquarters, found in the **north-east**, particularly in the low-lying **Caprivi Strip**.

The adult males are stately animals with shaggy coats and heavy horns almost one metre (three feet) long that sweep outward and upwards from the head. They are well known for their habit of escaping into water when chased by predators.

Somewhat smaller, at one metre (three feet) shoulder height and 120 kilos (260 pounds), **red lechwe** are more closely associated with swamps. In Namibia they are confined to the **wetlands** of the Caprivi Strip.

Lechwe generally occur in small groups of about twenty animals but occasionally gather in larger herds, feeding on grasses growing in seasonally flooded swamp margins. They spend much of the time in shallow water, but rest on dry land, often on islands in the swamps.

Lechwe take to the water if disturbed or pursued. Their hooves are elongated as an adaptation for walking in mud, and the males have large, lyre-shaped horns.

The *Tragelaphine* group of antelope are handsome animals which share a number of traits.

Eland, with males weighing up to 750 kilos (1,653 pounds), are the largest of all the antelope. They occupy a wide range of habitats in Namibia. Males have heavier horns than females although females' horns may be longer. Both sexes use the horns to break trees and shrubs when the foliage is too high to reach, by placing them on either side of the stem or branch and twisting the neck so that the branch breaks.

Widespread in Namibia, **Greater kudu** are a savannah woodland species, not found in forest, open grassland or desert. The adult males are magnificent animals, weighing up to 250 kilos (550 pounds) with curled, corkscrew-shaped horns measuring up to one-and-three-quarter metres (six feet) along the curve. They are almost entirely browsers and, like eland, great jumpers — they can clear a two metre (six foot) fence with ease.

Sitatunga are found only in dense

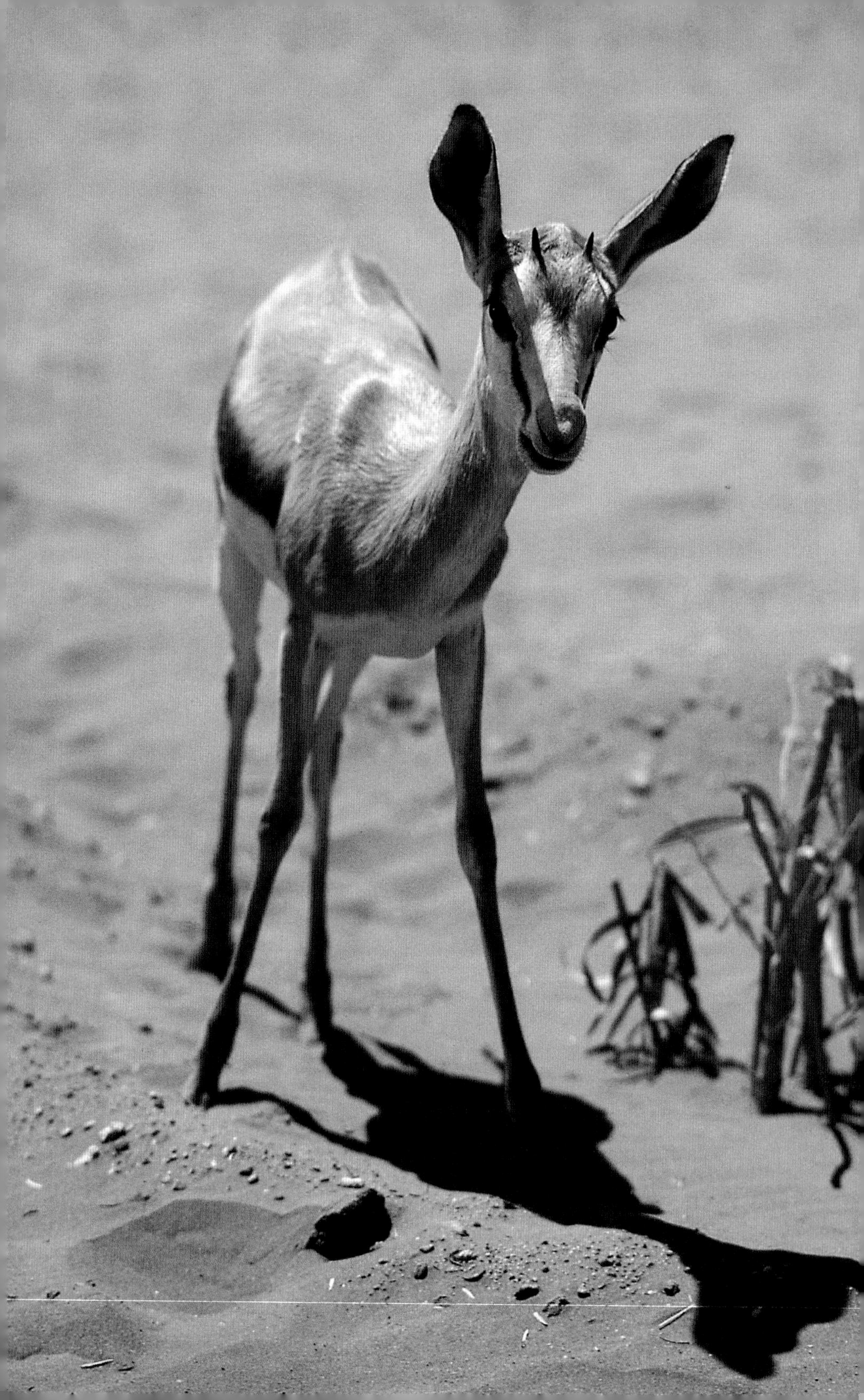

papyrus and **reedbeds** in the Caprivi Strip. Their basic food is young shoots of papyrus, reeds and other aquatic plants and they move out of the swamps at night to feed on the swamp margins.

They rest in the swamps on platforms of broken vegetation and like lechwe also use islands, where they are vulnerable to predation by lions and leopards which swim to the islands to hunt them.

The hooves of sitatunga are more elongated than those of lechwe, particularly the front hooves, which can be up to eighteen centimetres (seven inches) long as an adaptation for movement on the muddy swamp ground and for swimming.

Bushbuck, the smallest of the tragelaphine goup, with adult males weighing about forty-five kilos (100 pounds) are usually found in riverine thickets and are absent from the drier parts of Namibia. They are handsome animals with white stripes and spots on a reddish-brown background.

The *Hippotraginae* are a group of large, handsome, horse-like animals, in which both sexes carry horns. They are gregarious and primarily grazers.

The largest and, among the antelopes second in size only to the eland, are **roan**, with males weighing up to 270 kilos (595 pounds). Roan are associated with lightly wooded country with medium to tall grasses but are not common in Namibia.

Gemsbok, with their pale body colour, distinctively marked faces, long tails and straight rapier-like horns, are unmistakable inhabitants of the **desert** and **semi-desert** areas.

Zebra

Zebra are the only wild members of the horse family remaining in Namibia, apart from a herd of genuinely wild horses found in the southern Namib Desert. (See "Desert Horses and Diamond Mines", Part Two).

The only wild, desert-dwelling **horses** in Africa, they are rather docile and so thin that their ribs protrude through their thin coats. They can exist for as long as five days without water and by moving more slowly than other horses sweat less, thus reducing the number of trips to their one source of water, leaving more time to roam in search of sparse desert pasture.

Their numbers fluctuate according to the food available on the desert veld but never seem to be much more than 150, even in years of exceptional rain and grazing.

Common, or **Burchell's zebra** are almost entirely grazers. They inhabit open grassland and lightly wooded country where water is available, and often associate with other plains grazers such as wildebeest and tsessebe.

Burchell's zebra can be distinguished from the smaller mountain zebra by the presence of fainter dark stripes called shadow stripes, between the main stripes.

Hartmann's mountain zebra, endemic to Namibia and south-western Angola, has no shadow stripes and a distinct dewlap. The legs are striped to the hooves, the belly is white and there is a distinct grid-iron pattern on the rump.

As the name implies, they are associated with mountainous areas, where they have similar habits to Burchell's zebra. They mainly live on the transition zone between mountains and the surrounding plains, making use of both, according to grazing or water availability.

Mountain zebra are no longer confined solely to the traditional ranges, as introductions outside these areas have been made.

There are two species of the pig family in southern Africa, **wart hog** and **bush pig**. Wart hogs occur throughout the savannah areas of Namibia but are absent from the highveld and the arid Namib.

By no means handsome, wart hogs are dark grey with coarse bristles that form a crest along the back. Two growths on the face, from which the common name is derived, are much longer in males than

---

Opposite: Antelope of the arid plains, a newly born springbok calf takes a surprised look at its desert home. Gregarious creatures, springbok tend to move in small herds, occasionally forming immense herds of several hundred thousand animals.

Above: Burchell's zebra in Etosha National Park.

females, as are the curved, upper canines.

They are diurnal animals and retire to burrows at night, usually deserted antbear diggings, which the adults, but not the piglets, always enter backwards. Although they can modify existing burrows, they do not construct their own holes, and if burrows are in short supply, frequently use culverts under roads.

Bush pigs favour denser vegetation and are more typically pig-like in appearance. They have more hair and lack the facial warts and long tusks. Living in groups of up to about twelve animals they are active at night, lying up during the day in patches of forest, thickets or reedbeds.

The otters

The members of the **Mustelidae** family are represented in Namibia by five species — two aquatic — the **otters** — and three terrestrial, the **honey badger, weasel** and **polecat**.

Clawless otter occur both in fresh and salt water, while the **spotted-necked otter** only occurs in fresh water.

The clawless otter, the larger of the two species, weighing up to eighteen kilos (forty pounds), is found only in the **perennial rivers** and **permanent wetlands**.

Clawless otter are most active in the early morning and late afternoon and are very playful, preferring the quieter tributaries of major rivers. Once you can recognise their high-pitched whistle they are easy to find as they frolic in the water in search of crabs and frogs, their preferred diet.

The spotted-necked otter has a larger slimmer body than the clawless otter. The best place to find them is in the **wetlands** of the Caprivi Strip. More closely confined to their aquatic habitat than the clawless otter, they appear clumsy on land.

The honey badger

The **honey badger** is a pugnacious animal with a body built for fighting. Its very loose, tough skin and contrasting coloration of white crown, greyish-white upper parts and black make it unmistakable.

Honey badgers are found throughout Namibia, except in the Namib Desert. Although nocturnal, they are quite often seen during the day. Generally solitary, they are courageous animals and can become extremely aggressive, not fearing to tackle anything or anyone, even if unprovoked.

Weasels and polecats

The **black-and-white striped weasel** is apparently rare in Namibia, but it is easily overlooked in the short grassland it favours because of its short legs and low slung body.

The **striped polecat** is one of the most easily recognised of the small carnivores. An encounter with it will not be easily forgotten. The conspicuous coloration is a warning not to interfere, or one is likely to be tainted with the nauseating fluid which the striped polecat can release at will from its anal glands. These animals are widely distributed throughout Namibia.

Rodents

Rodents are the most successful of the modern mammals. Because they are small and often nocturnal, they are frequently overlooked in favour of the large herbivores and carnivores of Namibia. Ranging from the tiny **pygmy mouse** to the **porcupine**, their importance in ecology is usually underestimated.

Some rodents lead highly specialised lives. Perhaps the best example are the **mole rats**. Despite their name they are neither rats nor moles, but their fossorial habits have resulted in the evolution of features which are similar to moles.

Unlike moles, however, they possess tiny eyes and digging is done with their enormous incisors as well as the claws of their powerful forelegs.

Also unlike moles, mole rats are entirely herbivorous, feeding predominantly on roots and bulbs. Their eyesight is very poor, but their hearing and sensitivity for vibrations acute.

Only the common mole rat, *Cryptomys hottentotus*, is widely distributed throughout the region. Like most mole rats it lives in colonies, in underground tunnels whose existence is shown by mounds of surplus earth pushed out of the burrows. These mounds are often associated with exits from which the animals disperse to better feeding places.

The largest rodent in Namibia is a single species of **porcupine**, *Hystrix africaeaustralis* which is widely distributed. Its distinctive long black and white spines and quills are used for defence and, when raised, make the animal look larger. The long quills on the tail are rattled when the animal is threatened. It defends itself by reversing rapidly, often leaving quills embedded in its attacker.

In a family of its own, another distinctive rodent which occurs in Namibia is the **spring hare**, *Pedetes capensis*. Looking like a cross between a small kangaroo and a rabbit, the spring hare has long powerful hind legs, reduced forelimbs, a long tail, large eyes and long upright ears. It is nocturnal and spends the day in burrows from which it moves only a short distance to feed at night on grass, seeds and rhizomes.

Hares and rabbits

The **scrub hare** is common throughout Namibia except in desert areas, open grassland or forests. Its distribution appears to depend on its need for bushes under which to shelter during the day.

Like the **Cape hare**, found in drier regions, the scrub hare relies on its cryptic coloration to hide and does not dig burrows for protection.

As their name implies, the three species of **rock rabbit** occur only in rocky outcrops and *kopjies* where rock crevices provide cover during the day. They are all grazers, leaving their rocky habitat if necessary in search of grass.

Dassies

The most widespread of the dassies, or hyraxes, is the **rock dassie**, *Procavia capensis*, which is found in rocky outcrops throughout Namibia. The **tree dassie** is distinguished from the rock dassie by its

Above: Unmistakable because of its armour of heavy brown scales, the ant-eating pangolin resembles a fir cone when curled up in defence. Pangolin occur widely throughout Namibia except in the south and the Namib Desert.

longer fur and by its nocturnal and arboreal lifestyle.

The pangolin

Sometimes known as the scaly anteater, the pangolin, *manis temmincki*, is a highly specialised anteater which occurs everywhere except southern Namibia and the desert-proper. It is a distinct and unmistakable animal and has been described as an 'animated fir cone'. Its most distinct feature is the armour of heavy, overlapping scales on its back, sides, tail and legs..

Insectivores

As the name implies, this is a group of predominantly insect-eating animals — hedgehogs, golden moles, shrews and elephant shrews. Insectivores are mostly small nocturnal animals which have retained many of the features of the first mammals to evolve some 100 million years ago.

The earliest fossil insectivores, dated to thirty million years ago, are the **elephant shrews** which are found only in Africa. Being diurnal, these attractive animals are probably the most frequently seen of the insectivores, characterised by an extremely long, mobile snout. They have large ears and good eyesight, and the constantly moving nose tests the air for food and danger. Their hind legs are longer than their forelegs and they are easily distinguished from other shrews.

The **short-snouted elephant shrew** is the most widely distributed, occurring throughout Namibia, as does the **round-eared elephant shrew**.

The largest insectivore, the unmistakable South African **hedgehog**, occurs as a subspecies in Namibia. Its food comprises mainly invertebrates but it will eat lizards, mice and nestlings when the opportunity arises.

Although it does not truly hibernate, like the European hedgehog, it becomes inactive during cold weather and relies on fat reserves for up to two months at a time.

When rolled up, its spiny coat acts as an extremely good defence against predators.

Like the true moles of Europe, **golden moles** have adapted to a burrowing lifestyle. Although not closely related to moles, they look very similar.

Golden moles evolved in southern Africa and some are extremely confined. For example, **Grant's golden mole**, *Eremitalpa granti namibensis*, is found only on the south-west coast of Namibia.

First discovered in 1837 by Captain James Alexander, the animal was lost to science for 126 years until it was rediscovered in the Kuiseb River region in 1963.

Dormant during the day, usually at the base of a grass tuft or hummock, Grant's golden mole emerges at night to feed on insects and their larvae.

Bats

Six species of **fruit bat** occur in the region and have in common their relatively large size, two claws on the wings, large eyes, and their habit of feeding on fruit and flowers.

They fly long distances for food and use a variety of loud calls and squeaks to communicate. Almost all find their way around by sight and roost in groups during the day in large trees. The exception is the **Egyptian fruit bat**, *Rousettus aegyptiacus*, which rests during the day in caves where colonies of thousands of individuals may gather.

They are the only species of fruit bat to use a form of echo-location. Their eyesight is good but they use clicking sounds to echo-locate when in the total darkness of their roosting caves.

Some fruit bats are extremely difficult to identify in the field and, for example, two species of **epauletted fruit bat**, *Epomophorus wahlbergi* and *E. crypturus*, which are often found together, can only be distinguished by the number of ridges on their palate.

In fact the number of these ridges is the easiest way to differentiate between any of the four species of epauletted fruit bat occurring in the region.

Insectivorous bats in Namibia, divided into six families, are **sheath-tailed bats,**

Above: The six species of fruit bat found in Namibia are all relatively large in size, have two claws on their wings and feed on fruit and flowers.

free-tailed bats, vesper bats, slit-faced bats, horseshoe bats and **trident** and **leaf-nosed bats**. All use echo-location to navigate and to find and capture their prey, by emitting a sound which is reflected off surrounding surfaces.

The sounds produced in the throat of the bats are usually too high in frequency to be heard by humans. Many species have bizarre and sometimes grotesque facial features. Folded ears project outgoing sounds and ensure separation of outgoing and incoming sounds.

Bats are an important source of food for numerous reptiles and small carnivores which mainly capture them in their roosts. They form the exclusive diet of a species of bird, the bat hawk, which has specially adapted to hunting bats.

Bird Life: An Ornithological Treasury

Although the Dutch landed at Cape Town in 1652, it was not until the closing years of the eighteenth century, nearly 150 years later, that interest in the birds of the region developed. Since then, many species from southern Africa, including Namibia, have been identified.

There are professional government ornithologists in Namibia, mostly at work on conservation projects. High profile species for such attention include the blue swallow, jackass penguin, roseate tern, wattled crane, Cape vulture and bald ibis.

Southern Africa has also spawned three groups of people who are actively involved in species conservation and publicity — the African Seabird Group, Vulture Study Group and African Raptor Information Centre.

In addition to seabirds such as the **jackass penguin** and **albatross**, the Namibian coast offers breeding grounds to the **Cape gannet, Cape cormorant,** the endemic **bank** and **crowned cormorants, palm-nut vulture, black oystercatcher, roseate tern** and **mangrove kingfisher** among others.

But, far from the Equator, Namibia cannot boast Eastern Africa's great and diverse birdlife, although it does serve as home to gale-blown sub-Antarctic birds.

Many species of albatross, **petrel, shearwater** and **storm petrel** may be sighted off Namibia's Forbidden and Skeleton Coasts, as well as penguin. This is also the home of the jackass penguin which breeds in 'rookeries' on the flat islands off the coast.

The species, however, has suffered a dramatic ninety per cent decline this century, due to commercial egg- and guano-collection, and latterly the over-fishing of sardines.

In addition, oil spills, resulting from the closure of the Suez Canal in 1956 which drove oil tankers around the treacherous Cape route, have taken their toll. Now the jackass penguin is the subject of a concerted conservation programme.

The great arid zone that encompasses the Namib and Kalahari Deserts hosts a large number of endemic birds, adapted to the dry conditions and scattered low vegetation.

The **pygmy falcon, karoo** and **Rüppell's korhaans, Hartlaub's francolin** and various larks are examples, along with other species such as the **kori bustard**.

The Palaearctic migrants wing their way from Europe and Asia across 8,000 kilometres (5,000 miles) or more to Namibia. Two-thirds of these are **birds of prey, sandpipers, gulls, terns,** and **warblers**. Most migrants are insect-eaters or crustacea feeders, although quite a few eat fish.

About as many species come to Namibia from tropical Africa, conspicuous examples being the **cuckoo, carmine bee-eater,** and **paradise flycatcher.**

Also straddling the Namibian and **Angolan border** is southern Africa's last certain population of **Egyptian vultures** — seen occasionally at the **Etosha Pan** — one of eight species of vulture in the region.

The **jackal buzzard** and **black harrier** are endemic to Namibia while **Pel's fishing owl,** a secretive species, is found in the **Okavango Swamps** of the **Caprivi Strip** and along the **Zambezi River.**

For sheer gaudiness of colouring the families of **kingfisher, bee-eater** and **roller** (all rather closely related) must take the prize. The **malachite** and **pygmy kingfishers** are little feathered jewels, the one a fish-eater and the other a woodland insect-eater. Incidentally, half of the kingfisher species eat insects.

Similarly, the bee-eaters with their basically green colouring and the rollers with their blues and purples are astoundingly gorgeous, the rollers demanding extra attention by their raucous voices and diving and 'rolling' displays. The carmine bee-eater has one of nature's most unusual colours.

Not only are birds conspicuous by their bright colours or dramatic behaviour, but

Above: Pair of pale chanting goshawks scan the area for prey.

many of them also have beautiful or strident voices. Night birds and forest and woodland birds can, in fact, best be recognised by their calls or songs.

Cuckoos are good examples of this. Many species visit Namibia just before the rains and then set about calling, for weeks on end, in an effort, presumably, to locate and attract the opposite sex. They all have strikingly different voices. The **black** and **red-chested cuckoos** even call for long periods at night.

Some bird families are exceptionally well represented, while others are scarce, presenting a real challenge for bird watchers from around the world. Perhaps the easiest to spot is the **ostrich**, the largest of all living birds. Males are predominantly black with white wing and tail feathers, while females are brown with paler, greyish-brown wings and tail. They normally live in small family groups and, during dry seasons, gather at waterholes in large numbers.

While ostriches are rarely missed because of their sheer size, the **flamingo's** pink plumage is guaranteed to catch the eye, especially when their numbers create a colourful blanket across a lake.

The **lesser flamingo** is smaller and has a very dark red bill and face. The youngsters are dirty grey-brown with a uniformly dark

Below: Redwing starling.

Above: Lilac-breasted roller.

bill. They breed in vast numbers along the coast and in Etosha.

The **greater flamingo** is larger and almost entirely white when standing. With a pink bill and black tip, this is one of Namibia's most attractive birds.

As colourful as the flamingo is the **European bee-eater**, its upper parts a chestnut colour contrasted by a sky-blue breast and belly. It is a summer migrant from Europe, widespread throughout Namibia from October to mid-April. During this time it feeds on insects, including bees and wasps which, once caught, are beaten on a suitable perch so as to render them harmless, and then eaten.

Another eye-catcher is the **lilac-breasted roller** which has thin straight outer tail feathers and a lilac throat and breast. Its name comes from its habit of performing aerial acrobatics, particularly during the breeding season.

Some of Namibia's birds are renowned for their extraordinary bills. The **red-billed hoopoe** is perhaps the best example, occurring in well-developed woodland such as the mopane areas of the Caprivi Strip. The **red-billed hornbill**, along with his **yellow-billed** cousin, has broad head-stripes and lives in holes in trees.

Another woodland inhabitant is the stunning **golden-tailed woodpecker** which is about the size of a dove. The males are mottled, with red-and-black foreheads and moustache streaks, and the females have indistinct blackish moustaches which merge into dark mottles, throats, and black-and-white foreheads. They are shy, like all woodpeckers, and stay in pairs, making the occasional 'keeeh'.

As equally attractive as any of Namibia's woodland inhabitants is the **mariqua sunbird**. It has a green head with a blackish belly and is found most prominently in the **Daan Viljoen Game Park**. These birds usually build their nests high up in the middle of acacia crowns. Their favourite source of sustenance is the flower from mistletoe.

Moving away from the woodland to the swamps of the north, **Sandwich Bay** and other bodies of water, Namibia has an extensive variety of water birds.

The **black-headed heron**, as the name implies, is black on its neck. In addition it has a dark bill and two-tone underwing pattern. Most herons live in shallow water or marshy areas.

The **little egret** is a pure white heron, with black legs and yellow feet. It wades in shallow water hunting insects, frogs and small fish.

The **Marabou stork** grows to a full 120 centimetres (four feet) high, with a white body and slaty-black wings which contrast strongly in flight. Although usually regarded as repulsive and ugly due to its largely bare, pinkish head and neck, huge bill and feeding habits, it has a certain ponderous grace of movement both on the ground and in the air. Marabou commonly gather at carrion with vultures.

Similar in looks to storks is the peculiar **African spoonbill**. The adults are pure white with red legs, face, and bill. They live on bottom-dwelling worms, larvae, crustaceans and fish in shallow water, feeding with the sensitive 'spoon' on the bill.

Another water lover, also with a strange bill, is the **knob-billed duck**. This rather odd bird is usually seen in pairs or small groups, sometimes perching on trees. It has purple-glossed wings with contrasting white underparts.

Moving away from the confines of swamps and lakes, Namibia's skies are filled with busy traffic — some of it huge. The **white-backed vulture** is perhaps the most ominous looking bird found in Namibia. The adults are distinguished by their pure white backs, contrasting with otherwise dark brown wings and upperparts.

Like most other African vultures, the white-backed species searches for food while soaring at great heights. Despite its repulsive looks, it is probably the only vulture which cleans itself regularly, and can sometimes be seen flapping around at waterholes.

The **yellow-billed kite** is also a scavenger, feeding on whatever it can pick up, gathering at food sources such as termite mounds and locust flights. It has a longish, slightly forked tail and yellow bill.

Below: Ground hornbill.

Above: Yellow-billed hornbill.

Above: Social weaver birds and their communal nests in Eastern Namib.

The yellow-billed kite hunts on the wing, being a very accomplished flyer, sailing with characteristically bent wings and the tail constantly twisting and spreading as it banks and turns.

The **black-shouldered kite** is unmistakable. With a grey back and dark shoulder patches, it is common in Etosha, particularly in open country, but not in the desert. This little hawk is most often seen perched on some conspicuous vantage point, or hovering on rapidly-beating wings, watching for its prey below. From either position the bird will 'parachute' with its wings held above its back and its feet extended onto suitable prey such as small rodents, lizards, or large insects.

One of the best treats for bird watchers in Namibia is the thrill of watching the noble **tawny eagle**, with its rich cream to orange-buff neck, and dark wing-feathers and tail.

The extremely similar **steppe eagle** is an irregular visitor from central Eurasia during the Namibian rains. Both these eagles hunt for gamebirds and mammals up to hare size, but are also regular carrion eaters, often seen picking at carcasses with vultures. The tawny eagle's nests are always built at the very tops of trees, on the crown.

The **bateleur** is another eagle found in Namibia. With its striking feathers it often sails rapidly in rocking flight with seldom a flap of a wing. The name, of French origin, was given to the bird by the naturalist, Francois le Vaillant, in the last century, and refers to the aerial acrobatics which it performs, mostly when breeding.

Flora: The Great Survivors

Desert conditions in Namibia have provided the opportunity for desert flora to develop and persist. There are estimated to be between 4,000 and 5,000 seed-bearing vascular plants in the Namib and Kalahari regions.

Plants in desert areas grow in a number of diverse forms and adaptations for survival under hot, dry conditions. Annual or ephemeral plants escape the harsh conditions by their short life cycle, leaving seed reserves which germinate when conditions are suitable for completion of the next cycle.

Some forms are capable of withstanding extreme desiccation, while the majority possess a number of structural and physiological modifications to enhance the collection, storage and conservation of water.

Modifications include small leaves, hairiness, thick cuticles, and sunken stomata to reduce water loss by transpiration and evaporation. Lateral roots extend close to the soil surface over large areas to absorb as much rainwater as possible, or tap roots are sunk to great depth to reach underground supplies.

Swollen stems, leaves, or both, contain special cells which act as water reservoirs. Finally, many desert plants are spiny or produce poisonous secondary compounds as defences against herbivores.

Four broad vegetational zones may be distinguished on the basis of their dominant plant forms: dwarf and succulent shrubs in the coastal lowlands and low-altitude **Karoo;** stunted trees and tall succulent or semi-succulent plants of the rocky escarpment; savannah bushlands in the **Kalahari;** and dry riparian woodlands on the banks of perennial rivers and in dry riverbeds.

Within these zones a variety of types occur, as species composition changes in response to climate and soil differences.

In the **outer Namib,** dwarf succulent **shrubs** predominate but are accompanied by a sparse covering of desert **grasses** in areas of winter rainfall. Salt-tolerant species such as the **dollar bush** *Zygophyllum stapfii*, a succulent with coin-shaped leaves, and the **salt bush** flourish on the coastal dunes.

Apart from depressions and drainage lines, the extensive coastal plains are almost barren, although there is a profusion of more than seventy species of **lichens** which grow on stones or are unattached and thrive on moisture delivered as coastal fog.

Some species are adapted to growth on the underside of translucent stones which reduce the effects of desiccation while transmitting light for photosynthesis.

The dominant grass genus is *Stipagrostis* and the grass cover increases steadily eastward, particularly on deeper soils. A variety of small, two-leaved succulent species such as **Lithops ruschiorum,** which resemble pebbles, flourish in cracks on hard rock substrates.

Larger succulents such as *Euphorbia* and flowering *Aloe* species, predominate on shallow soils or softer rocks where more extensive fracturing traps sufficient water and provides access for roots. After rain, annual succulents like *Mesembryanthemum cryptanthum* and *Aizoanthemum mossamedense* may cover vast areas.

The moving dunes are almost completely barren, but some perennial grasses such as *Exagrostis cyperoides* and *Stipagrostis sabulicola* occur, as well as the thorny leafless Narra melon *Acanthosicyos horrida.*

The thorny stems of this plant are rich in chloroplasts allowing photosynthesis to take place even though there are no leaves. The flesh of its prickly fruit is a valuable source of water and the seeds provide a protein-rich food for animals and man.

Arborescent, semi-succulent to succulent plants, varying in height from less than one to five metres (three to sixteen feet) or more are characteristic of the escarpment regions of **Kaokoland** and **Damaraland.**

Representatives of this growth form include the paper bark tree, *Commiphora* species, the kokerboom or quiver tree, *Aloe*

Above: Colourful blooms in a Swakopmund garden.

dichotoma — the hollowed-out branches of which are used by bushmen to make quivers — and tall cactus-like *Euphorbia* species.

Three species of *Cyphostemma*, short, thickset, succulent trees with grape-like fruit are confined to Kaokoland and Damaraland. *Sterculia quiqueloba* is a striking tree with white bark to reflect heat.

Another characteristic species of arid, rocky places is the desiccation-tolerant resurrection plant *Myriothamnus flabellifolius* which appears dead until rainfall causes a flush of new leaves.

In the southern winter rainfall area of the escarpment, small and dwarf succulents represented by the *Mesembryanthemaceae*, *Asclepiadaceae*, *Crassulaceae* and *Euphoribiaceae* families are common.

When rainfall is more abundant, especially in Namaqualand, a profusion of flowering annuals of the *Asteraceae* and *Brassicaceae* families cover large areas. Seeds of these ephemeral species remain dormant in the soil for long periods of time, only germinating when there has been sufficient rainfall to ensure that they flower and set seed.

The most characteristic species of the arid plateau which comprises Namaland and Bushmanland is the driedoring, *Rhigozum trichotomum*, with its branches typically arising in threes and its golden yellow flowers in the spring. Dominant grasses belong to the genus *Stipagrostis*.

On the Kalahari sands, savannah grassland interspersed with tall shrubs or trees, occurs on dunes and sandy flats. A sparse dwarf shrub formation occurs on calcrete outcrops and riverbeds, and pan areas support very open grass communities.

The density of vegetation increases eastward and northward with rainfall. Communities include *Terminalia* shrublands, with *Acacia* species, *Boscia albitrunca*, *Bauhinia macrantha*, *Grewia*, *Lonchocarpus* and *Colophospermum mopane* woodlands.

Above: Brittle bush, wildflower of the Namibian deserts, known as Brosdoring in Afrikaans.

Above: Wild onion in all too brief flower in the Kalahari Desert.

Dry riverine forest is confined to the banks of perennial rivers and the courses of normally dry river-beds which occur throughout the region. *Acacia* is the best represented genus with *A. erioloba, A. albida* and *A. karoo* being most common.

Other common trees include *Colophospermum mopane, Combretum imberbe, Euclea pseudebenus* and *Ziziphus mucronata*. The palm, *Hyphaene ventricosa*, occurs along the Kunene River in northern Namibia. Reed species *Phragmites australis* and *Typha latifolia* are restricted to moist localities.

In truth, Namibia's flora does not provide a blaze of colour. What there is tends to be isolated in small areas. But many of the country's species are of considerable interest to experts around the world who, for decades, have pondered their survival techniques.

Among Namibia's great survivors, despite the onslaught of man, are its **lichens**. Indeed the country has some of the rarest and most interesting lichens in the world. They are always the first colonists of bare habitats and therefore form a ground-cover that prevents wind and water erosion.

An association between algae and fungi, these plants are able to survive under conditions that cannot be tolerated by the majority of plants, and are found in almost every environment, from the desert to cold sandy beaches, from the tropics to the arctic regions and from bare rock to fertile soil or living leaves and stems.

Lichens usually grow in conditions of high humidity, cool temperatures and low light intensity. Of these, moisture is the most critical factor because lichens apparently have no special mechanisms for the uptake or conservation of water. When it is available, they absorb it rapidly — and lose it just as quickly.

The sea fogs of the Namib Desert are especially favourable for lichen growth — and conditions along parts of the Namib coasts are ideal.

Growing extremely slowly, partly

because they are exposed to optimal conditions for a only a few hours in the morning, they can exist for tens of thousands of years, surviving long periods of drought. But when nature is disturbed, they are the first organisms to disappear.

That unique gymnosperm **Aloe dichotoma** — the **quiver tree** or **kokerboom** — found in a number of different vegetation formations from almost barren plains to fairly dense scrub or grassland with scattered trees, is perhaps the most characteristic plant of the hot, dry areas of Namibia and north-western Cape province. The Latin *dichotoma,* refers to the forked branches of the plant which are hollowed out by the San to use as quivers for their arrows. Koker is the Afrikaans word for quiver — hence the name.

It is extremely rare to find large groups of quiver trees. They are usually solitary but most live for several hundred years, in time reaching heights of between three and five metres (ten to sixteen feet), although occasionally they have been known to grow to nine metres (thirty feet) tall, extending two to three metres (six-and-a-half to ten feet) below the ground before the very large tap root starts.

Quiver trees grow mostly in black rock formations called *ysterklip* which absorb a vast amount of heat. The smooth trunks — often one metre (three feet) in diameter at ground level — are anchored to the rocks by an intricate, and often fragile, spread-root-system. Branching rootlets grow toward the surface where they absorb moisture, much of which originates as fog caught and condensed by the smooth broad leaves and channelled to the ground.

The kokerboom's yellow bloom is brilliant and beautiful, but can only be seen during June and July. And if that were thought to be all too short a time, it is only revealed for the first time when the trees are twenty to thirty years old.

Most visitors are attracted to Namibia by the abundant and diverse wildlife. But there would be no game without the even greater array of desert-adapted plants, feeding the animals and providing them with life-sustaining water contained in leaves, stems and trunks.

It is said that when Friedrich Welwitsch, an Austrian botanist and medical doctor, discovered the strange **Welwitschia mirabilis** plant in 1859 he fell upon his knees, hardly daring to touch it. He realized immediately that this unknown plant was unique. At about the same time the explorer and artist, Thomas Baines, found some near the **Swakop River.**

These simultaneous discoveries resulted in much conflict and confusion about choosing the correct botanical name. It was a difficult case to interpret under an international code of rules governing the naming of plants. Over time, the species name *bainesii*, often encountered in the literature, has been dropped.

Today, *Welwitschia mirabilis* is a well documented botanic oddity, continually studied by scientists from around the world. Each plant has two long, shredded leaves and is always separated from other plants by some distance. They appear as a tangle of foliage — some green, most a desiccated grey — emerging from a stubby wooden base.

Research suggests that most individual plants live for more than a thousand years. In fact, they are members of the conifer family. But it is still a mystery how these plants obtain moisture, despite the fact that their leaves spread across several metres, and their roots go over a metre (three feet) down.

One theory suggests that dew condenses on the leaves, only to drip into the sand where it is absorbed by the fine roots nearer the surface.

Another puzzle is how the trees reproduce. It is now thought that some of the specialist insects living in the plants act as pollinators, the wind then distributing the seeds far and wide. But young *Welwitschia* are rare indeed, only germinating during years of exceptional rain when conditions are right

Their ability to survive in such a harsh environment is amazing. There has even been a recent suggestion that the older plants change the chemical composition of the soil around them, making it harder for young plants to germinate nearby and compete for space.

Sporting Namibia

Sand skiing

A Frenchman pioneered the concept of cross-country sand skiing in North Africa and brought it to the highest sand dunes in the world. Indeed, the Namib is particularly suited to the sport as the dunes between Swakopmund and Sossusvlei are ideal.

Sand skiing involves the use of a cross-country ski with a light trainer-type shoe fixed only at the toe. The skis are lighter, longer and more flexible than those used for downhill snow skiing, and the surface underneath is fitted with fish scales. This makes it possible to ski downhill and up as well; the fish scales grip the surface without backsliding. Side skiing up a dune is far quicker than walking.

Athletics

Namibia's participation in the 1992 Olympics in Barcelona (where they won two silver medals) and the Africa Games in Cairo are seen in many ways as a milestone in the sporting history of this country. Not only did a Namibian team take part in the Games, but local athletes were given an opportunity to gauge the strength of their counterparts around the world. In the African Games in 1993, Namibian sprinter, Frankie Fredericks, won gold. The lessons learnt will serve to encourage all Namibian sportsmen and women.

The fact that Namibia won thirteen medals in Cairo and ended ninth overall of the forty-seven participating countries, indicated that Namibian athletes can compete with the best. More importantly, valuable ties were forged by the controlling bodies that participated. The ground was prepared for future participation and on an administrative level Namibia was heartily received into the various confederations.

Rugby

Since its introduction to Namibia at the turn of the century, rugby has become the most popular sport, and today it is played at all levels in schools throughout the country. The sport is run by the Namibian Rugby Union which celebrated its seventy-fifth anniversary by organising the Africa Cup tournament in Namibia.

Namibian teams have been touring internationally since Independence. Since then they have managed to win all twelve test matches played, including those against Italy, Ireland and Zimbabwe.

Angling

Namibia is well-endowed with a long coastline, inland dams, a superb climate and a good road network: all essential factors that have combined to make fishing a popular sport in the country, with countless angling clubs.

Fishing ranges from the cooler waters of the coast to the warm waters and dams of the Daan Viljoen Game Reserve, the Von Bach Dam, the Hardap Dam, the Goreangab Dam and the Fish River at Ai-Ais.

For most places anglers require a valid fishing licence. The total number of fish in the possession of a licence holder may not exceed thirty, while the number of galjoen that may be caught is eight. A permit is also required to catch rock lobster. Other popular species include large and smallmouth bass, carp, yellowfish, kurper and barbel.

Mountaineering and hiking

Despite the excessive summer temperatures, several areas in Namibia lend themselves to mountaineering, backpacking and trailing.

The Fish River Canyon in the south of the country is one of the most popular trails in southern Africa and is hiked by some 2,500-3,000 backpackers every year. Covering some eighty-six kilometres (fifty three miles), the trail, which ends at Ai-Ais, is usually walked in four or five days.

A popular area, of long standing with mountaineers and backpackers, is the Brandberg where Königstein is the highest point in the country. The mountain can be ascended along several routes, but because of the extremely rugged terrain and the limited water, excursions should only be undertaken by experienced and fit backpackers after careful planning.

One of the greatest challenges to mountaineers is the Spitzkoppe, known as the 'Matterhorn of Namibia'. Rising some 1,784 metres (5,852 feet) above the surrounding plains, the mountain, rated as an E-grade climb in some sections, was first ascended in 1946.

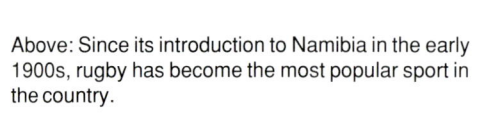

Above: Since its introduction to Namibia in the early 1900s, rugby has become the most popular sport in the country.

Opposite: One of the great challenges to mountaineers is the Spitzkoppe — the 'Matterhorn of Africa' which rises 1,784 metres above the plains.

Above: Hunting in Namibia as professional guide scans horizon for possible trophy.

Hunting

Hunting is not only a popular sport, but also helps to manage surplus game populations. In some areas controlled hunting is essential to proper wildlife management.

Though wildlife hunting is banned across much of the African continent, the thrill of big-game hunting is still available — at a price — for those seeking adventure in the style of old-time hunters. Free-spending 'great white hunters' can pay a fortune for the privilege of shooting lion, elephant, leopard and buffalo.

Very few areas are still untouched by man and his activities near the end of this century. The era of wildlife management has begun. Namibia's new model Democracy has a constitution that underwrites the utilisation of its 'renewable resources'.

Properly managed wildlife means, at some stage or other, the utilisation of wildlife by consumptive means to avoid over-population. Hunting, and especially Trophy Hunting, provides the maximum input with the lowest toll of animals.

All hunting in Namibia is exceptionally strictly controlled by laws and regulations to prevent over-exploitation, and the country prides itself on not having lost one species to extinction.

A very capable Ministry of Wildlife Conservation and Tourism is in control of all matters concerning wildlife and the environment, and also deals with the impact of general tourism on the country's sensitive environment.

Trophy hunting is available to visiting hunters on several levels. Hunting for plains game on registered hunting ranches, which include several registered guest farms, takes place in the commercial farming areas. Big game is available in more exclusive open Concession areas, mainly in the north-east of Namibia in the Bushmanland, Kavango and Caprivi regions, and is handled by safari operators with big-game-licensed professional hunters.

Plains game includes species like kudu, oryx, hartebeest, springbok, wart hog, duiker, Hartmann's and Burchell's zebra, southern and black-faced impala, blue and black wildebeest, giraffe, klipspringer and dik-dik. Predators include caracal, jackal, leopard and cheetah.

Depending on their international conservation status, various of the above-mentioned species are under very strict licensing, and official researchers allocate a quota for each hunting area.

The big game areas also offer a well-researched, restricted quota for elephant, lion, leopard, buffalo, crocodile, hippo, sable, roan and limited other plains game species.

Any visiting hunter can thus feel assured that any hunting permitted by license is justifiable in terms of conservation and management principles.

Accommodation for hunters has to be inspected and registered by the Ministry. In ranch areas, hunters are normally accommodated in small chalets, bungalows, or guest rooms. In the big game areas, accommodation is in traditional African tented style of the highest standard.

Namibia's hunting fraternity has a well-organised association, known as NAPHA. Every member is subject to the highest possible ethical standards and under a strict Code of Conduct. Violation can lead to the cancellation of the individual's registration and licence.

Visiting trophy hunters are, by law, only allowed to hunt under the guidance of a registered guide, master guide or professional hunter.

The trophy hunting season starts on 1 February and ends on 30 November each year. It is generally recommended to hunt in the cooler months, from April to September. The rainy season normally ranges from December to March. The hottest months are from November to March. Temperatures below freezing point at night can be expected in June and July.

Approximately 2,000 visiting hunters are handled by about 300 different outfitters every year. Hunters from all over the world visit Namibia. The main markets, however, are found in the German-speaking countries of Europe, USA, Spain, Italy, Netherlands, France and Scandinavia. Language has never really been a problem, as most of the outfitters are trilingual.

Some of the last remaining Bushmen live in Namibia and their phenomenal tracking abilities are utilised by hunters. Their knowledge of wildlife and bush lore is profound. They can read the spoor and signs in the drifting sands like a surveyor reads a map.

Namibia argues that controlled hunting is of more use to the environment than no hunting, and brings in badly needed foreign exchange, part of which is ploughed back into anti-poaching squads and conservation projects.

Not unnaturally the professional hunters also take this view. Many say that because of the ban on hunting in the late 1970s the once-flourishing wildlife sanctuaries of Kenya and Tanzania became a poacher's paradise. Hundreds of elephant and rhino were slaughtered, there was no money for anti-poaching patrols, and roads and tracks became totally overgrown.

Namibian wildlife authorities and hunters argue that they are the best protection against poaching, as the poachers remain far away when they and their clients are operating.

Unlike the poachers who kill as many animals as possible, including immature ones for their horn and ivory, hunters are interested in a trophy or perhaps a skin and will carefully select the animals they want.

Elephants are particularly popular, but cow elephants have thinner ivory and are ignored. Young breeding bulls are also passed by, though they may have tusks of perhaps twenty-three to twenty-seven kilos (fifty to sixty pounds).

Constantly checking the wind, trackers will often take hunters through, or around, perhaps 100 elephants in five or six herds until one is considered 'suitable'.

The most dangerous and exciting animals to hunt today are buffalo and leopard. The problem with buffalo is that they sleep in grass and you often do not see them until you are nearly on top of them.

Leopard present a different problem. Unlike lion, these cats tend to hunt and prowl at night, and spend most of the day sleeping. They have a keen sense of smell and excellent eyesight. Leopard move silently and will attack if wounded, cornered, or if someone inadvertently walks under a tree where they are resting.

Poachers catch leopard with cruel snares and traps, but the big-game hunter must lie in wait for his prey — a task which demands skill, iron nerve, and endless patience.

First the trackers search for a tree used by leopard. It will have claw marks on the bark, a long horizontal branch affording a view over a wide area, and be backed by thick bush or cover. Preferably the setting should also be near water.

Then a gazelle or wart hog is shot for bait and hauled up onto a branch where it hangs from a rope. Leopard generally take their kills into trees to eat and, in theory, a leopard will soon discover the dead animal, hook it up onto the branch with a paw, and start eating.

Hyena and most lions do not climb trees, and vultures, unable to hang upside down like bats, are also denied access to the bait.

The following day the hunters return to the tree to see if the lure has been touched. If it has, trackers build a hide of grass and branches. They carefully smear mud over the broken ends of the twigs so they do not show white wood and try to blend the construction into a bush.

A clear view of the branch from the hide is essential and, as the shot may be taken in almost total darkness, the leopard tree must also be silhouetted against the sky. The hide must be downwind of the heavy cover through which the leopard moves to approach the tree.

Hunter and tracker enter the hide in the afternoon. They must sit in total silence, not daring to move a limb, to sneeze, or to flick away biting tsetse flies or ants. There can be few more eerie experiences than squatting in a hide, surrounded by the mysterious, muttering night sounds of the African bush. Suddenly a leopard coughs nearby. The low grunt can carry a long way on the still air and it is impossible to tell how close the animal is.

The leopard moves silently to the tree. The hunter, with pounding heart, and hands slippery with sweat, almost fails to believe his eyes when the big cat appears like magic on the branch twenty metres (sixty feet) away. A well-placed shot from a small calibre, high velocity rifle will kill it. If, in his excitement, the hunter misses the lethal spot or his bullet is deflected by a branch, the leopard may leap to the ground wounded.

This is the most dangerous moment of all for any hunter. The cat will make for the long grass and the hunter must follow its trail of blood. The wounded beast can spring at him from only a few yards away.

One man who survived a leopard attack in such circumstances said all he recalled was blur of movement as, in total silence, the beast flashed towards him. Its tail appeared to windmill round and round as it kept its balance. The hunter had only a split-second to aim and fire his shotgun loaded with heavy double buckshot.

Much of the foreign currency earned from hunting in Namibia is ploughed back into wildlife protection and anti-poaching squads, to save many more animals from death, and Namibia was recently awarded the International Wildlife Conservation Award by the world body, SCI.

Rock Art: The Priceless Legacy

Thousands of years ago the San, those prehistoric pioneers of southern Africa, used rock faces and caves across the country as a 'canvas' for their unique and extraordinary art. These paintings are found throughout Namibia and, although hundreds of sites have been identified and catalogued, experts believe that many more priceless Stone Age art treasures have yet to be discovered.

The rock paintings, which are from a similar era to those discovered hidden deep in caves in France and Spain, are often found in Namibia on exposed granite faces, open to the wind, sun and rain.

The process of the earth's cooling, three billion years ago, affected the granite in many different ways. Some split in regular vertical and horizontal cracks that became enlarged over the centuries by water and weather.

In other instances upright sheets of granite fell away, leaving fresh, clean vertical faces — an ideal 'canvas' for those early artists. Another erosion process turned some of the granite slabs into large, shallow caves, whose smooth concave and convex walls and ceilings provided the San painters with their greatest opportunities. Such caves are the richest repository of these earliest art forms.

Almost inevitably, the views from these caves located high above the ground were panoramic, some stretching for at least 100 kilometres (sixty miles), providing a great deal of artistic inspiration.

The San artists belonged to the group of hunter-gatherers who lived in southern Africa 20,000 years ago. None of the paintings has been dated effectively but experts agree that they belong to the late Stone Age.

The most recent works incorporate different media used throughout the past: polychrome figures, and finally plastered kaolin works. When the kaolin clay fell off, etched in white among the black lichens were impressive and dramatic works of art.

The colours used in the rock art were derived from iron oxides: haematite provided the red, limonite the yellow, and the monochrome whites and greys came from various clays and organic matter.

How these were mixed and prepared is not fully understood, but the paint was not only remarkably smooth but incredibly durable. It had to be, to survive thousands of years of weathering.

While exact dating of the paintings is still to be confirmed, archaeologists have used stratified deposits to form educated guesses.

The sequential development of this art form through the millennia has been (and still is) the subject of much conjecture and postulation. There is, however, a clear line of evolution. The earliest monochrome forms depict animals in silhouette and matchstick people.

In a second form the animals are almost caricatured — depicted in outline profile only, while people are shown in much greater form and detail. A third style, which introduced the use of white pigment, had a great variety of animals and a wider use of colour.

Polychrome paintings, with a deft use of both colour and detail, are common. The fourth, more sophisticated style uses strong outlines and contrasts, subtle shading, and infilling. Many consider this to have been the apogee of rock art.

One constant theme in virtually all these works is the relationship between man and animal. Other common subjects include animal and human forms depicted with their tools, weapons, domestic goods, and crude jewellery.

Among the most frequent animal portrayals are antelope (particularly kudu and sable), elephant, rhino, zebra, and wart hog. In rare instances there are illustrations of reptiles, birds, fish and insects, along with surrealistic animal forms, and objects.

Namibia has one of the highest concentrations of rock paintings in Africa (found virtually throughout the country wherever there is bare granite). The Anibib Guest Farm, just south of Omaruru in central Namibia, boasts the largest collection. Not far away the Ameib Guest Ranch is home to Phillip's Cave in which can be found the famous white elephant painting. Twyfelfontein and the Brandberg Mountain are homes to some of the most famous in the world, including the White Lady.

Bound up with the life of prehistoric man — his hunting, dances, and spiritual beliefs — these paintings include the rituals that heralded puberty, circumcision, marriage, birth and death. Kudu, for instance, were a symbol of potency. Bees and honey also appear in San paintings, having a deep ritual or spiritual significance. It is thought that illustrations of elephants and abstract animals were linked to rainmaking celebrations and rituals.

More important than an understanding of what the pictures symbolise or narrate, however, is the need for an extensive and continuing survey to discover other rock art sites throughout Namibia — if indeed they exist.

Top: Ancient rock engraving at Twyfelfontein in Damaraland dates back to prehistoric times.

Above: The renowned 'Dancing Kudu' — one of the San paintings at Twyfelfontein.

Tastes of Namibia

Most Namibian hotels offer conventional European or German menus, and a visitor will be hard-pressed not to find one that does not serve a sauerkraut breakfast with spicy German sausages and cheese.

The *Schwartzwald-Torte* with whipped cream and *kaffee* constitution runs deep throughout this nation's culinary highways and byways. The best German confectionery includes delights like fruit in crisp pastry, creamy gateaux and cheesecake — to name just a few.

Visitors who wish to wander beyond the confines of German cuisine, steak (admittedly of excellent quality) and chicken, can find plenty to titillate their taste buds — if they look for more varied fare.

The finest kingklip, deep water hake, west coast sole and maasbanker come from Namibia's shores. A Swakopmund speciality is smoked barbel served with onion rings. When you think of a great Namibian starter, fresh oysters immediately come to mind, as they are rated amongst the world's finest.

Namibia is also famous for its lobster — often incorrectly called giant crayfish. The local rock lobster accounts for most of the 'crayfish' that are eaten in Namibian restaurants.

For visitors who are not great sea-food eaters, but still enjoy meat dishes, why not be adventurous? Crocodiles are not fish — in fact they prey on them — but the meat of this prehistoric reptile has become an interesting addition to the Namibian food scene in recent years. The meat comes from crocodile farms and ranches and is turned into an amazing variety of dishes, from meatballs to stew and soups.

While the uninitiated may blanch at the thought, crocodile meat is much nicer than it sounds, with a flavour variously described as resembling chicken, veal and fish. You can buy it smoked and sliced in Windhoek delicatessens and, increasingly, it is found on the menus of the country's best restaurants.

Above: Venison drying into biltong on a Namibian guest farm.

Several other species, traditionally regarded as 'wildlife', are farmed on ranches in Namibia and — again — their meat sometimes appears in supermarkets or on the menus of some hotels and restaurants. Impala meat, particularly a choice loin, is the most common. Provided it is well prepared — it usually needs marinading for a while — it compares well with the best venison. Eland, zebra, and buffalo meat (often more tender than prime beefsteak) are sometimes available and, depending on tastes, well worth a try.

And do not shy away from such local delicacies as mopane worms and flying ants if they are offered to you. They are nicer — much nicer — than you might think.

Vegetarians can delight in the fact that an incredible variety of fruit and vegetables is available, imported from South Africa. The citrus fruits include oranges, tangerines,

Above: One of the great tastes of Namibia — rock lobster from the depths of the Atlantic coast.

lemons and grapefruit. Apples, apricots, nectarines, peaches, pears, plums and quinces will probably be familiar to most visitors.

Those hailing from cooler climes may not have experienced the pleasure of tropical fruit, which is readily available — including kiwi fruit, superb avocados, guavas, bananas, lychees, grenadillas, mangoes, juicy pawpaws and pineapples.

Namibia also imports some first-class wines from South Africa. The producers have acquired the knack of turning locally produced grapes into a variety of wines with a surprisingly wide range of tastes and bouquets. Prices vary from 'reasonable' for a sturdy red and white house wine to substantial sums for an excellent vintage or pseudo-champagne.

The locally brewed beers are first class if you like the light, lager-type. All breweries still adhere to the *Reinheitsgebot*, a purity law laid down in 1516 by Duke William IV of Bavaria, which prohibits the use of any ingredients other than malt, hops, water and yeast.

Samples of the very excellent Windhoek Lager are sent to the world-famous Beer Institute in Munich, the Weinenstephen, three or four times a year, where their standards are confirmed through regular analysis.

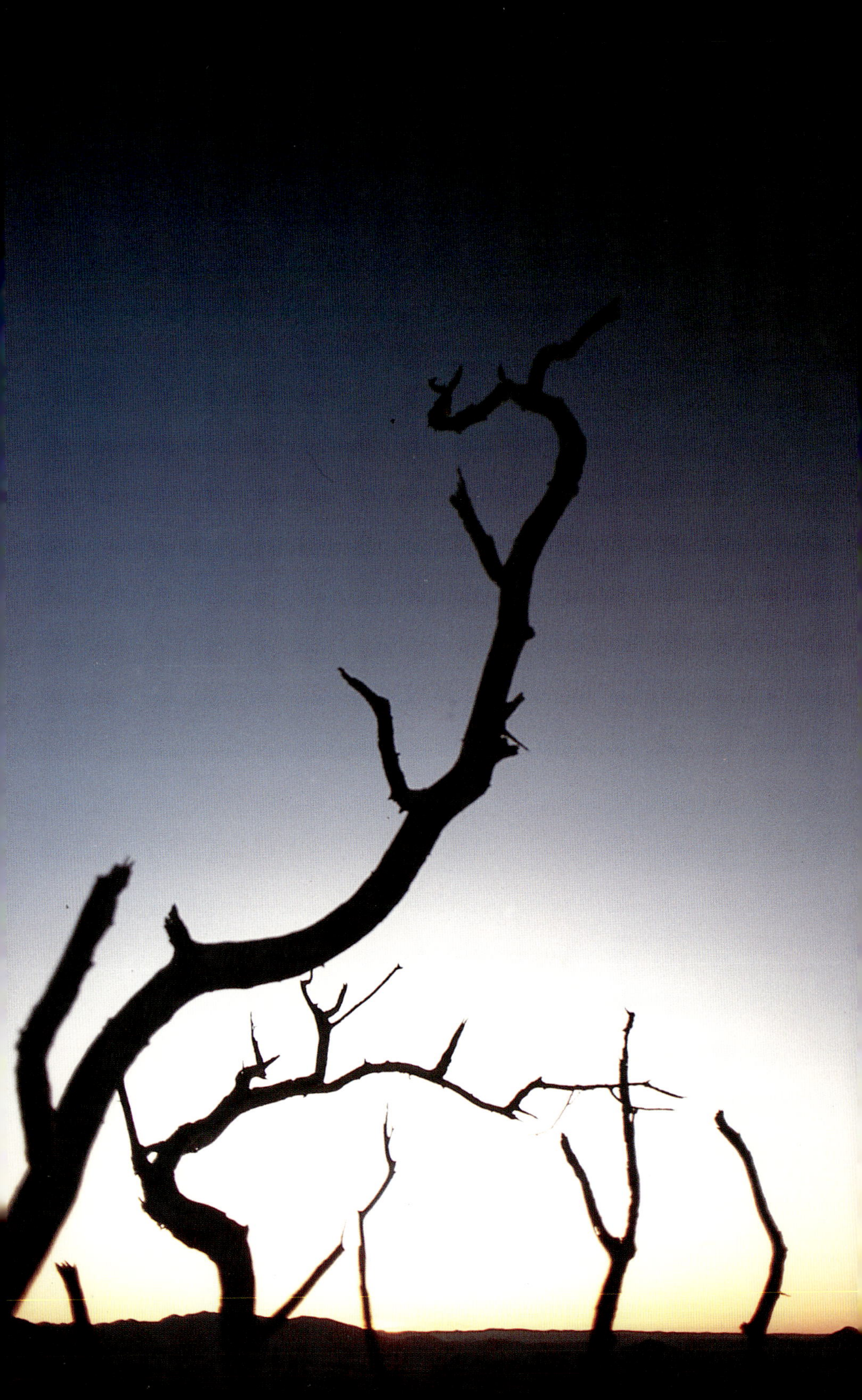

PART FIVE: BUSINESS NAMIBIA

The Economy

Namibia appears to be relatively prosperous in the African context and, economically, it is considered advanced by the standards of southern Africa. Per capita, Namibians enjoy a higher rate of income than any other country in the region, with the exception of South Africa.

The economy is based on mining, agriculture and fishing. The former is by far the most significant sector in terms of its contribution to GDP, but agriculture employs fifty per cent of the workforce. There has been a recent improvement in the net export of goods and Namibia also enjoys a relatively established infrastructure.

The country has a large and diversified mining sector, producing diamonds, uranium and base metals. Large ranches also provide significant exports of beef and karakul sheepskin. About ninety per cent of the goods that Namibia produces are exported and ninety per cent of the goods that are used in the territory are imported. This leaves the economy badly integrated.

The GDP increased in 1986, compared with a decline of 0.8 per cent in 1985, and further increased by 2.9 per cent in 1987, and 2.3 per cent in 1988. However, it declined in 1990 by two per cent owing to a number of factors including depressed international prices of Namibia's mineral exports.

In the 1980s South Africa was an important source of finance for Namibia. But in 1990 it ceased acting as guarantor of Namibian loans and, following Independence, the country received assistance from the international community. In July 1990 donors pledged US $696 million for the period 1990-93.

Germany was the largest bilateral donor, agreeing to provide US $186 million. Namibia is not permitted to borrow on concessionary terms owing to its higher per capita income (the fact that this is evenly distributed throughout the population as emphasised by President Nujoma).

It is likely that Namibia will continue to be economically dominated by South Africa in the initial post-Independence period. The Namibian dollar was introduced in September 1993. The country is a member (with Botswana, Lesotho, South Africa and Swaziland) of the Southern African Customs Union. At Independence, Namibia became a member of the Southern African Development Co-ordination Conference (SADCC) which aims to reduce the region's economic dependence on South Africa.

Namibia's abundant mineral reserves and rich fisheries form the basis of the nation's future economic prosperity, but it must expand the under-developed manufacturing sector. In September 1990 Namibia joined the International Monetary Fund. In December 1990, liberal legislation on foreign investment was introduced and, a year later, 140 potential foreign investors attended a conference in Windhoek.

There is a definite and urgent need for Namibian businessmen and women to establish themselves and set up joint ventures with richer and more experienced foreign investors. This will help to build capabilities for the implementation of the nation's development projects. The government is prepared to help local business people rise to the challenge and a Namibian Development Bank and Namibian Development Corporation have been formed.

Through these institutions the government has the necessary machinery to mobilise and channel financial resources to those Namibians who come up with worthy economic development projects.

Given the market economy system that

Namibia has opted for, the government hopes to create a favourable climate to encourage both local and foreign investors to put their money into the country's economy.

Agriculture

Namibia has a fragile ecology and most of the territory can support only livestock. The major agricultural activities are thus the processing of meat and other livestock products. More than ninety per cent of commercial agricultural output comprises livestock production, and the most important agricultural product is beef. The only large-scale commercial arable farming is in the Karstveld around Tsumeb, and on the Hardap irrigation scheme in the south. Subsistence crops include beans, potatoes and maize.

Colonial history bequeathed Namibia three different agricultural sectors: about 4,000 large commercial ranches, almost all white-owned; 20,000 African stock-raising households, compressed into central and southern reserves; and 120,000 black families practising mixed farming on just five per cent of the viable farmland in the far north. At the time of Namibia's Independence about half the country's commercial farms were owned by absentee landlords and the possible redistribution of such land was an important political issue. In mid-1991, a national land reform conference resolved that abandoned and under-utilised land would be reallocated and ownership of several farms by one person would not be permitted.

In 1990, following Independence, Namibia signed the Lome Convention, agreeing to supply an EC quota of 10,500 tonnes of beef in 1991 and 1992, rising to 13,000 tonnes in 1993. Some eighty-four per cent of commercial beef production had previously been exported to South Africa. Slaughtering and processing facilities were expanded during the 1990s.

Karakul sheep farming is a proven commercial success in Namibia. The lamb pelt is suitable for garment manufacture, the wool is used in the production of carpets and rugs, and the meat is excellent for human consumption. Karakul farming is viable even under adverse conditions such as drought.

Independence has opened up new avenues. One of the recent developments has been the establishment of a joint venture between the companies Nakara in Namibia and Grunstein of Finland. As a result of this, Nakara manufactures reversible Swakara garments, exclusively according to the Grunstein design.

Fishing

Potentially Namibia has one of the richest fisheries in the world — the industry was formerly second in importance to mining. There are, in fact, two separate fishery industries in Namibia: inshore and offshore. The inshore fishery, for pilchard, anchovy and rock lobster, is controlled by South African companies, based at Lüderitz and Walvis Bay.

However, the country's fishing resources were almost exhausted during the last two decades of unmanaged and irresponsible fishing practices by foreign fleets. The primary task of the government is, therefore, proper and sustainable management of marine resources. The declaration of the Namibian Exclusive Economic Zone (EEZ) was the turning point in the recovery of the fishing resource. The development of sound national fisheries policies is extremely important in the context of the industrial sector.

Walvis Bay is the main fishing harbour in Namibia, as well as the country's only deep water harbour. There are three canning plants with a combined capacity of 100 tonnes of pilchards per hour on one shift. This capacity far exceeds the market for the present products. A nucleus of processing capacity has been installed for freezing and other methods.

Mining

Several hundred minerals have been identified in Namibia, of which a number are exclusive to the country. Despite the vast diversity of minerals and commodities, only a limited number have been found in economically viable concentrations. About sixty have been exploited to date.

Base metal production in Namibia has

played a significant role in the country's history. Informal mining and primitive smelting of copper ores was conducted by indigenous people in the Otavi Mountainland during the early part of the 19th century. Large scale commercial extraction of copper and lead was carried out by OMEC and exported to Europe.

Non-metallic minerals have been produced sporadically in Namibia, although never on a large scale. Recent developments in the granite and marble quarrying industry, and the re-commissioning of the Okorusu mine in 1988, have provided a boost to the sector. A major recent development was the discovery of the Okanjande graphite deposit which is currently at pilot stage.

Semi-precious stones continue to be mined on a small scale. The potential for developing this industry, particularly amongst small-scale operators, is good. In addition to the expected increase in production, significant value-adding could be undertaken in Namibia and employment could be greatly boosted.

Namibia's mineral resources are vast and the country is under-explored, even by the standards of a developing country. In this regard, the government's approach is to encourage a broadening of the production base and to promote value-adding of mineral products within the country. Foreign entrepreneurs are most welcome to participate in this effort.

Tourism

Tourism is the fourth most important sector of the Namibian economy after mining, agriculture and fisheries. At least 6,000 people are directly employed in this sector.

With its sunny weather, very low population density, unspoilt landscape and unusual variety of fauna and flora, Nambia offers a wide range of attractions. More than ten per cent of the country consists of game reserves and conservation areas. There is abundant wildlife, fascinating indigenous flora and many places of historical, and archaeological, interest. Namibia offers mountains, the Atlantic Ocean, canyons, deserts and even a volcano. The Namib Desert covers fifteen per cent of the country's total area and runs along the coastline.

Almost twelve per cent of the total surface area of Namibia is managed and controlled by the Directorate of Nature Conservation and Recreation Resorts, as an arm of the Ministry of Wildlife, Conservation and Tourism. Most of this area is in the form of game parks, nature reserves and resorts, such as the Etosha National Park.

In addition to the reserves and game parks there are also about sixty hotels, thirty privately owned guest-farms and twenty safari companies. There are also more than 300 hunting farms under the control of the directorate. The private sector is well-organised into specialised organisations such as the Hotel Organisation of Namibia and the Federation of Namibian Tourist Associations (FENATA).

The present government policy is to improve the quality of tourism by providing new infrastructure and by creating a general tourist awareness about Namibia.

Industry

Namibia's manufacturing sector is extremely small. It provided 4.9 per cent of GDP in 1989 and consists mainly of processing meat and fish for export, and production of basic consumer products such as beer and bread. Food products account for about seventy per cent of all goods produced in Namibia. There are more than 300 manufacturing firms, which are located in or near the main urban centres. A cement plant, with a capacity of 200,000 tonnes, came into operation in 1991.

For a country like Namibia, just beginning to establish export manufacturing operations, EPZs (Export Processing Zones) will be an important tool in attracting investment. These will develop domestic capacity in new and more sophisticated industries and services.

The government policy objectives are to identify and encourage local processing and to add value to manufactured products, particularly in those areas where Namibia has an obvious comparative advantage. Emphasis will be placed on the development of small scale industries and the emerging sector in the short to medium term. For the long term, the Ministry is currently working on a comprehensive national industrial development policy. As mining, agriculture and fisheries are major economic activities of Namibia, the longer term policy will obviously be directed at ensuring efficiency in production.

Transport

Namibia has a well-developed and maintained road and aerodrome system. There are some 40,000 kilometres (24,856 miles) of proclaimed roads of which some 4,500 kilometres (2,800 miles) are surfaced, and some 34,000 kilometres (21,128 miles) of gravel and unsurfaced roads in the rural areas.

There are twenty-eight licensed aerodromes in Namibia and more than 300 unlicensed aerodromes and airstrips. Windhoek International Airport is the only international facility, and Air Namibia flies to the rest of the world.

The internal rail network extends over most of the country and the main rail network links up with the ports of Lüderitz and Walvis Bay. TransNamib Limited is the leading transport organisation operating rail, road, harbour and air services in, to and from Namibia.

Power

SWAWEK is the national power utility and is responsible for the supply of electric power throughout Namibia. The main sources of power supply to Namibia are the Ruacana hydro power-station on the Kunene River and the 120 MW coal-fired power-station near Windhoek.

The government has given permission for the construction of the Epupa Hydroelectrical Scheme, situated downstream of the Ruacana station. The project aims to satisfy the future demand for energy, and to make Namibia more self sufficient in the supply of power.

Telephone, radio and television

Eighteen automatic and 134 manual exchanges serve Namibia's 70,000 telephone subscribers who can also dial direct to more than sixty countries. An estimated ninety per cent of Namibia is served by FM radio stations through which NBC — the Namibia Broadcasting Corporation — relays programmes in English, German and nine other languages. Viewers in the larger towns receive a single-channel television service.

Water resources

Namibia's climate is governed by its geographical position in the southern tropics and the cold Benguela Current that flows along its coast. Its rainfall is seasonal, low and erratic. The annual rains are the only renewable water resource that the country possesses. Namibia's water resources are tapped by building sufficiently large dams on the more significant rivers, or by exploitation of viable underground sources.

Demand is on the increase and, by the year 2000, water will have to be imported from the rivers on the borders. Namibia in the 1990s is undergoing such a severe drought that the government has implemented an emergency rural water supply programme to complement the national rural water development plan. This programme will involve the repair and improvement of existing boreholes and wells, the extension of piped water systems in the worst-hit drought areas, trucked water delivery and construction of community storage tanks.

The government is presently spending about R35 million a year on capital works to provide water distributing systems. The most important and far reaching of these is the Eastern National Water Carrier Scheme which is designed to tap underground water in the Grootfontein area through a 350-kilometre (217-mile) canal to the Omatako Dam, from where it can be distributed to the Windhoek-Okahandja central area.

The country's largest water reservoirs are the Hardap Dam near Mariental, the Naute Dam near Keetmanshoop, Von Bach Dam near Okahandja, and the Omatako Dam, south-east of Otjiwarongo.

Labour

The Ministry of Labour and Manpower development is responsible for the development of Namibia's human resources. The Labour Act of 1992 represents one of the most significant and wide ranging enactments by Parliament since Namibia's Independence. The Labour Code, as it is known, provides a vital instrument for the promotion of social justice, economic development and national reconciliation in Namibia. The government has issued a national policy on labour and manpower development. The emphasis is clearly on involving its social partners, the employers' and employees' organisations, in the upgrading of labour matters. At present, the total economically active population in Namibia is estimated at about 600,000 and there are relatively well-organised Namibian unions.

Approximately thirty per cent of those who are eligible attend schools. Country-wide there are some 1,150 educational institutions, ranging from pre-primary to technical institutes, special schools, agriculture schools and industrial institutions.

The Namibian Academy for Tertiary Education was founded in 1980 to meet the tertiary educational needs of the people. The Academy, an autonomous institution, provides three forms of education through the University of Namibia, Windhoek. The Academy recognises and promotes the needs of a developing nation at every level of the labour force.

Investment

The strength of Namibia lies in a well-developed physical infrastructure and a spread of natural resources, particularly in minerals. The country also has the potential for diversified exports of both agricultural produce and minerals. In addition, there is the potential for further development in all economic sectors, especially the industrial sector, which offers numerous opportunities for import substitution. Since Independence the government policy has been:
• To dismantle an economic and social system built on apartheid.
• To redirect public expenditure to meet the health and educational needs of the majority.
• The immediate redistribution of assets and income versus long-term sustainable growth.
• The promotion of economic growth and provision of adequate social services for the poor and disadvantaged.
• To reactivate the economy by stimulating private investment, increasing public investment, and maintaining an enabling environment for private sector activity.

Foreign investment

The Foreign Investment Act of 1990 provides the legal framework within which investors can operate, creating an inviting investment and business climate. It makes provision for unhindered business activities of foreign nationals, investment eligible for the Certificate of Status Investment, and availability of foreign currency for the transfer of profits. This is all handled by the Investment Centre as a division within the Ministry of Trade and Industry.

The Bank of Namibia will ensure the availability of convertible currency for the holder of a Certificate of Status Investment. Foreign currency may be used for repayment of foreign loans, interest and service charges on such loans, and licence fees and royalties to persons ordinarily residing outside Namibia. Foreign currency may also be used for the transfer of profits, dividends or proceeds of sale. A certificate may also provide for the retention of foreign currency abroad for payments made outside the country.

Incentives

The government of the Republic of Namibia has adopted the concept of the Export Processing Zone (EPZ) as a policy option for meaningful industrial development in the country. The Namibian government grants the following industrial incentives to new companies.
• Exemption from corporate tax for a number of years and, thereafter, a substantially reduced standard corporate tax rate. The duration of the tax holiday and the level of the reduced tax rate thereafter are determined by negotiations between the

company and the government.
- Exemption from General Sales Tax on imported capital goods.
- Exemption from all import duties if the operation is geared for 100% export.
- Training grants in the form of reimbursement of up to seventy-five per cent of the total training cost incurred in training Namibian citizens.

Getting started

Business may be conducted in any of the following forms: Public or private company, branch of a foreign company, partnership, joint ventures and sole trader.

Registration of companies

Companies are regulated under the Companies Act, which covers both domestic companies and those incorporated outside Namibia and trading through a local branch. Both public and private companies are required to obtain, from the Registrar of Companies, approval for the name of the company before incorporation.

To obtain registration, the company's attorney must deliver to the Registrar:
- Certified copy of its memorandum and articles of association
- Address of the registered office
- A statement of capital
- A declaration of compliance
- Registration fee
- The company must also register with the Receiver of Revenue for the purposes of General Sales Tax.

Work permits

Although Namibia is endowed with well-trained and experienced professional people in various fields, there are sectors of the economy in which there is a shortage of skilled labour. The government has, therefore, opted for a policy of granting work permits to expatriates if the required skilled labour cannot be recruited locally.

All applications for work permits (temporary residence permits) are to be filed with the Ministry of Home Affairs. The Investment Centre in the Ministry of Trade and Industry has a permanent representative on the Immigration Selection Board. It is thus in a position to assist entrepreneurs to obtain work permits and to speed up the process.

Import/Export controls and procedures

Import controls operate under terms of regulations made by the Southern African Customs Union, of which Namibia became a member in 1990. The other members are Botswana, Lesotho, Swaziland and South Africa.

The essential ingredients of the SACU treaty are:
- No internal customs duties on the movement of goods and services between the member states.
- A common external tariff on all goods and services entering the common customs area from outside.
- Division between the member states of all customs and excise duties earned in the Common Customs Area (CCA).
- The right of a member state to prohibit or restrict imports for economic, socio-cultural or other reasons, but not to prohibit the importation of goods produced in the CCA for the purposes of protecting its own industries.

Namibia needs a larger market than its own market provides for the goods and services that it produces. This is an important consideration from the standpoint of attracting new industry to Namibia.

Finance

The Central Bank of the Republic of Namibia began its operations on 1 August 1990. Its activities as the Bank of Namibia are: acting as the lender of last resort and supervisory authority of the commercial banks; banker of the government and commercial banks; foreign exchange authority; issuer of notes and coins; and the monetary authority.

A wide variety of commercial banks is represented in the territory. The rand is legal tender and there is free movement of money between Namibia and South Africa. All the branches situated throughout the country provide a full range of services to their clients. There are two building societies - the SWA Building Society and the Namib Building Society.

Exchange control in Namibia

The exchange control policy of Namibia had to be consistent with that of the Common Monetary Area (CMA) until a Namibian currency was introduced in September 1993. All member countries of the CMA adhere to the same Exchange Control Regulations and Exchange Control Rulings which form the legal basis of the CMA whose members include South Africa, Lesotho, Swaziland and Namibia.

All the commercial banks in Namibia have been appointed as Authorised Dealers in foreign exchange. The Minister of Finance has authorised the commercial banks to administer the following type of applications:
- Outward payments for merchandise imports
- Outward payments for services (within certain limits)
- All receipts from abroad in payments for exports and services transfers between residents and non-residents based on the sale of Namibian assets owned by non-residents
- Interbank transactions in Commercial and Financial Rands
- Outward transactions of up to ND200,000 via Financial Rands
- Inward transfers by immigrants through Financial Rands for amounts of up to ND500,000 in total.

The Financial Rand System

The Financial Rand is a separate pool of currency created from the sale proceeds of South African and Namibian assets owned by non-residents. This pool may be used for certain approved capital investments, as opposed to the Commercial Rand which is used for current transactions. It provides an incentive for investments by non-residents in Namibia, since assets can be acquired at a discount. The Financial Rand mechanism must be used for outward capital disinvestments and inward capital investments.

Taxation

Corporate income tax is forty-two per cent and personal tax is levied on a sliding scale. A trust is taxed as an unmarried individual.
Income rebates : Individuals
- Unmarried/divorced person ND6,000
- Married/widow/widower ND8,000*
- One child ND1,500*
- Two children ND2,500*
- Three or more children ND3,000*
- Above 65 years-additional rebate ND1,000

(The above amounts are deductible from the taxpayer's income)
* Provided that, if a spouse earns taxable income, fifty per cent of these rebates will be allowed in respect of her/him.

Dividends received

- Dividends received by a Namibian resident from whichever source are taxable in Namibia.
- Companies are exempt from income tax on dividends received.
- Tax withheld by a foreign country is deductible from income tax payable on dividend income.

Non-resident shareholder's tax

The rate of non-resident shareholder's tax is ten per cent, in order to attract foreign investment in Namibia.

Write-off provisions

The cost of acquisition of machinery, implements, utensils, articles and motor vehicles (now also including the so-called 'passenger vehicles') will be allowed as a deduction from income as follows: one-third in the year such equipment was acquired, one third in the subsequent tax year and one-third in the year thereafter.

Fringe benefits

All fringe benefits received in terms of a contract of employment, whether in cash or otherwise are taxable. These fringe benefits are evaluated according to prescribed tax value tables and include meals, holiday accommodation, housing, advantageous sales of assets or donations, use of vehicle, housing loans, mortgage interest subsidies, and loans allowances.

PART SIX: FACTS AT YOUR FINGERTIPS

Visas and immigration regulations

A valid passport is required for all visitors and visas are required from all visitors except nationals of Angola, Austria, Botswana, Canada, Denmark, Finland, France, Germany, Iceland, Ireland, Italy, Japan, Lichtenstein, Mozambique, Netherlands, Norway, South Africa, Sweden, Switzerland, Tanzania, Russia, United Kingdom, United States of America, Zambia and Zimbabwe.

Visas are obtainable from Namibian missions in Angola (Luanda), Belgium (Brussels), Ethiopia (Addis Ababa), Nigeria (Lagos), Sweden (Stockholm), Russia (Moscow), United Kingdom (London), US (Washington) and Zambia (Lusaka).

Intending visitors from countries where Nambia has no mission may apply for visas to the nearest Embassy or High Commission in Angola, Austria, Belgium, Botswana, Canada, China, Ethiopia, Finland, France, Germany, Iceland, India, Italy, Japan, Kenya, Malawi, Mozambique, Nigeria, Sweden, Tanzania, Russia, the United Kingdom, USA, Yugoslavia, Zaire and Zimbabwe.

Entry is usually for one month. Immigration officials may also ask to see a return ticket and proof that you can support yourself during your stay. Consult the nearest Namibian mission abroad or your travel agent for the latest information regarding entry requirements.

Health requirements

Malaria is not widespread, but is endemic in northern Namibia. Visitors should start taking a recommended prophylactic two weeks before their arrival and continue for six weeks after their departure. Bilharzia is present in some rivers and lakes, but it is easily avoided by drinking treated water — tap water in major centres is safe to drink — and by not swimming in lakes and rivers, particularly where there are reeds.

International flights

There are direct flights on Air Namibia from Frankfurt and London, flying time 10-12 hours. South African Airways, Air Zimbabwe, Air Namibia and Air France have connections from South Africa and other neighbouring countries.

Air fares

The usual range of fares is available: business and economy class; excursion fares, bookable any time for stays of between fourteen and forty-five days; an APEX fare, bookable one calendar month in advance, allowing for stays of between nineteen and ninety days. The price of the cheaper APEX fares varies according to the season. Stop overs en route are possible when arranged with the airline for all but APEX fares. Reductions are available for children.

Departure tax

Namibia does not charge airport tax.

Arrival by sea

Cruise liners, and other passenger vessels on regular scheduled routes, do not call at Walvis Bay, although many dock at Cape Town where you may continue your journey to Namibia by road, rail or air.

Arrival by rail

There is one point of entry into Namibia by rail at Upington where the TransNamib connects with South Africa's TransNet. Journey time from Upington to Windhoek is between 29-34 hours. The train runs on Saturday, Monday and Friday.

Arrival by road

Namibia is bordered by South Africa in the south and south-east, Botswana in the east, Zimbabwe and Zambia in the north-east (Caprivi Strip) and Angola in the north.

There are many land entry points from all these countries.

On the South African border there are customs and immigration posts at Ariamsvlei between Upington and Nakop, at Rietfontein, Velloorsdrift and at Noordoewer. On the border with Botswana there are posts at Buitepos, Ngoma and Mohembo. The post between Zambia and Namibia is at Wenela on the Zambezi River and between Namibia and Zimbabwe at Kazungula.

Customs

Customs formalities are kept at a minimum. Unused personal effects, unexposed film, cameras and accessories may be temporarily imported duty free. You must declare firearms at the point of arrival and obtain a temporary import permit.

Road services

Long-distance road travel in Namibia is modern and efficient, but services are limited. Coaches leave Windhoek coach station — opposite the Kalahari Sands Hotel — for all major centres.

The Mainliner international service runs twice a week to Cape Town. There is also a twice weekly service to Johannesburg. The air conditioned coaches are comfortable, meals are served and they have reclining seats and video programmes.

Namibia is one of the few African countries with no cheap local buses — or equivalent — that the visitor may use.

Taxi services

Most taxis in Windhoek are positioned in the car park in front of the Kalahari Sands Hotel. Many are radio cabs and you may call them from your hotel. Most have meters and there is a fixed rate between Windhoek and the airport.

Car hire

Most car-hire companies in Namibia offer everything from small two-door sedans to spacious 4WD vehicles. While some offer a flat weekly rate, many charge a daily rate, plus mileage and insurance.

Vehicles may be hired on a self-drive basis or with a driver. All the major global companies including Avis and Hertz are found at the airport and in most major towns.

Driving

Drivers require a valid international driving licence. It is illegal not to wear a safety belt. There is a general speed limit of 120 kph (seventy-five mph) on open roads and sixty kph (thirty-seven mph) in built-up areas. Road signs are international.

Rail services

TransNamib's rail network is connected to all main towns. The trains are pleasant, rarely full, very slow and stop frequently. There are first, second and third class coaches. First and second have sleeping berths. In first class there are four persons to a compartment, and six in second. Food or drink is unavailable except for part of the way between Windhoek and South Africa. First and second class must be reserved in advance through the booking office at Windhoek station, Tel: 061-2982032.

TransNamib operates three passenger trains a week between Windhoek and De Aar, the rail junction in South Africa where passengers transfer to TransNet trains between Johannesburg and Cape Town. The *Southwestern* runs once a week between Windhoek and De Aar — a trip of about twenty-nine hours. Two other passenger trains a week take thirty-four hours to complete the journey. Passengers provide their own bedding or buy bedding tickets when making reservations.

Climate

The climate is typical of semi-desert country with hot days and cool nights. Temperatures in summer rise above 40°C (104°F). In winter the days are agreeably warm, although they often drop below freezing at night.

Temperatures are lower than the other inland regions over the high central plateau while, along the coast, the cold Benguela current moderates the desert heat, inhibits rainfall and causes fog. Characteristic of the coastal desert during autumn, winter and spring are dense fogs which occur generally from the late afternoon until mid-morning.

The interior of the country has two rainy seasons. The short rains fall any time between October and December. The long rains, when fairly frequent thunderstorms occur, are between mid-January and April. Dry and cloudless conditions mark the rest of the year. In all, the country enjoys more than 300 days of cloudless sunshine.

Currency

The unit of currency is the Namibian Dollar divided into one hundred cents. Notes are issued in denominations of 50, 20, 10, 5. There are 50, 20, 10 and 5 cents coins. The South African Rand is also in circulation.

Currency regulations

There is no limit to the amount of foreign exchange that overseas visitors may bring into the country. Travellers cheques and notes in foreign currency must be cashed at banks, whereas those in South African Rand are acceptable almost everywhere.

Banks

The major South African and Namibian commercial banks are represented in Windhoek and other major towns. Automatic telling machines have been installed in the capital and Swakopmund.

Banking hours are from 08.30 to 14.00, Monday to Friday. Some banks also open until 12.00 on Saturdays.

Credit cards

Master Card and Visa are widely accepted throughout Namibia. Some hotels, restaurants and shops accept American Express, but this is not common.

Government

Namibia is an independent republic within the Commonwealth, a member of the United Nations Organization of African Unity. It covers 824,268 square kilometres (318,250 square miles) mainly north of the Tropic of Capricorn. The population is about one-and-a-half million. The capital is Windhoek with a population of about 120,000. Other major towns include Walvis Bay, Swakopmund, Keetmanshoop, Lüderitz, Grootfontein, Tsumeb and Katima Mulilo.

The government operates under an executive President elected by universal ballot who is limited to two five-year terms in office. Constitutional amendments require a two-thirds majority of the seventy-two member National Assembly. The independent judiciary is presided over by the chief justice.

Namibia is divided into thirteen regional councils each with local authorities ranging from municipalities to towns and villages.

Language

English is the official language but all official documents and notices are also in Afrikaans. German is widely used and, being spoken throughout the country, enjoys a semi-official status as an important lingua franca.

There are many indigenous African languages and dialects in two main groups: Bantu and Khoisan. However, most people speak German, Afrikaans or English and — in many cases — all three.

Religion

Seventy-five per cent of the population is Christian. Of these most are Protestants of various denominations, German Lutheran being the dominant sect. As a result of early missionary activity, there is also a substantial Roman Catholic population, mainly in the centre of the country and spread throughout isolated mission stations in the north, especially Kavango. Most Portuguese-speakers are Roman Catholic.

Time

Namibia is two hours ahead of Greenwich Mean Time (GMT).

Business hours

Business operates from 08:00 to 13:00 and from 14:30 to 17:00, Monday to Friday. Some places also open on Saturday, and there are twenty-four hour petrol stations.

Security

Namibia is a friendly country and well-policed. Walking alone at night, however, is inadvisable. Preferably use taxis. Do not leave valuables in hotel rooms and do not carry large sums of cash. If you have valuables, use a safe deposit box.

Communications

Phones in Namibia are relatively efficient but

the lines may not be very clear. International phone calls may be made from post office booths or hotels. There are no phone boxes in the streets.

International telegraph, telex and facsimile services are available from most major hotels. Many, however, charge exorbitant rates and it is far cheaper to go to the international telephone bureau at Windhoek Post Office on Independence Avenue.

Media

Namibia has several newspapers, including the *Namib Times*, the *Times of Namibia*, *Die Suidwester* and the *Windhoek Observer*. South African daily papers and some European newspapers are available. German newspapers are available in Windhoek and Swakopmund, together with a full range of magazines and journals.

Energy

The electricity supply is 220/240 volts (50 cycles AC). Sockets are of the round three-pin, fifteen amp type.

Medical services

Medical services in Namibia are better than those in most African countries. Hospitals and clinics exist in all major urban centres. Standards range from private hospitals and clinics with sophisticated equipment and specialist personnel, to fairly basic government hospitals and clinics. Prices vary accordingly. The names and addresses of doctors are listed in the Namibian telephone directory.

Medical insurance

Cover can be bought in Namibia through locally-based multinational insurance firms, but it is usually cheaper and more practical to buy it in the country of departure.

Liquor

Licensing hours are liberal. Local spirits and wines, as well as imported brands, are available. The local beers are very good and South African wines, some of the world's finest, are readily available.

Alcohol is not sold in supermarkets. It must be bought in the local off-licence bottle store, *drankwinkel*.

Tipping

In the better restaurants and hotels a service charge is included in the tariff. If you should want to tip someone who has been especially helpful, ten per cent is reasonable. Otherwise, do as you see fit — remembering that while no tipping can result in poor service, too large a tip can make it difficult for the next customer.

Clubs

Clubs are a prominent feature of Namibian social life. Most have excellent facilities and welcome visitors, especially members of international clubs and societies with reciprocal arrangements. Others charge a temporary membership fee.

In Brief

Namibia National Parks, Game Reserves and Nature Sanctuaries

Namibia's national parks and reserves are wildlife and botanical sanctuaries which cover more than thirteen per cent of the country. They have been set aside for recreational and educational purposes and form the mainstay of the country's tourism industry.

Namibia has a superb system of national parks operated by the Directorate of Nature Conservation. The largest and best known is the Etosha National Park in the north of the country. It is a 200-kilometre-wide area of arid bushveld and savannah surrounding a dry calcrete pan or shallow lake. The other main park in Namibia, the Namib-Naukluft Park, includes part of the Namib Desert and its surrounding plains, the Sesriem-Sossusvlei area and Sandwich Harbour.

Parks and Reserves Legislation

The Federation of Namibian Tourism Association (FENATA) was founded in February 1991 to serve as a liaison between the government and the tourism industry. The complete spectrum of private sector tourism trade associations, together with governmental and non-governmental bodies in FENATA, provide an effective base for decision-making in the tourism industry. As a result of the open-door policy introduced by the Ministry of Wildlife, Conservation and Tourism, close co-operation has developed between the private sector and the State.

FENATA deals with matters such as the implications of Government Sales Tax legislation, especially for tour and hunting operators; travel agents and airlines; marketing campaigns to South Africa and Germany; the emergence of illegal accommodation and gambling establishments; visa and customs control.

In the field of selective tourism to Namibia, trophy hunting is an excellent example of a well-organised branch of the industry. All hunting in Namibia is under the supervision of the Directorate of Nature Conservation and controlled by the Namibia Professional Hunting Association.

Namibia Professional Hunting Association

The Association's Aims and Objectives are:
To look after game and nature;
To safeguard the client and particularly the non-resident hunter;
To apply the ethical conduct of hunting and to countenance only the fair chase; and
To promote and maintain a high standard of professional service by members.
Hunting with members of the association assures your protection and a high value of recreational time.

Namibia Hunting and Touring

Immigration and customs are simple and speedy, geared for hunters. Families are safe and may join the hunt or tour independently.

Hunting season: The season varies from year to year. Generally game can be hunted on game-proof-fenced farms from May to August, and on normally fenced farms from June to July. Bird-shooting is in August and September.

Generally you require light clothing with provision for occasional cool nights. Hunting is mainly on private land where a great number of antelope are available. Namibia meets the CITES international requirements, and trophies offered by the association can be taken home. There is a good range of taxidermy and shipment is done in a professional way.

Accommodation: This varies from tented safari camps to luxury lodges.

Firearms: Firearms present no problem and hunters are welcome in Namibia. On entering, arms are freely imported on a temporary permit valid for the duration of your hunt. No prior clearance is required — just arrive with your guns.

Non-resident protection: Namibian law requires that agents taking out hunting parties must be officially examined and tested. The standard is high regarding the selection of trophies, accommodation and hunting cars, and areas must fulfil minimum requirements.

Trophy Hunting

Namibia offers the following hunting categories:

Hunting Ranches (HR)

Owners of these ranches are cattle and sheep farmers. On the farms they also have natural game where certain numbers qualify as trophy animals.

Guest Farms (GF)

The same as hunting ranches, but the accommodation is on a higher level. The owner can be a hunting guide or a professional hunter, and can hunt on other ranches besides his own.

Game Ranches (GR)

These are safe-fenced areas where you find other African game besides the natural species.

Hunting Safaris (HS)
These are professional organisations which operate mostly on huge areas including hunting farms, guestfarms and game ranches. They occur to a limited extent on state owned land. Owners of hunting safaris are mostly professional hunters.

Heritage Sites
Namibia has a number of Heritage Sites and more than twenty national parks, game reserves and nature sanctuaries under the administration of the Directorate of Wildlife Conservation and Research, or the Directorate of Tourism and Resorts, Ministry of Wildlife, Conservation and Tourism, Private Bag. 13306, Windhoek. The parks and reserves are:
Ai-Ais Hot Springs
Brandberg
Cape Cross Seal Reserve
Caprivi Game Reserve
Daan Viljoen Game Park
Etosha National Park
Fish River Canyon Park
Gross-Barmen Hot Springs
Hardap Recreation Resort
Kaudom Game Reserve
Kokerboom Forest
Lake Otjikoto
Mahango Game Reserve
Mamili National Park
Mount Etjo Safari Lodge (private)
Mudumu National Park
Namib-Naukluft Park
National West Coast Tourist Recreation Area
Oanob Dam Nature Reserve
Otjiwa Game Ranch (priate)
Popa Falls Rest Camp
Reho Spa Resort
Skeleton Coast Park
Tsaobis Leopard Nature Park (private)
Von Bach Recreation Resort
Walvis Bay Nature Reserve
Waterberg Plateau Park

The Fish River Canyon
Karas Region.

Geographical location: Southern Namibia, south-west of Keetmanshoop.
Getting there: There is a west turn on the B1 — thirty-three kilometres south of Grünau and thirty-seven kilometres north of Noordoewer on the South African border — onto the D316 gravel road. Ai-Ais Hot Springs is eighty-two kilometres along this road.
Size: 161 kilometres (100 miles) long, twenty-seven kilometres (seventeen miles) wide, 550 metres (1,800 feet) deep.
Altitude: 1,000-1,800 metres (3,281-5,906 feet).
Vegetation: Small trees, shrubs and succulents.
Fauna: Hartmann's mountain zebra, klipspringer, gemsbok, springbok, chacma baboon, hyena.
Bird life: Prolific and varied, especially at the waterholes.
Climate: Extremely hot in summer and warm in winter.
Visitor facilities: There are 4-bed luxury apartments with all facilities at the Ai-Ais Hot Springs Resort, 4-bed huts, each with a refrigerator, cooker, bedding and shower and toilet block. Also a campsite and caravan park with shower and toilet block. Ai-Ais is open sun-up to sundown from mid-March to October, and the canyon is open from May to the end of September, which is the southern winter.
The canyon is one of the great natural wonders of Africa — a gigantic ravine gouged out over thousands of years by the force of the seasonal Fish River, which is Namibia's longest interior river. It flows intermittently, usually coming down in flood in late summer. When it ceases to flow, it becomes a chain of long narrow pools on the sandy rock floor of the chasm.

The Erongo Mountains
Erongo Region.

Geographical location: North of Usakos.
Getting there: From Okahandja on the B1 take B2 west to **Karibib**. There take the C33 north towards Omaruru. To reach the Erongo Mountains follow signposts on the west turnoffs.
Altitude: 1,000-2,000 metres (3,281-6,562 feet)
Vegetation: Scrub, semi-desert.
Climate: Extremely hot summers.
Visitor facilities: The caves and overhangs of these mountains contain many fine specimens of rock paintings. There is a 'white elephant' painting in the Phillip's Cave on the Ameib Guest Farm. Also on the farm is a curious jumble of large boulders known as the 'Bulls Party'.

The Spitzkoppe
Erongo Region.

Geographical location: North-west of Usakos and south of the **Omaruru River** on the Namib plain.
Getting there: One road from Henties Bay runs east through the Omaruru River Game Park to the south face of the Spitzkoppe. Another runs north-east again along the south face from the Omaruru-Khorixas road.
Altitude: 1,000-1,829 metres (3,281-6,000 feet)
Vegetation: Rare and unusual endemic plants such as *Euphorbia virosa* and *Welwitschia mirabilis*. The Spitzkoppe is a group of volcanic mountain peaks which rise from the flats of the arid Namib plain to a height of 1,784 metres (5,852 feet). Many ancient rock paintings and stone implements have been found in the vicinity of these precipitous peaks of weathered granite.
Climate: Extremely hot summers.

Visitor facilities: See "Damaraland: Land of Light", Part Two.

Waterberg Plateau Park
Otjozondjupa Region.

Geographical location: 300 kilometres (186 miles) north of Windhoek, sixty kilometres (thirty-seven miles) east of Otjiwarongo in the Central Region.
Getting there: There is an east turnoff to Waterberg Plateau Park thirty kilometres (eighteen miles) south of Otjiwarongo.
Size: 400 square kilometres (154 square miles).
Altitude: 1,700 metres (5578 feet).
Vegetation: Kalahari sandveld, broadleaf woodland, savannah grasslands, combretum, terminalia, acacia and thorn scrub.
Fauna: Twenty-five species including leopard, cheetah, caracal, hyena, eland, wildebeest, giraffe, black rhino, white rhino, buffalo, roan and sable antelope, red hartebeest, tsessebe, impala, duiker, kudu, steenbok, klipspringer, dik-dik and wart hog.
Bird life: More than 200 species including the last colony of Cape Vultures.
Climate: Warm dry summers and temperate winters.
Visitor facilities: There is an excellent new lodge with 100-seat restaurant, swimming-pool and luxury facilities, caravan park and thirty-two campsites. Three walking trails provide limited public access to the 100-metre (328-foot) sandstone plateau with its vertical cliffs on the western and eastern boundaries of the park. It is renowned for its rock engravings, and for plants found nowhere else in the country.

The mountain is also associated with an historic event, for it was on the plain in 1904 that the Germans and Hereros fought their final battle which resulted in a victory for the German forces.

Burnt Mountain
Kunene Region.

Geographical location: South of Tywelfontein.
Getting there: Seventy kilometres (forty-three miles) west from Khorixas on the C39, follow the signposted turnoff to the north for Petrified Forest and Burnt Mountain.
Size: The mountain is part of a twelve-kilometre (seven-mile) long east-west ridge.
Altitude: 200 metres (656 feet) above the surrounding area.
Vegetation: The mountain slopes have hardly any vegetation, but the rocks are vividly coloured, mostly in shades of red and purple, and glow like fire in the sun.
Climate: Extremely hot year-round but cold at night.
Visitor facilities: Refer to Khorixas.

Petrified Forest
Kunene Region.

Geographical location: West of Khorixas.
Getting there: Follow the C39 seventy kilometres (forty-three miles) west from Khorixas and take the signposted turnoff to the north. It is a few kilometres to The Burnt Mountain.
Size: Three hectares (seven acres).
Altitude: 1,200 metres (3,937 feet).
Vegetation: Barren rock and scrub. The 'forest' consists of a number of recumbent and broken petrified tree trunks, some up to thirty metres (ninety-eight feet) long scattered over the open veld. The age of the fossil trunks is estimated to be over 200 million years, and evidence suggests that the trees did not grow in this area but were uprooted by some gigantic flood. A number of *welwitschia* grow amongst the fossilised trunks. The area has been declared a national monument.
Climate: Extremely hot all year round, cold nights.
Visitor facilities: Refer to Khorixas.

Kokerboom (Quiver Tree) Forest
Karas Region.

Geographical location: Southern Namibia, north-east of Keetmanshoop on the road to Koes.
Getting there: From Keetmanshoop, travel fourteen kilometres (nine-and-a-half miles) north-east along the Koes road. The reserve is signposted.
Altitude: 1,300 metres (4,265 feet).
Vegetation: Kokerboom woodlands. The forest, one of the rarest in the world, is on Gariganus Farm and is open to the public. It is a national monument. It consists of a dense stand of about 300 of the strange tree plants, *Aloe dichotoma*, which grow to a height of eight metres (twenty-eight feet).
Climate: Hot dry summers, cold winter nights.
Visitor facilities: Refer to Keetsmanshoop.

National Parks, Game Reserves and Nature Reserves

Brandberg Mountain Massif
Erongo Region.

Geographical location: Western Namibia, north of Swakopmund.
Getting there: From Swakopmund follow the C44 (C34) for sixty-seven kilometres (forty-one miles) to Henties Bay. Seven kilometres (four miles) beyond Henties Bay, to the north-east, turn onto the C76 (C35), and then 116 kilometres (seventy-two miles) to Uis Mine. From there travel approximately fourteen kilometres (nine miles)

and turn left onto the D2359. It is another twenty-eight kilometres (seventeen miles) along this road to Brandberg. From Henties Bay the gravel roads vary in condition.

Uis Mine may also be reached on the C64 (C36) via Omaruru and via Outjo and Khorixas on the C65 (C39) and the C76 (C35) from the north. All are graded gravel roads.
Size: 500 square kilometres (193 square miles).
Altitude: 2,000-2,579 metres (6,562 - 8,462 feet).
Vegetation: Thick-stemmed succulents, small-leaved bushes, grasses and annuals.
Fauna: Springbok, steenbok, smaller species.
Bird life: A number of bird species live in the bushy gorges, and rarities such as Rüppell's korhaan occur on the plains surrounding Brandberg.
Climate: Extremely hot in summer. Little rainfall. Mild winters.
Visitor facilities: Although not an official reserve, this beautiful mountain is a national monument. There is no accommodation but many visitors camp at the foot of the mountain. Walking is allowed. The Brandberg is famous for its large number of Bushman paintings, said to be more than 15,000 years old. The nearest filling stations are at Henties Bay, Khorixas and Omaruru. You must carry water and all other supplies you need. Brandberg is open 24-hours a day throughout the year.

Cape Cross Seal Reserve
Erongo Region.

Geographical location: Namib Desert, north-west of Swakopmund.
Getting there: Follow the C44 (C34) northwards from Swakopmund past Henties Bay to the turn onto the D2301 (C34). From there it is approximately sixty-four kilometres (forty miles) to the Cape Cross signpost and a left turn onto a good brine road to the reserve.
Size: One square kilometre (one-third of a square mile).
Altitude: Sea level.
Vegetation: Rocky shores, desert plains with little or no vegetation.
Fauna: The cape protects one of the largest Cape fur seal colonies in southern Africa — between 80,000 and 100,000 seals. Black-backed jackal and brown hyena frequent the area, to prey and scavenge on young seals.
Bird life: Cape Cormorant and other birds.
Climate: Extremely hot but subject to sudden, dense, chilling and long-lasting fogs when easterly winds blow. Cold nights.
Visitor facilities: There is no accommodation but there is a large campsite with toilet blocks at Mile 72, twenty kilometres (twelve miles) south of the reserve. The reserve is open every day between 10.00 and 17.00 all year-round from Saturday to Thursday. Cape Cross is named for the cross raised there in 1486 by the Portuguese navigator Diego Cão. From mid-October the bull seals return from their ocean travels to establish territories and harems. At the end of November and in early December the pups are born.

Caprivi Game Reserve
Caprivi Region.

Geographical location: East of Rundu, between Angola and Zambia in the north and Botswana in the south.
Getting there: Follow the B8 eastwards from Rundu for 165 kilometres (102 miles) to Kangongo on the banks of the Okavango River. From there it is another thirty kilometres (eighteen-and-a-half miles) to Mukwe Andara, gateway to the Caprivi Game Reserve. The same road runs through the reserve. There are control points at Bagani in the west and Kongolo in the east. There are some good waterfalls on the Okavango near Andara.
Size: 6,000 square kilometres (2,316 square miles).
Altitude: 500-1,000 metres (1,640-3,281 feet).
Vegetation: Dense, broad-leafed woodland.
Fauna: Elephant, buffalo, giraffe, hippo, crocodile, lion, hyena, kudu, and roan antelope.
Bird life: More than 200 species, including some rare endemics.
Climate: Hot, humid summers, warm winters with cold nights.
Visitor facilities: There is a camp for forty people on the east bank of the Okavango River and also a campsite. There are no other facilities. The park is open throughout the year from sun-up to sundown. Hippo and crocodile abound, therefore it is advisable to swim only in designated bathing places near the camps. Popa Falls rest camp near Bagani is close to the eastern end of the park and to Mahango Game Reserve.

Daan Viljoen Game Park
Khomas Region.

Geographical location: Central Namibia, north-west of Windhoek.
Getting there: Follow the C52 (C28) towards Swakopmund from Windhoek for twenty kilometres (twelve miles), then take the signposted turn north for a short distance to the Daan Viljoen Game Park entrance gate.
Size: Fifty square kilometres (nineteen square miles).
Altitude: 1,500-2,000 metres (4,921-6,562 feet).
Vegetation: Grasslands with occasional low trees and bushes.
Fauna: Hartmann's mountain zebra, red hartebeest, blue wildebeest, gemsbok, kudu, springbok and eland.
Bird life: There are many species, including helmeted guineafowl and red-billed francolin.

Climate: Summer day temperatures are high but nights are cool. Mild winter but cold and often frosty nights.
Visitor facilities: The park is a small game reserve on the shores of a dam in the hills of the Khomas Hochland overlooking Windhoek. Two-bed bungalows have refrigerator, hotplate and handbasin and a communal toilet block. There is also a large campsite and caravan park with toilet block and communal kitchens. Visitors may go game-viewing by car or on nature walks which are allowed along marked trails. There is fishing in the dam. Permits are available at the office. There is a picnic site, swimming pool and restaurant. The reserve is open throughout the year from sun-up to sundown. The best places for birdwatching are around the dam and the rest camp.

Etosha National Park
Kunene Region.

Geographical location: North-central Namibia, north-west of Tsumeb.
Getting there: From Windhoek to Okaukuejo follow the B1 for 242 kilometres (150 miles) to Otjiwarongo. There turn west and north on to the B2 (C33) to Outjo. There take the C68 (C38) north for 117 kilometres (seventy-two miles) to the Okaukuejo gate. From there it is eighteen kilometres (eleven miles) to Okaukuejo.

From Windhoek to Namutoni continue north-east from Otjiwarongo along the B1 for 182 kilometres (113 miles) to Tsumeb, and then another seventy-three kilometres (forty-five miles) along the B1 to the west turn onto the C84 — it is not numbered so look for the signpost — to the Namutoni gate. Namutoni camp is another eight kilometres (five miles). Mokuti Lodge is half a kilometre from the Van Lindequist Gate at Namutoni. Halali camp is reached by internal Etosha roads only. There are charter flights to all three camps and to Tsumeb.
Size: 22,270 square kilometres (8,600 square miles).
Altitude: 1,000-1,500 metres (3,281-4,921 feet).
Vegetation: Soils are shallow and alkaline which, together with low and erratic rainfall, result in sparse annual grasslands with small acacia and combretum shrubs. The area around the pan consists of short, open grassland with belts of deciduous trees and bushes. Mopane woodland covers large areas in the east towards Namutoni.
Fauna: Elephant, Hartmann's zebra, springbok, giraffe, zebra, kudu, eland, duiker, gemsbok, blue wildebeest, black-faced impala, Damara dik-dik, black rhino, lion, leopard, cheetah, hyena, honey badger, scaly anteater and many others.
Bird life: More than 300 species, including ostrich, secretary bird, guinea fowl, crimson-breasted shrike, lilac-breasted roller, many waterfowl and greater and lesser flamingo.
Climate: Extremely hot all year-round. Summer temperatures rise to 43°C (109°F)
Visitor facilities: One 3-star lodge, three rest camps with restaurants, shops, fuel supplies, rondavels, bungalows, caravan parks and campsites. An extensive network of game-viewing roads. The park is open from sun-up to sundown throughout the year. The pan from which the park takes its name covers 6,133 square kilometres (2,368 square miles) and is the park's focal point. In years of exceptional rainfall the lake fills with water but depth rarely exceeds a few centimetres.

Gross-Barmen Hot Springs and Von Bach Recreation Resort
Khomas Region.

Geographical location: North of Windhoek.
Getting there: Take the B1 north from Windhoek for seventy kilometres (forty-three miles) to the signposted west turnoff to the resort. Gross-Barmen is to the left, Von Bach Dam to the right.
Size: Five hectares (twelve acres).
Altitude: 1,350 metres (4,429 feet).
Vegetation: Highland savannah, mountainous thorn veldt savannah.
Fauna: Greater kudu, Hartmann's mountain zebra, eland, gemsbok, red hartebeest, wart hog, steenbok, common duiker, chacma baboon.
Bird life: Around 200 different species, with large variety of non-passerines, near passerines and passerines.
Climate: Close to temperate with dry summer days.
Visitor facilities: The resort is open throughout the year from sun-up to sundown. Gross Barmen has bungalows, a caravan park, campsites, shop, restaurant, swimming pool, spa, tennis courts, and nature trails. Von Bach has only camping and picnic sites. You can fish in the dam.

Hardap Game Reserve
Hardap Region.

Geographical location: South-central Namibia.
Getting there: Take the signposted west turn off the B1 twenty kilometres (twelve miles) north of Mariental.
Size: 255 square kilometres (ninety-nine square miles).
Altitude: 1,200 metres (3,937 feet).
Vegetation: Savannah shrub with thorn trees.
Fauna: Black rhino, kudu, gemsbok, springbok, ostrich, mountain zebra.
Bird life: More than 260 species including white-breasted cormorant, flamingo, fish eagle, pelican, and Goliath heron.
Climate: Close to temperate, with hot dry summer days.
Visitor facilities: There is a modern rest camp

with 2-bed and 5-bed bungalows, the latter with bathroom and kitchen, and a restuarant. Caravan parks and campsites are also available. It also has a shop and filling station. There is a network of free-walking nature trails.

Kaudom Game Reserve
Otjozondjupa Region.

Geographical location: North-east Namibia, east of Tsumeb and Grootfontein on the Botswana border.
Getting there: Follow the B8 north of Grootfontein for fifty-seven kilometres (thirty-five miles) to the east turnoff on the gravel C74 (C44). Follow this for 222 kilometres (138 miles) to Tsumkwe. There turn north and follow the signposts some distance to the reserve.
Size: 3,840 square kilometres (1,483 square miles).
Altitude: 1,000-1,500 metres (3,281-4,921 feet).
Vegetation: Dry savannah Kalahari woodland.
Fauna: Elephant, buffalo, giraffe, blue wildebeest, red hartebeest, tsessebe, roan, gemsbok, kudu, eland, wild dog, zebra, lion, leopard and cheetah.
Bird life: Varied and interesting desert avifauna.
Climate: Hot dry days and cold nights.
Visitor facilities: The reserve is open throughout the year from sun-up to sundown. Kaudom is completely undeveloped with only basic 4WD trails meandering through the bush. There are two campsites — at Sigaretti in the south and Kaudom in the north with 4-bed huts. Bookings must be made in advance. Those without bookings should stay at Popa Falls in the Caprivi Strip.

Mahango Game Reserve
Okavango Region.

Geographical location: North-east Namibia, between the Angola border in the north, Botswana in the south and Caprivi Strip in the east.
Getting there: Follow the B8 227 kilometres (141 miles) from Rundu to the signposted turnoff — just before Bagani — to Popa Falls and Botswana. The gate is twenty-five kilometres (sixteen miles) south of this turnoff.
Size: 250 square kilometres (100 square miles).
Altitude: 1,000-1,500 metres (3,281-4,921 feet).
Vegetation: Extensive wetlands of reed and papyrus beds, narrow belt of riverine forest, dense broad-leaf woodlands and open grasslands.
Fauna: Elephant, hippo, crocodile, tsessebe, oribi, duiker, steenbok, roan, sable, buffalo, kudu, bushbuck, sitatunga, lechwe, reedbuck, blue wildebeest, wart hog, leopard, lion, cheetah, wild dog, brown and spotted hyena, Cape clawless otter and banded mongoose.
Bird life: Rich and varied with many water birds.
Climate: Hot, humid summer and warm winter, but cold winter nights.
Visitor facilities: The only accommodation available is a rustic rest camp at Popa Falls twelve kilometres (seven miles) north of the gate. There is another private camp seventeen kilometres (ten-and-a-half miles) from the gate. The reserve is open throughout the year from 07.00 to 18.00.

Mamili National Park
Caprivi Region.

Geographical location: South of Sangwali.
Getting there: The internal road is not in good condition therefore the Ministry of Wildlife, Conservation and Tourism in Windhoek or the office in Katima Mulilo should be contacted before making a visit.
Size: 350 square kilometres (135 square miles).
Altitude: 940 metres (3,084 feet)
Vegetation: The area around the reserve with islands of trees such as apple-leaf and wild date palms, is surrounded by open, grassy flats during the dry season.
Fauna: Buffalo, elephant, hippopotamus, crocodile, red lechwe, sitatunga, lion, spotted hyena, leopard and hunting dog are seen around the reserve.
Bird life: This is the major attraction, with species such as fish eagle, wattled crane, swamp boubou, collared palm thrush, Bradfield's hornbill, white-crowned plover, slaty egret and Pel's fishing eagle.
Climate: It is uncomfortably hot and humid in the summer. Summer temperatures rise to 43°C (109°F).
Visitor facilities: There is no accommodation in the park but information on camping may be obtained from the Ministry of Wildlife. Telephone Katima Mulilo 27.

Mount Etjo Safari Lodge
Central Region.

Geographical location: North of Windhoek.
Getting there: Follow the B1 northwards from Windhoek for approximately 210 kilometres (130 miles) and turn left onto the D2483 to Kalkfeld. The lodge is situated north of the road and is clearly signposted.
Vegetation: Area of mixed woodland grassland.
Fauna: There is a wide range of game species including elephant, white rhinoceros, roan antelope, kudu, gemsbok, impala, blesbok, red hartebeest, eland and Hartmann's mountain and Burchell's zebras. Leopard and cheetah are indigenous to this area.
Climate: Summers are hot; winter nights can be cold.
Visitor facilities: Open throughout the year from sun-up to sundown. A swimming-pool; conducted game viewing walks; game viewing by going in open vehicles and from hides at waterholes.

Mudumu National Park
Northern Region.

Geographical location: In eastern Caprivi, east of the Kwando River, in the extreme north-east of Namibia.
Size: 750 square kilometres (290 square miles).
Altitude: 940 metres (2,952 feet).
Getting there: The main gate into Mudumu National Park is forty-five kilometres (twenty-eight miles) south of Kongola on the main B8 Grootfontein-Rundu-Katima Mulilo road but prospective visitors should report to the Directorate of Nature Conservation offices, the Ministry of Wildlife, Conservation and Tourism in Windhoek, or get information from the local office in Katima Mulilo. Telephone Katima Mulilo 27. It is possible to arrange charter flights to Lianshulu.
Vegetation: The area, covered with riverine woodland and reedbeds, is dominated by mopane.
Fauna: Elephant, sable, hippopotamus, bush-pig, leopard, buffalo, kudu, lion, leopard, spotted hyena and wild dog.
Bird life: The park's prolific birdlife numbers more than 200 species, some of which are endemic.
Climate: Summers are hot and humid with mild winters.
Visitor facilities: Lianshulu Lodge, with twin bed chalets, can accommodate sixteen people and there is another luxury lodge. There are accompanied game-viewing drives, walks and boat trips. It is not advisable to wander off alone because of potentially dangerous game. It is best to contact the conservation authorities.

Namib-Nauklahft Park
Hardap and Erongo Regions.

Geographical location: South-central Namib Desert between the Kuiseb and Swakop Rivers.
Getting there: From Maltahöhe the C14 leads south a few kilometres to a turnoff along a minor gravel road leading west to the Naukluft Mountains of the Namib-Naukluft Park.
Size: 49,768 square kilometres (19,215 square miles).
Altitude: Sea level to 2,100 metres (6,890 feet).
Vegetation: A variety of lichens, halophytes such as *Zygophyllum* on the dunes, succulents including *Aloe*, *Euphorbia* and *Lithops* and woody genera such as Acacia and *Euclea* occur in riverbeds. The most unusual single species is the unique gymnosperm *Welwitschia mirabilis*, first discovered in 1863 near the Swakop River. In the mountains there are sparse tufts of perennial grass and scattered shrubs including *Commiphora* and *Boscia* with *Ficus* and Acacia in riverbeds.
Fauna: Three species of elephant shrew, the desert golden mole, three species of gerbil, black-backed jackal, bat-eared fox, hyena and springbok. Mountain fauna includes baboon, leopard, cheetah, mountain zebra, gemsbok, rock hyrax, kudu, klipspringer.
Bird life: There are two endemic bird species, Bradfield's swift and Gray's lark, as well as a number of raptors and the black eagle. Sandwich Harbour and Walvis Bay attract large numbers of gulls, cormorants, waders and waterfowl.
Climate: Extremely hot but subject in parts to dense, cold fogs. Nights are cold.
Visitor facilities: There are camping facilities at Sesriem and Naukluft and at various points in the Namib, with some regions open for day visits only. The campsite at Sesriem has facilities for caravans. There is a walking trail at Naukluft. Guided tours of the southern dune area are available from Lüderitz. The park stretches from the Atlantic Ocean south of Walvis Bay, rising to over 2,000 metres (6,562 feet) in the Naukluft mountains 179 kilometres (111 miles) to the east. Extensive sand dunes run parallel to the coastline for up to 120 kilometres (seventy-five miles) inland, and at Sossusvlei, where they tower 350 metres (1,148 feet) above the river-bed, they rank among the highest in the world. Four dry rivers rise in the eastern plateau, cross the desert and provide a source of underground water. In the case of the Kuiseb, this gave rise to important wetlands at Sandwich Harbour and Walvis Bay where water seeps through the coastal dunes.

Lake Otjikoto
Northern Region.

Geographical location: North of Tsumeb.
Getting there: Follow the B1 north-eastwards for twenty-eight kilometres (seventeen miles) from Tsumeb. The lake lies just west of the road.
Vegetation: Lush vegetation and magnificent trees like the jacaranda.
Visitor facilities: Open throughout the year from sun-up to sundown. The only hotels and camping and caravan sites are in Tsumeb. Lake Otjikoto is home to the very rare, blind cave catfish. This fish only comes to the surface at night, and fish seen during the day are bream. The lake makes an interesting stop on the way to Etosha National Park.

Oanob Dam Nature Reserve
Central Region.

Geographical location: North-west of Mariental.
Getting there: Follow the B1 northwards to Rehoboth from Mariental; from there take the D1237 north-westwards and drive one-and-a-half kilometres (almost a mile) to the entrance gate.
Size: Seventy square kilometres (twenty-one square miles).

Altitude: 1,000-1,500 metres (3,281-4,921 feet)
Vegetation: Most of the area consists of rugged broken country. The vegetation consists of highland savannah and dwarf shrub savannah.
Fauna: Kudu, eland, gemsbok, springbok and Hartmann's mountain zebra occur in this reserve.
Visitor facilities: Open throughout the year from sun-up to sundown. The only accommodation nearby is the Reho Spa which has self-catering bungalows and a camping and caravan site. Another camping and caravan site is planned. A picnic area is being developed and the existing tracks will be upgraded.

Otjiwa Game Ranch
Northern Region.

Geographical location: Between Okahandja and Otjiwarongo.
Getting there: It lies adjacent to the B1, between Okahandja and Otjiwarongo.
Altitude: 1,000 - 1,500 metres (3,281 - 4,921 feet)
Vegetation: Located in typical northern Namibian thornveld.
Fauna: Twenty-eight game species occur including white rhinoceros, kudu, eland, gemsbok, Burchell's zebra and waterbuck
Visitor facilities: Open throughout the year, the main camp has four-person park homes. Two exclusive camps are self-contained and accommodate up to eight people. Walking trails, game viewing drives, horse riding, restaurant and a swimming-pool are all available.

Skeleton Coast Park
Kunene Region.

Geographical location: 110 kilometres (sixty-eight miles) north of Cape Cross between the Ugab River in the south and the Kunene River in the north.
Getting there: The park's two zones can be reached by road either from Swakopmund via the coastal salt road or from Khorixas along a gravel road which crosses the park's eastern boundary north of the Koigab River. The northern section of the park has been left as a complete wilderness area, the only access to it for tourists being by way of exclusive fly-in safaris which operate from Windhoek and are available throughout the year.
Size: 16,390 square kilometres (6,328 square miles).
Altitude: Sea level to 650 metres (2,133 feet).
Vegetation: Typical desert plants such as Salsola and Zygophyllum species, and a number of endemics.
Fauna: Black-backed jackal, brown hyena, cheetah, lion, seals, elephant, giraffe, black rhino, springbok and gemsbok.
Bird life: Cormorants and other sea birds including various species of gull. Ostrich, bustards, larks in the interior.
Climate: Summer heat tempered by the cold Benguela Current. Subject to sudden, dense, cold and persistent fogs.
Visitor facilities: The Skeleton Coast is divided into south and north zones. The southern section is more accessible to tourists than the northern area. No visitor is allowed to enter without a permit from the Directorate of Nature Conservation and Recreation Resorts. At Terrace Bay a converted mining camp offers accommodation complete with restaurant, shop and airstrip. The camp is open throughout the year. There is a caravan park and campsite at Torra Bay which has tent sites, but the resort is only open during the December-January school holidays.

Fishing along the coast is excellent. A regular shoreline of sandy beaches stretches northward from the Ugab River north of Swapokmund to the Kunene River on the Angolan border. Barchan dunes reach inland for forty kilometres (twenty-five miles) and this is the only area in Africa south of the Sahara where such dunes occur.

A number of rivers, which rise in the mountains of Damaraland and Kaokoland to the east, cross the park and in several cases form perennial pools where their mouths are blocked by dunes. Precipitation from coastal fog generated by the mixing of cold and warm sea currents provides the equivalent of forty millimetres (one-and-a-half inches) of rain a year.

Tsaobis Leopard Nature Park
Khomas Region.

Geographical location: Khomas Hochland west of Windhoek
Getting there: Follow the B2 from Windhoek towards Swakopmund. At Karibib take the C32(G77) towards Anschluss and Otjimbingwe. Then follow the C32 (G77) south to the Swakop River for about fifty-two kilometres (thirty-two miles). The park is ten kilometres (six miles) from the main road on the south bank of the river.
Size: 350 square kilometres (135 square miles)
Altitude: 1,500 - 2,000 metres (4,921 - 6,562 feet)
Vegetation: Rugged mountainous country.
Fauna: This park was established as a sanctuary for leopard. Other game such as springbok, kudu, gemsbok and Hartmann's mountain zebra occur.
Bird life: The birdlife is interesting and includes a number of species.
Climate: Summer days are hot and nights are mild. Winter days are mild but nights are cold.
Visitor facilities: Open throughout the year from sun-up to sundown. It has ten fully-equipped bungalows with bedding, and a swimming-pool. Unaccompanied walks and tours of the park are available by arrangement.

Walvis Bay Nature Reserve
Namib Region.

Geographical location: South of Walvis Bay.
Getting there: The road southwards from Walvis Bay to Sandwich Bay passes through the reserve.
Size: 450 square kilometres (174 square miles)
Bird life: Walvis Bay Nature Reserve forms a link on the route of many migratory birds. During the summer months more than 100,000 birds of forty species inhabit the area.
Visitor facilities: Open throughout the year, there is no accommodation here but there are hotels, camping and caravan sites in Walvis Bay. Fishing from the beach and hiking trails are planned.

Namibian Museums

The Namibian Heritage is preserved in the seventeen recognised museums in Namibia. They are found in towns established as colonial settlements, because they were first formed to preserve collections assembled by settlers.

The bulk of collections in most Namibian Museums comprise artifacts and specimens reflecting human endeavour in the region. Most exhibits display these items for their intrinsic beauty and interest as products of indigenous cultures. The State Museum of Namibia is the only museum to devote large portions of its resources to collections and research concerned with natural sciences.

Addresses
The President
FENATA
P.O Box 3900
Windhoek

The Permanent Secretary
Ministry of Wildlife, Conservation and Tourism
Private Bag 13346
Windhoek

Windhoek Information and Publicity
P.O Box 1868
Windhoek

National Museums and Historical Sites

State Museum
Location: Alte Feste (Old Fort), Robert Mugabe Avenue, Windhoek
Tel: 2934362
Contents: Cultural items, Independence display.
Open: Monday to Friday from 09.00 until 18.00 except on Saturday and Sunday when the hours are 10.00 to 12.30 and 15.00 to 18.00.

Closed: Public holidays.
Features: Housed in a modern building, the complex comprising the State Museum, Library and Archives are of interest to any visitor. In the library are many rare books on the early days of 'South-West' and the museum section contains exhibits of the country's natural history and examples of tribal crafts and utensils.

Owela Museum
Location: Robert Mugabe Avenue, Windhoek
Tel: 2934358
Contents: Mainly natural history, 'Touch room' for children.
Open: Monday to Friday from 09.00 until 18.00 except on Saturday and Sunday when the hours are 10.00 to 12.30 and 15.00 to 18.00.

Transnamib Museum
Location: Above the railway station, Bahnhof Strasse, Windhoek
Tel: 2982186
Contents: A history of the railway and transport in Namibia.

Duwisib Castle
Location: On the edge of the Namib
Features: In 1908, Baron von Wolf and his American bride built their sandstone castle. Open for day visitors, a unique collection of furniture, weapons and portraits can be seen.

Martin Luther
Location: Swakopmund on the road to Windhoek
Features: The old steam engine was ordered from Germany in 1896 to convey goods between Swakopmund and the interior. It still stands in the same place where it once broke down.

Railway Station
Location: On Bahnhof Street in Swakopmund
Features: The station building is a striking example of German architecture and was built in the nineteenth century. It was a terminal of the state railway line from the harbour of Swakopmund to the interior. The station is now a monument.

Swakopmund Museum
Location: Old Customs House, The Strand, Swakopmund
Tel: 2982186
Contents: Natural history, cultural history and Kavango display.
Open: Monday to Sunday from 10.00 until 12.30 and 15.00 to 17.30.
Features: The Swakopmund Museum started as the scientific collection of Dr Alfons Weber in 1951. Special exhibits include panoramas of desert and sea life, a collection of semi precious stones, an extensive historical collection, and a modern

technical exhibit of Rössing Uranium Ltd, the largest open-cast uranium mine in the world.

Swakopmund Military Museum
Location: Woermannhaus, Bismarck Strasse, Swakopmund
Tel: 0641 2411 (Municipality, Key on request from Tourist Information Office in Woermannhaus)
Contents: Small collection of military memorabilia relating to military occupation of Namibia.
Open: Monday to Friday from 09.00 until 13.00 and 14.00 to 17.30. It is open on Saturdays from 09.00 util 11.00.

Woermannhaus
Location: Bismarck Street in Swakopmund
Features: Erected in 1894 by the Damara and Namaqua Trading Company. In 1903/04 the Woermannhaus was extended with wood panelled offices. The Damara Tower served as a water tower, landmark and navigation point for the ships of the Woermann line. A fund raising campaign was launched which provided the financing for the Woermannhaus to be restored and transformed into a public library and art centre.

Die Kaserne
Location: Corner of Bismarck and Lazerett Streets in Swakopmund
Features: A typical German Colonial style building was erected in 1905 to provide living quarters for the engineers' regiment sent to Swakopmund to fight the Herero and build a landing pier and railway line to the interior. The entrance hall is decorated with crests of the then German federal states and a plaque with the names of the men who died. It was declared a National Monument in 1973.

Marine Denkmal
Location: West end of Post Street, Swakopmund
Features: The Marine Denkmal (monument) sculptured by a Mr Wolf, was built to commemorate members of the German naval expedition killed in action. The monument was intended for Windhoek but stands in Swakopmund.

Helmeringhausen Museum
Location: Adjacent to the Helmeringhausen Hotel
Contents: Open air display of farm implements, wagons.
Open: Key from Hotel

Grootfontein Museum
Location: Alte Feste, Erikstrasse, Grootfontein
Tel: Phone number on door
Contents: History of the locality, mineral collection, restored carpenters and blacksmith shop.
Open: Tuesdays from 16.00 until 18.00,
Wednesdays from 0900 to 11.00 and Fridays from 16.00 until 18.00. Other times on request.

Powder Tower
Location: Otjimbingwe
Features: Built in 1872 by the Rhenish mission for defence purposes it withstood thirty attacks by hostile Namas. It is now an historical monument.

Mission House
Location: Seventy-two kilometres north of Windhoek, in Okahandja
Features: An historic mission house and church dating back to the 1870s, also public gardens in which are the graves of several Herero chiefs. Towards the end of August every year the Hereros hold a memorial service there.

Tsumeb Museum
Location: Main Street, Tsumeb
Tel: 0671 21538
Contents: History of locality, especially Herero history, minerals and mining and display of items raised from Lake Otjikoto.
Open: Monday to Friday from 09.00 until 12.00.

Shambyu Roman Catholic Mission Museum
Location: Shambyu, thirty kilometres east of Rundu
Tel: 067372 1111
Contents: Mainly woodcarving, traditional crafts of the Kavango area and southern Angola and some stone artifacts.
Open: Open on request.

Omaruru Museum
Location: Rhenish Mission House
Tel: 062232 277
Contents: A brief history of the mission.
Open: Key from Municipality Building in Main Street.

Outjo Museum
Franke House
Tel: 06542 13

Walvis Bay Museum
Location: Adjacent to the Civic Centre
Tel: 0642 5981
Contents: History of the town including large collection of photographs, costumes, furniture, archaeology, minerals and natural history.
Open: Monday to Thursday from 09.00 until 13.00 and 15.00 to 19.00. It is open on Fridays from 09.00 to 13.00 and Saturdays from 10.00 to 12.00.

Lüderitz Museum
Location: Diaz Street, Lüderitz
Tel: 06331 2582
Contents: Early history of the area, Diaz display, natural history of the seashore, Namib Desert,

minerals and diamond mining, Namibia's indigenous peoples, history of the town, outdoor courtyard with whale bones and wagons.
Open: Monday to Friday from 16.00 until 18.00. (other times possible by arrangement).

Kolmanskop Outdoor Museum
Location: Ten kilometres east of Lüderitz on B4
Tel: 06331 2582
Contents: Museum and history, diamond mining plus many houses and workshops to visit, all subject to drifting sand and wind erosion.
Open: Monday to Saturday from 09.30 until 10.30
Permits needed from Lüderitz Foundation Office on Bismarck Street.

Rehoboth Museum
Location: Signposted from B1 road. Adjacent to Post Office and Police Station, Rehoboth.
Tel: 06721 2954

Contents: History of Rehoboth Basters, local archaeological finds, natural history, ecology and traditional houses.
Open: Monday to Friday from 10.00 until 12.00 and 14.00 to 16.00.

Rhenish Mission Church Museum
Location: Keetmanshoop
Tel: 0631 3316 extn 134
Contents: History of Keetmanshoop, interesting garden with local plants e.g Quiver trees, farm implements and Nama hut.
Open: Monday to Friday from 08.00 until 12.00 and 16.00 to 18.00 except on Saturday when the hours are 08.00 to 12.00.

Schmelenhaus Museum
Bethanie (Bethanien) National Monument
Location: Signposted in Bethanie
Contents: History of the mission
Open: Collect key locally as stated on door.

Monuments

1. Grave of Jonker Afrikaner (Okahandja)
2. Fort Namutoni (Etosha Game Park, Tsumeb)
3. Gibeon Meteorites (Meteorite Fountain, Windhoek)
4. Petrified Forest (Outjo, Damaraland)
5. Powder Magazine (Otjimbingwe)
6. Phillip's Cave (Ameib, Usakos)
7. Paula Cave (Okapekaha, Omaruru)
9. Cottage of Dorsland Trekkers (Rusplaas, Kaokoveld)
11. House of Josef Frederiks (Bethanien)
12. Branderg Area (Damaraland)
13. Baobab Tree (Grootfontein)
14. Footprints of Dinosaurs (Otjihaenamaparero, Kalkfeld)
15. Reverend Schmelen's Cottage (Bethanien)
16. Rock Paintings and Engravings (Twyfelfontein, Damaraland)
17. Old Railway Engine (Walvis Bay)
18. Bushman Paradise Cave (Damaraland)
19. Hoba Meteorite (Hoba West, Grootfontein)
20. Mukorob Rock (Keetmanshoop)
21. Quiver Tree Forest (Gariganus, Keetmanshoop)
23. Waterberg Plateau (Otjiwarongo)
24. Farm Verbrandeberg (Damaraland)
25. Von Francois Fort (Khomas Hochland, Windhoek)
26. Alte Feste (Windhoek)
27. Stone Tower (Outjo)
29. Fish River Canyon Farm (Warmbad)
30. Windmill (Otjimbingwe)
31. Relics of Pre-Historic Elephant (Zoo Park, Windhoek)
33. Franke-Tower (Omaruru)
34. Eagle Monument (Keetmanshoop)
36. Rock Engravings (Peet Alberts Koppie, Kamanjab)
37. Grave of John Ludwig (Klein Windhoek)
40. Boundary Post (Kusieb, Walvis Bay)
41. Old German Fortresses at Naiams (Seeheim, Keetmanshoop)
43. Monument at Kub (Kalkrand, Mariental)
44. Replica of Original Cross (Cape Cross, Swakopmund)
45. Equestrian Statue (Windhoek)
46. War Memorial (Zoo Park, Windhoek)
47. 'Marine-Denkmal' (Swakopmund)
48. Memorial In Old Cemetery (Lüderitz)
49. Cemetery on Farm Mooifontein (Helmeringhausen)
50. Cemetery at Nomtsas (Maltahöhe)
51. Stone Rondavel (Quellort, Aroab)
52. Naulila Monument (Outjo)
53. Woermann House (Swakopmund)
54. Battle Field around Franke Tower (Omaruru)
56. 'Moordkoppie' (Okahanja)
57. Otjikoto Lake (Tsumeb)
58. Railway Station (Swakopmund)
59. Rhenish Mission Church (Walvis Bay)
60. Site of Original Diaz Cross (Lüderitz)
61. Prison Building (Swakopmund)
62. Khorab Memorial (Kilometre 500, Otavi)

63. Old Barracks (Swakopmund)
64. Historical Gateways (Forts) (Warmbad)
65. Grave of Axel Eriksson (Urupupa, Grootfontein)
66. Christus Kirche (Windhoek)
67. German Lazarett (Gobabis)
68. Rhenish Mission Church (Otjimbingwe)
69. 'Martin Luther' (Swakopmund)
70. Old Fort (Grootfrontein)
71. Omeg-Haus (Swakopmund)
72. Magistrate's Residence (Lüderitz)
73. 'Prinzessin Rupprecht Heim' (Swakopmund)
74. Station Building (Swakopmund)
75. Kramersdorf Building (Swakopmund)
76. Regimental Badges (Swakopmund)
77. Regimental Badges (Badges 158, Swakopmund)
78. Okaharui War Memorial (Okahanja)
79. Edward Cook's Commemorative Stone (Warmbad)
80. Rhenish Mission Church (Keetmanshoop)
81. Ev. Luth. Church Complex (Bethanien)
82. Ev. Luth. Church (Lüderitz)
83. Ev. Luth. Church (Swakopmund)
84. Ovikokorero War Memorial (Harmonie, Okahandja)
85. Façade of Rösemann Building (Karibib)
86. Krabbenhöft & Lampe Building (Lüderitz)
87. Two Historic Dwellings (Lüderitz)
88. Grave of Kahimemua Nguvauva (Okahanja)
89. Deutsche Afrika Bank Building (Lüderitz)
90. Kreplin House (Lüderitz)
91. 'Hohenzollern' Building (Swakopmund)
92. Roman Catholic Cathedral (Windhoek)
93. Kubas Station Building (Karibib)
94. Prisoner-of-War Camp Site (Aus)
95. Old German School Building (Klein Windhoek)
96. Semi-Det. House, (Lüderitz)
97. Rhenish Mission House (Omaruru)
98. Old Prison Building (Windhoek)
99. 'Hälbitch Buidings' (Karibib)
100. 'Haus Woll' (Karibib)
101. 'Hotel Zum Grünen Kranze' (Karibib)
102. 'Proviantamt' (Karibib)
103. Elisabeth Haus (Windhoek)
104. Kaiserbrunnen (Karibib)
105. Ten Man House (Windhoek)
106. Old Post Office (Keetmanshoop)
107. Second Director's House (Tsumeb)
108. Omeg Minenüro (Tsumeb)
109. German Private School Building (Tsumeb)
110. Roman Catholic Church Building (Tsumeb)
111. Herero Graves (Okahandja)
112. Fort Sesfontein & Cemetery (Damaraland)
113. Old Hotel Building (Otjimbingwe)
114. Old Windhoek Cemetery (Leutwein Street, Windhoek)
115. 'Old Location' Cemetery (Windhoek)
116. Erkrath-Gathermann-Kronprinz Façade (Windhoek)
117. Roman Catholic Church (Omaruru)

Animal checklist

Mammals

INSECTIVORES
(*Insectivora*)
Swamp Musk Shrew
Tiny Musk Shrew
Reddish-Grey Musk Shrew
Giant Musk Shrew
Lesser Red Musk Shrew
Round Eared Elephant Shrew
Short-Snouted Elephant Shrew
Smith's Rock Elephant Shrew
Bushveld Elephant Shrew
South African Hedgehog
Grant's Golden Mole

BATS
(*Chiroptera*)
Angolan Epauletted Fruit Bat
Straw-Coloured Fruit Bat
Nigerian Free-Tailed Bat
Pale Free-Tailed Bat
Little Free-Tailed Bat
Egyptian Free-Tailed Bat
Schreibers' Long-Fingered Bat
Angola Hairy Bat
Rusty Bat
Banana Bat
Butterfly Bat
Long-tailed Serotine Bat
Somali Serotine Bat
Cape Serotine Bat

Yellow House Bat
Lesser Yellow House Bat
Schlieffen's Bat
Damara Woolly Bat
Common Slit-Faced Bat
Rüppell's Horseshoe Bat
Geoffroy's Horseshoe Bat
Darling's Horseshoe Bat
Cape Horseshoe Bat
Dent's Horseshoe Bat
Commerson's Leaf-Nosed Bat
Sundevall's Leaf-Nosed Bat

BUSHBABIES, BABOONS, MONKEYS & PANGOLINS
South African Lesser Bushbaby

Chacma Baboon
Vervet Monkey
Pangolin (*Pholidota*)
Pangolin

HARES AND RABBITS
(*Lagomorpha*)
Cape Hare
Scrub Hare
Smith's Red Rock Rabbit
Natal Red Rock Rabbit
Jameson's Red Rock Rabbit

RODENTS
(*Rodentia*)
Damara Mole Rat
Cape Porcupine
Springhaas
Rock Doormouse
Woodland Doormouse
Cape Ground Squirrel
Mountain Ground Squirrel
Striped Tree Squirrel
Tree Squirrel
Greater Cane Rat
Dassie Rat
Brants' Whistling Rat
Littledale's Whistling Rat
Single-Striped Mouse
Striped Mouse
Woosnam's Desert Rat
House Mouse
Setzer's Pygmy Mouse
Desert Pygmy Mouse
Natal Multimammate Mouse
Multimammate Mouse
Shortridge's Mouse
Tree Rat
Namaqua Rock Mouse
Red Veld Rat
House Rat
Brown Rat
Short-Tailed Rat
Hairy-Footed Gerbil
Dune Hairy-Footed Gerbil
Setzer's Hairy-Footed Gerbil
Bushveld Gerbil
Highveld Gerbil
Pouched Mouse
Large-Eared Mouse
Grey Climbing Mouse
Brants' Climbing Mouse
Tiny Fat Mouse
Fat Mouse
Pygmy Rock Mouse

CARNIVORES
(*Carnivora*)
Aardwolf
Brown Hyena

Spotted Hyena
Cheetah
Leopard
Lion
Caracal
African Wild Cat
Small Spotted Cat
Serval
Bat-Eared Fox
Wild Dog
Cape Fox
Side-Striped Jackal
Black-Backed Jackal
Spotted-Necked Otter
Honey Badger
African Weasel
Striped Polecat
African Civet
Small-Spotted Genet
Large-Spotted Genet
Suricate
Selous' Mongoose
Yellow Mongoose
Large Grey Mongoose
Slender Mongoose
Small Grey Mongoose
Bush-Tailed Mongoose
White-Tailed Mongoose
Water Mongoose
Banded Mongoose
Dwarf Mongoose

AARDVARK
(*Orycteropodidae*)
Aardvark

ELEPHANTS
(*Probiscidae*)
African Elephant

DASSIES
(*Hyracoidea*)
Rock Dassie

ODD-TOED UNGULATES
(*Perissodactyla*)
White Rhinoceros
Black Rhinoceros
Hartmann's Mountain Zebra
Burchell's Zebra

EVEN-TOED UNGULATES
(*Artiodactyla*)
Wart hog
Giraffe
Black Wildebeest
Blue Wildebeest
Red Hartebeest
Common Duiker
Springbok

Klipspringer
Damara Dik-Dik
Steenbok
Impala
Black-Faced Impala
Roan
Gemsbok
African Buffalo
Kudu
Bushbuck
Eland
Reedbuck
Sharp's Grysbok

Reptiles

TERRAPINS
(*Pleurodira*)
Helmeted Terrapin
Cape Terrapin
Huge-flapped Terrapin
Soft-shelled Terrapin

TORTOISES
(*Testudinidae*)
Angulate Tortoise
Leopard Tortoise
Namaqualand speckled padloper
Aus Tortoise
Hingeback Tortoise
Kalahari Tortoise
Tent Tortoise

TURTLES
(*Chelonia*)
Nile Turtle
Okavango Mud Turtle
Variable Mud Turtle
Black Mud Turtle
Serrated Mud Turtle
Green Turtle
Loggerhead Turtle
Hawksbill Turtle
Olive Ridley Turtle
Leatherback Turtle

LIZARDS
(*Sauria*)
Thick-Tailed Rock Gecko
Kalahari Burrowing Gecko
Kaokogecko
Palmatogecko
Banded Barking Gecko
Common Barking Gecko
Tropical House Gecko
Festive Gecko
Marico Gecko
Leaf Toad Gecko

AGAMA
(*Agamidae*)
Etosha Agama
Damara Rock Agama
Tree Agama

CHAMELEONS
(*Chamaeleonidae*)
Namaqua Dwarf Chameleon
Common Chameleon
Namaqua Chameleon

SKINKS
(*Scincidae*)
Mopane Skink
Cape Three Lined Skink
Western Three Lined Skink
Common Striped Skink
Koppie Skink
Common Variable Skink
Variegated Skink
Wahlberg's Dwarf Skink

Lacertidae
Shovel Nosed Sand Lizard

Cordylidae
Dune Plated Lizard
Blue Tailed Plated Lizard
Yellow Throated Plated Lizard
Rough-Scaled Plated Lizard
Giant Plated Lizard
Angola Plated Lizard
Leguaans
Veld Leguaan
Water Leguaan

Amphibians

FROGS & TOADS
Tropical Platana
Common Platana
Mottled Frog
Guttural Toad
Karoo Toad
Raucous Toad
Pygmy Toad
Yellow Swamp Toad
Red Toad
Common Rain Frog
Desert Rain Frog
Namaqua Rain Frog

Mocambique Rain Frog
Red-Banded Frog
Red Marbled Frog
Bull Frog
Striped Sand Frog
Knocking Sand Frog
Marmorate Pyxie
Cape Sand Frog
Cape Rana
Golden-Backed Frog
Angola Rana
Gray's Frog
Ornate Frog
Plain Grass Frog
Broad-Banded Grass Frog
Sharp-Nosed Grass Frog
Dwarf Grass Frog
Mascarene Grass Frog
Speckled Grass Frog
Striped Grass Frog
Snoring Puddle Frog
Common Caco
Namaqua Caco
Foam Nest Frog
Mottled Burrowing Frog
Bocage's Tree Frog
Running Frog
Sharp-Nosed Reed Frog
Marmorate Reed Frog

SNAKES
(*Serpentea*)
Cape Worm Snake
Slender Worm Snake
Damara Worm Snake
Long Tailed Worm Snake
Western Worm Snake
Beaked Blind Snake
Brown House Snake
Spotted House Snake
Cape Wolf Snake
Damaraland Wolf Snake
Cape File Snake
Black File Snake
Angola File Snake
Mole Snake
Western Keeled Snake
Eastern Striped Marsh Snake
Olive Marsh Snake
Bark Snake
Spotted Skaapsteker
Striped Skaapsteker
Grey Bellied Grass Snake

Rufous Beaked Snake
Dwarf Beaked Snake
Lined Olympic Snake
Pygmy Sand Snake
Cross-Marked Snake
Fork-Marked Sand Snake
Karoo Sand Snake
Leopard Sand Snake
Western Striped-Bellied Sand Snake
Western Sand Snake
Dwarf Python
African Python
Cape Centipede Eater
Reticulated Centipede Eater
Common Purple Glossed Snake
Quill Snouted Snake
Common Burrowing Asp
Kalahari Burrowing Asp
Angola Shovel Snout
Twin Striped Shovel Snout
South Western Shovel Snout
Semi-Ornate Snake
Angolan Green Snake
Green Water Snake
Ornate Water Snake
Spotted Bush Snake
Barotse Water Snake
Red-Lipped Snake
Namib Tiger Snake
Damara Tiger Snake
Boomslang
Vine Snake
Egg Eater
Cobras
Angola Garter Snake
Kalahari Garter Snake
Coral Snake
Shield Nose Snake
Egyptian Cobra
Mocambique Spitting Cobra
Black-Neck Spitting Cobra
Cape Cobra
Black Mamba
Adders and Vipers
Snouted Night Adder
Rhombic Night Adder
Horned Adder
Namaqua Dwarf Adder
Desert Mountain Adder
Many Horned Adder
Namib Dwarf Sand Adder
Puff Adder

Wildlife Profile

Elephant, *Loxodonta africana*: Occurs in northern and north-eastern Namibia. Huge concentrations are seen in the Mahango Game Reserve.

Black Rhinoceros, *Diceros bicornis*: They still exist in Kaokoland and Damaraland in the north-west and in the eastern parts of the Etosha National Park.

White Rhinoceros, *Ceratotherium simum*: Grazer, mainly confined to smaller wildlife areas and subjected to heavy poaching pressure.

Burchell's zebra, *Equus burchelli*: Common in grasslands and open savannah woodlands, confined to the northern and north-eastern areas from Kaokoveld to the Botswana border.

Hartmann's mountain zebra, *Equus hartmannae*: Occur in the mountainous transition zone between the Namib Desert and an extensive area of occurrence on the escarpment from the Swakop River to the Naukluft Mountains. Also seen in the Fish River Canyon.

Aardwolf, *Proteles cirstatus*: Widely distributed throughout Namibia except on the Namib Desert coast.

Hyena, *Hyaena brunnea*: Brown hyenas have had a restricted distribution, historically found along the extremely dry west coast, but today spotted hyenas (Crocuta crocuta) are confined narrowly to the central Namib Desert and to the north and the north-east of the country.

Cheetah, *Acinonyx jubatus*: In Namibia they occur widely but sparsely throughout, as far as the Orange River mouth.

Leopard, *Panthera pardus*: Has a wider distributional range and is widespread in Namibia, except in the coastal desert.

Lion, *Panthera leo*: Largest of the African carnivores, is widespread in the northern and north-eastern parts, including Etosha National Park, and also occur in Kaokoland and along the Namib Desert coast.

Caracal, *Felis caracal*: They occur widely in Namibia and are predominantly nocturnal.

African Wild Cat, *Felis lybica*: Occurs widely except in the coastal Namib Desert and has a wide habitat tolerance. The small spotted cat, *Felis nigripes*, are confined to the central and southern parts of the eastern areas of the country.

Bat-Eared Fox, *Otocyon megalotis*: Occur widely in Namibia and are associated with open country.

Cape Fox, *Vulpes chama*: These are widespread in Namibia, except in the coastal Namib Desert and in parts of the northern and north-eastern parts of the country.

Side-striped jackal, *Canis adustus*: Have a fringing distribution in the extreme northern parts in the vicinity of the Okavango Delta favouring thickly wooded country.

Black-backed Jackal, *Canis mesomelas*: Have a wide habitat tolerance and can be seen throughout Namibia including the Namib Desert.

Spotted-necked otter, *Lutra maculicollis*: In Namibia they are confined to the Kunene River in the north.

Honey badger, *Mellivora capensis sagulata*: These are widespread in Namibia and are common in and around the Okavango Swamp.

Clawless Otter, *Aonyx capensis helios*: Nocturnal, partly diurnal, occurs in rivers, streams and swamps.

Striped polecat, *Ictonyx striatus*: Occurs throughout the country and is one of the most easily recognised species of carnivores because of its black and white colour and long hair.

Small-spotted genet, *Genetta genetta*: These are widespread in the country occuring in open, arid conditions.

Suricate, *Suricata suricatta*: Absent from the greater north-eastern parts of the country but occuring in the Namib and pro-Namib Desert at least north of Swakopmund.

Mongooses, *Viverridae*: Yellow mongoose and the slender mongoose are probably the most often sighted and are widespread in Namibia.

Rock Dassie, *Procavia capensis*: Occur in the inland escarpment and adjacent rocky areas.

Hippopotamus, *Hippopotamus amphibius*: Occur marginally in the extreme north-east and some may still be seen in the Kunene River. They are common in the Okavango Swamp.

Giraffe, *Giraffa camelopardalis*: They occur in the extreme north-eastern parts of the country, with two isolated populations in the Kaokoveld.

Blue wildebeest, *Connochaetes taurinus*: They have a restricted distribution in Namibia, only occuring in parts of the northern and north-eastern sectors and along the Botswana River.

Red Hartebeest, *Alcelaphus buselaphus*: Occur in a belt of country from the Angola border south-eastwards to the Botswana border.

Common (or bush) duiker, *Sylvicapra grimmia*: Distributed throughout the country penetrating the coastal Namib Desert along dry watercourses.

Waterbuck, *Kobus ellipsiprymnus:* Occur marginally in the wetlands of the eastern Caprivi Strip.

Red lechwe, *Kobus leche:* Common in the Linyanti Swamp of the Caprivi Strip and on the Chobe and Zambezi floodplains. They also occur in the Okavango Swamp.

Sitatunga, *Tragelaphus spekei:* Occur widely throughout the Caprivi Strip in the swamps associated with the Chobe and Zambezi and are common in the Okavango Delta of Botswana and Namibia.

Bushbuck, *Tragelaphus scriptus*: Occur in north-eastern Namibia, particularly in the savannah plains along the Caprivi Strip.

Roan antelope, *Hippotragus equinus:* Found only in the extreme north-east, along the Caprivi Strip.

Springbok, *Antidorcas marsupialis*: Widespread in Namibia, except in the north and north-east, moving in small herds during dry months.

Klipspringer, *Oreotragus oreotragus*: They are confined to the mountainous escarpment and broken plateau regions of central Namibia.

Damara (or Kirk's) dik-dik, *Rhynchotragus damarensis*: Occur from Kaokoland southwards to Brukkaros mountain in the central hilly parts of the country; in the north they occur as far east as the Grootfontein district also penetrating into the coastal Namib Desert.

Steenbok, *Raphicerus campestris*: Widely distributed, where they narrowly penetrate the coastal Namib Desert down avenues of dry watercourses.

Impala, *Aepyceros melampus*: Recently introduced onto Namibian game ranches for hunting and also occur in the extreme north-west, west of the Etosha Pan.

Gemsbok, *Oryx gazella*: Occur widely in Namibia in open grasslands, open bush savannah and in light open woodlands.

Blesbok, *Damaliscus phillipsi — albifrons*: Occur in the grasslands of central Namibia in the Mount Etjo vicinity.

Kudu, *Tragelaphus strepsiceros*: Persist in the face of heavy hunting pressure and settlement and occur widely and locally in Namibia, except in the coastal Namib Desert.

Eland, *Taurotragus oryx*: They are confined to the north-eastern parts of Namibia and southwards along the border.

Vervet monkey, *Cercopithecus aethiops*: Occur in northern, north-eastern and southern Namibia.

Chacma Baboon, *Papio ursinus*: Spread throughout the country and can occupy virtually any habitat except desert.

Pangolin, *Manis temminckii*: These occur widely except in the southern parts of the country and in the coastal desert.

Cape Hare, *Lepus capensis*: These are found from the Kunene River, in the north, narrowly southwards along the coast and throughout the southern parts of the country.

Scrub Hare, *Lepus sexatilis*: Widely spread throughout the country occuring in savannah woodlands and scrub.

Lesser bushbaby, *Galago senegalensis*: Habitats include acacia, mopane, and other woodlands. Found in Etosha region.

Birds

OSTRICH
(*Struthionidae*)
Ostrich

GREBES
(*Podicipidae*)
Great Crested Grebe
Black-Necked Grebe
Dabchick

ALBATROSS
(*Diomedeidae*)
Wandering Albatross
Shy Albatross
Black Browed Albatross
Grey Headed Albatross
Yellow-Nosed Albatross

PETREL
(*Procellariidae*)
Southern Giant Petrel
Northern Giant Petrel
Antarctic Fulmar
Pintado Petrel
Great Winged Petrel
Atlantic Petrel
Corry's Shearwater
Great Shearwater
Sooty Shearwater
Manx Shearwater
European Storm Petrel
Leach's Storm Petrel
Wilson's Storm Petrel

PELICANS
(*Pelecanidae*)
Great White Pelican
Pin Backed Pelican
Brown Booby
Cape Gannet

CORMORANTS
(*Phalacrocoracidae*)
White Breasted Cormorant
Cape Cormorant
Bank Cormorant
Reed Cormorant
Crowned Cormorant

DARTER
(*Anhingidae*)
Darter

HERONS, EGRETS & BITTERNS
(*Ardeidae*)
Grey Heron
Black Headed Heron
Goliath Heron
Squacco Heron
Green Backed Heron
Rufous Bellied Heron
Black Crowned Night Heron
White Backed Night Heron
Purple Heron
Great White Egret
Little Egret
Yellow-Billed Egret
Black Egret
Salty Egret
Cattle Egret
Little Bittern
Dwarf Bittern
Bittern.

HAMMERKOP
(*Scopidae*)
Hammerkop

STORKS
(*Ciconiidae*)
White Stork
Black Stork
Abdim's Stork
Woolly Necked Stork
Open Billed Stork
Saddle Billed Stork
Marabou Stork
Yellow-Billed Stork

IBISES & SPOONBILLS
(*Plataleidae*)
Sacred Ibis
Glossy Ibis
Hadada Ibis
African Spoonbill

FLAMINGOS
(*Phoenicopteridae*)
Greater Flamingo
Lesser Flamingo

DUCKS & GEESE
White Faced Duck
Fulvous Duck
White-Backed Duck
Egyptian Goose
South African Shelduck
Yellow Billed Duck
African Black Duck
Cape Teal
Hottentot Teal
Red-Billed Teal
European Shoveller
Cape Shoveller
Southern Pochard
Pygmy Goose
Knob-Billed Duck
Spurwinged Goose
Maccoa Duck

SECRETARY BIRD
(*Sagittariidae*)
Secretary Bird

VULTURES
(*Accipitridae*)
Bearded Vulture
Egyptian Vulture
Hooded Vulture
Cape Vulture
White Backed Vulture
Lappet Faced Vulture
White Headed Vulture

BIRDS OF PREY
(*Accipitridae*)
Black (Yellow-Billed) Kite
Black-Shouldered Kite
Cuckoo Hawk
Bat Hawk
Honey Buzzard
Black Eagle
Tawny Eagle
Steppe Eagle
Lesser-Spotted Eagle
Wahlberg's Eagle
Booted Eagle
African Hawk Eagle
Ayre's Eagle
Long Crested Eagle
Martial Eagle
Crowned Eagle
Brown Snake Eagle
Black Breasted Snake Eagle
Western Banded Snake Eagle
Bateleur
Palmnut Vulture
African Fish Eagle
Steppe Buzzard
Long-Legged Buzzard
Jackal Buzzard
Augur Buzzard
Lizard Buzzard
Ovambo Sparrow Hawk
Little Sparrow Hawk
Black Sparrow Hawk
Little Banded Goshawk
African Goshawk
Gabar Goshawk
Pale Chanting Goshawk
Dark Chanting Goshawk
African Marsh Harrier
Montagu's Harrier
Pallid Harrier
Black Harrier
Gymnogene

OSPREY
(*Pandiomidae*)
Osprey

FALCONS
(*Falconidae*)
Peregrine Falcon
Lanner Falcon
Hobby Falcon
African Hobby Falcon
Sooty Falcon
Red-Necked Falcon
Western Red-Footed Kestrel
Eastern Red-Footed Kestrel
Rock Kestrel
Greater Kestrel
Dickinson's Kestrel
Pygmy Falcon

FRANCOLIN & QUAILS
(*Phasianidae*)
Coqui Francolin
Crested Francolin
Orange River Francolin
Redbilled Francolin
Cape Francolin
Hartlaub's Francolin
Swainson's Francolin
Common Quail
Harlequin Quail
Helmeted Guineafowl
Crested Guineafowl
Kurrichane Buttonquail
Blackrumped Buttonquail

CRANES
Wattled Crane
Blue Crane
Crowned Crane

CRAKES, GALLINULES & RAILS
(*Rallidae*)
Corn Crake
African Crake
Black Crake
Spotted Crake
Baillon's Crake
Striped Crake
Buffspotted Flufftail
Purple Gallinule
Lesser Gallinule
American Purple Gallinule
African Rail
Moorhen
Lesser Moorhen

FINFOOTS
(*Heliornithidae*)
Redknobbed Coot
Finfoot

BUSTARDS & KORHAANS
(*Otididae*)
Kori Bustard
Stanley Bustard
Ludwig's Bustard
Karoo Korhaan
Rüppell's Korhaan
Red-Crested Korhaan
Black-Bellied Korhaan
Black Korhaan

JACANAS
(*Jacanidae*)
African Jacana
Lesser Jacana

OYSTERCATCHERS
(*Haematopididae*)
European Oystercatcher
Black Oystercatcher

PLOVERS & TURNSTONES
(*Charadriidae*)
Ringed Plover
Whitefronted Plover
Chestnut Banded Plover
Kittlitz's Plover
Three Banded Plover
Mongolian Plover
Greater Sand Plover
Caspian Plover
Lesser Golden Plover
Grey Plover
Crowned Plover
Blacksmith Plover
White Crowned Plover
Wattled Plover
Long-Toed Plover
Turnstone

SANDPIPERS & SNIPES
(*Scolopacidae*)
Terek Sandpiper
Common Sandpiper
Wood Sandpiper
Redshank
Marsh Sandpiper
Green Shank
Knot
Curlew Sandpiper
Dunlin
Little Stint
White Rumped Sandpiper
Baird's Sandpiper
Temminck's Stint
Sanderling
Buff Breasted Sandpiper
Broad-Billed Sandpiper
Ruff
Great Snipe
Ethiopian Snipe

Bartailed Godwit
Curlew
Whimbrel

PAINTED SNIPES
(*Rostratulidae*)
Painted Snipe

PHALAROPE
(*Phalaropidae*)
Grey Phalarope
Red-Necked Phalarope
Wilson's Phalarope

AVOCETS & STILTS
(*Recurvirostridae*)
Avocet
Blackwinged Stilt

DIKKOP
(*Burhinidae*)
Spotted Dikkop
Water Dikkop

COURSER
(*Glareolidae*)
Burchell's Courser
Temminck's Courser
Double-Banded Courser
Three-Banded Courser
Bronze-Winged Courser
Red-Winged Pratincole
Black-Winged Pratincole
Rock Pratincole

SKUA
(*Stercorariidae*)
Arctic Skua
Long-Tailed Skua
Pomarine Skua
Sub Antarctic Skua

GULLS & TERNS
(*Lariidae*)
Kelp Gull
Lesser Black-Backed Gull
Grey Headed Gull
Hartlaub's Gull
Franklin's Gull
Sabine's Gull
Caspian Tern
Royal Tern
Swift Tern
Sandwich Tern
Common Tern
Arctic Tern
Roseate Tern
Damara Tern
Little Tern
Black Tern

Whiskered Tern
White-Winged Tern

SKIMMER
(*Rynchopidae*)
African Skimmer

SANDGROUSE
(*Pteroclidae*)
Namaqua Sandgrouse
Burchell's Sandgrouse
Yellow-Throated Sandgrouse
Double-Banded Sandgrouse

PIGEONS & DOVES
(*Columbidae*)
Feral Pigeon
Rock Pigeon
Green Pigeon
Red-Eyed Dove
Mourning Dove
Cape Turtle Dove
Laughing Dove
Namaqua Dove
Emerald Spotted Dove

PARROTS & LOVEBIRDS
(*Psittacidae*)
Cape Parrot
Meyer's Parrot
Rüppell's Parrot
Rosy-Faced Lovebird
Black-Cheeked Lovebird

LOURIE
(*Musophagidae*)
Knysna Lourie
Grey Lourie

CUCKOO
(*Cuculidae*)
European Cuckoo
African Cuckoo
Red-Chested Cuckoo
Black Cuckoo
Great Spotted Cuckoo
Striped Cuckoo
Jacobin Cuckoo
Thick-Billed Cuckoo
Emerald Cuckoo
Klaas's Cuckoo
Didrik Cuckoo
Black Coucal
Copper-Tailed Coucal
Senegal Coucal
Burchell's Coucal

OWLS
(*Tytonidae*)
Barn Owl
Grass Owl

Wood Owl
Marsh Owl
Scops Owl
White-Faced Owl
Pearl-Spotted Owl
Barred Owl
Cape Eagle Owl
Spotted Eagle Owl
Giant Eagle Owl
Pel's Fishing Owl

NIGHTJARS
(*Caprimulgidae*)
European Nightjar
Fiery Necked Nightjar
Rufous Cheeked Nightjar
Natal Nightjar
Freckled Nightjar
Mozambique Nightjar
Pennant Winged Nightjar

SWIFTS
(*Apodidae*)
European Swift
Black Swift
Bradfield's Swift
White Rumped Swift
Horus Swift
Little Swift
Alpine Swift
Palm Swift
Boehm's Spinetail

MOUSEBIRDS
(*Coliidae*)
White-Backed Mousebird
Red-Faced Mousebird

TROGON
(*Trogonidae*)
Narina Trogon

KINGFISHER
(*Halcyonidae*)
Pied Kingfisher
Giant Kingfisher
Half Collared Kingfisher
Malachite Kingfisher
Pygmy Kingfisher
Woodlands Kingfisher
Brown Hooded Kingfisher
Grey Hooded Kingfisher
Striped Kingfisher

BEE-EATER
(*Meropidae*)
European Bee-Eater
Olive Bee-Eater
Blue Cheeked Bee-Eater
Carmine Bee-Eater

White-Fronted Bee-Eater
Little Bee-Eater
Swallow Tailed Bee-Eater

ROLLERS
(*Coraciidae*)
European Roller
Lilac Breasted Roller
Racquet-Tailed Roller
Purple Roller
Broad-Billed Roller

HOOPOE
(*Upupidae*)
Hoopoe
Red-Billed Hoopoe
Violet Wood Hoopoe
Scimitar-Billed Wood Hoopoe

HORNBILL
(*Bucerotidae*)
Trumpeter Hornbill
Grey Hornbill
Red-Billed Hornbill
Yellow-Billed Hornbill
Crowned Hornbill
Bradfield's Hornbill
Monteiro's Hornbill
Ground Hornbill

BARBET
(*Capitonidae*)
Black Collared Barbet
Pied Barbet
Yellow Fronted Tinker Barbet
Crested Barbet
Greater Honey Guide
Lesser Honey Guide
Slender-Billed Honey Guide

WOODPECKER
(*Picidae*)
Bennet's Woodpecker
Golden-Tailed Woodpecker
Cardinal Woodpecker
Bearded Woodpecker
Olive Woodpecker

BROADBILL
(*Eurylaimidae*)
African Broadbill

LARKS
(*Alaudidae*)
Monotonous Lark
Rufous Naped Lark
Clapper Lark
Flapper Lark
Fawn Coloured Lark
Sabota Lark
Long-Billed Lark

Karoo Lark
Dune Lark
Dusky Lark
Spike-Heeled Lark
Red-Capped Lark
Pink-Billed Lark
Sclater's Lark
Stark's Lark
Bimaculated Lark
Gray's Lark
Chestnut-Backed Finch Lark
Grey-Backed Finch Lark
Black-Eared Finch Lark

SWALLOWS
(*Hirundinidae*)
European Swallow
Angola Swallow
White-Throated Swallow
Wire-Tailed Swallow
Pearl-Breasted Swallow
Red-Breasted Swallow
Mosque Swallow
Greater-Striped Swallow
Lesser-Striped Swallow
Rock Martin
House Martin
Grey-Rumped Swallow
European Sand Martin
Brown-Throated Martin
Banded Martin
Black Saw-Wing Swallow

SHRIKES
(*Campephagidae*)
Black-Cuckoo Shrike
White-Breasted Shrike

DRONGO
(*Dicruriidae*)
Fork-Tailed Drongo

ORIOLES, RAVENS & CROWS
(*Oriolidae*)
European Golden Oriole
African Golden Oriole
Black-Headed Oriole
Black Crow
Pied Crow
White-Necked Raven

TITS
(*Passeriformes*)
Southern Grey Tit
Ashy Grey Tit
Southern Black Tit
Carp's Tit
Rufous-Bellied Tit
Cape Penduline Tit
Grey Penduline Tit

BABBLERS
(*Timaliidae*)
Arrow-Marked Babbler
Black-Faced Babbler
White-Rumped Babbler
Pied Babbler
Bare-Cheeked Babbler
Titbabbler
Layard's Titbabbler

BULBULS
(*Pycnonotidae*)
Red-Eyed Bulbul
Black-Eyed Bulbul
Terrestrial Bulbul
Yellow-Bellied Bulbul
Yellow-Spotted Nicator

THRUSHES, CHATS & ROBINS
(*Trurdidae*)
Kurrichane Thrush
Olive Thrush
Ground-Scraper Thrush
Short-Toed Rock Thrush
Mountain Chat
Capped Wheatear
Familiar Chat
Tractrac Chat
Sickle-Winged Chat
Karoo Chat
Arnot's Chat
Ant-Eating Chat
Stone Chat
Whin Chat
Heuglin's Robin
Natal Robin
Cape Robin
Collared Palm Thrush
Rufous Tailed Palm Thrush
Thrush Nightingale
White-Browed Robin
Karoo Robin
Kalahari Robin
Bearded Robin
Herero Chat

WARBLERS
(*Sylvidae*)
Garden Warbler
White Throat
Icterine Warbler
Great Reed Warbler
African Marsh Warbler
European Marsh Warbler
European Sedge Warbler
Cape Reed Warbler
African Sedge Warbler
Willow Warbler
Yellow-Breasted Apalis
Long-Billed Crombec

Yellow-Bellied Eremomela
Karoo Eremomela
Green-Capped Eremomela
Burnt-Necked Eremomela
Bleating Warbler
Barred Warbler
Stierling's Barred Warbler
Cinnamon-Breasted Warbler
Rock Runner
Fan-Tailed Cisticola
Desert Cisticola
Grey-Backed Cisticola
Tinkling Cisticola
Rattling Cisticola
Red-Faced Cisticola
Black-Backed Cisticola
Chirping Cisticola
Croaking Cisticola
Neddicky
Tawny-Flanked Prinia
Black-Chested Prinia
Spotted Prinia
Namaqua Prinia
Rufous-Eared Warbler

FLYCATCHERS
(*Muscicapidae*)
Spotted Flycatcher
Blue-Grey Flycatcher
Collared Flycatcher
Fan-Tailed Flycatcher
Black Flycatcher
Marico Flycatcher
Mouse-Coloured Flycatcher
Chat Flycatcher
Chinspot Flycatcher
Pririt Batis
Fairy Flycatcher
Paradise Flycatcher

WAGTAILS, PIPITS & LONGCLAW
(*Motacillidae*)
African-Pied Wagtail
Cape Wagtail
Yellow Wagtail
Grey Wagtail
Richard's Pipit
Long-Billed Pipit
Plain-Backed Pipit
Buffy Pipit
Tree Pipit
Fülleborn's Longclaw

SHRIKES
(*Laniidae*)
Lesser-Grey Shrike
Fiscal Shrike
Red-Backed Shrike
Sousa's Shrike

Long-Tailed Shrike
Tropical Boubou Shrike
Swamp Boubou Shrike
Crimson-Breasted Shrike
Puff-Back Shrike
Brubru Shrike
Three-Streaked Tchagra
Black-Crowned Tchagra
Bokmakierie
Orange-Breasted Bush Shrike
Grey-Headed Bush Shrike
White-Tailed Shrike
White-Helmet Shrike
Red-Billed Helmet Shrike
White-Crowned Shrike

STARLINGS
(*Sturnidae*)
European Starling
Wattled Starling
Plum-Coloured Starling
Burchell's Starling
Long-Tailed Starling
Cape-Glossy Starling
Greater Blue-Eared Starling
Lesser Blue-Eared Starling
Sharp-Tailed Starling

OXPECKERS
(*Buphagidae*)
Yellow-Billed Oxpecker
Red-Billed Oxpecker

SUNBIRDS
(*Nectariniidae*)
Malachite Sunbird
Coppery Sunbird

Marico Sunbird
Purple-Banded Sunbird
Lesser-Double Collared Sunbird
White-Bellied Sunbird
Dusky Sunbird
Scarlet-Chested Sunbird
Black Sunbird
Collared Sunbird

WHITE-EYES
(*Zosteropidae*)
Cape White-Eye
Yellow White-Eye

SPARROWS & WEAVERS
(*Ploceidae*)
Red-Billed Buffalo Weaver
White-Browed Sparrow Weaver
Sociable Weaver
House Sparrow
Great Sparrow
Cape Sparrow
Grey-Headed Sparrow
Yellow-Throated Sparrow
Scaly-Feathered Finch
Thick-Billed Weaver
Spectacled Weaver
Speckled-Backed Weaver
Chestnut Weaver
Masked Weaver
Lesser Masked Weaver
Golden Weaver
Brown-Throated Weaver
Red-Headed Weaver
Cuckoo Finch
Red-Billed Quelea
Red Bishop
Golden Bishop

Red-Shouldered Widow
White-Winged Widow
Pintailed Whydah
Shaft-Tailed Whydah
Paradise Whydah
Broad-Tailed Paradise Whydah

WAXBILLS & FINCHES
Blue Waxbill
Violet-Eared Waxbill
Common Waxbill
Black-Cheeked Waxbill
Cinderella Waxbill
Orange-Breasted Waxbill
Melba Finch
Jameson's Fire Finch
Red-Billed Fire Finch
Brown Fire Finch
Quail Finch
Red-Headed Finch
Purple Widow Finch
Violet Widow Finch
Steel-Blue Widow Finch

CANARIES & BUNTINGS
(*Fringillidae*)
Yellow-Eyed Canary
Black-Throated Canary
Black-Headed Canary
Yellow Canary
White-Throated Canary
Golden-Breasted Bunting
Cape Bunting
Rock Bunting
Larklike Bunting
Cut-Throat Finch
Bronze Mannikin
Pied Mannikin

Birdlife Profile

Namibia's Kaokoveld wilderness supports an abundant variety of birds. Many are dependent on the nutrient-rich coastal waters of the cold current and many depend on the desert rivers. Others survive in the arid savannahs. The avifauna of the Kaokoveld, includes 382 species of birds. The seabirds and waders are found along the coast and at the Uniab delta.

The desert avifauna of the Namib are the larks, which include the most highly adapted desert birds. Birds are also found in higher rainfall areas to the north and east of the Kaokoveld on the Central African Plateau, in the southern African subregion, and in the arid and semi-arid areas of southern Africa.

Ostrich: This large bird, *Struthio camelus*, is widespread, living in grasslands and lightly wooded areas. Ostrich farming and ranching is popular in Namibia.

Pelicans: The **White pelican**, *Pelecanus onocrotalus*, and the **Pink-backed pelican**, *Pelecanus rufescens*, occur along pools and stretches of shallow water. The latter are found in Caprivi.

Cormorants: The **Cape cormorant**, *Phalacrocorax capensis* occur along the coastal waters, while the **Reed cormorant**, *Phalacrocorax africanus* is widespread except the dry south-east. The **darter**, *Anhinga melanogaster* is widespread.

Herons: Namibia has nine species of herons. The **Goliath heron**, *Ardea goliath*, is the largest African heron and is found along Hardap Dam and Ovambo-Etosha eastwards. The **Grey heron**, *Ardea cinerea*, is widespread. The **Purple heron**,

Ardea purpurea, occurs in Caprivi and along the Okavango River.

Egrets: Of Namibia's six egret species the **Little egret**, *Egretta garzetta*, is the most common in Namibia. The **Cattle egret**, *Egretta ibis*, is found in Caprivi. The **Black egret**, *Egretta ardesiaca*, occurs in the north and is easily identified by the distinctive way it curves its wings over its head while fishing.

Hammerkop: This is a well-known and common bird. **Hammerkop**, *Scopus umbretta*, can be seen around the dams or temporary pools of water.

Storks: Abdim's storks, *Circonia abdimii*, arrive in large numbers from North Africa during summer. The **White stork**, *Ciconia ciconia*, is also common, while the **Open-billed stork**, *Anastomus lamelligerus* is seen east of Ovambo-Kamanjab.

Ibises: The **Sacred ibis**, *Threskiornis aethiopicus*, occurs in Etosha and Mariental while the **Glossy ibis**, *Plegadis falcinellus*, is becoming more widespread. The **African spoonbill**, *Platalea alba*, is distributed in the Kavango-Caprivi area.

Flamingos: The **Greater flamingo**, *Phoenicopterus ruber*, is common and the **Lesser flamingo**, *Phoenicopterus minor*, occur along the coast and the north.

Geese: The **Egyptian goose**, *Alopochen aegyptiacus*, is seen throughout, while the **Spurwinged goose**, *plectropterus gambensis*, occurs in the north-east of Ovambo and Hereroland. The **Southern pochard**, *Netta erythrophthalma*, is widespread. Three teal occur in Namibia, of which the **Red-billed teal**, *Anas erythrorhuncha* and **Cape teal**, *Anas capensis* are seen throughout.

Vultures: Seven species of vulture have been recorded in Namibia, of which the **Lappet-faced vulture**, *Torgos tracheliotus*, is most common. The **Cape vulture**, *Gyps coprothers*, is found south of Etosha-Bushmanland. **White-headed vulture**, *Trigonoceps occipitatis*, is quite common. **Hooded vulture**, *Necrosyrtes monachus*, occur in the north-east of Kavango-Hereroland.

Secretary bird: The **Secretary bird**, *Sagittarius serpentarius*, is found throughout Namibia foraging for insects, small rodents and reptiles in grasslands and lightly wooded areas.

Kites and Buzzards: The **Black-shouldered kite**, *Elanus caeruleus*, is Namibia's most widespread bird of prey. The **Black (yellow-billed) kite**, *Milvus migrans*, are divided into two races. The **Honey buzzard**, *Pernis apivorus*, occurs in Eastern Caprivi while the **Jackal buzzard**, *Bueto rufofuscus*, is seen in Daan Viljoen.

Eagles: Namibia has fourteen species of eagles. The **Martial eagle**, *Polemaetus billicosus*, is most common. The **Western banded snake eagle**, *Circaetus cinerascens*, occurs around Okavango River and Caprivi. The best known is the **African fish eagle**, *Cuncuma vocifer*, which thrives in the north.

Hawks: Three sparrowhawks and five goshawks occur in Namibia. The **Ovambo sparrowhawk**, *Accipiter ovambensis*, is seen between eastern Kaokoland and Gobabis. Of the goshawks, the **Gabar goshawk**, *Micronisus gabar*, is the most common.

Harriers: The **harriers**, long-legged raptors with large wings and owl-like faces, are represented by four species, of which the **African marsh harrier**, *Circus ranivorus*, occur along Okavango River-Caprivi. The **Gymnogene**, *Ployboroides radiatus*, belongs to this group and may be seen clambering about on tree trunks in the north and east of Namibia.

Falcons: Namibia has seven species of falcon. The **Lanner falcon**, *Falco biarmicus*, is widespread while the **Peregrine falcon**, *Falco peregrinus* is a race minor seen throughout. The **African hobby falcon**, *Falco cuvierii* is a summer visitor occuring in north Kavango and Caprivi.

Kestrel: Out of Namibia's seven species of kestrel, the **Rock (European) kestrel**, *Falco tinnunculus* and the **Greater kestrel**, *Falco rupicoloides* are the most common.

Quails: The **Common (European) quail**, *Coturnix coturnix*, are found around Ovambo-Orange River and **Harlequin quail**, *Coturnix delegorguei* is seen in the northern half. The **Black-rumped-button quail**, *Turnix hottentotta*, occurs only in eastern Caprivi.

Cranes: The **Wattled crane**, *Grus carunculata* and the **Blue crane**, *Anthropoides paradisea* are inhabitants of Etosha. The **Crowned crane**, *Balearica regulorum* is seen in the south to Otjiwarongo.

Crakes: Baillon's crake, *Porzana pusilla*, lives in the swamps from Etosha to Caprivi. **Striped crake**, *Aenigmatolimnas marginalis* occurs in Ovambo. The **Black crake**, *Amaurornis flavirostris*, is seen in the north.

Bustards: The **Kori bustard**, *Ardeotis kori*, is the heaviest flying bird in the world. It occurs throughout Namibia. **Stanley (or Denham's/ Jackson's) bustard**, *Neotis denhami*, is seen in the extreme north while **Ludwig's bustard**, *Neotis ludwigii* occurs in the west.

Jacanas: The **African jacana**, *Actophilornis africanus*, is sometimes called the 'lily-trotter' and is seen around Caprivi, Swakopmund and Windhoek. **Lesser jacana**, *Microparra capensis* is vagrant and will be found in Caprivi.

Oystercatcher: The **European oystercatcher**, *Haematopus ostralegus*, occurs around Sandwich Harbour and Walvis Bay. The **Black oystercatcher**, *Haematopus moquini*, is seen along the coast.

Plovers: Namibia has fifteen species of plovers. The **three-banded plover**, *Charadrius tricollaris*, and **Blacksmith plover**, *Vanellus armatus*, are most common. The **Grey plover**, *Pluvialis squatarola*, is uncommon inland but occurs along the coast. The **Crowned plover**, *Vanellus coronatus*, lives in grasslands, burnt veld, and other open spaces.

Sandpiper: **Terek sandpiper**, *Xenus cinereus*, is rare inland but found at the coast. **Common sandpiper**, *Tringa hypoleucos* and **Wood sandpiper**, *Tringa glareola* are migrants visiting. **Greenshank**, *Tringa nebularia*, are winter visitors.

Dikkop: The **Spotted dikkop**, *Burhinus capensis*, is widespread, while the **Water dikkop**, *Burhinus vermiculatus*, occurs along Ovambo and Caprivi.

Coursers: The **Three-banded courser**, *Rhinoptilus cinctus*, is endemic to Namibia, found along the northern borders. **Double-banded courser**, *Rhinoptilus africanus*, are quite common.

Skua: There are four migrant species of skuas. **Arctic skua**, *Stercorarius* and **Longtailed skua**, *Stercorarius longicaudus*, are migrant on coastal and offshore waters.

Gulls and Terns: These are seen on Namibian waters. The **Kelp gull**, *Larus dominicanus*, is vagrant in Hardap. The **Grey-headed gull**, *Larus cirrocephalus*, occurs along the coast and inland in Caprivi and Etosha. Out of the twelve species of tern, the **Royal tern**, *Sterna maxima*, is rare. **White-winged tern**, *Chlidonias leucopterus*, are found throughout.

Pigeons and Doves: The **Feral pigeon**, *Columba livia*, breed wild in several towns. The distinctive call of the **Emerald-spotted dove**, *Turtur chalcospilos* can be heard in the northern part of the country. The **Cape turtle dove**, *Streptopelia capicola*, occurs throughout Namibia while the **Mourning dove**, *Streptopelia decipiens* are seen only in the extreme north. Both the **Cape turtle dove** and the **Laughing dove**, *Stigmatopelia senegalensis*, inhabit the woodlands throughout the country.

Parrots: Namibia has three parrots and two lovebirds. **Meyer's parrot**, *Poicephalus meyeri* is most commonly seen. **Rüppell's parrot**, *Poicephalus rueppellii* occurs on the northwestern hills south to Windhoek. The **Rosy-faced lovebird**, *Agapornis roseicollis*, is most common while **Black-cheeked lovebird**, *Agapornis nigrigenis* occur in Caprivi.

Lourie: The **Grey lourie** or Go-away bird, *Corythaixoides concolor*, is seen throughout except in the Namib and drier south. The **Knysna lourie**, *Tauraco corythaix*, is found only in eastern Caprivi.

Cuckoos: Cuckoos lay their eggs in other birds' nests, while coucals build their own. The **African cuckoo**, *Cuculus gularis*, is most common. **Senegal coucal**, *Centropus senegalensis* and **Burchell's coucal**, *Centropus supercilliosus* are both found in Caprivi.

Owls: There are twelve species of owl in Namibia of which the **Barn owl**, *Tyto alba* and **Spotted eagle owl**, *Bubo africanus* are widespread. The **Giant eagle owl**, *Bubo lacteus* is also common. The **Wood owl**, *Strix woodfordii* occurs only in Caprivi.

Nightjars: The **Fiery-necked nightjar**, *Caprimulgus pectoralis*, is seen in the north eastern region and is easily identified by its call, said to resemble 'Good-Lord-deliver-us'. **Rufous-cheeked nightjar**, *Caprimulgus rufigena* and **Freckled nightjar**, *Caprimulgus tristigma*, are most common. The **European nightjar**, *Caprimulgus europaeus*, is a visitor to Kavango-Caprivi and the extreme southeast.

Swifts: Of the country's eight swifts the **European swift**, *Apus apus*, is a common migrant. **Bradfield's swift**, *Apus bradfieldi*, are found on the hills of the west and south. The **Palm swift**, *Cypsiurus parvus*, glues its nest to the underside of palm fronds and is a prevalent resident.

Kingfishers: The **Pied kingfisher**, *Ceryle rudis*, is a permanent resident in fresh water throughout. The **Giant kingfisher**, *Megaceryle maxima*, is the largest kingfisher in the world and occurs in the tree-lined permanent rivers, the Orange, Kunene and Okavango. **Grey-headed kingfisher**, *Halcyon leucocephala* is a summer migrant in Okahandja.

Bee-eaters: The **European bee-eater**, *Merops apiaster* is a summer migrant throughout. The **Olive (Madagadcar) bee-eater**, *Merops superciliosus*, occurs along the Kunene and

Okavango rivers. The **Swallow-tailed bee-eaters**, *Merops hirundineus*, are local residents and occur throughout.

Rollers: The **European roller**, *Coracias garrulus*, is a summer migrant occurring in the north. The **Lilac-breasted roller**, *Coracias caudata*, is a common and spectacular species, often seen perching on poles or dead branches overlooking open ground. The **Purple roller**, *Coracias naevia* is fairly common except in Namib and southern Namaqualand. The **Racquet-tailed roller**, *Coracias spatulata*, is often seen in eastern Caprivi.

Hoopoes and Woodhoopoes: The **African hoopoe**, *Upupa epops*, closely resembles the European and Senegal species and is found throughout Namibia. The **Violet woodhoopoe**, *Phoeniculus purpureus*, breeds in Kaokoland south to Khomas Hochland whereas the **Scimitar-billed woodhoopoe**, *Phoeniculus cyanomelas*, is fairly common.

Hornbills: Namibia has eight hornbill species, all characterised by their raucous voices and huge bills. The **Trumpeter hornbill**, *Bycanistes bucinator*, lives in riverine woods in eastern Caprivi. The **Grey hornbill**, *Tockus nasutus*, are widespread except in the dry west. The **Crowned hornbill**, *Tockus bradfieldi*, is found in riverine woods along Okavango River and in Caprivi.

Barbets: The **Pied barbet**, *Lybius leucomelas*, are the most common. The **Crested barbet**, *Trachyphonus vaillantii*, is often seen in parks and gardens and has a call said to resemble an alarm clock with the bell removed. The **Black-collared barbet**, *Lybius torquatus*, make woodpecker-like nest holes in trees and occur in Caprivi.

Woodpeckers: There are five species of woodpecker. The **Cardinal woodpecker**, *Dendropicos fuscescens*, is the most common throughout except Namib. The **Olive woodpecker**, *Mesopicus griseocephalus*, and the **Bearded woodpecker**, *Thripias namaquus*, are both seen in the north.

Larks: Namibia has a big lark population. There are twenty species. The **Red-capped lark**, *Calandrella cinerea*, is the most common and seen throughout. The **Flappet lark**, *Mirafra rufocinnamomea*, is found only in Kavango and Caprivi. The **Dusky lark**, *Pinarocorys nigricans* is a summer migrant found in the north. **Sclater's lark**, *Spizocorys sclateri*, occurs in the south east.

Swallows and Martins: Out of the twelve species of swallows in Namibia, the **Greater striped swallow**, *Hirundo abyssinica*, is a migrant which comes to breed in summer. The **Wiretailed swallow**, *Hirundo smithii*, occurs in the extreme north and Caprivi. **Rock martins**, *Hirundo fuligula* are present throughout the year. The **House martin**, *Delichon urbica*, is a common migrant except in the extreme south.

Drongos: The **Forktailed drongo**, *Dicrurus adsimilis*, are shiny black birds with strongly forked tails and are common at Daan Viljoen and indeed throughout in open woodland or bushveld, slinging their flimsy hammock-like nests in the forks of large trees.

Tits: The **Ashy Grey tit**, *Parus cinerascens*, is an active little bird generally seen creeping around in trees in search of food. They are fairly noisy birds and their typical call sounds like 'pietjoutjou'. The **Rufous-bellied tit**, *Parus rufiventris*, occurs in north Ovambo and Kavango.

Bulbuls: The **Red-eyed bulbul**, *Pycnonotus nigricans* is most common and is easily recognised by its black crest. It has a cheerful whistling call, 'tiptol'. The **Black-eyed bulbul**, *Pycnonotus barbatus* and The **Terrestrial bulbul**, *Phyllastrephus terestris*, occur in Caprivi and north Kavango.

Thrushes: The **Groundscraper thrush**, *Turdus litsipsirupa*, occur in the north in pairs or small groups and prefer the dry river valleys where there are big trees. The **Short-toed Rock thrush**, *Moticola brevipes*, are found in rocky places and usually perch on some conspicuous bare trees.

Chats: **Mountain chat**, *Oenanthe monticola*, are common on hillsides and cliffs, where they nest during the warmer months under rocks and in crevices. **Tractrac chat**, *Cercomela tractrac*, are most common. **Familiar (Red-tailed) chat**, *Cercomela familiaris*, are fairly common and can be distinguished from other 'little brown birds' by the orange rump and tail.

Flycatchers: The **Marico flycatcher**, *Melaenornis mariquensis*, is one of the commonest birds at Daan Viljoen and generally one of the most nondescript. The **Black flycatcher**, *Melaenornis pammelaina*, occurs in Okavango woodland and Caprivi. The **Fairy flycatcher**, *Stenostira scita*, is seen in Namaqualand north to Rehoboth.

Wagtails: The **Cape wagtail**, *Motacilla capensis*, is the common 'Kwikkie' with its characteristic bobbing tail and dark bib. It is well accustomed to human habitation and is common in town gardens. The **African pied wagtail**, *Motacilla aguimp* is seen along permanent rivers, the Kunene-Okavango-Caprivi, and Orange.

Pipits: Pipits are ground dwelling birds and the

most common is **Richard's pipit**, *Anthus novaeseelandiae*. The **Tree pipit**, *Anthus trivialis*, is a summer migrant often found near Swakopmund.

Shrikes: The **Fiscal shrike**, *Lanius collaris*, is wide ranging. **Lesser grey shrike**, *Lanius minor*, is a summer migrant and **Brubru shrike**, *Nilaus afer*, are most common. The **Tropical boubou shrike**, *Laniarius aethiopicus*, has a preference for riverine woodlands but is also seen in urban gardens. The **White helmet shrike**, *Prionops plumata*, is a resident of the country's woodlands. The **Crimson-breasted shrike**, *Laniarius atrococcineus*, is the bird of the savannah.

Plant profile (by family)

Because of its climate and topography the south-western section of Africa has some of the most unusual plants in the world. The diverse and relatively unresearched lichen fields of the Namib are of the world's richest. In the vicinity of Cape Cross small areas have been put aside as reserves.

Protection of plants has become necessary because of scarcity, in some cases natural, in more cases unnatural, due to the activities of collectors and unscrupulous plunderers who sell them in South Africa. Plants are also protected because of their endemism. There are approximately 200 species endemic to south west Africa.

Asclepiadaceae (*stapeliads*; 2000 species)
Stapeliads are represented by approximately 200 genera. They are unassuming low-growing plants which only produce their beautiful flowers on new growth. A genus of this is *Trichocaulon* found in the arid regions of Namibia.

Proteaceae (1 species)
There is only one species of protea in Namibia, the *Protea gaguedi*. It occurs in Kavango. It is usually a shrub or small gnarled tree two-to-three metres high, often with several main stems. The flowers are silvery white and have a typical protea shape.

Welwitschiaceae
Welwitschia mirabilis, occurs in the Namib from Swakopmund northwards to Mossamedes in Angola and nowhere else on earth. The Welwitschia is dioecious, meaning that the male and female flowers are on separate plants. The cones are brightly coloured, the male cones salmon pink and the female greenish yellow banded with redish brown. These plants are certainly among the oldest in the world.

Vitaceae (700 species)
Members of this family are perennial herbs, climbing shrubs and, occasionally, trees. They have thick yellow stems, large green leaves and small red fruits which resemble grapes. *Cyphostemma currorii*, grows up to four-and-a-half metres high. None of the wild genera produce particularly palatable fruit.

Portulacaceae (several species)
These plants range from dwarf to large woody shrubs with clusters of flowers, some of which are herbaceous. The *Portulacaria* species are known as *spekboom, haaskos* or elephant's food. These plants have thick supple stems with dense growths of small fresh-green leaves and tiny pink flowers.

The species of this family belong mainly to the genus *Anacampseros*. They occur in the most arid parts of the country in the west and in the south. They have flowers of white, pink and red.

Moringaceae (1 species)
This is a monotype family and the only genus is the Moringa. Twelve species of Moringa occur throughout Africa. The *Moringa ovalifolas* occurs in Namibia, in the vicinity of Maltahöhe, Okahandja, Karibib and the Etosha National Park. They have branched sprays of attractive white flowers. The *Moringa ovalifolia* can be cultivated from seeds and is ideally suited for bonsai growing.

Geraniaceae (250 species)
The genus which typifies this family is the Geranium. A considerable number of these are aromatic. Several species have medicinal qualities. Most of the Pelargonium species are used as a remedy against dysentery and diarrhoea. *Pelargonium radula* and some of its local relatives yield geranium oil which is used in the perfume industry. The Sarcocaulon genus has species which excrete a type of resin.

Crassulaceae (31 species)
All members of this family are succulents. The Crassulas are adapted to a wide range of habitats from cool shade to dry exposure. Their flowers are small and congested into white, pink and, less often, scarlet heads.

Thelypteridaceae
There are several species of fern in south west Africa of which one, *Thelypteris chaseana*, is protected. Most species grow in localities where there is water all year round. Apart from Caprivi and Kavango there are luxuriant growths of fern at Naukluft along the river course and around the rock-pools, and at Waterberg in the vicinity of the springs and under the cliffs. There are also a surprising number of fern species which grow in the drier and desert areas of the country.

Zygophyllaceae (4 species)
Zygophyllum stapfii is found from the northern boundary of the Namib Desert Park to west Kaokoland. It is a semi-deciduous shrub with white flowers which grow into succulent fruits.

Fabaceae (11 species)
The best known tree in Namibia is the *Acacia erioloba*, or camelthorn. Its most distinctive feature is its thick, curiously shaped pods, sometimes more than ten centimetres long and covered with grey, velvety felt.

Sterculiaceae (Hermannia 93 species)
One of the most beautiful species, *Hermannia amabilis* is found in gorges and dry river-beds of the Namib, and is often an eye-catching mass of hanging flowers. The flowers hang down like little bells, and the five petals vary from white to pale pink, with a coloured patch below the middle which may be pink, red or mauve.

Convolvulaceae
The only member found is *Ipomoea adenioides* which has been utilised by many people from Namibia to Somalia because it has an underground tuber like a potato. Found throughout Namibia, but particularly in the sandveld of the eastern parts, raw tubers are eaten by the Pedi people of northern Transvaal when food is in short supply.

Ophioglossaceae
Ophioglossum polyphyllum, also known as adder's tongue fern is, amazingly, found at greatly varying altitudes and rainfall ranges. It is a small, somewhat fleshy plant which propagates itself vegetatively by means of root buds. It is eaten raw by Bushmen as a wild spinach.

Demographic Profile

In 1991, the population of Namibia was estimated at 1,401,711, of which 48.6 per cent were male and 51.4 per cent were female.

The bulk of the population (about sixty per cent) lives in the northern districts, with only a small proportion, about seven per cent, living in the districts in the south. The rest of the population live in the central part of the country. The annual population growth is three-and-a-half per cent, and population density is 1.8 persons per square kilometre.

The bulk of Namibia's people live in the districts of Oshakati/Ondangwa, Windhoek, Kavango and Caprivi. Windhoek has about eleven per cent of the population, and the north of the country about sixty per cent.

The combined districts of Oshakati and Ondangwa have forty-four per cent of this total population. The southern districts of Mariental, Maltahöhe, Namaland, Bethanien, Karasburg, Keetmanshoop and Lüderitz, with about seven per cent of the population, are the least populous areas in the country. This may be attributed to the prolonged drought in these parts.

Data from the 1991 Population and Housing Census shows that about thirty-three per cent and sixty-seven per cent of the population live respectively in rural and urban localities.

The proportion of urban and rural population in the various districts shows considerable variation. This pattern may reflect the differing types of urban locality which are in the commercial, farming and mining areas.

The country has various cultural groups: Wambo, Damara, Nama, English, Coloured, Baster, German, Herero, Afrikaner, Tswana, Portuguese, Bushmen, Caprivian and Kavango. English is the official language. Afrikaans is one of the national languages. There are Namibian Afrikaners and Standard Afrikaners. The term Namibian Afrikaners is used when referring to any of the varieties owing their origins to Orange River Afrikaners.

Historical factors have contributed to the existence of different varieties of Afrikaners in Namibia today, each with its own status and function in Namibian society.

Then there are the Basters, who are divided into three groups: The Vilanders, Klaas Swart-Basters and the Basters of Rehoboth. The Basters regard it as an insult to be called Coloureds. Among themselves the inhabitants speak of each other as Burgers.

They originate from the Cape Colony to the south, and are descendants of white fathers and Khoi-Khoi or Hottentot mothers. The home language of the Basters is Afrikaans.

The Coloureds are neither Whites nor Blacks. They are a mixture of Namas, the Hereros and Whites (especially Germans) in Namibia. The Coloureds of Namibia are chiefly Afrikaans-speaking and maintain a Christian way of life.

Then there are the Caprivians, the Wambo, and the Tswanas. All these are divided into many tribes and speak different tribal languages.

Population by the major ethnic groups (1992)

Wambo	641,000
Kavango	120,000
Herero	97,000
Damara	97,000
Whites	82,000
Coloureds	52,000
Caprivians	48,000
San	37,000

Basters	32,000
Tswana	8,000

Population by regions (1991)

Kunene	58,500
Omusati	158,000
Oshana	159,000
Ohanguena	178,000
Oshikoto	176,000
Okavango	136,000
Liambesi	92,000
Erongo	98,500
Otjozondjupa	85,000
Omaheke	55,600
Khomas	161,000
Hardap	80,000
Karas	93,000
TOTAL	1,401,711

Namibia population by sex (1991)

Males	680,927
Females	720,784
TOTAL	1,401,711

Population by Districts (1991)

Bethanien	2,911
Bushmanland	3,828
Caprivi	70,782
Damaraland	32,938
Gobabis	27,844
Grootfontein	34,905
Hereroland East	25,255
Hereroland West	18,824
Kaokoland	26,313
Karasburg	11,284
Karibib	12,147
Kavango	136,592
Keetmanshoop	20,804
Lüderitz	16,721
Maltahöhe	4,110
Mariental	24,892
Namaland	16,820
Okahandja	20,118
Omaruru	7,446
Otjiwarongo	23,326
Outjo	12,377
Oshakati/Ondangwa	615,057
Rehoboth	34,372
Swakopmund	20,757
Tsumeb	22,511
Windhoek	158,609
TOTAL	1,401,543

Gazetteer

(First lines indicate kilometre distances from major towns)

BETHANIE
Johannesburg 1,489, Ruacana 1,477, Rundu 1,317, Cape Town 1,011, Swakopmund 975, Walvis Bay 708, Windhoek 618, Lüderitz 259, Mariental 356, Keetmanshoop 157. Alt: 700m. Post Office. Police Post. Clinic. Petrol and diesel available. Landing strip. Pop: 1,769.

GOBABIS
Johannesburg 2,176, Cape Town 1,698, Walvis Bay 1,185, Ruacana 1,065, Lüderitz 1,021, Walvis Bay 938, Rundu 905, Keetmanshoop 687, Swakopmund 563, Windhoek 205. Alt: 1,200m. Post Office. Police Post. Hospital. Petrol and diesel available. Airfield. Railway station. Pop: 10,024.

GROOTFONTEIN
Johannesburg 2,411, Cape Town 1,993, Lüderitz 1,268, Keetmanshoop 934, Swakopmund 578, Ruacana 494, Windhoek 452, Rundu 248. Alt: 1,350m. Post Office. Police Post. Petrol and diesel available. Airport. Railway station. Pop: 18,151

KARASBURG
Johannesburg 1,281, Ruacana 1,550, Rundu 1,390, Walvis Bay 1,079, Swakopmund 1,048, Windhoek 690, Lüderitz 471, Keetmanshoop 208. Alt: 900m. Post Office. Police Post. Petrol and diesel available. Airport. Railway station. Pop: 7,109.

KARIBIB
Johannesburg 2,152, Cape Town 1,674, Lüderitz 999, Rundu 741, Ruacana 686, Keetmanshoop 665, Walvis Bay 206, Windhoek 181, Swakopmund 175. Alt: 900m. Post Office. Police Post. Petrol and diesel available. Railway station. Pop: 7,168.

KATIMA MULILO
Johannesburg 3,332, Cape Town 2,854, Swakopmund 1,485, Windhoek 1,361, Grootfontein 909, Rundu 661. Alt: 900m. Customs. Immigration. Border area for Angola, Botswana, Zambia and Zimbabwe. Post Office. Police Post. Hospital. Petrol and diesel available. Airport. Pop: 15,004.

KEETSMANHOOP
Johannesburg 1,489, Ruacana 1,342, Rundu 1,182, Cape Town 1,011, Swakopmund 840, Walvis Bay 814, Windhoek 482, Lüderitz 334, Mariental 221. Alt: 1,000m. Post Office. Police Post. Museum. Petrol and diesel available. Airport. Railway station. Pop: 17,475.

LÜDERITZ
Johannesburg 1,823, Ruacana 1,676, Rundu 1,516, Cape Town 1,345, Windhoek 816, Swakopmund 731, Walvis Bay 722, Keetmanshoop 334. Alt: sea level. Customs. Immigration. Seaport and point of entry. Hospital. Post Office. Police Post. Museum. Petrol and diesel available. Airfield. Railway station. Pop: 16,601.

MALTAHÖHE
Johannesburg 1,599, Cape Town 1,343, Ruacana 1,232, Rundu 1,072, Swakopmund 482, Walvis Bay 451, Lüderitz 374, Windhoek 372, Keetmanshoop

332, Mariental 111. Alt: 1,200m. Post Office. Police Post. Petrol and diesel available. Landing strip. Pop: 2,137.

MARIENTAL
Johannesburg 1,710, Cape Town 1,232, Ruacana 1,121, Rundu 961, Walvis Bay 650, Swakopmund 619, Lüderitz 555, Windhoek 261, Keetmanshoop 221. Alt: 1,200m. Post Office. Police Post. Petrol and diesel available. Airfield. Railway station. Pop: 12,458.

NOORDOEWER
Ruacana 1,646, Rundu 1,486, Johannesburg 1,185, Walvis Bay 1,175, Swakopmund 1,144, Windhoek 786, Cape Town 707, Lüderitz 609, Keetmanshoop 304. Alt: 300m. Post Office. Police Post. Petrol and diesel available. Customs. Immigration. Border post with South Africa.

OKAHANDJA
Johannesburg 2,042, Cape Town 1,564, Lüderitz 889, Ruacana 789, Rundu 629, Keetmanshoop 553, Walvis Bay 318, Swakopmund 287, Windhoek 71. Alt: 1,400m. Post Office. Police Post. Landing strip. Railway station. Pop: 12,473.

ORANJEMUND
Johannesburg 885, Cape Town 407, Windhoek 1,086, Lüderitz 270. Alt: sea level. Post Office. Company hospital and health clinic. Airfield. Pop: 8,000.

OTJIWARONGO
Johannesburg 2,216, Cape Town 1,738, Lüderitz 1,061, Keetmanshoop 727, Ruacana 615, Rundu 455, Walvis Bay 403, Swakopmund 371, Windhoek 245. Alt: 1,300m. Post Office. Police Post. Hospital. Petrol and diesel available. Airfield. Railway station. Pop: 17,028.

OUTJO
Johannesburg 2,289, Cape Town 1,811, Lüderitz 1,134, Keetmanshoop 800, Ruacana 688, Rundu 500, Walvis Bay 476, Swakopmund 444, Windhoek 318. Alt: 1,300m. Post Office. Police Post. Health clinic. Petrol and diesel available. Airfield. Railway station. Pop: 7,055.

REHOBOTH
Johannesburg 1,884, Cape Town 1,406, Ruacana 876, Rundu 787, Lüderitz 729, Walvis Bay 476, Swakopmund 445, Keetmanshoop 395, Windhoek 87. Alt: 1,500m. Post Office. Police Post. Hospital. Museum. Petrol and diesel available. Railway station. Pop: 21,654.

SWAKOPMUND
Johannesburg 2,372, Cape Town 1,849, Keetmanshoop 840, Rundu 826, Lüderitz 731, Ruacana 684, Windhoek 356, Walvis Bay 31. Alt: sea level. Customs. Immigration. Port of entry. Post Office. Police Post. Hospital. Museums. Petrol and diesel available. Airfield. Railway station. Pop: 19,319.

TSUMEB
Johannesburg 2,397, Cape Town 1,919, Lüderitz 1,242, Keetmanshoop 907, Walvis Bay 673, Swakopmund 552, Ruacana 434, Windhoek 426, Rundu 308. Alt: 1,300m. Post Office. Police Post. Hospital. Museum. Petrol and diesel available. Airfield. Railway station. Pop: 16,190.

WALVIS BAY
Johannesburg 2,362, Cape Town 1,884, Rundu 947, Lüderitz 938, Keetmanshoop 814, Ruacana 715, Windhoek 389, Swakopmund 31. Alt: sea level. Customs. Immigration. Main port of entry into Namibia. Post Office. Police Post. Hospital. Petrol and diesel available. Airport. Railway.

WINDHOEK
Johannesburg 1,971, Cape Town 1,493, Ruacana 860, Lüderitz 816, Rundu 700, Keetmanshoop 482, Walvis Bay 389, Swakopmund 357. Alt: 1,640m. Customs. Immigration. Main entry point by air. Police HQ. Post Offices. Hospitals. Museums. Seat of Parliament. Petrol and diesel available. Two airports. Railway station. Pop: 144,588.

Public Holidays

January 1	New Year	May 12	Ascension Day
March 21	Independence Day	May 25	Africa Day
March 22	Public Holiday	August 26	Heroes Day
April	Good Friday	December 10	(variable)
Easter Monday	(variable)		Human Rights Day
May 1	Workers' Day	December 25	Christmas Day
May 4	Cassinga Day	December 26	Family Day

LISTINGS

Airlines

Windhoek
Air Namibia
PO Box 731
Tel: (061) 38220/
229630/35
Fax: (061) 36460/
228763
Telex: (0908) 657

Cape Town
Air Namimbia
PO Box 739
Cape Town
Tel: (021) 216685/
216692
Fax: (021) 215840

Johannesburg
Air Nambia
PO Box 11405
Johannesburg
Tel: (011) 331-6658
Fax: (011) 331-2037

Air Namibia
Jan Smuts Airport
Tel: (011) 970-1767
Fax: (011) 970-1847

Air France
PO Box 20975
Tel: (061) 227688
Fax: (061) 32944

Lufthansa German
Airlines
PO Box 3161
Tel: (061) 226662
Fax: (061) 227923
Telex: (0908) 663

Air Charter

Windhoek
Air Namibia
PO Box 731
Tel: (061) 38220
Fax: (061) 36460
Telex: (0908) 657

Namibia Commercial
Aviation (NCA)
PO Box 30320
Tel: (061) 223562/3
(A/H 51897/223185/
31369/227043)
Fax: (061) 34583

Swakopmund
Pleasure Flights
PO Box 537
Tel: (0641) 4500
Fax: (0641)5325

Art Galleries

Swakopmund
Hobby Horse Picture
Framers & Art Gallery
PO Box 1275
Muschel Die
32 Breite Street
PO Box 17
Tel: (0641) 2874/5

Reflections
Swabou Bldg 1
Moltke Street
PO Box 933
Tel: (0641) 5484

Windhoek
Klein Gallery
Sübel Street
PO Box 20757
Tel: (061) 227846

Modern Picture
Framers
14 Volans Street
Tel: (061) 225991

Banks

Aranos
Standard Bank
Namibia Ltd
PO Box 44
Tel: (06442) 11
Fax: (06442) 229

Bethanie
Standard Bank
Namibia Ltd
PO Box 132
Keetmanshoop Street
Tel: (06362) 3
Fax: (0681) 2710

Gobabis
Standard Bank
Namibia Ltd
Voortrekker Street
Tel: (0681) 2512

Bank Windhoek Ltd
80 Church Street
PO Box 58
Tel: (0681) 2061
Fax: (0681) 3815

Grootfontein
Standard Bank
Namibia Ltd
6 Bismarck Street
PO Box 29
Tel: (06731) 3051
Fax: (06731) 3052

Bank Windhoek Ltd
Tel: (06731) 3165

Helmeringhausen
Standard Bank
Namibia Ltd
26 Goethe Street
PO Box 1081
Tel: (06362) 3

Kalkfeld
Standard Bank
Namibia Ltd
PO Box 16
Tel: (06672) 7

Karbib
Standard Bank
Namibia Ltd
Tel: (062252) 14

Karasburg
Park Street
PO Box 55
Tel: (06342) 136

Katima Mulilo
Bank of Windhoek Ltd
PO Box 166
Tel: (67352) 107

Keetmanshoop
Commercial Bank of
Namibia Ltd
The Khabuser Street
PO Box 166
Tel: (0631) 3354
Fax: (0631) 3814

Bank of
Windhoek Ltd
24 Fenchal Street
Po Box 415
Tel: (0631) 3291
Fax: (0631) 3946

Standard Bank
Namibia Ltd
Kaiser Street
Tel: (0631) 3274

Khorixas
Standard Bank
Namibia Ltd
Tel: (0020) 243

Kombat
Standard Bank
Namibia Ltd
Bank Hoof Street
Tel: (067362) 26

Leonardville
Standard Bank
Namibia Ltd
Tel: (06822) 31

Lüderitz
Standard Bank
Namibia Ltd
Bismarck Street
PO Box 65
Tel: (06331) 2316
Fax: (06331) 2986

Maltahöhe
Standard Bank
Namibia Ltd
Ampt Street
PO Box 14
Tel: (06632) 11
Fax: (06632) 141

Mariental
Standard Bank
Namibia Ltd
Marie Brandt Street
PO Box 2009
Tel: (0661) 2371
Fax: (0661) 586

Bank of
Windhoek Ltd
48 Marie Brandt
Street
PO Box 108
Tel: (0661) 2381
Fax: (0661) 746

Okahandja
Standard Bank
Namibia Ltd
Main Street
PO Box 35
Tel: (06221) 2047
Fax: (06221) 2760

Omaruru
Standard Bank
Namibia Ltd
Main Street
PO Box 73
Tel: (062232) 7
Fax: (062232) 34

Oshakati
Standard Bank
Namibia Ltd
Po Box 379
Tel: (06751) 20911
Fax: (06751) 20582

Otavi
Standard Bank
Namibia Ltd
Union Street
PO Box 29
Tel: (06742) 12
Fax: (06742) 232

Otjiwarongo
Standard Bank
Namibia Ltd
29a Voortrekker
Street
Tel: (0651) 2051
Fax: (0651) 2330

Bank of
Windhoek Ltd
Vootrekker Road
Po Box 441
Tel: (0651) 2541
Fax: (0651) 2810

Outjo
Standard Bank
Namibia Ltd
Voortrekker Street
PO Box 1
Tel: (06542) 16
Fax: (06542) 42

Bank of
Windhoek Ltd
Voortrekker Street
PO Box 45
Tel: (06542) 73
Fax: (06542) 71

Swakopmund
Commercial Bank
of Namibia Ltd
The Kaiser Wilhelm
Street
Tel: (0641) 4925
Fax: (0641) 2274

First National Bank
of Namibia
Moltke Street
PO Box 1
Tel: (0641) 5055
Fax: (0641) 4081

Bank of
Windhoek Ltd
5 Moltke Street
PO Box 608
Tel: (0641) 4070
Fax: (0641) 4084

Tsumeb
Standard Bank
Namibia Ltd
Main Street
PO Box 211
Tel: (0671) 20956
Fax: (0671) 21871

Walvis Bay
Commercial Bank
of Namibia Ltd
The M & Z Bldg 8
Street
Tel: (0642) 6006
Fax: (0642) 2457

**Standard Bank
of South Africa Ltd**
The 7 Street
PO Box 36
Tel: (0642) 5825
Fax: (0642) 5636

Bank of
Windhoek Ltd
9th Street
PO Box 7
Tel: (0642) 2311
Fax: (0642) 4846

Windhoek
Bank of Namibia
10 Göring Street
PO Box 2882
Tel: (061) 226401
Fax: (061) 227649

Bank Windhoek Ltd
262 Independence
Avenue
PO Box 2121
Tel: (061) 31850
Fax: (061) 225813

Boat Charter

Walvis Bay
Namib Marine Services
PO Box 899
Tel: (0642) 2620
Fax: (0642) 5545

Bus Companies

Swakopmund
Mainliner
Booking Office
11 Post Street 176
PO Box 882
Tel: (0641) 4031
(A/H (0641) 228353/
227259/225828)
Fax: (0641) 2114

Windhoek
Mainliner
5 Nordland St Lafrenz
PO Box 5673
Tel: (061) 6 3211
(A/H (061) 228353/
227259)
Fax: (061) 6 1422

Business Associations

Windhoek
Chamber of Commerce
and Industry (CCI)
PO Box 191
Tel: 222000
Fax: 33690

Nambia National
Chamber
of Commerce and
Industry (NNCCI)
PO Box 9355
Tel: 228809
Fax: 228009

Chamber of Mines in
Namibia
PO Box 2895
Tel: 37925
Fax: 222638

Clearing Bankers
Association
PO Box 31067
Tel: 2942400
Fax: 2942409

Electrical Contractors
Association
PO Box 3163
Tel: 37920
Fax: 38795

Federation of
Namibian
Tourist Associations
PO Box 3900
Tel: 38560
Fax: 35652

Guild of Woodworking
and Allied Trade and
Industries of Namibia
(TISCHLERINNUNG)
PO Box 5597
Tel: 227737

Hotel Association of
Namibia
PO Box 2862
Tel: 33145
Fax: 34512

Institute of Estate
Agents of Namibia
PO Box 23306
Tel: 34177
Fax: 33204

Insurance Association
of Namibia
PO Box 417
Tel: 229207

Jewellers Association
of Namibia (JASSONA)
PO Box 946
Tel: 36100
Fax: 35955

Life Assurers
Association
of Namibia (LAAN)
PO Box 23159
Tel: 37337
Fax: 34874

Master Builders and
Allied Trades
Association
PO Box 1479
Tel: 63101
Fax: 63545

Motor Industries
Federation of Namibia
PO Box 1503
Tel: 38280
Fax: 33690

Namibia Estate Agents
Board
PO Box 2588
Tel: 34177
Fax: 33204

Namibia Information
Technology
Association
(NITA)
PO Box 24280
Tel: 37190
Fax: 32201

Namibia Institute for
Economic Affairs
PO Box 1503
Tel: 35528
Fax: 228504

Namibia Road Carriers
Association
PO Box 5673
Tel: 63211
Fax: 61422

Namibian Chamber of
Printing
PO Box 363
Tel: 37905
Fax: 222927

Namibian
International
Business
Development
Organisation (NIBDO)
PO Box 82
Tel: 37970
Fax: 33690

Project Management
Institute
PO Box 9659
Tel: 226557
Fax: 225332

Car Hire Firms

Windhoek
Avis Rent-a-Car
PO Box 2057
Tel: (061) 33166/7,
(A/H 52222)
Fax: (061) 223072

Budget Rent-a-Car
(Namibia)
PO Box 1754
Tel: (061) 228720,
(A/H 52222)
Fax: (061) 227665

Imperial Car Hire
PO Box 1387
Tel: (061) 227103,
(A/H 52222)
Fax: (061) 222721

Kessler Car Hire
PO Box 20274
Tel: (061) 33451,227638,227222
(A/H 52222)
Fax: (061) 224551/227665

Namib 4x4 Hire
PO Box 9544
Tel: (061) 220604
Fax: (061) 220605

RK 4x4 Hire
PO Box 31076
Tel: (061) 223994
Fax: (061) 223994

Woodway Camper
Hire
PO Box 11084
Tel: (061) 229918
Fax: (061) 222877

Zimmermann Garage
PO Box 2672
Tel: (061) 37146 (A/H 51578)
Fax: (061) 37207

Swakopmund
Avis Rent-a-Car
Tel: (0641) 2527
Fax: (0641) 5881

Budget Rent-a-Car
(Namibia)
PO Box 180
Tel: (0641) 4118
Fax: (0641) 4117

Imperial Car Hire
PO Box 748
Tel: (0641) 61587

Namib 4x4 Hire
PO Box 4048
Tel: (0641) 61791
Fax: (0641) 62184

Tsumeb
Avis Rent-a-car
Tel: (0671) 2520

Walvis Bay
Imperial Car Hire
PO Box 1591
Tel: (06742) 4624
Fax: (06742) 2931

Clubs

Swakopmund
Swakopmund Club
Breite Street
PO Box 199
Tel: (0641) 2047

Windhoek
Windhoek Country
Club
Eros Airport
Tel: (061) 51668
Fax: (061) 51460

Namibian Missions Abroad

ANGOLA
Rua Rei Katyavala 6
PO Box 953
Luanda
Tel: (09244)-2-339.234

BELGIUM
Stephanie Square
Business Centre S.A
69 Avenue Louise
1050 Brussels
Tel: (0932)-2-535.7801
Fax: (0932)-2-535.7766

CUBA
5th Avenue No. 4406
Between 44 & 46 St
Miramar
Havana
Tel: (0953)-7-331.427/8/9
(0953)-7-204.403
Fax: (0953)-7-3069

ETHIOPIA
Higher 17, Kebel 19
House No. 002
PO Box 1443
Addis Ababa
Tel: (09251)-1-611.966/612.055
Fax: (09251)-1-612.677
Telex: (09251)-2-1032

FRANCE
224/226 Rue de
Faubourg
Saint Antoine
Paris
Tel: (0933)-143-48.30.80
Fax: (0933)-143-48.30.47

GERMANY
Konstantintrasse 25a
5300, Bonn 2
Tel: (0949)-228-359.091/95
Fax: (0949)-228-359.051

NIGERIA
PMB 800015
Victoria Islands
Lagos
Tel: (09234)-1-619.323
Fax: (09324)-1-619.323
Telex: 50905-22650
EKOHTL

RUSSIAN
FEDERATION
2nd Kazachy Lane
House No. 7
Moscow
Tel: (097)-95-230.0113
Fax: (097)-95-230.2274/(097)-502-222.1428

SWEDEN
Luntmakargatan 86-88
111 22 Stockholm
PO Box 26042
S 100 31 Stockholm
Tel: (0946)-8-612.7788
Fax: (0946)-8-416.6655

346

UNITED KINGDOM
34 South Molton Street
London WIY 2BP
Tel: (0944)-71-408.2.333
Fax: (0944)-71-
409.7.306

UNITED STATES OF
AMERICA
1605 New Hamshire
Ave, N.W.
Washington D.C. 20009
Tel: (091)-202-986.0540
Fax: (091)-202-986.0443

ZAMBIA
6968 Kabanga Rd/
Addis Ababa Drive
Rhodes Park
PO Box 30577
Lusaka
Tel: (09260)-1-252-250
Fax: (09260)-1-252-497

Foreign Representation and Consuls

AFRICAN NATIONAL
CONGRESS
(South Africa)
1st Floor Kenya House
134 Leutwein Street,
Windhoek Central
PO Box 24505
Windhoek
Tel: 33412
Fax: 228321
Telex: 724 WK

CONSULATE OF
AUSTRIA
60A Jan Jonker Road
Klein Windhoek
PO Box 3163
Windhoek
Tel: 37934
Fax: 38795

BELGIUM
Defco Namibia (Pty)
CDM Centre
4th Floor
Bülow Street
PO Box 22584
Windhoek
Tel: 38295
Fax: 36531

HUNGARY
5 Denis Shepherd St
Olympia
PO Box 586
Windhoek
Tel: 37728, Fax: 52033

REPUBLIC OF SOUTH
AFRICA
RSA House
Corner Jan Jonker
& Klein Windhoek Rd
PO Box 23100
Windhoek
Tel: 229765, Fax: 224140
Telex: 701

SWITZERLAND
2nd Floor, Southern
Life Tower
Post Street Mall
PO Box 22287
Windhoek
Tel: 222359, Fax: 227922
Telex: 869 WK

Foreign Diplomatic Missions

AFGHANISTAN
Embassy
26 East Road
PO Box 1227, Harare
Zimbabwe
Tel: (092634) 720083
Telex: 22276 ZW

ANGOLA EMBASSY
Angola House, 3
Ausspann Street
Windhoek Central
P/Bag 12020
Ausspannplatz
Windhoek
Tel: 227535, Fax: 221498
Telex: 897 WK

AUSTRALIA
High Commission
4th Floor,
Karingamombe Centre
53 Samora Machel Ave
PO Box (907) 4541,
Harare
Zimbabwe
Tel: (092634) 794591
Fax: (092634) 704615

AUSTRIA EMBASSY
Room 216, New Shell
House
30 Samora Machel
Avenue
PO Box 4120, Harare
Zimbabwe
Tel: (092634) 702921
Fax: (092634) 70396
Telex: 22546 EMBAUS
ZW

BANGLADESH
HIGH COMMISSION
98 Klein Windhoek
Road
Klein Windhoek
PO Box 9123
Windhoek
Tel: 32301
Fax: 34570
Telex: 650 BDTWK

BELGIUM EMBASSY
Tanganyika House 57
23 Third Street
PO Box 2522, Harare
Zimbabwe
Tel: (092634) 793306/7
Fax: (092634) 703960
Telex: 24788

BOTSWANA
HIGH COMMISSION
101 Klein Windhoek
Road
Klein Windhoek
PO Box 20359,
Windhoek
Tel: 221942, Fax: 36034
Telex: 894

BRAZILIAN EMBASSY
52 Bismarck Street
Windhoek, West
PO Box 24166,
Windhoek
Tel: 37368/9
Fax: 33389
Telex: 498 BREMB WK

BURUNDI EMBASSY
Development House
Moi Avenue
PO Box 44439, Nairobi
Kenya
Tel: (092542) 728340/
729275
Fax: (092542) 729275
Telex: 22425

CANADIAN
HIGH
COMMISSION
111-A Gloudina Street
Ludwigsdorf
PO Box 2147
Windhoek
Tel: 222941/222966
Fax: 224204
Telex: 402 WK

EMBASSY
OF CHINA
13 Wecke Street,
Klein Windhoek
PO Box 22777
Windhoek
Tel: 222089
Fax: 225544
Telex: 675 WK

CONGO EMBASSY
9 Körner Street
Windhoek Central
PO Box 22970
Windhoek
Tel: 226958/9
Fax: 228642
Telex: 405 WK

EMBASSY
OF CUBA
31 Omuramba Road,
Eros
PO Box 23866
Windhoek
Tel: 227072/227153
Fax: 31584
Telex: 406 WK

ROYAL DANISH
EMBASSY
5th Floor, Sanlam
Centre
154 Independence
Avenue
PO Box 20126
Windhoek
Tel: 229956
Fax; 35807
Telex: 461 WK

EMBASSY OF EGYPT
10 Berg Street
Klein Windhoek
PO Box 11853
Klein Windhoek
Tel: 221501/2/3
Fax: 228856

EMBASSY OF FINLAND
5th Floor, Sanlam Centre
154 Independence Avenue
PO Box 3649
Windhoek
Tel: 221355
Fax: 221349
Telex: 671 WK

FRENCH EMBASSY
1 Goethe Street
Windhoek Central
PO Box 20484
Windhoek
Tel: 229021/2/3
Fax: 31436
Telex: 715 WK

GERMAN EMBASSY
6ht Floor, Sanlam Centre
154 Independance Avenue
PO Box 231, Windhoek
Tel: 229217/8/9
Fax: 222981
Telex: 482 WK

GHANA HIGH COMMISSION
5 Klein Windhoek Road
Klein Windhoek
PO Box 24165
Windhoek
Tel: 221341/2
Fax: 221343

HUNGARY EMBASSY
20 Lanark Road
Belgravia
PO Box 3594, Harare
Zimbabwe
Tel: (092634) 733528
Telex: 24237 ZW

INDIA HIGH COMMISSION
97 Klein Windhoek Road
Klein Windhoek
PO Box 1209,
Windhoek
Tel: 226036/7/8
Fax: 37320
Telex: 832 WK

INDONESIA EMBASSY
103 Klein Windhoek Road
Klein Windhoek
PO Box 20691
Windhoek
Tel: 52912
Telex: 600 WK

IRAN EMBASSY
81 Klein Windhoek Road
Klein Windhoek
PO Box 24790
Windhoek
Tel: 229974/5
Fax: 220016
Telex: 637 WK

ITALIAN EMBASSY
Corner Anna and Gevers Streets
Ludwigsdorf
PO Box 24065
Windhoek
Tel: 228659/228602
Fax: 229860
Telex: 620 WK

JAMAICA HIGH COMMISSION
Plot 77, 303 Road
Victoria Island Annex
PO Box 75368
Victoria Island, Lagos
Nigeria
Tel: (2341) 611085
Fax: (2341) 612100

JAPAN EMBASSY
18th Floor,
Karigamombe Centre
53 Samora Machel Avenue
PO Box 2710, Harare
Zimbabwe
Tel: (092634) 727500/727618/727769
Fax: (092634) 727769

KENYA HIGH COMMISSION
5th Floor, Kenya House
134 Leutwein Street
Windhoek Central
PO Box 2889
Windhoek
Tel: 226836/225900
Fax: 221409
Telex: 823 WK

KOREA (North) EMBASSY
2 Jenner Street
Windhoek West
PO Box 22927
Windhoek
Tel: 220279
Fax: 220328
Telex: 631 KT WK

KOREA (South) EMBASSY
10th Floor, Sanlam Centre
154 Independence Avenue
PO Box 3788
Windhoek
Tel: 229286/7/8
Fax: 229847
Telex: 801

LIBYA
69 Burg Street, Luxury Hill
Klein Windhoek
PO Box 124
Windhoek
Tel: 34454/34464/34381
Fax: 34471
Telex: 868

MALAWI HIGH COMMISSION
56 Bismarck Street
Windhoek Central
PO Box 23384
Windhoek
Tel: 221391/2/3
Fax: 227056
Telex: 469 WK

MALAYSIA HIGH COMMISSION
70 Orange Grove Drive
Highlands
Harare
Zimbabwe
Tel: (092634) 796200
Fax: (092634) 728450

MEXICAN EMBASSY
3rd Floor, Southern Life Tower
39 Post Street,
Windhoek
Private Bag 13220
Windhoek
Tel: 229082
Fax: 229180

ROYAL NETHERLANDS EMBASSY
47 Enterprise Road
PO Box HG 601
Highlands
Harare
Zimbabwe
Tel: (092634) 731428/734528
Fax: (092634) 790520
Telex: 24357 ZW

NEW ZEALAND HIGH COMMISSION
57 Jason Moyo Road
PO Box 5448
Harare
Zimbabwe
Tel: (092634) 728681
Fax: (092634) 790693
Telex: 22742 ZW

NIGERIA HIGH COMMISSION
4 Omaramba Road,
Eros Park
PO Box 23547
Windhoek
Tel: 32103/4/5
Fax: 221639

ROYAL NORWEGIAN EMBASSY
5th Floor, Sanlam Centre
154 Independence Avenue
Windhoek
PO Box 9936, Eros
Tel: 227812
Fax: 222226
Telex: 432 WK

PAKISTAN HIGH COMMISSION
10 Klein Windhoek Road
PO Box 9123
Windhoek
Tel: 221463/220388
Fax: 229031
Telex: 491 WK

PALESTINE EMBASSY
5 Sanderburg Street
Luxury Hill
PO Box 24823
Windhoek
Tel: 227002
Fax: 221624

PORTUGAL
28 Garten Street
Windhoek Central
PO Box 443
Windhoek
Tel: 228736
Fax: 37929
Telex: 409 WK

EMBASSY OF
ROMANIA
3 Hammerkop Street
Hochland Park
PO Box 6827
Windhoek
Tel: 224630
Fax: 221564
Telex: 435 ROMAN
WK

RWANDA EMBASSY
PO Box 2918
Dar es Salaam
Tanzania
Tel: (0925551) 30119/
30120
Fax: (0925551) 20115

EMBASSY OF
SPAIN
58 Bismarck Street
Windhoek West
PO Box 21811
Windhoek
Tel: 224409
Fax: 223046
Telex: 672 ESNAM WK

EMBASSY OF
SUDAN
6 Johann Albrecht
Street
Windhoek West
PO Box 3708
Windhoek
Tel: 228544
Fax: 228617
Telex: 818 WK

EMBASSY OF
SWEDEN
9th Floor Sanlam
Centre
154 Independence
Avenue
PO Box 23087
Windhoek
Tel: 22905/22973
Fax: 222774
Telex: 463 WK

EMBASSY OF
SWITZERLAND
9 Lanark Road,
Belgravia
PO Box 3440
Harare, Zimbabwe
Tel: (092634) 703977
Telex: 24669 AMSWIS
ZW

TANZANIA HIGH
COMMISSION
Luanda, Angola
Tel: (092442) 335205/
333686
Fax: (092442) 393486
Telex: 3448

EMBASSY OF
TUNISIA
5 Ashton Road,
Alexander Road
PO Box 4308,
Harare, Zimbabwe
Tel: (092634) 791570/
791555
Fax: (092634) 701392

UGANDA
HIGH COMMISSSION
PO Box 33557
Lusaka, Zambia
Tel: (092601) 227916/
7/9
Fax: (092601) 226078
Telex: ZA 40990

EMBASSY OF RUSSIA
4 Christian Street,
Klein Windhoek
PO Box 3826
Windhoek
Tel: 228671
Telex: 865 WK

BRITISH HIGH
COMMISSION
116A Leutwein Street,
Windhoek Central
PO Box 22202
Windhoek
Tel: 223022
Fax: 228895

AMERICAN EMBASSY
14 Lossen Street,
Ausspannplatz
P/Bag 12029
Windhoek
Tel: 221601
Fax: 229792

EMBASSY OF
VENEZUELA
3rd Floor
Southern Life Tower
Post Street Mall
P/Bag 13353
Windhoek
Tel: 227905/227907
Fax: 227804
Telex: 862 VENEM WK

EMBASSY OF
VIETNAM
Luanda
Angola
Tel: (092442) 323388/9

EMBASSY OF
YUGOSLAVIA
10 Chateau Street
Klein Windhoek
PO Box 3705
Windhoek
Tel: 227896
Fax: 31660

EMBASSY ZAIRE
24 Van Praagh Avenue,
Nilton Park
PO Box 2446
Harare
Zimbabwe
Tel: (092634) 724494/
45827
Telex: 22265 ZR

ZAMBIA
HIGH COMMISSION
22 Curt von Francois
Street
Windhoek Central
PO Box 22882
Windhoek
Tel: 37610
Fax: 228162
Telex: 485 WK

ZIMBABWE
HIGH COMMISSION
Corner Independence
Avenue
& Grimm Street,
Windhoek Central
PO Box 23056
Windhoek
Tel: 228134/227738/
227204
Fax: 226859
Telex: 886 WK

Guest Farms for Tourists

Aus
NAMTIB DESERT
LODGE
PO Box 19
Tel: (06362) 6640

Gobabis
HETAKU
PO Box 24575
Windhoek
Tel: (06202) 3504
(061) 36674
Fax: (061) 227841

OHLSENHAGEN
PO Box 434
Tel: (0688) 11003

STEINHAUSEN
PO Box 23
Omitara
Tel: (06202) 3240

Helmeringhausen
DABIS
PO Box 15
Tel: (06362) 6820
Fax: (061) 32300

SINCLAIR
PO Box 19
Tel: (06362) 6503

Kalkfeld
MOUNT ETJO SAFARI
LODGE
PO Box 81
Tel: (06532) 1602
Fax: (06532) 44

Kamanjab
HOBATERE LODGE
PO Box 110
Tel: (0020) 2022

EPAKO KAMEL
GAME RANCH
PO Box 108
Tel: (06221) 2141
Fax: (06221) 2141

Karibib
ALBRECHTSHÖHE
PO Box 124
Tel: (062252) 1222
Fax: (062252) 230

AUDAWIB
PO Box 191
Tel: (062252) 1631
Fax: (062252) 240

Maltahöhe
BURGSDORF
PO Box 28
Tel: (06632) 1330
Fax: (06632) 66

DAWEB
PO Box 18
Tel: (06632) 1840
Fax: (06632) 66

NAMIB NAUKLUFT LODGE
PO Box 22028
Windhoek
Tel: (061) 63082
Fax: 215356

OU KAMKAS
PO Box 191
Tel: (06632) 4413
Fax: (061) 226412

Mariental
ANIB LODGE
PO Box 800
Tel: (0668) 12421
Fax: (0661) 746

DONKERHOEK
Private Bag 2145
Tel: (06662) 3113

Okahandja
HAASENHOF
PO Box 72
Tel: (06228) 82131/ (061) 32748
Fax: (061) 228461

J+C LIEVENBERG
PO Box 66
Tel: (062252) 3112
Fax: (061) 34470

MATADOR
PO Box 214
Tel: (06228) 4312

OKOMITUNDU
PO Box 285
Tel: (06228) 6403
Fax: 41186

OTJIRUZE
PO Box 297
Tel: (06228) 81621
Fax: (061) 223585

OTJISAZU
PO Box 149
Tel: (06228) 81640
Fax: (061) 37483

OTJISEMBA
PO Box 756
Tel: (06228) 82103
Fax: (061) 217026

WILHELMSTAL-NORD
PO Box 641
Tel: (06228) 6212/ 6321

Omaruru
BOSKLOOF
PO Box 53
Tel: (06532) 3231

ERINDI ONGANGA
PO Box 20
Tel: (061) 32624
(06532) 1202
Fax: (061) 224863

IMMENHOF
PO Box 250
Tel: (06532) 1803
Fax: (061) 227021

OKOSONGORO
PO Box 324
Tel: (06532) 1721

OTJANDAUE
PO Box 44
Tel: (062232) 1203 255
Fax: (062232) 209

OTJIKOTO
PO Box 404
Tel: (062232) 2102

OTJUMUE-OST
PO Box 323
Tel: (062232) 1913

SCHÖNFELD
PO Box 382
Tel: (06532) 1831
Fax: (061) 227021

Otavi
KUPFERBERG
PO Box 255
Tel: (06742) 2211
Fax: (06731) 2611

Otjiwarongo
OKONJIMA
PO Box 793
Tel: (0658) 18212
Fax: (0651) 3242

WATERBERG BIG GAME HUNTING LODGE
PO Box 973
Tel: (0658) 15313
Fax: (0658) 15313

Outjo
BAMBATSI HOLIDAY RANCH
PO Box 120
Tel: (06542) 1104

BERGPLAAS SAFARI LODGE
PO Box 60
Tel: (06542) 1802

OTJITAMBI
Private Bag: 2607
Tel: (06542) 4602

TOSHARI INN
PO Box 164
Tel: (06542) 3602
Fax: (06542) 182

Tsumeb
LA ROCHELLE
PO Box 194
Tel: (0678) 11002, 11013

Usakos
AMEIB RANCH
PO Box 266
Tel: (062242) 1111
Fax: (061) 35742

WÜSTENQUELL DESERT LODGE
PO Box 177
Tel: (062242) 1312
Fax: (062252) 277

Windhoek
ELISENHEIM
PO Box 3016
Tel: (061) 64429
Fax: (061) 64429

FINKENSTEIN
PO Box 167
Tel: (061) 34751
Fax: (061) 38890

HOCHLAND
P.O. Box 22221
Tel: (061) 32628
Fax: (061) 32628

HOPE
PO Box 21768
Tel: (0628) 3202

HUAB LODGE
PO Box 21783
Tel: (061) 226976

INTU AFRICA GAME LODGE
PO Box 40047
Tel: (0642) 4742/6120

KAMAB
PO Box 3873
Tel: (061) 31614
(06228) 5313
Fax: (061) 35936

KARIVO
PO Box 11420
Tel: (0628) 1321
Fax: (061) 221647

KUZIKUS GAME FARM
Private Bag 13112
Tel: (0628) 3102
Fax: (061) 225000

MONTE CHRISTO
PO Box 5474
Tel: (061) 32680

NIEDERSACHSEN
PO Box 3636
Tel: (0628) 1102

OKAPUKA RANCH
PO Box 5955
Tel: (061) 34607/ 227845
Fax: (061) 34690

SILVERSAND
Private Bag 13161
Tel: (06202) 1102
Fax: (061) 35501/ 228751

SWARTFONTEIN
PO Box 20113
Tel: (0628) 1112

VILLA VERDI
PO Box 6784
Tel: (061) 222574

WEISSENFELS
Private Bag 13144
Tel: (0628) 1213

Guest Farms for Hunters Only

Gobabis
KALAHARI
HUNTING LODGE
PO Box 21
Witvlei
Tel: (0628) 3422
Fax: (061) 44010

Karibib
KHOMAS
PO Box 954
Walvis Bay 9190
Tel: (0642) 4129
(062252) 4202
Fax: (0642) 6850

Okahandja
MORINGA
PO Box 65
Tel: (06228) 6111
Fax: (061) 61619

OKATJURU
PO Box 207
Tel: (06228) 1521
Fax: (061) 226266

Windhoek
BELLERODE
PO Box 5185
Tel: (061) 35485

IBENSTEIN
PO Box 20
Dordabis
Tel: (0020) 8
Fax: (061) 34635

MOUNTAIN VIEW
GAME LODGE
PO Box 9061
Tel: (0628) 1131

ONGORO-GOTJARI
PO Box 20129
Tel: (0628) 1312
Telex: (0908) 3201

PANORAMA
HUNTING
LODGE
PO Box 2992
Tel: (061) 33345
Fax: (061) 52922

Accommodation

Hotels, Guest Houses, and Self-Catering

Aranos
ARANOS HOTEL
PO Box 315
Tel: (06642) 31/133
Fax: (06642) 229

Aroab
AROAB HOTEL
PO Box 5
Tel: (06352) 27

Asab
ASAB HOTEL
PO Box 7
Keetmanshoop
Tel: (0668) 15441

Aus
BAHNHOF HOTEL
PO Box 27
Tel: (063332) 44

Bethanie
BETHANIE HOTEL
PO Box 13
Tel: (06362) 13

Gobabis
CENTRAL HOTEL
PO Box 233
Tel: (0681) 2094/5
Fax: (0681) 2092

GOBABIS HOTEL
PO Box 942
Tel: (0681) 2568/3068
Fax: (0681) 2703

Gochas
GOCHAS HOTEL
PO Box 117
Tel: (06662) 44

Grootfontein
METEOR HOTEL
PO Box 346
Tel: (06731) 2078/9, 3071
Fax: (06731) 3072

NORD HOTEL
PO Box 168
Tel: (06731) 2049
Fax: (06731) 2049

Grünau
GRÜNAU HOTEL
PO Box 2
Tel: (0020) 1

Helmeringhausen
HELMERINGHAUSEN
HOTEL
PO Box 21
Tel: (06362) 7

Henties Bay
HOTEL DE DUINE
PO Box 1
Tel: (06442) 1

Hochfeld
HOCHFELD HOTEL
PO Box 454
Okahandja
Tel:(06228) 1703
NHFD

Kalkrand
KALKRAND HOTEL
PO Box 43
Tel: (06672) 24

Karasburg
KALKFONTEIN
HOTEL
PO Box 205
Tel: (06342) 172/23
Fax: (06342) 172/23

VAN RIEBEECK
HOTEL
PO Box 87
Tel: (06342) 23/172
Fax: (06342) 172/23

Karibib
HOTEL
ERONGOBLICK
PO Box 67
Tel: (062252) 9

HOTEL STROBLHOF
PO Box 164
Tel: (062252) 81
Fax: (062252) 240

Katima Mulilo
ZAMBEZI LODGE
PO Box 98
Tel: (067352) 203
Fax: (067352) 203

Keetmanshoop
CANYON HOTEL
PO Box 950
Tel: (0631) 3361
Fax: (0631) 3714

TRAVEL INN
PO Box 141
Tel: (0631) 3344/5/6
Fax: (0631) 2138

Koes
HOTEL KALAHARI
P/Bag 1042
Tel: (06322) 14

Lüderitz
BAY VIEW HOTEL
PO Box 387
Tel: (06331) 2288
Fax: (06331) 2402
Telex: (0908) 846

KAPPS HOTEL
PO Box 100
Tel: (06331) 2701
Fax: (06331) 2402
Telex: (0908) 846

ZUM SPERRGEBEIT
HOTEL GARNI
PO Box 373
Tel: (06331) 2856
Fax: (06331) 2976

Maltahöhe
MALTAHÖHE HOTEL
PO Box 20
Tel: (06632) 13
Fax: (06332) 133

Mariental
SANDBERG HOTEL
PO Box 12
Tel: (0661) 2291 738

Noordoewer
CAMEL LODGE
PO Box 1
Tel: (0020) 13
Fax: (0020) 43

Okahandja
OKAHANDJA HOTEL
PO Box 770
Tel: (06221) 3024
Fax: (06221) 2259

Omaruru
CENTRAL HOTEL
PO Box 29
Tel: (062232) 30

HOTEL STAEBE
PO Box 92
Tel: (062232) 35
Fax: (062232) 339
Telex: (0908) 3554

Omitara
OMITARA HOTEL
PO Box 641
Tel: (06202) 4
Fax: (06202) 20

Oshakati
INTERNATIONAL
GUEST
HOUSE
PO Box 542
Tel: (06752) 20175/
21001

Otavi
OTAVI HOTEL
PO Box 400
Tel: (06742) 229 & 5
Fax: (06742) 73

Otjiwarongo
HOTEL BRUMME
PO Box 63
Tel: (0651) 2420
(Temporarily closed)

HOTEL HAMBURGER
HOF
PO Box 8
Tel: (0651) 2520
Fax: (0651) 3607
Telex: (0908) 3841

OTJIBAMBA LODGE
PO Box 510
Tel: (0651) 3133/3139
Fax: (0651) 3206

Outjo
HOTEL ETOSHA
PO Box 31
Tel: (06542) 130
Fax: (06542) 130

HOTEL ONDURI
PO Box 14
Tel: (06542) 14/165
Fax: (06542) 166

Rehoboth
RIO MONTE HOTEL
PO Box 3257
Tel: (06271) 2161

SUIDWES HOTEL
PO Box 3300
Tel: (06271) 2238

Rehoboth-Rail
BAHNHOF HOTEL
PO Box 540
Tel: (06271) 5350

Swakopmund
ATLANTA HOTEL
PO Box 456
Tel: (0641) 2360
Fax: (0641) 5649

HANSA HOTEL
PO Box 44
Tel: (0641) 311
Fax: (0641) 2732
Telex: (0908) 3560

HOTEL
EUROPA HOF
PO Box 1333
Tel: (0641) 5898, 5061
Fax: (0641) 2391

HOTEL GARNI
ADLER
PO Box 1497
Tel: (0641) 5045/6/7
Fax: (0641) 4206

HOTEL GRÜNER
KRANZ
PO Box 211
Tel: (0641) 2039
Fax: (0641) 5016

HOTEL
JAY JAY'S
RESTAURANT
PO Box 835
Tel: (0641) 2909

HOTEL SHÜTZE
PO Box 634
Tel: (0641) 2718
Fax: (0641) 2718

HOTEL-PENSION
DEUTSCHES HAUS
PO Box 13
Tel: (0641) 4896/7/8
Fax: (0641) 4861

HOTEL-PENSION
DIG BY SEE
PO Box 1530
Tel: (0641) 4130
Fax: (0641) 4170

HOTEL-PENSION
PRINZESSIN-
RUPPRECHT-HEIM
PO Box 124
Tel: (0641) 2231
Fax: (0641) 2019

HOTEL-PENSION
RAPMUND
PO Box 425
Tel: (0641) 2035
Fax: (0641) 4524

HOTEL-PENSION
SCHWEIZERHAUS
PO Box 445
Tel: (0641) 331/2/3
Fax: (0641) 5850

PRIVAT-PENSION
D'AVIGNON
PO Box 1222
Tel: (0641) 5821
Fax: (0641) 5542

STRAND HOTEL
PO Box 20
Tel: (0641) 315
Fax: (0641) 4942
Telex: (0908) 3557

Tsumeb
HOTEL ECKLEBEN
PO Box 27
Tel: (0671) 21051
Fax: (0671) 21575
Telex: (0908) 3842

MINEN HOTEL
PO Box 244
Tel: (0671) 20171/2
Fax: (0671) 21750

MOKUTI LODGE
PO Box 403
Tel: (0671) 21084
Fax: (0671) 21084
Telex: (0908) 749

Usakos
USAKOS HOTEL
PO Box 129
Tel: (062242) 259

Walvis Bay
CASA MIA HOTEL
PO Box 1786
Tel: (0642) 5975
Fax: (0642) 6596

FLAMINGO HOTEL
PO Box 30
Tel: (0642) 3011/2/3
Fax: (0642) 4097

HOTEL ATLANTIC
PO Box 46
Tel: (0642) 2811/2
Fax: (0642) 5063

MERMAID HOTEL
PO Box 1763
Tel: (0642) 6211/2/3
Fax: (0642) 6656

Windhoek
ARIS HOTEL
PO Box 5199
Tel: (061) 36006

CONTINENTAL
HOTEL
PO Box 977
Tel: (061) 37293
Fax: (061) 31539

TUCKERS TAVERN
PO Box 5374
Tel: (061) 223249
Telex: (0908) 3891

HOTEL
FÜRSTENHOF
PO Box 316
Tel: (061) 37380
Fax: (061) 228751

HOTEL
KAPPS FARM
PO Box 5470
Tel: (061) 34763/36374
Fax: (061) 38936

HOTEL-PENSION
CELA
PO Box 1947
Tel: (061) 226294/5
Fax: (061) 226246

HOTEL-PENSION
HANDKE
PO Box 20881
Tel: (061) 34904
Fax: (061) 225660

HOTEL-PENSION
STEINER
PO Box 20481
Tel: (061) 222898
Fax: (061) 224234

HOTEL SAFARI
PO Box 3900
Tel: (061) 38560
Fax: (061) 35652
Telex: (0908) 438

HOTEL THÜRINGER
HOF
PO Box 112
Tel: (061) 226031
Fax: (061) 32981
Telex: (0908) 3227

KALAHARI SANDS
HOTEL
PO Box 2254
Tel: (061) 222300
Fax: (061) 222260
Telex: (0908) 3174

SOUTH WEST STAR
HOTEL
PO Box 10319
Khomasdal
Tel: (061) 213205

Witvlei
WITVLEI HOTEL
PO Box 13
Tel: (06832) 4

Rest Camps & Caravan Parks

Caprivi
LIANSHULU LODGE
PO Box 6850
Windhoek
Tel: (061) 225178
Fax: (061) 239455

ZAMBEZI LODGE
PO Box 98
Katima Mulilo
Tel: (067352) 203
Telex: 0908-3391

Damaraland
ETENDEKA
MOUNTAIN CAMP
PO Box 6850
Windhoek
Tel: (061) 226174
Fax: (061) 239455

PALMWAG LODGE
PO Box 339
Swakopmund
Tel: (0641) 4459
Fax: (0641) 4664

Gobabis
WELKOM
PO Box 450
Tel: (0688) 12213

Grootfontein
Municipality
PO Box 23
Tel: (06731) 3100/1/2/3
Fax: (06731) 2930

Henties Bay
DIE OORD
PO Box 82
Tel: (06442) 239 165

JIMMY REA BEACH
ANGLING LODGE
PO Box 154
Tel: (06442) 323

Karasburg
OAS HOLIDAY FARM
PO Box 4
Tel: (06342) 4321
Fax: (06342) 75

Karibib
TSAOBIS LEOPARD
NATURE PARK
PO Box 143
Tel: (062252) 1304
Telex: 0908-669
Fax: (061) 33690

Keetmanshoop
Municipality
P/Bag 2125
Tel: (0631) 3316
Fax: (0631) 3818

Khorixas
REST CAMP AND
RESTAURANT
PO Box 2
Tel: (065712) 196
Telex: 0908 3512

UIS REST CAMP
PO Box 2, Uis
Tel: (062262) 21 153

Koës
KALAHARI GAME
LODGE
PO Box 22
Tel: (06662) 3112

Lüderitz
LÜDERITZ
PO Box 377
Tel: (06331) 3351/2/3/4
Fax: (06331) 2869

Maltahöhe
HAMMERSTEIN
PO Box 250
Tel: (06632) 5111

NAMIB
REST CAMP
PO Box 1075
Swakopmund
Tel: (06632) 3211

Omaruru
OMARURU
PO Box 190
Tel: (062232) 337

Otavi
Municipality
PO Box 59
Tel: (06742) 22

Otjiwarongo
Municipality
P/Bag 2209
Tel: (0651) 2231
Fax: (0651) 2098

OTJIWA GAME
RANCH
PO Box 1231
Tel: (0658) 11002
Fax: (0658) 11002

Outjo
Municipality
PO Box 51
Tel: (06542) 13 205

Rundu
KAISOSI SAFARI
LODGE
PO Box 599
Tel: (067372) 265

SARASUNGA
LODGE
PO Box 634
Tel: (067372) 13 244
Fax: (067372) 13

Swakopmund
ALTE BRÜCKE
PO Box 3360
Tel: (0641) 4918
Fax: (0641) 4918

HAUS GARNISON
PO Box 1228
Tel: (0641) 5246

Tsumeb
Municipality
PO Box 275
Tel: (0641) 21056
Fax: (0671) 21464

Usakos
AMEIB RANCH
PO Box 266
Tel: (062242) 1111

Walvis Bay
Municipality
PO Box 86
Tel: (0642) 5981

LANGSTRAND
PO Box 86
Tel: (0642) 5981

ESPLANADE PARK
Private Bag 5017
Tel: (0642) 6145
Fax: (0642) 452

Media Directory

Magazines

Agri Forum
Private Bag 13255
Windhoek
Tel: 37838
Fax: 220193

CNN Messenger
PO Box 41
Windhoek
Tel: 217621
Fax: 62786

Flamingo
PO Box 39143
Bramley 2018
South Africa
Tel: (011)-4633350
Fax: (011)-4633091

Monitor
PO Box 2196
Windhoek
Tel: 34141
Fax: 229242

Namibia Brief
PO Box 2123
Windhoek
Tel: 37250
Fax: 37251

Newspapers

Abacus
PO Box 22791
Windhoek
Tel: 35596
Fax: 36467

Action
PO Box 20500
Windhoek
Tel: 62957
Fax: 216375

Die Republikien
PO Box 3436
Windhoek
Tel: 33111
Fax: 35674

Namibia Economist/ Ekonoom
PO Box 49
Windhoek
Tel: 221925
Fax: 220615

Namibia Press Association (NAMPA)
PO Box 61354
Windhoek
Tel: 221711
Fax: 221713

Namibia Today
PO Box 24669
Windhoek
Tel: 225436
Fax: 31484

Namib Times
PO Box 706
Walvis Bay
Tel: (0642)-5854
Fax: (0642)-4813

New Era
Private Bag: 13364
Windhoek
Tel: 34924
Fax: 224937

Tempo
PO Box 1794
Windhoek
Tel: 225822
Fax: 223110

The Namibian
PO Box 20783
Windhoek
Tel: 36970
Fax: 33980

The Namibian Worker
PO Box 61208
Windhoek
Tel: 216186
Fax: 216816

The Windhoek Advertiser
PO Box 2255
Windhoek
Tel: 221737
Fax: 226098

Radio

Namibian Broadcasting Corporation (NBC)
PO Box 321
Windhoek
Tel: 215811
Fax: 217206

Television

Namibian Broadcasting Corporation (NBC)
PO Box 321
Windhoek
Tel: 215811
Fax: 217206

Museums

Helmeringhausen Museum
PO Box 85
Bethanien

Altes Fort Museum
PO Box 22
Groofontein

Keetmanshoop Museum
Post Bag 2125
Keetmanshoop

Kolmanskop Elizabeth Bay & Sperrgebiet Museums
PO Box 45
Lüderitz

Lüderitz Museum
PO Box 512
Lüderitz

Okahandja Fort
Private Bag 13186
Windhoek

Rhenish Mission House Museum
PO Box 14
Omaruru

Otjiwarongo Museum
Private Bag 2208
Otjiwarongo

Outjo Museum
PO Box 171
Outjo

Rehoboth Museum
Private Bag 1017
Rehoboth

Kavango Museum
Ministry of Education & Culture
Rundu

Swakopmund Museum
PO Box 361
Swakopmund

Swakopmund Military Museum
PO Box 678
Swakopmund

Tsumeb Museum
PO Box 5
Tsumeb

Walvis Bay Museum
PO Box 86
Walvis Bay

Namibian Scientific Society
PO Box 67
Windhoek

Namibian Arts Association
PO Box 458
Windhoek

State Museum of Namibia
PO Box 1203
Windhoek

Transnamib Museum
Private Bag 13204
Windhoek

Taxis

Windhoek
Taxi
Kaiser Street
Independence Avenue
Tel: (061) 3 7966

Windhoek Radio Taxis (PTY) Ltd
Independence Avenue
Tel: (061) 3 7070

Namibia Radio Taxi
David Bezuidenhout Drive, PO Box 10706
Khomasdal
Tel: (061) 21 1116/22 5222

Travel Consultants

Windhoek
African Extravaganza
PO Box 22028
Tel: (061 63086/7/8
Fax: (061) 215356
Telex: (0908) 802

Azur Travel Consultant
PO Box 11020
Tel: (061) 228427
Fax: (061) 221647
Telex: (0908) 400
AZUR

Encounter Namibia
PO Box 23066
Tel: (061) 228474
Fax: (061) 34017
Telex: (0908) 721 ENNAM

The Namib Travel Shop
PO Box 6850
Tel: (061) 226174/225178
Fax: (061) 33332
Telex: (0908) 614

Top Travel Information
PO Box 80205
Tel: (061) 51975
Fax: (061) 51975

Tour Operators

Windhoek
Africa Adventure Safaris
PO Box 20274
Tel: (061) 34720
Fax: (061) 227665

Bushland Safaris
PO Box 11880
Tel: (061) 33977/32507
Fax: (061) 225003

Ermo Safaris
PO Box 80205
Tel: (061) 51975
Fax: (061) 51975

Kaokohimba Safaris
PO Box 11580
Tel: (061) 222378
Fax: (061) 222378

Namib Wilderness Safaris
PO Box 6850
Tel: (061) 221281/220947
Fax: (061) 239455
Telex: (0908) 614

Ongwe Safaris
PO Box 6088
Tel: (061) 230869
Fax: (061) 230797

Ondese Travel
PO Box 6196
Tel: (061) 220876

Oryx Tours of Namibia
PO Box 2058
Tel: (061) 217454/217480
Fax: (061) 63417
Telex: (0908) 877

Otjimburu Trails
PO Box 5144
Tel: (061) 32738
Fax: (061) 228461

Safaris Unlimited
PO Box 6013
Tel: (061) 64521/51975
Fax: (061) 51975

Skeleton Coast Fly-in Safaris
PO Box 2195
Tel: (061) 224248
Fax: (061) 225713

Sun Safaris
PO Box 80226
Tel: (061) 230287

SWA Safaris & Southern Cross Safaris
PO Box 20373
Tel: (061) 37567
Fax: (061) 225387
Telex: (0908) 649

Toko Safaris
PO Box 5017
Tel: (061) 225539
Fax: (061) 222319

Trans Namib Tours
PO Box 415
Tel: (061) 298-2388/9, 221549
Fax: (061) 298-2033
Telex: (0908) 3034

Windhoek City Tours & Hiking
PO Box 80205
Tel: (061) 51975
Fax: (061) 51975

Gobabis
Owingi Adventure Safaris
Private Bag 2245
Tel: (0688) 17330

Lüderitz
Lüderitz Safaris and Tours
PO Box 76
Tel: (06331) 2719/2622
Fax: (06331) 2863

Maltahöhe
Namib Sky Adventure Safaris (PTY) Ltd
PO Box 197
Tel: (06632) 5703

Namutoni
Etosha Fly-in Safaris
PO Namutoni via Tsumeb
Tel: (0671) 21199
Telex: (0908) 3550

Outjo
Rafidim Safaris
PO Box 231
Tel: (06542) 4312

Swakopmund
Charly's Desert Tours
PO Box 1400
Tel: (0641) 4341
Fax: (0641) 4341

Desert Adventure Safaris
PO Box 339
Tel: (0641) 4459/2027
Fax: (0641) 4664

Historical Sight-seeing Tours
PO Box 871
Tel: (0641) 61647

See Africa Tours
PO Box 4123
Tel: (0641) 4311
Fax: (0641) 4203

Walvis Bay
Gloriosa Safaris
PO Box 212
Tel: (0642) 6300
Fax: (0642) 2455

Hunting

Namibia Professional Hunting Association
PO Box 11291, Windhoek
Tel: (061) 34455
Fax: (061) 222567

Camping Equipment

Gav's Camping Hire
PO Box 24074, Windhoek
Tel: (061) 38745
Fax: (061) 38745

Bibliography

A Guide to Namibian Game Parks (1993), by Willie and Sandra Olivier, published by Longman Namibia (Pty) Ltd, Windhoek.

Deserts, Paths and Elephants: Travel Guide Southwest Africa Namibia (1986), by Michael Iwanowski, published by V & S Verlag Johanna Iwanowski, Dormagen.

Economic Development Strategies for Independent Namibia (1985), based on the work of Harbans S. Aulakh and Wilfred W. Asombang, published by United Nations Institute for Namibia, Lusaka.

Guide to Southern African Game & Nature Reserves (1989; 2nd edition), by Chris and Tilde Stuart, published by Struik Publishers (Pty) Ltd, Cape Town.

Guide to Namibia & Botswana (1991), by Chris McIntyre and Simon Atkins, published by Bradt Publications, Chalfont St Peter.

Independent Namibia: Succession to Treaty Rights & Obligations (1989), based on the work of Julio Faundez, published by the United Nations Institute for Namibia, Lusaka.

Insight Guides: Namibia (1993), by Dr Beatrice Sandelowsky, Dr Hans Jenny and Eberhard Hofmann, published by APA Publications (HK) Ltd, Singapore.

Journey Through Namibia (1994), by Mohamed Amin, Duncan Willetts and Tahir Shah, published by Camerapix Ltd, Nairobi.

Kaokoveld — The Last Wilderness (1988), by Anthony Hall-Martin, Clive Walker and J. du P. Bothma, published by Southern Book Publishers (Pty) Ltd, Johannesburg.

Karakul the Industry: Policy Options for Independent Namibia (1989), based on the work of L. Neubert, published by United Nations Institute for Namibia, Lusaka.

The Mammals of the Southern African Subregion (1983; 2nd edition), by J. D. Skinner and R. H. N. Smithers, published by University of Pretoria, Pretoria.

Namib (1991), by David Coulson, published by Sidgwick & Jackson, London.

Namibia in History (1988), by Nangolo Mbumba and Norbert H. Noisser, published by Zed books Ltd, London.

The Namib — A Shell Guide (1987), by Dr. Mary Seely, published by Shell Namibia Ltd, Windhoek.

Namibia The Struggle for Liberation (1983), by Alfred T. Moleah, published by Disa Press, Inc., Wilmington.

National Atlas of South West Africa (1983), edited by J. H. van der Merwe, University of Stellenbosch, Stellenbosch.

Rocks, Minerals and Gemstones of Southern Africa — A Collector's Guide (1976; softback edition), by E. K. Macintosh, published by Struik Publishers (Pty) Ltd, Cape Town.

Skeleton Coast (1984), by Amy Schoeman, published by Macmillan South Africa (Publishers) (Pty) Ltd, Johannesburg, (Reprinted).

Snakes — A Struik Pocket Guide for Southern Africa (1986), by Rod Patterson and Penny Meakin, published by Struik Publishers (Pty) Ltd, Cape Town.

Snakes of South West Africa (1980), by P. J. Buys and P. J. C. Buys, published by Gamsberg Publishers, Windhoek.

Southern African Spiders — An Identification Guide (1991), by Martin R. Filmer, published by Struik Publishers (Pty) Ltd, Cape Town.

Southern, Central and East African Mammals A Photographic Guide (1992), by Chris and Tilde Stuart, published by Struik Publishers, Cape Town.

Southern African Travel Guide (1971; 23rd edition), published by Promco (Pty) Limited, Cape Town.

This is Namibia (1992), by Gerald Cubitt and Peter Joyce, published by Struik Publishers (Pty) Ltd, Cape Town.

To Be Born a Nation — The Liberation Struggle for Namibia (1981), by the Department of Information and Publicity, SWAPO of Namibia, published by Zed Press, London.

Top Birding Spots in Southern Africa (1992), compiled by Hugh Chittenden, published by Southern Book Publishers (Pty) Ltd, Johannesburg.

Walvis Bay (1984), by Richard Moorsom, published by the International Defence and Air Fund for Southern Africa in co-operation with the United Nations Council for Namibia, London.

Waterberg Flora Footpaths in and Around the Camp (1989), by Patricia Craven and Christine Marais, published by Gamsberg Publishers, Windhoek.

Zimbabwe, Botswana & Namibia — a travel survival kit (1992), by Deanna Swaney and Myra Shackley, published by Lonely Planet Publications, Hawthorn.

All photographs taken by Mohamed Amin and Duncan Willetts except the following:-

Debbie Gaiger 151 (bottom), 195, 196, 197

Dennis Rundle 217

Amy Schoeman 147, 148, 169, 171, 174, 176 (top)

Ministry of Information 51 (bottom), 296 (top)

John Reader 71, 72

Mani Goldbeck 99, 301 (bottom)

Mike Griffen 177, 284

INDEX

(Illustrations are indicated in bold.)

A

Aardwolf 186, 271, 330
Aba-Huab River Valley 188
Acacia 146, **154**, 157, 201, 292
Acacia, flame 146
Accommodation 26, 351-353 see also Caravan Parks, Guest Farms, Rest Camps
Adder, puff **220**
Adder, side-winding 118, **177**, 177
African Improvement Society 44
African National Congress (ANC) 44, 47
Afrikaners 43
Afrikaner, Jager 36
Afrikaner, Jan Jonker 36, 38, 251
Afrikaner, Jonker 36, 137, 138, 228
Agate Mountain 170
Agriculture 305, 306
Ai-Ais Hot Springs 23, 75, 77, 78, 79, 80, 295
Aigamas Farm 155
Air Charter 344
Air Namibia 18, 20, **26**, 83, 308
Airlines 344
Albatross 286
Albatross Island 73
Albrecht, Abraham 38
Albrecht, Christian 38
Alexander Bay 71
Alexander, Captain James 120, 228, 233, 255, 284
Alte Feste Museum **45**, 154, 234
Ameib Guest Ranch 140, 301
Amethysts, mining of 170
Amphibians, checklist of 329
Andara 215, 218
Andersson, Charles John 34, 135, 138-139, 147, 153, 196, 199
Angling see Fishing
Anglo-Boer War 153
Angola 49, 52, 54, 211, 214
Anibib Guest Farm 140, 301
Animal checklist 327-329
Antelope, roan see Roan
Antelope, sable see Sable
Apartheid 43, 44
Appleleaf, Kalahari 146
Arandis 130
Arbeid Adelt Valley 111
Art Galleries 344
Art, Namibian **239**
Art, prehistoric **31**, 36, 58, 140, 141, **147**, 184-185, **186**, 186, 187, 189, 190, **191**, 300-301, **301**
Athletics 295
Atlantic Ocean 30, 32, 56, 70, 93, 118, 126, 158, 164, 179, 241, 244, 255, **259**, 264
Atlantic Pride 178
Auas Mountains 135
Augeigas River 133
Augrabies-Steenbok Nature Reserve 80-81
Auob River 101
Aus **84-85**, 87, 88
Avis Dam 238
Avocet 175
Ayre, Chris 180

B

Babbler, white-rumped 219
Baboon, chacma 78, 81, 108, 133, 136, 146, 175, 219, 277, 331
Badger, honey 282-283, 330
Bagani 218, 220
Baines, Thomas 294
Banks 314, 344-345
Bantu 21, 36
Baobab tree 156, **223**
Barbel 80, 104, 133, 136, 295
Barbet, black-collared 339
Barbet, crested 339
Barbet, pied 225, 339
Baskets **221**
Bass, black 133
Bass, large-mouth 136, 295
Bass, small-mouth 295
Basters 23, 37, 62, **65**, 106
Bat, Egyptian fruit 285
Bat, epauletted fruit 285
Bat, free-tailed 285
Bat, fruit 285, **285**
Bat, horseshoe 285
Bat, leaf-nosed 285
Bat, sheath-tailed 285
Bat, slit-faced 285
Bat, trident 285
Bat, vesper 285
Bauhinia, white 146
Bause, Albert 259
Bause, Heinrich 259
Baynes Mountain 195
Bee-eater, carmine **217**, 286
Bee-eater, European 108, 288, 338
Bee-eater, olive 338-339
Bee-eater, swallow-tailed 339
Bee-eater, white-fronted 225
Beer 303
Beetle, tenebrionid 118, 177, **179**
Beetle, white 178
Benguela Current 162, 172, 176, 251
Bergdama see Damara
Bethanie 87, 96, 342
Bibliography 356-357
Biltong **302**
Bird checklist 332-336
Birdlife 78, 104-105, 108, 129-130, 133, 147, 148, 165, 179, 186, **208**, 208-209, **211**, **217**, 219, 222, 224-225, 238, **248-249**, **252**, 253-254, **262**, 286-290, **287**, **288**, **289**, 290
Birdlife profile 336-340
Black Nossob River 107
Black Rock Island 73
Blacktail 165, 177
Blesbok 331
Boat charter 345
Bobabis 107
Boers 37, 38

Bogenfels rock 72
Bokmakierie 78, 108, 175
Bondelswarts 43
Bosua Pass 132, 133
Botha, General Louis 42, 75, 149
Botha, Roelof (Pik) 52
Botswana 214
Bottlenose, western 225
Boubou, swamp 219, 222
Brackbush 173
Brandberg Mountain 58, 161, 181, **182-183**, 184, 185, 186, 190, 295, 301, 318-319
Brandberg, White Lady of the 30, 58, 184-185, 301
Brandt, Hermann 103
Breuil, Abbé Henri 185
British, the 37, 38, 39, 216, 240, 251, 255
Brits, Jacobus 150
Britz, Superintendent 217
Brukkaros volcano 98, **99**, 99, 100
Buffalo, Cape 146, 219, 222, 265, 267, 298
Bulbul, black-eyed 339
Bulbul, red-eyed 78, 175, 186, 339
Bulbul, terrestrial 339
Burnt Mountain 180, 187, 190, 191, 192, 318
Bus companies 345
Buses 20
Bush baby, lesser 148, 277, 331
Bush, brittle **293**
Bush, coffee 146
Bush, cork 146
Bush, dollar 173, 291
Bush, lavendar 146
Bush, Nama 173, **176**
Bush, salt 291
Bush, wild camphor 133
Bushbuck 281, 331
Bushman's candle 173
Bushman's Paradise 184
Bushmanland 292
Bushmen see San Bushmen
Bushpig 222, 281, 282
Bushwillow, red 133, 136, 146
Bushwillow, silver 146
Business 305-311
Business associations 345-346
Business hours 314
Business, getting started in 310
Bustard 108, 176, **211**, 286, 337-338
Bustard, kori **211**, 286, 337-338
Bustard, Ludwig's 108, 176, 338
Bustard, Stanley 338
Butterfly **104**
Buxton, Lord 149
Buzzard, augur 108
Buzzard, honey 337
Buzzard, jackal 286, 337

C

Camels **120**, **121**, 130

Camping 26
Camping equipment 355
Cão, Diego 30, 33, 34, 158, 161, 167
Cape Cross **8-9**, 158, 161, **162**, **163**, **164**, 165, 166, 167, 276
Cape Cross Seal Reserve 165, 166, 319
Cape Frio 170, **174**, 176
Cape of Good Hope 37
Caprivi Game Reserve 214, 218, 220, 221, 319
Caprivi Strip **12-13**, 17, **24**, 26, 30, 32, 47, 56, 63, 146, 156, **198**, 211, 214, 215, 216, 217, 218, 221, 222, 223, **223**, 224, **224**, **225**, 264, 267, 279, 281, 286; map of **214-215**
Caprivian, East 62, 63
Car hire 313, 346
Caracal 147, 175, 267, 270, 298, 330
Caravan Parks 353
Carp 80, 104, 136, 295
Carp Cliff viewpoint 126
Cat, black-footed 267, 271
Cat, small-spotted 267, 271
Catfish, cave 155
Central Bank 310
Central Escarpment 17
Chat, familiar 339
Chat, Herero 108, 186
Chat, mountain 78, 108, 175, 186, 339
Chat, red-tailed 339
Chat, sickle-winged 78
Chat, tractrac 339
Cheetah 143, 146, 162, **204**, 206, **263**, 267, 268, 270, 298, 330
Choate, Tom 146
Chobe River 211, 222
Chovuma Falls 214
Christuskirche **38**, 233
Church on the Rock **258**, 259, **261**
Cisticola, chirping 219
Cisticola, fan-tailed 104
Civet 272
Clay, Crispin 83
Climate 23, 313-314
Clothing 24 see also Dress, traditional
Clubs 315, 346
Cob 165, 177
Coetse, Jacobus 38
Colonialism 37, 39, 42, 43
Commiphora tree 173
Communications 314-315
Companies, registration of 310
Conservation and Research, Directorate of 105, 170, 317
Consolidated Diamond Mines (CDM) 43, 70, 72, 73, 92, 258
Cook, Edward 74
Coot, red-knobbed 105, 175
Copalwood 157
Copper, mining of 135, 149, 150, 153, 307
Cormorant 105, 176, 179, 286, 336
Cormorant, bank 286

358

Cormorant, Cape 176, 179, 286, 336
Cormorant, crowned 286
Cormorant, reed 105, 336
Cormorant, white-breasted 105, 179
Coucal, Burchell's 338
Coucal, coppery-tailed 219
Coucal, Senegal 338
Courser, double-banded 338
Courser, three-banded 338
Crab, ghost 176, **179**
Crafts **82, 221,** 232, 238
Crake, Baillon's 337
Crake, black 337
Crake, striped 337
Crane, blue 337
Crane, crowned 337
Crane, wattled 222, 337
Crater Hills 105
Crayfish 260
Credit cards 314
Cricket, dune 118
Crocodile 196, 219, 222, 224, 267, **269,** 298
Crow 165
Crow, pied 176
Cuckoo 108, 209, 286, 287, 338
Cuckoo, African 338
Cuckoo, black 108, 287
Cuckoo, Didric 108
Cuckoo, Klaas's 209
Cuckoo, red-chested 287
Curlew 253
Curoca River 178
Currency 314
Currency regulations 314
Customs 313

D
Daan Viljoen Game Reserve 133, 288, 295, 319-320
Dabchick 130
Damara **16,** 36, 62, 63, 107, 147, 149, **189,** 189
Damara and Namaqua Trading Company 242
Damaraland 56, **58,** 164, 180, 181, **184,** 187, 192, 264, 291, 292
Damaraland Wilderness Reserve 191
Damaraland-Kaokoland Desert Project 180
Darter 105, 336
Dassie, rock 78, 108, 133, 147, 148, 186, 283, 330
Dassie, tree 283-284
De Cuellar, Dr Javier Perez 55
De la Bat, Bernabé 146
De Pass, Spence and Company 128
Democratic Turnhalle Alliance (DTA) 51, 52, 53, 54, 137
Demographic Profile 341-342
"Desert rose" 92, **129**
Deutsche Diamanten Gesellschaft 42
Diamond Area One 88, 92
Diamonds, mining of 42, 59, 70, 71, **72,** 72, 73, 89, 91, 170,

255, 305
Diaz Point **93,** 96
Diaz, Bartholomeo 30, 251, 255
Die Kaserne 325
Die Valle Waterfall 111
Dik-dik 143, 147, 205, 206, 278, 298, 331
Dik-dik, Damara 143, 205, 206, **274,** 278, 331
Dikkop, spotted 338
Dikkop, water 338
Dinosaurs 143, 149
Diplomatic Missions, foreign 347-349
Dog, wild 148, 156, 157, 219-220, 222, 273-274
Dolphin 257, 276, 277
Dolphin, common 277
Dom João II, King 161
Doros Crater 192
Doros Crater concession area 192
Dorsland Trekkers 150, 195
Dove, Cape turtle 338
Dove, emerald-spotted 338
Dove, green-spotted 225
Dove, laughing 338
Dove, mourning 338
Drakensberg Mountains 71
Dress, traditional **16, 32,** 32, 54, **63,** 64, **235**
Driving 19, 313
Drongo, fork-tailed 225, 339
Duck, knob-billed 289
Duiker 146, 148, 206, 228, 278, 297, 331
Duiker, blue 278
Duiker, bush 278, 331
Duiker, common 148, 206, 278, 331
Duiker, grey 278
Duiker, red 278
Duminy, Captain 251, 255
Dunedin Star 163
Durban Light Infantry, Second 131
Düsternbrook Farm 135, 268
Dutch Reformed Church **102,** 103
Dutch, the 37, 255
Duwisib Castle **97,** 97-98, 324

E
Eagle, African fish 55, 105, 222, 224, 337
Eagle, bateleur 290
Eagle, black 108, 148
Eagle, booted 148
Eagle, martial **262,** 337
Eagle, Pel's fishing 222
Eagle, steppe 290
Eagle, tawny 290
Eagle, Wahlberg's 209
Eagle, western-banded snake 219, 337
Eastern National Water Carrier Scheme 308
Eberlanz, Friedrich 260
Economy 305-309
Egret, black 337
Egret, cattle 337
Egret, little 289, 337
Egret, slaty 222

Eidelweiss, desert **173**
Ekuma River 203, 209
Ekuma River Delta 209
Eland 104, 107, 133, 136, 141, 143, 146, 157, 206, 208, 228, 279, 331
Elders' Council 48
Elephant 143, 156, 157, 162, **169,** 175, 180, 191, 192, 195, 205, **207,** 219, 222, **224, 225,** 225, 264-265, **266,** 298, 330
Elephant Commission of 1956 199
Elephant's foot 173
Energy 315
Epako 141
Epupa Falls 195
Epupa Hydroelectrical Scheme 308
Eriksson, Alex 141
Erongo Mountains **57,** 140, 158, 164, 181, 264, 317
Eros 58
Eros Regional Airport 19, 20
Etemba Cave 140
Etemba Guest Farm 140
Etjo Formation 148-149
Etorocha Mountains 194
Etosha Ecological Institute 201, 206, 208, 278
Etosha National Park 18, **24,** 24, 30, 32, 56, 143, 150, 154, 199-211, **201, 202, 203, 204, 206, 207, 208, 209, 210, 212-213,** 264, 265, **266,** 267, 268, 278, 316, 320; map of **200**
Etosha Pan 56, 58-59, 199, 208, 286
Euphorbia **58,** 173, 291
Europeans 64, **65**
Evangelical Lutheran Church 41, 44, 96, 233, 258, **258,** 259, **261**
Exchange control 310
Export Processing Zone (EPZ) 307, 309

F
Falcon 108, 286, 337
Falcon, African hobby 337
Falcon, lanner 108, 337
Falcon, peregrine 337
Falcon, pygmy 286
Federation of Namibian Tourist Associations (FENATA) 307, 316
Fenchel, Reverend Thomas 81
Fern, adder's tongue 341
Fern, Waterberg 146
Finance 310
Financial Rand System 310
Finfoot 219
Finger of God *see* Vingerklip
Finnish Missionary Society 38, 44
Fischer's Pan 209
Fischer, Lieutenant 210
Fish 80, 104, 105, 133, 136, 154, 155, 165, 177, 196, 214, 225, 295
Fish River **29,** 74, 78, 87, 103, 105, 118, 295
Fish River Canyon **14-15,** 17,

23, 30, 58, 75, **77,** 77-78, 80, **86,** 87, 268, 295, 317
Fish River Canyon Conservation Area, map of **76**
Fishing 80, 104, 133, 136, 165, 177, 250, 251, 295, 306
Fisons Albatross Fertilisers 128
Flamboyant 150
Flame tree **232**
Flamingo **128,** 129, 208-209, **248-249, 252,** 253, 287-288, 337
Flamingo, greater 96, 129, 176, 208-209, 253, 288, 337
Flamingo, lesser 129, 176, 208-209, 253, 287-288, 337
Flights, international 312
Flora **58,** 70, 78-79, **104,** 108, 115, 117-118, **122-123,** 125, **127,** 127, 130, 133, 136, 146, 150, **151, 154,** 156, 173, **173,** 175, **176,** 203, 205, **232, 233,** 260, 291-294, **292, 293,** 340-341
Flycatcher, black 339
Flycatcher, fairy 339
Flycatcher, Marico 339
Flycatcher, pallid 147
Flycatcher, paradise 286
Food 302-303, **302, 303**
Forbidden Coast 70, 72, 73, 286
Foreign representation and consuls 347
Four Finger Rock 79, 80
Fox, bat-eared **273,** 273, 30
Fox, Cape 273, 330
Francolin, Hartlaub's 147, 286
Francolin, red-billed 133
Franke House 144
Franke Tower 141, **142**
Franke, Captain Victor 141, 144, 149
Fredericks, Captain Joseph 96, 255
Fredericks, Frankie 295
Fresh Water Fish Institute 105
Fruit 301-302

G
Gaap River 78
Gai-Ais fountain 192
Galago, lesser *see* Bush baby, lesser
Galjoen 165, 177
Gallinule, purple 78
Galton, Sir Francis 147, 153, 199
Game Ranches 316
Game Reserves 316-324
Gamsberg 132-133
Gamsberg Pass 125, 126, 132-133
Ganna 173
Gannet, Cape 286
Gariganus Farm 87
Garnets, mining of 170
Garvey, Marcus 44
Gathemann, Heinrich 233
Gaub River 125
Gazetteer 342-343
Gecko, web-footed 118

359

Geelbek 165
Gellap Ost Karakul Farm 83
Gemsbok 81, 104, 107, 108, 111, 130, 133, 139, 143, 146, 157, 162, 163, 175, 178, 186, 191, 192, 195, 205, 208, 219, 281, 331
Gemsbokvlakte plains 208
Genet 175, 272, 330
Genet, large spotted 272
Genet, small spotted 272, 330
Geography 56-61
Geology 59, 148-149
German Lutheran Church 228
German Missionary Society 81
German South West Africa 39, 43, **45**, 138
Germans, the 17, 34, **35**, **37**, 38, 39, 41, 42, 43, 75, 87, 88, 96, 99, 100, 101, 103, 106, 128, 131, 138, 141, **144**, 144, 147, 149, 150, 154, 210, 216, 240
Giant's Playground 68, **75**, 87
Gibeon 100, 101, 141
Gibeon Meteorite Shower, the 101, 233
Giraffe **Half title**, 141, 143, 146, 156, 162, 175, 192, 195, 205, 206, **206**, 220, 267, 298, 331
Go-away bird *see* Lourie, grey
Goageb 87
Gobabis 155, 342
Gochas 101
Goerke, Hans 258
Goose, Egyptian 78, 105, 175, 337
Goose, spurwinged 337
Gorbachev, Mikael 53
Goreangab Dam 238, 295
Göring, Dr Heinrich 138
Goshawk, pale chanting **287**
Government 314
Grasplatz 42, **92**
Grass, Bushman 78
Great Escarpment 126
Grebe, blackened 253
Green, Lawrence G 34, 161
Greenshank 338
Griess, Professor A 185
Griffith Bay 96
Grootfontein 32, 149, 150, 154, 342
Grootfontein Museum 325
Gross Barmen 137
Gross Barmen resort 138, **139**, 320
Gross Nabas Farm 103
Gross Otabi 149
Grosse Bucht 96
Grosse Dom Ravine 190
Grünau 74, 80
Guano 167, 255
Guano Bay 96
Guano Platform **250**
Guest Farms 316, 349-351
Guest Farms, hunters 351
Guest Farms, tourist 349-351
Guinea fowl, helmeted 133
Gull 104, 165, 176, 253, 286, 338

Gull, Cape 176
Gull, grey-headed 253, 338
Gull, Hartlaub's 253
Gull, kelp 104, 165, 253, 338
Gymnogene 209, 337

H
Hahn, Carl Hugo **35**, 136, 138
Hainabis 81
Halbich, Eduard 139
Halifax Island 73, 96, 257
Hammerkop 78, 337
Hardap Dam 103, **105**, 295
Hardap Game Reserve 104, 320-321
Hardap Recreation Resort 105, 295
Hare, Cape 175, 283, 331
Hare, scrub 283, 331
Hare, spring 283
Harrier, African marsh 337
Harrier, black 286
Harrier, Montagu's 209
Hartebeest 104, 133, 141, 143, 146, 157, 206, 278, 297, 331
Hartebeest, Coke's 278
Hartebeest, Jackson's 278
Hartebeest, red 104, 133, 141, 143, 146, 157, 206, 278, 331
Hartebeest, Swayne's 278
Hartebeest, Tora 278
Hartebeest, Western 278
Hartmann Mountains 196
Hartmann, Dr George 161
Haruchas Farm 101
Haunted Forest 205
Hawk 337
Health 25, 312
Hedgehog, South African 284-285
Hell's Bend 79
Helmeringhausen 97
Helmeringhausen Farmers' Association 97
Helmeringhausen Museum 325
Henties Bay 165, 166, 187
Herero **16**, 23, **32**, 32, 36, 37, 38, 39, 41, 42, 43, 51, **54**, 62, 63, **63**, 64, 75, 107, 128, 136, 137, 138, 139, 141, 143, 147, 199, 228, **235**
Herero Uprising of 1904 210
Heritage Sites 317
Hermann, Ernst 106
Herodotus 30, 33
Heron, black-headed 289
Heron, goliath 104, 336
Heron, green-backed 104, 133
Heron, grey 78, 336
Heron, purple 336-337
Heusis River Valley 135
Highland Savanna Veld 133
Hiking 80, 110-111, 178, 295-296
Himba 64, 162, 170, 193
Hippopotamus **12-13**, 219, 220, 222, 223, 224, **266**, 267, 298, 330
History 30-55, **31**, **32**, **33**, **35**, **36**, **37**, **38**, **39**, **40**, **41**, **42**, **46**, **50**, **51**
Hoanib River 165, 175, 177,
180, 192, 195, 199
Hoarusib Canyon 170, 172
Hoarusib River 114, 164, 175, 194, **195**, 195, 199
Hoba Meteorite 32, 150
Hobatere Game Park 192
Höft, Friedrich 242
Hohenzoller Mountain **86**
Holidays, public 343
Home Affairs, Ministry of 310
Hoopoe, African 339
Hoopoe, red-billed 288
Hop, Hendrik 38, 81
Hornbill, Bradfield's 147, 222
Hornbill, crowned 339
Hornbill, grey 339
Hornbill, ground **289**
Hornbill, Monteiro's 108, 133, 148
Hornbill, red-billed 288
Hornbill, trumpeter 339
Hornbill, yellow-billed 288, **289**
Horses, wild desert **84-85**, 89
Hotel Organisation of Namibia 307
Hottentot Memorial 228
Hottentots 66, 228, 255
House, H-shaped 237
Huab River 175, 178, 179
Humphries, Jayta 98
Huns Mountains 36, 75
Hunsberge Mountains **29**
Hunt, William Leonard 155
Hunting 297-299, **297**, 316, 355
Hunting dog, Cape 147
Hunting Ranches 316
Hunting Safaris 317
Hyena 127, 130, 146, 157, 165, 175, 176, 179, 191, 206, **210**, 222, 271-272, 330
Hyena, brown 127, 130, 146, 165, 166, 176, 178, 179, 206, 271, 272, 330
Hyena, spotted 127, 157, 206, 222, 271, 272, 330
Hyrax, rock *see* Dassie, rock

I
Ibenstein Farm 107
Ibis, glossy 337
Ibis, sacred 337
Ichaboe Island 73
Immigration regulations 312
Immigration Selection Board 310
Impala 141, 146, 192, 205, 219, 278, 297, 331
Impala, black-faced 141, 192, 205, 278, 297
Impala, southern 297
Import/export controls 310
Independence **50**, 55
Industrial and Commercial Workers Union (ICU) 44
Industry 307-308
Insects 118, 177, 178, 179
International Court of Justice (ICJ) 44, 47, 48
International Monetary Fund 305
Investment 309-311

Investment Centre 310
Investment incentives 309-310
Investment, foreign 309
Ipumbu, Chief 44

J
J G Strijdom Airport 238
Jacana, African 338
Jacana, lesser 338
Jacaranda 150, **233**
Jackal 127, 130, 147, 148, 157, 165, 166, 176, 179, 186, 191, 206, **269**, 274, 330
Jackal, black-backed 127, 130, 147, 157, 165, 166, 176, 179, 186, 206, 274, 330
Jackal, side-striped 148, 157, 274, 330
Jacobs, Erasmus 71
James, Christopher 153
Jochmann Shelter 185
Jochmann, Hugo 185
John II, King 30, 34, 158
Jones, Captain R 71

K
Kahitjenne, Chief 138
Kalahari Desert 32, 33, 42, 56, 59, 155, 156, **208**, 218, 264, 268, 270, 272, 286, 291, 292
Kalkfeld 141
Kamanjab 192, 193
Kambazembi, Chief 143
Kaoko Otavi 195
Kaokoland 164, 180, 193, 194, 195, 210, 264, 268, 291, 292; map of **159**
Kaokolander 62
Kaokoveld 36, 52, 64, 67, 158, 161, 180, 199
Kapuuo, Chief Clemens 51, 137
Karakul Carpet Weaving Centre 107
Karakuwisa 201
Karanab 135
Karas Mountains 74
Karasburg 74, 75, 342
Karibib 138, 141, 180, 342
Karoo (bird) 286
Karoo 291
Karree 133
Karstveld 154
Kartoffel River 184
Katima Mulilo 216, 217, 218, **221**, 222, 223, **223**, 224, 225, 342
Katutura 45
Kaudom Game Reserve 156-157, **157**, 214, 321; map of **214-215**
Kavango (people) 48, 62, 64, 66, 214, 215, 216, **219**
Kavango 49, 52, 56, 67, 264
Keetman, Johan 81
Keetmanshoop 38, **68**, 70, 74, **75**, **79**, **80**, 81, 83, 185, 255, 257, 342
Keetmanshoop museum 81, 83
Keetsmanshoop Airport 80
Kerina, Mburumba 47
Kestrel, greater 337

360

Kestrel, rock 78
Kestrel, rock 337
Khan River 140
Khoikhoi 36, 63, 66, 99, 103, 106, 107, 128, 147, 193
Khoisan 21
Khomas Hochland 58, 126, 132, 133, 268
Khorab 149
Khorab Treaty 149
Khorixas 32, **69**, **187**, 187, 188
Khumib River 161, 175
Kingfisher, giant 338
Kingfisher, grey-headed 338
Kingfisher, greyhooded 209
Kingfisher, half-collared 225
Kingfisher, malachite 286
Kingfisher, mangrove 286
Kingfisher, pied 338
Kingfisher, pygmy 286
Kite, black-shouldered 290, 337
Kite, yellow-billed 289-290, 337
Klein Spitzkoppe 181
Kleinschmidt, Heinrich 106, 136, 138
Kleynstuber, Udo 146
Klipspringer 78, 81, **86**, 108, 133, 147, 186, 278, **279**, 298, 331
Knot 254
Knudsen, Reverend Hans 96
Koch und Schultheiss Dam 133
Koichab River 175
Koigab River 178
Koigab Valley 178
Kokerboom Forest see Quiver Tree Forest
Kokerboom tree see Quiver tree
Kolbe, Friedrich 136
Kolman, Jani 91
Kolmanskop 71, **88**, **89**, **90**, 91, 92
Kolmanskop Outdoor Museum 326
Kololo 216
Kombat 149
Kombat Mine 149
Kongola 221
Königstein 58, 295-296
Konkiep River 97
Korhaan, Rüppell's 176, 286
Korn, Hermann 127
Kramer, Friedrich 257, 258
Kreplin, Emil 257
Krone Canyon 192
Kudu Memorial 236
Kudu, greater 78, 103, 104, 107, 108, 133, 136, 139, 143, 146, 156, 157, 192, 195, **205**, 206, 219, 220, 222, 228, **270**, 279, 297, 331
Kuhlmann, August **33**
Kuhlmann, Elizabeth **33**
Kuiseb Canyon 126, 127
Kuiseb Pass 125, 127
Kuiseb River 114, 117, 120, 125, 126, 127, 129, 251, 284
Kuiseb Valley 126, 251
Kunene 158, 164, 170, 194, 264

Kunene River 32, 34, 56, 105, 114, 126, 158, 161, 163, 167, 170, **172**, 180, 195, **196**, 196, **197**, 199, 267, 275, 276
Kupferberg 149
Kurper, blue 80, 104, 133, 136, 295
Kutako, Hosea 44, 137
Kwando River 211, **217**, 218, 219, 221, 222

L
Labour 308-309
Labour and Manpower Development, Ministry of 308-309
Labour Code 309
Lake Guinas 154-155
Lake Liambesi 214, 218, 222
Lake Otjikoto 153, **154**, 154, 322
Lambert's Bay 276
Lambert, Tom 144
Lampe, Lieutenant 107
Lang, Ferdinand 153
Language 314
Large Bay 96
Large-mouth, brownspot 225
Lark, dusky 339
Lark, flappet 339
Lark, Gray's 108, 175
Lark, red-capped 339
Lark, sabota 108
Lark, Sclater's 339
Le Vaillant, Francois 290
League of Nations 43
Leather fish 196
Lechulatebe 21
Lechwe, red 219, 222, 279, 331
Leopard 78, 108, 127, 143, 146, 157, **157**, 175, 186, 206, 220, 222, 267, 268, **271**, 298-299, 330
Leutwein, Governor 141
Leutwein, Major Theodor **35**, 107
Levin, D 189
Lewala, Zacharias 42, 91
Lianshulu **198**
Lichen 173, 175, **176**, 187, 291, 293
Liebig House 135
Lily, red flame 146
Linyanti River 222
Linyanti Swamp 222
Lion 143, 156, 162, 175, 179, 191, 192, **201**, **202**, **203**, 206, 220, 222, **265**, 267-268, 298, 330
Liquor 315
Litfass, E. 246
Livingstone, Dr David 216, 217
Lizard, desert-plated 177
Lizard, sand-diving 118
Lizard, shovel-nosed 177
Lizuali **65**
Lobster, rock 295
Lome Convention 306
London Missionary Society 81, 96, 136
Lourie, grey 38
Lourie, Knysna 338

Louw, Captain Peter 130
Lovebird, black-cheeked 38
Lovebird, rosy-faced 186
Lovebird, rosy-faced 338
Löwen River 81, 87
Lozi 216, 217
Lucerne, dune 173
Lüderitz 44, 70, 73, 83, 87, 88, 89, 93, **94-95**, 255-260, **258**, **259**, **260**, **261**, 306, 342; map of 256
Lüderitz Bay 37, 42
Lüderitz Museum 259-260, 325-326
Lüderitz, Adolf **35**, 39, 96, 255
Lukonga 216
Lupala Island 222

M
Maack, Reinard 185
Mackerel 177
Mafwe 216
Magic 64
Mahango Game Reserve 214, 218, 220, 321
Mahango River 218
Mahereo, Willem 137
Maherero, Chief **35**
Maherero, Samuel 137
Mahler, Anna-Maria 103
Maltahöhe 106, 110, 342-343
Mamili National Park 214, 218, 222, 224, 321
Mammals, checklist of 327-328
Manassa, Chief 141
Manketti tree 157
Mariental **101**, **102**, 103, 105, 343
Marine Memorial (Denkmal) 245, 325
Maroelaboom 156
Martin Luther **245**, 324
Martin, Henno 127
Martin, house 339
Martin, rock 339
Matchless Mine 133, 135
Mbau 237
Mbukushu 216
McKenzie, Brigadier-General Sir Duncan 100
Meat, game 302
Media 315, 353-354
Media Directory 353-354
Medical insurance 315
Medical services 315
Meercat 272
Mercury Island 73
Messum Crater 161, 186, 187
Messum River 186, 187
Messum, Captain W 34, 161
Meteor Fountain 101, 232
Metje, Hermann 257
Mimosa, coffee 146
Mining 42, 59, 70, 71, **72**, 72, 73, 89, 91, 130, 133, 135, 149, 150, 153, 170, 184, 305, 306-307
Mission House 325
Mole rat, common 283
Mole, Grant's golden 118, 120, 285
Mole, The 242, 244, 245

Mongoose, banded 272, 273
Mongoose, bush-tailed 272
Mongoose, dwarf 272, 273
Mongoose, large grey 272
Mongoose, Selous 272
Mongoose, slender 272, 273, 330
Mongoose, small grey 272, **274**
Mongoose, water 272
Mongoose, white-tailed 272
Mongoose, yellow 272, 330
Monkey, vervet 219, **277**, **277**, 331
Monuments, listing of 326-327
Moordkoppie 137
Moorhen 130
Mopane 157, 203
Mopane, large false 157
Morenga, Jacob 41
Mount Etjo Safari Lodge 143, 321
Mountaineering 295-296
Mouse, pygmy 283
Mousebird 78, 175
Mousebird, white-backed 78
Mouthbrooder, southern 154
Movimento Popular de Libertacao de Angola (MPLA) 49
Möwe Bay 163, 164, 170
Mudfish 104
Mudge, Dirk 51
Mudumu National Park 214, 218, 221, 222, 268, 322
Mukurob 100
Mulambwa 216
Mullet, mud 104
Munutum River 175
Museums, Namibian 324-326, 354
Mwanambinyi 216

N
Nachtigal, Dr Friedrich 96
Nadas River 175
Nama 36, 37, **37**, 38, 39, 41, 43, 62, 63, 64, 66, 75, 80, 81, 96, 101, 103, 106, 128, 137, 138, 228, 233, 251
Namaland 66, 292
Namaqualand Metamorphic complex 78
Namaqualand, Great 66, 292
Namib Building Society 310
Namib Desert Park 108
Namib Desert **Title page**, 17, **20**, **24**, 24, 28, 30, 32, 33, 42, 56, 57-58, 72, **84-85**, 88, 108-131, 110, **112-113**, **114**, 119, **120**, **122-123**, **124**, **125**, 158, **166**, 168, 173, **173**, **176**, 178, 211, 240, **252**, 255, 257, 260, 264, 268, 286, **290**, 291, 293, 316
Namib-Naukluft National Park **22**, 32, 108-131, **112-113**, **114**, 316, 322; map of **109**
Namibe River 56
Namibia Broadcasting Corporation (NBC) 308
Namibia Commercial Aviation 320

361

Namibia Commercial Aviation 236
Namibia Professional Hunting Association 316
Namibia Rugby Union 295
Namibia Wildlife Trust 180
Namibia, coat of arms of 51, 55
Namibia, flag of 45, 55
Namibia, map of 14-15
Namibia, regions of 15
Namibian Academy for Tertiary Education 309
Namibian Crafts Centre 232, 238
Namibian Development Bank 305
Namibian Development Corporation 305
Namibian Exclusive Economic Zone (EEZ) 306
Namibian Missions abroad 346-347
Namibian National Front 52
Namibian Women's Day 45
Namutoni 201, 206, 209, 210, 211
Namutoni Fort 210
Nasilele, Moses 225
National anthem 27
National Assembly 235
National Convention of Non-Whites 48
National Monuments Council 150, 167
National Parks 316-324
National Party 44
National West Coast Tourist Recreation Area 162, 164, 165, 170, 187, 250, 276
Nature Conservation, Directorate of 26, 146, 148, 161, 177, 178, 180, 222, 250, 257, 307, 316
Nature Sanctuaries 316-324
Naukluft Mountains 22, 108, 110, 186
Naukluft River 111
Naute Dam 80, 87
Necho II 30, 33
Neudam 83
New-Heusis Farm 135
Newspapers 315
Nightjar, European 338
Nightjar, fiery-necked 338
Nightjar, freckled 338
Nightjar, rufous-cheeked 338
Nkasa Island 222
Nkrumah, Kwame 47
Nomtsas Farm 106
Noordoewer 73, 74, 343
Noorsdoring 78
North Long Island 73
Nujoma, Shafiishuna Samuel 45, 47, 51, 54, 55, 236
Numas 186
Numas Ravine 186
Nyamboma Gorge 214

O
Oanab Dam 107
Oanob Dam Nature Reserve 107, 322-323
Odendaal Commission 146, 199
Odondojengo River 175
Okahandja 136, 137, 138, 141, 343
Okanjande 143
Okarakuvisa 147
Okarukuvisa cliffs 148
Okaukuejo 201, 205, 206, 208, 209, 210
Okaukuejo Fort 201
Okaukuejo Rest Camp 144
Okavango Delta 107, 156, 216, 221, 222
Okavango River 17, 30, 32, 58, 64, 105, 198, 208, 211, 214, 215, 218, 219, 220, 267
Okavango Swamp 214, 286
Olbrich, Joseph 153
Oldani 193
Oldham, Lieutenant 128
Olifants River 56
Omaruru 141, 142, 180, 301
Omaruru Museum 325
Omaruru River 34, 140, 141, 161, 165
Omaruru River Game Park 180
Omatako River 155
OMEG 153
OMEG Minenburo 153
Omingonde Formation 148, 149
Omitara 107
Omusema River 138
Ongongo Waterfall 193
Ongulumbashe 47
Onion, wild 293
Onjoka 149
Oorlam 36, 66
Opuwo 194 Karoo 56
Orange River 32, 36, 37, 38, 42, 56, 66, 70, 71, 72, 73, 74, 78, 89, 106, 114, 118, 126, 255, 267, 276
Oranjemund 71, 72, 73, 343
Organ Pipes 187, 190, 190
Organization of African Unity (OAU) 314
Oribi 278
Orupembe 161
Oryx 55, 114, 115, 168, 297
Oshigambo River 203
Osprey 104
Ostrich 100, 101, 103, 104, 136, 173, 176, 191, 195, 219, 287, 336
Otavi 149, 153, 154, 155
Otavi Mountains 33, 149
Otjihaenamaparero Farm 141
Otjihipa 195
Otjihipa Mountains 194
Otjikango 138
Otjimbingwe 38, 39, 138
Otjitunduwa 195
Otjitunduwa fountain 195
Otjiwa Game Ranch 143, 323
Otjiwarongo 134, 136, 143, 144, 178, 180, 343
Otjosondjupa 155
Otjovasandu 201, 208
Otjozonjupa 147
Otter, clawless 219, 282, 330
Otter, spotted-necked 282, 330

Outjo 144, 178, 180, 264, 343
Outjo Museum 325
Ovamboland 194
Owambo 47, 48, 49, 52, 53, 67, 154, 194, 264
Owambo Campaign Memorial 42, 228, 236
Owambo People's Organization (OPO) 45
Owela 237
Owela Museum 237, 324
Owen-Smith, Garth 180
Owl, barn 338
Owl, giant eagle 338
Owl, Pel's fishing 219, 286
Owl, spotted eagle 338
Owl, wood 338
Oyster-catcher, African black 254, 286, 337
Oyster-catcher, European 254, 337
Oysters, cultivation of 165

P
Padloper, Namaqualand speckled 275
Pager, Harald 185
Paintings, rock see Art, prehistoric
Palgrave, W C 141
Palm Beach 242
Palm Springs 79
Palmatogecko see Gecko, web-footed
Palmwag 178, 192
Pangolin 284, 284, 331
Parrot, Meyer's 338
Parrot, Rüppell's 108, 148, 186, 338
Parsley, desert 173, 173
Pelican 103, 104, 253, 336
Pelican, pink-backed 336
Pelican, white 104, 253, 336
Penguin 257, 286
Penguin Island 73
Penguin, jackass 286
People 16, 17, 21, 23, 50, 54, 62-67, 63, 65, 66, 67, 193, 194, 219, 341
People's Liberation Army of Namibia (PLAN) 48, 49, 52, 53, 54, 217
Pepperkorrel Farm 107
Petrel, storm 286
Petrified Forest 32, 180, 184, 187, 188, 318
Petroglyph see Art, prehistoric
Phillip's Cave 140, 301
Phoenicians 33
Photography 25-26
Pienaar, Pieter 38
Pigeon, feral 338
Pigeon, rock 78
Pipit, Richard's 339-340
Pipit, tree 340
Plant profile 340-341
Plover, blacksmith 78, 338
Plover, chestnut-banded 253
Plover, crowned 338
Plover, grey 179, 254, 338
Plover, Kittlitz's 130
Plover, Mongolian 254
Plover, ringed 130

Plover, sand 254
Plover, three-banded 338
Plover, white-crowned 222, 224
Plover, white-fronted 179, 254
Plum 254
Plum Pudding Island 73
Plum, wild 146
Poaching 180, 195
Pochard, Southern 337
Polecat 282, 283, 330
Polecat, striped 283, 330
Pomona Island 73
Pond, George; grave of 96, 259
Pondok Mountain 181, 184
Popa Falls 30, 156, 218, 219, 224
Population 30, 55, 341-342
Porcupine, crested 175, 283
Portuguese, the 17, 30, 33, 34, 39, 49, 144, 158, 251
Possession Island 73
Potgieter, Hennie 237
Powder Tower 325
Pratincole, rock 219

Q
Quail, black-rumped-button 337
Quail, common 337
Quail, harlequin 337
Quiver Tree Forest 87, 318
Quiver tree 70, 77, 78, 87, 99, 100, 291-292, 294

R
Rabbit, rock 108, 283
Radford Bay 93
Radford, David 93
Radio 308
Railways 21, 21, 83, 136, 143, 150, 152, 153, 228, 232, 236, 246-247, 254, 257, 313
Range, Dr P 101
Rathm, Johannes 138
Reagan, Ronald 52, 53
Redecker, Gottlieb 83, 233, 234
Redshank, common 254
Reedbuck 157, 219
Rehoboth 37, 38, 43, 62, 106, 343
Rehoboth Museum 106-107, 326
Reinhardt, Oswald 257
Reiterdenkmal 228
Religion 314
Reptiles 177, 328-329
Reptiles, checklist of 328-329
Resin tree, Namibian 133
Rest Camps 353
Rhenish Mission Church 96, 137, 254
Rhenish Mission Church Museum 326
Rhenish Missionary Society 38, 44, 96, 138
Rhinoceros 143, 146, 162, 175, 180, 191, 192, 204, 265, 330
Rhinoceros, black 175, 180, 192, 204, 205, 265, 330

Rhinoceros, white 143, 146, 162, 265, 330
Richwater Oyster Company 165
Rider Memorial 235
Rietfontein 155, 210
Ringwood tree 136
Road services 313
Roan 143, 146, 156, 157, 205, 219, 220, 281, 298, 331
Roast Beef Island 73
Robert Harbour 257
Robin, Cape 78
Robin, white-browed 225
Rodents 283
Roller 228, 286, 288, **288**, 339
Roller, European 339
Roller, lilac-breasted 228, 288, **288**, 339
Roller, purple 339
Roller, racquet-tailed 339
Rooibank 251
Rössing 180, 240
Rössing Country Club 130, 250
Rössing Uranium 59, 130, 150
Rotse 217
Ruacana 196
Ruacana Falls 194, 195
Rugby 295, **296**
Rundu 214, 215, 218
Runner, rock 108, 133, 148
Rusplaas 195
Rust, Heinrich 101

S

Sable 146, 219, 222, 298
Safaris 27
Salt works 165
San Bushmen 17, 32, 36, 62-63, 66, 147, 155, 156, 220, 300
San, Dzuwazi 62
San, Kung 62
Sander, August 98
Sander, Willi 233
Sanderburg Castle 237
Sanderling 179, 253
Sandgrouse, Namaqua 176
Sandpiper 130, 179, 253, 286, 338
Sandpiper, broad-billed 179
Sandpiper, common 130, 338
Sandpiper, curlew 179
Sandpiper, marsh 130, 179, 254
Sandpiper, terek 179, 254, 338
Sandpiper, white-rumped 179
Sandpiper, wood 338
Sandwich Harbour 126, 127, **128**, 128, 129, **252**, 288, 316
Sarusas 170
Schinz, Hans 209
Schlettwein, Dr C A 193
Schmelen, Heinrich 38, 96, 136
Schmelenhaus (Schmelen House) Museum 96, 326
Schmidt, Etemba 184
Schroder, John 81
Schultze, Lieutenant George 185

Schutztruppe **35**, 39, 41, 42, 98, 147, 233, 234
Schwerinsburg Castle 237
Scott, Michael 44
Seal Island 73, 276
Seal, Antarctic fur 276
Seal, Cape fur **8-9**, **94-95**, **160**, **162**, **163**, **164**, 166-167, 170, 176, 179, 276
Seal, Sub-Antarctic fur 276
Sebitwane 216, 217
Sechomib River 175
Second Lagoon 93, 96
Secretary bird 337
Security 314
Seeheim 78, 87
Seitz, Dr 149
Seringa tree 157
Serval 267, 270-271
Sesfontein 193, 201
Sesriem Canyon 111, **116**, 120, 121, 125, 316
Shambyu Roman Catholic Mission Museum 325
Shark Island 96
Shearwater 286
Sheep, karakul **82**, 83, 306
Shelduck 130
Shortridge, Captain G C 180
Shrew, elephant 186, 284
Shrew, round-eared elephant 284
Shrew, short-snouted elephant 284
Shrike, brubru 339
Shrike, crimson-breasted 339
Shrike, fiscal 339
Shrike, lesser grey 108, 339
Shrike, tropical boubou 339
Shrike, white-helmet 225, 339
Shrike, white-tailed 133
Sinclair's Island 73
Sitatunga 219, 222, 279, 281, 331
Skeleton Coast 17, 19, 30, 32, 56, 158-179, **160**, **166**, **169**, **171**, **174**, 250, 268, 277, 286; map of **159**
Skeleton Coast Park 161, 163-164, 165, 167, 177, 323
Skiing, sand 295
Skimmer, African 219
Skoogi *see* Lizard, desert-plated
Skua, Arctic 338
Skua, longtailed 338
Smithsonian Institute 99
Smuts, General Jan 42
Smuts, General Jan Christian 44
Snakes 118, **220**
Solitaire 125
Sossusvlei 30, 56, **60-61**, 110, 111, **112-113**, 114, 115, 118, 120, 121, **125**, **126**, 126, 316
South Africa Engineering Corps 131
South Africa, Union of 42, 43
South African Food and Canning Workers Union 45
South African Railways 47
South Africans, the 17, 42, 43, 44, 45, 47, 48, 49, 50, 51,

52, 53, 54, 75, 88, 100, 131, 154, 165, 210, 216, 217, 240, 251
South Long Island 73
South West Africa Company 128, 150, 153, 161, 255
South West Africa People's Organisation (SWAPO) 45, 46, 47, 48, 49, 50, 51, 52, 54, 216, 217
South West Africa, UN Committee on 47
South West African National Union (SWANU) 44
Southern African Customs Union (SACU) 305, 310
Southern African Development Co-ordination Conference (SADCC) 305
Southern Tourist Forum 83
Sparrow, Cape 175
Spider 118, 177
Spider, trapdoor 177
Spitzkoppe 180, 181, 184, **185**, 296, **296**, 317-318
Spoonbill, African 105, 289, 337
Sports 295-299
Sports Club 250
Springbok 103, 104, 107, 108, **110**, 111, 133, 136, 139, 162, 173, 175, 178, 186, 191, 192, 195, 205, 208, 278, **280**, 297, 331
Springer 196
Stamps **46**
Starling, pale-winged 78
Starling, redwing **288**
Stauch, August 91, 255
Steenbok 108, 133, 146, 186, 192, 206, 278, 331
Steenbras 165, 177
Stengel Dam 133
Stilt, black-winged 254
Stint, little 179, 254
Stone Age 189, 300
Stork, Abdim's 337
Stork, Marabou 289
Stork, open-billed 337
Stork, white 337
Strepie 177
Stuhlmann, Eugen 101
Stump-nose, white 177
Stumpfe, Sergeant E. 103
Sturmvogelbucht 96
Subiya 216
Suclabo 219
Sulphur Springs 79
Sulphur, mining of 135
Sunbird, dusky 78, 108, 186
Sunbird, mariqua 288
Sunbird, white-bellied 209
Sundano 216
Suricate 272, 330
SWA Building Society 310
Swakop Canyon 127
Swakop River 38, 114, 117, 127, 130, 135, 138, 240, 247, 294
Swakop River Valley 130
Swakopmund 32, 42, 59, 91, 117, 130, 131, 132, 133, 153, 164, 165, 175, 181, 228, 233, 240-250, **243**, **244**, **245**, **246**,

247, **292**, 343; map of **241**
Swakopmund Military Museum 325
Swakopmund Museum 130, 242, 324-325
Swakopmund Railway Station 324
Swallow, greater striped 339
Swallow, wiretailed 339
SWAWEK 308
Swift 108, 130, 147, 338
Swift, alpine 147
Swift, Bradfield's 108, 338
Swift, European 338
Swift, palm 338
Syringa, wild 146

T

Table Mountain 79
Tamarisk, wild 78
Taxation 311
Taxi services 313, 354
Tchagra, three-streaked 225
Teak, wild 157
Teal, Cape 175, 337
Teal, red-billed 337
Telephone 308, 314-315
Television 308
Terminalia, silver 146
Tern, Caspian 104, 130, 253
Tern, Damara 165, 176, 253
Tern, roseate 286
Tern, royal 338
Tern, swift 253
Tern, whiskered 130
Tern, white-winged 130, 338
Terrace Bay 178, 179, 250
Terrapin, Cape 275
Terrapin, soft-shelled 275
Thorer, Paul Albert 83
Thorn, black 136
Thorn, blue 136
Thorn, buffalo 133
Thorn, camel 78, 133, 136, 341
Thorn, candle 133
Thorn, devil's 79
Thorn, hairy umbrella 203
Thorn, mountain 133
Thorn, red umbrella 203
Thorn, sweet 78, 133, 136
Thorn, umbrella 203
Thorn, water 203
Thrush, collared palm 222
Thrush, groundscraper 339
Thrush, short-toed 339
Tiger fish, fighting 196, 225
Tilapia 143, 154, 225
Tilapia, Mozambique 154
Tilapia, Otjikoto 143
Time 314
Tin, mining of 184
Tipping 315
Tit, ashy grey 339
Tit, rufous-bellied 339
Tit-babbler 175
Tit-babbler, Layard's 108
Tjamuaha 137
Tjimba 64
Tjokwe 156
Toivo ja Toivo, Andimba Herman 45, 47
Tonnesen, T 150
Torra Bay 178

363

Tortoise, angulate 275
Tortoise, hingeback 275
Tortoise, leopard 274-275, 275
Tortoise, mountain 274-275
Tour operators 355
Tourism 307
Tourism and Resorts, Directorate of 317
Trade and Industry, Ministry of 310
Trans-Kalahari Highway 107
Transitional Government of National Unity (TGNU) 53
TransNamib Limited 308, 313
TransNamib Museum 324
Transport 308, 312-313
Transvaal Scottish Regiment 131
Travel consultants 354-355
Trekking, camel 120, 130
Trekkopje, Battle of 131
Troost, Lieutenant Edmund 247, 257
Trougoth 137
Tsams River 111
Tsaobis 135
Tsaobis Leopard Nature Park 139, 268, 323
Tsauchab River 30, 116, 118, 120, 121, 126
Tsessebe 146, 156, 157, 219, 278
Tshekedi, Chief 47
Tsisab Gorge 58
Tsondab River 111
Tsumeb 150, 151, 152, 153, 154, 154, 155, 343
Tsumeb Corporation 135, 149, 154
Tsumeb Museum 152, 153, 325
Tsumkwe 156
Tswana 62
Turnhalle Conference 49, 236
Turnhalle, Lüderitz 259
Turnhalle, Windhoek 236
Turnstone 130, 179
Turtle, Hawksbill 276
Turtle, leatherback 196, 276
Turtle, loggerhead 276
Turtle, marine 275-276
Turtle, Nile 275
Twyfelfontein 31, 180, 186, 187, 189, 190, 190, 191, 301, 301

U
Ugab River 34, 146, 161, 165, 167, 170, 175, 177, 178, 179, 180, 199, 250
Uis 184
Ukuambi 44
Uniab River 175, 178, 192
Uniab Valley 178
United Nations 44, 47, 48, 52, 53, 137
United Nations Security Council Resolution 435 53, 54
United Nations Transition Assistance Group (UNTAG) 52, 54

Universal Negro Improvement Association 43-44
Upingtonia, Republic of 150
Uranium, mining of 59, 130, 240, 305
Usakos 59, 117, 140

V
Van Wyk, Hermanus 106
Van Zylsgat 192
Versailles, Treaty of 43, 88
Viehe, Gottlieb 141
Viljoen, D T du P 133
Vingerklip 30, 69, 100, 144, 145, 146
Visa regulations 312
Visagie, Gert 225
Vogelsang, Heinrich 255
Von Bach 136
Von Bach Recreation Resort 135, 295, 320
Von Bismarck, Chancellor 39
Von Byrgsdorff, Malta 106
Von Caprivi di Caprara di Montecuccoli, General Count George Leo 216
Von Estdorff, Major 144
Von Estorff, Ludwig 233
Von Francois Fort 135
Von Francois, Captain Curt 39, 135, 141, 228, 241, 244; statue of 237
Von Kleist, General 100
Von Lindequist, Friedrich 199
Von Trotha, General 41
Von Trotha, Lieutenant Thilo 80
Von Wolf, Baron Hans-Heinrich 89, 98
Vulture, Cape 148, 337
Vulture, Egyptian 285
Vulture, hooded 337
Vulture, lappet-faced 148, 175, 337
Vulture, palm-nut 286
Vulture, white-backed 148, 289
Vulture, white-headed 148, 337

W
Wagtail, African pied 339
Wagtail, Cape 78, 339
Waldheim, Kurt 48
Walvis Bay 32, 37, 38, 39, 48, 49, 127, 128, 250, 250, 251-254, 253, 306, 343
Walvis Bay Mining Company (WBM) 135, 138, 139
Walvis Bay Museum 325
Walvis Bay Nature Reserve 324
Wambo 36, 38, 48, 49, 62, 63, 66-67, 72, 150, 194, 209, 210
Warbler 78, 286
Warbler, African marsh 78
Warehouse Theatre 238
Warmbad farm 193
Warmquelle 192
Warren, Captain W B 34, 161
Wart hog 146, 219, 222, 281-282, 297
Wasp, dune 177

Water resources 308
Waterberg Plateau 146, 148, 211
Waterberg Plateau Park 146-149, 147, 268, 318
Waterbuck, common 143, 278-279, 331
Waxbill, blue 225
Weasel 282, 283
Weasel, black-and-white striped 283
Weaver bird 108, 119, 290
Weaver, chestnut 108
Weaving 82
Weber, Dr Alfons 242
Weeping-wattle 146
Weissrand Plateau 100
Welwitsch, Friedrich 294
Welwitschia mirabilis 55, 56, 115, 130, 131, 131, 175, 294, 340
Welwitschia plains 130
West Caprivi Game Park 146
Whale 179, 276-277
Whale, baleen 277
Whale, beaked 277
Whale, killer 277
Whale, sperm 277
Whimbrel 179, 254
White Temples 194
Whydah, pin-tailed 133
Wild cat, African 175, 267, 271, 330
Wildebeest 133, 141, 146, 156, 157, 206, 208, 209, 219, 220, 278, 298, 331
Wildebeest, black 141, 298
Wildebeest, blue 133, 141, 146, 156, 157, 206, 208, 219, 220, 278, 298, 331
Wilderness Area 164
Wildlife Half title, 8-9, 12-13, 78, 84-85, 86, 94-95, 104, 107, 108, 110, 114, 115, 133, 136, 139, 141, 143, 146-147, 148, 156, 157, 157, 160, 162, 163, 164, 169, 177, 179, 180, 186, 191, 192, 195, 201, 202, 203, 204, 205, 205-206, 206, 207, 208, 210, 219-220, 222, 224, 225, 263, 264-285, 265, 266, 269, 270, 271, 273, 274, 275, 276, 277, 279, 280, 282, 284, 285, 330-331
Wildlife Conservation Award, International 299
Wildlife profile 330-331
Wildlife Society of Namibia 238
Wildlife, Conservation and Tourism, Ministry of 149, 297, 307, 316, 317
Wilhelm II, Kaiser 233, 235, 259
Wille, Hermann 246
William V of Orange, Prince 71
Windhoek 18, 20, 24, 32, 33, 36, 38, 38, 39, 40, 42, 45, 45, 48, 51, 58, 62, 101, 132, 133, 135, 138, 226, 227, 228-238, 230, 232, 233, 234, 235, 237, 238, 239, 343; map of 229
Windhoek Conservatoire 238

Windhoek International Airport 18, 19, 26, 27, 228, 308
Windhoek massacre 45
Windhoek State Museum 154, 234, 236, 324
Windhoek Theatre 238
Witbooi, David 44
Witbooi, Hendrik 37, 41, 44, 49, 103, 106, 233
Witbooi, Pastor Hendrik 49
Witvrou 184
Witwatersrand 153
Wlotzkasbaken 165
Woermann and Brock 242
Woermann Line Shipping Company 246
Woermannhaus 325
Women's Council 48, 50
Wondergat 191
Woodhoopoe, scimitar-billed 186, 339
Woodhoopoe, violet 339
Woodpecker, bearded 339
Woodpecker, cardinal 339
Woodpecker, golden-tailed 288
Woodpecker, olive 339
Work permits 310
World War, First 75, 131, 153, 210
World War, Second 44, 153, 216, 217

Y
Yellowfish, large-mouthed 80, 295
Yellowfish, small-mouthed 80, 104, 136, 295
Yezi 216
Youth League 48, 50, 52

Z
Zambezi Queen 225
Zambezi River 211, 214, 216, 218, 223, 224, 286
Zambezi tree 157
Zebra 78, 81, 104, 107, 108, 133, 136, 139, 141, 143, 162, 175, 186, 191, 192, 195, 205, 207, 208, 220, 281, 282, 297, 330
Zebra, Burchell's 141, 143, 205, 208, 220, 281, 282, 297, 330
Zebra, Hartmann's mountain 78, 81, 104, 107, 108, 133, 136, 139, 162, 175, 186, 191, 192, 195, 205, 208, 281, 297, 330
Zeraua, Chief 139
Zoo Park 233
Zwraua, Wilhelm 141